CW01394440

Hebrews: A Commentary

The Faith that Endures

By

William H. Bicksler

1663 Liberty Drive, Suite 200
Bloomington, Indiana 47403
(800) 839-8640
www.AuthorHouse.com

First published by AuthorHouse 07/07/05

ISBN: 1-4208-5593-X (sc)

Printed in the United States of America
Bloomington, Indiana

This book is printed on acid-free paper.

Table of Contents

Genre:

"Unlike most other NT epistles, Hebrews does not begin like a letter. There is no introductory salutation, the writer is not identified, and no mention is made of those to whom the document is addressed. The author characterizes the work as a "word of exhortation" (13:22) which suggests a sermon or oral homily (Cf. . Acts 13:15). The phrase "time would fail me to tell" (Heb 11:32) suggests a spoken rather than a written discourse. Yet although the general character of Hebrews is sermonic, its conclusion is that of a conventional letter (13:22–25).Some have detected a gradual transition in the document from an 'essay' to a more specifically 'epistolary' form (Cf. . 2:1; 4:1; 13:22–25).[1] The effort to conform genre designation to one category hampers study of the book. From the last chapter only it is an epistle. However, theological essays plus exhortation is a homily format. Use of OT quotes is exposition, not merely citation. Portions of exhortations border on the prophetic genre of warning or threat. The use of 'we' often could be called an apostolic type of coherence use, to create bonding with those addressed. The use of historical allusions is more than illustrations of truth, but is the truth itself. Hidden in both the doctrinal and hortative are various needs or errors of the addressed and these showing the pastoral concerns. The contrastive use of OT allusions and citations show a dispensational and definitive clarification of the NT Gospel in its uniqueness. However, the same use of the OT also shows the effort to present a philosophy of history focusing on historical or Heilsgeschichte continuity of God's revelation, acts, and People throughout history. Aileen Guilding shows links between the content of Hebrews and Pentecost, since Gen 14 and Ps 110 were prescribed for that season in the triennial lectionary of Palestinian and western synagogues.[2]

Outline for the Book #1

If we use these quotations as a guideline for discerning its structure, the following picture of Hebrews emerges.

"*Chapter One* is an introduction. This chapter is full of Old Testament quotations demonstrating Jesus' superiority over angels.

"*Chapter Two* appeals to Psalm 8. Jesus rescues man by coming down beneath angels, joining man in flesh and blood, dying, and then returning to his place of exaltation above the angels. All who cling to him in faith return with him to the throne.

"*Chapters Three and Four* deal with Psalm 95. God offers rest to all who trust him. The land of Canaan was not that rest, for this Psalm spoke of a rest long after the Israelites who wandered in the desert hardened their hearts and lost the rest which God offered to them. God's rest is still available for all who believe him.

"*Chapters Five, Six and Seven* are organized around Psalm 110. Jesus is a priest like Melchizedek, who was also superior to the priesthood of the old covenant. Jesus, in fact, is a priest forever by God's oath.

"*Chapter Eight* introduces Jeremiah 31. The new covenant, created by Jesus our great high priest, is superior to the old covenant. It is founded on better promises than the old covenant, which was a mere copy and shadow of this new covenant.

"*Chapters Nine and Ten* treat Psalm 40. Jesus' living sacrifice of himself through obedience is far superior to the Old Testament sacrifices of dead bulls and goats repeatedly offered in the old tabernacle. Jesus took this sacrifice into the very presence of God, thus fully taking away sins and cleansing our consciences.

"*Chapter Eleven* develops a theme from Habakkuk 2, that the righteous will live by faith. This principle by which we live is illustrated by numerous examples of people living by faith.

"*Chapter Twelve* treats Proverbs 3. We must accept the discipline God brings upon us, for God disciplines those he loves.

"*Chapter Thirteen* is the conclusion. It is full of exhortations on how to give ourselves to God in the life of faith.

"Remove the introductory and concluding chapters for a moment and an interesting picture of the structure of the main body of thought emerges. The new covenant (chapter 8) is central, tying together his priesthood (chapters 5–7) and his sacrifice (chapters 9–10). This is prepared for by the offer of rescue (chapter 2) and rest (chapters 3–4) and followed by the response of faith (chapter 11) and the endurance of discipline (chapter 12) which he expects from us.

"There are many other uses of the Old Testament woven into this main structure of the book but the central focus is on Jesus the superior priest who brings his superior sacrifice to God. This is the core of the new covenant. By this means he offers rescue and rest. From us he expects faith and endurance."[3]

Outline from College Press NIV Commentary: #2

I. JESUS IS SUPERIOR TO THE ANGELS — 1:1–14
   - A. The Preeminence of the Son — 1:1–4
   - B. The Son Superior to the Angels — 1:5–14

II. JESUS RESCUES MAN — 2:1–18
   - A. Warning Not to Ignore Such a Great Salvation — 2:1–4
   - B. Jesus Became a Man to Bring Men to Glory — 2:5–18

III. GOD OFFERS REST TO ALL WHO TRUST HIM — 3:1–4:16
   - A. Jesus Is Superior to Moses — 3:1–6
   - B. Psalm 95:7–11 — 3:7–11
   - C. Hold Firm to the End — 3:12–15
   - D. Unbelieving Israelites Fell in the Desert — 3:16–19
   - E. A Sabbath-Rest for the People of God — 4:1–5
   - F. A Sabbath-Rest Remains — 4:6–11
   - G. The Message from God Does Its Part to Save Us — 4:12–13
   - H. Jesus, the Great High Priest — 4:14–16

IV. JESUS IS SUPERIOR TO THE PRIESTHOOD OF THE OLD COVENANT AND A PRIEST FOREVER BY GOD'S OATH — 5:1–7:28
   - A. Requirements of the High Priest — 5:1–4
   - B. Jesus Fulfills the Requirements and Offers Eternal Salvation — 5:5–10

VII. GOD EXPECTS US TO SHOW FAITH — 11:1–40

A. The Nature of Faith — 11:1–3

B. Faith Illustrated by Abel, Enoch, and Noah — 11:4–7

C. Faith Illustrated by Abraham — 11:8–19

D. Faith Illustrated by Isaac, Jacob, and Joseph — 11:20–22

E. Faith Illustrated by Moses — 11:23–28

F. Faith Illustrated in Israel — 11:29–38

G. God Planned to Make Them Perfect with Us — 11:39–40

VIII. GOD EXPECTS US TO ENDURE DISCIPLINE — 12:1–29

A. A Call to Perseverance — 12:1–3

B. The Word of Encouragement — 12:4–6

C. God Disciplines His Children — 12:7–11

D. Practical Actions — 12:12–17

E. Terrifying Mt. Sinai — 12:18–21

F. Mt. Zion, the Heavenly Jerusalem — 12:22–24

G. A Kingdom which Cannot Be Shaken — 12:25–29

IX. CONCLUDING EXHORTATIONS — 13:1–25

A. Keep Loving Each Other — 13:1–3

B. Stay Pure — 13:4–6

C. Remember Your Leaders — 13:7–8

D. Counterparts to Old Covenant Practices — 13:9–16

E. Obey Your Leaders and Pray for Us — 13:17–19

F. Benediction and Closing Exhortations — 13:20–22

G. Personal Greetings — 13:23–2[4]

THE AUTHOR'S METHODS OF INTERPRETING SCRIPTURES:

His methods of interpretation are varied. They include:[7]

- Etymology (determining the meaning or significance of a word by dividing it into its constituent parts) and/or the literal sense of a word of phrase
- *qal wa-homer*, a rabbinical method of arguing from lesser to greater

- *gezerah shawah*, another rabbinical method which established a relationship between two passages of Scripture on the basis of similar wording, using one passage to expand the meaning of the other
- Typology, a method of viewing a place, person, event, etc. in the Bible as a pattern (or "type") of a later place, person, event, etc. ("antitype"). The "type" takes on a significance beyond its historical referent which is later recognized as a result of its similarities with the "antitype"
- Homiletical Midrash, a kind of hortatory running commentary which applies a passage to the experience of an audience[5]

Importance of the Book:

"John Owen, the English Puritan, appropriately remarked: "No doubt the Epistle next in importance to Romans is this to the Hebrews." The letter is doctrinal and practical, theological and pastoral. In short, it builds a compelling case for the finality of Christianity. Yet in addition to the excellence of its doctrine and apologetic, Hebrews reflects the impassioned concern of a pastor's heart. Those who have experienced God's ultimate work of grace in Christ are urged to hold fast to God's final word of revelation in his Son. [6]

1. Hebrews offers an alternative to Pauline and James theology as well as the eschatology of Revelation. New insights are observable from the biblical perspective of antithetical or contrasting ideas and realities. His description is of the tabernacle not the subsequent temples of Solomon, Haggai or Herod. .This doesn't seem to be a Palestinian situation for the writer.
2. Hebrews, except for Rome, may have a different set of cultural entities than those Paul's missions reached and so the manner of presenting the Gospel and follow-up in the assemblies may differ in unusual respects.
3, Hebrews uses terms in unique ways and thus forms a world in and of itself, by which to see an emerging theological system.
4. Hebrews' world still is experiencing the dynamic of the Spirit but there is a development both in what is expected of catechumens, what spiritual experiences they have, and what works they must manifest so as to not backslide back into the old ways. Some are similar to Paul's and others are uniquely expressed and some unique.

5. Hebrews is in touch with the Jewish thought world largely for many who have never made a trip to Jerusalem and have only heard about the specific customs. As such, it is a reminder of their heritage and this serves then as a basis for building a new structure of belief on the old structure.
6. Hebrews only in the last chapter has the features of a letter. In chapters 1-12 it is a theological treatise with exhortations interspersed, and hence the whole is a homily or sermon because of these strongly worded applications.
7. Hebrews' theology and administrative features together with its history is not dependent upon certain apostolic authority, some original disciples or their disciples, but does not depart from their message. The affinity with Paul is the closest but with many unique deviations in keeping with the recipients and message. The freedom of the Spirit to assert the truth and apply it to the situation gives a hint of preaching in his time.
8. Hebrews does not reject the Old Testament or Hebrew Scriptures and customs but sees them coming to fruition and in the process of passing away because of fulfillment of types, of prophecies, and substitutes 'the will of God' for the legal system of Judaism

AUTHOR:

1 .Argument from language: Clement of Alexandria (d. 220) theorized that Paul wrote the letter in Hebrew for Jews and that Luke translated it into Greek from Aramaic or Hebrew, but was skeptical, but with Origen felt the style was sufficiently Pauline. Calvin surmised that either Luke or Clement of Rome was responsible for the letter.It is definitely not translation Greek, but closer to Luke's writing.

2. Argument from Style: Clement's pupil Origen (ca.230, d. 254) stated more generally that the thoughts of the letter are Pauline, but that the style is unlike that of the known writings of the apostle."Only God knows who really wrote it." Scholars have noted that the Greek of Hebrews resembles the language and style of the third Gospel and Acts.
3. Argument from necessity of canonicity for apostleship: Jerome (d. 419) and Augustine (d. 430), persuaded that canonicity demanded apostolic authorship, likewise affirmed that Paul was the author.

4. |Argument from Anonymity: The anonymity of the letter is contrary to the consistent pattern of Paul's introduction in the opening salutation of his letters. Bruce notes that the western church, up to the 4th century, resisted attribution t Paul and this early tradition did not present a handicap to a Jewish readership. Ambrosiaster did not include it in a Pauline corpus because he considered it anonymous. Pelagius considered it Pauline, but perhaps not on the same level as the other 13. Jerome and Augustine viewed it as Pauline through the 16th century.[7]
5. Argument from testimony: 2:3 indicates the writer was discipled by eyewitnesses of the Lord. Yet Paul insists that his knowledge of Christ was gained from an encounter with the risen Christ (Cf. . Gal 1:12).
6. Argument from multiple factors: F.F. Bruce evaluates the authorship of Hebrews as follows: "We may say with certainty that the thought of the epistle is not Paul's, the language is not Paul's, and the technique of OT quotations is not Paul's."
7. Argument of Tertullian (d. 220), "many early authorities believed that Barnabas was responsible for the letter. Acts 4:36 speaks of him as a "son of exhortation" (Cf. . Heb 13:22). Furthermore, as a Levite, Barnabas would have been familiar with the Jewish sacrificial ritual so prominent in the letter." The book has many exhortations and content has to do largely with priestly matters. Silas would also have been knowledgeable of Levitical protocols. . Silas is described as one of the "chief men among the brethren" (Acts 15:22). He was a co-worker with Paul in the gentile mission, and apparently was known in Rome as well as in Jerusalem (1 Pt 5:13).
8. Argument from Alexandrian conventions: Luther was the first to suggest that Hebrews may have been penned by Apollos, "an excellent man of learning, who had been a disciple of the apostles and learned much from them, and who was very well versed in Scripture." As a native of Alexandria (Acts 18:24), Apollos would have been familiar with the typological interpretation evident in Hebrews. Clearly Apollos was the sort of man who was qualified to write Hebrews. The arguments in the book show 'Platonizing tendencies of Alexandrian Judaism.'
9. Argument from associations. Ruth Hippon suggests Priscilla, one of Paul's intimate circle, awareness of Paul's patterns of thought and use of scripture, even though theology was divergent as seen in Acts 18.19. She could have traveled with Timothy, but unwilling to day the trip on his account. References to church leaders give a locus of Rome 13.7,17,24. the Salutation 'those from Italy' 13.24 and the fact Hebrews was known

and circulated in Rome and may have influenced Roman liturgy. Some manuscripts name Rome or Italy as the place of origin. Priscilla was leader of a house church in Rome. Tradition says she was of nobility, with training in rhetoric, philosophy and oratory. Priscilla had a ministry to Ephesus and this would correspond to Timothy's homecoming. Apollos was taught by her as Chrysostom notes. Because of this instruction Apollos presented from scripture the messiahship of Jesus, a major theme in the book. Apollos came to Priscilla only knowing the baptism of John Acts 18.25. She taught him the difference between John's and Christian baptism. The masculine participle diegoumenon 'telling' in Heb 11.32 in the accusative has the same form in the neuter as in Classical usage. The stress on parent-child relations shows tenderness, while there is an interest in education. She names women as models of faith, and alludes to others. Loss of the tradition of a woman author could be seen as a witness to the fact. Note Hunter's discussion of Apollos q.v.There is sympathy for women expressed 11.1,31,35. In 11.11 Sarah has faith while in Gen 18.11-15 she laughs in unbelief. If Priscilla and Aquila wrote it the shift from 1st person sg to 1 person plural is understandable.[8]

10. Theoretical considerations: He appears to be a second generation Jewish-Christian 2.3. He knows interpretation of the LXX. Probably a Hellenist he was probably one with Jerusalem Hellenists as in Acts 6-8 and 11.19ff. Thus he probably was associate to Stephen and Philip, pioneers in Gentile mission. The Recipients knew him and so he did not need to talk about himself.
11. Argument from Trimm: "For a number of reasons this author is persuaded that Paul was the author of Hebrews. The Church Fathers; Clement of Alexandria (150-212 C.E.) and Eusebius (315 C.E.) maintain Pauline authorship of the book (see quotations below under Language). In addition, the most ancient New Testament manuscripts place Hebrews with the Pauline Epistles, as does the Peshitta Aramaic New Testament. From 2Peter 3:15 it appears that Paul had written a letter to the Hebrews (compare 2Pt. 1:1 and James 1:1). Pauline authorship is supported by the fact that the author was in bonds (10:34) in Italy (13:24) and Timothy was one of his companions (13:23). Further support for Pauline authorship may be found in the fact that Heb. 6:1-2 gives an outline for the whole of the General Pauline Epistles (see note to 6:1-2). The author treats the subject of inheritance in detail, Paul had been commissioned to teach on the topic of inheritance (Acts 26:12-18) and only in the Pauline epistles is the concept of inheritance dealt with in such detail. Finally, the authors' expert use of the Seven Rules of Hillel and complex forms of Homiletic Midrashic Exegesis

point to Paul (Saul), who had been a student of Gamaliel (Acts 22:3) the grandson of Hillel."[9] The use of Pauline data sets the foundation for finding pertinent information in Hebrews. The use of many-faceted points, none of which is certainly found in Hebrews makes the argument seem irrefutable. But the one point of attitude toward the Law and the Judaism of the time as well as the author's relation to Judaism and lack of any antagonistic spirit toward Jewish tradition speak volumes against Pauline authorship.[10]

12. In conclusion, it is probable that the author of Hebrews was a second-generation Jewish-Christian, a master of classical Greek whose Bible was the Septuagint, conversant with first-century Alexandrian philosophy, and a creative apologist for the Christian faith. As to the identity of that author, we can affirm no more than Origen did in the 3rd century: "But as to who actually wrote the Letter, God alone knows."[11]

Historical Background Issues:

1. While not as specific as the epistles of James and Peter, these recipients seem to be living in the Diaspora: The very early title of the letter, "To Hebrews," suggests that the book concerns Jewish Christians living in the dispersion.
2. Not long after becoming Christians, were the readers of the letter were exposed to severe persecution (10:32–36) and what kind of persecution? Possibilities arise from: 1. Non-Christian Jews which could be involved; 2. Roman authorities who are peacekeepers; 3. Romans who recognize Christian practices as cultic and have no official standing in the empire; 4. Local defenders of synagogues who involve Jews and non-Jews in persecuting Christians. 5. Gentile converts would not respond to 'If perfection had been attainable through the Levitical priesthood…' with 'We never thought it was.'.[12]..But converted Jews might think of returning to a practicing Judaism.
3. Did these believers, during their trials or public trials, of which there is no indication, endured imprisonment, confiscation of personal property, and public ridicule and contempt. How much of this is unknown. The

dangers of apostasy were real for them and for the future, they were what Bruce called 'the horror of the irretrievable sin of apostasy.'[13]

4. The persecution had not been fatal, since they had apparently not yet been called upon to lay down their lives in martyrdom (12:4).
5. When they believed there was excitement of their new-found faith in Christ and spiritual gifts and experiences, and they had demonstrated practical concern and love by ministering to fellow believers in need (6:10) and comforting others who had been harassed for their faith (10:34). But were these established congregations or only places of occasional assembly?
6. Had the passage of time, since those earlier trials, led to the readers into making very little progress into Christian maturity (5:11–13)? Is this referring to the recipients in general as if they were in one location such as Rome, or to a group among the larger group of recipients?
7. Were they facing a new wave of persecution, and was there despondency caused by an apparent delay in the Lord's coming, and are these connected to the believers who may have begun to waver and abandon hope. Did they actually threaten to renounce Jesus Christ and to revert to the security of the Jewish religion, which enjoyed the protection of Roman law? Alternatively, is this using extra-biblical evidence to suggest a possible scenario since we know a little bit about the history of the early church?
8. Was there false doctrine or "diverse and strange teachings" of certain Judaizers who sought to draw them back to their former religion (13:9), the wavering believers have neglected to assemble together (10:25) and have lost confidence in their spiritual leaders (13:17). Faced with the possibility that these Jewish Christians might abandon their faith altogether, the writer sternly warns them of the tragic consequences of renouncing the Son (13:12–19; 6:4–6; 10:26–31) and urges them to renew their commitment to Christ, God's foremost and final revelation. Each of these items must stand alone, and their total of disparate things does not equal a majority opinion that these things actually happened.

The Recipients:

The prior question is a balancing of the synchronic view that sees scripture as directed to all men and the diachronic that seeks a particular group of people, Christians or not, Jewish or Jewish-Christians in the first century that had certain needs and were in great peril.

Snell represents a view that the recipients were Palestinian Jews who had been exposed to the Christian message but not converted. He is dealing with the exhortation and 'lest' passages of warnings. Every allusion to basic doctrine is a problem for the unbeliever faced with a choice of the new versus the old. There is no circumcision party or rejection of Judaism, but a focus on fulfillment in Christ alone. Snell's points are a labored effort to identify the recipient's as 'not yet' believers or 'catechumens' so 'enlightened' is awakening not a new birth, and 'baptisms' are ablutions of Judaism, and repentance is a change of mind of one who had the light but walked away. The treatise is then a letter of concern to a Jewish community in Palestine that show none of the overseas Jewish issues.

But The viewpoint of this commentary is more congenial to a group of believers in Rome who had been persecuted and would face much more. They were largely Jewish believers since detail about Jewish customs was minimized consciously. They had been baptized and experienced all the basic gifts and graces of believers, but now were on the verge of succumbing to testing and temptation to deny the Lord to save their lives, and therefore needed to know that martyrdom was good and right. Or they were Jewish believers under pressure to legitimize their rights to live in Rome, save their families, and not identify to the radical Pauline doctrine. By not assembling as believers they may have returned to a synagogue type fellowship. The concerns for them addressed as 'brothers' in keeping with apostle habit would refer to Christian believers. The cup and bread is not passover, but the Lord's Supper. So the scope still is narrow but by no means to believers only. The subject matter of the letter presents the complete Gospel. For Gentile believers, and there is no indication of this distinction, there are faithful examples from all biblical history, not only from Jewish history and it was their faith that won God's approval, not the doctrinal contents of that faith, but simply faith as faithfulness to God.

The fact the letter plus treatise that are conjoined as part of the canon is such excellent Greek, comparable only to Luke, points to a wider constituency that needed the whole message. A synchronic approach does not use historical criticism and determination of a time, place and constituency to determine meaning but the writing itself. This respect for the text and its message regardless of readership makes this a Gospel treatise or tract with a letter appended, a unique structure comparable to Romans. By reading it as scripture it is the message and all the smaller messages explcit and implicit that allow the book to speak, not only scholars.

Date:

1. Generational data: We have already noted that the author of Hebrews, and probably his readers as well, had been discipled by those who were personally acquainted with Jesus (2:3). Does further evidence in the letter suggests that Paul probably was not still living? Timothy, Paul's younger associate, was still living (13:23).
2. Does missing information provide a basis for dating? The absence of any mention in Hebrews of the destruction of the Jerusalem temple is significant for dating the letter. In terms of his argument that the old covenant had passed away and the legal priesthood had been superseded, the writer would scarcely have omitted mention of the temple's destruction had he written the letter later than A.D. 70. Hebrews 9:6–10 and 10:1–4, 11–14 plainly suggest that the Jewish sacrifices were still being offered. Hence it may be concluded, with some degree of certainty, that the letter was written prior to A.D. 70. But nothing of the war and struggles from 66-68 are mentioned either. There is imminent expectation of the parousia.10.25,36-39. Timothy's release from prison 13.23 could indicate an early date. 10.3234 could describe persecution under Claudius, while 12.4 predicted that under Nero in 64.A.D.
3. Numerical considerations: Some scholars point to Hebrews 3:7–19 (quoting Ps 95:8–11) and suggest that the argument of Israel's 40 years wandering in the wilderness would be more forceful if the 40th year from the Lord's death was approaching. Such a scheme of reckoning would date Hebrews about A.D. 66. The use of 40 years is in the context of the generation that died in the wilderness because of rebellion and nothing is that pessimistic that the first 40 years of the church would repeat that history. In conclusion, the various strands of evidence suggest that Hebrews was written between A.D. 60 and 70, possibly near the middle of the decade.[14]

Theological Issues of these believers:

1. The exaltation of angels does not recognize their subordinate position as servants of God. There are ministering spirits.
2. The deity of the Son of God includes his eternity, unchangeableness, role as creator, terminator, ruler and conqueror. There is Deity
3. The thought that obedience to the tradition and law was sufficient so that ignoring the message of Christ and the apostles could not destabilize their position as a part of the People of God. There are a People of God.
4. The relationship of the mandate of man to rule, links to the incarnation of Christ as a man that did not seem to be fulfilling that original role. There is a Prime Directive.
5. The relation between suffering and death, and the bringing of grace to mankind, really depend on Christ tasting death for every man, not only for Jews. There is Universal provision.
6. The humanity of Christ, seeing he is now glorified, no longer has relevance to the church, while it does for the intercessory work of Christ as priest.. There is constant Intercession.
7. The real possibility of unbelief and rebellion results in hardness of heart, and a repetition of the rebellion that happened at Kadesh. There is a break with historical patterns.
8. The real danger of the converted and those experiencing grace, was a returning to a full-orbed Judaism, with its devaluing of the cross and atonement accomplished once for all. They must be prepared for the destruction of city and temple. There is Closure
9. The understanding of suffering as within the divine plan and not merely attacks by believers, unbelievers or Satan. There is acceptance.
10. The gradual failure to meet for sharing and worship would undercut the community of the faith in a pagan world and is not merely an individual matter. There is a community..
11. Various inadequate views about the pre-history of the Son of God could cut away at the many aspects of Redemption inherent in his deity and humanity and rule over all. There is the Truth about Christ

.12. The focus of faith on faithfulness and obedience as a total response to God could counter Paul's influence as well as the use of every effort to achieve the rest promised by God. There is Centering.

Chapter One:

CHRIST IS GREATER THAN THE PROPHETS AND ANGELS

God's Message, Angels, Son and Eternity.

1.1 'God spoke' ho theos lalesas includes the man who writes it down[15] as well as one who translates it. The antithesis is 'in the past' to 'in these last days,' and this affirms another antithesis of 'God' and 'Son' and 'prophets' versus 'Son.' The former is through 'prophets', which in this period could be used of early leaders from Abraham onward, although the Zohar begins with Moses. The offices of poet, musician and sage are not mentioned, although the rabbis of the Zohar place sages above prophets in rank. The parallel 'by prophets' and 'to fathers' place those events in deep history.

'Many times' indicates a lack of historical continuity, but events not processes. 'Various ways' may include audio-aural, written, dreams, oracles, visions, drama etc. In this is another antithesis of instruments plural versus agents. There is also an assumed discontinuous presence of prophets up to the coming of the Son. This divides sacred history into two periods, the one already closed and the second opened by the revelation through the Son although the phrasing is that the latter was a completed solitary event. Two words polymerws fragmentary, often, many ways corresponds to Louw-Nida's 63.19, 67.11 and 89.81 domains. polytropws means about the same but many different ways. This appears to deny strict continuity or completeness of the OT revelation.

'To the ancestors' has no antecedents to designate Hebrew ancestors nor to designate the patriarchs. A kind of dispensationalism, by way of revelation, shows God speaking through prophets many different ways [acted out, varied genre, dreams, visions,text, oracle, music etc] and times, hence not continually. But the Son wasn't involved in that. According to this verse all revelation is now given through the Son, who did not speak in the OT.[16]

Does the author exclude poets, kings, priests, wise men and women as being instruments God uses for revelation? Sitz im Leben of the author would see 'prophet' as being all inclusive. The OT uses 'prophetess' eight times.[17] While none of the masculine form texts in the OT refer to women linguistically the feminine is marked while the masculine is a lexical form and thus unmarked. Since the masculine of 'prophet' occurs 173 times in the OT the simple proportion would rule for the inclusiveness of use here. The role of women as prophets and their function in society and God's plan needs more study, along with the wise women.[18] 'Wise man' occurs 25 times while 'wise woman' only 3 times. Textual--would this tell us there is only one avenue of revelation through human beings. Angels are skipped over. He does not apparently recognize wise men and priests as media for God to speak since the former are men speaking to men and to God traditional values, while the latter are applying the exhortations and judgments based on canonical law. This verse is simplifying and indirectly asserting the belief in the intertestamental cessation of prophecy. Now there is a new messenger. Note that wise men were sent with oracles and words of wisdom and wisdom in Proverbs is revelation itself. The usage of generic 'prophet' here also is reflected in 1 Pet 1.10-12 and 2 Pet 1.19-21. God is the major topic in the book next to his son, who is the focus of the book.[19] What emphases about God can be gathered from these footnoted verses? Is anything new, which is not found in the OT? The splendor of God is found in Ezekiel 1-3 and 40-48 as well as in Isa 6. But here it is asserted not only that his face glowed, but that Christ was the splendor of the Godhead. Nothing is said of 'glory' in the creation story and so the comparison in this case is not with man, but with God himself. Such language is never used of the Angel of Yahweh. The past is from the "beginning," probably Abel 11.4, through the message of God's son. Variously, the OT 'forefathers' can begin with Abram, Jacob/Israel or Moses, or even David. Note that 11.4 delimits the scope of this, and thus 'forefathers' includes Enoch Gen 4.26. In terms of 'revelation' there are two dispensations, before and after Christ.[BCE, CE[20]]. The two agents are prophets and the Son. Note Judaism reckoned Abraham David and Solomon all as prophets, thus God speaks in the OT era solely through prophets. The two words I thus interpret. I refer multifariously to a diversity as to times and methods. The Greek word polumerows is usually "in many parts." On the other hand, polutropws points out a diversity, in the very manner of revelation. And when this author speaks of the 'last times,' he intimates that there is no longer any reason to expect any new revelation, for it was not a partial word that Christ brought, but the final conclusive word. It is in this sense that the Apostles understand the last times and the last days. Paul means the same when he says, "Upon whom the ends of the world are come." (1 Corinthians 10:11.) Isaiah 40ff mentions all the many times God has predicted events that came to pass and Amos says the pattern is to predict, and then interpret what happened. en with force of dia with the genitive.[21][22] There is a contrast of agents so is it possible that the stress on the Son's position and nature makes 'in' a better and more comprehensive translation. God is speaking not only as a revelation event, such as with other prophets, but in and was the argument by which Aaron and Miriam's complain was answered. through the unique person of Christ. This compares somewhat to Moses in Numbers as uniquely one who saw the face of God, denying any ordinary prophet role to Moses. This It is the person, as in 'you shall be my witnesses' more than simply the witness-message and Paul, in alluding to his calling as apostle is very clear that the person stands behind the verbal message.

1.1-2 en tois profetais is parallel to en huiw v.2., and the Greek would indicate 'in' the person but the Hebrew background shows it is 'through' not en huiw, Compare 2 Sam 23.2 dabar be indicates the agent God used to convey the word. The contrast is thus of media not of word as opposed to the person. Question arises of a comparison of the two Greek phrases whether the definite article in one case is contrasted to its absence in the second case. "In a son' is literal but Buchanan translates "through a Son." [23] Without the monitoring of Hebrew idiom we might suppose God spoke in a different way "in a Son" and not using words. But, while contrast[24] is here in evident, the basic contrast is the finality of the revelation in the Son. Polymerw kai polytropws The previous revelation was 'at many times' and 'various ways' [history, oracle, dreams, visions, wise men etc]. But now [time: an era as well as a literary contrast] the last days are here and it is 'through /in his son.' This is the only time and only way. The book thus begins with evaluation, contrast, climax. Still the idea of 'fulfillment' has not been mentioned.

1.1-ch.2 Dodd analyzed NT citations of OT texts into: ,[25] 1. Apocal-eschatological; 2. Scriptures of the New Israel [this text]; 3. Servant of the Lord and righteous sufferer; 4. Unclassified scriptures. Fitzmyer,[26] 73n. To these should be added biblical allusions that are rooted in historical events of Israel's history and the coming of the Son of God. Events and dialogue in heaven or just before the birth of the Son are also used from Psalms without historical context except for the birth of a king. Poetry that is at the heart of

Israelite worship in the Psalms, all these are the basis of his presentation of the Gospel of the Son.

1.2 'At the end of these days.' 'Last' or 'end' are both correct. But the end of the days or era of the prophets may be in mind and also as an indicator that the End-Time was here. 'Heir of all things' is for a Son only, and as believers we are sons and daughters by adoption. But 'appointed' indicates the Son is not heir by virtue of physical generation, but by God's designation. This use of terminology is almost better than adoption, since the latter has many earthly counterparts that do not correspond to this unique event. The OT designation of Isaac, not Ishmael and Jacob not Esau is similar in the divine action referred to here, and in both divine and human domains the designating occurred before the person's history. The closest parallel is 1 Chronicles 28.7 "He said to me 'Solomon your son is the one who will build my house and my courts. For I have chosen him to be my son, and I will be his father.'"

'Appointed'....'through whom' is a heavenly pattern of apostleship and servanthood. A later argument shows Jesus being appointed High Priest, for no one takes it on himself. Here the pattern is found before creation even began. God commits responsibility and privilege to his Son first including empowerment and then the Son does the same for those He would use. Agency is not an afterthought but part of the very pattern. The Great Commission reflects the same appointment and empowerment to preach the Gospel to all men and cause them to become disciples and new creations. It is for this reason that ch.13 stresses honoring those who have leadership over them because they are so appointed by God. 'heir of all things;' sounds strange except that Israel inherited the land and the promises and the blessings all came through their position as son. 'Let my Son go'. The entrance of the Mosaic covenant rather changed that paradigm. In the NT believers as children of God receive eternal life as their inheritance. God has 'his inheritance in the saints.' In the OT the blessings of Isaac, Jacob and Joseph along with Moses in which they bless in the position of father of Israel, gives a context. Since God cannot die, yet did in Christ, those through whom he transmits his inheritance do, and Moses is the chief example of the last person to die and because of that death Joshua was freed to cross the Jordan. Martyrs inherit and pass on the inheritance of the faithful. Eternal life is not earned but is inherited. the last of these days' reflects Semitic idiom and attitude toward time.[27] But this is definitely NT not OT. From Peter's address in Acts 2 onward there is universal recognition that the last days had arrived.

'Through whom' The scripture never tells us the how of the Son being Agent of God's creating power. In Proverbs Wisdom chokmah is the Agent or instrument of creation, and the parallels, along with John 1 are close indeed. In the NT period one could be tempted to see Aristotle's four kinds of causation or three. Efficient cause, Teleological or final cause, The best analogies are found in how God uses people, making things happen through the orally delivered word of command. Why have an agent, instrument, helper to do what one can do himself? In what sense is 'the Son' the actual creator? How does this correspond to wisdom in Prov 8?;

'To us' indicates to the Jewish people although v.2-13 is universal in scope. The question of the recipients of this treatise includes Jews but may not be limited to them owing to the explanations given for some Jewish rituals and other information non-Jews might not be aware of. Narrowly speaking 'us' could be the original apostles.

'In these last days' is not the 'Day of the Lord' but a time period including Christ's earthly ministry and, based on Christ's word in John 15-17, continued through his apostles.

"Appointed heir" is a problem of chronological sequence, either before or after creation or before and after redemption. In Phil 2 the glory follows the cross. If Christ was 'heir' before creation the inheritance required the death mentioned in Heb 9.16 for it to be valid and the inheritance made available. If the order of these lines chronologically is the reverse sequence, then 1. Spoke; 2. Appointed 3; made takes us backward to the dawn of creation. In this way it is as heir that the son speaks to us. Is the life and ministry of

'The Son' [not 'Christ!!'] in a nutshell. 1.2B His prehistory; 1.3 the cross as an altar for the purification of sins; 1.3 the session of 'the Son' at God's right hand. But in the OT [Deut] the cross or tree is a place of curse in an unclean place! Similar to the brass serpent poisons save lives. Is the cross based on Persian 'exposure' or Assyrian 'hanging' of dead bodies without burial? Can the cross be considered an altar? The phrase is Hebraizing as in Mt 1.11; 1 Pet 1.20 Heb 7.11[28] The reflex of the son as creator is in 11.2. Themes in this chapter will recur as this is a table of contents of a sort, not an index or outline of the book. The Universe, in Hebrew called 'The All' ▯ is not only the galaxy or solar system of earth or the earth system. Nor is the connection to Gen 1.3 absolutely clear, except that there God 'said' and hence 'through the Word' is the same thought as 'The Son.' Note v.2 stresses God speaking through the son now, not aforetime, and thus creating an 'aforetime' and a 'now'. In a sense the work of creation is ongoing, but here what is ongoing is called 'sustaining'. [29] aiwn from Hippocrates on has the sense of 'world' The sense of 'the... course of the world' can easily pass over to 'World'. Mk 4.19; 1 Cor 1.30; 2.6; 3.19. Hellenistic mysteries equated aiwn with kosmos. Late Hebrew developed the concept of universe, in addition to 'heaven and earth'. Hence ha-kol and 'olam sufficed. IV Ezra gives a spatial aspect. II Baruch has both meanings. Rabbinic writings hardly ever document a spatial use for 'olam or 'alma before the First Century CE. The plural aiwnes changes the meaning. Here and in 11.3 'worlds' or 'spheres' are spatial. Note Wisd 13.9 'search out the course of the world' and 14.6 'the later time of the world'; 18.4 could also reflect a Hellenistic deity Aiwn, God of Eternity. Centered in Alexandria. But Philo notes "time is considered a god by the wicked men, who would conceal the really existing One. For which reason Scripture says 'The time of all mankind has come against me.' The Book of Revelations:.

'Who is and was and is to come' reflects rather YHWH, The Eternal. Winston, 257. The reference to past time as an era before the Gospel was stressed in early Christianity in Mk 1.15; Eph 1.10; Heb 1.2[30] Paul's treatment is clear in Gal 4.3-5 called 'the weak and beggardly stoicea'. Note Gal 3-4. The law was temporary.[31]. The law was guardian or regent. Law filled the time between promise and fulfillment Gal 3.16-25; 4.1-5; It was intended to end with the coming of faith Gal 3.23-25 and the arrival of Christ 3.16; 4.4. The promise to Abraham is much broader than the law can encompass, just as a negative command is always narrower than a positive one. Note Gen 12.3,7; 13.15-16;15.5,18; 17.7-8,19;18.18;22.17-18; 26.4; 28.14.[32], Paul understood the resurrection to mean the ushering in of the last days and a new age. Rom 1.4 'resurrection of [not from] the dead.' Acts 2.17; Heb 1.2; Jas 5.3; 1 John 2.18. In 1 Cor 4 9 it is the last act in the amphitheatre; 10.11; 15.45; 1 Thess 2.16 'to the end?' Note Ezek 37 and its relation to apocalyptic chs 38-39, he last war.[33] Use of dia of agency without the force of hypo, thus Jesus is not the absolute independent creator, but the intermediate agent.[34]

Whom he has appointed, heir, etc. He honors Christ with high commendations, in order to lead us to show him reverence; for since the Father has subjected all things to him, we are all under his authority. He also intimates that no good can be found apart from him, as he is the heir of all things. It hence follows that we must be very miserable and destitute of all good things except he supplies us with his treasures. He further adds that this honor of possessing all things belongs by right to the Son, because by him have all things been created. At the same time, these two things are ascribed to Christ for different reasons. The world was created by him, as he is the eternal wisdom of God, which is said to have been the director of all his works from the beginning; and hence is proved the eternity of Christ, for he must have existed before the world was created by him. If, then, the duration of his time be inquired of, it will be found that it has no beginning. Nor is it any derogation to his power that he is said to have created the world, as though he did not by himself create it. According to the most usual mode of speaking in Scripture, the Father is called the Creator; and it is added in some places that the world was created by wisdom, by the word, by the Son, as though wisdom itself had been the creator, [or the word, or the Son.] But still we must observe that there is a difference of persons between the Father and the Son, not only with regard to men, but with regard to God himself. But the unity of essence requires that whatever is peculiar to Deity should belong to the Son as well as to the Father, and also that whatever is applied to God only should belong to both; and yet there is nothing in this to prevent each from his own peculiar properties.

'The effulgence of His glory. While the Son is built upon Wisdom 2-4, Prov 8.22ff, wisdom is the apaugasma of 'everlasting light' or glory. Cf. John 1.1ff; Col. 1.15. Peter refers to this in the Transfiguration experience 2 Pet 1.16-18. This impression is testimonial and a second witness besides the resurrection. See also Ezek 1-2; Rev.1, and Isa 6. Moses halo, in art described as horns, may represent glory.

1.3 Hypostasis "This meaning, however, is not attested in the NT, apart from Heb 1:3, where the Son is the imprint or effigy of the substance of the Father." "the essence of an entity, that which is hidden beneath the appearances."[35] This is the philosophical meaning, since it is not material or physical substance. The same word appears later in Heb 11.1.

'Exact representation of his being' Compare with Phil 2 and Gen 1, no longer is man in the image of God, only the Son is, and more so, the exact representation.' It is clear that idols are the gravest insult to Almighty God. As in John 1.18 the only way to know God is to know Jesus. Jesus said 'I am the Way, Truth and Life. 'exact representation' No Christian will ever have the same glory, and power, even in a derived sense. Adam did not have the glory and power or knowledge. Thus this is not a statement linked to 'Second Adam' theology, but an altogether new sense.

'For sins' and not 'for the sinner'. The sinner needs reconciliation and forgiveness, a declaration of cleanness and restoration to fellowship in the worshipping serving community. But sins need something as separate from the sinner. The mass of sins does exist as an entity and the 'sins' of the Amorites and aborigines is quantified in those passages that speak of eliminating the people from the sacred land of Israel. In Christ 10.14,11 says this mass has been dealt with in Christ's sacrifice once and for all. 'glory' 'nature' and 'word' are somehow parallel here. The glory is the presence of God revealed on crucial occasions to select persons, such as Jacob at Peniel, Moses, at Sinai, the three apostles in Caesarea, and possibly Elijah at Horeb. Isaiah saw the glory and was told it fills the whole earth. So the presence of God in power is the glory. But the Son is only a reflection of this glory much as the reflection of God's grace transforms the believer. The 'image of the nature' is related to Titus chapter one, where we are told that we have been made partakers of the divine nature. The only original image of God was Adam or man; now the only image is in the Son. The implication is that so much other than the nature of God is active in man that only one person is truly the image of God. God is invisible, but without holiness [ch.12] no man can see God'. The implication is that peace on the horizontal plane and holiness on the vertical restore the image of God so that we can see that which we reflect. The 'Word' here is that which allows history and nature to go on. It is the word of power and 'upholding' must be read understanding the ANE background of pillars of cosmology and the OT image of Rock or Foundation. Since it is the Word of power it is not passive at all but consists of God's decrees for every day.

'His powerful word' is continued later as a two edged sword that opens the heart and mind through the Gospel. This is the initial phase of taking out the heart of stone and imparting a heart of flesh. The Word is powerful in creation, sustaining and in redeeming. 'made purification for sins' is not for people but corresponds to the Day of Atonement when purification is made for the sanctuary, utensils, Levites and priests and the whole of the people, an act of kipper to normalize their use as avenues of worship and reconciliation.

Kypru is the cover of the ark, or mercy seat, the throne of God. The verb could be to cover, rub on[oil] or from another root 'purify.' The Day of Atonement is the type for which Christ's atonement is the antitype. The purification took place and then came the session at the Father's right hand. Did this purification take place in the heavenly sanctuary? If so it was accomplished and need not per SDA theology, wait till 1840 or some other date, which in fact, separates this event from the cross and resurrection and makes Christ's rule postponed till the end time. This confirms two persons in the Godhead, the throne and the seat on the right side of the Majesty on high. This is in heaven not in the tabernacle on earth. While Hebrews reflects the temple is still standing the first chapter might indicate it is not. For the Diaspora it is good to know that the throne room is in heaven and thereby unshakeable. The Son is both the radiance of God's glory, the divine aspect and the representation of his being, a role originally conferred on Adam. Paul called Christ the last Adam. The glory was revealed to the apostle on the mount of transfiguration. Nothing is said about it after the resurrection event. But 'I and the Father are one' and the expression egw eimi must confirm the meaning of YHWH. But Jesus himself used the term 'Son of Man' or 'human' and as God in flesh he condemned sin in the flesh. John 1 deals with this revelation defined not as a mere phenomenon but as 'grace and truth.' Cf. also John 17. The Son was not only the agent of creation but is the current sustainer of all things by his word. This eliminates Deism as a theology. The 'by his ...word' goes back to the initial creation of Gen 1.2-3 and here includes creation and sustaining. Without God's Word this universe could not continue as such.

'Sat down at the right hand of the Majesty in heaven.' Both Phil 2 and Heb 1.3 make this a result of the redemptive work, a culmination of his emptying himself and not seizing equality with God, which he still does not seize it. The OT Dan 7 shows this same Son of Man coming to the Ancient of Days and being given all power and authority, still the Ancient of Days is the one on the throne. There still are no two thrones or more. 'Sat down at the right hand' indicates subordination in any kind of metaphor, yet to nothing but God Himself. It is by virtue of completing purification for sins that he is now seated in power. Paul, in 1 Cor 15 indicates Christ must rule till all enemies are placed beneath his feet and then the kingdom will be handed back to the Divine Majesty. The previous verses indicate full divinity, and the following indicate a break with any equivalent stature with angels. "he sat down' is adduced by F.F. Bruce[36] to be founded on OT analogies, first of words spoken to the Davidic king in Ps 110.1, and then in the regular preaching of the apostles. Acts 2.33ff; Rom 8.34; 1 Pet 3.22; Rev 3.21b. Here it speaks of the perfect and unrepeatable quality of the redemptive sacrifice, never to be repeated. Note it was the royal prerogative of David and his descendants to admit men to sit in the presence of God. 2 Sam 7.18; Ezek 44.3. Note that Hebrew can mean to sit or lie down, and in the plural

'Inhabitants of' and except where a throne is mentioned the usage can be ambiguous. [37]Ex. 12:29.; 1Kings 2:12.; 1Chr. 29:23 So Solomon sat on the throne of the LORD as king in place of his father David. He prospered and all Israel obeyed him.[38]. This material suggests the worthiness of a study to see links between the Book of Revelation and Hebrews. Here the focus may not be position relative to the throne but to the right hand of God. The following verses give a framework, while the footnote[39] gives a broader context. A preliminary judgment is that the right hand is the executor or executive function. Psa. 77:10 Then I thought, "To this I will appeal: the years of the right hand of the Most High." "the 'session' of Christ here and in Phil 2 followed the purification for sins. This verse contradicts SDA claims that the heavenly atonement only took place in 1840. There is no OT model for a ruler to be seated after functioning as high priest, except possibly for Melchizedek. apaugazw

"Shine out, emit rays of light and perceive emitted rays"; apaugasmos= "shining rays of light. "In its choice of the word apaugasma, Hebrews suggests rays of light emanating from a bright fire, with the idea of splendor, magnificence, beauty; the brilliance of Majesty. Hence, in the passive sense: refulgence, as Littre said:": the great brilliance formed by the expansion, the reflection of light." Perceptible by mortals."[40] eikwn This brings in the theme of conformity to the image of the son in Rom 8.29[41]. 2 Cor 4.4.;[42] "Glory [doxa] is participation in the divine nature [2 Pet 1.4; Heb 1.3] and puts the emphasis on luminous manifestation Matt 17.2; Mk 9.2. Cf. . 1 Cor 6.17;419; contrasts with in that it is only of God not men[43] karaktēr the exact representation of his being'-Louw&Nida. NT "the One on whom God has stamped or imprinted his being. This means that the NT use is entirely different from our modern concept of 'character' which develops itself by a will that seeks to conform to principles." NIDNTT. This is not English character' but approaches 'nature.'. Note that in derivation it is like the original; "is a noun derived from charassw 'notch,' 'indent,' and means 'one who sharpens, scratches,' and later 'one who writes in stone, wood or metal.' Thence it came to mean an 'embosser' and a stamp for making coins, and from this, looking to the result, the 'embossed stamp made on the coin,' character in writing, style. Finally, it came to mean the basic bodily and psychological structure with which one is born, which is unique to the person and which cannot be changed by education or development, though it may be hidden or effaced. Hence, it also means 'individuality, personal characteristics.' In Philo the human soul is called the charaktēr of divine power and the Logos is entitled the charaktēr of God." NIDNTT. megalwsynē does not appear in the papyri and is a divine attribute. Ps 145.3; Enoch 5.4 "Yahweh is great and worthy of praise, and his majesty is unsearchable." It is associated with his power in Ps 79.11[44]. In Sir 2.18 it is associated with God's mercy "as is his majesty, so also his mercy' 18.5 "who can measure the strength of his greatness? And who will attempt to tell of his mercy.?" Ep.Arist. 192;[45] megaloprepēs in the Bible is always a designation for God as in Deut 33.26; 2 Macc 8.15. At the transfiguration the voice comes from the 'magnificent glory' meaning the divine glory. A similar word is here in Heb 1.3 megalwsyne. But in secular Greek megaloprepes is the opposite of tapeinwteron. In Hermias, the year 112 BC he asks Horus to receive the Roman senator Lucius Memmius with 'special magnificence.' Megalopreses_is an adjective used of Jeremiah in 2 Macc 15.13 and in the 5th through 7th centuries of anyone being honored or asked for a favor, of a benefactor, master, archwn, consuls. In the 8th century it is a formula in letter writing 'your magnificent Brotherliness' and 'I embrace your Magnificence through this letter.' The noun megaleiotes expresses the grandeur of God Dan 7.27 reflecting Hebrew rebu, and Solomon in 2 Esdr 4.10. It is used of the greatness of pyramids, first century, an honorific title, and of the emperor from the first century on. Claudius wrote to the Alexandrians in 41"Each one reading this letter individually will wonder at the majesty of our god Caesar and show gratitude."[46]. Rabbis called God megale doxa. Gen 43.34 uses rabah ''surpass, become more abundant' Zech 12.7; Am 8.5 of making a weight bigger, having worth 1 Sam 26.24; Jdt 12.18; Eccl 2.9 'I became great and surpassed those before me in Jerusalem.' 1.16; 2.4. In 1 Sam 2.21,26;3.19 and Ezk 16.7 gadal expresses greatness.As a verb it refers to glorifying someone or something.[47] Cf. . Ps 69.31 and Lk 1.46. Phil 1.20 and T.Levi 18.3 "his star rises in the sky...the light of knowledge shines...kai megalunthesetai en te oikoumene. 1 QM 11.15 says "to show your greatness and holiness in the eyes of the rest of the nations."For megalwsyne, unknown in papyri, gedolah is found in Ps 145.3 reads "Yahweh is great and worthy of praise, and his majesty [gedolah] is unsearchable" In Ps 79.11 "By the greatness [godel] of your arm, preserve those condemned to death." Prov 18.10 Sir 2.18 "as is his majesty, so also his mercy." 18.5. "who can measure the strength of his greatness?" At Qumran "Words of the Book that Michael spoke to the Angels" calls God "the Majesty, the Master of the world." And Sir 44.2 "this majesty from eternity."; Enoch 5.4 "you offend his majesty" Wis.18.24 18.24; "your majesty was on the diadem of his [Aaron's] head." T.Levi 3.9 "the face of his majesty." 18.8.[48] Purification for sins reflects the Day of Atonement, where sins create the need not only for forgiveness, but for cleansing. Here 'purification' defines kipper not as a covering over, but as a cleansing. He is both the gift offered for cleansing the holy [place and things from long-term defilement, but also the Azazel to the rid of the sins from the midst of the dwellings of the covenant people. Purification of sin and the Son's session on the throne are joined almost as if the purification took place in heaven. The SDA Church sought a future time for this heavenly purification, which this text will not allow. Whenever and wherever it happened it is past tense and completed. Purification in the OT involves all sacred things and locations, but the one great purification on the Day of Atonement was in the Most Holy Place. The context of this paragraph does not seem to have this one line only as located on earth, while all other lines are in heaven. But if it occurred on earth the heavenly real temple is still a fact, while the earthly one does not seem to be the place of atonement in this Epistle's soteriology. 1.1-4 all seem to happen in heaven. But on earth, to sum up the Son's whole saving work as making purification then becomes the reason why the saving work is finished, and 'sat down' could indicate some sort of Sabbath after all the other work has been done. Chapter 4 stresses the completing of the work and the rest that follows. Refers to Ps 110.1 often quoted in Hebrews. His place is at God's right hand. How this correlates with disciples for whom it is prepared to sit on Jesus left and right is unclear. Clearly the place of honor the quote still subordinates the king of Israel, or the Messiah who is the Son to 'The Majesty.' In this case the position is gained by his redemptive work so the Redeemer is enthroned. According to Revelation there are many thrones and crowns and believers will reign with him; just what this means is never specified. V.4 'having become' points to a change in the Son whereas change could never be predicated of God Himself. Several times the content of Ps 68.18; is mentioned in the NT. "When you ascended on high, you led captives in your train; you received gifts from men, even from the rebellious--that you, O Lord God, might dwell there." The events seemed to be connected first of all, with the wilderness and Israelite history. V.8 speaks of earthquakes and rain even though v.7 speaks of the wastelands. God is 'the One of Sinai' and he brought about settlement, no conquest [in vv 8-10]. The conquest seems to follow settlement vv.11-14.Then the Gilead earlier conquest vv.15-16 is called to look at mount Zion.V.17. Here God is coming to reign, to dwell, from Sinai, into his sanctuary. Thus the ark represented God ascending on high into the sanctuary on Zion v.18. The 'captives' are possibly people like the Gibeonites. The 'gifts' would be David and Solomon's extravagant offerings v.18. And it is recognized that Israel and even David and Solomon were 'the rebellious.' The Psalm is a national Psalm, mentioning the tribes, and both petition and praise abounds; petition for victory and supremacy over nations; praise to 'the one 'who rides the ancient skies above.'

God is in his sanctuary and is worthy of the praise of all peoples. Note that in view of the Book of Hebrews' heavenly antitype and earthly type theology the sanctuary can easily be transferred to a heavenly sphere. The one riding the clouds is the Lord of the Ascension. And the entering of the sanctuary is His Session. The fact that 'He gives power and strength to his people' would be recognized by the early church as descriptive of the Day of Pentecost and outpouring of the Spirit. Eph 4.8 changes the verb "He led captives in his train and gave gifts to men.' It is redirected to the gift of the Spirit and the orders of ministry that the Gifts of the Spirit created. The 'captives' are referred to those who heard the Gospel through Christ in Sheol, before the resurrection.

"When he ascended on high" no longer is 'riding the clouds' but a direct reference to the ascension. Thus the NT converts the text to prophecy, and more so, as an historical prologue, harbinger, preview and type of the acts of Jesus in redemption. spaugasma .according to Louw and Nida, could be active 'radiance' or passive 'reflection.' The latter would be appropriate for the Son of Man or man as anointed or as Moses' face shown. The former would be the shine as the source of light that has no difference from God's glory. Cf. . John 17.

The 'right hand' is God's, not the 'Son's'. Thus Jesus could not give this position to any two of his disciples. But The 'Son' also has a throne and he said there are those selected to bit on his left and right. The Principle is that the one on the throne is appointed under God's plan and appointment and hence this is not a momentary decision or choice. It is not based on prior commitment to James or John, but is in the decision -making prerogative of the 'Majesty.' The powerful word appears again in 4.12-13, here as having sustaining force. 11.1 asserts the Word power in creation. 12.4 is rather the word of encouragement, but in a context of the disciplines of God in the 'sons' lives. Note the contrast there between the 'Son' and 'sons.' The presentation of the Son as equal to God required delicacy lest a dualism or pluralism or polytheism should be created. God made man in his image, which was originally true of Adam. Otherwise, only David is a man after God's heart and Ps 2 celebrates the authority, power, respect, honor, position, of the Son as equal to God's.

The quote repeatedly of Psalm 110 [Here Ps 110.1], just as Ps 1, seems to be an oracle on the accession of earthly king to the throne, pronouncing God's plan and blessing. In the ANE this would normally come at New Years, or when a new king moves from the year of accession to the first year of his reign, presumably at New Years. But later this is declared as spoken by God Father to the Son, since the same person is addressed as high priest after the order of Melchizedek, not Levi. As addressed to the human/divine Son of God the reign as Priest-King is eternal. The Psalm omits Zion and Israel, because, as addressed to the Son of God, the 'nations' here includes all nations, much in the vein of Daniel's prophecy. If a prophet speaks this Psalm to the earthly king quoting God's words, then v.7 affirms that God is Immanuel, is with the king, and God will bring the victory. V.7 reminds us of Jonathan eating honey before battle and Samson also having honey and at Lehi God opening a fount of water for him. Jesus found a well in Samaria, and the conversion of the woman and many in that village is a first-taste of the judging of nations and crushing of kings.

For this reason the Acts of the Apostles stresses the conversion of certain Samaritans. The word apaugasma means here nothing else but visible light or refulgence, such as our eyes can bear; and charakter is the vivid form of a hidden substance. By the first word we are reminded that without Christ there is no light, but only darkness; for as God is the only true light by which it behaves us all to be illuminated, this light sheds itself upon us, so to speak, only by irradiation. By the second word we are reminded that God is truly and really known in Christ; for he is not his obscure or shadowy image, but his impress which resembles him, as money the impress of the die with which it is stamped. But the Apostle indeed says what is more than this, even that the substance of the Father is in a manner engraven on the Son. The word which, by following others, I have rendered substance, denotes not, as I think, the being or essence of the Father, but his person; for it would be strange to say that the essence of God is impressed on Christ, as the essence of both is simply the same.

But it may truly and fitly be said that whatever peculiarly belongs to the Father is exhibited in Christ, so that he who knows him knows what is in the Father. And in this sense do the orthodox fathers take this term, hypostasis, considering it to be threefold in God, while the essence (ousia) is simply one. Hilary everywhere takes the Latin word substance for person. But though it be not the Apostle's object in this place to speak of what Christ is in himself, but of what he is really to us, yet he sufficiently confutes the Asians and Sabellians; for he claims for Christ what belongs to God alone, and also refers to two distinct persons, as to the Father and the Son. For we hence learn that the Son is one God with the Father, and that he is yet in a sense distinct from him, so that a subsistence or person belongs to both. And upholding (or bearing) all things, etc. To uphold or to bear here means to preserve or to continue all that is created in its own state; for he intimates that all things would instantly come to nothing, were they not sustained by his power. Though the pronoun his may be referred to the Father as well as to the Son, as it may be rendered "his own," yet as the other exposition is more commonly received, and well suits the context, I am disposed to embrace it. Literally it is, "by the word of his power;" but the genitive, after the Hebrew manner, is used instead of an adjective; for the perverted explanation of some, that Christ sustains all things by the word of the Father, that is, by himself who is the word, has nothing in its favor: besides, there is no need of such forced explanation; for Christ is not wont to be called rhma, saying, but logon, word.

Hence the "word" here means simply a nod; and the sense is, that Christ who preserves the whole world by a nod only, did not yet refuse the office of effecting our purgation. Now this is the second part of the doctrine handled in this Epistle; for a statement of the whole question is to be found in these two chapters, and that is, that Christ, endued with supreme authority, ought to be head above all others, and that as he has reconciled us to his Father by his own death, he has put an end to the ancient sacrifices. And so the first point, though a general proposition, is yet a tea of old clause. When he further says, by himself, there is to be understood here a contrast, that he had not been aided in this by the shadows of the Mosaic Law.

He shows besides a difference between him and the Levitical priests; for they also were said to expiate sins, but they derived this power from another. In short, he intended to exclude all other means or helps by stating that the price and the power of purgation were found only in Christ. Sat down on the right hand, etc.; as though he had said, that having in the world procured salvation for men, he was received into celestial glory, in order that he might govern all things. And he added this in order to show that it was not a temporary salvation he has obtained for us; for we should otherwise be too apt to measure his power by what now appears to us.

He then reminds us that Christ is not to be less esteemed because he is not seen by our eyes; but, on the contrary, that this was the height of his glory, that he has been taken and conveyed to the highest seat of his empire. The right hand is by a similitude applied to God, though he is not confined to any place, and has not a right side nor left. The session then of Christ means nothing else but the kingdom given to him by the Father, and that authority which Paul mentions, when he says that in his name every knee should bow. (Philippians 2:10) Hence to sit at the right hand of the Father is no other thing than to govern in the place of the Father, as deputies of princes are wont to do to whom a full power over all things is granted. And the word majesty is added, and also on high, and for this purpose, to intimate that Christ is seated on the supreme throne whence the majesty of God shines forth. As, then, he ought to be loved on account of his redemption, so he ought to be adored on account of his royal magnificence[49].

1.3 This reflects Gen 1.27 'exact representation of his being' bout not created, as Adam was. The 'radiance of his glory' was not a part of OT creation theology, since man is made like God in two respects, not in all respects. The'Glory' is what God bestows on man through salvaticn, realized and anticipated. No man by nature, before or after the 'Fall,' has 'Glory.' John 1.14. the Glory of the One and Only is interpreted to mean 'full of grace and truth'. But he 'became flesh'. Jesus' earthly life is described in John in drastic contrast to the solitary event of the Transfiguration and Ascension [a minimalist interpretation.' But Peter was greatly impressed by the Transfiguration on the mount and speaks of that event as 'having seen his glory' on the mount. The 'Mount' recalls Ancient Near Eastern common theology about Mount Zaphon and the Bible about Sinai, Horeb, Zion, Nebo, Hermon, Gerizim and Ebal. The place God reveals himself in theophany is 'on the mountain'. John 17 has a word play on 'Glory' as a prayer 1. T once again possess the eternal glory v.5; 2. To share that glory with the disciples; 3. And to bring glory to God. Possession of the Glory alone makes one capable of glorifying God. The purpose of Jesus' prayer has widespread ramifications for his disciples, Paul also used this text directly or indirectly in Rom 8.34; 1 Cor 15.25; Col 3.1 and Eph 1.20. Cf. . Mk 12.36; 14.62; Acts 2.34-35; Heb 8.1; 10.12; 12.2; 1 Pet 3.22. Based on Ps110.1 'my lord' is known by early Christians as Jesus the Messiah. He was now God's vice-regent.

The installation to Lordship is linked to the resurrection Rom 8.34. The resurrection began Christ's reign as Lord 1 Cor 15.23,24-25 and included is the 'Session' in Col 3.1. The clearest is Eph 1.20, [50] , The potency of the Word of God comes out in Isa 11.4; 55.11; Ps 18.8,13; Rev 11.5; 19.15; 2 Thess 2.8; Ps.Sol 17.27; 1 En 62.2; Jer 5.14 and II Esdras 13.10"...he did not so much as raise his hand, or take a spear, or any other weapon of war, I saw only how he discharged from his mouth, as it were, a torrent of fire and from his lips a 'flaming blast'; and from his tongue he poured forth a 'gust of sparks.' All of these were joined together--the torrent of fire, the flaming blast, and the powerful gust. Then it descended upon the onrushing host that had determined to fight and cremated all [of them]."

Suddenly nothing of the innumerable host was apparent except powdery ashes and the smell of smoke, so that I was astonished when I saw it. Afterwards I saw the man himself come down from the mountain and summon to himself another, peaceful host. Many persons of [different] appearances joined themselves top him--some were joyful, some sad, some in shackles, some leading [others] of them as offerings" Note 'the man came from the sea and was flying with the clouds of heaven[51] Note that apaugazw "shine out, emit rays of light and perceive emitted rays' relates to apaugasmos 'shining, rays of light' Hebrews uses apaugasma rays of light emanating from a bright fire, with the idea of splendor, magnificence, beauty; the brilliance of Majesty., and passively "refulgence" the "great brilliance formed by the expansion, the reflection of light" as perceived by mortals[52] ,Theognostus, head of school in Alexandria from 265-282 used Wisd. Saying "the Logos is also called the radiance of the glory of God' an unspotted mirror [Wisd 7.26]. Athanasius preserved another fragment: 'The ousia of the Son originated from the ousia of the Father like radiance from light, like vapor from water' [Wisd. 7.25-26]. Silvanus's hymns allude to Wisd 7.25-26 "For he [the Logos] is a light from the power of God, and he is an emanation of the pure glory of the Almighty, and he is the spotless mirror of the activity of God, and he is the image of his goodness. For he is also the light of the Eternal Light' [53]. Who being the brightness of his glory, etc. These things are said of Christ partly as to his divine essence, and partly as a partaker of our flesh. When he is called the brightness of his glory and the impress of his substance, his divinity is referred to; the other things appertain in a measure to his human nature. The whole, however, is stated in order to set forth the dignity of Christ. But it is for the same reason that the Son is said to be "the brightness of his glory", and "the impress of his substance:" they are words borrowed from nature. For nothing can be said of things so great and so profound, but by similitudes taken from created things. There is therefore no need to discuss to refinedly the question how the Son, who has the same essence with the Father, is a brightness emanating from his light. We must allow that there is a degree of impropriety in the language when what is borrowed from created things is transferred to the hidden majesty of God. But why is he so described as only a representation, precisely what man-Adam was supposed to be? Is it because the essence of the godhead cannot be described in words that humans use? Or is it because as Phil.2 says the elevation of Jesus to the highest position of equality with God was a result of his redeeming work and person.? So now in these verses we see the glorified Lord in his native element and all of this is 'God's glory' revealed in him. 'Through whom' occurs 12 times.Rom 5.2,11; 1 Cor 3.5; 8.6 have to do with the Christ.

If man's productivity commanded in Gen 1 is a continuation of God's creation, then the Jewish concept that creation was left unfinished so that man might complete it. In harmony with this exegesis is the command to rule all animal life forms, which was later interpreted to rule and manage the world as in Ps 8 cited in Heb 2.6-8. In this case God the Father as a team created the structure, infrastructure, life forms, and man, while God and man create and classify the names and use the botanical forms. The two witness rule, two apostles together, and husband-wife pair, with emphasis in Gen 1 and ch.6 on 'by twos' can be elucidated.Christ will judge the world and believers will judge the world are not a contradiction. Earthly society depends on the relation of a man and God and a man with husband if creation is to be finished. The 'Good' of creation is not our 'good' but God's making the world and man precisely as he wanted it, not as we want it. Therefore challenge, tests, temptations, goals, purpose, and effort are built in to original creation. A concept of Rabbis that the evil tendency and good tendency are not the result of the 'Fall' but are part of the original plan. Without which man cannot become complete.Oswald Chambers[54]for Dec 11,12 focuses on personality versus individuality, an antagonism necessary for growth. The creative power of two is seen in Peter and John at the temple Acts 3.1. It is seen in the witness of The Spirit with my spirit' in Rom 8.16. and the fruit of the Spirit of Gal 5.16-25. Linking Wisdom of James 3 and Spirit creative things can happen. Jesus did miracles which the Father did 'for My Father works hitherto and I work.' Prov teaches as does Amos on the power of two. If two or three agree on earth as touching any thing is shall be done.' Often 'The Spirit and the Word' or 'Spirit and the Bride.' The Father's witness, Christ's witness and the miracles witness. In Paul's words so much was done 'through someone' 1 Kgs 22.8 to inquire of the Lord; Lk 17.1 through a person causing others to sin and the others sinning. ! Pet 3.19 Through the Spirit Christ preached to the spirits in prison. In Proverbs creation is God through Wisdom.

1.3 Purification for sin and session at the right hand are the priestly and kingly roles of the Messiah. In 12.28 'We receiving a kingdom' explicitly closes the argument portion of the book. Luke closes Acts also on the note of Paul preaching the kingdom in Rome. But the features of the kingdom do permeate this book. Christ's prophetic role is minimized here. The Second Coming is not a topic as such. The relation of priest and purification is very clear in many chapters, but the priestly and kingly relation isn't really clarified except that the reward for the sacrifice of himself is the resurrection and session on God's right hand. Session does emphasize the finality of his work without discussing the next phase. He is the Davidic king of Ps 110. Cf. Acts 2.33ff; Rom 8.34; 1 Pet 3.22; Rev 3.21. Priest's never sat while ministering, but Eli did, but at the time he wasn't sacrificing. Samuel was sleeping in the holy place when her heard God speak, but not yet a priest. Cf. . 2 Sam 7.18; Ezk 44.3.

1.3-13 The term kurios in "the use..of Ps 110.1 elsewhere in the NT clearly emphasizes Jesus' exaltation to Lordship and heavenly glory[see Mk 16.19; 1 Cor 15.25; Eph 1.20; Col.1.3; Heb 8.1; 10.12,13; 12.2] and at times stands in contrast to his Davidic relationship [Acts 2.29-35; 13.23-39; Heb 1.3-13.Fitzmyer,[55] Jesus is now and always superior to angels, human and more, and subordinate in his person to God the Father, since he sits at the Father's right hand. All authority has been given him until the Father makes all enemies subject to him after which Jesus will turn the kingdom over to the Father.

1.4 'Angels' is never used of bad angels in Pauline writings except hypothetically in Galatians. Sensuality is never attributed to good angels in and Christian or Jewish writings of the period. 1 Cor 13.1; Mt 13.49; 25.31; Lk 16.22; Fitzmyer,[56]197a. .

'Superior' is a basic theme of the book and here is initially applied to those who elevated angels in worship. Col 2.18 and Rev 19.10. Kreittwn 'more excellent' appears 13 times in Hebrews. Thus long before the second century the worship of angels was in evidence. The comparative used as such and also as superlative is found in many proverbs in the Books of Proverbs 4.

'He became as much superior..' is a change of status from the preincarnational Son. But is the 'Son' v.3 preincarnational or post-ascensional? Did this change only begin at the resurrection or did it begin with the inauguration of Jesus' ministry in his baptism in Jordan when the father spoke to him in John's hearing 'This is my beloved son.'?

When did He inherit the' Name'? Is it YHWH or Jesus? If most of this occurred post-incarnational then very little speaks to the situation before it. v.2 refers to the past and v.3 the present—after the ascension. What Name did he inherit that is superior to all the names of all the angels? The only unique name in the Hebrew Scriptures is the tetragrammaton. The short form yw might appear in Ugarit, and does in Hebrew personal names as yo- or –ya. But in the times of the writing of this book it was pronounced Adonai and translated kurios.. The various representations in Mari as ya- are verbal preformatives not names. YHWH does not correspond to hyh in verbal form. But in Ugarit yesh, a noun is used of Baal's resurrection, but merely means 'exists'. Some say this name is a mystery but also that He will in that time receive a new name. Phil. 2 says 'at the name of Jesus every knee shall bow.' Yah-is Savior' is a name in the Hebrew Scriptures but not so used of God. "That point is called Ani (I) (Lev. XIX, 30), and upon it rests the unknown, the Most High, the unrevealed One which is TETRAGRAMMATON (the Lord), both being one.'"[57] YHWH belongs to Israel. It is also a mystery.

'He became:' in what sense is the 'Son' the God who does change, not the immutable? Why was it necessary for God to change, and to do it through the Son.?

'Inherited' is not because God died, but means 'received' by virtue of being a Son and believers being joint heirs. The genre requires 'received' in a non-gift and non-inheritance sense. In the Near East besides distribution of property at a death there was also distribution before death as was the case of the Prodigal son

'The name he obtained' The OT background is the name change for Jacob, Sarah, Abraham and even Jerubbabel, although differing in many particulars. The changes in the name of the true God are indicated by a change from El to Elohim or El Shaddai to YHWH. The name 'Jesus' was given by God and man. While certain kings had two names, in the case of Zedekiah the name change indicated a different superior monarch as one's lord. But in Phil 2 the name is given after atonement is accomplished. In Revelation a new name is promised to Jesus and to every believer. To obtain a new name indicates completion of a certain role that was divinely ordained. So just as Jesus now has a body, a glorified body, so he also received a new name. Usually in historical narrative a new name is a new phase of personal and salvation history and if in heaven new names are given that would indicate heaven has an eternal history.

'The name' inherited must be 'Jesus,' since it is as a person the name was given by revelation from God and also from angels and the earthly legal father. This name continues in heaven. So while 'Son' existed from eternity, 'Jesus' did not. The use of 'inherited' is unique here perhaps indicating the first gift of the Father to the Son.

"He became" indicates a growth and phase in the life of the Eternal Son. This was due to the name "Jesus" and the completion of redemption? Phil 2 also indicates a cause-effect relationship between what Jesus did in the incarnation and atonement and his exaltation. On the one hand, he didn't seize equality with God, on the other he was rewarded with the name above all other names. Do we know that name? Both texts stress the result of death on the cross and the suffering that entailed as preliminary to Christ's exaltation, in Phil 2.9 with a name above every name, worthy of obeisance and honor and confession as Lord and in Heb 1.4, being made superior to all angels. Both texts have an heavenly aspect ['in heaven and on earth and under the earth' which apparently includes angels, men and any other beings with knees, while Hebrews stresses the session on God's hand far above all names and honor. The 'Name' theology enters here. The 'name he has inherited' par' autou keklēronosmēken onoma is not clear. Phil 2.9,10 makes it clear the name 'Jesus Christ is Lord' goes beyond a simple name theology. Does this imply that at one point he was not greater than angels by much? What is the 'name' the author is speaking of? Kreittwn 'superior' occurs 13 times in the epistle, of Christ and the new order and is a buzz word for the message being conveyed, but perhaps not the outline of salient points.. The basic OT pattern is in Proverbs where the son/student/disciple is instructed to choose the better of two options, stressing really the choice of the best. The writer cannot win Jews to the Gospel if he/she rejects the validity of the old order; but he must make clear the contrast to demonstrate that type and prophecy fulfillment were occurring.

'Inherited' requires a death of the bequeather, is this translation in error? Why is this language used? The 'better' name, and inheritance are not original but occur within historical processes. Note this word used in a certain type of proverb., Instrumental case of measure 'for a long time' Acts 8.11. here 'degree of difference' [58] The NT stresses Jesus as kurios, and the name Jesus. Bousset asserted:" As the cohesiveness and the knowledge of God of the old covenant were conditioned and determined by the sacred name of Yahweh, so is the unity of the new religious fellowship dominated by the name of Jesus. In this sense it is meant that the Father has given his name to the Son." Cf. John 17.11,6,26. Eph 1.21; Heb 1.4; Baptism is in the name of the kurios Jesus Christ 1 Cor 6.11; Acts 19.5.[59]Parke-Taylor,104[60]

1.5 'This day I have become your father.' This is in the OT and not prophecy, since it is in the past tense, the author uses seven quotations from the OT to prove to Jewish readers that Jesus was superior to angels. Were some Jews worshipping angels? The church refused to see this verse as indicating that Christ was created somewhere this side of eternity, a view that will not hold up in this context. If not at baptism or birth was it in eternity? The 'I come to do thy will O Lord' would indicate the son's obedience to the Father began in eternity at a point where the role of 'Son' was conferred on the 'Son.'

There is no theogony but Adoption and Assignment to a role of the most complete seeking to complete all the will and desire of the Father. This asserts the Son never was an 'angel' even though he was 'sent' nor is he called 'Apostle'. The word mala'k except in the phrase 'Angel of YHWH' is not used clearly of Jesus. This cites 2 Sam 7 on Christ's divine Sonship, Fulfillment [per.13] is as in 2 Sam prophecy #12. Payne,[61]573; Fitzmyer,[62]33n, Composite citation formula.appears in 67n, 86, 197n; 'Will be my son' is this contingent on events historically or in a declarative mode should the translation be revised.? Originally this was said to Solomon and also in Psalm 2. Does this go back to a moment in prehistory or to the eve of the birth of Christ, or to his baptism when a voice from heaven declared this? If the latter, was sonship just then initiated? How do declarations of this sort grow out of an ANE background? Could God have said 'from today on you are my Son.'?

According to ANE law a formula would make it true. Then the relationship would be adoptive. Theoretically it would be possible. But v.1 identifies this one as 'His Son' and not adopted. But ANE usage is for adoption as heir usually and 'adoption' as king occurs in a different genre of hymns or royal domain about the king and God. This is not strictly 'adoption.' Cf. . Ps 2. Note in Hosea 1.8-11. If the believer is adopted and Jesus is elder brother, what makes him unique except that he really is God's son in a much deeper way. God's words to Solomon are still not deep enough. relates to Ps 2.7, which is in the Sitz im Leben of a new king being seated on his throne as God's son, God's anointed v.2. At times of a new king foreign satellite kings frequently regarded all treaties as null and void, which they were not, and sought to relieve themselves of the obligations of tribute. The early days of Darius and Haggai exemplified the tendency for the whole empire to be in turmoil. But God has installed his king, there is an installation decree pronounced v.7 announcing sonship, a legal formula 'you are my Son." There are promises, such as those offered to Solomon, but in this case the entirety of the earth. The prophecy and promise is to rule with an iron scepter. Therefore all kings and rulers must be warned. "Kiss the Son" would correspond to the 'footstool' ritual. The Psalm closes with a blessing on those who take refuge in the Son. The concrete situation in the OT period and the formulas do not becloud the fact that it is only the Christ that will actually rule all the kings of the earth.

The thrice repeated Hebrew stresses an eternally present fact huios mou ei su, removed from the Semitic legal formula to assert Christ's eternal sonship not an installation ritual. The next line egw semeron gegennekas se declares a present fact and in context refers to Christ's birth in Bethlehem. Part of the scenario in Heb 1-2 is the birth of the Savior, his humanity. The third line Egw esomai autw ei patera is the same promise made to Israel as 'Son' reiterating similarly the mutuality kai auto estai moi ei uios of that relationship. The 'Son,' namely the Christ, has now come to substitute for Israel. None of these lines stresses the eternal Sonship but rather the decision to come to earth as Savior, which reappears later in the book. The promise in 2 Samuel is to David for his son Solomon, and is conditional both on man's side and God's. God will never again remove his love from Solomon [David's heirs??] as He did to Saul, nor is the promise without condition, since it is prophesied that Solomon will do wrong. In contrast to this v.15 "My love will never be taken from him" cannot be fully fulfilled except on the Son of God Himself, who never causes anything to break the fellowship of obedience. V.16 asserts the kingdom and 'house' will last forever. From other texts it is understood Jesus Christ is the heir of David who fulfills this and other prophecies and promises. Here that is not a part of the argument. The promise and fact depends upon the cross and not descent. Later in the book descent is raised as an argument and denied; Christ is priest not according to Levi but Melchizedek. 2 Sam 7.14. The quote may allude to David or Solomon but in this context the words are Messianic and spoken to the Son. 'You are my son' is a legal formulation of adoption or of designating a son among many, not always the eldest, as heir apparent. Church history has stood behind the great councils of the church as to the two natures of Christ and thereby the rulings and creeds have become the standard to read many biblical texts. The initial occasion is the case of David and Solomon and this is reflected in the quote from the Psalm. So initially the contrast is angels versus human, and a special human by election. Except for Israel the collective these words were not spoken as such to any other. In the Gospel God said these words to Jesus as his baptism. 'I have begotten you' is used for establishing the 'firstborn' status and in the sense of 'I have become your father' could presumably be used as an adoption formula, since' You are my son' is often so used in cuneiform documents of the ANE. The birth narratives do not directly affirm the use of this psalm, but the words of Mary and Elizabeth could allude to them and to the connection to David and Solomon as Messiah. If the context for the 'time' of hypothetically saying these words to the Son as being pre-incarnation there are verses in Hebrews that detail some of pre-incarnation decisions, decrees and events. But v.2 'His Son' goes back to pre-creation. Was the appointment as heir of all things also pre-creation or rather post resurrection? What rituals of adoption in the OT, ANE and Roman world would have a divine application to The Son?,[63]

"You are my son" quotes Ps 2.7, an oracle addressed to the Davidic king on enthronement, but was fulfilled in prophecy and antitype at Jesus' baptism Mk 1.11. Ps 2 was applied to the Messiah in Ps.Sol. 17.26 and later in acts 4.25f; 13.33; Rev 12.5. v.5b comes from 2 Sam 7.14, where God promises David that his son will build the temple. Qumran Cave 4 a messianic anthology has a fragment applying the words to the Messiah.[64], Based on Rev 12.2 the early church used 'resurrection' as a kind of birth metaphor and therefore used Ps 2.7 'You are my son; today have I begotten you' in this light. Acts 13.33; Rom 1.4?; Heb 5.5; Linking passion, resurrection and childbirth are Gal 4.18; Rev 1.5; John 12.24; 1 Cor 15.36; Acts 2.24. Ps 38.6; Ps 96.8 2 Sam 22.6 refer to the bonds of death, but with change of pointing the Hebrew could point to pains of childbirth. Ford,[65] 190 , Father-Son expressions appear regarding Israel and God, God and David in 2 Sam 7.14 and to Christ in Heb 1.5.

Usually this is a protocol for a king's relation to God. Is it related to the doctrine of the adoption of believers into the family of God.? Myers,[66]155. 'avenge'//'take vengeance'//'make atonement' are parallel as are 'his people'// 'his servants'// 'his enemies'// 'his land and people'. Dt 32.43 LXX DSS;

Lindars[67] investigates the son of man in the Gospels as a unique concept and role based on Daniel. I John shows the early church did have problems with a truly human Jesus and Messiah. But Paul and Hebrews establish the divine son of God, a doctrine already in John 1. But Hebrews moves from heaven to earth and from pre-incarnation to present so 'Son' appears to be eternal in heaven before it appears in the baptism of Jesus on earth. These trajectories are all wrestling with the God-man nature of the beloved.

'Firstborn' is a status and position as heir and representative of the second generation legally and ethically before God. 'into the world' refers to the birth of the Son. But 'Firstborn' was the status of the Son before he was born. It is specifically the Son as firstborn that came into the world. This verse also alludes to Luke's story of the angels praising God at the birth of the Messiah. He cites Dt 32.43 LXX on angels worshiping Christ, when "God brings the firstborn into the world"[68] Fulfilled at the first advent per Payne,[69]573. Does this poetic line refer to the birth of Christ and the songs of the angels in that event? How can a man be designated as worthy of worship by heavenly beings? His deity is asserted in the incarnation night on the birth of the Christ in that all the angels were to worship Him. If the 'firstborn' coming into the world is mentioned here in v.6, was v.5 speaking of a time preceding that event? Kai proskynesastwsan autw pante aggeloi theou' as in Phil 2 does stress that everything will be made subject, namely will bow to him. This verse quotes Dt 32.43,LXX, having a longer text as in Qumran. In Deuteronomy God is worshipped at the conclusion of his work. Ps 97.7. This quote is from Dt 32.43, agreeing with the LXX against the MT; Fitzmyer,[70]87-8n The incarnation or birth of Christ is here recounted as a decree of God that all the angels of God are to worship him. On earth the wise men and shepherds responded similarly. Here is a case where God permits and orders that all beings worship the Son, who is a man but not only man. Monotheism compromised? Or is this rather a conferring of power, authority and honor beyond that of mortal men? prwtokos[71] and Heb 11.28 Cf. . Ps 78.51 are literal, all other occurrences are figurative in the NT. "All expressive of honor, dignity, or eminence. Christ "has a primacy of excellence in the order of creation that could be described as cosmic. He is also firstborn with respect to the dead. Prwtokos primacy in the order of resurrection, not simply because he was the first to come forth from the grave, but because he came forth as the all-powerful sovereign, the prince of a new humanity. Rev 1.5 ho archwn. Finally, Christ is honored with a primacy in the eschatological order, because in glory he will be' firstborn among many brethren' prwtokos Rom 8.29." Spicq, 212n12. Philip Segal, '"Begotten' Messiah,"[72] traces all the birth notions surrounding the birth of Joshua of Nazareth to the previous history of the Jews and the model Moses. Enoch 48.2-3,6;62.7 gives the name, the Son of Man, who is precreation, relating to Ps 72.17 '[His name] existed before the sun.' Babylonian Pesahim 54a is a proto-rabbinic view and links Ps 72.17 exegesis to Enoch 48, where either his identity was secret, or that the person, not only his name, was pre-existent. In this case the pre-existent messiah must be incarnated.

The Jew Trypho in Justin's Dialogue with Trypho expressed the view that 'all Jews expect the Messiah to be anthrwpon ex anthrwpou 'a man from men.' So we must set this in the context of second-century polemic in which ;the argument for a human Messiah would be part of the argument against the Messiahship of Jesus....the originators of Christianity were Jews, and they found their notion of a divine Messiah in their own heritage.' Contrary to Klausner, Brown and Grelot the writings of Philo 'On the Cherubim' and Jubilees do give ground for pre-Christian divine conception. Evidence alluded to are types of Christ 1. Abraham's wife was in Gen 21.1 'in her solitude' so it is divine impregnation not removal of barrenness. Paqad here is not 'visit' but 'remember.' 2.Jesus as the aqedah in the Isaac sacrifice story shows Isaac born the 15th of Sivan Jub.16.13 the day of first fruits Cf. . 1 Cor 15.20. While post-apostolic writers stressed the deity of Christ more so than Paul or the Gospels, and Jewish writers could consider Moses half-god half-man, and the Greek world considered poets and some philosophers or generals divine, none of this compares to the tradition of a divine messiah truly becoming a human being. Late Christianity only had a genetic relation of Jesus to God. Pythagoras and Plato were conceived to be of divine conception but not genetically related to God, which only appears in Greek myth.

The question for Heb 1.5 is 'Was this said to the Son' at a pre-existent time, or at the birth in Bethlehem? If the latter, then the link to the baptism witness is very close. 'You are my son' also links to Hosea and OT texts where God adopts or elects Israel into a special relationship to him. In this case the miraculous birth of Isaac and unusual election of Jacob are followed by Moses' birth and calling as well as Samuel's, and Samson's. While in relation to man the protocols of the ANE allowed for a proclamation of divorce or adoption or dis-adoption, this could not be with the Son.[73] 1.5

'I will be his father and he will be my son' taken from 2 Sam 7.14 and 1 Chr 17.13 is a legal formula for full adoption or installation into sonship. In

Sumer the same was expressed by the new born being placed in the lap of the father or in the lap of the image in dedication. The Hebrew could have been read 'I am his father' as a performative verb. But here it refers to the future relationship from one point onward. In the NT the Spirit bears witness with our spirit that we are the sons of God' whereby we cry Abba Father. The child can recognize and bond even better than a shepherd's sheep can know their shepherd.

1.6 'God brings the firstborn into the world.' Not 'God brings the son into the world as firstborn'.Evidently firstborn here has a heavenly aspect from all eternity and an earthly aspect from the birth in Bethlehem. This intervention is not by angels but by God himself. The time of this birth on earth, the angels are commanded to sing worship of the new born and the shepherds heard their singing. The role of angels vis a vis the Messiah is clear here, in the pre-birth narratives, the temptation in the wilderness and in Gethsemane. After the resurrection they appear at the tomb.

1.7 'Angels..winds...fire' Both wind and fire were evidences of God's presence at Pentecost. Perhaps the lack of one story in the OT where wind and fire appear in a theophany might cause us to reflect on Acts 2. Was that room filled with angels, with apostles speaking with the tongues of angels [1 Cor 13], when the Holy Spirit baptized and filled the apostles? The reverse analogy is incorrect. Wind and fire are natural phenomena. Here wind and fire are analogies of an unusual occurrence of power in the world. Both are destructive and both are cleansing. The activity of good angels in this role is outstanding, since we usually think of their protective roles. But this again is not what angels are, but what they are 'made' for the tasks of serving the son.

'winds...fire.' Elijah's experience at Horeb thus could have been that of angels. Elisha experienced armies of angels and let his servant see them too. But both are destructive as well as purifying and protective and could easily not be viewed as heaven-sent angels. This is especially true of the dry south wind portending drought and famine or the burning down of a city in war.

To see angelic beings in destructive events means faith to see beyond judging what God is doing is right or wrong. God is doing it and this is no accident. Does this poetic line de-personalize angels, making them winds or fires? In Rev 4.5; 5.6 and Zech 6.5 angels are spirits. Wind, fire and spirit are immaterial forces. From Ps 97.7 and Deut 32.43 a quotation:" Let all the angels of God worship Him.' This does not seem to be used in the preaching that Christ was the divine Messiah. Worship must not be given to anything created, so this affirms the Deity of the Son.

The OT text stresses the nature metaphors for the revelation of God within process, hence natural light v.2, 'heavens,' probably 'clouds'; 'upper chambers' the ancient 'structural' pattern and its language, mainly of this solar system. The 'winds' are parallel to 'fires' as two forces of nature, which in this context are two classes of angels, celestial and, presumably, terrestrial. Ps 14.4 The subsequent text of the Psalm confirms the immanence of God within the processes of nature. Hebrews confirms ho poiwn tou aggelou autou pneumata that these angels are spirits not winds and they are created by God himself and designated ['making...to be spirits'] or reading 'making his spirits to be angels.' The Greek prefers the former reading. Thus angels not yet sent out can be described as 'Holy Ones." But as sent ones they are aggeloi . Here the second line cannot deal with fire made into servants of him but his servants made into fire kai tou leitourgou autou' pyro floga. This explains the Job disasters involving wind and fire, both sent on embassies of disaster upon Job's household

The relationship of angels to natural disasters of wind or storm and fire are paralleled by the study of religion in Babylonia where the various gods are said to represent various powers of the natural world which is perhaps different from saying they control the aspects of wind and rain, thunder and lightning. The Greek and Hebrew expression is that 'God thundered on the earth' or 'God rained.' Is there other data that angels are involved in natural phenomena except the 'Death' angel concept possibly derived from the Last Exodus Plague? Or is there here no connection to natural phenomena and rather focuses on forces that occur and may be either a blessing or a tragedy? Are angels unbound by nature and yet at work in nature? As in nature do they bring cooling as well as heat? Or are they simply part of the mystery of John 3 that we don't know where the wind is coming from or where it is going and so is everyone who is born from above? These do seem to be political or military and natural disasters. Were the winds and flames of Elijah's Horeb really angels? In what sense are angels apparent in the natural world as a driving force behind natural phenomena? Which is the metaphor? Are winds really angels, is fire really ministers? Or do angels function sporadically like the wind and in crises events such as war as fire.? "All of the Greeks' great national festivals, and especially the Olympic Games, had a religious character. The crowd came together with the priests around a common sanctuary where sacrifice was offered.

Paneguris or 'sacred festival' is constantly associated with qysia . This meaning of liturgical observance is clearly present in Heb 12.22, where the heavenly joy is tinctured by religious seriousness and reverence. On the one hand, the epistle [of Hebrews] pictures heaven as a place of worship, where the great high priest and leitourgos officiates [8.2]; on the other hand the myriads of angels are leitourgika pneumata [1.14], born agents of divine worship, occupying themselves with praising God and proclaiming God as sovereign and universal judge: "and let all the angels of God worship him." Kai proskynesatwsan autw pantes aggeloi theou 1.6. "; [74] Cf. Ps 14.4 In T.Abr. A 15 God calls Michael ho emos leitourgos . Note Heb 2.14 leitourgika pneumata, literally liturgical or officiating spirits [Philo Virtues 74]; aggeloi leitourgoi. T.Levi 3.5: archaggeloi oi leitourgountes kai exilaskomenoi pros Kurion. Jub 2.2. "According to Philo, the angels are consecrated and assigned to the worship of the Father, who uses them as servants and ministers in charge of mortals [Giants,12]. The adjective leitourgikos, unknown in secular literary texts, refers in the papyri to a sum due for a work, the tax to support statute [75]but also 'service days' during which the priests officiate...Its six occurrences in the LXX are all religious: Aaron's sacred vestments,[Ex 31.10; 39.1]; the objects used in worship services [Num 4.12,26], the ceremonies in the tabernacle 7.5; so it could be defined as 'pertaining to the worship services." Heb 9.21 it is 'the tabernacle and all the liturgical vessels."[76] , Rev 1.4 'the seven spirits' are thought to be the seven mighty throne angels of Jewish tradition. The apocrypha and Pseudepigrapha mention them as in Tobit 2.15; 1 Enoch 20.1-8 by names of Uriel, Raphael, Raguel, Michael, Saraqael, Gabriel, and Remiel. 'Spirits' almost never refers to angels I OT or NT [exception: 1 Kings 22.21-23; Heb 1.7m14. The seven spirits could be correlated to seven churches in terms of angelic tutelage 1.4; 1.20. But in Ezekiel several angels engage in destroying Jerusalem and they are in the shape of men. An alternate viewpoint is that the Holy Spirit is mentioned in his seven gifts Isa 11.2-3 LXX MT only has 6; This fits better with Rev 4.5; 5.6 and Zech 3.9; 4.10. Swete considers diversified ministries of the Holy spirit as seen in older Latin commentators and Heb 2.4; 1 Cor 12.10; 14.32; Rev 22.6. 4Qserek at Qumran speaks of Chief Princes and seven words of blessing, which could be the enthroned angels.[77]Ford,[78]377

1.8 'O God' is addressed in the singular to the Son. His kingdom and throne are eternal and apparently will not and cannot conceptually be turned over to the Father, since the Son himself is God. But conferred authority, position and essence are three different aspects of the Christ. In this verse his kingdom is the Kingdom of God and not only David's kingdom and the scenario is the Millennium. Especially in this verse it is God who declares these things of His Son in praise and commission. God speaks to the Son as God. The context has many things about creation and history but only 'provided purification for sins' having to do with the atonement. So nothing specifically speaks to the post resurrection and post-session situation, but rather seems to reflect more easily the eternal status, role, and acts of the Son as the eternal king. The prediction 'will be' an eternal throne, 'a scepter of righteousness' as the one feature of his rule, and in v.9 an absolute antithesis of loving righteousness and hating wickedness as an absolute attitude and commitment. It is based on the merit of this holiness that places him above all others through the anointing with the oil of joy. 'The kingdom of God is righteousness joy and peace in the Holy Spirit.' When was this anointing made except by John by a body of water following the Hebrew Scriptures pattern for anointing of Solomon? How are 1.5 'my Son' 1.6 'worship him' and 'your throne O God' related? Is there progression or intensification? RSV has a footnote to read 'God is thy throne'. This avoids imputing deity to the Son and seems theologically motivated. But the two cola of this verse are addressed by God to the Son as is the following context. Clearly such alternate translation does not consider context. There are 75 verses in the Bible(38 in the OT) with 'throne' and 'God' in the same verse. The obvious parallel is David or Solomon referring to his son to succeed him on the throne. The following seems to be even closer to this meaning: "2Chr. 9:8 Praise be to the LORD your God, who has delighted in you and placed you on his throne as king to rule for the LORD your God. Because of the love of your God for Israel and his desire to uphold them forever, he has made you king over them, to maintain justice and righteousness." Psa. 45:6 Your throne, O God, will last for ever and ever; a scepter of justice will be the scepter of your kingdom. Psa. 47:8 God reigns over the nations; God is seated on his holy throne." But God and throne do not seem interchangeable as are 'White House" and "president."

The kingdom is spiritual; God reigns "in our midst through the virtues and his gifts, the evidences of his presence. Rom 14.17; 1 Cor 15.50; Cf. . 1 Cor 4.9-10; Gal 5.21; Eph 5.5; Col.1.13; "Christ's scepter is a scepter of righteousness" [79] Jesus' words about the kingdom are definitive John 18:36. 'Is not from in here' and ek tou kosmou 'not of this kosmos'. Spicq 1.269n65 The link of 'throne' and 'righteousness and truth' is found in OT prophecy Isa 51.4-8 and 1 Kgs 9.5 with a link of 'heart' 'throne' v.5 and justice. The truth is that no power can last if it is not based on truth and justice.The throne and kingdom, exude stability; the antithesis is angels as winds or fire, the utmost of instability. Any permanent good must come from God. The earliest wind or spirit was at the dawn of creation in Gen 1.1 when all was still chaos. The earliest fire was in the flaming sword, preventing man's gaining of eternal life. The next was at Noah's altar and the destruction of Sodom. Altars and covenants have fire because of the oath that can be destructive, a matter of life and death. The juxtaposition of being and becoming, of stability and instability, or of structure and dynamo is a heavenly contrast between the Son and angels. The Son is addressed as God, in Ps 45.6, and his throne is everlasting [Eternity], and it is righteous government that has won supremacy over other rulers. RSV took this as 'your divine throne' and doesn't uphold the correct understanding of the vocative "God". The Son is called 'God' and he has an eternal throne. The evidence for deity is based on Ps 45 and other texts. In ch.1 the deity of Christ must be demonstrated, and so the OT quotations are many. In ch.2 and following the humanity of Jesus must be fully explicated and how this relates to the earlier institutions. The writer clarifies that the OT speaks of the Son as God with an eternal throne. Most Royal Psalms begin with a sentence reading either 'Our God is king' or 'our God [just now] reigns' as if reflecting the New Years accession to the throne practice. This verse would indicate that these psalms should not be read as a repeated event by which the rule of the earthly king is guaranteed, but as a hymn of praise that in fact, God always rules and this is unchangeable: Read 'Our God is king'. The Ps 45.6 context is of riding forth to war v.4 and piercing with arrows the hearts of the king's enemies. His riding forth is victoriously, for truth, humility, righteousness, with awesome deeds. The Psalm focuses on the aftermath of war and the glory while here the war hasn't begun. He is God, Son, firstborn, worshipped, eternal, righteous, anointed, creator, and ruling monarch. Cf. . Ps 104.4,LXX. 'God' is a vocative addressed to the Son not that God is supporting the Son as in the RSV 'God is your throne.'

1.8-9 'Forever and ever' in the OT and ANE carry what signification? Does this deny a 1000 year millennium and 1 Cor 15 where Paul has Christ turn the kingdom over to the Father? He cites Ps 45.6-7 on the anointing of Christ. Fulfilled.#3. Payne,573,[80] This is a case where the original context gives way to the NT speaker's situation. Fitzmyer,33n,[81] These verses apply v.6-7 to Jesus, while Pal Tg.Gen 49.8, influenced by Psalm 45, reads 'How beauteous in the King Meshicha, who is to arise from the house of Jehuda' Other early interpretation took Ps 45 as describing the king as beautiful. Evans, 235[82]

1.9 'Above your companions' in context is the angels.. The angels seem to be a better 'companion-context' than the prophets. In the OT, when angels are not on missions they are usually called 'sons of 'Elohim' meaning 'supernatural beings' less than divine or having a divine nature.'. But if the entire chapter grows out of real history it may point to the apostles or John the Baptist and others. The 'oil of joy' reflects back to Jesus baptism and anointing by the Spirit in real time. In the quotations original setting David is the one chosen. The companions are angels or heavenly messengers on the one hand and prophetic messengers on the other.

'Anointing' in heaven seems to be the reality for which anointing on earth is the shadow. Anointing in the Bible seems to have begun with priests but was extended to kings and probably prophets, often linked in Isaiah with prophetic and leadership gifts. Just as whoever is bound or loosed on earth is so in heaven the fact of anointing cannot be undone by men here. 'The anointing remains on you' in 1 John indicates a permanent gift not event-oriented as in the Book of Judges.[83]

'Oil of gladness' goes back to the OT passage in Isaiah: Is. 61:3 and provide for those who grieve in Zion — to bestow on them a crown of beauty instead of ashes, the oil of gladness instead of mourning, and a garment of praise instead of a spirit of despair. They will be called oaks of righteousness, a planting of the LORD for the display of his splendor In context opposite of depressed and mourning the anointing made Jesus one who attracts the multitude, it was the factor prior to the miracles and teaching that drew men.

'Therefore' indicates merit or cause for the anointing. 'comrades' could reflect the heavenly counterpart to Heb 2 'brethren' among whom the Son is present, preaching and praising. The time element in this contrastive analysis would be heavenly 'comrades' 'companions' or <u>mutacheous</u> As a heavenly event we lack information, but as the event at Jesus' baptism, the <u>mutacheous</u> are all those who came to the Jordan to receive baptism, of which only one person received the Spirit and the oracle 'This is my Son'. Hos 4:17; Ps 44(45):8; 118(119):63; Prv 29:10; 3 Mc 3:21; companion of <u>[tinos]</u> Ps 44(45):8; companion of, being in the companionship of, partaking in the cult of (idols) <u>[tinos]</u> Hos 4:17; accomplice with <u>[tini]</u> 1 Sm 20:30 'men who participate in bloodshed, bloodthirsty men'; Prv 29:10. The OT background is the hapiru that could be related to 'Hebrew' 'ibri not through the genealogical line but through the concept of those who are bonded, allied by covenant, and hence diverse peoples who confederate for good or evil goals. In the case of Jesus it could refer to all the servants of God throughout history or especially to his own chosen disciples, who initially were chosen when they responded to the call for repentance in John's baptism. Louw and Nida link the only other verse in the NT containing the word to specifically link it to the life of Christ: "4.8 'one who shares with someone else as an associate in an enterprise or undertaking' — 'companion, partner.' 'and they signaled to their companions in the other boat' Lk 5:7; 'therefore, God, your God, anointed you with the oil of gladness more than he did your companions' He 1:9." Jesus apparently did not use this terminology but rather that of servants, disciples, apostles, and friends. In Heb 1 the context is one and many and hence haber is the appropriate background for the usage.

"Anointing with joy" Cf. . Ps 134 linking praise [joy?] with servants/ministers who presumably are anointed ones. Ps 135.2 says "sing praise to his name for that is pleasant." Rom 14.17 declares "The Kingdom of God is not a matter of eating and drinking but of righteousness, peace and joy in the Holy Spirit." This conception of the Kingdom is missing from the OT except for Psalms celebrating God as king. Ps 97.2 and v.8 "Zion hears and rejoices." V.11 "joy on the upright in heart." V.12 the joy links to the Lord who v.1 says reigns. Rom 14.17 could read "the rule of God..." based on a presumed Aramaic usage. Is 'anointing' dependent upon loving righteousness and hating wickedness? Jews and people around the world think of merit or meritorious acts and rewards that should follow. Here love of righteousness and hatred for wickedness are rewarded by a higher rank than others and by the anointing of joy. In the NT 'joy' or 'rejoice occur 93 times; in the Gospels 31 times. Jesus himself rejoiced in Luke 10:21 "At that time Jesus, full of joy through the Holy Spirit, said, "I praise you, Father, Lord of heaven and earth, because you have hidden these things from the wise and learned, and revealed them to little children. Yes, Father, for this was your good pleasure." John 15:11; John 3:29 "The bride belongs to the bridegroom. The friend who attends the bridegroom waits and listens for him, and is full of joy when he hears the bridegroom's voice. That joy is mine, and it is now complete." John 17:13; In 3.29 Jesus apparently takes the role of the friend and God is the bridegroom as in Jewish thought. In the first instance joy is linked to the fullness of the Spirit Love and hate represent character and spirituality that are also absolutes and uncompromising and here the basis for the anointing and exaltation over the "companions." David was "a man after God's heart." 1 Sam 16.7 since God looks at the heart. Calling depends on character v.10, and David also had a fine appearance v.12. The anointing with oil v.12-13, was followed by the outpouring of the power of the Holy Spirit. 16.18 interprets from a laity-standpoint: 'He is a brave man and warrior. He speaks well and is a fine looking man, and the Lord is with him." Cf. . 1 Sam 13.14 "after his own heart." metehw and words of this family indicate a sharing, participating, and partner, even as Hebrew haber, which signifies a link, attachment, a joining' But Spicq relates Ps 45.8=Heb 1.9 to anointing Moses 'in preference over his companions' princes, heads of families or other sovereigns who also had their anointing, such as colleagues in the priesthood. He also relates haber to 'the confederates, the Hebrews', while the Bible usually relates Hebrews to an eponym Heber of Gen 10, written with an ayin not a heth. But if this would be accepted the relation to covenanted people and also to the hapiru would be even closer especially if the word came from outside NW Semitic, in which case the 'ayin/heth variation could be explained.[84] Note Ps 45. 6-7 which combines the accession to the throne while the father is still alive, a unique situation except for the eternal Messiah, and coregencies, along with the wedding of the king. Referring in Ps 45.7; to the king, he is separated above his companions by the anointing, true of Saul and David. The Psalm apparently is the wedding of the king. In v.10 the 'daughter' or bride is addressed. The description in these verses may be useful to inter-interpret the Song of Solomon. Isa 61.3 rather points to a declaration of amnesty, of release from debts, possibly a Jubilee, definitely more than a seventh year. The Eschatological meaning 'year of the Lord's favor' could be the idea of the accession year as opposed to the first year, and a year in which political prisoners such as Jehiachin could be and was released. The anduraru was a Babylonian custom and did have a reflex in Israel. But as' Day of grace' this era is really that 'day'. The anointing on earth was at Jesus' baptism or was it accomplished in heaven before coming to earth. This anointing qualified Him for the Messianic task. Surely this is a fair reading of the Gospels, and is not historicizing a pre-incarnation event. We know little of Jesus before his baptism although various apocryphal traditions did arise. But here is a forthright statement that the Son always loved righteousness and hated lawlessness, in good wisdom tradition. Knowing the Rom 5 background we understand the anointing brought the love of God for people and hence ushered Jesus into public ministry. Who are Jesus' companions here? God and Christ judge the world as sovereigns Heb 7.2, under the analogy of Melchizedek, king of justice/righteous. But Spicq's use of "judges and prophets" is rather out of the ch.1 context. The sovereigns can "distribute their benefits 2 Pet 1.1, punishment and rewards Acts 17.31; 2 Tim 4.8; but does not mention the aspect of ministering that the book brings up later, which is in the temple. For it was the priest that could exclude people due to uncleanness. But Spicq seeks to make a case based on Heb 5.13 that 'justice/righteousness' is a word pair with God and the sphere of natural law as well as moral prescriptions of the NT world were in the foreground. Hence Num 10.35, Acts 24.25; 2 Pet 2.5; Acts 17.31 recall to mind a basic ma'at or ME or mishpat in this world, and this is established by God in Christ.;[85] . How does 'anointing of joy' relate to the believers' anointing in 1 John? Are there evidences in the Gospels of Jesus' joy? There was the instance when Jesus said 'You have hidden these things... and revealed them to babes.'

1.10 'Head' as ro'sh: The NT naturally uses kefale objectively, e.g., in descriptions of visionary appearances of Christ (Rev 1:14; 14:14; 19:12), of the 24 elders around God's throne (4:4), and of other figures (e.g., 12:1). kefale is used metonymically in the curse formula translated from the Hebr. in Acts 18:6. Fig. usages are dominated by the social use to the extent that it facilitates one of Christ's majestic titles: Christ is kefale in relation to the church (Eph 4:15; 5:23; Col 1:18; 2:19), which is his body (Eph 1:22f.; 4:16), and in relation to the cosmos (hyper panta Eph 1:22, developed in v 23b) and to its archai and exousiai (Col 2:10). Just as Christ is the "head" of the church, the husband is the "head" of the wife (Eph 5:23); according to 1 Cor 11:3, God, Christ, the husband, and the wife are arranged hierarchically as kefale. Rosh, ro'sh and re'sh in temporal use are represented in the LXX and the NT by arch, both for the "beginning" of an objectively demarcated period of time and for the beginning of time per se, the latter in the phrases ap arch ktiseou (Mark 10:6; 13:19; 2 Pet 3:4), (Matt 24:21), or in the abs. usages en (John 1:1) and (Heb 1:10). Rev 3:14 calls Christ "the beginning of God's creation" (Cf. . Acts 3:15; 5:31; Heb 2:10; 12:2). In Jude 6 seems to mean "office," corresponding to reshit. 1:57b.Note all are the human body metaphor.

'Foundations of the earth' is usually interpreted from the standpoint of literary references showing ANE cosmology and mythological understanding of the universe in which the earth rests on pillars. But if a geological reading is made 'foundations' is truly a meta-textual plurality and indicates creation by extended process that had to precede the creating of the heavens. 'You laid the foundations' is a finished work but the heavens continue to be God's ongoing work and 'upholding all things' is a continuing task dependent on God moment by moment. Does 'foundations of the earth' and 'heavens are the work of your hand' equal 'the universe of 1.2? Does 'foundations' correspond to Gen 1 or is this more ANE oriented? If it doesn't equal 'earth' is the earth a given in this world view? Why is the division of water and land, water and sky, upper and lower waters omitted? Is 1.2 more universal than 1.10 as geocentric or earth-centric?

If Egyptian terminology or cosmology has influenced this book through the Alexandrian school then 'foundations' is based on Hebrew but basically reflects Egyptian 'pillars.' This verse asserts the priority of the earth over the heavens which would be scientific fact in that the earth is related to the formation of the complex of gasses and oxygen necessary to sustain life. By beginning with earth and then referring to heavens is the author geocentric? V.6 seems to show the world as secondary with heaven or its equivalent as primary. Indeed Gen 1.1 shows 'heavens and the earth' in that order. The passage cannot be used by critics to show geocentrism, rather the passage is Christocentric.

This contrasts to John 1 in that the Lord [Yahweh] creates, while 12 God does this through the Son. The 'beginning' of creation points to the end, when the visible heavens and foundations will wear out, rolled up and changed, discarded. In contrast to the physical universe God and the Son remain the same [immutability] and never end [eternity]. The exegetical question concerns the foundations, since the metaphor is about the heavens. But the contrast between what remains and what changes or passes away remains. The word 'change' implies possibly, the new heaven and new earth. Ps 12.25-27 The alternating between 'God' in 5,6,9 and 'Lord' in v.10 could indicate an identifying of YHWH with Gen 1 instead of Elohim, and also that YHWH is the Son. The impact this has is on reading Exodus. God says 'let my people go' or 'let my Son go' and if it is the eternal creating Son speaking he is speaking not to brethren by virtue of one father, but as Son to his earthly 'Son' the Israelites. The death of the firstborn of Israel and later of pharaoh links to the Son demanding that Israel grow in to their elective position as 'Son.' The beginning of all things and ending of all things are accomplished by one and the same 'Son'. But why are the 'heirs' not called sons' and only in ch.2 called 'brethren.?' Who is called 'companions' in 1.9. What Hebrew would express the concept in <u>para tou metachou sou</u>.? The root <u>h</u>br can indicate friend, companion, neighbor, what of colleague? Can this relate at all to the parable of the Samaritan and his neighbor? Or should <u>metachou</u> be sought rather in <u>h</u>br [86] 'a cohort, member of a clique or informal covenant.' Use of <u>kai</u> as short formula of citation meaning 'and he said' Fitzmyer, 392[87] Most of David's psalms were laments or confessions and only a few rose to joy. David's heir the Lord Jesus has the gift of joy that helps define the kingdom in Paul's writings.

1.10-12 Corresponds to Ecclesiastes 3.14 everything God does will endure forever and nothing is or can be added or taken from in. So do these lines mean the same thing, or are

1. Perishing things;
2. Worn-out things;
3. Rolled up things;
4. Changed things distinguished.

Then 'remain the same' is not on his eternality, but on not changing. 'Never end' then corresponds to 'perish'. By contrast the heaven and earth are viewed in the Psalms as permanent. Ps 14.5. Several scriptures use the OT into a new context. When Paul writes, 'As God's fellow-worker, I appeal to you too, not to accept the favor of God and then waste it. For He says 'I have listened to you at a welcome time, and helped you on a day of deliverance!' Now the welcome time has come' 2 Cor 6.1-2 from Isa 49.8. Paul here quotes the words of Deutero-Isaiah, which refer immediately to the return from exile, but which are general enough to be applied to his own preaching and apostolic activity among the Corinthians. Note similar scriptures: Lk 22.37; Jn 12.38; 13.18; 19.24; Acts 3.25; 13.33-34; Rom 9.29; 10.15-16; 15.21; 2 Cor 6.2; Heb 1.5,8-9,10-12,13; 3.7-11; 4.3,7; 5.6; 8.8-12; 10.16-18. Fitzmyer, 33n,[88] The new garment Mk 2.21f; Matt 9.16f; Lk 5.36-38 Gospel Thomas 47b are linked to the wedding figure. The foolishness of mending an old garment, or pouring fermented wine into worn-out or damaged wine skins. All of these are The New Age figures. In the history of religions the cosmos can be described as a garment or world-garment. Here Psa. 12.26-28 and this text describes the Parousia as a date when Christ rolls up the cosmos as a garment and unfolds a new cosmos. Note Acts 10.11ff and 11.5 where Peter sees the symbol of a sheet let down full of every kind of creature, and in effect, sees the new cosmos cleansed by God. Tent, sheet, garment are figures of the cosmos. Thus in Mk 2.21 the old world's age has run out. The old world is no longer worthy of patching. Jeremias,118,[89] 'You will roll them up' is the Son as Creator and Terminator of the world as it is. Do the words about the Son's eternity mean that these words of the Father are illocutionary and make it a fact in the act of speaking? If so then the Father is truly Lord of all including the eternal life of the Son. But in v.8 the son's kingdom is forever indicating that it is the living God's eternity conveyed to the Son that becomes the one who bestows eternal life on his brothers and children. Is there a contrast between the 'foundations of the earth' thought of as permanent and the heavens that 'will all perish'?

1.11 "It is the sovereign Lord who helps me, who then will bring charges against me'? Cf. . Rom.8. "Let us face each other' reflects Job's prayers. "Who is my accuser'. Paul develops this theme. V.9 "They will all wear out like a garment. The moths will eat them up.' Here it is not the natural world but the accusers in terms of their mortality. Isa 50.9; 51.6. Jesus' words about the Word of God are hypothetical in that if the heavens and earth could pass away the Word of God will not and will be fulfilled. Here is a clear clarification that the earth and heavens of Gen 1, the creation, will perish. In v.10 'Thou Lord' is another vocative that the Psalmists like to use and in context Cf. . V.13 still is referring to the Son. The Son is Eternal and unchangeable.[90] The heavens and earth have a beginning and an end. V.10-12 assert that everything changes except for the Son, unless the switch to 'Lord' in v.10 is a switch to the Father in keeping with 1 Cor 15 where Jesus rules till all enemies are subdued and then turns the kingdom back to the Father. 'they will perish' views creation dynamically, as having a life of its own and therefore a death. Viewing creation as a garment that wears out or a robe that is rolled up or changed as a garment approaches 'phenomena' in that what is seen is appearances. That which gives it an appearance will be done away with. How this blends with a new heaven and new earth is a connection not made. Only God's very being is unconditionally eternal.

1.11-12 Is the figure of rolling up a garment, a phenomenological view of the sky and clouds, and not a canopy or inverted lid concept of a geosystem, Ps 17.25-27. the latter was modeled on that of Ptolemy and pictures of it are found in various textbooks as representing the cosmology of the Ancient Near East and Israel. Both anachronism and literal reading of metaphorical language are involved in this error. This Psalm says nothing except that they experienced phenomena on the seas during a storm. Ps 12.25-27 Cf. . V.19

"Sanctuary on high" is parallel to "heaven" and hence not Mt. Zion. The language is the same as is developed in the Book of Hebrews. Sacred language places God in heaven, from which he "looks down." It possibly is derived from Near Eastern conceptualization in the scope of religion or myth but not cosmology. The word could be derived either from 'up' or 'high God' or from Sumerian ANU "Heaven."

"The "foundations of the earth"v.25 make the universe to center not on Palestine or Israel or even man, as in later Jewish thought. Subsequently "heaven" follows the order of creation in Gen 1, where no subsequence is clear.

Both are gods doing, his work, and all will perish, all are temporal and will wear out. The metaphor of an old garment changed and discarded lays the foundation for the NT doctrine of a new heaven and new earth. God never changes [Immutability], and He is eternal, immutable and present, clearly not a part of the created world at all. The figures of speech hardly apply to the layers of the earth but rather to the layers of shy and clouds that form an analogy more and more striking as man has probed into the Ionosphere and beyond. A speeded up. The language is not of cessation of existence but of putting away, rolling up, and change. If this is the new heaven and new earth the foundations of the earth and heavens both encompass all things. But contrasting the created order to God, God does not perish, change or come to an end. Ps 12.26b-27 on the eternity of Christ. Ps 12.26 and Hag 2.6 on the passing away of heaven and earth, 'the removal of those things which can be shaken, as of all created things."[91]

1.12 'Your years never end' clarifies what eternity is about. There is no absence of time in Eternity, but endlessness. This goes with God's eternity, a term never used to describe men, but linked here to God's unchanging nature. 'they will be changed; does mean they cease to exist but that they exist in a new form. from Ps 12.25-27 'Years never run out' is a statement of deity and not merely a statement about an eternal soul or rituals to secure freedom of movement in the next life. God alone is eternal on the ground of his very being. God and the Son are eternal, why can the material world not be eternal? 'Changed' does this mean continuing indefinitely? Or is the point of the first line that God never changes? In Rev 6.14 'rolled up' elissw means to 'split, separate, rend' but can apply to the rolling up of a cloak. Isa 34.4; Heb 1.12 or a scroll or even an inscribed lead tablet. "The ancient Hebrews thought the firmament of heaven [Gen 1.7] was composed of solid material. Thus, heaven's having 'been wrenched apart like a scroll that is rolled up' leads to an image not of papyrus or leather scroll, but rather a scroll like the two copper ones found in Qumran. The idea of noise is conveyed more dramatically if the reader is meant to picture a metal scroll suddenly snapping shut."Ford,[92]100

1.13 'Footstool' in ANE iconography the defeated foes are under the feet of the victorious. Joshua had the warriors of Israel act out the victory ritual over the kings of the Jerusalem coalition and then he personally killed these kings. Paul in his letters promises that God will shortly put Satan beneath their feet. So the icon, art work, word, ritual, concept and cultural milieu over many centuries is one message. There is complete victory and submission to His Lordship.

'Spoke to angels' Clearly God did speak to angels in Ezekiel 8-11 and 40-48. Daniel records speeches between angels in 10-11. But clearly the Pseudepigraphic literature may be in mind here and not simply the biblical.

'To which' indicates that God's messages are directed specifically to certain people and particularized, whether to Nebuchadnezzar, Abraham, Moses, Israel, Saul or Samuel, whether part of the chosen people or not. So there were messages to angels not given to men and vice versa. In the OT pre-exilic books this question would be meaningless, but by NT times many of the angels had names and profiles. 'until I make your enemies' not only asserts that God the Son has enemies, at the same time it neither affirms nor denies that these enemies are also such to God the Father. But the 'until' does not say what happens after all enemies are subdued. In this current time-frame God the Father is prayed to by the disciples and apparently the Father subdues the Son's enemies through the church-in-prayer.

God's promise to the Son is to make all of the Son's enemies a footstool, using the symbolism of ancient Egypt and representations of the pharaoh's feet on a decorated stool. In this verse the Father is executive in the final spiritual warfare to subdue all evil persons and powers. This is not a militant Son nor a militant church. In the times-and-book-context the church is suffering and a martyrs church. But this verse alone only has subjection not Phil 2 in its acclamation by all creation that Jesus is Lord YHWH to the glory of God the Father. Nor are the enemies destroyed but subdued. The Hebrew for 'angels' often is bene ha'elohim, while the singular is mala'k. As 'sons of the gods' the collective reference usually appears in poetic literature. The singular in Mal 4 is messianic in context. As 'messenger' he is apostle but never is he called disciple, although in Hebrews Jesus 'learned obedience through what he suffered.' But God never called the angels 'my son' only Solomon. 'I will put my trust in Him' are the words of Jesus. Some psalms of confidence have similar resolve and consequences. But If Jesus, as any son, is disciplined and learns obedience by what he experienced than the sons will also. But did Jesus need to make this discovery and commitment? Was it at the temple, at baptism, or Gethsemane? Believers bond with God's promises in the Bible. But there is a whole sphere of promises the Father gave to the Son and to him alone that we also share in. Here, as in most scriptures, the promise is set forth in a command first of all, and based on fulfilling that command God will act in certain ways. Here God acts through a time frame 'till thy enemies,' the Son's enemies, are totally subdued. The meaning is deeper than Egyptian art showing a huge pharaoh standing with one foot on a small enemy on a footstool. This is total victory over every enemy, and throughout the process of accomplishing this the Son is on the throne. From NT theology we know that Christ is seated till He returns. And so in this present age the Spirit, sent from the father and the Son is enabling God's people to make war. This content corresponds to Daniel 7 where God is ruling and hands the kingdom over. Here God is the Holy Warrior and The Son is the recipient of conquering grace, almost in a passive sense. As growing out of Psalm 2, an oracle spoken on the day of a new king's accession, it sets an agenda for his rule, and from this background the promise of God to the Son does not show the Son as passive, and as acting on the agenda. The picture of Sennacherib seated in a kingly-throne chariot outside Lachish, while the city is being taken and burned, the dead hung on poles [an early form of the cross, but for corpses not the living]. He is judging those brought before him, indicates that his role is not that of Narmer's Palette where the pharaoh is standing, wielding weapons and apparently engaged in hand to hand combat before cringing little foes. This heavenly king can 'sit' and in that posture achieve victory. This presents the problem of Revelation's horsemen, in which one is the Word of God.' David mentions a conversation between 'The Lord' Yahweh' speaking to 'my Lord' --the Messiah. Here the enemies are not David's and the time span is not one man's lifetime. Here is final victory in view, which David saw as a prophet. Ps 110.1.

"Footstool": Besides the iconography, there are 13 references to footstools in the Bible :1Chr. 28:2 King David rose to his feet and said: "Listen to me, my brothers and my people. I had it in my heart to build a house as a place of rest for the ark of the covenant of the LORD, for the footstool of our God, and I made plans to build it. Here the temple or house is viewed as the footstool, and hence the permanent place of God's session 2Chr. 9:18. The throne had six steps, and a footstool of gold was attached to it. On both sides of the seat were armrests, with a lion standing beside each of them. Since the throne and footstool were of one piece, to speak of the footstool includes the throne, and hence God's rule. Psa. 99:5 "Exalt the LORD our God and worship at his footstool; he is holy." This is either Jerusalem, Mount Zion, the temple or the heavenly throne. The LORD says to my Lord: "Sit at my right hand until I make your enemies a footstool for your feet." This verse is cited in Hebrews and comes under the domain of subjugation, where the enemies, even as Gideon placed his foot on his enemies' neck and killed them, this is subjugation. The foot cannot be placed on their necks long-term unless it is on a replica of enemies designed into an actual footstool Psa.

132:7 "Let us go to his dwelling place; let us worship at his footstool — Is. 66:1 Lam. 2:1 [93] Heb. 1:13 "To which of the angels did God ever say, 'Sit at my right hand until I make your enemies a footstool for your feet'"? Heb. 10:13 Since that time he waits for his enemies to be made his footstool, The last sent of verses are all prospective, promises and prophecies awaiting the time of complete victory. Since the NT scriptures use them, they cannot be considered fulfilled already. The Encyclopedia of Judaism cites the use of anthropomorphisms as follows: "(From the Greek meaning "human form"). The description of God in human terms is an anthropomorphism. There are numerous anthropomorphisms in the Scriptures, e.g. such phrases as "the image of God," "the hand of the Lord," "His outstretched arm," "the eyes of the Lord," or "His footstool." The prevailing view has always been the one expressed in the rabbinic phrase "the Torah speaks in the language of men" (Ber. 316); in other words, that the Bible uses such terms because they are the only kind of language which humans can understand. This is a clear affirmation that the biblical anthropomorphisms must not be taken literally, but should be viewed as metaphors to describe the otherwise impossible-to-describe Divine Presence and God's involvement in the history of Israel and of mankind. When the Bible refers to the "outstretched arm" of God, it is taken to indicate something of His power. Similarly, the expression "the eyes of the Lord" is interpreted as a metaphor for Divine omniscience. The first Aramaic translation of the Bible by Onkelos (first cent. CE) attempted to avoid some of the strongest anthropomorphisms by means of paraphrase. The rabbis of the Talmudic Period, while frequently using anthropomorphisms homiletically, were also keenly aware of the potential danger to the purely spiritual concept of God, should such anthropomorphisms be taken literally. They therefore had recourse to several phrases which sought to diminish such a possibility, for example, their use of the term ki-ve-yakhol, "if it were possible to say this..." Three responses are needed: 1. God did appear in human form in several accounts in the OT and only revision of actual text can eliminate these scriptures. 2. God is not raw force, and as Person must be described in human forms. In addition 3. the belief that the earthly corresponds to the reality in the 'heavenlies' means that there is a footstool and a throne in actuality, far more glorious than anything one can conceive of on earth. From Ps 2.7

'You are my son. Today I have fathered you.' Greek 'begotten you'. Said of Solomon, it is clear since at birth David promised the throne to him via his mother, a fact the prophet bore witness to. The death of the illegitimate child gave way to Solomon as God's gift. The birth is not in glory but upon the earth. Generally though, such terminology was used of adoption formula and not literal progenitor relationships. How does this picture differ from Dan 7? In some Jewish tradition and repeated by many in later years, there was one who was a special angel, and that in a non-messianic context. Lucifer was the most beautiful angel or star and he fell. Ezekiel 28 gives a little hint of that pre-history. But Satan never heard these words. Motivated by jealous wrath he then sought to destroy all that God was doing, and sought to be equal with God. Phil.2. But only to the Son did God make such a promise as this. In contrast to Gen 1, where man is to manage all higher mammals and life forms and arrange for the earth as territory for scattered mankind, man turned his energy on the environment and man himself. But that mission was not given to man, only to the Son. So beginning with Cain who sought to control Abel, and his descendants who established the first higher civilization in a network of rivers and canals requiring government to manage the territory and laws to manage people, man entered into a control era only punishable by making a situation possible where man cannot control things. Is this a rhetorical question? In modern 'Satan' theory the Lucifer, Bright and Morning Star, was a son of God and fell from a prominent position. But this verse would assert that being declared firstborn gave the father's blessing to him, and this blessing was victory in all conquests and lordship over all enemies ... Did the Son before creation already have enemies? This line is eschatological in focus, and hence eschatology precedes creation. Salvation is viewed as an inheritance, not merely a gift or grace and it is still future, in the not so distant future. Ps 110.4 is used in 1.13 then 5.5-10 to contrast Jesus and Aaron. "The role of high priest was not usurped in either case, but bestowed by divine appointment. Fitzmyer,223,[94] The ascended and glorified Christ at God's right hand has the promise that God will eventually make 'your enemies a footstool for your feet.' The continued existence of enemies as an interpretation would follow Egyptian representations of a conqueror. But the intent is to declare total victory, not their conversion to non-life forms. Perhaps this situation fits the Millennium. This is said of no earthly king except perhaps the one in Isa 9, and implies a period between session of Christ and the victory over all the enemies, namely the church age. G. Campbell has said the OT has no inkling of a church or church age. At least here is a time between session and when God gives the Son the complete victory. Catholic eschatology has seen the church establishing the city of God on earth gradually; this verse hardly allows this to happen mainly through human effort. ,2.6-9 the former citation of Ps 110.1b, the latter Ps 8.4-6 on Christ's ascension Fulfilled in per.13 as Ps #8. Payne, 573[95] 1.13b,2.5; 10.13 First and last cite Ps 110.1c on Christ's Messianic kingdom. 2.5 of making 'the world to come' subject to Christ. This is the new world order inaugurated by Christ's enthronement at his ascension.

1.14 'All angels'[not aggelos word but simply 'all,' either includes fallen ones or not. An example of ministering leitourgika is found in Daniel's account. The definition is that angels in heaven are 'spirits' pneumata, but on earth 'sent ones'; apostellomena on earth 'sent' and in function ministering' eisin leitourgika; pneumata to serve eis diakonian. Those served are the heirs, placing the heirs above the rank of angels. If Satan in Job was one of the bene 'elohim and these were angels, was he on a mission to investigate all mankind and to test the limits of endurance of Job? If so the limits of his duty were clearly set. But in the End Time Satan is cast on earth and then are those limits removed? Nothing is said about non-heirs so this is a deterministic problem of interpretation based on the other side of the coin. In that case nothing even implicit is said about the non-heirs in this verse.

'Inherit salvation' as a phrase goes back to nahalot YHWH referring to both the land and to Israel. The inheritance in this book links to interpreting the covenant as really a Last Will and Testament. Christ, the first party has died and therefore the party of the second part, believers inherit. Thus salvation is not due to merit, or mere gift or grant but is within the Father-Son inheritance law pattern. In the ANE it is possible to use a divorce formula and forever declare performatively 'you are not my son' as well as disinheriting a son. The other possibility is that believers inherit because of brotherhood with Christ the Son we are heirs, but then the problem is one of the death of the testator. In the OT the testament aspect of the covenant is barely touched upon. This is an inner-Greek problem. 'inherit salvation' kleronomein swterian... corresponds to 1.4 'inherited a name' keklerono meken onoma. Where Christ is in the 'already' and believers in the 'not yet'. 'inherit' goes back to the OT use and at least 14 references in the Encyclopedia of Judaism and 45 occurrences in the OT. Under the root, which includes 'seasonal river' there are 196 occurrences, usually with a preposition beth or definite article attached. Ex. 32:13 Remember your servants Abraham, Isaac and Israel, to whom you swore by your own self: 'I will make your descendants as numerous as the stars in the sky and I will give your descendants all this land I promised them, and it will be their inheritance forever.'" is an oath or covenant context referring to the land or promise. Ex. 34:9 "O Lord, if I have found favor in your eyes," he said, "then let the Lord go with us. Although this is a stiff-necked people, forgive our wickedness and our sin, and take us as your inheritance."shows the inheritance to be Israel, God's inheritance as in Eph 1.18. 'inherit' salvation is the Hebrew Scriptures background of the land as nachal or inherited portion, based on adoption of Israel as God's

Son. Within election and adoption context, not covenant, there is no salvation by merit even here in Hebrews. Salvation in this view is still future since it encompasses so much already realized as Hebrews presents it, but also so much still to come that could be lost through unfaithfulness or neglect of the saving word. The role here of all angels without exception is as ministering spirits to serve those who will inherit salvation. While these people are serving God and men angels are serving them. But what is this service? Isa 6 is an illustration where seraphim serve God in worshipful song and proclamation and serve Isaiah by a powerful cleansing applied by the seraphim. All angels serve the elect, all are sent. These 'who will inherit salvation' presents the tension of the book that the ministering is absolutely necessary because they have not inherited their final salvation of their souls yet. Later the theme of apostasizing is introduced in various degrees, and the theme of perseverance in faith is asserted in many ways. 'Inherit" implies that diathēkē meant 'Testament' and the death of the Testator. The OT word is nhl 'inheritance' but is used of land, and if stretched, it is used of descendants as heirs of the promise. Here 'inheritance' is not related to Adam's 'soil' but to the 'tree of life' not to 'toil' but to 'rest from labors.'

'Ministering servants' might be broader than angels, but here only the good ones are included. All of these sent forth to serve, possibly including pastors and teachers and missionaries and so on, are to serve for the sake of those who will be saved. Man's role is to serve God and the angels' role is to serve the redeemed 'who are to obtain salvation.' Hebrews paints salvation as still future. The serving and receiving that service is strongly joined to obtaining the goal in the end, almost as cause and effect. The process of pressing toward this goal is everywhere set forth in this book. But salvation is not through dead works but through serving the living God. Faith is the total response of the Servant to the Lord and those he is seeking to save and helping them obtain this. According to this verse there is no sent angel or minister whose goal is other than aiding these people to obtain salvation at last.

"All": are all angels good and ministers for good? Or are temptations ultimately for good? How do they minister or "serve"? A study of angels in Daniel, Ezekiel, Zechariah, Jesus [temptation and Gethsemane] etc., should yield some information about this. Should people pray to angels as Ezekiel, Daniel and John, Joshua, Abraham and Gideon dialogued with angels? But in 2.18 temptation is wrong and hence not done by angels but by Satan 2.15; Angels do not deliver; only the high priest does Cf. . 2.15,18. There is no other intercessor or Saviour under the Gospel. Angels are called guardians of the created order and assisters at gatherings of public worship. Note Ps

137[138].1 where LXX reads enantion aggelwn ...soi. Rev 8.3 shows an angel as mediator of the prayers of the saints. Two Qumran writings show the presence of angels in sacred gatherings. War Scroll col.7 "for holy angels accompany their armies." 1QM 7.4-6. Rule of Congregation: "for holy angels are [present] in their [congregation]. This precludes anyone unclean from entering the assembly. Fitzmyer,[96]198n. Is this rhetorical [answer yes] or a moot question[some angels may not be ministering angels but of another kind]. Ministering ei diakonian is used of service rendered to man, self or God.[97] Besides the NT to act as deacon [1 Tim 3.10,13], that is to wait on tables in the early church relief program, it is used to act as servants in Plato, to render a service[98] To act as servants' requires the middle voice. The parallel of angels to mighty ones, to heavenly hosts, and 'his servants' is extended to 'his works everywhere.' While this begins in heaven it extends to all creation. 'Who do his bidding'//'who obey his word'//'who do his will' are parallel. It is the obedient that can worthily praise God. In v.22 the author includes himself 'praise the Lord, O my soul' as one of the obedient ones. Ps 13.20. This is one of the few declarations that all angels are ministering spirits, invisible aids, for those who will inherit salvation, to help them on the way. They serve believers. But Jesus' role is different indeed. The form of a question is that it stimulates the answer 'yes'. While Daniel and Zechariah and Genesis have narratives about angels here is a declarative statement about them.. Myriads of angels are called leitourgika pneumata, agents of divine worship, "occupying themselves with praising God and proclaiming God as sovereign. On earth the leitourgika officiates 8.2, as in Heaven 'the Son' does, since this epistle portrays Heaven as a place of religious seriousness, reverence, worship, and praise. Thus in 1.6 "and let all the angels of God worship kai prosknesatwsan autw pantes aggeloi theou. Much of this comes from Isaiah 6.[99]. Cockerill[100] argues a common tradition accounts for the use of archiereus' high priest' as a title, and possibly from a liturgy, but ignores the Gnostic use of terms beginning with arch- . In the OT 'priest' suffices for the high priest in many places.

Chapter Two:

Christ is Greater than the Angels and Apostles

God's Message, Miracles, Creation, and High Priest

2.1 'Drift away' is from the message heard but was it acted on? The 'we' is inclusive of speaker and hearers. Assuming that the treatise is a presentation of the Gospel to all men believers or not and Jews or Gentiles, the basic Gospel portions must be distinguished from those that are warning believers to not fail in their faith or worse, to deny the Lord. But as a working hypothesis, if it is directed to all men then every part of the treatise is important for their faith. Since the faith chapter Memorial of Heroes has those who had earthly successes as well as others who did not. Some delivered others and others were not delivered. Still they remained true. 2.6-7 asserts the universality of the scope of creation and v.9 that He died for 'everyone.'

'drift away' mepote pararuwmen < pararrew 1 pl.aor.pass.subj. 'to drift away.' "Flow by, slip away, be washed away' a nautical metaphor. A-G,622. 'lest / so that we do not drift away[from them]' , mepote pararuwmen Several illustrative uses are apropos: 1. 'Many points escaped you' Plato Legus 781a. "Disappeared from memory' Gp.Prooem.4. Of persons: 'slip away from one's senses' Eup.357.6; 'to be careless, neglect advice' LXX,Pr 3.21 and Heb 2.1. The subjunctive with me pote gives a negative possibility and consequence. 'Dia; touto dei ' therefore,' placed first in Greek stresses the logical connection with all the content of the first chapter, which stresses the finality of 'The Son's' message v.1, as possibly made available by angels v.14. So read v.14 'ministering' is defined by the role in these last days of the Son. But it is not the role of angels that presents the urgency.

Elsewhere in the book the urgency is that after the son there is no further possibility of grace. Here dei' already expresses 'necessity' and this is intensified by perissoterw" 'more' careful attention' 'to hold before one'[101].

Hearing is not enough. The action as accusative is subject of the infinitive and includes the speaker as part of the 'we'. He is not elevating himself into a separate status in grace. The commonality of 'what had been held' expressed in the infinitive toi'" akousyeisin, is essentially what is presented in this book by way of remembrance, a motif repeated often. The urgency is not toward an apostle or living witness but to what they had heard, which is viewed as a body of truth. The comparative is frequently used for the superlative, which was in decline, hence endings in -rws in Heb 7.15; 2.1,13; 13.19 'much more' increases the comparative per. mallon. [102]

The pattern for the book and almost all NT epistles is to place Christology or doctrine first, as in ch.1 and follow this by an exhortation. 'Therefore' expresses the immediate connection between what we would call the sermon or homily and the invitation or appeal. The appeal, as in this case, and more so in Paul's, carries the expressive mode of speech, whereby the concern, feeling, urgency comes through in verses 1-3. It matters what happens to those who read this treatise. Amelein is the opposite of prosexein "to fix one's attention, attach oneself' Cf. 1 Tim 4.14; Heb 2.1,3 "Do not neglect the spiritual gift that is in you'.

The negative appears frequently me amelei "to express a psychological orientation of zeal and urgency or application to a task." Amelew is used in medicine of neglected parents, lost for lack of care, of functionaries in public administration who default of obligations. It is used of a proxy who shirks his obligations. Cf. . 1 Tim 4.14. The expanded verb epimeleomai in 1 Tim 3.5 is used "to busy oneself, take care, direct' a public function of the minister in pastoral role including the devotion needed with respect to his task. He must 'look after the church of God." It can be used of any role in the ekklesia, but the task must require personal devotion, effective leadership and diligent application. Spicq,1.88n5; 3.39

2.1-3 The use of 'we' includes the leadership but also all those who read the treatise, Christian or non-Christian, Jew or Gentile, Messianic Jew or Circumcision Party Jew. The inclusiveness of the recipients of the treatise needs further study. But by using 'we' and 'us' the author is identifying common concerns, not simply that he has heard information about these people, but that he has not heard but yet is concerned for their spiritual welfare.We may mean 'any of us Hebrews while 'us' could mean 'all of us Hebrews.' Snell is thus not narrowing the recipients yet to mainly Christians.Ch.13. reflects the shepherd's heart and in 13.20 Jesus is called the Great Shepherd.

"The word used here —pararruew— occurs nowhere else in the New Testament. The Septuagint translators have used the word only once. Proverbs 3:21."Son, do not pass by (mh pararruhv) but keep my counsel;" that is, do not pass by my advice by neglect, or suffer it to be disregarded."[103] 'To slip beside' or 'by the side of'' from 'flow' would mean to drift by theside of' like driftwood. Had these people drifted past the centrality of Christ.[104] As aorist this may be finished action, and a result or a whole event if they aren't careful.

It is necessary dei involves logical as well as necessary to survive connection.The truly necessary things fill the pages of Hebrews both in regard to doctrine, reality, God, the Messiah, the present and eternity, and especially faithfulness versus apostasy.They must receive Christ's atonement for the old sacrificial animals no longer are pertinent.

2.2 'By angels' contrasts to 1.1 and 1.2 and refers to the Jewish belief that angels communicated the Law to Moses at Sinai. In Hebrew or Aramaic malakh could refer to malakh YHWH and thus to the Lord himself. But Jewish belief had removed God from his presence as a person in every-day affairs. Still if God so revealed himself then, how much more important to obey now. Note that angels did appear to Abraham, Jacob, Joshua, Ezekiel, Daniel and others. Respect, not worship was due them.

'Every word binding' bebaiw" is 'firm' as used of a root, a belief religiously, of declaration by a mantis-prophet, of hope, promise, confidence, and the dependable effect of the Eucharist and its validity. Subjectively it can mean confidence Heb 3.14, putting up a dialectic between the objective firmness of the Faith and the subjective experience of it as a result. In Phaedo "the word was valid." 2 Pet 1.19 the prophetic word is altogether reliable.' The Testament is valid To 'confirm the call' means to not let it elapse. Faith can be steadfast; a church well-established.[105]

"Every violation and disobedience received its just punishment" could refer to the major transgressions of Israel in the wilderness or the punishment on the cumulative sins by means of Exile. This belief is close to Job's friends that truly every single transgression is punished. Arndt and Gingrich: 'just penalty' while noting it can also mean 'reward.' Heb. 11.26 and 2.2 10.35 are the only citations, the usage being confined to Biblical and Ecclesiastical use. In view of the two parts to the composite noun 'recompense' might be more suitable. There was a great deal of forgiveness in the OT period, and some following 'recompense,' not instead of it. David's child by Bathsheba, his census, Hezekiah's[106] patronizing with Babylonians, all had some 'recompense' but not severe punishment.

"The message spoken by angels" is usually identified with the 'messenger of YHWH' and the giving of the law in Judaism, here called law or covenant. Perhaps the intent is to include all revelation in the OT through angels, including the 'messenger of YHWH' and hence the inconclusive language with focus on the latter books of Ezekiel, Daniel and Zecharaiah. And Malachi, which bear witness to the punishment of Israel. 2.1 confirms the reading to give attention "to what we have heard."

"Was every violation justly punished" Historical books would say no, but Jeremiah make the exile punishment for all the accumulated violations in all generations. So the truth holds that God always and justly gives punishment, the "drift" or ignore" is spoken to by the writer using 'We" and "us." This may include both Jewish and Jewish Christian readers. "Ignore" seems too light a word if directed to unbelievers, but the evidential character of:

1. Eyewitnesses;
2. The lord's own words;
3. The signs wonders and miracles;
4. The gift of the Holy Spirit, would all indicate 'unbelievers' here. So the polemic is also apologetic. The pastoral homily to believers is also a preached Gospel. The gospel is clearly being presented to believer and unbeliever alike. Bruce compares the description of the Son to Wisdom in Prov 8.22f, Wisd 2-4; Wisd 7.26 where wisdom is the effulgence apausgasma v.3 of everlasting light. Cf. Jn 1.1ff; Col 1.15ff Thus pre-eminence is in terms of wisdom and communication. 1 John 1.5-6 says God is light and in him is no darkness at all. But in describing wisdom in Proverbs little of this language is used. The fire of God on the altar and glory on Moses' face and tabernacle are better references to this effulgence. If reference is made to Gen 1.1-2, "let there be light" there would be then a time when this light came into being and in harmony with the description of wisdom in Prov 8. But Christ was with the Father in the beginning. John 1.1. 1 John 1.1-5. If viewed as a projection of the godhead actualizing itself in the created universe then the beginning of light, wisdom and the son are not a time-when or before when, but the moment of creation when this aspect of deity breaks into chaos. Similarly Paul was awakened by light and came to know Christ, just as the blind people found healing and this is compared to spiritual sight. Paul especially emphasizes wisdom as one aspect or realization of deity in Christ 1 Cor 1. This declares that every sin received just punishment as an historical fact for the Exodus or OT period. Many of these must have been temporal. But punishment must be

distinguished from the later topic in ch.12 on chastisement. Here the reason is disobedience not sanctification as in ch.12.

Similarly the prophets speak of punishment but wise men of chastisement. logos corresponds, in large, to dabar. The stress on the 'word' brings out many nuances, the main of which is the message, oracle, revelation of God. The source and gravity of this word is greater than any other. The point isn't 'salvation or punishment' but salvation and if neglected there is awesome punishment, but the punishment is not specified. The usual exegesis begins with the post-biblical conviction among rabbis that the Law was given through angels. Within the Exodus and wilderness time-frame it is true that every violation was punished in its time but usually after considerable patience on God's part or intervention on Moses' part.

But that as a general truth all disobediences is always punished this seems to ignore the data of Job and Ecclesiastes that God's will does not always correspond to man's sense of justice nor with God's program of mercy. The punishment concept is the same for OT or NT faith if people reject the Word of salvation. The stress is 'even more so' under the age of grace. Logos bebaios is used of a revelatory word or oracle through Moses that is 'valid and authentically divine.' The veracity of these prophecies in the OT is guaranteed by the transfiguration of Jesus. Bebaioteron...logon 2 Pet 1.19. Note that bebaios 'that on which one can walk' hence' solid, firm, durable" and then 'sure, certain.' If it modifies logos it means an utterance that is well-founded, authorized and thus convincing.' Thus firmness implies immutability of a promise, institution or Word of God Papyris have considerable uses in the legal domain meaning 'valid, guaranteed'. Cf. . Rom 4.16 bebaian ten epanggelian The promise is not only firm and immutable, assured for all posterity, but is guaranteed to them. Cf. . Mk 16.20 ton logon bebaiountov The Lord confirms the word, but authenticates and guarantees it. [107]Spicq,1.281; 3.29, The mediation of Angels at Sinai is based on Dt 33.2[108] .

> 'Angels' is not mere avoidance of Anthropomorphism or denial that the law came from God. Dunn,140nn.65,67. The word spoken by angels was God's word just as the prophets' words were and this is from God. So they had to be fulfilled since they were the message of God Himself albeit not a loud voice from Sinai.

2.3 'First...by the Lord' Thus not 'covenant' but God's word speaking of salvation theology. Not 'God' but 'Jesus' here. From now on the kingdom is preached to you. Before and after Christ's person and message is the proper division of history. This links directly to 1.1. Here the word is confirmed by miracles, a first witness; the second is the apostles and the third God. 'How shall we escape' again is inclusive of believer and unbeliever alike because the backslider will be neglecting salvation for his ability to endure and the unbeliever neglecting the one salvation that is available. The only alternative is punishment not chastisement, which comes in ch.12 and is addressed to believers only. There is nothing in the Hebrew Scriptures allusion to the sanctions of the covenant, only the decrees of judging punishments more in keeping with prophetic words. The Lord, then the first generation and now the third generation is passing it on to the fourth generation. The pattern is similar to Luke's Introduction. Faith involves not only faith in the Lord but faith in the apostles, 'those that heard him' a past and closed experience, but the third generation as well, without the authority of 'apostle.' Still the word is that spoken by the 'Lord' as distinguished here from 'God.'

'How shall we escape' includes author, co-workers and readers in the 'we' style that might be more than epistolary rhetoric. In the argument of this context and the whole book the 'we' should be Gospel-Era people, of whatever faith and background. Ekfeugw is categorized by Arndt-Gingrich as 'escape by flight' making this a resultative verb. Other uses .'run away, seek safety in flight' make it a process verb. But meaning 3 'shun, avoid' used of 'the world', would simply be lack of engagement with kakian or maxen . The meaning would then be determined by the preceding lines: avoid punishment. [109]

Note that simple feugw covers a broader field[110] Gen 19.17 is the warning to Lot to flee to the mountains so as to escape the conflagration. Heb 6.18 is flight 'to take hold of the promises'of God, not from God. Cf. Isa 17.13; 21.15; Lk 21.21. Most OT uses, and there arem any, deal with war-flight situations and not the final judgment. 'ignore' amelesante" swtheria",[111] is for any person, believer or not. The concept, not the word amelew,[112] in the following references shows the seriousness of it.[113] This seems to refer to the Nazareth incident in lk 4.18-19, which deals with the proclamation of salvation without that key word appearing in the text. The reference of the whole 'to the Lord' [Jesus= YHWH) rings of 'salvation' not the 'kingdom' and this migh be due to the politics of the speaker's situation. It sounds as if it is directed to non-believers. But anyone may ignore' or 'neglect' this great salvation. The rest of the book through ch.12 explains why one must not neglect it and also the greatness of this salvation. This then, is the topic paragraph. In view of many exhortations that speak of drifting away or backsliding it is clear that believers are included in this reference. Ch.10.25 speaks of forsaking the assembling together. This plus the stress in chapter 13 on respecting their leaders might indicate pressure from without to deny Christ, coupled with pressure from within over leaders in the church or societal unit that they can't agree with.[114] Again on amelew and epimeleomai 'to not matter'; and 'to busy oneself with,see to'. The [a] is a negation. The base verb is melei 'to care for someone with respect to someting, to take an interest in, or busy oneself with a matter. Meletaw 'think about, mediate on' and 'to be busy about, exert oneself, practice'.

'To be careless, negligent, to to put oneself out.' But amelew Cf. . Matt 22.5; Jer 48.10 curses this kind of attitude. [115] çonditional participle "from which, if ye keep yourselves' Acts 15.29,[116] The theme here is salvation. Later in the book 'covenant' is the dominant theme. What is the relation to them?Compare 'salvation' in Isaiah and Hosea with 'covenant' in Hosea and Jeremiah along with Deuteronomy. The urgency of appeal in Isaiah 55.6-13 'Do not delay' " may well make one poem with the preceding paragraph. Delay in responding to the divine invitation may be fatal. Divine grace is no excuse for human complacency. Ps 95.7-11; Rom 6.1f; Heb 3.7-19. "Let the wicked man abandon his way of life and return to the God whose forgiveness is 'abundant' yarbeh."v.7 Note that 'seek...call to' qa2ra æ are in sacrifice and public or private vocal prayer 'call aloud'. The urgency in Isa 55 lies in a time-window 'while he may be found' behimmats Niphal tolerativum 'while he lets himself be found' "Man must not presume upon God's patience."

'Turn back shub is 'repentance' Hos 6.1. Wesley preached a sermon in his collected sermons called "The Repentance of Believers" so this truth is important for everyone in any congregation, believers or non-believers. North[117] 259 'God also testified to it by signs' fits the pattern of 'message spoken' the law, 'first announced' the revelation first through Christ; 'was confirmed to us by those who heard him' the second witness, and then God's testifying the third witness. The original message was sent by God, then spoken by angels or messengers, possibly including Moses, and the extraordinary punishments are the third witness. The role of the disciple is to confirm what Christ announced, and this role uses the scripture, logic, personal testimony, rhetoric, exposition and every means possible to bring about faith in the hearers.

2.4 'Gifts of the Holy spirit distributed according to his will.' corrresponds to 1 Cor 12.3-4 both for plurality of gifts and v.11 that God distributes according to His own plan. Eph 4.7 makes these gifts the chief evidence of the 'Session' of Jesus at the Father's right hand. The link to Joel 2.28 where the gifts are different: prophecy, dreams, visions. 'Gifts...His will.' Paul urged people to seek the best gifts, those that will establish the church. Here the apostles and second generation apostles receive these gifts only according to God's will and not unilaterally across all those meeting together as in Acts 2. Here the gifts are evidences of Christianity and powerful proofs of the truth of the faith.

'His will' The words 'distributed' do not appear, since the focus is not on the gift but the witness. Boulh appears in 6.17 . Note qelema appears in 10.7,9,10,36 and 13.21; the verb qelw in 10.5; 10.8; 12.17; 13.18;and qelesis in 2.4 . How do these 4 evidences of Christianity differ? The miracles gifts and witnesses are reflected from Ex 15.11 'wonders' 'power' and Ps 89.5 among other passages. The gifts of the Holy Spirit are listed with signs, wonders and miracles, all of which are confirmations and evidences to confirm the word spoken by Christ. They are' distributed according to his will' although the number and kinds of gifts are not listed here.

Here perhaps the confirmation is not for unbelievers but believers in the body of the church.[118] Semeion was a prodigy that is recognizable and provides proof for everyone. In the NT it is a category of miracle, together with mighty works dynamically and wonders terata, Acts 2.22; 2 Thess 2.9; 2 Cor 12.12; Heb 2.4.; but it retains its value as a sign or demonstration. n.19.3.252. The command to tell all His wonders links the OT to the words of Jesus to his disciples and to people recently healed. The immediate witness is crucial. Myers,[119]153,

Amelew 'neglect' 'to not care' or 'placed no value' on what Christ had done.The tragedy of moving from a message of salvation and drifting off because of no interest in it is a danger to recent catechumens or hearers of the message.Cf. .Matt 22.5 'made light of' seems to indicate they had become unaware of the seriousness of what they are doing.

2.5 'The world to come' is Jewish terminology, and may not fit the New Jerusalem concept. "world to come" is inclusive of

1. God's original plan for man v.6-8;
2. Bring many sons to Glory v.10;
3. A whole family 2.11;
4. The presence of God v.12;
5. The destination of the Devil v.4;
6. Freedom from fear and death v.15;
7. It is for Abraham's descendants v.16. This is part of the eschatology of this book. 'World to come' or 'coming inhabited earth' the world of People and their civilizations. The Dan 7 paragraph of the holy People indicates that

with the Son of Man they will reign forever. Scriptures vary in the on-earth administration of the millennium or beyond. Some point to the Jews, Christians will judge the world, Christ will rule on earth, Finally Christ will turn the kingdom over to the Father, etc. Definitely the angels, good or evil, will have a part in the final war but not in ruling this kingdom.

'World to come' would mean something different to early Christians, or Qumran and other sectarians, main line official Judaism of the pre- or post-70 CE destruction, and the major political parties and persuasions before 70 CE such as Sadduccees, Pharisees, Zealots, Herodians, or others. Several things are not shared with angels 1.13 or authorized for angels to do. The world-to-come, a phrase from Hebrew or Aramaic, which may not correspond to the concept of Millenium.

2.5-10 hadar splendor: Jenni-Westermann:[120]

1. Extra-Hebr. words related to hadar "ornament, splendor, majesty" may be identified with certainty only in Aram. On Ug. hdrt see 3b; on Old SArab. hdr "ornament(?)" on Eg. hdrt [121] . A relationship to Hebr. 'dr addir or Arab. hdr "to effervesce" (GB 175a), which is sometimes posited, is rather doubtful. The verbal forms are apparently denominatives from the subst. hadar [122] . In addition to hadar (in Dan 11:20 with a segholate cs. form heder instead of the more common hadar,[123] a fem. hodara "finery, grandeur" occurs (see 3b); Bibl. Aram. has hadar "majesty" amd hdr pa. "to glorify." Imp. Aram. has hdr "majesty" (AhΩ. 108) and hdyr "majestic"[124]

2. The root occurs 42x in the Hebr. OT it is represented 6x in Aram. The verb appears 6x in Hebr., 4x in the qal and 1x each in the ni. and the hitp. (see 3c). The subst. hadar occurs 31x (incl. heder in Dan 11:20; pl. only in Psa 110:3), hodara 5x. The word group occurs most often in the Psa (15x; Isa 8x; Prov 4x; Lev 3x); it is entirely absent from narrative texts. Aram. occurrences are limited to Dan (noun and pa. 3x each).

3. (a) The subst. hadar characterizes nature's grandeur (Lev 23:40; Isa 35:2a) and human beauty (Isa 53:2; Psa 8:6; Prov 20:29; 31:25). In reference to God, the declaration of beauty acquires the meaning "glory, grandeur, majesty" (Cf. . Isa 35:2b with v 2a; see 4). In the sense of "majesty," hadar is also an attribute of the earthly king (Psa 21:6; 45:4, 5; Aram. Dan 4:27, 33; 5:18; Prov 14:28). The pl. in Psa 110:3 may more likely refer to the royal finery (consisting of various ornamental pieces;[125]. hadar

also pertains, however, to cities (Isa 5:14; Ezek 27:10; Lam 1:6) or a tribe (Deut 33:17). According to Dan 11:20, Israel is heder malkut "an ornament of the kingdom." Several passages describe God or a person as "clothed" with hadar (Yahweh, Psa 104:1; Job 40:10; housewife, Prov 31:25; Jerusalem, Ezek 16:14; qal ptcp. Isa 63:1). Par. terms for hadar are hod "loftiness" (Psa 21:6; 45:4; 96:6; 104:1; 111:3; Job 40:10; 1 Chron 16:27), kabod "glory" (˘ kabod; Isa 35:2; Psa 8:6; 21:6; Cf. . Psa 145:5, 12), pahad "terror" (Isa 2:10, 19, 21), ˘ koah "might" (Psa 29:4), {'oz "strength" (˘ {zz; Psa 96:6; Prov 31:25), tiperet "ornament" Psa 96:6; Prov 20:29), and to'ar "stateliness" (Isa 53:2). Other synonyms for hadar include 'eder 'addiîr,..... This interpretation should be maintained with Donner[126] on the basis of Ug. hdrt in KTU 1.14.III.51, which parallels hlm "dream" and could mean something like "vision, face"; the derivations in UT no. 752 and WUS no. 817 remain uncertain in any case. (c) The qal verb means "to adorn someone's appearance, honor someone" (Lev 19:32 "you should stand up in the presence of a gray head and honor the aged"). In juridical terminology it acquires the nuance "to give preference (in judgment)." Lev 19:15 demands impartial judgment: "You should not regard the person of the poor nor favor the mighty" The apodictic saying in Exod 23:3 is also usually emended as an apodosis[127] Exod 23:6 represents the protasis). The Aram. pa. always means "to honor (God)" The hitp. refers to self-attributed honor ("before the king" Prov 25:6, par. to "to assume the place of the mighty.") The ni. should be rendered "to come to be honored" or the like (Lam 5:12).

4. hadar plays a special role in Israel's praise (Psa 96:6; 104:1; 111:3; 145:5, 12; 1 Chron 16:27) as an expression of God's royalty.[128] Hymnic praise of Yahweh's "beauty"[129] grows out of the experience of his historical deeds (Psa 111:3; 145:5, 12). The communal prayer (Psa 90:16) is based on it. The association of God's splendor with his activity in history is broadened to include Yahweh's glory revealed in his creation (Psa 104:1). Even when Israel speaks of God's majesty as unwavering (Psa 96:6; 1 Chron 16:27), it means that which takes place at God's impulse (Isa 35:2b; Cf. . 63:1). The "splendor of his majesty" is experienced even in Yahweh's judgment, Isa 2:10, 19, 21; the combination of two synonymous words has superlative force, Joüon §141m). Yahweh's chosen, Israel's king (Psa 21:6; 45:4f.; Prov 14:28), the pious (Psa 149:9; Cf. . Mic 2:9), Jerusalem (Ezek 16:14), and Zion (Lam 1:6), participate in his majesty. Israel also recognizes God's grandeur in creation and consequently praises the

creator (Psa 8:6). But Israel knows that it cannot obtain divine glory for itself (Job 40:10). Perfect beauty exists only insofar as God grants hadar (Ezek 16:14). The use of Ps 8 with its singular refers not to a collective but to the sovereign Christ.

2.6 'What is man' deals with anthropology of adam[earth bound], enosh[weak], ben-adam[human], n'philim[dead men], gibbor [heroes] and meth- as well as 'ish [males]. As for 'Adam' he is part of earth and part of God. Thus ruach, is opposed to adamah, and nefesh is life shared with other creatures. But yetser is the 'frame, constitution or character' of man as with a good and evil tendency. It is diffiicult to not read modern categories into analysis of biblical psychology.

"There is a place" [naturally a situation, geography, time, culture, context, event] and a 'someone' nameless. We read in Ps 8 'David" in the superscription. Here only 'someone.'. The person, authority, history, motivation are divorced brom its eternal meaning. The WORD is a 'Stand-Alone Application.' It is not pertinent from the standpoint of authority or meaning. New Criticism looks carefully at background; here the Text is all that matters.

In context with martyrdom, accusation, pressure, death, suffering, while others are backsliding and denying the Lord does not negate the care of God for all mankind because of what man is, however that is defined. pou means 'where ever' here and 4.4 an indefinite, but 'approximately' in Rom 4.19[130]. This line in the OT is answered positively and negatively in Psalm 8 and 144.3.

2.7 'led to glory' here v.10 is heaven or is it 'perfect' which is 'holy'? 'Glory' translates many words, but as the Encyclopedia of Judaism says it may involve a spiritual attainment to see the Transcendence of God: "mysteries of the Divine Chariot, and other kabbalistic themes. Eleazar held that the Divine light or glory (Heb. kabod) once revealed to the prophets can still become visible to chosen mystics, thus bridging the void between God's transcendence in the realms above and mortal man here below. To attain this vision, one must continually seek God through a life of piety (Hasidut) demanding saintliness and humility, prayerful devotion and contemplation, altruism, religious example, and love of fellowman. According to Eleazar, the formulation of each blessing enables man to approach God as an intimate friend, while "no monument sheds such glory as an untarnished name." Glory also can stand for the Person of God: "The word qadosh ("holy") applied to God means metaphysical transcendence, while the word kabod ("glory") refers to the indwelling experienced presence of God. Thus the hymn, "Holy, Holy, Holy is the Lord of Hosts, the whole world is full of His glory" (Isa. 6:3), expresses the paradoxical nature of God's utter transcendence coupled with His constant immanence. God is beyond the world, far removed from it ontologically and conceptually (Ps. 97:9), yet He is very much the ground of all being (Ex. 3:12- 15), the "soul of our soul," accessible to man at all times (Ps. 145:18). He is God who reveals Himself to man, yet often appears to be a "hidden God" (Isa. 45:15). The biblical concept of God is personalistic, i.e., He is portrayed in terms of personality. He appears as a moral will who engages in dialogue with men, demanding and commanding, judging, punishing and rewarding. God contemplates and plans, decides and chooses, and acts purposefully. He is aware of the human condition (Ex. 2:24) and reaches out to man in love. Elsewhere Glory is an explicative, a shout, and a title for God himself, or for heaven and all that entails. Jesus was lower than the angels for a time, not God. So the argument for humanity of chapter 2 must read Ps 8 as 'angels'. Thus he goes through the process of being 'cared for' by God and brought to glory just as any man must also experience. Psalms are prophecy for man in general, and here is both poetry and prose. Man already has a lot of glory and power. But originally it was over 'everything.' God still has a purpose for man as seen in Dan 7 where the Messiah takes the throne followed by the Holy Ones taking the throne to rule. The destiny of man is to be crowned with glory and honor with everything under his feet, and this is not fulfilled as yet. Men who seek glory are seeking to preempt God and thus are children of Satan. But Jesus is the first of the line of humanity that is now crowned with glory and honor. The connection with suffering and death brings Jesus into a line of martyrs who through death share in the promise of glory. The original literally was lower than 'elohim' and does have contextual variants. But the context here requires 'than angels' in an age when angels were emphasized. What is the MT problem?[131] Based on 1 Cor 2.8 and Jas 2.1 "Here kyrios is a title of supremacy and even divinity. Here Ps 8.5-7 is quoted, where doxa and time are a lordly crown. His glory is greater than Moses' glory[132]

2.8 'Put everything under his feet.' While scholars differ as to the referent, man in general or Jesus in particular the 'But' in v.9 is the shift from general to particular. Thus 'man' and 'son of man' are taken as equivalents for humankind. If 'Son of man' is particularized on the basis of Jesus' usage referring to himself then the shift takes place here. The 'But' contrast is between mankind in particular and one descendant of Adam, Jesus, for whom it is ordained to suffer for all mankind in order to bring sons to glory. Nor can 'man' refer to Adam alone and 'son of Adam' except in this reading 'Cain' is the obvious elder son with one chapter of detail on his descendents and almost no mention about Abel or Seth. But 'everything' either is an extension of the promise in Gen 1 or a reading of Gen 1 as a merism to include all things. What Gen 1 says is that man he is given authority and enabling to govern all animal forms of life, which by extension would later include ruling power over mankind. What is not stated is that the air or heavens, sea, fish or plant life is subject to him. Plant life is rather 'given' to him and other animals for food. Is this in Hebrews an extension of the original mandate in a context of the history of revelation and salvation or is it merely a clarification of a merism—an expression of two or more elements to include within it everything? In this context the prime mandate to mankind, which man has failed to achieve or assume would then be contrasted to Jesus, who will rule all things, but only as he suffers to redeem all mankind. I prefer to retain the quote v.6-7 as referring to mankind in poetic form and v.8 as a comment on that quote. 'We don't see' because it hasn't happened because of man's need of redemption. But through the route of suffering, not of mankind's suffering or of Israel's suffering, as some Jewish scholars would maintain, but through the suffering of one man, Jesus, reconciliation and adoption occur, not ruling or subjugation, but rather the contrast of brotherhood. This implies the 'ruling' authority of Gen 1, and includes more than can be seen. Cf. . 11.3. An invisible world plus a world not yet in existence is 'the world to come'. Implied is that the original mandate to rule had not been cancelled.[133] 1 Cor 14.27-28 cites Ps 8.7. Note in Eph 1.22; Phil 3.21; Heb 2.8; 1` Pet 2.24 God puts all creation in submission to himself. [134]

2.9 ''But we see Jesus' The community of speaker-hearers is speaking, but by contrast the pivot turns to one representative man, the man Jesus. The other contrast is pain and glory contrast. Again everything has been placed under him and still we do not see all that has been placed under him. It is an 'already' 'not yet' scenario.

'A little lower than the angels' is the Godward aspect of the incarnation, and 'like his brothers' is the human. But in Ps 8.5 'than heavenly beings' is the word Elohim which can be used of judges or spirits of the dead as in the case of Samuel. 'made' a little lower refers to the creation of the man Jesus in the womb of Mary. According to Phil 2 this follows the decision to 'empty himself' and not seek equality with God. For Jesus to suffer death is cause for Him to be crowned with glory and honor because it accomplished 'death for everyone.' The message of 'the grace of God' is not 'grace of Jesus.' It is the higher that gives grace to the lower. The message of how one dies as a martyr was important and emulation of Jesus also was likewise. 'taste death' means 'experience death' and must not be forced into a 'little taste' only. The sentence that all die goes back to Adam. But the death for every person is universal also as contrasted to Romans 5. This suffering and death were by the grace of God not anger or merely judicial decision. In Hebrews suffering is added to sacrificial concepts and makes Him worthy of all honor and glory.

'By the grace of God' has a mss harder reading 'apart from God' xoris theou. This was probably a marginal note to limit the scope of 'everything' or 'every one' that is 'everything [or every one] apart from God.' The OT Psalm 'I have no good apart from You' and sense of isolation in Psalms of lament point to the cross where Christ sensed man's sense of alienation from God as God caused humanity's sins to be laid on him. This may very well be an ambiguity with double entendre here. 'Apart from me you can do nothing' is reflected that before the cross Jesus did nothing apart from God Is. 43:11 I, even I, am the LORD, and apart from me there is no savior. Christ is Yahweh in the flesh, the only Savior. Is. 44:6 "This is what the LORD says — Israel's King and Redeemer, the LORD Almighty: I am the first and I am the last; apart from me there is no God. The Trinity does not compromise basic monotheism. The rods in Isa 44 have a reflex in Rev 22.13 Rev. 22:13 I am the Alpha and the Omega, the First and the Last, the Beginning and the End, which acts as an envelope structure to the entire book of Revelations: Rev. 1:17 When I saw him, I fell at his feet as though dead. Then he placed his right hand on me and said: "Do not be afraid. I am the First and the Last. Rev. 2:8 "To the angel of the church in Smyrna write: These are the words of him who is the First and the Last, who died and came to life again. The meaning is that the church is nothing apart from Christ and end things depend totally upon Him. The basis for this 'sole Christology' is in Isa 45.5 a 'sole monotheism':Is. 45:5 I am the LORD, and there is no other; apart from me there is no God. I will strengthen you, though you have not acknowledged me, Is. 45:21 Declare what is to be, present it — let them take counsel together. Who foretold this long ago, who declared it from the distant past? Was it not I, the LORD? And there is no God apart from me, a righteous God and a Savior; there is none but me.This verse declares the two roles of God and Christ as God and Savior in one. Heb. 7:26 Such a high priest meets our need — one who is holy, blameless, pure, set apart from sinners, exalted above the heavens. This was not true while on earth. Hebrews stresses equally Christ's keeping the law and his identification with sinful humanity. It is after the resurrection and ascension that the separation from sin in exaltation can be mentioned yet he still dwells in the midst of his brethren.[Heb 2];

'By the grace of God' relates to suffering or 'for everyone'? It could not be efficacious in any other way. 'By'....'for' is the pattern, Note 'for everyone' is not a limited atonement. Glory is not by creation but by vicarious suffering. The contrast from man ruling to Jesus' redemptive work[not ruling] involves a change of referrent and a change of topic. In 2.9 glory, honor imply ruling without that becoming a substitute topic, here for man's ruling. Man gets honor, Christ gets suffering. Since "they are all sons of God[2.9,13] belonging to the same family [2.11], brothers of Christ [2.12], Christians share Christ's lot, have common use of riches [6.4] and are associated with him in the closest possible way."[135] huper with ablative case 'for, for the sake of, in behalf of' [136]

2.10 "'The sons to glory' v.7 is the goal of creation and redemption. Glory is what God has and is. The goal is a full return to God, but transcending Gen 1-2. In those verses no mention is made of glory, only of 'God's image.'

"The goal of Jesus' advent on earth was 'to lead many sons to glory." Similarly Moses' goal was to lead Israel to the land flowing with milk and honey. The goal of the servant is to bring Israel from all their nations back to Mount Zion. In Malachi the goal of 'My messenger' is to turn the hearts of the fathers to the sons and the sons to the fathers.' [137] How can suffering make someone perfect who is already perfect?,[138] If the Son is made perfect through suffering suffering must be needed for all men in order to be perfected. It is hard to see how else to relate suffering to God's purposes. But in Job's case he is called perfect before the troubles came but not afterward. 2 Peter seems to refer this to persecution and torture but the principle, in view of the Psalms, must be applicable to all men. But what of Job? He was perfect before the trial similar to Adam. But this seems a convenient starting point for the reader, the friends, the consciousness of Job and the barbs of Satan. Actually he was innocent and still not knowing God and it is through suffering and response to all of God's giving and taking away that we see a Job made perfect. ,Acts 3.14; 7.52 'the coming of the Just One' 22.14; 1 Pet 3.18. "Christ died...the just for the unjuust.' 1 John 2.1 "we have an advocate with the Father, Jesus Christ the Just." Enoch 46.3 "the Son of Man who possesses justice and with whom justice dwells." Christ is a 'saint', a holy one. one consecrated to God Ps 16.10; Mk 1.24; Lk 4.34; John 6.69. If he is 'just' he is so inasmuch as he fulfills the divine will, and also because he is totally innocent; but this designation also means that he is perfect to an absolute, limitless degree that belongs to the divine realm"_teleiow_2.10; 5.9; 7.28; 12.2 teleiwtes; [139] God brings sons to glory since all things exist for Him. He made the author of salvation perfect through suffering. This is in line with Isa 53 'The Lord has laid on him the iniquity of us all' and the use of passives to express God raising Jesus from the dead. God is 'the Holy One of Israel and is the one who makes holy. But the assertion is that God and believers are of the same family. This is a veiled extension of the 'Son' theology and recalls to readers Jesus use of 'My Father' and the Lord's Prayer 'Our Father.' In contrast to Abraham or Adam and others the believer's 'Ancestor' is God himself. Because the Father's work is perfect, Jesus, who has perfect confidence in the Father v.13, is 'not ashamed to call them brothers.' The OT use of 'House' is both an administration, building and dynasty, but also Family. The use of 'brothers' is not gender specific and includes both genders.

'For whom and through whom' here and in 1.2 is used of the Son. The proper understanding is not of subordination or a secondary instrumentation but of Agency. Both Father and Son are so described as are Logos in John ch.1 and Wisdom in Prov 8-9. Jesus said 'My Father works hitherto and I work.' This is not a Demiurge or Prime Mover but the concept of two persons working totally in harmony, a concept quite foreigh to humanity. Paul both claims to have done things and also that God did them, but in fact Paul and God were more than Co-workers, they were a creating team, just as the Word in Gen 1 and the Spirit. Often the Spirit is linked to the word is because both are working in tandem.

2.11 'Brothers' so above the translation 'family'. This implies family by redemption but more so adoption, and hence 'calls them brothers' by imputation and adoption.

'Of one' is translated 'family' because of the next lines. Here the answer is 'God.' Holiness is derived. Isaiah saw the holy God and was cleansed, part of what holiness was and is. The OT commands men to be holy as man's act. Adam is not called 'holy' but 'in God's image.' Enoch walked with God. Abram was commanded to be perfect. But here in the NT God in Christ imparts and imputes holiness.

'Shame' and 'ashamed' are OT topics. The willingness to identify with the underdog is seen in Jonathan and David, Samuel and Eli's sons, Boaz and Ruth's rendezvous and Rahab and the spies. This is 'The One" God or Jesus? "if Jesus is given by God as a pledge of his eternal covenant, then he must take on himself all the obligations[140] of a contract of guarantee and is possibly even called upon to give his life. Is he not in solidarity with the parties to the contract--ex henos pantes 2.11f, and the archegos of salvation v.10? [141] The sanctifier and sanctified are of the same family. Why not say 'nature' as in 2 Peter 1.? But calling them brothers fits the 'family' designation. Does this mean something like genetically or DNA, in a spiritual sense? The analogy fits. 'brothers' appears in many epistles and perhaps goes back to haber 'colleague''compatriot' in relation to each other and 'disciple' 'apostle' in relation to Jesus. The weakness of this interpretation is that haber isn't used much in the OT. But 'brother' is directly because of our relation to Jesus the Son.

2.12 Name Theology: 'Your name' might be YHWH or ABBA, but then might be a secret name to be revealed. But 'Name' can stand for 'person'. 'EHYEH is another. Rev 1.8 may reflect this name 'who is, and who was, and who is to come,' the Almighty.' Many names for the true God are given in the Hebrew Scriptures such as Shaddai, El, Elyon, but the new name might very well be 'Jesus' the one who will save his people from their sins. John uses the name LOGOS but for the son. Rev 22.4 has his name on their foreheads. In Rev 19.16 the rider of the white horse has a name written on robe and thigh 'king of kings and lord of lords.' But in v.13 it is 'the Word of God.' Cf. ., Rev 3.12. The ambiguity of the phrase 'Spirit of Jesus' the Lord allows for the presence of the Triune God with his people individually and collectively, and in the latter, the Spirit participates along with God's people in giving praise to God and in the preaching which is 'to declare your name.' Here 'congregation' is not the synagogue but is rather reflective of the temple worship with God's people. As a model of worship 'declaring God's Name' takes precedence over praise, but the model is God's revelation to his people followed by their response to Him in praise. Christ is the preacher model, the subject of the sermon is God; Jesus is a participant in worship. Declaring the name might include revelation of a new name. It is Jesus that is revealer of the holy name, possibly YHWH, since in this time it would not be pronounced and adonai would be spoken instead. Since they are brethren of the Lord it is only they who get to receive this revelation of the name. Jesus in the midst corresponds to his promise to be with the two or three gathered together in his name. The added factor is that for some who in ch.10 are no longer meeting together with the others they are being deprived of the revelation. It must be Jesus in the church, among believers, and in the hearts of the brethren that is singing praise to God. Pauline thought would speak of the Spirit in these terms; here it is mainly Christology not pneumatology that is the focus of the message. 'Declare your name' suggests the scholarly theory that not only is the Tetragrammaton YHWH not pronounceable but is also untranslateable. This text suggests a revelation of this secret name. While originally 'I am who I am' is secretive, here the deeper significance becomes known. The Exodus' variance between third person and first person 'ehyeh supports this view. The background of fist century Judaism refused to pronounce audibly the sacred name YHWH. Does this mean that Jesus in the church is now authorizing its use? Or is there now a new name, since YHWH only concerned the first covenant? Isa 62,2 You will be called by a new name the mouth of the Lord will bestow.' 'You' sg is Mt Zion. Rev. 2.17 'I also will give him a white stone with a new name written on it; known only to him who receives it.' This is the overcomer's reward. Rev 3.12 'I will write on him my new name.' 3 occurrences. Therefore God will have a new name to some, according to this verse.

Christ's being with his people in worship is more than mere presence of the promise 'I will never leave you nor forsake you.' It includes 'Where two or three are gathered in my name. there am I in their midst.' But beyond this Christ is head of the church so that whatever any believer does for a needy person is done for Christ. Who believes such a disciple believes in Christ. More so, the inspiration to worship is present in the declaration of God's name: preaching; in singing praises: praise; in affirmation of trust and faith: Confession, and in confession of being sons, a gift from God to the Son:: Assurance. These are characteristics of NT worship.

2.13 Spiritual waiting: The prophet, during a time of waiting for initial prophecies to be fulfilled, is waiting for God to act, and committing the message, the teaching [not law] to his disciples. Linked to v.18 the prophet is with his disciples and recognizes them as signs and symbols from the Lord, that are not 'sealed.' The sealing seems to be a message that men of the time cannot profit from v.14-15. So while this written message is a sealed torah, his disciples or sons are an open book because of their names. In this context he says "I will put my trust in him.' Now the antitype is glorified but still within the church or brethren, worshipping, teaching, compassionate and causing them to be signs and symbols. The verse implies not only Immanuel [Isa 7] but 'Christ in you' the hope of glory. As such Christ's very love that constrains and the faith he himself gives through his indwelling presence, express a worship of trust that is actually that of the Son Himself. Isa 8.17,18; 2Sam 22.3;

'Children' comes from Isa 8, where Isaiah is a type of Christ's presence standing with, on the side of, the family of God. Cf. . V.11. Christ is in each believer saying "I will put my trust in Him' [God]. Jesus commitment and expression of it through testimony and assertion 'I will put my trust in Him' namely the Father, is the expression of a sanctified and sanctifying Redeemer. This could be read as a performative verb as well

'I put my trust in Him.' As Son and man the decision and commitment to trust God implicitly was made for his own sake and for ours. It is part of the decision 'to fulfill all righteousness.' Jesus said as Scriptures say he would 'I will put my trust in him.' This is a discovery from baptism, temptation to Gethsemane. 'Here am I and the children God has given me' may have been declared after the ascension but is a discovery of identification with him in his victory. Periphrastic future perfect 'I shall have believed on him' Dana-Mantey,233

2.14 'Destroy him who has the power' Will Satan be destroyed? Does the Lake of Fire mean a destruction without end? In 1 Cor 15 the last enemy is Death, an allusion to Satan's other name Apollyon. In Isaiah Israel made a covenant with Death, really Satan, and thus sought to control their own lives and deaths. God said it would not stand since life and death are always in God's hands. 1 John simply speaks of destroying the works of the Devil. But will stark evil force be totally and finally eradicated? Once the one controlling death is gone, would there then be no more Death? The language is suggestive of God's plan not allowing any perpetuation of any evil in all the visible and invisible universe, a total victory. Believers begin sharing in this the moment they believe.[142]

'Share flesh and blood' seems to ignore the spiritual aspects of man. Here the flesh is what returns to dust and evidently the 'blood' is the life or soul that continues beyond death. It is improper to read this as if Jesus did not share in man's humanity from the standpoint of spirit, since the very point is 'in all points' and this paragraph only stresses mortality. 'Flesh' here has none of the sinfulness connotation of Paul, and rather reflects only on man's mortality.

'Through death' as a means or a path? Is there a concept that death conquers death? Or if 'path' is adopted, then this is the Way Jesus spoke of in part in John 14-16. While poison can counteract poison the analogy here is using Satan's worst weapon, the weapon that controls people through fear, to conquer death. My conclusion is that both viewpoints seem to be concurrent in this text.

"The Devil" is he "who holds the power of death." The theological question is in Job 1-2 and the degree of power and authority conferred by God. In Lk 4 Satan arrogantly says "I will give you all their authority and splendor for it has been given me, and I can give it to anyone I want to. So if you worship me all these will be yours." Jesus later said, about prayer, about the same words. Here Jesus did not reply to the substance of the temptation, but 'to not tempt/test the Lord your God." Satan's God must not be tested by either Satan or man. "Fear him who has the power to destroy soul and body in Hades." But would Jesus ever ask people to fear Satan? I think not. In Mk 8.33 "He rebuked Peter" is the narrative line; "get behind me Satan" is to Satan. "You??" do not mind the things of God but the things of men" is partly Satan and partly Peter in that the world flesh and Devil are the unholy threesome. This motif recurs in John 21 after Peter had led other disciples to go fishing. Cf. . 9.43 'enter into life' is contrasted to 'go into Hades where the fire never goes out. "Be thrown into Hades" v.47 has passives as opposed to 'enter into life' or 'enter the kingdom.' In John 8.44 "you belong to your father the Devil, and you want to carry out your father's desire. He was a murderer [he killed Adam and Eve] from the beginning, not holding to the truth, for there is no truth in him. When he lies, he speaks his native language, for he is a liar and the father of lies." Cf. . Matt 12.43-45; 13.37-39. Lk 11.14-26; "Do not fear" Lk 12.32 contrasts with 'fear him." The conclusion is that Satan lied. Jesus said 'all power is given to me in heaven and on earth." So Satan has nothing to give.

Death destroys death? [As in poison and antidote made from poison?] Or 'by his death': The relation of the cross to the end of Satan is clear 'Destroy' Can this mean 'no longer exist'? It is unclear how dying destroys the Devil who holds the power of death, unless Satan's rule is through the power he uses in the negative forces within man, one being fear of death. Could Satan exist with his tools, persons, sphere and power totally denied any point of connection. If 'magnifying' the name of God extends his rule effectively among men the disallowing Satan any anger, fear, hate, jealousy, anxiety, mistrust or the like actually shrinks his rule. Where chaos breaks out in war, street unrest, mistrust of a partner, fear of terror, mobilization to resist evil regimes –all of these and more extend confirmation of Satan's rule. People are on both sides part of his army because they are not driven by reason, love, faith, patience and the like. The saving work of Christ is here through his humanity to destroy 'him who holds the power of death—that is the Devil, and free those who all their lives were held in slavery by their fear of death.' 1 John repeats part of this 'to destroy the works of the Devil.' Jesus work is not to help angels but those of Abraham's descendents, his brothers. Here nothing is said of those who are descendents of Abraham in having Abraham's faith. 'Shared in their humanity //have flesh and blood'. In what sense define what is human? Or are these used in antithesis to angels? 'Flesh' here really means 'body' not Paul's technical use. Both body and blood are in the communion ritual. Do these represent the total person or do they define 'human' but not the individual person who has mind, heart, kidneys[bowels of compassion], etc? The imperishable soul is not mentioned, only that which dies and which awaits the resurrection as a complete person. 'children have flesh and blood' uses the word 'children' because the quote in v.13 does. Biblical physiology varies, but for this verse 'flesh and blood' is equated with 'human.' Jesus became a human not to destroy Satan, which might be foundi n Revelations or 1 John, but to through his death dsestroy the one who holds the power of death, the devil, and free humans from slavery. In this view fear of death alone is the handle Satan uses to control humans, and from this all other negative forces within human nature develop and grow. 'All their lives; points to the dynamite of fear. The Gospel sword or Word, the Spirit, and the community plus many other things are hear to provide an alternate reaction to circumstances besides fear. According to 3.13-14 sin's deceptiveness aim directly at one's confidence.

2.15 'Free'; The second verb paired with 'destroy'. Here liberty is not from the law but from fear of death and dying and the resultant servitude. The articular infinitive, here with an attributive in the same case: dia pantou tou zen[143] Here the genitive 'throughout life' 403 The nexus of the Devil or Satan with the power of death makes him the Angel of Death. In Job Satan was expressly forbidden to take Job's life, but nevertheless wreaked devastation on his family. The link to fear of death is the chain of bondage for all men. Paul called death the last enemy. Some words used for death are personifications of Satan himself. 2 Peter says that those who have faced suffering and death are ready for heaven and also for martyrdom since they don't fear what man can do to them. Those baptized into Christ's death are in union with Christ's death and resurrection and are free to be as Paul, who was equally desiring to leave this world and be with Christ and to remain so as to be a benefit to the church. In Christianity baptism most closely is linked to Classical usage, not Jewish, because in secular usage the use of baptw or baptizw usually ended in the death of those who experienced it.[144] In this way baptism also prepared believers for their martyrdom. The doctrine and experience of union with Christ in crucifixion, death, burial, resurrection, ascension, session is the 'in Christ' context for this deliverance. It is Jesus that frees who are on bondage, a task of the Messiah, since Jesus read the specific text in Nazareth listing the tasks of the Messiah. The usual approach is to take this chapter in Isaiah to refer to the gradually emerging Cyrus. Suggestive of this approach is an allusion to 'justice to the nations' v.1 and the title 'my servant'.The scope in universal in v.5-6. The context of 'new things' brings up the New Covenant and Age to Come. The acts of Christ to establish the new law in Matt 5-7, his avoiding the streets v.2; his care with those accused or hurting v.2; his covenant v.6; the use of 'light to the gentiles' my that Synoptics, and specifically causing the blind to see v.7. Perhaps not being able to free John from prison v.7 was a preview of his own not being able to ask for deliverance from the cross. Specifically 'whom I delight' in is reflected in the baptism of Christ and 'I will put my Spirit on him' was recognized by John the Baptist and fulfillment of this passage of Scripture. Only once did he shout v.2 at the great day of the feast. But that was linked to a synagogue not to the streets. He is an antitype to 'Wisdom" in Proverbs in that he went into people's houses. Isa 42.7[145] , 2.16 Cf. dhpou 'here[hither] in Heb 2.16BDF, BDF, 103, here a hapax legomenon. 107, dhpou 'of course, certainly' to soften an assertion, here classical and literary use.441[3], Antistrophe by repeating a word that need not be so: epilambanetai.491 the Passover Seder mentions the Angel of Death in connection with the Exodus:[146] "The Seder concludes with the cheerful singing of table hymns, most of them jingles for the delight of the children present, such as Had Gadya' (One Kid), constructed on the same lines as This Is the House That Jack Built, the cat devouring the kid, the dog devouring the cat, and so on until the Angel of Death devours the final slaughterer and then God slays the Angel of Death. Commentators to the Haggadah have read into this theme various mystical ideas about the survival of Israel and the ultimate overcoming of death itself in eternal life." Islam has an angel of death.: "'Izra'il is the angel of death; Isafal places souls in bodies and sounds the trumpet signaling the Last Judgment".[147] "(2 En. 3-9).130: "Elsewhere within the same book, the Angel of Death inquires of Jehoshua whether there are any gentiles (or "descendants of Esau") in Paradise or any Children of Israel in Hell. Included in the reply is the observation that those descendants of Esau who performed righteous deeds on earth are rewarded here but sent to Hell after death; Israelites on the other hand receive punishment while living and inherit the joys of Paradise after death." [148] In the Bible 'Death' is often personified and in Revelations is equated with Satan, the Devil, the serpent.

2.16 Is this grace limited to Abraham's descendants? Or is this directed to these at the time? The limitation to descendants of Abraham does not exclude others who become children of Abraham by faith in Christ but here is in contrast to angels. This assumes that some angels need help and reconciliation but are promised none. Salvation is described as help. It is the resurrected Lord to helps believers overcome the fear of death and that slavery. Interestingly studies show that a major drive in man is for survival, and the one who puts survival first, according to Jesus, will not survive. The text does not specifically say that the Devil is a fallen angel or what angels are his, only that there is no help for them. To accept help or not often is a crux for those converting to Christ, since the need to use one's own effort to achieve goals is also a basic need of human nature. This runs counter to the surrender in faith to Christ. , Quoting Ps 8.5 'What is man that you should remember him' God's remembering is mentioned 4 times: Mary Lk 1.54; Zech Lk 1.72; Ps 98.3; 16.8; and here. Jer 31.34. Much more has to do with human's remembering. or forgetting.,de 'really' climacteric, the point is clear and assumed to be true.[149] Christ doesn't help angels. Is this because they don't need help, which is not true in Daniel 9, or because they are sinners or redeemable because as angels there can be no blood of atonement.

2.17 'Become a merciful and faithful high priest.' Clearly this involves a process of growth and is not ready made. The growth in spirituality of Jesus and equipping for the ministry is stressed as part of the human side of the 'Son' equation. A person must learn to balance these opposites. Eli was merciful to his sons and Hannah, but not faithful to God and the law in dealing with his sons. Law and grace, love and justice, judgment and forgiveness must coexist. For these two sides of his personality to develop there had to be experiences along the way to make this outcome possible. Gray[150]focused on Jesus' role as brother as prerequisite to being hgh priest. His starting point is 13.1, an admonition to let brotherly love continue. Plutarch described the close relationship of fraternal and filial devotion, and how to overcome impediments. Here is not only a brotherhood but Jesus' relation to each believer. There is an ethos, a sibling conflict possibility, and the sociology of individuals of 'liminal status' in light of conflicts in the family created by the newly found faith. As 'children of God' in relation to the 'firstborn' Jesus is the older brother. This involves not only Christology but ecclesiology. Gray assumes an immediate connection between Greco-Roman ideals of fraternal devotion and the earliest readers. Jesus is the seed of Abraham as are these readers, so there is physical and spiritual relationship to complicate the meaning. But it is this Psalm 22 cited by Jesus here and on the cross in Matt 27.46= Mark 15.34. arxegos in 2.10; 12.2 and prodromos in 6.20 indicate priority of the elder brother, and this while based on Isa 8.18. His brothers are a gift of the Father entrusted too him. 2.11,12,17. He is the appointed guardian John 6.37,39; 17.6,12,24 or tutor who was the eldest brother. What makes for a brother relation is that both have one Father. .Gudɔrf[151] reads 'for it [the fear of death] clearly does not seize angels, but it does indeed take hold of the seed of Abraham.' Epilambanw 'to seize, take hold of, gripping' indicate enslavement.

2.17 'In every way'? Does this include original sin or the yetser hara;/hatob? 'merciful and faithful' In man this is usually a contradiction and so these are paired together. In pastoral ministry this combination is so important.. A basic problem of Hebrew Scriptures priests was lack of faithfulness and lack of righteousness. The latter is what Jesus had throughout from heaven to earth and to glory. But he must 'become' a merciful and faithful high priest in service to God, and that he might make atonement for the sins of the people.' The word 'become' is in keeping with Jesus 'learning obedience' and enduring temptation. The growth of character and experience in Jesus' life is manifold. In this case the forbidding of fire from heaven on Samaritans, the first putting off the Syro-Phoenician woman and then praising her for her faith may be aspects of this growth which began when Jesus at age 12 was found in the temple and at the first miracle when he replied to his mother 'what-to-me-is-to-you' ?! But then goes on to solve the problem. The tests of mercy are seen with the Samaritan woman and in patience when only two of ten returned to give thanks. Jesus 'grew' in favor with God and men as did Samuel. Like classical 'to reconcile with oneself' In Plato Lg.9.862c exilasyen 'atone for'

"Blessed are the merciful" Matt 5.7 elemones. Root: elemwn 25 of 30 occurrences in the LXX refer to an attribute of God, Christ in Heb 2.17. and usually it translates hannun . God punishes sin but has mercy on the sinner Jon 4.2; Joel 2.13; Isa 55.7; Col 3.12. especially on the person who is compassionate Lk 6.36-38; Eph 4.32; Col 3.12 and forgiving Matt 6.12; Lk 11.5-6. Cf. .Matt 25.31-46. [152]

2.18 "help" implies salvation, but not apart from human response and involvement. Ps 140 requires deliverance and not only help. Ps 37.24 'uphold him' ; 37.40 'The Lord helps them...they take refuge in him" So reciprocating is implied in the usage of 'help'.[153] 'Help' seems help to atone: He accepts people as eligible for atonement. Help is also for the tempted. Thus as high priest Jesus has the gift of helps. Most theories of the atonement and the cross, and all of them have elements or aspects of truth, don't discuss the role of suffering in the atonement since in the paschal lamb or other sacrifices the death comes quickly. Substitutionary death to fulfill the law of 'eye for eye' or for 'shedding blood' or any capital crime really have no element of suffering in them. 'By him blood will be shed' treats of the need for blood in atonement or cleansing but again suffering is another thing. In Deuteronomy 'cursed is anyone who hangs on a tree' at the time was not that of a live person, but was done by Assyrians and others to the corpse as a warning to others not to rebel against the great king. Only Job and Isaiah 53 give detail of vicarious suffering and offer clues to what it means. Zech 11.17 'strike the arm' is pain, the 'right eye' also is pain and infection with never again being able to approach God. 'the arm withered' and 'totally blinded' may not be mortal injuries but are only punishment for dereliction of duty. Zech 12.10 'they will look on me, the one they have pierced' but the focus is on the emotional pain to mourners and on his death. Zech 13.6 'wounds I was given at the house of my friends' are painful but not ending in death. But Isa 53 is a single person subjected to pain before dying. V.3' a man of sorrow and familiar with suffering' involves suffering rejection. V.4 'stricken by God, smitten by him and afflicted' belongs to the near eastern category of disease of unknown causes or attributed to a curse or evil griffin. V.5 only has wounds not death. V.7 the lamb does not react but death is immediate. V.10 'It was the Lord's will to crush him and cause him to suffer' but as a guilt offering which does not involve suffering per se. It is the guilt offering where that offered is a recompense or payment for a debt and involves some loss. But 52.14 stresses not suffering but marring, disfigured, causing people to be appalled, none of which are suffering per se. But if Jesus death answers Abraham's plea 'will the judge of all the earth destroy the righteous with the wicked' and the uniform belief that the judge of all the earth only does right, then one aspect of Jesus suffering is to answer the questions of seeming injustice in this world.

The answers to suffering offered by Hebrews are

1. Jesus had to suffer to be a sympathetic high priest.
2. He had to suffer because it was God's will which Jesus came to fulfill;
3. He had to suffer to fulfill as 'Son of Man' all the testings and temptations mankind undergoes.
4. He had to suffer to be made perfect as a person.
5. He had to suffer for men to realize the horrendous crimes mankind has endured or perpetrated.
6. He had to suffer in order to experience and accept injustice in its full flower as involving the good will of God. The other case is Gethsemane, where Jesus prayed that 'this cup be taken from me.' Since his being 'lifted up' was already predicted and known it must have been the suffering in the garden. If so was he fearing he could not survive to get to the cross? But Hebrews says he learned obedience by what he suffered and was delivered

because he 'feared God.' Did the three times of extreme prayer all without a single person supporting him, only angels after a time, indicate this full surrender as the ultimate temptation in his life?

The temptations

1. of Peter's exhortation to not go to suffer and die.
2. of a brother's sarcasm to go early to Jerusalem;
3. of desert Satanic attack and offer that doesn't seem to be aware of a cross;
4. of argumented attacks by Jewish lawyers and biblical scholars;
5. of the particular events on the cross 'why have you forsaken me' uttered in pain;
6. of Pilate to get him to talk, which a lamb cannot.
7. of appeals for the Son of David or Son of God to do or not do something.

These are only backdrop, while Gethsemane and the cross are crucial as tests and suffering. 'He bore my sorrows' is, in effect, the Day of Atonement goat, bearing injustice, sorrow, pain, sin, uncleanness etc into the wilderness of Death. "Since compassion was indispensable for the high priest of the new covenant, the Son of God had to take on human nature in order to acquire it, because participation in the same sufferings makes companions in misfortune compassionate and devoted. In addition, Christ henceforth lends his aid to humans. After Peter's undergoing temptation and failure he did rise to 'strengthen your brethren.' Jesus 'suffered temptation' recalls the temptation in the desert 40 days, replicating Moses and a whole generation, and in Gethsemane the 'sweat as drops of blood' and on the cross 'I thirst' etc. This suffering aspect doesn't belong to the topic atonement but preparation for being a high priest deliverer.

Chapter Three:

CHRIST IS THE HIGH PRIEST AND APOSTLE GREATER THAN MOSES

God's House and Oath

3.1 Jesus is first apostle and then high priest 'whom we confess' not 'to whom we confess.' This call to fix on Jesus echoes in 12.1-2 under the race-track metaphor. So does 'the heavenly calling' which echoes Paul in Phil 3.14. 'holy brothers' takes one back to 2.11. 'Turn your thoughts on Jesus' also reflects Phil 2.2,5. Since he has established the humanity of Christ in 2.12-18 he now uses the name Jesus. Is there avoidance of using 'Christ' the anointed one as king? The "Lord" role as king, warrior, God v.3b, resurrected one, priest forever, judge, and anti-type to Samson or Jonathan, places this king beyond David, Solomon or Uzziah who attempted some priestly things. Hebrews stresses the promise as backed up by oath, as if swearing by himself was another witness to the word. Ps 110.4[154]

3.1ff-ch.4 may be compared to Num 13-14.

1. Hebrews: stress rests on 'rest' not on war and challenge;
2. Hebrews: stress is on 40 years long testing and rebellion, not on one act of disobedience;
3. Hebrews: stress is on the voice at Sinai not on Kadesh, where there was no voice.
4. Hebrews: focus is not on the spies or 20 years age, but on 'generation' 3.10;
5. Hebrews: Focus is not on lack of faith in the NT believer but on 'holding confidence firmly to the end' 3.14;
6. Hebrews: 'the rebellion' 3.15 cites Ps 95.7,8 as a NT possible scenario.
7. Hebrews: stresses unbelief, disobedience, rebellion and hardening.
8. Hebrews: shows no forgiveness. But in Num 14.20 God does forgive.
9. Hebrews: has 'testing' compared to Num 14.22 10 times.

10.Hebrews: does not mention Caleb or Joshua Num 14.24,30.
11.Hebrews: does not mention the collective reaction to the report, while Num 14.1ff does.
12.Hebrews: takes 'hardening' as a cause of rebellion not the details of the spies' report. Thus a character problem is involved, not a detailed job description and sense of inability. The 'voice' is thus the voice of the report.

They could not enter due to disobedience/disbelief, while in Num 'we are not able' is reflected in Hebrews as 'they were not able'. Note in Num 13. Caleb mistakenly stood on a faith platform saying 'we are more than able' which everyone knew was not true, rather than pointing the crowd to God who is able.

3.2 The parallel of the Son and Moses is on the question of faithfulness. Both were faithful. Either this glosses over Moses arrogant anger and hence blasphemous words that did not honor God, or, this instance did not rank as unfaithfulness, or, Moses long term faithfulness made amends for this, or, the fact that once the true atonement was concluded all of Moses sins were wiped out of the record book. 'In all God's house' means that only Moses was truly faithful. Just as Lot was one righteous man in Sodom and Noah in his generation, and Ezekiel refers to Job, Daniel and Samuel in their generations. If antithesis occurs here 'with reference to all God's house' would translate the many times Moses interceded for Israel and finally placed himself in their stead, which God took him up on. But contrariwise, Jesus was faithful to the one appointing him.' 'Whom we confess' is the Christian confession. The other element of the pair does not mention Moses whom we confess since all Jews did confess him already. Moses is contrasted to all other prophets. God did not use visions, dreams, or riddles, but spoke to Moses face to face. The function of v.7 is to clarify the reason for Moses having the special status and privilege of seeing the form and speaking to God face to face, although the scripture writer says he only saw God's 'back'.The reason is that Moses was 'faithful in all my house.' Num 12.7 Part of this is used in John 16.29-30 of the disciples vis a vis Jesus. Hebrews omits the application of this fact to Aaron and Miriam "why did/do you[pl] not fear to accuse/speak against my servant against Moses."[155] Heb 3.2 adds a line to stress this special position , 3.2 piston onta tw poiesanti auton stressing personal faithfulness, not dealing with his transgression whatsoever, since that debt had been paid in full by Moses' death or/and by Calvary, and the second difference 'in all my house' versus 'all his house' which NIV and Union Bible both add 'in God's whole house.' The Levites, a stress of this book, were faithful, but actually, Caleb and Joshua were the only faithful ones. If en is taken as 'in respect to' the faithfulness to the people and the abstract entity 'God's house' was clear for Moses. The other possibility is that the rashness and dishonoring act of Moses as not considered unfaithfulness but wanton dishonoring of God. Perhaps his greatest act of faithfulness was offering to die for the people and his one-mind to be able to see the land, a faithfulness to the prime objective that brought him the commendation of this verse. It is hard to see in this a commendation for high priests or priesthood in each generation because of Moses' standing as federal head in a covenant with Levi, which covenant is mentioned by Malachi. The whole story cannot be told till it is over and in that Moses' story is over, Hebrews is telling us the final revised edition--the only edition totally from God's perspective. The rhetorical effect is that if Moses was so great in God's sight then the greatness of the builder of the house is obviously prior to and greater than the house.

3.3 Jesus is of greater honor because he is builder of the house and creator of all things. He is God the creator of His house. The house as a creature cannot have more honor than God or his Christ. In a Greek-Roman world 'honor' is very important, but the parallel doesn't hold up as if to say that Augustus is greater than the Empire since he created the empire. Moses is only reckoned to be part of God's house, the one faithful one.. This deflates the balloon of how Moses is usually viewed and venerated. 'worthy of more glory' seems to be a wisdom mode of thinking as in Proverbs with its 'better than' sentences. 'worthy' is also found in Jesus teachings about evangelizing a village and entering and staying in the home of one who is worthy. It also fits into the idea of greater or lesser punishments or rewards that was expounded by Jesus. The relativizing of character and performance is also found in the author's comments to various kings of Israel and Judah. This prophetic act placed a crown on the high priest's head. But the prophecy is not about Joshua, but about the Branch, who will build the temple, bear the honor and rule as priest on his throne. Both offices will merge "the counsel of peace will be between the two offices." This prophecy will establish Zechariah's credentials and establish Helem, Tobijah, Jedaiah and Hen as a reminder in the temple. People from afar will build the temple. The relation .f v.15 to v.13 is similar to Daniel 7, where the Son of Man rules and yet at the end of the chapter it is the people of the Most High who will rule. Zech 6.12,13. The merging of priest and king was not a counsel of peace in Samuel's time with Saul, but under David in the Nob and sacrificing incident, and later when Solomon officiated at worship the barrier seems to be breaking down. Was Uzziah's sin more than the act of entering the temple? Here one anointed one will unite the people under God alone. What does 'house stand for? In a monarchy it can stand for dynasty. In a clan society it can stand for the extended family and in a patriarchial society the head of the tribe or people. Does this stand for 'the whole house of Israel' as a visible-invisible entity, including but transcending any moment in history? Is this at all related to 'church'?[156]

3.4 The customary present tense 'every house is built by someone'[157] Every king in Babylon and Assyria had large building projects they boasted about. Saul did not. But David, Solomon, Rehoboam, Uzziah, Ahaz, Jeroboam I, Jeroboam I, etc., all did even if many were merely refortifying or rebuilding. In contrast to the Davidide Dynasty in Judah the 'house' of Omri and others were notorious. But if the Lord not build the hoouse they labor in vain, whether of stone or of flesh and blood.

3.4-6 Moses role as 'servant' in God's house, based on Isaiah, could be said for Jesus. But the antithesis here is 'as a Son over God's house..'We are his house if we hold on.' There is one house not two for different covenants. Christ is faithful over God's house and in addition 'we are his house if we hold on to our courage and hope.' Is this last sentence substituting for 'faithfulness' and its equivalences? Or is the house secure because of Jesus faithfulness, one firm foundation, while the 'we' are only His house in so far as they hold on to courage and hope. The two uses of 'house' would be different, perhaps one is an eternal entity guaranteed by the Messiah, while in the latter case the constituents of the house individually must hang on in faith.

3.5 This testimony does not seem to know of Moses failures, or does 'faithful' really zero in on the most important factor in keeping with ch.11 and its stress of faith? Moses was faithful to God, but was also arrogant in the rock incident, not giving glory to God, and brash in asking that his name but wiped out of the book of the living. and that the people not be destroyed. Faithfulness to the people 'God's house' may be one reason he could not enter the land since God took him up on his offer. He could not enter in because of identification with the people and hence he died that they might live. Faithfulness thus could be viewed as the cause of his failure to enter or one of the causes, apart from the brash arrogance in the Rock incident. His also was a type of the substitutionary sacrifice of the Christ. Note that neither NT nor OT view Moses' failure to be allowed to enter the land as due to his old age, his incapacity to lead an army, the need for new leadership, or new leadership with gifts to lead an army, or lack of faith on Moses' part, or any rebellion or disobedience on his part. [158] It was brash anger and assuming an authority before the leaders that only God had, and thus corrupting Moses role as a servant only. But this was unwise and foolish but not rebellion. Faithfulness probably is really what faith pistis means in Hebrews. Both Moses and the Son were faithful. But Moses was part of the 'House' which is susceptible to temptation from peers, leaders, and mass hysteria, but he overcame these. Especially he was faithful to Israel in being willing to die for them. Christ as faithful over God's house is another kind of temptation, that of usurping authority beyond what God had ordained. Moses did not presume to be over God's house or his act of striking the Rock would be one of unfaithfulness to the basic mandate, which it was not. It was simply a dishonoring to God not unfaithfulness. We might see unfaithfulness to his God ordained role as leader and mediator, intercessor and inspirer where he did fail, but God interpreted it differently.

3.6 'Courage and hope' are other terms for faith in a situation of persecution and stress. Faith in this book is not merely belief one time for ever, but a firm attitude of the inner man that enables one, much as an inner agent and instrument, to keep on keeping on. 'if we hold fast..' The 'if' is used in the OT of case law and also in covenant formulations.[159] The 92 occurrences of 'if' in the covenant book Deuteronomy are used in many ways of hypothetical situations, commitments, warnings, case laws, etc. Deut. 11:13 "So if you faithfully obey the commands I am giving you today — to love the LORD your God and to serve him with all your heart and with all your soul" — Deut. 11:22 "If you carefully observe all these commands I am giving you to follow — to love the LORD your God, to walk in all his ways and to hold fast to him" — Deut. 11:27 "the blessing if you obey the commands of the LORD your God that I am giving you today;" Deut. 11:28 "the curse if you disobey the commands of the LORD your God and turn from the way that I command you today by following other gods, which you have not known. Note the conditional aspect is not to do with merit but an acted-out faithfulness to the God of covenant promises. Faith and faithfulness are to be concretely expressed even as 1 John and James insist on. [160] 'faithful'....'faithful'....'hold on' the structure Moses, Christ, 'we' makes the phrase 'hold on' the emphatic point and a stylistic variant of the theme of faithfulness. 'we are his house if...' seems to make the 'People' of God or' Church' a tentative and insubstantial entity. But this is consistent in both

Testaments. The abstract 'People' or 'House' or 'Church' is continuous but not necessarily each individual or each generation, otherwise the 'Remnant' doctrine wouldn't have developed, creating an 'Israel after the flesh' and 'Israel as a remnant.'

3.7 'As the Holy Spirit says' in lieu of a particular prophet or judge leader. In this case the Spirit is speaking using Ps 95.7-11 and this is repeated in Heb 4.3,5. The prime example of rebellion here does not mention Kadesh but the testing in the desert forty years, not only the first part of that period since it began at Sinai and ended at Kadesh twice. A citation formula Fitzmyer,[161] 10 Note Assyrian or Amarna umma corresponds to hen or 'thus says the Lord' in the prophetic books. "1 Tim 4.6 concludes an (elaborated) oracle 4.1-5 introduced by the formula, 'the Spirit says,' a phrase occasionally used elsewhere for the citation of a prophecy or a prophetic writing." 2 Sam 23.2; Acts 21.11; Heb 3.7; Rev 14.13; 22.17; 1 Clem 13.1; Justin I Apollo. 39,1 etc. Evans,[162] 243

3.7-8 Hardening of heart in the OT, as in Isaiah 6, is an accumulative condition and loge-term rejection of God's word. Pharaoh's hardening also showed progressive resistance, but not to the point of killing Moses. The theology of not 'touching' God's anointed one to hurt him was observed by the pagan pharaoh as well as David. Proverbs takes 'stiff-necked' as resulting from repeated warnings ch.20. Here in Hebrews it can happen at one time, contrasting to the wilderness situation of accumulated rebellions. Stephen's audience killed him after hearing the message one time, but the fact mentioned in Stephen's message is that every generation became hardened and Stephen's generation was no different. So their reaction was still as a result of accumulative rebellion. Radical evil is capable of desperate responses.

3.8 'As in the rebellion' indicates an historical event that served as a model for behavior to be avoided It also points to a repetition of history as an real possibility. Recurrence of such an event is a hardening due to severe testing or temptation as well as to a mass hysteria. But the command in Hebrew Scriptures and Gospels comes to believers as well as to all men, to not let the testings of life turn one against God so as to test God by verbally abusing Him followed by a decision to forsake God. A subjunctive of prohibition 'lead us not into temptation' Mt 6.13. 1 Cor 16.11 includes being tested and testing God.[163] Both God and man have a limit of testing beyond which erratic behavior results.

3.9 God's Great Expectations: One reading of Scripture is that God was looking for positive response for the whole 40 years implying that perhaps a whole generation[reckoning 40 years] was not really needed to fulfill the punishment. Specifically those males 20 age and above had to die before the rest of the people could enter the land. In Numbers the 40 years probation and 'treading-water' followed the sin and judgment. God was willing to make salvation possible once again. If the 40 years was truly a probation then God's providing food shoes and shelter all during that period was pure grace since God still honored His Covenant. But if God was seeking amenability and submission, then their response, at least with the bronze serpent and the women of Moab, simply demonstrates the fact of their hardened hearts.

Tests of God: Does this time period mean that they were testing God and He them throughout the 40 year period? Cf. . 3.17 Most of this period has no record in Numbers or Deuteronomy. But clearly the events of the generation that died left an impression on the following one whereby they became very obedient to Moses and Joshua. This was the generation of adult males that rebelled, while many youth and women also came out of Egypt and became faithful to God. But in that 40 years that generation saw God's acts and miracles continue. The OT does not indicate testing of God all 40 years, except for the Psalms reference. After Kadesh Numbers seems to see a generation 'marking time.' Here in Hebrews their behavior never changed for the better and this is spite of miracles continuing all during that time. God tests man often allowing temptations and hardship, but man must never test God to see if he really will punish or not. The complaints and unhappiness each time developed into rebellion, and always started over dissatisfaction, attributing killer motives to God, and ending in rebellion and punishment. Jeremiah questioned God, was accusing him, and finally was given the ultimatum in Jer 15.19. Often children with a new parent or guardian or even a teacher will seek to test the limits of the adult's patience, faithfulness to his or her word, love and self-control. Often they feel success if they cause the adult to unravel. But a prime directive in the Bible is to 'never test the Lord your God.' God is not simply a more powerful version of a human adult. Often faith and presumption are hardly distinguishable. But adventuresomeness is like what Satan did in tempting Jesus to jump of a high place and see whether God would fulfill his word to protect his Son, when Satan knew nonintervention by God was the arrangement for the Son of Man. Testing God is not faith because 1. The act was not commanded by God; 2. The test of common sense and responsible action, two witness rule, is not followed. 3. The purpose is not to glorify God and his word. 4. The danger is a quick way to get to a legitimate end. 5. Some point is present where the man refuses to surrender to God.

3.10 Extent of guilt and punishment: 'with that generation' points to a collective guilt of all Israel but only punishment for those adult males, even though all Israel suffered the delay, and patiently or not waited till the last rebel died. Accountability was based on being part of the twelve tribes plus those others that left Egypt. Liability was based on being part of the adult-male collective. The spies' influence was not pointed out as especially condemned, even though their not directly reporting back to Moses was largely responsible for the fear that their haphazard reporting to the others, including their wives and families, was responsible for the rebellion. 'They have not known my ways' is not that they didn't see God's manifestations, graces and punishments, his word and warnings. 'To 'know' is deeper than information and knowledge, ability to tell the story or reflect on historical events. For that society to know God's ways but be to understand the reasons for laws, punishments and graces and to be part of their deep structure civic religion at least. Throughout Hebrews what 'God' does and what 'Jesus' does are very separate. God brings sons to glory .For God all things exist. God makes the author of salvation perfect. God makes men holy. Jesus declares God's name to his brothers. Jesus sings praise to God in the congregation on earth. God is the object of Jesus declared trust. God gives children to Jesus. The relation of Jesus to God in this book requires an in depth study since it is the Son that is pre-existent. Jesus is not ashamed to call them brothers because God is making them holy. God evaluated that generation saying 'their hearts are always going astray.' This is comparable to the Noah and Sodom generations and words in Jeremiah before the demise of the nation.

Sinning as a lifestyle: The reason for their dying in the wilderness was not due to a one time event here, as it is in Num 13 at Kadesh. It is rather the incessant going astray and harsh words toward God and Moses that betrayed their total lack of spiritual knowledge[not information] of God's ways.[164] To describe a whole people and generation as those 'whose hearts are constantly going astray' touches on inherited depravity, but rather is the dominance of the evil tendency over these particular families. It is later theology that defines inherited depravity or original sin, which is not a Jewish concept. But applied to the readers in v.12 they might develop a 'sinful, unbelieving heart that turns from the living God' and finally v.13 'be hardened through the deceitfulness of sin.' Neither a concept that man is good or total evil, corresponding development that baptism removes original sin, or that sanctification occurs only shortly before death, really are dealing with the biblical concept of dynamic evil and good. Only the blood of Christ's atonement applied through faith in his blood and the Spirit can deal with the sin in man. Christ came, according to Rom 8.-13 'condemned sin[resident in]the flesh' to enable the righteous decrees of the law to be fulfilled in our mortal bodies'

3.11 'An oath in my anger' does not seem to be the self-control of the Spirit and seems more like a human monarch in the heat of anger. Among men an oath even uttered in anger stands firm. How is this to be understood. First, God does not merely rule without personal feeling, concern, and emotion. This is not merely an anthropopathism as a matter of style and medium of communication, which would mean God doesn't have anger, nor does it mean that God corresponds to redeemed man in everything. God does have patience, a fruit of the Spirit, but makrothumia indicates that there is a point beyond which anger must be expressed. Nor is God coldly managing the universe with no personal feelings at all. But contrasting to anger is Jesus as high priest who feels with the infirmities and weaknesses because he has personally experienced these things. Does this mean God does not feel pity? Alternatively, is God's expression of pity in Jesus different qualitatively since in Christ God has experienced pain and suffering and he can be a faithful high priest both in matters of justice and discipline as well as in redemptive grace?

3.11-4.11 'Rest'and 'Sabbaths' are emphasizing the nuances of rest and inviolable peace, to which panegyris adds the idea of brotherly harmony. As Philo says concerning the sacred Sabbath:[165] "All the festivals of the year are in reality daughters of the sacred Sabbath, which is like a mother...In their ceremonies and in the joy that they stir up, one tastes pleasures unmixed with anxiety and bitterness, filling both body and soul, the former with the pleasures of life, the latter with the teachings of philosophy."[166]. Note that Heb 12 stresses the problem of holiness versus bitterness and this is in parallel to those passages reflecting rebellion at Kadesh which climaxed all Israel's bitterness. It is even a motif at a place called Marah, that extended throughout their journey. Thus the Christian's Sabbath of the soul excludes bitterness. The panegyris assembly may be seen in an equivalence with the use of katapausin and sabbatismos "emphasizing the nuances of rest and inviolable peace, to which panegyris adds the idea of brotherly harmony. 'brothers' means that believers must be on guard. Cf. . 12.15-17. A 'sinful, unbelieving heart, turning from' is a cluster that gloss each other. 'Hardening' v.13 is first due to being deceived, and all are part of 'an interacting together' for no good whatever. Note the possibility of turning from God can only be countered by the 'encouragement' v.13 as part of the function of the church. Wesley's care groups called societies were essentially places and times where mutual accountability laid bare any sham and spiritual wavering, so that "turning away' might be avoided and effort toward holiness were impressed on those in attendance..

'Sinful unbelieving heart in departing...' If one's theological system interferes with direct reading of scripture one might say that everyone has such a heart of unwillingness to count all individual scriptures as equal and simply read what is there. and the only question is to not allow it to control to the point that one departs from God. But a direct reading here indicates change-of-state. A departing event can occur if one does not notice and control the nature of one's own heart. The address 'brothers' is clarified in v.14 as believers in Christ. The basic issue is that a 'sinful unbelieving heart that turns away from the living God' can be created in the believer so that hardening will occur owing to 'sin's deceitfulness' The antidote is for the brothers to daily encourage one another. There is no system of original sin or inherited depravity or even Satan here in this text but could lie further back in biblical theology.. Hearts can become unbelieving and sin can deceive and always does. Some scholars would say 'sinful heart' is the given, but here it is qualified in its occurring as unbelief and as deceit. But 'sinful' is only known in its effects. Anything that deceives through attacking faith can turn one from God. This sinful force destroy the share a believer has in God. Truly converted people may follow the OT rebellion pattern and this is the real danger that each person in the NT era must be aware of and face responsibly. This is not talking about original sin, but a condition of the heart that can and must be avoided. Believers are not in 3.10 'always going astray' but may do so. Believers may develop unbelieving hearts as at Kadesh.[167] 'Believers' describes those who continue to believe and obey.

3.12 The 'brothers' must take responsibility for their hearts. The command is to each believer. It is possible. The 'sinful, unbelieving heart, that turns away from the living God' are three aspects of backsliding or two that describe it as unbelieving and turning away. Repentance in the OT is to 'turn toward,' or 'turn around.'shuv. Usually sar is to turn away. Only a rejection of truth must precede a walking away. Suicide of a Christian may be due to not being able to believe or walk away, and the sinful heart compromises one into mere escapism.

3.13 'Encourage' is probably too weak a translation, although it is a resultative verb, since this is the main external power to avoid being deceived and thus hardened by sin. This is a 'buddy-system' as in AA, where each person sees to it that his partner does not backslide.

'Sin's deceitfulness' is a personification of sin as deceiver, which elsewhere is used of Satan. Elsewhere sin is a force with many products:

Rom. 1:29 They have become filled with every kind of wickedness, evil, greed and depravity. They are full of envy, murder, strife, deceit and malice. The NT does make the link to Satan: Acts 13:10 "You are a child of the devil and an enemy of everything that is right! You are full of all kinds of deceit and trickery. Will you never stop perverting the right ways of the Lord? Here cause-effect is the logical link between the two verses. In the Talmud and Zohar the evil inclination/tendency is sometimes equated with Satan and sometimes made part of man's original composition before the fall of Adam. But in the NT Eph. 4:22 You were taught, with regard to your former way of life, to put off your old self, which is being corrupted by its deceitful desires, speaks of the evil inclination as a force that must be put off and cancelled out. The clearest OT text is in Jeremiah, and here the 'heart' is described as to one aspect only Jer. 17:9 "The heart is deceitful above all things" and beyond cure. Who can understand it? The second line clarifies the first making the first line mean a contagious malignant infecting sickness.

'Today' and 'daily' point to the antithesis of Mosaic religion and stipulations for one or three annual festivals.. The Passover as a New Years Day naturally remained central for Jews even in the Diaspora and the later song and prayer before and after meals filled the same need. But even then it is only the father or head of household that aided in the remembrances. Here. Linked with 'forsake not the assembling of yourselves as the manner of some is' points to the need for community, even a small group of non-professionals and on a daily basis as necessary to stimulate to faithfulness in martyrdom. Every day has temptation and testing in which hardening can happen.

3.13-14 'Have come to share'[168] is a fact not a goal, but a dynamic state that depends on holding faith and confidence steadfast to the end. One act of faith 'at first' saves as in regeneration and justification, but must be lifelong for one to finally share in Christ.[169] The conditional aspect of sharing 'in Christ' depends on holding fast confidence from the first time of believing the Gospel to the end, which may mean death, martyrdom or the end of the world. 'If we hold firmly' includes the writer and all believers. There is no 'believe' once and that suffices for all future situations, but a confidence held firmly through it all. Later the writer deals with persecution and martyrdom and even apostasy. Here the inner problem is the primary one. The only means to this end is the encouragement of fellow believers.

3.15 Hardening is done by people to themselves in response to hearing God's voice. The best and earliest illustration is in Adam and Eve after they sinned, as they hide from God and cover up verbally their full responsibility for their actions. On hearing the sound of God in the garden they hid themselves from God. Without a sound they earlier had hidden themselves in the garden and their bodies with fig leaves. How did Israel and NT believers differ? Perhaps the voice of God is clearer and the tendency to rebellion less. But the danger of hardening is still real. It belongs to man as man. Isaiah 6 speaks of hardening not as the mission of Isaiah, but the infinitive+verb format means that Isaiah will surely cause them to hear, but their hearts will become hardened, a stative verb in hiphil used as a change of state verb. God clearly wants them to hear, but the oft repeated message will simply not be heeded.

The Hebrew Scriptures citation was originally addressed to Israel in the wilderness of Sinai, and at Kadesh after the covenant had been reconfirmed Ps 95.7,8; Num 14.2,29. Originally they hardened their hearts in unwillingness to hear God speak directly. Then in assuming Moses was dead or had deserted they rebelled in the golden calf event. The crux came at Kadesh where they believed that they were not able to take the land and that God had and would still forsake them attributing to God unfaithfulness. Hardness is a false belief that forsakes God. It is a mindset that rebels and stakes out one's own path of security. It accepts the majority rule for the rule of God.

This Psalm is a call to worship God as the great king who is creator of everything. It is the covenant [:"he is our God"] that is the basis for the conditional clause and exhortation ['we are the people of His pasture"]. "Today, namely the day of worship, do not harden your hearts as at Massah. Evidently in the synagogue there was not only worship [no sacrificing is mentioned] but the preached or read word. The word to the wilderness generation is valid now. Hardening of heart is related to 'testing' God: "when your fathers tested Me, they tried me, though they had seen My work."Ps 95.7,8 'Work here stands for miracles and providences.' God's oracle to worshipers v.9-11 focus on two problems: one is God's reaction to their evil: "loathed" 'in my anger' and on a problem in the people with two aspects: 'who err in their heart' and "do not know My ways." They saw his deeds but did not know his ways. The judgment is clear they shall not enter into my rest. This, in a sense, is another case of "Adam forfeiting eternal life." "Adam" was like the collective Israel.

3.16 Justice, Testings and punishments: According to this revision of the historical record all those coming out of Egypt with Moses rebelled at Kadesh. In this reading those whose lives would survive 40 years in the wilderness who were women or not 20 or older were saved as a result of mercy and the larger plan to fulfill the promise to Abraham, and not because these people were any 'better' than those who died. The readership of Hebrews would be aware of Num 14.2,11,30 and thus the abridgement would be supplemented as they read. There was:

1. Emotional outburst;
2. No sleep;
3. Weeping was not directed to God;
4. The next day v.2 they grumbled to Moses and Aaron;
5. There was mass hysteria v.2;
6. They express hope [or despair] by past condition contrary to fact sentences;
7. They focus on death as a benefit that has escaped them;
8. They question the motive of the Lord;
9. They attribute intent to murder to God;
10. They pass a resolution to do a political act and elect a new leader;
11. In response to prayer they take stones to execute Moses and Aaron v.10;
12. The grumbling and complaints v.27 were against God; escalation of violence
13. The punishment for the spies is immediate, for all other adults for 40 years according to the days spent in the land.
14. After forgiveness v.20, God is not with them v.42. and defeat followed.14.45.[170]

3.17 God's ways are not our ways: 'angry 40 years' is unusual for humans, even though some anger continues generation after generation as with the Samaritan animosity. But in this case it was not merely a sentence of death to the rebels, but a passionate carrying out of it while at the same time showing mercy and provisions for God's people throughout that time. The 'people' were not slaughtered, but preserved while the rebels eventually died even while God was providing their needs and keeping them from diseases.

The OT depicts anger of God as lasting for a moment, while the judgments of God are continuing. In Psalms, Lamentations and Daniel the felt experience of believers, in times when blessing is withheld, is that the wrath is continuing. Hosea 11 separates the notion of personal wrath that can 'turn around,' from the judgment that justice demands. There the result of love is that God does not punish but follows a rational pattern leading toward the repentance and restoration of those being disciplined. As a metaphor 'wrath' cannot be sustained as an emotion and attitude, but a course of punishment that is salvific can be. This theology is repeated several times. Human anger does not usually last that long. But that whole time God protected them, fed them, their clothes and shoes didn't wear out. So the meaning is not a rejecting anger. but a trial by ordeal. disciplined anger, so that they could not move toward the promised land during those years. At the same time the inhabitants of the land were changing and the fear of God was settling on them.

3.18 'Unbelief' is a summary of 'unbelieving heart, falling away, evil heart, v.12, hardened through sin v.13, but then in v.18 'disobedient' describes the same thing. The crux is their refusal to go up at God's command.. The heart of basic character center may be good or evil and may shift to either. Hardening creates a fixed Gestalt whereby the person cannot conceive of a different way of perceiving things. God told Joshua to 'be strong' and Pharaoh's heart 'became strong' but one for obedience and one for disobedience.

Punishments with oath: The oath that they would never enter into rest differs from usual punishments in that it is an oath and cannot be changed. This is tantamount to the unpardonable sin. Moses at that time did not intercede and God did not repent. Moses was immediately commanded to pronounce the verdict and this eliminated his fear and depression, but still he didn't intercede. Israel would survive, but not that generation. God's promise is fulfilled, not on all Israel, but on a remnant. While the word 'remnant' is not used the concept is present. In this case the innocent are spared as when Abraham had questioned God about executing both the wicked with the good. [Gen 18];Num 14.30[171] Is this kind of punishment extra-covenantal?

The link of unbelief and disobedience makes them almost equivalent. One deceived disbelieves and one who disbelieves disobeys. James also spoke of the process that leads to over sinning 1.14 "Each one is tempted when, by his own evil desire, he is dragged away and enticed. Then, after desire has conceived, it gives birth to sin; and sin, when it is full-grown, gives birth to death.;'

3.19 Punishment fulfilling wrong belief: The cause of their death was not a divine decree only, but a decree that fulfilled the negative faith they had often expressed that they would die in the desert. The crux is unbelief, taking God's command and promise as a lie and acting contrary to the will of God. In the end the large numbers of leadership and males who had come out of Egypt were incorrigible, and a momentary punishment would not resolve their problem of unbelief, that reared its head in every new crisis. But the Joshua generation was not of this mindset. Did they learn fear of God and learn faith in God's word in a situation with few tests so that it was not tests only that changed them?

Chapter Four:

Christ is Greater than the 'Rest' of Joshua and Aaron the Priest

God's Oath, Promised Rest and Word.

4.1 Partial and full fulfillments: The promise, whether to Abraham or Joshua or David may have had partial fulfillments earlier, but the same promise of 'entering his rest still stands.' The 'us' divides responsibility and the concern is for 'none of you' who had fallen short of it. In context the recipients here are those who have heard the preaching of the gospel. To fall short is to not yet believe and actually enter into that rest.

'Therefore' builds on the entire narrative as expressing the truths of:

1. Israel's rebellion;
2. The nature of rebellion as testing God;
3. The 40 years of perpetual testing of God and God testing them;
4. The miracles in the wilderness during those 40 years;
5. The judgment, similar to that of Noah's day that 'their hearts are always going astray and they have not known my ways'
6. The oath that that generation would not enter into 'my rest'. Apparently 'my' here indicates more than promised to them in the wilderness.
7. The urgency of 'Today' comes from Psalm 95.7,8 referring to the same incident, and thus builds on a homily on the Psalm.

'A promise' is what is left behind for the Gospel generation. To not experience the promise is called:"lest any one from your midst should appear, seem to come short [of it]. [172] But more than the promises to Abraham, Moses, David and prophets are the promises of Christ in his lifetime and through the apostles in the NT Scriptures. Have any promises been abandoned? Is the projected temple of Ezekiel a promise or merely a plan to stimulate faith? There are 'aids to faith' in scripture.

The exhortation can be obscured in English because 'Let us fear lest' is not merely possibility of fearing, but the antithesis to the words to Joshua and Gideon not 'to fear.' 1 John speaks of 'perfect love casts out fear, for where there is fear of death there is torment.' But it was fear that originally led to the rebellions! But this was not fear of God, but fear of failure and wrong motives on the part of God. Here is a command to fear similar to those verses in Proverbs 'the fear of the Lord is the beginning of wisdom.' But there it is an attitude and here an act and entering into [inchoative] that are expressed in the cohortative. The writer includes himself. Watchfulness of oneself and one's attitudes may only be starting to fulfill God's plan for one's life. The promise is still valid, still stands, still remains or is left behind, not 'deserted, abandoned,'[173] While Joshua took Israel into the land, the history accounted in ch.3 does not extend into Joshua's work. In ch.4 Joshua's work is recounted, but Joshua did not give them rest. This builds not on the summaries of the book of Joshua that declare all the land was in Israelite control, but on the accounts from ch.11 onward and Judges that must land remained to be taken. But taking land does not mean rest. 4.9 is speaking of more than a weekly Sabbath or 7 years or Jubilee, but an inner rest. 2 Esdras 8.119 'immortal time...promised to us' sounds like Titus 1. Cf. . 7.113; Myers,[174]240. There is a semantic jump from 'ceasing from labor' to 'entering into rest,' and, in fact, the domains differ. The domain of the conquest was followed by the domain of occupation and settlement. But the rest remaining for the believer now goes beyond these to a spiritual or psychological domain on inner rest.

4.1-9 'Sabbath of rest' in Lev 23.32 you must 'deny yourself', which is probably fasting and related elements of self-control. Hebrews 4 focuses on God's rest and v.9 'a Sabbath rest' borrowed from the Sabbath observance domain into a new domain.. 'Rest' is broader that 'deny oneself' Lev 23.32 corresponds more to Lk 9.23 'come after me' also linked to 'deny oneself' and 'take up one's cross' and 'follow me,' with the stress on doing something in positive self denial. This is not a single religious ritual related to a single act. In Lk 9.23 the connection to Hebrews is closer than to Lev 23.32, in the sense that it is inchoative in entering into a new lifestyle and spiritual experience and not a single act. Robert North[175] wrote of the Derivation of the Sabbath. He concludes the verb ''cease' derives from a cultic noun 'sabbath.' It then represents a dual od Shabbat 'seven-er' adjective and originally the seventh of the month. Two-sevens was the fullmoon. Babylonians made this a day of appeasement, with distressing and agreeable aspects. Thus Babylonian shapattum did influence the Hebrew Sabbath.[176] The prohibition of fire-making on the Sabbath may have derived from work-cessation of the Qenites, a humanitarian concern. Thus rest, cultus, and appeasement all were infused new significance based on Creation and the Exodus. The footnote cited gives Information from cuneiform that the 15th or full moon called shappatu was not auspicious and this use may have spread to every seventh. In this sense a day of ceasing activity would be least likely to incur problems with God or man or nature. Some elements are left over from this background but centered now on the Lord, maker of heaven and earth not on superstition. The substitute made the Sabbath one of the most distinguishing features of Judaism. This book says the Sabbath and Joshua never brought about what Sabbath pointed to. 'Take my yoke andl earn of me' is the answer.

4.2 'Good news' is not only the Gospel in the NT period, but began in the OT. Preaching also did not begin in the NT period. The use of bisser is not too wide-spread, but the promises, predictions, and those elements that need to be believed, acted on and responded to are essentially good news, because they specify a way to take.

'No value to them' introduces not a contrast clause but an exceptive clause or a contrast to the whole promise of the good news, in that 'it did not profit them.' This is contrary to Ecclesiastes, since there there is no preached word, only personal discovery, but the final result and its cause are the same, a lack of mixing faith with data. Qoheleth ended in a 'Vain Universe" because he did not look at it through the eyes of faith, but through observation, recording, experience, classifying, deducing, without bringing God into this process at all except as a final appeal. God was always peripheral to both Qoheleth, his experimentation, and his conclusions.

"Gospel" covers the OT and NT. 4.2: could be read "we also are 'good-news-ized' as they were." This is also called 'the heard message.' In OT and NT the word is good news, a promise and also a command and failure to mix it with faith can be disastrous in either dispensation.

4.2 Recipe for the hearing-acting recipe: 'mixed with faith': Liddell-Scott,1664[177] i1. Temper pleasure; mixture of pain; 2. Mix together,co-mingle; 3. Attempter,compose;I 4 Be mixed or blended with, coalesce; ii 5. Be commingled, blended of woes; 6. Of friendships: top be formed by close union; form a close friendship with someone; 7. Of persons: to be closely attached to, be close friends with; to become closely acquainted with, deeply involved in, 8. Of a wife: III. Medicine: mix with or for oneself. The dative of persons would preclude a medical or pharmaceutical use. The sun- requires another sun, in this case with a dative as substitute. The word must be -x- with those hearing. This is then, very close to James and Peter 'receiving the engrafted word' which is able to save your souls. The word must be coalesced with those hearing. The OT verse is Isaiah 6 where the senses all aren't functioning or contributing "ever hearing, but never understanding, ever seeing, but never perceiving [reading infinitive absolutes not imperatives]. 'The heart of this people has become calloused, their ears dull, their eyes closed, otherwise they might see with their eyes, hear with their ears, understand with their hearts, and turn and be healed." The purpose or goal of v.10 not realized precludes using an imperative to translate these verbs. Note that all of these are verbs of state and the hiphil in this case indicates a change of state; the forms could be infinitives or imperatives, but in view of v.9 they should be infinitives for the sake of a reading preserving continuity. The message or word has power v,12, but can become 'of no value' to those who don't mix it with faith. The human and divine must mix in this recipe. But had Moses faith in Israel and did they have faith in him as they later did in Joshua? Had he democratized too early in the Kadesh spy episode and thus decentralized authority? Had this action made the conquest not one of God's miracle but of human common sense? Is this proven by Moses and Aaron prostrate before God in hopelessness because in the report scene even they had lost faith in God and Israel. Moses wasn't even able to encourage Aaron! Did even Moses' final address in Deuteronomy, his last will, and his blessings reveal faith in God and in Israel? There never was mutuality but the covenant was a step toward this and a structure and clear instructions were a second, along with Moses' intercessions not known clearly in Exodus but enunciated so in Deuteronomy. Growth in faith, 'from faith to faith' must be on both sides of a relationship. Here the ingredient lacking was 'faith.' What 'Gospel' did the wilderness generation hear? The word pair has 'message.' 'We also have had the Gospel preached to us as they did.' The Gospels have the message of the Kingdom. The Hebrew Scriptures is a message of covenant. Or was the crisis at Kadesh in mind where the message of predicted victory the point of rebellion. A parallel of situations is that at Kadesh Israel did not want to die in the wilderness outside the land, while the martyrs were definitely outside the land of promise willing to die for another land. The fear led to a demonic wave of rumor, stories, nay-saying till rebellion set in politically. Not 'word of hearing' but 'the heard word' 'which they heard' The pure genitive in adjective sense.[178]

4.3 'His work has been finished since the creation of the world' alludes to the seventh day and God's resting from his work.. What work was finished?

Did man undo God's work? Does this mean that the Sabbath preceded Moses and that early man rejected it? Or does it mean that all things pertaining to mankind, nature, Israel, sin and salvation were already authorized so there were no surprises even though man's free will was also taken into consideration. If this rest begins after man's creation but doesn't predate natural history than the earliest challenge to finding a partner is a situation 'not good' and the 'effort' led to God providing one, which should have led to rest. After sin work does not have rest till Noah's blessing descends. But the unfolding of what was accomplished at the beginning is within a time-history continuum. In Enoch it was a walk with God that became eternal. In 'Noah' meaning rest, comfort, sin intervened. From that point the promises multiply but also focus the meaning of rest and it becomes a goal and promise requiring faith throughout. 'that rest' is that left to new covenant believers. It is further defined as 'my rest' and 'Sabbath-rest.' God 'rested' from his work and the believer 'rests from his own works. The works of God were those of creation in the seven-day format after which initial creating work ceased. Man's work began in Gen 2-3 and involved 'naming,' like God named things, and in 'keeping' a garden, while the prophetic books use the same metaphor for God and Israel, and in 'tilling' the soil in order to survive. Man 'does' or 'makes' evil also and 'makes sacrifice.' It is this work that man must cease in order to enter God's Rest. Woman's 'work' is not work, but 'making'[banah is give birth to a son or create] children and productivity is always a part of man's role. God's Rest is linked to the Sabbath observance as a symbol and sign and type, not of death and heaven but of the rest of faith in God. 'Do the first works' in Heb 6.1-3 and Rev 2.5 have to do with the response of faith.

'Make every effort to enter that rest' has to do with that response to faith of belief and repentance that brings the gifts and graces of the Spirit mentioned in ch.6.4-5. God's Rest was only for one day, and even so man 'must work if he should eat' and the command to work six days has never been rescinded. But man's own works, replying on his own effort apart from surrender to God must cease. When asked 'what must we do to do the works of God'" Jesus replied 'This is the work of God to believe on him who He sent.' The 'work of faith' and 'labor of love' are not man's works, but believers' works wrought in the realm of faith and that rest God gives now. This fulfills the meaning and symbol of the seventh day partially, but the sevens of scripture must await eschatological events to be completely fulfilled.

An oath sworn in anger is a contingent circumstance and only God can keep his head [anthropopathism] in the heat of a rage. The oath in this case is the opposite of what God had promised before. The reason is not that the purpose had changed, the people, the times, nor that worship and sacrifice had failed or the covenant. What changed is the permeating effect of unbelief, bringing rebellion and the judgment of God. Ps 95.11.

The present includes anyone who has believed or heard the word; the 'we' implies the church age believer, gentile or Jew. This is a present fact-in-progress in contrast to the Wilderness Generation, and by implication every subsequent generation. 4.3 indicates 'we enter' probably in a gnomic sense, since the action of 'entering' cannot be that of a process., and at most action-process.

Ei not 'as if',or 'whether' but 'not.' Gen 14.23; Num 14.28 in LXX[179] The use of 'My rest' linking creation, God's resting, Moses, Joshua, and the NT believer points to a transcendent quality to entering into a state God has prepared for believers. What do these have in common? Some may never enter and this is for this life and the next. Some experienced the promises fulfilled as in Joshua's taking the land but still did not partake of God's Rest. This rest is 'for the People of God' with no indication at all whether Jew or Gentile Christians are designated. But the man who believes ceases from his own works as God did from his. But 'cease' must be preceded by 'every effort to enter.' The 'cease from his own work [not works] follows.

So the issue of not dealing with inner matters of disobedience, unbelief, rebellion, and thoughts, attitudes, of soul and spirit focus attention on allowing the Word of God a thorough work of exposing everything hidden to the very essence of the person. Only by such intense and deep scrutiny and repentance can one enter this rest. At this point one's own work counts for nothing, and never will again. From this point on he has rested and ceased from his own work. There must be a point when Caleb no longer will think 'we are able to do it.' There is no contradiction between 'work' that they are praised for and 'rest' or 'cessation.' People asked Jesus 'what might we do to do the works of God'. Jesus replied 'This is the work of God that you believe in him whom God has sent.' The crux is believing not working, so that what the believer does is 'a work of faith' and done through God not for God.

4.4 'For somewhere he has spoken' is strange since this occurs in Genesis and Exodus. God's work is finished so he rested from His works. But what is the parallel, is it that 'having done all stand' applies to the loyal believer and therefore only faith in addition to the law, is needed to enter the rest? Actually, the application is that God finished the work of creation and redemption and therefore we must enter by faith. God's rest for Him is not that God now does nothing, a kind of Deistic and mechanistic view, but that before our work of faith actually begins along with God's we must enter his rest by faith and be co-laborers with God. God is not resting now in the sense of not doing anything, since he sustaining all that is. The parallel is that being sustained by God depends on imitation of God. Hebrews does not attribute the Gen 2.2 verse to Moses 'somewhere' but to God himself. The first part of the verse is omitted since "and by the seventh day God completed His work which he had done; and He rested on the seventh day from all His work which He had done."

Hebrews does not acknowledge that 'completion' had occurred. The Hebrews context of 'works were finished from the foundation of the world"[180] is the promised and denied rest 4.3, 4.5. The 'works' that were completed were not creation per se but the provision for a rest for man of which Canaan is a type only. But if a whole generation died because of rebellion in the case of the type, they send a mixed message to the people of the anti-type era that the latter is not unconditionally prepared for man but in the same way and even more so has conditions attached to it.

4.5 "They will never enter my rest' Ps 95.11 is later qualified as all the males of military age and over representing the Assembly and delegated responsible persons that refused the direct order. Repetition enforces it, forty years completed the term, and it appears in the Psalms of worship as part of sacred history they must never forget. The antithesis of 'God rested from all his work becomes 'my rest' and because of disobedience they shall never enter it and through Joshua's time never did.

This rest now is available if one makes' every effort to enter that rest.' This effort is to stop working as God did from his work. The 'every effort' is a behavioral therapy against backsliding. Note that nothing involves 'merit' and so this effort is a spiritual exercise and not salvation by works. In fact, it is a cessation from one's own works,. Can it be abstracted from God resting from his work that God does this periodically even as man should, so that there are seasons of intensive activity by God and other times of greatly lessened activity having nothing to do with sin and punishment? The lesson of the Sabbath should be that man, like God, needs to dedicate the seventh to God, not merely to avoid an originally unlucky day of the month shipmate, which was extended to the seventh day, but to 'plateau', to 'cease' from the work that daily sustains a man's earthly life.

4.6 'Some will enter that rest; follows the pattern of history that even now in the church age some of God's people will enter and others will not. This message is data to say the book is an evangelistic message for unbelieving

Jews and believing Jews alike and some extended descriptions of ritual matters may also be for Non-Jewish readers. Note that 'unbelief' is linked not to intellectual questions or debatable options but to 'disobedience.' In holy war this is non-submission to orders and worthy of a court martial and possibly execution. Here is a concession clause by use of participle, kaiper, 'although he was a son'[181] In the crime of Kadesh 'disobedience'peith-, and 'unbelief' pist- are interchangeable. 'Some will enter that rest' is present-future indicating that some Jews will become believers. There is nothing deterministic about this since this is the response to the gospel based on free will.

4.7 'God again set a certain day' David's words in Ps 95.7,8 are David's day, while v.8 is Joshua's day and now the 'Today' is the present time. The second chance set by God is a verbal call in this case through David. It did not occur immediately after the Kadesh incident; Why? Was God waiting for the fourth generation punishment or probation to expire or 400 years, taking us to the time of David? The hearing elicits hardening as a knee-jerk reaction as in the story of two sons where one said to his father 'I go' but did not, while the other said 'no' but later went. The initial reaction of the sons did not involve reflection and thought, while after a time and thought the change of response meant repentance, a change of mind. Hebrews is meant to make this reversal possible for Gospel believers. But change of mind metanoia, can be for the good or bad. God 'again' sets a 'certain day' a special time of challenge and grace. This helps to lay the foundation for the actual initiation of a New Covenant in history as God's work not Paul's.. Ps 95.7,8 According to Hebrews God ordained this special day to take the land and hopes they will listen and not harden their hearts. The author applies this to the Gospel age probably in the sense of The Day of the Lord. So far as philosophy of history is concerned the author jumps from creation to Moses to David. In terms of new revelations are concerned and Melchisedek and Abraham in terms of types.

4.8 'If Joshua had given them rest' denies that the meaning of Sabbath-rest was exhausted at that time. But it does not deny the accuracy of Joshua as an account the way some liberal scholars do. Actually it is a re-reading of the text from the standpoint of subsequent history, that the major sweeps of Palestine followed by the dispersion of tribes to their territory left a major task of occupation up to the individual tribes and clans. The Period of Judges was periodically one of rest from war, but also sin and failure. The full import of Joshua's successes and failures are recorded in his book. But here the author says the promised rest was for another day thus belonging to the future of prophecy. Jos 22.4 The 'rest' in Joshua is for the two and half tribes who fought with Israel west of Jordan and now they may return to their wives and flocks for their job is done. No more wars E of Jordan are given till later in the Judges Period.

4.9 Corporate versus individual: Being part of the people of God and having the experience of entering God's rest are entirely different things. Just as Israel came out of Egypt it was the obedient generation that entered into the land. God's people is a transgenerational entity. Experiencing rest is a synchronic or same generation gospel. Of those who hear some will enter in and others will not.. But can this be applied to the church in that baptized members of the church are God's people, but only those who hear the promise of rest and have faith do, in fact, enter in. They may have collective rest and the security of belonging and being baptized with pardon, but have they entered the Second Rest, as some call it, where they cease from their own personal reliance on their works and discover imitating God and His Rest for living and serving in this world? In 2 Esdras 2.34 'eternal rest' goes beyond Hebrews 4.9; Cf. Matt 11.29; 2 Esd 7.91; Rev 14.13 'rest from their labors'. Gnostics also used the concept of anapausis. Myers,[182]151

4.9-11, A symbolical happening need not necessarily have been a prediction of the future[Ezk 8.3; 10.1; 10.18-19;11.23][183]it can rather be a simultaneous reality. "The Sabbath institution, insofar as it serves as a symbol of heavenly rest, provides a final OT illustration; for this aspect of it is not specifically predictive. The Sabbath existed as symbolical from the date of its hallowing by God [Gen 2.3], even before heaven had been revealed as man's destiny; and it continues thus timelessly symbolical on into the NT era [Heb 4.9-11] Only when considered as a type of rest in Christ [Mt 11.28] may the Sabbath be assigned a truly predictive value." Payne,[184]48

4.10 The Gospel is always for 'anyone'. This anyone must first enter God's rest and then will discover he has rested from his own works. This doesn't mean he isn't working, but it is the sphere of God's rest. This is the author's way of expressing 'in Christ' and being a 'co-worker' with God. The author does not distinguish between Jewish or Jewish-Christian people. If the promise has not been realized the exhortation is applicable no matter of their spiritual condition.

4.11 'Make every effort to enter' is not reliance on human energy but rather focus, singlemindedness in seeking and pursuing a goal, the forerunner to loving God with all one's heart. The effort to enter as well as the entering are the safeguard against falling into disobedience. If one is distracted by predecessors one will follow the example of 'their disobedience.' Focus on Jesus only allows one to actually enter God's rest. God's Rest is a new level of grace called establishing grace. The problem is when one has entered God's Rest and then feels secure in his position and experience and not in the person of God. Several scriptures are a call for whole-hearted pursuing and seeking with intense effort: 4.11; 6.1; 6.11; 4.1; 3.11; 2.3; 10.22-24;35; 12.1; 12.12,14. How can this be reconciled with Paul? In Paul 'works'= 'things done for merit that will justify'. Here the supreme effort is made to lay hold of salvation, not merit. Barring burnout the focused living of effort to please God is an aid to not stagnate and lose out. This is not living on emotion but pursuing what God has promised those who lay hold of it.

4.12 The living and active sword has been portrayed in movies with a 'life' of its own, a realm of magic, myth, incantation and divination. But the Word brings creation and life and is powerful to the tearing down of strongholds. The double edged sword wasn't used for piercing or penetrating as with a saber but to slice and slash with horizontal and vertical movements. But the figure given in of a surgeon, penetrating in order to divide pieces of meat as a butcher does. Dividing entered in to the original creation account of heaven and earth, sea and land, mammals and man etc. Soul and spirit become an open revelation to a man so dealt with by the divine surgeon so he becomes deeply aware of the soul or life mystery and of the eternal spirit mystery. The issue of life and death and eternity suddenly dawns on him. 'joints and marrow' goes to the skeletal structure and mobility, the stuff that fails the elderly and the stuff that rebuilds blood cells. Then in a third step it judges the thoughts and intents of the heart. These are two witnesses to inner activity in the heart of man. The three-fold cuts of six elements of man's nature leave him uncovered and bare before God and the individual who must give account. As in the prophetic gift unbelievers will hear and say 'God is truly among them' and be convinced of his sins. The Word brings a man's sins beforehand to judgment. The instrument, surgeon, quality, organs operated on, all are for this prosecutor to bring conviction now. Nothing in all creation is hidden from God now that the last citadel of secrecy is exposed. The offerer, who in context is the priest, doesn't cut open an animal, but the very innards of the worshipper. We immediately think of Goliath's sword as being unique, and the legend of Excaliber. In the Ezk 36 passages the heart is a rock and the word breaks rocks asunder. The only verse having 'heart' and 'sword' is in Lamentations:

> Lam. 1:20 "See, O LORD, how distressed I am! I am in torment within, and in my heart I am disturbed, for I have been most rebellious. Outside, the sword bereaves; inside, there is only death. Probably the 'sword of Goliath' is a background but its qualities are not described. 1Sam. 21: 1Sam. 22:10 Jer. 17:10 "I the LORD search the heart and examine the mind, to reward a man according to his conduct, according to what his deeds deserve." While military and medical metaphors abound the use of the double edged sword is not so specified. Metaphors for the Word abound: Deut 32.42 the sword has a mouth Dt 13.15 that devours or eats. Dt 11.4 'the rod of his mouth' slays the wicked. Rev. 1.16; 2.16; 2 Thess 2.8. In Jer 23.29 it is like fire and a forge-hammer that shatters rock, a prophet-context. Hos 6.5; Eph 6.17; The sharp word of the Servant is of a prophet not edict of a king. A polished arrow ch<u>ets baru </u>Isa 49.2 Cf. . Jer 51.11 may not read 'sharpen the arrows' which should be c<u>hets shanun</u> Isa 5.28; Ps 45.6; 120.4; Prov 25.18. Arrows, shaft and spears, so the tip has to be sharp. [185], The sword of Rev 6.8 is the <u>rhomphaia,</u> a large broad sword used by barbarians and in Philo of the angel's flaming sword as in Gen 3.24; Rev 2.16; 18.15. Lk 2.35 it is the sword that will pierce Mary's soul. There is pain and anguish. The prophetic word pierces as a sword. Note The Sibylline oracles 3.316 and Ezk 14.17. Ford,[186]99,This is an image of Christ's word, found frequently in varying forms, all of which intend to suggest the irresistible power and unfailing force of his judgment, punitive or otherwise. Isa 11.4; 49.2; Wisd.Sol 18.15; Eph 6.17; Heb 4.12; 2 Thess 2.8; Ps of Sol 17.39; 1 Enoch 62.2; 2 Esdras[=IV Ezra] 13.10.383,For the appearance of the resurrected Lord [187]

4.12-13 Inspiration doctrine could well use these verses as a basic statement of the living and active Word of God. If this is a personification the reality is that it is 'organic' partaking of the life forms of creation yet functioning as creator not the created 'Active' could mean 'ambulatory' or 'functional' or 'mobile.' Sharpness has to do with tempering and materials as well as manufacturing skills and secrets. The two-edged sword was used for horizontal or angular strokes, seldom vertical. But what is described is surgery of a most painful slow and agonizing movement. It does 'penetrate but also 'divides' the total person soul and spirit, joints and marrow, and 'judges' the thoughts and intents of the heart. The person is left 'uncovered and laid bare' before God, what is known as conviction of the Spirit. Thus the Word of God does not only reveal God to us but reveals what is inside us. We immediately think of Goliath's sword as being unique, and the legend of Excaliber. In the Ezk 36 passages the heart is a rock and the word breaks rocks asunder. The only verse having 'heart' and 'sword' is in Lamentations.: Lam. 1:20 "See, O LORD, how distressed I am! I am in torment within, and in my heart I am disturbed, for I have been most rebellious. Outside, the sword bereaves; inside, there is only death. Probably the 'sword of Goliath' is a background but its qualities are not described. 1Sam. 21:9 The priest replied, "The sword of Goliath the Philistine, whom you killed in the Valley of Elah, is here; it is wrapped in a cloth behind the ephod. If you want it, take it; there is no sword here but that one." David said, "There is none like it; give it to me." 1Sam. 22:10 Ahimelech inquired of the LORD for him; he also gave him provisions and the sword of Goliath the Philistine." As a motif in the David narrative, from taking it to using it there is a continuity but if the sword were commensurate to Goliath's size David would hardly be able to wield it. As for scriptures where God searches the heart, the means is not given Jer. 17:10 "I the LORD search the heart and examine the mind, to reward a man according to his conduct, according to what his deeds deserve." While military and medical metaphors abound the use of the double edged sword is not so specified.

Metaphors for the Word abound: Deut 32.42 the sword has a mouth Dt 13.15 that devours or eats. Dt 11.4 'the rod of his mouth' slays the wicked. Rev. 1.16; 2.16; 2 Thess 2.8. In Jer 23.29 it is like fire and a forge-hammer that shatters rock, a prophet-context. Hos 6.5; Eph 6.17; The sharp word of the Servant is of a prophet not edict of a king. A polished arrow chets barur Isa 49.2 Cf. Jer 51.11 may not read 'sharpen the arrows' which should be chets shanun Isa 5.28; Ps 45.6; 120.4; Prov 25.18. Arrows have shaft and spears, so the tip has to be sharp. North 187,260. The sword of Rev 6.8 is the rhomphaia, a large broad sword used by barbarians and in Philo of the angel's flaming sword as in Gen 3.24; Rev 2.16; 18.15. Lk 2.35 it is the sword that will pierce Mary's soul. There is pain and anguish. The prophetic word pierces as a sword. Note The Sibylline oracles 3.316 and Ezk 14.17. Ford,[188]99,"This is an image of Christ's word, found frequently in varying forms, all of which intend to suggest the irresistible power and unfailing force of his judgment, punitive or otherwise. Isa 11.4; 49.2; Wisd.Sol 18.15; Eph 6.17; Heb 4.12; 2 Thess 2.8; Ps of Sol 17.39; 1 Enoch 62.2; 2 Esdras[=IV Ezra] 13.10.383,For the appearance of the resurrected Lord see Ford: 385. The unmasking of sin' appears very frequently: Hos 7.1; Lam 2.14; Isa 59.12; Job 20.27; Ps.Sol 8.8; 2 Bar 83.3; Lk 12.2; 1 Cor 4.5; 4QpNahum 3.3 The opposite 'conceal your sins' in 2 Esd 16.15 appears in Ps 69.5; Jer 16.17; Ezk 8.16f Myers,[189]348. Ps33.13-15;90.8;Job 26.6. Rev 19.12 mentions 'eyes are a flame of fire' His judgment is incapable of deception or fraud, it penetrates all things, even the secrets of the heart, and consumes the enemies. 1.14; Heb 4.13; Note this 'face' of God may be the reason for God denying Moses the vision, for the divine 'lasor' would have destroyed Moses and he was the closest person to God in history.. Thus clouds and all were for protection, precisely what God stresses at Mount Sinai, lest the people transgress the barrier and die. Ford, 313[190].

The unmasking of sin' appears very frequently: Hos 7.1; Lam 2.14; Isa 59.12; Job 20.27; Ps.Sol 8.8; 2 Bar 83.3; Lk 12.2; 1 Cor 4.5; 4QpNahum 3.3 The opposite 'conceal your sins' in 2 Esd 16.15 appears in Ps 69.5; Jer 16.17; Ezk 8.16f, Myers, 348[191]. Buchanan[192] 'Soul' psyche and spirit pneuma can be used synonymously but not here. They are in contrast to soma 'body.' According to Paul Adam was made a living soul; and the last Adam 'a life-giving spirit.' Philo said 'spirit is the essence of the soul.' And names the soul of man 'spirit' Wis 15.11. To separate between soul and spirit is as difficult as distinguishing 'designs and intentions of the mind.' This exceeds the limits of the 'Intentional Fallacy' since God knows but we don't. 'Joints and marrow' can be separated but hardly put back together again. God keeps body soul and spirit 1 Thess 5.23 and Odes of Sol. 12.5 says 'For the swiftness of the Word is inexpressible and like his expression is the swiftness and his sharpness.' But is psychē physical life like zoē, and pneuma religious and thought, affection, commitment and realm of surrender to the One and the larger good?

4.13 God's omniscient awareness and knowledge over all creation in parts and as a whole follows so who can zero in on the use of the Word as a sword to do surgery and open up one's innards? It is clear God already knows but we don't. This helps us understand the Psalmist's petitions as well as Jeremiah's. Ps 19.7-8 places God's word as the primary instrument of searching and then in v.12 confesses 'Who can discern his errors'? Forgive mi hidden faults.' In Ps 139.1 the Psalmist confesses that God has searched and known him' v.1-4. But he closes in v.23-24 he prays 'Search me O God, and know my heart; test me and know my thoughts, see if there is any offensive way in me, and lead me in the way everlasting.' Past searchings aren't enough because a human constantly needs new light. For Jeremiah he is the tester and refiner but it is through the word. In the midst of a plot against him Jeremiah 11.20 prays "But, O Lord Almighty, you who judge righteously and test the heart and mind,' It is in reactions to God's word that both God and Jeremiah know the situation. 12.3. 17.9-10. Ps33.13-15"From heaven the Lord looks down and sees all mankind; from his swelling he watches all who live on earth; he who forms the hearts of all, who considers everything they do." Hebrews adds the line about God forming motivations and the idea of an accounting time ;90.8;"You have set our iniquities before you, your secret sins in the light of your presence.' Job 26.6 "Death is naked before God; Destruction lies uncovered." ,Rev 19.12 mentions 'eyes are a flame of fire' His judgment is incapable of deception or fraud, it penetrates all things, even the secrets of the heart, and consumes the enemies. 1.14; Heb 4.13; Note this 'face' of God may be the reason for God denying Moses the vision, for the divine laser would have destroyed Moses. Thus clouds and all were for protection, precisely what God stresses at Mount Sinai, lest the people transgress the barrier and die. Ford,[193]313. Nothing hidden' but some poetry in the OT indicate death and Sheol are beyond his presence. Others strongly assert omnipresence especially Psalm 139. For us God does surgery with a scalpel; but for himself everything is already uncovered.

4.14 'Gone through the heavens' implies a seven or fourteen layered heaven concept but not the Platonic scheme. Jesus the priest is in the highest heaven and thus Lord over all. This priest is again identified as 'Jesus the Son of God' and therefore we must hold on to our faith. Trials on earth are no reason to have negative nay-thinking, doubts and fears that ch.2 has already shown come from the Devil. 'The faith we profess' is now not only subjective but a body of beliefs and commitments. These verses contain a tradition that Jesus went through the heavens, not only into heaven. This might reflect the Elijah account or some apocryphal ascension or flight accounts. In Jewish thought there are upwards of 14 heavens. But this has nothing to do with Neoplatonic thought of levels of purity or Gnosticism and aversion to material per se. Just as in Greek myth the River Styx takes one to Hades by going 'through' a route to arrive there finally, so Jesus went by a route and finally arrived at God's right hand. Ezekiel also was transported just as Elijah's disciples feared Elijah, who had earlier disappeared, had been whisked away by the Spirit and may have landed on some hill. The presence of this high priest in God's presence is motivation to hang on to faith. Never in the OT is a high priest's role or stature or influence on personal piety so described. The contrast between the description of the high priest and his garb in Exodus and Leviticus along with ordination and job description links him to the Day of Atonement and sacrificial roles or his role as one who blesses only. The role here is transformed to a perpetual presence before God with the one sacrifice finished. The closest OT text is in Isa 53.12. Here in Hebrews the role of the high priest has been expanded to 'help' 2.18 and not just 'making atonement' 2.18. It also includes 'freeing from bondage' and 'destroying him who has the power of death'. Here the ability 4.15 to sympathize is especially stressed. 'mercy' is to sinners but 'grace' is to help in time of need. This high priest actually enables. The case of Melchizedek comes to mind but his was only a pronounced blessing. Eli enabled Hannah to have faith and rejoice before the prayer was fulfilled. The enabling role of the high priest needs a thorough study since Aaron and others enabled Israel to sin and Jehoida enabled a coup to put out an evil queen. "One is tempted to find an intentional antithesis between the awe-inspiring description of the word of God in the previous verse and the tender language of the verse that follows. Is the word a living, energizing power? The High-priest too is living and powerful, great and dwelling above the heavens. Does the word pierce to our innermost being? The High-priest sympathizes with our weaknesses, or, in the beautiful paraphrase of the English Version, "is touched with a feeling of our infirmities." Does the word judge? The High-priest can be equitable, inasmuch as He has been tempted like as we are tempted, and that without sin. Hebrews 4:15)[194]

4.15 We don't have much information about priests who cannot sympathize with weakness. This may simply be a human characteristic of those whose lives are steady, but often is a behavior of ministers and politicians who have a 'physician save yourself' belief at the same time they identify with the Savior of the Bible. Assigning penance, alms, gifts, time, service, or other behavioristic therapy may cover a basic unfeeling heart and expression. We do know that only Aaron and Phinehas and Jehoiada were proactive for the right. We do know Eli was weak, and sons of Moses and Aaron died because of rebellions. We do know priests opposed all the prophets and the prophets opposed them almost without exception. They belonged to the prophet, priest, king, elder, wise man, judge configuration, a system perverted by idolatry and efforts to use the world's methods to resolve problems initiated by God as disciplinary actions. We also know they were implicated in murders, Cf. Hosea, and did not seek the Lord. Jesus was tempted but did not yield. A minister who is tempted and yields doesn't sympathize but is totally compromised in feelings and actions and unable to sense people's weakness and needs. Chwris 'without, separate from' links real temptation which focuses on individuality and personal needs with sinlessness, that Philo attributes to the Logos and Messiah.[195] Philo distinguishes the spiritual from the natural man: "Such men attribute to God these three things: the soul, the external sense, and speech. For they have received all these things, not for themselves, but for him, in whose favor they naturally and appropriately confess that the energies according to each of these three things depend upon him, namely, the imaginations and apprehensions of the mind, the explanations of speech, and the perceptions of the outward senses. (109) Those, now, who attribute these things to themselves, have received an allotment worthy of their own perverseness, namely, a soul fond of plotting against others, polluted with irrational passions, and enveloped in a multitude of vices; at one time eager to indulge in violent insolence through its gluttony and lasciviousness, as though it were in a brothel; at another time held fast by the multitude of its iniquities as in a prison, with wicked (not men but) actions which deserve to be led before all the judges. Secondly, speech insolent, loquacious, sharpened against the truth, injurious to all who come in its way, and bringing disgrace upon those who possess it. Thirdly, the external sense, insatiable, always filling itself with the objects of the outward senses, but through its immoderate appetites never able to be satisfied, disregarding all its monitors and correctors, so as to refuse to look upon or listen to them, and to reject with disdain all that they say to it for its good. (110) But those who take these things not for themselves but for God, attribute each one of them to him, guarding that which they have acquired in a truly holy and religious manner, keeping their mind, so that it shall think of nothing else but the things relating to God and to his excellencies, and their speech so as to make it, with unrestrained mouth, and with encomiums, and hymns, and announcements of happiness, honor the father of the universe, collecting together and exhibiting all its power of interpretation and utterance in this one office; and regulating the external senses, so that forming a conception of the whole of that world which is perceptible by them, they may, in a guileless, honest, and pure manner, relate to the soul all the heaven and earth, and the natures whose home is between the two, and all animals and plants, and their respective energies and faculties, and all their motions and their stationary existence." In this analysis Jesus, as the Son, did create all things, but avoided temptation by attributing all to the Father. <u>Asthenia</u> in 5.2; 7.28 11.34 of the OT priests is in contrast to dynamis of Christ, and is not only physical weakness, but of intellectual and moral weakness, which leads to failure to do God's will. Again the errors of Eli just weren't 'tough love.' The case of the priests of Nob were not strong enough to say know on the basis not of a situation but of the law of separation of priestly from laity. <u>Sympathew</u> is used of family affection in 4 Macc 14.13-20 and Christian Family Heb 10.34. Here it is of the relation of Christ as high priest, and believers. Perhaps empathize might be more accurate with an added compassion component. Sumpaschw are in a context of imprisonment, which Christ did not experience, temptation, which he did, and shared suffering as in Rom 8.17; 1 Cor 12.26. Cf. . metriopathew in 5.2. [196]

4.16 The exhortation to approach the throne of grace with confidence 'so that we may receive mercy and find grace to help us in time of need.' The arrangement is not automatic. Jesus brings the believer into a network on heaven and earth that is set up to pray and receive actual help in time of need. They are already believers and have received grace but grace and mercy are always needed and prayed for in times of crisis.

Chapter Five:

Christ is greater than Aaron and Melchisedek

God's Son and Word

5.1-3 Atonement in context of purification offering denotes 'purge', but with burnt offering and other sacrifices it means 'atone' to reconcile the individual or community with God so as to 'become at-one' The inclusive reading is the case here. Note that in Lev 9.7 'to make atonement for them' is a matter of an important sequence: Priests must first atone for themselves before they can do so for others. [B.Yoma 43b] Milgrom,[197]578; 7.23-28,Milgrom,578; ba'adka ub'ad if the object is a person a preposition is requires, either 'al or be'ad or both, meaning 'on behalf of' Lev 16.6,24,33;Num 8.12,21]'al can only be used of others. Be 'ad can include the subject in the act Cf. Lev 16.6,11,24; Ezek 45.22. Note in Job 42.28 "offer a burnt offering for yourselves be 'adkem and Job, my servant, will intercede on your behalf 'alekem. 8.1-7,Milgrom,578.

Atonement in context of purification offering denotes 'purge', but with burnt offering and other sacrifices it means 'atone' to reconcile the individual or community with God so as to 'become at-one' The inclusive reading is the case here. Note that in Lev 9.7 'to make atonement for them' is a matter of an important sequence: Priests must first atone for themselves before they can do so for others. [B.Yoma 43b] Milgrom,[198]578; 7.23-28,Milgrom,578;ba'adka ube'ad if the object is a person a preposition is requires, either 'al or be'ad or both, meaning 'on behalf of' Lev 16.6,24,33;Num 8.12,21] 'al can only be used of others. Be'ad can include the subject in the act Cf. Lev 16.6,11,24; Ezek 45.22. Note in Job 42.28 "offer a burnt offering for yourselves be'adkem and Job, my servant, will intercede on your behalf 'alekem. 8.1-7,Milgrom,578. The high priest leads the nation of individuals in sacrificing for his own sins. No one knows more how he does it than other priests and Levites. He cannot pretend he isn't a sinner. But with so much sin, his and others, would there be a tendency to take sin for granted and not aim at sinlessness? Would compromise simply be viewed from a hierarchy of laws and justified for the greater good? If his basic work is sin-work would the conscience about ethics, love, righteousness and justice ob obscured?

5.2 The priest could deal gently with transgressors, perhaps too gently. His own weaknesses could interfere with objective ministry to those who are ignorant and going astray. That is why priests cannot divorce or marry a divorced person because then his own unhappy experience would interfere with those undergoing the same. Eli is a case in point with his sons, but for Hannah this gentle approach turned out to be a real ministry. The priests of Nob were gentle with David and caused their execution. The laws of particular cases was very specific so it was necessary for the priest to apply them consistently and with no animosity. Moses' and Aaron's sons turned out to be rebellious and others joined the coup de tat. Caiaphas was not gentle. Jehoiada wasn't either but otherwise he could not rid the land of evil Athaliah. The extent the king controlled the priesthood in the time since Solomon and centralization took away from the impact the priest could have on original lives.

5.4 'No man' takes this honor ..but must be called by God.' For those descendents of Aaron did this call consist of the father's designation or the role of the firstborn? As in the kingship role the initial kings of Saul, David and Solomon had experiences with God but they are not mentioned for those subsequently in the kingly line. Or was there such an experience for some at the moment of the anointing with oil or only through the messages of prophets? This is a tradition that Jesus went through the heavens, not only into heaven. This might reflect the Elijah account or some apocryphal ascension or flight accounts. In Jewish thought there are upwards of 14 heavens. But this has nothing to do with Neoplatonic thought of levels of purity or Gnosticism and aversion to material per se. Just as in Greek myth the River Styx takes one to Hades by going 'through' a route to arrive there finally, so Jesus went by a route and finally arrived at God's right hand. Ezekiel also was transported just as Elijah's disciples feared Elijah, who had earlier disappeared, had been whisked away by the Spirit and may have landed on some hill. Ex 28.1 "Have Aaron your brother brought to you from among the Israelites, along with his sons Nadab and Abihu, Eleazar and Ithamar, so they may serve me as priests." The focus is one-on-one, namely Aaron and Christ. The OT account is rather considering a line of priests serving forever. Therefore ministers in the church are shepherds, pastors, deacons, elders, disciples, apostles but not priests, for there was only one priest in the NT pattern.

5.5 'Today I have become your Father' must refer to either Jesus' birth apart from Joseph, or baptism when similar words were pronounced in what might be called an adoption formula. So while pagan religions had AB and AB.BA and other references to the Father such as AD or Adab, the relation of the pre-existent messiah only became 'SON or 'my son' in the incarnation thus fulfilling the type that found its antitype in Solomon. Thus, except for Malachi, the use of Father was confined to the collective 'Israel' or creator of all beings, and in the incarnation the basis is laid for the eternal 'Son' and his sons. Ps 2.7 The decree in both texts establishes the authority of the king, not his own initiative except to die for mankind, leaving disciples an example that exultation only comes from serving men. Instrument use of infinitive 'Christ glorified not himself by becoming a high priest.' Burton:conceived result [199] 'Christ did not take on himself of becoming a high priest,' thus is not linked to emptying himself in Phil 2, or Heb 10.7 'I come to do your will o God.'. Evidently the text links this to Sonship. Being willing the whole plan may not have been in Christ's mind all during his lifetime even though sacrifice was. He was made high priest. This was prefigured by his relationship to John the Baptist, son of a priest and baptism, a symbol of death, but become clear from John 13-21. The lesson is that commitment opens new understanding of suffering and glory that were not apparent at the call to be a Son in relation to God. The connection of the first quote in v.5 to the related one in v.6 is that it was the High Priest's son who was established by his father or God as the successor. God here designates his son as Son and then on this basis declares his priesthood and the eternity of that priesthood. In Hebrews church leaders are not called priests so there is no succession such as with Aaron. But in Peter he conceives of the church as a kingdom of priests in which every believer is such.

5.5-10 Jesus is shown from Ps 110 to have all the qualities of the 'perfected' or 'qualified' high priest. He cites Ps 2.7 'you are my son' and joins it to Ps 110.4 'The Lord has sworn...' E.Lövestam has proven that all the clear uses of Ps 2.7 in the NT relate to the Resurrection.[200] "As of the time of his resurrection Christ became a 'son of God' in a special sense--God's son endowed with universal and everlasting royal dominion [Rom 1.4]. To this notion derived from Ps 2.7, Hebrews now links another from Ps 110.4: God's appointment of the risen royal Son as the possessor of the eternal priesthood of Melchizedek.";[201] Note that Ps 2.7 establishes the risen Jesus as having royal inheritance, and Ps 110.4 establishes his eternal priesthood. The phrase 'al dibrati is a problem.

1. 'For the sake of' Eccl 3.18;8.2;7.14 does not suit the context;
2. A modal sense is favored;
3. LXX uses kata ten taxin Melchizesek is followed by Heb 5.6; 6.20; 7.11,17 and Vulgate. Taxis can mean many things. 3. 7.15 paraphrases: homoiothta M. 'According to the likeness of M.'
4. Peshitta in Ps 110.4 reads badmuteh de Melkizedek 'in the likeness of M.'[202] Fitzmyer,[203]223

5.6 In vv5-10;"Jesus is shown from Ps 110 to have all the qualities of the 'perfected' or 'qualified' high priest. He cites Ps 2.7 'you are my son' and joins it to Ps 110.4 'The Lord has sworn...' E. Lövestam has proven that all the clear uses of Ps 2.7 in the NT relate to the Resurrection.[204] "As of the time of his resurrection Christ became a 'son of God' in a special sense--God's son endowed with universal and everlasting royal dominion [Rom 1.4]. To this notion derived from Ps 2.7, Hebrews now links another from Ps 110.4: God's appointment of the risen royal Son as the possessor of the eternal priesthood of Melchizedek.";[205] Note that Ps 2.7 establishes the risen Jesus as having royal inheritance, and Ps 110.4 establishes his eternal priesthood. The phrase 'al dibrati is a problem. 1. 'For the sake of' Eccl 3.18;8.2;7.14 does not suit the context; 2. A modal sense is favored; 3. LXX uses kata ten taxin Melchizesek is followed by Heb 5.6; 6.20; 7.11,17 and Vulgate. Taxis can mean many things.3. 7.15 paraphrases: homoioteta M. 'According to the likeness of M.'4. Peshitta in Ps 110.4 reads badmuteh de Melkizedeq 'in the likeness of M.'[206] Fitzmyer,[207]223. Ps 110.4 The promises or rbd of God in both cases also involve direct speech declaring a present fact performatively 'you are [forthwith] a priest forever…' This is not the same degree as the oath which is unilateral, while covenant involves two parties.

5.7 'Save from death' The tears of Jesus are the antitype of the type in the Psalms of lament where one is facing death. Ps 13.3 16.10; Psa. 9:13 O LORD, see how my enemies persecute me! Have mercy and lift me up from the gates of death, Psa. 13:3 Look on me and answer, O LORD my God. Give light to my eyes, or I will sleep in death; Ps 9.0 speaks of Christ's death as prefigured by David's son dying. Psa. 9:0 For the director of music. To [the tune of] "The Death of the Son." A psalm of David. Elements of Messianic content include

1. He requires blood v.12;
2. God makes himself known v.16 in executing judgment.
3. v.19 speaks of the resurrection and
4. God's throne is a current factor in life v.4.
5. God is a God or Lord kurios of grace v.13;
6. v.18 shows that because of the Lord's resurrection he abides forever v.7 in contrast to mortals and gives a hope that does not perish.
7. The second coming is spoken of as a future event in v.20 and in the meantime v.10 urges the NT motif of trust and faith in 'Thy name'. As v.13 is a prayer to avoid death, Gethsemane can be so interpreted, but the 'hour' and 'cup' may mean not avoidance of death but of dying before the hour had arrived, standing in contrast to the hour of darkness or 'my hour' and 'your hour' Psa. 68:20 Our God is a God who saves; from the Sovereign LORD comes escape from death. 72.13;78.31;78.50;88.15;89.48;90.5;94.17;94.21 etc. Only Eli shows concern of a priest in the case of Hannah and his words to erring sons. Samuel for God's concerns but hardly shows concern in accompanying backslidden Saul back to the city. Jehoida does for the kingdom and the new regent but not for Athaliah. Josiah's priest does for God's word but this does not relate to people. More so is Ezra, who is only concerned about the law. in the NT Caiaphas and Annas show a little, that one should die and not all die. Some Psalms show responding oracles that show personal concern for the worshipper, but other mainly a concern for holiness in the worshipper. Aaron and Phinehas both stepped in to stop the wrath of God.. apo 'on account of' emphasizing source 'heard on account of his devotion' Dana-Mantey,101. Attridge[208] notes eulabeias can mean reverence or godly fear and traces the motif to a pattern of ideal prayer of a pious man in Hellenistic Judaism. Apo as 'from' would be 'saved from fear' while 'because'of his reverence'.The latter would fit the Son of Man role of salvation because of submission, while the former would be salvation from the strangle-hold of Satan using fear of death. Was Jesus heard? If he was he would be saved from death, or death in the garden. Others believe he was not heard so that as 5.9 says he ;was made a cause of eternal salvation to all obey him.' 'Deliverance from death' was through resurrection and ascension. Harnack does not situate the verse in Gethsemane. Attridge then uses Philo to connect parresia 'boldness' and 'loudness' before a terrible despot because he has words and frankness are proper but at the

same time Abraham in Gen 15.2-18 had reverence calling God 'Master' Thus as Abraham submitted to the divine will so did his seed Jesus.. It was 'religious awe' that caused his prayers to be heard. Lane notes "The noun εὐλάβεια, which occurs in 5:7 and 12:28 (and not elsewhere in the NT), can mean "fear, anxiety" or "reverence, piety." If in v 7 εὐλάβεια connotes an emotion of fear felt by Jesus when faced with the prospect of impending death, ἀπό will mean "from" and the phrase will signify "he was heard (and rescued) from fear." This was the understanding of the latter. Ambrose: "he was heard [and rescued] from that fear") mss: cop[sa] cop[bo] sy. It involves, however, a rather harsh ellipsis, which is unexpected in a writer so skillful. Moreover, he has already spoken of the "fear of death" in 2:15, where he wrote φόβος θανάτου, and not εὐλάβεια. It is difficult to perceive how Jesus could have rescued others from the fear of death (2:14–15) if he had himself been shaken by that fear. The ptcp εὐλαβηθείς occurs in 11:7, where it signifies careful attentiveness within the context of a godly life. In 12:28 the noun εὐλάβεια connotes attentiveness to the divine will or godly reverence. This would seem to be the nuance of the term in v 7 as well. This understanding precludes the proposal that ἀπό means "from" or "after" and supports the translation "heard because of his godly fear"[209]

5.8 'He learned obedience from what he suffered.' The event of v.7 is Gethsemane and the crisis does not seem to be desire to avoid death on the cross but to avoid death in the garden due to extraordinary stress. God heard his prayer granting angels to strengthen him. But his reverent submission 'not my will but yours be done' is the reason he was heard. The prayer's answer may have included strength to go through judgment halls and events leading up to his death as well. His learning obedience as a son, not The Son, was necessary for him to be a perfect priest and perfect sacrifice. As a righteous man he would normally do the right thing but to learn obedience means that suffering and pressure bring to bear what his human nature desire, 'not my will but thine be done.' But if this only involved premature death in Gethsemane the subject of death is curtailed and since the Son did not know the time of the End perhaps he was praying that the offering of himself was sufficient as it was in the type, Abraham and Isaac. Three times praying to avoid death seem to be a broader issue of allowing death to win and evil triumph. The intentionality of obedience corresponds to that of Isaac. The lesson is that of Jesus needed to learn obedience at age 12 in the temple, and at Cana and in the temptation so do believers need to learn obedience within suffering. From the background of Jewish theology of the good tendency and evil tendency if a person has no evil tendency and merely acts according to nature it is a-moral and no obedience is learned. Surrender utterly to God in particulars contrary to one's own feelings is learned obedience. A Son of God and the image of God he becomes a son in the flesh. But by nature is not sufficient, he must endure suffering, as in Isa 53, where suffering is a separate subject from substitutionary death and atonement. Only through all man's experiences can incarnate God become fully man. Note Adam, Enosh, and 'Iysh are all words for man. Adam through manual labor, Enosh through sickness, which the word implies and calling of Yahweh, and 'Iysh through being tempted. All three had to be experiuenced including Adam's death. Learning, such as in the motif of Proverbs, is also a common feature of man per se as well as enduring the temptations of the wayward woman, a common feature to Proverbs and the Gospels that stress the prostitutes that were transformed through knowing Jesus.

5.9 'Once made perfect' may refer to the resurrection or glorification for it is in heaven that the prediction about Jesus' being high priest in the order of Melchizedek is fulfilled at the heavenly sanctuary. It is the resurrected Jesus who is the source of eternal salvation.

'Perfect' comes through learning obedience, making him fully qualified for his role in God's plan. Job was such a person, since God considered him adequate to the testing based on righteousness, avoidance of evil, the fear of God and concern for family and society. But in Job and here 'mature' is not the right word and is an anachronism, since in Roman and Israelite society usually 20 or 30 is the age of adulthood as well as the bar mitzva age of 13. But Job was not mature, and this only came through suffering. This then qualified him to pray for and atone for his friends. The fact he was willing to plead for forgiveness for them shows his acceptance of them in spite of all they said about him. Jesus is the source and only source of salvation, but only to those who obey him. Matt 7.21-23 begins with 'everyone' who confess 'Lord Lord' and the 'Many' to bear witness to faithful preaching and exorcisms in Jesus name and miracles, but they are rejected as evil-doers because they did not do the will of 'my father, who is in heaven.' Fulfilling the will of God in the individual, the church, society, world, must start with the individual believer. 'Not my will but thine be done' is the model forever.

5.10 'Designated by God' is in lieu of an inherited position. It is similar to the call or commission. At each new phase of history some new beginnings were in order for which we have precedent. Joshua was raised up and David replaced Saul. Elijah brought Elisha into ministry. While illegal tampering with the system occurred in the John Hyrcanus period of the Maccabees, this was quickly recognized by the faithful. The precedent the author alludes to is not in the historical books but an incident reported in the Psalms.. Ps 110.4 The words do not occur in narrative or historical writing but the Psalm. The formula constitutes the act. Just as Saul's anointing did not require witnesses so God the Father and God the son both witnessed the event that is recorded here.

5.11-12 This rebuke 'slow to learn' hides the knowledge of impending persecution under Nero and other emperors. The teacher must teach to the ability to receive and comprehend of the students. The reason given is that the foundations of their faith and experience and doctrines were not firm. The expectations for these disciples is that they should have been teachers. The need for 'milk' means enzymes needed are not there and meat is not assimilated. Here the repeat of 'Elementary Truths of God's Word' course needs to be repeated. Locative of sphere 'babes in hearing'[210] ' 'hard to explain' is because a commonly used hermeneutic among rabbis is being used with new connect points and content, some of which run counter to established 'Truth' such as 'only Aaron's descendents can serve as priests.'

5.12 'First principles' stoicheia is 'letters of the alphabet.' not 'elementary powers' as in Gal 4.9; Col 2.8. These are the ABCs that one needs to move beyond. Isa 28.10,13 use letters of the alphabet in repetition to mimic the rote memorization exercise of a child in school Is. 28:10 For it is: Do and do, do and do, rule on rule, rule on rule; a little here, a little there" and Is. 28:13 So then, the word of the LORD to them will become: Do and do, do and do, rule on rule, rule on rule; a little here, a little there — so that they will go and fall backward, be injured and snared and captured. The alliteration adds to the pun or metaphor or even irony and incongruity that adults physically should need grade school rote training. Did they memorize by alliteration or the letters of the alphabet as in Psalms that are acrostic in nature? causes us to reflect on the 'sword of the Lord and of Gideon' and the sword of Goliath used to decapitate the warrior. But in the prophets Israel's enemies wield God's sword in disciplinary action against Israel. Perhaps the most visceral is the special sword of Ehud that could be concealed under his robe and used with the left hand--an act no one could prepare against. It was used for surgery.

Logoi in the NT Apocrypha designates the sayings of Jesus. Logia is not used. From the time of Herodotus on logion meant 'oracle' 'A Saying Derived From A Deity'. The Lxx Uses It For 'Word Of God', So It Is No Longer 'Oracle' But 'Revelation' Cf. Actas 7.38; Rom 3.2; 1 Pet 4.11; Heb 5.12. Fitzmyer,[211]366-7 Concession, kaiper, 'although' Dana-Mantey,94,213,227, 228, 293.peirazw belongs to the family peira, peirasmos, apeirastos. [212] Peira can mean in Classical Greek 'attempt, trial, experience' putting to the test. Zeno knows from experience whether or not the potter Pettukamis is capable. Ammonius asks his brother, 'Try to do this for me.' 'Proof' is found: "He found a man to supply the proof.'[213] "you have given me sufficient proof of your character' [Dysk.770] Moschion: "gave proof of a gifted mind' hence an athletic trial. It translates massah Dt 33.8 for an experience. Philo: "Every day we have experience of it.' [Worse Attacks Better,131]. These experimentations are sources of knowledge for Philo. Neither Philo nor Josephus use <u>peirasmos</u>. Josephus for peira gives 'proof', 'test' [Ant.20.28] 'trial' and attempt' as well as 'means, occasion, expedient'.<u>apeiros</u> ''without experience, inexpert'; <u>apeirastos</u> 'having no experience.' <u>Empeirikos</u> 'experienced' <u>empeiraomai</u> 'make trial of' Chantraine: 'an attempt to seduce a woman.' Spicq,3.80n1

5.13 'We must give account.' Here and ch.12 present God as the final judge of all men and believers as well. Considerable motivation is derived for holiness since we must all be judged. A similar picture is found in Job ch.1-2 where Satan is called in to make an account, to answer questions and to explain his report. Job also hoped to be able to give an account. But the firends considered this blasphemy.. The prayers in Ps 139 and elsewhere for God to 'search me' here are put in a surgical context, not exactly a trial context. It is the operation of the sword that allows visual inspection, with the hope that if God knows the true condition of the inner man then the man will come to know as well. The inscrutableness of the inner man is a prior assumption on psychoanalysis.

Genitive of reference 'heart evil with reference to unbelief' [214] Why would an infant continue on milk? Usually this means he is hungry all the time. Growth and development of brain function is slowed, he isn't challenged by baby language. Was lack of receptivity, of relational thinking, of Christian education the blame? Or did the leaders not give them responsibility as teachers, not knowing that by teaching what they knew they would become inquisitive about what was unclear? Was the method of teaching substantive ideas inadequate to stir the mind and create a hunger for the new food? Was the basic truth insufficient so that for the 'mature' class there was a whole realm of truth that was not, in fact, taught to novices? Did this atttitude represent a lack of faith in the new converts? Paul was able to leave new church plants after a few weeks because he had confidence in them and the Holy spirit even in the absence of ordained elders.

5.13-14 'The Word of righteousness' is a set of instructions using wisdom terminology and non-judicial in import. It must have involved test cases to give skills in distinguishing good from evil. Note that wisdom is the most universal of application and yet the conflict of cultural norms of Rome, Alexandria, Palestine, Syria, Greece and elsewhere might make for differences of opinion between church and community or even within the church, especially on ethical situations where there no longer is an immediate support of fellow believers. The Book is preparatory for facing martyrdom as are Revelations and 2 Peter. To do the right thing may be illegal in places but to be arrested for wrong doing besmirches the Gospel, so training was necessary. Early Church Fathers give many instructions in which rightness is the interface between Christian culture and pagan culture. How can one relate the elementary truths to training to distinguish good and evil? You cannot.! They must have real food. Adam and Eve knew the difference but in practice really did not act on the basis of that knowledge. The application of basic truth is not enough. There is a level of training and critical thinking needed and not blind acceptance of whatever is taught. Paul commended the Bereans for not believing every word, but rather they daily searched the scriptures to see if those things were so. Gifts of the Spirit enable those with these gifts to distinguish the spirits. The Devil as a lion is seeking to deceive the very elect.

5.14 Isa 7.15 The prophet refers to the 1. Pregnancy; 2.birth; 3. Naming; 4. Eating curds and honey; 5. Knowing to reject the wrong and choose the right. Before the last mentioned Ephraim and Aram will be destroyed. In Hebrews these are infancy up to step four. Solid food of doctrine requires discernment to distinguish good and evil, right and wrong in what is taught. The OT only has 'high priest' not great high priest. In fact, frequently the high priest is merely called priest. Here the author is seeking to distinguished Jesus from all others. In the historical books kings are rated but not priests, possibly because of their office and anointing. But what is maturity in a spiritual biblical sense? Present psychology has influenced the readings of scripture so what the scriptures intend in sometimes obscured. In context maturity has a path based on Jesus ;we have much to say about this' v.7-10. Essentially this:

1. Path has prayers and petitions with loud cries and tears;
2. reverent submission;
3. learning obedience in suffering;
4. understanding the exulted position of Jesus as high priest. But in addition
5. a gift to teach v.12,
6. a strong hold on elementary truth of God's word v.12;
7. knowing teaching about righteousness v.14;
8. personal training oneself to distinguish good from evil. It is these who must go on to maturity or perfection. They already have received five gifts from God 6.4-7.

Chapter Six:

Christ's Gifts and teaching are Greater: Greater hope and promises

God's Promise and Oath

6.1 The foundation in the NT is usually building on rock not sand in Matt 7.24f, Christ, the chief cornerstone, the apostles, the 'Rock' of the confession of Peter as Lord, or the knowledge of Christ of those who belong to him and that such depart from iniquity. But in the OT the foundation is not the pagan foundation ritual of putting a blessing or curse into it, as possibly occurred at Jericho, with Joshua's curse, but rather the foundations of Zion. Of the 39 references many are specifically the foundation of the literal temple in Jerusalem of Solomon or Haggai. The metaphorical uses are many, but apparently none refer to a system of doctrinal teaching as in Hebrews. God himself as Rock is usually not a foundation but a refuge, taken from fugitive experience and becoming a fugitive motif. In Revelations the Heavenly Jerusalem has many foundations and a differing set of 12 gates. So the idea of plurality or unity in plurality is not foreign to scripture. 2 Esdras 7.119 uses the phrase 'death-dealing works' nekra erga. In the translation death is taken to bean agent, a pesonification, while the descriptive use of the genitive simply describes the works as dead, much as Rom 7 describes the body as under the control of sin to be a corpse. Myers,[215]240

6.2 Bruce cites A Nairne that 1. 'repentance' is consistent with the creed of a Pharisee creed; 2. Ablutions is not Christian baptism, but ceremonial purifications; 3. elementary doctrines of Christ could be evangel not catechetical; 4. 'Enlightened' could be baptism Cf. . 10.32; Eph 5.14; and concludes 'this does not mean that our author 'will allow no forgiveness for Christian sinners.' Per Tertullian, but that repudiation of the faith leaves one like Isa 5.1ff; Lk 13.6-9; John 15.6.[216]

6.3 'God permitting' involves extended time for becoming mature in Christ. In the crazy world of Nero this may not permit much time to really go beyond the basic truths and experiences. The exhortation is not only for the recipients but also for the writer: 'let us'...'we will do'.

6.1-3 Give a list of initial acts done by men who turn to God or are assisted to do so which theology calls 'prevenient grace:

1. 'Laying the foundation of repentance from acts that lead to death' is an interpretive translation of the NIV. 'dead works' are those things unpleasing to God since a holy person must avoid all appearance, contact or connection with dead things, people or animals. Dead works also are works that contaminate, pollute, infect and produce nothing that lives and reproduces itself. Without God all the works of a life are dead and not pleasing to God unless wrought in God and for God's glory. They also lead to death.
2. 'Faith in God' is basic John 14.1 but is not directly the focus of the Hebrew Scriptures, where 'faithfulness' 'hope' and 'obedience' are more central. Heb 11,1ff is the focus of Hebrews and for even non-believing and believing Jews a two-fold definition is given and a two-fold object of faith specified. This gives a uniquely Christian basis, structure and system for theology that includes a whole world view that differs in most details from that of the world.
3. 'Instruction about baptisms' include kerygma and didache, and the plural is either believers' baptism and baptism for the dead, a reference to the Corinthians as a hapax in scripture, or to water and Spirit baptism, in keeping with Lk 3.16, which has a greater scriptural base than the other choice.
4. 'The laying on of hands' is to receive the gifts of the Spirit as is the case with Paul, Cornelius and others.
5. 'The resurrection of the dead' a central tenet of early Christianity.
6. 'And eternal judgment' according to Acts 17, the sermon at Athens, a central element of kerygma and in Acts 2 an intentional extension of a quote from Joel to include end-time events.
7. begins the chapter and may link both lists 'to go on to perfection.' 'maturity' derives from current educational and psychological theory and thus limits a key word of the book. 'Maturity' is suitable for 5.11-14. But 5.1ff does not link to educational theory but to a completeness that can hold a person steady when family members are having their eyes put out,

their skin peeled, and their bodies mauled by viciously trained and half-starved beasts. This is more than maturity or a natural process of growth and entails a spirituality that can endure.

6.4, In Esd 8.4 Ezra is expressing doubts and seeking intellectual solutions for his problems, and his vocabulary reflects wisdom such as in Prov 3.5; Ps 34.8; 1 Pet 2.3 He is probing the ways of the Lord. In Hebrews there is the opposite problem of having been enlightened and rebelling against the light. Myers,[217]242. The early church under persecution and martyrdom had many who would not deny their faith and were saved martyrdom, but rejected any route of salvation by the church. This verse may have had some part in this ostracism. If the church would not reach out to these it would be impossible for them to come back to restoration. If the early church took the view that the Kingdom had a military structure and mission then a deserter could only be executed, which the church did not do. What is the 'heavenly gift' as other than the Holy Spirit? If this is a list genre then it should be eternal life or the gift of speaking in tongues, of election to salvation or of the Savior Himself. The experiential aspect of salvation brings a higher level of accountability since it is all of grace as seen by the verbs: enlightened, tasted, shared. "It is impossible for them…to be brought back to repentance.' According to v.1 it is a fact that some are 'laying again the foundation of repentance.' Often in scripture the passive involves more than one agent, instrument, means, or people. Here first God brings people to repentance but usually through concerned people of the church and other communities. The impossibility is first psychological, cognitive, a question of shame, and secondly the appearance of repentance if not real brings even greater shame to the Lord, a fact the offender and those in the communities who are also the offended are deeply aware of. Just how do Christians forgive and accept a person who has fallen? For this reason often Jesus reiterated the necessity to forgive. Forgiveness opens the possibility of the forgiver being forgiven as well as the offender being forgiven. So this verse must be read in the light of the four Gospels.

6.4-5 The sequence of elements entering into becoming a believer and experiencing salvation are given here. Rom 5.1-5; 2 Pet 1.5-8 also 1 Cor 13 and Gal 5.22-26 can be adduced for the changes in the newly born child of God.

1. 'Enlightened' is the awakening of which the shining of a light on the soul follows Paul's own Damascus experience. After awakening, which

belongs to prevenient grace, or the grace that precedes salvation, there is the understanding at the time of receiving Christ as Savior.

2. 'Tasted the heavenly gift' is a spiritual experience of salvation as the free gift of God. This is not specified, but could include the cleansing of the conscience from dead works, which is mentioned elsewhere as the basic grace.
3. 'Shared in the Holy Spirit' is the receiving of the Spirit that is often connected with one's baptism as in the case of Samaritans. Ephesian disciples, Samaritan believers and Acts 2. and Paul's baptism. The fruits and gifts of the Spirit and presence of Christ in the heart of the believer. 13.5-6;
4. 'Tasted the goodness of the Word of God ' links to Ps 19 and 119 and those Psalms of witness to fulfillment of promises.
5. 'The powers of the coming age' points to the Millennium and the miracles of long life, health, healings, and special gifts of the Spirit. These are graces received and experienced. The powers of this age are free will, community, healing arts, wisdom from earth, prevenient grace, conscience etc. The coming age does have eternal life and peace on earth, the rule of Christ over all, and subjugation of Satan.

6.6 The impossibility is not salvation, but impossible to bring the fallen away back to repentance, a social, psychological, and theological problem. In Galatians Paul urges the church to restore the brother. But official and public denial of the faith and the atonement is tantamount to crucifying the Son of God all over again which subjects the Lord to public disgrace. Shame and disgrace are powerful motivations in most societies but survival and honor are more so. The goal of Rome was to discredit Christian faith as was local Jewish reaction to the message of Paul. A key phrase is 'because to their loss' indicates that Christ cannot be offered again and atonement is no longer valid for them. the first three centuries of the church took this seriously for 'turncoats'. They refused to restore such to the church until Tertullian in N Africa began to lay out a plan for restoring them. Evidently the real problem was the unwillingness of the church to forgive and to realize Christ died for all. The problem for a person to accept forgiveness from the church and God points to a theology that totally misunderstood the grace of the atonement. In those circumstances how hard it would be to commit perjury against Rome and accept pardon. This double bind left the survivor without a support group, a religion, a hope, and an avenue for salvation. The double mindedness can't conceive God would forgive, can't forgive himself, is shamed, and without the

Spirit of prayer, humility, seeking, willingness, and concentration on this one thing. He has lost a good support group and knows the old sacrifices won't work anymore. The first coming of the Messiah was for disgrace as part of his sin and abuse-bearing role. The second time is with glory, beginning with the resurrection. To subject Jesus to public disgrace is blasphemy and an utter desecration of his person. The absolute punishment is commiserate to the number and kinds of graces just listed that the individual has received, but most directly related to how they are treating the crucified Lord.

6.7 Ps 65.10 Psalms deals with preparing the field by leveling almost with terraces in mind and inundated like rice fields since the land is soften with showers. Hebrews tends toward the vegetation produced and the blessing experienced. Isa 55.12-3 is similar but stresses the kind of produce. Palestine is a land that depends totally on rain and dew, and that is given by God. So the presupposition is that the land is blessed by God not cursed and the heavens respond to the earth in the sense of Hosea 10.12; 6.3; 2.21-22. Not mentioned are plowing here or insects, because rain softens the soil and God protects from infestation and the result is a good harvest.

6.7-8 The believers can become either good land or bad land in which both receive the gift of rain but one produces a crop that is useful and that continues to receive blessing from God. That which produces thistles and thorns is worthless, in danger of being cursed. In the end it will be burned. The lesson is similar to John 15. The use of burning is a farming practice for tobacco and rice as it destroys infestation, weeds and provides fertilizer. But the intent here approaches more closely to the curse on Jericho and Babylon, to never again be used by man. In this analogy the antithesis and form follow wisdom protocols. The constant is the rain, good farmers with no mention of seed. Similar analogies of the vineyard and gardens appear in the prophetic books. Land is a receiver of grace and a producer, but it is accountable for what it creates. The parable of the Sower shows sowing on every possible kind of soil without discrimination, giving opportunity to all, but the thistles hadn't come up yet. In that parable plowing, fertilizing, weeding, alternating crops, and care to not use the seed on bad land must have brought smiles to Jesus' audience. But even with care the corn crops show a rise in the land doesn't have much water and the plants are much smaller. Only soil not used for some time or cared for will become such useless land.

6.8 Isa 5.6 God makes a wasteland as well as a fruitful land. If it is fruitless it may be cursed, abandoned and burned. Here the reason is God's control over the rain. Many kinds of farming do burn the land to restore its original state, kill the weeds and infestation. So the end of the field, as the world, is to restore the world through fire. Cursed land goes back directly to the land outside the Garden of Eden into which Adam and Eve were cast plus the curse on that land instead of on Adam and Eve.

6.9 'Things which accompany salvation' are expected confidently of these recipients that the author evidently knows in a trust relationship. This exhortation follows the typical New Covenant pattern of transforming legal expressions into personal ones. The effort toward self-control and witness to salvation is appealed to, even though the warnings are real and are increasing in severity. Still no broken covenant is mentioned or any security as being part of the historical Israel. The appeal is to the individual catechumen or believer to follow through in his faith. Rom 15.14 includes all Roman Christians without a single exception. 'We are persuaded that you are in a better situation, favorable for your salvation." Pepeismetha. This is thus one way to express confidence and faith in the believers. Spicq,3.77n66; The problem of faith compromised is found in 1 Cor 3.15; 5.5; Heb 2.3; 6.9; 1 Pet 4.18. Thus good works 1 Tim 4.16; knowing the truth 1 Tim 2.4; and Scriptures 2 Tim3.15, and prayer Rom 10.1; 11.14 help one not to fall. Spicq,350n30 . The of Hebrews is carefully to strongly warn and urge obedience of faith giving all the possible and indeed firm consequences should they leave the message and their faith aside. But he also affirms them and in these asides he shows his faith and confidence in them, a factor missing in almost all the OT prophetic books.

6.10 'God will not forget your work and the love shown him…' It is hard to conceive of Paul even hinting at this idea. But the work is apart from the old rabbinic system of merit and the work and love grow out of personal relationship to Christ. Nehemiah prayed using his works for God as the basis for asking God to remember and protect him. This was salvation through faithfulness not through a fixed merit system mathematically calculated. Aorist in contrast: 'for God is not unrighteous to forget your work and the love which you showed toward his name' you ministered to the saints and continue ministering. Dana-Mantey,195,230. Nehemiah also called on God to remember him and his work and faithfulness and the same basis of appeal appears in Job and Psalms. But these are not appeals to merit but to faith as faithfulness to God. God's not forgetting does not mean that the person will not be martyred, but that he will inherit his reward. 'God is not unjust' is a strange remark in this place. But for the wavering God will remember their work and love shown to God in helping God's people. Remembering means rewards, even though a present there is no evidence of God's remembering.

6.11 'Make your hope sure' The 'hope' is Christ is secure, but for each generation, each group of believers as in Rev ch.1-3, and each believer it is possible so to act as to have an insecure hope. 'same diligence to the very end' means death. The diligence is not said to be for helping others see Christian testimony or for purposes of proselytizing or evangelizing but for believers each individually. Thin joins with v.10 and the truth needed is that God is not unjust. Their work for God and love to God and help for God's people will be rewarded, and will also hold them steady. Epiqumein with infinitive in Luke indicates an unfulfilled desire. Lk 15.167; 16.21; 17.22; 22.15. Matt 13.17; 1 Pet 1.12. Rev 9.6; and Heb 6.11. Jeremias,[218]184[219] Repeatedly perseverance is urged 'to the end' so as to make their hope sure. Faith hangs on and in this way hope does also.

6.12 Here 'inherit what has been promised' must be martyrdom. Those who have died in the faith are the models to follow. 'Lazy' is from the perspective of Proverbs, where it is linked to 'sinners'. 'faith' and 'patience' or endurance are needed. 'Courage' is avoided because of Roman idolizing those dying in battle. has motifs of the Book of Proverbs and wisdom aphorisms. The fool is lazy noqroi, not something born as, but that which one anyone may become. The antithesis is also change, but for the good, but this positive change comes through imitation 1 Cor 11.1 and the inward work of the Spirit using God's Word. - Louw-Nida. The counterpart in our terms is a model and modeling. The conscious reproducing of character traits of faith and patience from those who are in a process of reaching out, running, hoping, 'hanging on,' Louw-Nida about makrothumia said 'a state of emotional calm in the face of provocation or misfortune and without complaint or irritation — 'patience.' 'but imitators of those who through faith and patience inherited the promises' He 6:12. 'fellow believers, take the prophets as an example of suffering and patience' or '... patience in the face of suffering' Jas 5:10. In a number of languages 'patience' is expressed idiomatically, for example, 'to remain seated in one's heart' or 'to keep one's heart from jumping' or 'to have a waiting heart.'" A near synonym is hupomone,: capacity to continue to bear up under difficult circumstances — 'endurance, being able to endure.' hupomone 'endurance inspired by hope in our Lord Jesus Christ' 1Th 1:3."Louw-Nida. Actually inheriting is not for certain elect persons, but for those who center on the promises of God, not men, and persevere in faith. Walvoord assumes all the exhortations are toward one group of people: "The warnings the writer gives against apostasy are found in four different expressions. He warns against letting New Testament truth slip away (Heb. 2:1-4), hardening the heart against the Holy Spirit (Heb. 3:7-19), falling away (Heb. 5:11--Heb. 6:12), committing the willful sin of treading under foot the Son of God, counting His blood as common blood, and doing insult to the Holy Spirit (Heb. 10:26-29). This is one sin, the act of an unsaved Jew in the first century renouncing his professed faith in Messiah as high priest, and returning to the abrogated sacrifices of the First Testament, doing this under the pressure of persecution from apostate Judaism (Heb. 10:26-34)."[220] Is imitation the best advice? Paul asked people to imitate him and not only once. With a clear modeling goal it might help one to avoid laziness in regard to self-improvement. But what of the foibles that abound in ministers' and rabbis' lives that are fully documented? Truly, wisdom would be needed to distinguish what was right and what wrong in the life of their leader while showing respect and honor at the same time. Rabbi stories show how this works out in mentor-disciple relations. The linking of faith and patience to inherit the promises doesn't seem to be salvation by faith alone. But 'we are saved by hope' is linked to faith as when the woman Jesus helped: 'Her love saved her.' If salvation is to restore the image and character of God, then faith results in praise, glory and honor through suffering grief 1 Pet 1.7. Heavenly wisdom works toward good fruit of peace and righteousness. James 3.17-18. God's gifts of divine power and promises are to enable the believer to participate in the divine nature, having escaped the corruption in the world through lust 2 Pet 1.3-4. To faith goodness, knowledge, self-control, perseverance, godliness, brotherly kindness, love must be qualities added to be effective and productive in the knowledge of Christ. 'If you do these things you will never fall, and you will receive a rich welcome into the eternal kingdom.' 2 Pet 1.5-11. Another way of saying this is the fruit of the Spirit which displace the works of the flesh and their desires. Paul's evangel to unbelievers was also different; 'to turn to God from idols to serve the living God.' The rich young ruler had to sell all and give to the poor and 'come and follow' Jesus. The common elements involve a whole-souled response to Jesus and allowing all that He has worked for us to be worked out in us. Any response to the still small voice, in readings, scriptures, attending a meeting, making things right, or like Cornelius sent for Peter, or the widows alms, are a first response and a real response. But the continued of faith and love and obedience and repentance affirm and move the believer to fill out the faith, hope and love that save the soul. Cornelius is an interesting case, for as Peter began to speak he reached the words 'that whosoever....' And immediately the Holy Spirit fell on them and they were immediately baptized. Salvation includes justification, sanctification, character transformation and so much more to prepare one for the heavenly kingdom in which he is already a citizen.

6.13 Faith is not gullibility or incredibleness but an evaluating of who is speaking and how. God promises over and over again and swears by himself. God adheres to the two or three witness rule in his dealings with the men he calls to be servants and takes time to convince them through testing, pain, fear, challenge. The oath refers to the Abrahamic covenant that is more important in this book than that of Moses. What is used in not Gen 12.1-3 but 22.16-17 'I swear by myself.' 'Surely I will bless you' is a summary of the promises of the entire covenant.NIBC. Gen 22.16,17 The background of the Akeda [binding] of Isaac is not related, only the oath the Angel of the Lord makes that God will multiply Isaac's descendants. The motivation for an oath is not related, and so the overwhelming significance and comfort of the oath is missed.

6.14 The crises of Adam, Noah and Abraham is that they are the beginning of a line or several lines and reproduction from this time becomes the obsession of the race long after there is no shortage of humans. The two needs for place and posterity are reiterated, but only for the future. But the timing of obtaining the entire eastern Mediterranean with all its political complexity would have to wait and due to sin and exile with diaspora further put off all but the multiplication of progeny and pagan preoccupation with reproduction in the pagan cults and image making. The problem of faithful loyalty to the promise is not to be countered through imitation, not only of the living but the dead who were faithful and patiently pressing on. Blessing is not earned but bestowed to faithful believers. , ei mhn 'assuredly/ above all blessing I will bless you' Dana-Mantey,261. The expressive mode with Hebrew duplication of the same verbal root is rather missed and the 'assuredly' could belong to the speaker giving assurance, or to the certainty that it will happen. The oath is expressive enough so the latter certainty should be the point of it all.

6.15 'Abraham received what was promised.' V.14 limits this to descendents and to the birth of Isaac. But the list of descendents of Ishmael gives the impression of fulfillment. Abraham waited patiently and then received what was promised. No mention of land not received or of land purchased as a burial site. But elsewhere in Heb 11 it declares that none of the men of faith received what was promised since all this is collectively experienced in the End. Abraham waited and received the promises but not what was promised. NIV adds 'what was promised.' If like Moses and Abraham and David these are alive in heaven then truly land and posterity were received, the portion of the vast multitude of witnesses. But this is going beyond what is stated. Gen 12.4; 21.5 Hebrews attributes persevering as the reason for inheriting the promise. The Genesis account simply relates life as usual until ch.18 when God told him next year at this time. This is more than process but rather crisis of believing God's specific words and doing what will make it happen. But Abraham on earth was not patient and only got a son. This Abraham in heaven was waiting and patiently and saw the multitude of descendents and the land in possession of Israel He inherited but not in this lifetime. He is one of that multitude of onlookers, witnesses, cheerleaders that 'surround us.' 6.12 again refers to these witnesses 'who receive' what has been promised but this includes those on earth and those in heaven. God is waiting and believers on earth and in heaven are waiting alike. The joy of one saint in seeing a promise fulfilled can be imagined.

6.15-20 Christ brings the blessings of 'uprightness' Isa 9.5-6; 32.1; Jer 23.5-6; Dn 9.24; Mal 3.20; Acts 3.14; 1 Cor 4.30; and of peace Isa 9.5; 32.17; Zech 9.9-10; Epg 2.14. "As king and priest forever he establishes the new order of hope, and in him the fruits of the traditional priestly blessing Num 6.23-26 take in a new nuance." Does this use of the OT and the OT texts themselves prove that the OT writers never saw the church age and hence linked the First Coming and Second Coming together? Or were two comings an afterthought, which can hardly be true in light of Jesus' sayings in the Gospels. Or in the kingdom within/among you a concept for the present church age, since Paul in Rome preached their the Kingdom or rule of God.

Note that justification by faith of the individual, or peace of mind regarding sins, is inadequate to account for the one atoning and blessing to bring on a righteous society. If this is applicable to the church to which the writers of Hebrews is speaking than there must be a genuine change to righteousness so that the scriptures can be fulfilled in terms of their own original meaning. Snell denies the book is written to Christians, only to Jews. To apply this all to the Millennium also makes it irrelevant for the original readership unless they believed the End of the word was at hand, which it wasn't. But in terms of hope and 'The City' process of being it serves a faith function. Another approach would be that the End Time is here and in the realized [not already realized] in that old structures are passing away but have not passed away. In the same sense the new structures are in place but are they fully operative in the here and now? Fitzmyer,[221]233

6.16 Ex 22.11The use of an oath among People regarding a suspected theft is used in Exodus to show how valid an oath is perceived by all parties so that it actually settles the issue. Hebrews understands this but focuses on God's oath taking, important in a world where the polytheistic and Greek Gods were capable of lying. The power of the oath in the ANE was not a formality but a binding contract on a par with a signed and witnessed document. The oath would establish fact. As to gods and men making promises the veracity of God in that milieu could only be established through an oath. Besides, the promise is one witness and the oath a second one, and in Israel the two or three witness rule maintained.

6.17 No doubt because of Paul and others Jews had doubts about the intent of the Christian movement and thought it was severing connections with Judaism. But 'the unchanging nature of his purpose is clear' answers that question. While Paul's writing might be needed to see the purpose of the Law here the purpose of God predates Moses. Why is an oath necessary? Because this is a self-inflicted curse on self if one does not honor his own word. Only God could contemplate a universe without God, since history begins with chaos, water, darkness, wind, all basic elements without life at all. Man cannot conceive of this. People of Nuzi in Iraq chose the river ordeal than an oath before God so awesome that would be. But God uses the oath, but only once or twice, not very often. Jesus forbad using oaths since the focus is not on protections against unfaithfulness but on the veracity of believers who imitate God who is true and faithful. How can God affirm something of verbal content in such a way that man must believe? In the ANE 1.documents were written; 2. witnesses names with their fathers were added; 3. This was done on a certain date with all present; 4. copies were made; 5. the cuneiform tablet or papyrus was sealed' 6. A copy was stored in the temple or administrative archive; 7. An oath was taken according to certain formula before God in the temple; 8. Curses were added should the document be changed or not fulfilled. 9. Messengers knew the content of the document to repeat by heart; 10.The concluding of the document was done publicly. Hebrews, in a much later period stresses the promise and oath and a written covenant with writer and readers as witnesses.

6.18 The two evidences are God's word the promise and the addition of the vow. In Titus 1.2 'God who cannot lie' does not present an illustration. It is this which gives the believer hope or expectation. There is a link between covenants sealed by the promise and oath[222]. " swzw has to do with the salvation of the soul Mk 8.35; 1 Pet 1.9, which is already actual [semeron Lk 19.8; kaq hmeron Acts 2.47; hemera swthrias 2 Cor 6.2; eswthemen Rom 8.24; Eph 2.5,8; eswsen Tit 3.5] and continues to become effective [swsomenoi 1 Cor 1.18; 2 Cor 2.15], but will not be complete and definitive until entrance into heaven: eternal life [1 Tim 12.16; 6.12], which is still an object of hope [Rom 8.24; Titus 3.7; Heb 6.18; 1 Pet 1.3]. Two major conditions are required: faith and perseverance, because the undertaking is difficult in the midst of tribulations [Mk 13.20] and its success can be compromised: so much so that one may wonder whether in the end 'there will be few saved.' Cf. Lk 18.27.Spicq:3.43n10; 112n7; 350. 'Impossible for God to lie' appears also in Titus 1.2. Is this a universal truth or a NT truth? There was Micaiah, but when God permitted lying spirits to move false prophets it was for God's purpose, to destroy the king. But then Micaiah told the whole story that God is doing this so God's purposes will be accomplished. But Jesus is the Truth and Pilate who asked 'What is Truth' did not realize this. Because 'promise' and 'oath' are separate legal genre they count as two witnesses. The promise is by the first agent; the oath is essentially by the second person, not necessarily the second person of the Godhead. Those written are for Abraham's sake and for our sake also, but what of the generations in-between? Bruce uses 11.8-19 to say both to Abraham and to use the promise of heavenly bliss was given, namely 'the same heavenly blessings to which Christians look forward. Genesis only says Abraham was promised Canaan and a posterity of millions. Is this the equivalence of a city and country? Or did the promise to Abraham on earth extend to Abraham's eternal life in heaven so that 'he saw Christ's glory and rejoiced.' The continuing hope would continue to have modified content as thousands of years passed and thus would include all who are children of God by faith in Christ. Abraham's faith in God in heaven became faith in Christ and in all the subsequent promises made to God's people of every ethnic background. Jesus is 'yesterday, today and forever the same' and he 'never' leaves or forsakes his own.

6.19 The metaphor of sliding away is used in the context with an anchor. Without functionality the anchor would allow the ship to crash into the rocks. But the Christian hope has an anchor and he is secure. 'we have fled –the refugee role—to take hold of the hope—spiritual initiative. This hope, then, is integral to worship, since bridges the present and the future, the existential only in this way can be turned into power for facing the future. Just as faith is the infrastructure and proof of things unseen and is a gift of God (Eph 2.8) so hope is the anchor of the soul is a gift of God through 'character'(Rom 5.5) process and the outpouring of the Spirit of love in the heart. We are saved by hope, faith and love, the latter as in the woman Christ forgave 'for she loved much.' John Wesley distinguished the verb 'believe' pisteuw from the noun pistis 'faith' since the former is our response to God and the second is the gift of grace. It is conceivable that one who only believed cognitively, or emotionally or under pressure, or without commitment might assent to Christian truth but without receiving the gift of faith. So hope is an anchor and a proper translation may approach 'expectation,' 'anticipation,' 'visualization,' and 'confidence' as in the corresponding Hebrew qawwah. 'Behind the curtain' into the inner sanctuary of the tabernacle. Does heaven have a curtain? Actually the point is that hope is the enabling of prayer by whch we go to Jesus where he is in the holiest of all. It is this immediate presence before Him that makes this subjective anchor and objective and effective instrument for spiritual stability and avoid dragging the ship into the rocks.

6.20 Jesus has gone before us. This links to 12.1 and the Memorial of the Faithful and to those that speak of Jesus going to heaven and inside the curtain. Martyrs are not mentioned in the same breath!!. The focus is not on the dead but the living Lord. 'He entered on our behalf.' His help is as high priest, although the connection isn't clear. Perhaps the last sentence simply is for coherence to where it was previously mentioned and a closure to the section. Since here the tabernacle is only symbolical of God's eternal presence in heaven and not predictive of events to be fulfilled in subsequent human history. It is here the Seventh Day Adventists consider it predictive, not only symbolical. Payne,[223]575n;8.1-2; 9.11,24,

Chapter Seven:

Christ is Greater than Levi and the Law:

God's priest, tithe, Availability and Perfection

7.1 Melchizedek is introduced and is used in a midrash on Gen 14.18-20. "Introducing his implicit quotation of Genesis by houtos gar Melchisedek, the author of Heb first gives a brief resume in vv.1-2 and afterwards takes up various elements of it for comment. Thus in this section of Heb are verified the five characteristics of midrash, poi nted out by R.Bloch, viz,., its

1. Point of departure in an OT passage [Gen 14.18-20 is implicitly quoted],
2. Its homiletic character [here for apologetic purposes],
3. Its attentive analysis of the text [the interpretation of the names and explanation of the blessing and tithes],
4. Its adaptation of the OT text to a present situation[the priesthood of Christ],
5. And its haggadic character [an elaborative expose in which the interest is centered on the biblical account rather than on the historical figure as such.]" It resembles the classic midrash in Genesis Rabbah 43.6. [224]Fitzmyer,[225]221-2, n, 253-4,n, 267. Gen 14.18-20 The 'met' of Hebrews doesn't show the food that Melchisedek brought out with wine and the blessing pronounced in this context. Clearly Abram was giving the tenth as a response to the food, wine and blessing, paying the minister, as it were. Hebrews relates a discovery, that in Salem there was a worshipper of the true God and as Abram gave the tithe it was to God who will bless him. Melchisedek is not treated as a pagan or one worshipping improperly. He is both king of Salem 'Peace' and probably Jerusalem, and priest of' God Most High.' Melchizedek is introduced and is used in a midrash on Gen 14.18-20. "Introducing his implicit quotation of Genesis by houtos gar ho Melchisedek, the author of Heb first gives a brief resume in vv.1-2 and afterwards takes up various elements of it for comment. Thus in this section of Heb are verified the five characteristics

of midrash, pointed out by R.Bloch, viz,., its 1. Point de depart in an OT passage [Gen 14.18-20 is implicitly quoted], 2. Its homiletic character [here for apologetic purposes], 3. Oits attentive analysis of the text [the interpretation of the names and explanation of the blessing and tithes], 4. Its adaptation of the OT text to a present situation[the priesthood of Christ], 5. And its haggadic character [an elaborative expose in which the interest is centered on the biblical account rather than on the historical figure as such.]" It resembles the classic midrash in Genesis Rabbah 43.6.[226] Fitzmyer,[227] Melchizedek: {mel-kiz'-uh-dek}Although mentioned only twice in the Old Testament, Melchizedek is a prominent name in the New Testament Epistle to the Hebrews. In Genesis 14, Melchizedek is apparently a Canaanite priest who blesses Abraham. In Psalm 110 he is the head of a messianic order of priests. In Hebrews 5-7 he typifies the priesthood of the Messiah and is identified with Jesus Christ. Melchizedek's priestly preeminence is applied to Christ, who is thus the heavenly high priest, "of the order of Melchizedek for ever." Grolier Encyclopedia..

II Esdras has 'Most High' 68 times, [Lord, Lord ten times;] It does not appear in chs 102, 15-16 but does in Mk 5.7; Lk 8.28; Acts 16.17; Heb 7.1 from Gen 14.18-20 El Elyon. 1 QH 4.31; 6.33. Myers,[228]121 "→ Elyon ('lywn), 'Most High', mentioned in the Hebrew Bible. Elyon is a well documented divine name or epithet in biblical traditions and poetic passages like 2 Sam 22:14 (= Ps 18:14) and Ps 21:8 unequivocally associate Elyon with the divine name YHWH (→Yahweh). Nevertheless, modern scholarship has identified Elyon as originally the name of an ancient Canaanite deity or as a divine epithet, that only with the passage of time made its way into early Yahwistic religious traditions. In support of this reconstruction, interpreters have cited the Ugaritic texts, the Hebrew onomastica, Philo of Byblos' treatment of the history of Kronos where Elyon is apparently mentioned, as well as the biblical form *'ly*.[229] Melchizedek: {mel-kiz'-uh-dek}Although mentioned only twice in the Old Testament, Melchizedek is a prominent name in the New Testament Epistle to the Hebrews. In Genesis 14, Melchizedek is apparently a Canaanite or Jebusite priest who blesses Abraham. In Psalm 110 he is the head of a messianic order of priests. In Hebrews 5-7 he typifies the priesthood of the Messiah and is identified with Jesus Christ. Melchizedek's priestly preeminence is applied to Christ, who is thus the heavenly high priest, "of the order of Melchizedek for ever."[230] Demonstrative pronoun outos gar 'for this Melchizedek' the immediate demonstrative. Dana-Mantey,127. This shows the remarkable element in the passage is the priest-king himself who is the figure of the priest-king Messiah. The name Melchi-zedek is apparently West Semitic 'My King is just' or 'My king is Zadok'.[231] This could give support that Zadok the priest derived from this source before the time priests had to be of Aaron. But this line of argumentation is not followed. This would legitimize a priest, especially one from Jerusalem. Amarna read URU Salim 'City of Salim.' But not uniformly so. Normally in Amarna the Uru sign would be read alu. The blessing is first given with food and then Abraham requites this with the tithe.as professionals in the ANE were priests above ethnicity, which changed later on. This priest is king and priest, and therefore is uniquely the forerunner of the Christ. There is discussion whether there was a deity Zadok or not in this time and region. Baker's Commentary notes "Largely on the basis of this uncertainty, some scholars have suggested that Zadok's origins were completely outside the family of Aaron, and that the genealogy was a fabrication designed to support his eventual position as high priest. Zadok also has been viewed as a young military hero (1 Chr 12:28), whose elevation to the priesthood was a reward for his outstanding services in David's cause. An obvious objection to this, and to the following views, is that David throughout appears concerned not to alienate the religious traditions of the tribal confederation. Such an appointment would surely have offended his own established priesthood. Another suggestion is that David appointed Zadok as priest in charge of a second major sanctuary at Gibeon (16:39–42), which is later called "the most famous of the hilltop altars" during Solomon's reign (1 Kgs 3:4). Zadok is thought to have been a Gibeonite priest whom David elevated to the high priesthood at Jerusalem in the furtherance of his centralization policy, the prominence given to the sanctuary at Gibeon being in the interests of national unity.Equally conjectural is the view that Zadok was the leading priest of the Jebusite Jerusalem captured by David. Indeed, it has even been suggested that Zadok revealed to David the city's vulnerability if attacked via its water tunnel (2 Sm 5:8). The connection of the name Zadok with Melchizedek and Adonizedek, another king of Jerusalem (Jos 10:1), has led to the view that this was the traditional name of the chief priest or priest-king of the Jebusite city. David may have allowed Zadok to continue in office to facilitate Jerusalem's integration into his kingdom. There are many grave objections to this view. David's animosity to the Jebusites following their taunts is apparent (2 Sm 5:6–8). The adoption of the Jebusite cult and the elevation of its priest above the native Israelite priesthood would be a tactless action in a period when David displayed remarkable diplomacy in uniting the two sections of his kingdom. In fact when the ark was brought to Jerusalem, it was not placed in the Jebusite temple, but in a tent shrine (6:17). Similarly, in David's elaborate plans for the building of the temple, there is no hint that the existing Jebusite temple cult had any part. When the temple was built, it was completely outside the walls of ancient Jerusalem, but within Solomon's extension of the city."[232] While the writer doesn't stress this, Melchisedek is the only analogy where the king is also the priest. The significance is that usually the king is the judge and punisher while the priest is reconciler. In this case there is no one to condemn the elect.

7.2 'Tenth' here the tithe is not from produce, but plunder. This expands the tithe of the law and is an example of taking the tithe before dedication, gross not net, from all income, even that later refused and given back to colleagues and the rest returned to Sodom. v.4 defines all of this as plunder. More logical would be to take it as a thanksgiving offering.. 'Tenth' here the tithe is not from produce but plunder. This expands the tithe of the law and is an example of taking the tithe before dedication, gross not net, from all income, even that later refused and given back to colleagues and the rest returned to Sodom. v.4 defines all of this as plunder. More logical would be to take it as a thanksgiving offering. Gen 14 is read as 'king of righteousness' but this does not enter the argument of the book. From Northwest Semitics the following possibilities emerge: 1. Malki-tsedeq could mean '[the god] tsedeq is my king' or 2. 'My king is upright' Philo Byblius gives the Phoenician divinity as Sydyk which Damascius writes as Sadykos. It can also mean 'righteous'. Note the Jerusalem king's name at the time of Joshua was 'adoni-tsedeq 'tsedeq is my Lord' or 'My lord is upright' Jos 10.1,3. The Amorite king in the 16th century, a king of Babylon, was named Ammi-tsaquqa. Josephus and Philo both record popular etymology of the day as basileus dikaios. Targums read basileus dikaisynes. 'King of uprightness'. Genesis Apocryphon writes it as one name not two. Neofiti I and Pseudo-Jonathan write mi_kætsdyk' Fitzmyer does not mention the possibility of 'My king is Zadok' to raise up the new priesthood from David's time onward. Fitzmyer,[233]229-31,231-3, 239,n,265. In Gen 14.20 'he paid him a tithe of everything' is unclear as t who paid whom. Jerome saw both interpretations were possible. MT and LXX express no subject. The subject of the preceding verb is Melchizedek. But in 18-20 are an insertion, then Melchizedek as vassal paid tithes to his ally

Abraham. Hebrews inserts Abraam. Genesis Apocryphon 22.17 reads" And he gave him a tithe of all the goods of the king of Elam and his companions--which can only refer to Abram. Josephus read 'Abram then offered him the tithe of the spoil, and he accepted the gift.' From current interpretation the writer stresses that Christ as high priest is greater than Levi, since Levi was the collector of tithes in Dt 10.8-9; 12.2 and Heb 7.10. The patriarch paid tithe not to a kinsman but to an outsider.[234].....a certain drop which He joined with the flame, and from the two He created the world. The flame ascended and encircled itself with the Left, and the drop ascended and encircled itself with the Right. They then crossed and changed places, going up and down alternately until they were closely interlocked, and there issued from between them a full wind. Then those two sides were made one, and the wind was set between them and they were entwined with one another, and so there was harmony above and harmony below; the grade was firmly established, the letter he was crowned with vau and vau with he, and so he ascended and was joined in a perfect bond. This is alluded to in the words "Melchizedek (lit. king of righteousness) king of Salem" (lit. completeness), i.e. the king who rules with complete sovereignty. When is he completely king? On the Day of Atonement, when all faces are illumined. According to another explanation, "Melchizedek" alludes to the lower world, and "king of Salem" to the upper world; and the verse indicates that both are intertwined inseparably, two worlds like one, so that the lower world also is the whole, and the whole is one. "Brought forth bread and wine": signifying that both of these are in it. And He Was Priest Of God Most High: i.e. one world ministers to the other. "Priest" refers to the Right, and "Most High God,' to the upper world; and hence a priest is required to bless the world. For this lower world receives blessings when it is associated with a High Priest; hence there is a special force in the words "and he blessed him and said, Blessed is Abram to the Most High God". After this model it behoves the priest on earth to intertwine his fingers when blessing in the synagogue in order that he may be linked with the Right and that the two worlds may be linked together. "Blessed Is Abram". The words of the text are a prototype of the formula of blessing (used by the Israelites). "Blessed is Abram" (in the sense we have given to it) corresponds to "blessed art Thou ". "To the Most High God" corresponds to "O Lord our God". "Possessor of heaven and earth" corresponds to "king of the universe. Further, and he blessed him indicates the course of blessing from below to above; blessed is the Most High God indicates from above to below. and he gave him a tenth of all: so that he should cleave to the place where the link was formed with the lower world. As they were going along they came across

R. Yesa and a certain Judean with him who was explaining the text "To David: Unto thee, O Lord, do I lift up my soul" (Ps. XXV, 1). He said: 'Why is the inscription of this psalm simply "to David" and not "A Psalm of David"? It is because the real meaning is "for the sake of David", i.e. of his grade. "Unto thee, O Lord", i.e. upward-striving; "my soul", i.e. David himself, his original grade; "I lift up": to wit, I cause to ascend, since David was ever striving to rise to a higher grade and to link himself to it firmly. Similarly it was for the sake of his grade that David uttered the words "To David: Bless the Lord, O my soul" (where the word eth indicates his desire to be linked above) "and all that is within me bless his holy name" (Ps. CIII, 1), referring to the "beasts of the field" which are called "inwards".' Said R. Eleazar to R. Yesa, 'I see that you have come in company with the Shekinah.' He said, "Assuredly it is so. I have been walking with him three parasangs, and he has told me ever so many excellent things. I hired him as a porter, not knowing that he was the shining light which I have discovered him to be.' R. Eleazar then said to the man, 'What is your name?' He said: 'Joezer'. Whereupon he said: 'Let Joezer and Eleazar sit together.' So they sat down on a rock[235] Sedeq is here not Sadduccee, since they had ceased after 70 AD, or the divone name Sedeq, but the ruler who is in charge of what is right. In Paul it might have to do with 1 Cor 1 or justification by faith. Here 'right' and 'peace' are joined. Gen 14 is read as 'king of righteousness' but this does not enter the argument of the book. From Northwest Semitics the following possibilities emerge: 1. Malki-tsedeq could mean '[the god] Tsedeq is my king' or 2. 'My king is upright' Philo Byblius gives the Phoenician divinity as Sydyk which Damascius wrires as Sadykos. It can also mean 'righteous'. Note the Jerusalem king's name at the time of Joshua was 'adoni-tsedeq 'Tsedeq is my Lord' or 'My lord is upright' Jos 10.1,3. The Amorite king in the 16th century, a king of Babylon, was named Ammi-tsaquqa. Josephus and Philo both record popular etymology of the day as basileus dikaios. Targums read basileus dikaisunes. 'King of uprightness'. Genesis Apocryphon writes it as one name not two. Neofiti I and Pseudo-Jonathan write mlkætsdyq. Fitzmyuer does not mention the possibility of 'My king is Zadok' to raise up the new priesthood from David's time onward. Fitzmyer,[236]229-31,231-3, 239,n,265. In Gen 14.20 'he paid him a tithe of everything' is unclear as t who paid whom. Jerome saw both interpretations were possible. MT and LXX express no subject. The subject of the preceding verb is Melchizedek. But in 18-20 are an insertion, then Melchizedek as vassal paid tithes to his ally Abraham. Hebrews inserts Abraam. Genesis Apocryphon 22.17 reads" And he gave him a tithe of all the goods of the king of Elam and his companions--which can only refer to

Abram. Josephus read 'Abram then offered him the tithe of the spoil, and he accepted the gift.' From current interpretation the writer stresses that Christ as high priest is greater than Levi, since Levi was the collector of tithes in Dt 10.8-9; 12.2 and Heb 7.10. The patriarch paid tithe not to a kinsman but to an outsider. Fitzmyer,239. Melchizedek:[237] .....a certain drop which He joined with the flame, and from the two He created the world. The flame ascended and encircled itself with the Left, and the drop ascended and encircled itself with the Right. They then crossed and changed places, going up and down alternately until they were closely interlocked, and there issued from between them a full wind. Then those two sides were made one, and the wind was set between them and they were entwined with one another, and so there was harmony above and harmony below; the grade was firmly established, the letter he was crowned with vau and vau with he, and so he ascended and was joined in a perfect bond. This is alluded to in the words "Melchizedek (lit. king of righteousness) king of Salem" (lit. completeness), i.e. the king who rules with complete sovereignty. When is he completely king? On the Day of Atonement, when all faces are illumined. According to another explanation, "Melchizedek" alludes to the lower world, and "king of Salem" to the upper world; and the verse indicates that both are intertwined inseparably, two worlds like one, so that the lower world also is the whole, and the whole is one. "Brought forth bread and wine": signifying that both of these are in it.

And he was priest of God Most High: i.e. one world ministers to the other. "Priest" refers to the Right, and "Most High God,' to the upper world; and hence a priest is required to bless the world. For this lower world receives blessings when it is associated with a High Priest; hence there is a special force in the words "and he blessed him and said, Blessed is Abram to the Most High God". After this model it behoves the priest on earth to intertwine his fingers when blessing in the synagogue in order that he may be linked with the Right and that the two worlds may be linked together. Blessed is Abram. The words of the text are a prototype of the formula of blessing (used by the Israclites). "Blessed is Abram" (in the sense we have given to it) corresponds to "blessed art Thou ". "To the Most High God" corresponds to "O Lord our God". "Possessor of heaven and earth" corresponds to "king of the universe. Further, and he blessed him indicates the course of blessing from below to above; blessed is the most high god indicates from above to below. And he gave him a tenth of all: so that he should cleave to the place where the link was formed with the lower world. As they were going along they came across R. Yesa and a certain Judean with him who was explaining the text "To David:

Unto thee, O Lord, do I lift up my soul" (Ps. 25. 1). He said: 'Why is the inscription of this psalm simply "to David" and not "A Psalm of David"? It is because the real meaning is "for the sake of David", i.e. of his grade. "Unto thee, O Lord", i.e. upward-striving; "my soul", i.e. David himself, his original grade; "I lift up": to wit, I cause to ascend, since David was ever striving to rise to a higher grade and to link himself to it firmly. Similarly it was for the sake of his grade that David uttered the words "To David: Bless the Lord, O my soul" (where the word eth indicates his desire to be linked above) "and all that is within me bless his holy name" (Ps. 103, 1), referring to the "beasts of the field" which are called "inwards".' Said R. Eleazar to R. Yesa, 'I see that you have come in company with the Shekinah.' He said, "Assuredly it is so. I have been walking with him three parasangs, and he has told me ever so many excellent things. I hired him as a porter, not knowing that he was the shining light which I have discovered him to be.' R. Eleazar then said to the man, 'What is your name?' He said: 'Joezer'. Whereupon he said: 'Let Joezer and Eleazar sit together.' So they sat down on a rock... Soncino Zohar, Bereshith, Section 1, Page 87a.   Sedeq is here not Sadduccee, since they had ceased after 70 AD, or the divine name Tsedeq, but the ruler who is in charge of what is right. In Paul it might have to do with 1 Cor 1 or justification by faith. Here 'right' and 'peace' are joined. The writer of Hebrews does not draw the connection between this tithe as a thanksgiving tribute in its original setting since the Levites collected tithe as their support from God, a tax on the households so that a system of education and ministry could be grounded in local autonomy.

Was Salem Jerusalem?. "Commonly regarded as the site of Jerusalem. It has also been supposed to represent Salei>m *Salim,* mentioned in >John 3:23. Jerome says that the place retained that name in his day, and that the ruins of Melchizedek's palace were shown there. The ancient name of Jerusalem was Jebus. Others, again, suppose that Salem is not the name of a place, but is merely the appellation of Melchizedek. The passage in Genesis, however, points to a place, and the writer might naturally have desired to indicate the typical meaning of the city over which Melchizedek reigned." If not Jerusalem, where URU-salim could represent Amarna reading, there would be no connection with David's city, throne, kingship and those promises. But this isn't the author's point. He wants to show difference not compatible points. ABD notes ". A town near Aenon where John the Baptist preached repentance during the latter half of his ministry and baptized converts since there was a copious supply of water (John 3:23). Salim appears to have been located W of the Jordan River (John 3:26; 1:28; 10:40). The identification of this site is further assisted by its association with Aenon, which means "place of springs." The number of major spring sites along the W side of the Rift Valley is limited. Three of these locations have been identified as the Aenon near Salim. Eusebius *(Onomast.)* and Jerome *(De situ et nom. loc. heb. 165)* in the 4th century locate the site 8 Roman miles S of Scythopolis (Beth-shan, M.R. 197212) near the Jordan River. The Medeba Map affirms this tradition by locating springs in that region. Modern advocates of this position point to Tell Sheikh Salim as retaining the ancient name and also to Umm el-Umdan (M.R. 199199). W. F. Albright (1924:193) and others have argued for a site which retains the name "Salim," located 4 km away from springs named Ainun in the Wadi Farah. This site in ancient Samaria is rejected by some scholars as it is argued that John the Baptist would have avoided the area. A proposed S site of Salim in Judea is located 10 km NE of Jerusalem in the Wadi Salem near an important waters" [238]

7.3 Analogies are only partially so. Jesus had a genealogy, beginning and end and a legal earthly father, but Jesus died and lives again. Melchizedek is a break-in into history, and Jesus is to but more naturally. His greatness is that he represented the true God and came to bless Abraham and so Abraham was obligated to offer a gift. It was the plunder. The tithe doesn't quite fit except that it was the tenth and offered to a priest as it later was offered for support of Levites and priests. But Rabbinic law exclusively deals with tithe of produce of fields and trees or nuts, not from business or other profit such as plunder. In Gen 14 narrative context Abraham seems piqued at Melchizedek's taking advantage of the situation, and then at the Sodom king's suggestion and implies he will make no profit at war and will never again go in league with the Amorites. Later he does associate with Hittites but will pay his own way, owing them nothing. So the motive of Abraham notwithstanding, probably is hard to ascertain since this is the only religious part to the war, and a detailed confession of Abraham's faith. Perhaps it was merely a thank you to Melchizedek and god. But even so Melchisedek had no genealogy records and probably escaped the stigma of being a native of the land. 'Just like the son her remains a priest forever' may possibly not be a hypothetical case for the sake of argument, but a fact, that Melchizedek was in fact a converted and saved priest. But nothing in other scriptures would indicate he functions as a high priest in heaven.

7.4 'How great [was] this one.' There is no verb or copulative so it is tenseless. In keeping with wisdom literature there is a strong emphasis on greatness of God,. The Son, and the faithful, including Moses and the martyrs. In the case of God His greatness is that of creator and sustainer of all there is, and his designating his son and angels to minister in His name. The greatness of Abraham was faith and Moses faithfulness and martyrs faithful obedience to death as witness to the truth. Church leaders have honor. Aaron did not assume to be priest but was appointed and continued in this calling. But Melchizedek is only second to the Son, and perhaps Elijah and Elisha. Bruce notes that in receiving the blessing and in giving the tithes Abraham was acknowledging Melchisedek as superior.[239]

7.5 Num 18.21-26 Hebrews makes collecting a tithe from the People an administrative matter while Numbers makes the tithe a gift from God for the special situation of the Levites whose inheritance is God Himself. The law--from brothers, descendants from Abraham. ;though' -the law contradicts the Abraham pattern. Christianity returns to the original promise pattern.

7.6 'blessed him' How does blessing add to the promises? Gen 15 and 17 follow from 14, in which the blessing is realized in terms of the sign of the covenant and the covenant itself, with promises and prophecies., cause and effect. He evidently had to find righteousness and peace before he could have the blessing and covenant. This had to come through a human being first. The blessing is validated by being from priest and king and through his character. Cf. . Matt 5 for the eight blessings awarded to people of a certain character. The writer uses extensively the Gen 14 tradition about Melchizedek. He identifies El 'Elyon with Yahweh, and adopts Melchizedek into Israelite tradition along with Genesis 14.18. He is Canaanite. El is the name of the henotheistic deity in the second millennium BC. In Sefire ! A 11 El and 'Elyan appear as a pair of Canaanite gods in this Aramaic inscription in the 8th century. Eventually this deity revealed himself by the name Yhwh, to the patriarchs of the chosen people, although the earliest explicit reference is that revelation to Moses in Gen 3 abd 6 unless in the offering of Isaac God revealed himself as YHWH. Note that in Gen 14.22[240] Abraham contradicts Melchizedek's[241] Most High God by using YHWH, but identifying him as The most High God. Abraham's prayer in Gen 15 also testifies in another situation, in another narrative and in a speech act Abraham's knowledge of YHWH. In fact 'YHWH' appears throughout the narrative except in 22.1-2,v.8,12, but it is 'The angel of the Lord YHWH that saves Isaac, and then Abraham confesses YHWH as 'On the mountain of YHWH it will be provided.' Note the angel of YHWH appears twice, and God's Words ne'um

Yhwh are part of the divine words, where YHWH identifies himself to Abraham. Usually source analysis is used to separate the use of the divine names. But besides an insider versus outsider perspective, where 'God' is used with non-covenant peoples, and YHWH is used for those in the covenant, another principle appears to be involved, and that is the spiritual growth of Abraham involving in part a knowledge of YHWH by name. This is further stressed in Gen 14 by the number of times that El 'Elyon is used in two verses. Since Melchizedek had not formal relations with Abraham it would be appropriate for Abraham to use the same divine name, which he does not. He intentionally, not the author's intention, uses YHWH to clarify that he is not worshipping a pagan God. Fitzmyer suggests:" It has been proposed that the hero of these verses (or of the whole saga) was Melchizedek, and that it was a hieros logos of the Jerusalem sanctuary with the aetiological purpose of showing Abram paying tithes to the Jerusalem priest-king.[242] It is rather more likely that the saga told of the cooperation of Melchizedek, an allied king, who went forth to refresh Abram and his troops, to bless him and give him 'a tithe of everything' i.e. pay him tribute. Such a hypothesis accounts at least for the choppy character of the three verses and their relation to the whole. With the insertion of the Melchizedek verses in Gen 14 and the identification of El 'Elyon as Yahweh, Melchzedeq was adopted into Israelite tradition. By the time of the establishment of the Maccabean royal priesthood Melchizedek's designation becomes the official title of the Hasmonean dynasty.[243] Josephus, who calls Melchizedek Canaanite dynasty 'a lord of the Canaanites', mentions that he was the first to officiate as the priest of God,[244] and according to Philo God made him both 'king of peace, for that is the meaning of 'Salem', and his own priest hierea heautou.[245] This Jewish adoption of Melchizedek underlies the treatment of him in Hebrews, for the author knows that Melchizedek does hot have a common ancestry with Abram 7.6 . Note in Genesis nothing is said that he will live forever, rather is part of the promise to the Israelite king that he will be priest forever Ps 110. Thus Melchizedek did was not in a hereditary line and did not transmit it to others. The implication is that Melchizedek and the Son both have heavenly descent or antecedents. In the account the OT could be read that Melchizedek paid tribute to Abram as part of the victory celebration. If Abraham paid tribute the reasoning is unclear unless Melchizedek and Jerusalem were the sacred site of the allied troops and if so then Melchizedek should have been Amorite not Canaanite as Josephus called him. Fitzmyer,[246]235. The writer uses extensively the Gen 14 tradition about Melchizedek. He identifies El ;Elyon with Yahweh, and adopts Melchizedek into Israelite tradition along with

Genesis 14.18. He is Canaanite. El is the name of the henotheistic deity in the second millenium BC. In Sefire ! A 11 El and ;Elyan appear as a pair of Canaanite gods in this Aramaic inscription in the 8th century. Eventually this deity revealed himself by the name YHWH, to the patriarchs of the chosen people, although the earliest explicit reference is that revelation to Moses in Gen 3 abd 6 unless in the offering of Isaac God revealed himself as YHWH. Note that in Gen 14.22[247] Abraham contradicts Melchizedek's[248] Most High God by using YHWH, but identifying him as The most High God. Abraham's prayer in Gen 15 also testifies in another situation, in another narrative and in a speech act Abraham's knowledge of YHWH. In fact 'YHWH' appears throughout the narrative except in 22.1-2,v.8,12, but it is 'The angel of the Lord YHWH that saves Isaac, and then Abraham confesses YHWH as 'On the mountain of YHWH it will be provided.' Note the angel of YHWH appears twice, and God's Words ne æum Yhwh are part of the divine words, wherev YHWH identifies himself to Abraham. Usually source analysis is used to separate the use of the divne names. But besides an insider versus outsider perspective, where 'God' is used with non-covenant peoples, and YHWH is used for those in the covenant, another principle appears to be involved, and that is the spiritual growth of Abraham involving in part a knowledge of YHWH by name. This is further stressed in Gen 14 by the number of times that El ;Elyon is used in two verses. Since Melchizedek had not formal relations with Abraham it would be appropriate for Abraham to use the same divine name, which he does not. He intentionally, not the author's intention, uses YHWH to clarify that he is not worshipping a pagan God. Fitzmyer suggests:" It has been proposed that the hero of these verses (or of the whole saga) was Melchizedek, and that it was a hieros logos of the Jerusalem sanctuary with the aetiological purpose of showing Abram paying tithes to the Jerusalem priest-king.[249] It is rather more likely that the saga told ofvthe cooperatiohn of Melchizedek, an allied king, who went forth to refresh Abram and his troops, to bless him and gve him 'a tithe of everything' i.e. pay hm tribute. Such a hypothesis accounts at least for the choppy character of the three verses and their relation to the whole. §With the insertion of the Melchizedek verses in Gen 14 and the identification of El ;Elyon as Yahweh, Melchzedek was adopted into Israelite tradition. By the time of the establishment of the Maccabean royal priesthood Melchizedek's designation becomes the official title of the Hasmonean dynasty.[250] Josephus, who calls Melchizedek cananaiwn dynasthß 'a lord of the Canaantes', mentions that he was the first to officiate as the priest of God,[251] and according to Philo God made him both 'king of peace, fr that is the meaning of 'Salem', and his own priest hierea heautou.[252] This Jewish adoption of Melchizedek underlies the treatment of him in Hebrews, for the author knows that Melchizedek does hot have a common ancestry with Abram 7.6 . Note in Genesis nothing is said that he will live forever, rather is part of the promise to the Israelite king that he will be priest forever Ps 110. Thus Melchizedek did was not in a hereditary line and did not transmit it to others. The implication is that Melchizedek and the Son both have heavenly descent or antecedents. In the account the OT could be read that Melchizedek paid tribute to Abram as part of the victory celebration. If Abraham paid tribute the reasoning is unclear unless Melchizedek and Jerusalem were the sacred site of the allied troops and if so then Melchizedek should have been Amorite not Canaanite as Josephus called him. Fitzmyer,[253]235

7.7 'The lesser is blessed by the greater' But in Gen 47.8 has Jacob blessing pharaoh which was followed by the question 'How old are you'? indicating that age would be the only factor to make Jacob greater than pharaoh. But 'bless' in Hebrew in piel conjugation with a direct object means 'curse.' That is why late Hebrew uses baruk the passive form to begin prayers 'Blessed art thou O God.' A prayer wish expressed to God. The role of a father is one that may use the blessing formula.

7.8 "As the clause stands, all the emphasis falls on the startling assertion that Melchizedek is "one to whom witness is borne that he is alive." The term μαρτυρούμενος, "witness is borne," almost certainly has reference to Scripture (Cf. . v 17; 10:5). In this context the declaration must refer back to v 3, which the writer considered to be exegetically established on the basis of Ps 110:4 and Gen 14:18–20. Scripture announces of Melchizedek only his living and the administration of a priesthood that is free from temporal limitation"[254] Scriptural assertions of this type assume that after death Melchisedek, Abraham and David are still living in heaven among the cloud of witnesses. But of the lists of genealogy in Gen 5 and of priests and kings only Enoch didn't die and Melchisedek's 'he lives' with no record of his death corresponds to Jesus who lives forevermore. If Jesus' priestly office only began after the resurrection then from that point on hs cannot die. But the Gospels show John 14-17 where Jesus has already entered His intercessory office and this book shows Jesus functioned as priest when he offered up himself.

7.9 'One may even say' is based on historical fact that Levi grandson of Abraham, but actually paying tithes began with the descendents of Levi.

But in Federal Headship Theory descendents share in the acts of their first father. Rom 5 expresses this that in Adam all sinned and all died. In the Ten Commandments punishment is limited to the third or fourth generation 'of those who hate me.' Stephen, among others, recounts the sins of Israel and punishments throughout history. But some accounts go back to a sin at Gibeah. As a fact Levi was grandson, it is a fact then that he is one with Abraham's act and takes priority over a later practice. Precedent rules. The original situation is a controlling factor in biblical thought, but contrary to a restoration of Paradise the book of Revelation teaches a new heaven, earth and holy city. But the author of Hebrews is using this legal argument to establish the priority of Melchisedek even over Levi and the law.[255]

7.10 This is not reincarnation but expresses that Levi had not yet been born Fitzmyer,[256]239. If Melchizedek then the tithe has predated the Mosaic legislation by many years. He could also have used Jacob's vow at Bethel. 'Levi was still in the body of his ancestor' does not only deal with issues about abortion, but about the whole plan of God and superintendence over life in a transgenerational manner. This is affirmed by Jesus birth and prophecies hundreds of years prior to it and others such as Samuel and especially Jeremiah. 'God will raise up another' said by Moses in Deuteronomy could point to Samuel or the Christ, as it is so interpreted in the NT. But clearly the genetic and DNA make up of the future servant of God goes back further than Transactional Analysis which sees patterns in the grandfather generation of parents. It is possibly for cthis reason the genealogies and rule against mixed marriages is harshist for priests and levites. Purity of line was a doctrine in the priestly documents.

7.11 Why does he suppose 'perfection' can come through a priesthood? Did he have a sacerdotal faith that the efficacy of sacred rites depended upon the holiness of the priest and his assistants? The following verses mention the 'order' of Melchizedek or Aaron; the 'tribe'and ancestral background. The 'law' change was necessitated since Jesus came from Judah. 'Moses' words, and 'precedent' are lacking in Jesus' case. The new high priest has one qualification among many: 'the power of an indestructible life.' Is there a theory or fact that a properly ordained priesthood can forgive sins, purge iniquity, and communicate grace? Was all perfection only in terms of what the priest did as a person in prayers and offerings so that all access to God was only through the priesthood derived from Aaron with official genealogical proofs? The issue of Jesus forgiving sins may be that the priests either no longer perceived this as valid since this awaited the Messiah. But if God only can forgive then Jesus must be God or his is invalid? But then He authorized by the gift of the Spirit that the apostles forgive not, bind or loose on earth and commanded his disciples and apstles to fiorgive as a condition to their own forgiveness. Does this mean that forgiveness can only come through a minister as some churches would teach? Actually, there is one door and only one and it is only through the Son nand no other. But the minister can be used by God to inspire saving faith

7.12 'Change of the law' is a major theme in the book, not a discarding of the law. This one change is into the order of Melchizedek, the tribe of Judah, the negating ancestry and proclaiming the resurrected Jesus as sufficient evidence. If it is appointed to men once to die and after that the judgment, then Jesus died once and the judgment follows. But this paragraph says nothing about serving an earthly altar. Paul doesn't talk of change of the law but its replacement with a new foundation. Paul also was not speaking of laws but of the whole 'tradition of the elders.' This change is in the sacerdotal domain only.

7.13-14 'Is said to belong to a different tribe':The Lord sprang from Judah according to the flesh, a non-:Levitical tribe, thus without qualifications to be a priest; But in Judah was Jerusalem, and Melchizedek came from there, but not with heirs or ancestry, hence with 'a life which cannot end' zwh akatalutos. Is this merely a comparison or is it also saying something about Melchizedek? Jerome thought he was Shem [Ep.73 Ad Evangelum]#5. Fitzmyer,238; Isa 1.1

7.16, 'Power of indestructable life' could only apply to post-resurrection Christ and not to Melchizedek, who has no history before or after this event. [257] So the validity of Melchizedek's office is taken for granted as a fait accompli. But the use of Melchizedek must reflect OT backgrounds where kingly families and speciialized guilds stayed within their speciality for hundreds of years and were accepted across the boundaries of all nations and peoples by virtue of that background. Note the Levite in judges and Balaam in Numbers, along with the Assyrian and biblical records of the specialized People taken into captivity, along with historical documents showing these family guilds could be sold intact to the highest bidders.[258]

7.17 Another evidence is the call or election of the Son after the order of Melchizedek forever. The call initiates a new order as with Moses, Joshua, Gideon, Samuel, Saul, Aaron, Zadok, David, Paul. Testimony is a matter of record and thus may be quoted and cited as a precedent. The Word of God is God's testimony and that of prophets, kings and priests, apostles and wiise men to what transpired when God had the testimonyt written Fitzmyer,[259]222,226; Ps 110.4

7.18 'Change of regulations' has to do with the priesthood. The evidence could go to Acts 1.20 from Ps 19.8. Pater is claiming the OT forecast Judas' defection and also his replacement. But the Psalm context 'may...' is a wish prayer or curse. Since Peter's purpose is not to curse the dead Judas he probably was unaware of the context. 19.14 his sins were and are remembered before the Lord in an eternal biblical record. v.15 says there is no forgiveness even as Jesus called him 'son of perdition'. His rejecting the women who would do good to Jesus usnder the pretense of wanting to use the money to help the poor was essentially rejecting and cursing those women, including Mary. v.17.. The former law was useless and weak, for it, the law, made nothing perfect.

7.19 'Law made nothing perfect.' Ps 19.7-11 1. reviving, making, joy, light, warned, etc. 2. law is perfect 9-10. 3. The law fails v.12 at 7 things: v.13cd. 1. errors 2 hidden faults, hidden stuff'; 3. wilful sins 4. ruling sin. words 6. meditations of the heart 7. The great transgression 3-4-7 are in a progression. The goal in Ps 19 is 'perfection' Paul would not criticize the law to this extent since in Rom 4 he calls it good and perfect and links this in Rom 12.1-2 to the good and perfect will of God. So perhaps Paul is thinking of 'law' and not torah per se. Ps 19 uses many terms to encompass the whole revealed will of God. The latter in Rom 8.1-3 is the stated to be the purpose of the law of the Spirit of life to fulfill 'in' us the requirements of the 'law', namely the law of Moses. The difference is a broad or narrow understanding of law and the fact that torah cannot be represented rightly in Greek..' Ps 19.7-11;

A. reviving, making, joy, light, warned, etc.;
B. law is perfect 9-10.
C. The law fails v.12 at 7 things: v.13cd.
   1. errors;
   2 hidden faults 'hidden stuff';
   3. wilful sins;

4. ruling sin ;
5. words ;
6. meditations of the heart
7. The great transgression□□□□3-4-7 are in a progression. The goal in Ps 19 is 'perfection' □□Paul would not criticize the law to this extent since in Rom 4 he calls it good and perfect and links this in Rom 12.1-2 to the good and perfect will of God. So perhaps Paul is thinking of 'law' and not torah per se. Ps 19 uses many terms to encompass the whole revealed will of God. The latter in Rom 8.1-3 is the stated to be the purpose of the law of the Spirit of life to fulfill 'in' us the requirements of the 'law', namely the law of Moses. The difference is a broad or narrow understanding of law and the fact that 'torah' cannot be represented rightly in Greek. It isn't clear what 'better hope' is contrasted with except for an eternal life as opposed to a long temporal life.

7.21 Here it is not the virtue of being a Son, being God or a priest, but by virtue of an oath and the ensuing role he is authorized to fulfill. There is a grand plan in the unveiling. Ps 110.4. Aaron was made priest by Moses, and may have been of such a clan earlier.Feinberg notes :" Because it marked the beginning of the priesthood in Israel, the consecration of Aaron to his office was both instructive and solemn. Nothing was left to human ingenuity; all was precisely commanded of God. There were three ceremonies: washing, clothing, and anointing. When the tabernacle was finished, Aaron and his sons were set apart to the priesthood by washing (to signify purification), clothing with official garments (for beauty and glory), and anointing with oil (to picture the need of empowering by the Spirit; Cf. . Ex 28; 40:12–15; Lv 8). Aaron thus became the first high priest, serving nearly 40 years." [260] Levite in Nabnataean mean 'one joined to, adherent of' and could be in the sense of a devotee or official in a cult. Eli was rejected. Abihu had merit of executing a Hebrew man copulating with a Moabite woman. Zadok was simply chosen by David and later Ezra. But Jesus was directly designated by God. The omission of any reference to Aaron being ordained as involving an oath is here an antithesis emphasizing Jesus' ordination as priest with an oath. Therefore the new order is superior. Legal matters are not easily changed and accepted so this argument is very pertinent for new believers.

7.22 Aaron was designated priest and Melchisedek was a priest of the true God, but Zadok come through David and others. Christ was through being designated as priest, a new beginning. David was also a new beginning but designated by Samuel, and with Saul as father-in-law and Saul's daughter as wife he had more than one ground of kingship. The army acknowledged and won battles and character confirmed it. Paul also fits the 'designated category' contrary to the Apostles electing Mathias as a replacement for Judah. But this oath makes Jesus' priesthood unique.

7.23 The focus on the high priest as the bearer of reconciliation to God calls to mind rabbinic thought where they believed that God raises up one righteous man in each age or era and if none the world would come to an end. Their application was not directly on the priest. Also their thought takes the initiative on providential rule over the world and history is taken from God and humanized. Still, the pre-creation Christ, the OT Yahweh-Lord, is the Righteous one of the Psalms and Acts. It is because of Christ the righteous one that the world can continue.

7.24, Christ's priesthood once conferred cannot be revoked but is permanently his. This leads to the laws pertaining to distribution and ownership of tribal and clanal land and office in Israel. It is his, it belongs to him. Possessive by use of the article. Dana-Mantey,131,151.Possessive by use of the article. Dana-Mantey,131,151. The rebellions of Aaron never were punished. Aaron's death is not said to be a punishment. But two of his four sons died as a result of punishment but the remaining sons were preserved in theirs. The elimination of Abiathar was linked to politics and a transition due to Jonathan. In Ezra's time derivation from Aaron with genealogical proof was necessary. Later it was believed the genealogies would not be restored till the Messiah came[261] aparabatos 'permanently, untransferable, indefectible and unsupersedable' and thus is final both in this new priestly office and it the priest himself. "He can guarantee their total and final salvation' such as the earlier priests could not.[262]

7.25 'Save completely' is individualized either time wise 'utterly' 'to the end' or existentially, 'fully' as in 1 Thess 4.This salvation meets current needs, because Jesus is ever interceding for those who 'come to God through him.' Jesus continues in office and lives forever, and 'has a permanent priesthood.' Both meanings can be established from Hebrews. "intercede for them" is a role and a task forever? V.21,24,25. Isa 53.12 in the past tense context might allude to the two criminals, not only the one. This is a model for the completed event, not a type or symbol. He fulfills Moses' role in Ex 32.31-34, except that in trhe Son's case God accepted the free substitutionary offer of himself to atone for their sins. eis to panteles 'completely'[263] There is unceasing availability of grace.

'He always lives to make intercession for them' evidently is not only for believers' forgiveness which the atonement has covered, but for 'grace to help in time of need' and all other subject material of prayer. Jesus told his disciples to ask largely 'that your joy may be full.' Hebrews so stresses the sacrifice and atonement that is a concluded event so the stress on intercession in this book theoretically doesn't concern forgiveness which is a concluded transaction. On the other hand 1 John 1-2 indicate Jesus as guarantor and 1.7,9 does include confession of believers. 'Whoever calls upon the name of the Lord shall be saved' indicates an intercession ministry to sinners and believers who turn to the Lord. Lk 22.32. To Peter Jesus said 'I have prayed for you.'

7.26 The criteria for man as high priests, as set forth in Hebrews in relation to Jesus, are 1. holy; 2. blameless; 3.pure;4. set apart from sinners; 5.offers sacrifices for himself and people; 6. weak; 7. designated ancestry; Jesus was sinless, but not set apart from sinners in his earthly life but savior of sinners. His ancestry is not of Levi. He was weak. He did not need to offer for himself. In addition Jesus was designated priest after the Melchisedek line, was sinless,[264] and was eternal. 'Separate from sinners' doesn't correspond to the Gospel record of Jesus seeking to save that which was lost. But for the high priest image and in keeping with Pharisee expectations Jesus is portrayed as a good pharisee. In Hebrews it isn't the life Jesus lived on earth that saves but the atonement-redemption of the cross and present ministry of intercession. The qualifications for priests were the background for choice of bishops and deacons in the church. All high priests were to be 'holy, blameless, unstained' having one wife, not a widow, and thus above reproach. Still he had to offer for his own sins. This one, Jesus, is 'exalted above the heavens; 4.14 which he passed through, to the throne of God. This doesn't refer to the staggered and elevated height of the holy place and Most Holy Place in the temple.

7.27 Lev 9.7; 16.6 The stark contrast to the OT places the priest on the same level as the People needing sacrifice although his sacrfice is usually once a year officially. Christ made this once for all but not for himself at all and once for all for all the People. It is very serious to refuse its merit. It is more serious to once receive the sacrifice and to turn from it since this cannot be sacrificed again. ,In Lev 6.13 'Aaron and his sons' is solely done by the high priest, and the sons could be successors only. [Sir 45.14; Tg.Ps.J]. Philo says every day the daily cereal offering must be offered by every priest [Laws

I.255-56]. Josephus "The priest a his own expense, and that twice a day, offers meal soaked in oil and hardened by a little cooking' [Ant.3.257]. Rabbis referred this to every priest individually on the dayof his consecration [t.Seqal 3.25;Sipra Saw 3.3; b.Menah 51b]Milgrom,396. the present practice of many denominations for the minister or co-ministers in a communion service to first partake of the sacred elements may derive from the high priest's role as first offering for himself and then the people. This identification of the role of the Christian minister as a priest is not universally accepted among church groups, but many of these continue to have the minister serve himself and co-workers first.

7.28 'Who has been made perfect' cannot refer to moral attainment. It could refer to 1. the resurrection since all other peoples are still awaiting for the completion of the promises in thwe events surrounding the general resurrection. 2. The other possibility that could be equally valid from Hebrews is the completing of all qualifications for Jesus to have learned obedience through the things suffered. It is the suffering, enduring temptation, running the race, enduring verbal and physical abuse and accusation that he did not take in the wron g way that he is perfectly able, including his eternal life, to save all who come to him forever. 3. He is alive and perfected for ever. Never again subject to all the temporal limitations of earth. And Satan's attacks. James said that God is not tempted with evil, but Jesus on earth was tempted. In Israelite history God was tested but it may be that he no longer is since his patience in this era may indicate that response to outrageous affronts in this age seem to do not elicit the immediate response, but rather await the final judgment. The OT judgments almost all except in apocalyptic literature, seem limited within the history framework and usually are centered around the promises to Israel without global implications.

Chapter Eight;

CHRIST'S TABERNACLE AND WORSHIP MINISTRY ARE GREATER; NEW COVENANT GREATER THAN THE FIRST COVENANT.

God's Majesty, Covenant and Laws

8.1 The high priest's role[265] is the mediator of 1 John 2.1 and Isa 53.12; Job 9.33-34; 16.20-21; 19.25; 31.35-37. But his main work is described here only in the offering of sacrifices and offerings. The latter encompasses all of the worship offerings. Is this a summary or highlighting? What is found on his role, person, session, sanctuary? The 'throne of Majesty' is strongly monotheistic, no mention is made of a Trinity. The true sanctuary is set up or was set up by the Lord YHWH, not man. Thus the earthly sanctuary is man-made, making thel ikeness of something in heaven, which is forbidden in the 10 Commandments, but at God's command.

8.1-10.ff" In Christianity the sacrificial system has been consummated and, in its cruder forms, abolished. But Christianity, no less than Judaism, must have its cultic expressions, its body as well as its soul."On Isa 52.10 North,224. the Catholic Mass and related Anglican and some Lutheran churches call the Lord's Supper a sacrifice. Serving God is urged on believers as a sacrifice, and giving time and funds to God's work beyond one's ability is considered 'sacrifice' but not not linked to the biblical pattern. But church furniture have a table altar or prayer rail often called 'altar' and on these the Elements of Communion or offering plate are placed. The Protestant church follows the synagogue floor plan and furniture, but not universally so. Occasionally the dedication of babies is with serving God in mind much as Hannah presented Samuel to God for service. Again, the cross is more the emblem of Christianity than an altar, and it is there Jesus suffered outside the gate, serving as an altar nonetheless.

8.2 The heavenly throne and the sanctuary [Most Holy Place] and tabernacle are united at the throne of God. The 'true sanctuary is real, but corresponds to that on earth. Was there a curtain in heaven? Did heaven have to wait for the veil to be rent for the veil to be removed? Was there such a separation of God from angels in heaven; and before the High Priest Jesus took office was there no one to act as mediator and reconciler? Did all this have to wait till redemption had been purchased? Was the tabernacle set up 'by man'? What is inferior about that? When did the Lord set up the 'heavenly tabernacle'? v.5 shows a pattern and there the heavenly tabernacle on which the pattern is based. Does 2 Peter's new heaven and new earth indicate a doing away with that heavenly tabernacle? What does Jesus do in serving in the heavenly temple? As a role not action this can be explained. But Hebrews stresses Jesus' heavenly role as intercessor to deliver from testing. Where is this sanctuary? Is this an 'Alexandrian' idea or is there actually a sanctuary in heaven? When was it set up by God?[266] Revelation has a heavenly altar, heavenly incense, heavenly curtain, heavenly ark and holy of holies. But nothing of sacrifices unless the 'souls under the altar are such. But if the counterpart on earth is fulfilled and not needed is the heavenly still needed. Revelation shows no temple or altar in the New Jerusalem. But Why, in the last days, must the earthly temple be rebuilt if reconciliation in the new covennant has been accomplished? 'set up by man' But wasn't the plan and its execution under the close supervision of Moses and providences of God? Still it was manmade. The detail of the construction through anointed specialists and free contributions along with some materials from Egypt do stress the human participation component. 'Sat down' is the session of Christ, priests never sat down in the Most Holy Place. 'Serves in the sanctuary' is clear from historical priests, but how is it applicable to Jesus? Is there a parallel heavenly ministry now with sacrifices or only the intercessory ministry which sums it all up.

'Set up by the Lord' indicates the heavenly tabernacle was set up by God and Jesus serves in it. As 'tabernacle' it should be temporary. ' Num 24.6 LXX read 'like tabernacles which the Lord pitched.'. When would this be set up?

8.3 'Every high priest' is appointed, a present gnomic truth, and so as the writer writes the temple is still standing, men are still being appointed as priests. One task is to offer sacrifices and offerings, even after all that has been fulflled. The larger question is how much of OT religion is stil being done after all has already been fulfilled in Christ? The OT shows the worshipper offering the sacrifice and the priest with the believer carries out the procedure.

Jesus, rather, offers himself for the people and not for himself. The stress in the NT is on what God has provided by grace through Christ and not on human efforts to pacify or please a holy God. [267]

8.4 The Jerusalem temple seems to be standing at the time of writing. Payne, 571[268]But the OT has passages referring to the tabernacle long after they had a temple and to Israel's tents long after they lived in houses. Of course those passages were where the army was in bivouac. Why could Jesus not be a priest on earth? Does this mean 'The Law' is not applicable in heaven? Nothing is said of 'church' or of 'kingdom'. 'offer gifts' The word for 'gift' in OT mattan, and NT, can include all the sacrifices as a general term.

8.5 Is there a distinction between 'copy' and 'shadow'? Do they correspond to type or symbol? In Alexandrian thought there is a reality in heaven corresponding to the copy on earth. In scripture outside of Hebrews the clearest foundation for this is in the heavenly sanctuary in Revelation and in the tabernacle made according to the plan revealed to Moses 'on the mount.' What is the broader truth in 'pattern'? What hermeneutic should control the interpretation of this? This isn't allegory or parable but is it analogy? Why can all sacrifices be called 'gifts'? Originally that mattan pertained to a political assessment of Assyria along with fines and taxes. Would this include freewill offerings and thank offerings only and later be applied to all offerings except for the tithe?, In II Esdras 10.49 'her figure' is the heavenly pattern of her' Heb 11.10,16; 1.22; 13.14 refer to the hevenly city. Cf. Ex 25.9,40 for the original copy or model. Myers,[269]276 R"Who serve in the temple, which had not yet beendestroyed? After the pattern and shadow of heavenly things - Of spiritual, evangelical worship, and of everlasting glory. The pattern - Somewhat like the strokes pencilled out upon a piece of fine linen, which exhibit the figures of leaves and flowers, but have not yet received their splendid colours and curious shades. And shadow - Or shadowy representation, which gives you some dim and imperfect idea of the body, but not the fine features, not the distinguishing air; none of those living graces which adorn the real person. Yet both the pattern and shadow lead our minds to something nobler than themselves: the pattern, to that holiness and glory which complete it; the shadow, to that which occasions it[270]

8.5, Note that in Rev 15.5, Heb 9.11; 13.10 the tabernacle plan is alluded to. "In [rev 15.5] the seer receives another vision, that of the sanctuary or shrine of the tent of witness in heaven. This must be distinguishes from the vision in [Rev] 11.19 where the ark of the covenant was seen. The tent was the shelter for the ark and it was here that Moses went to find God and to receive orders and revelatiobns. It was believed that when Moses constructed it in the desert he did so on a model of the tent in heaven. Its appearance does not seem fortuitous here, for the manifestation of the ark and the tent and the altar of incense had eschatological significance. In II Macc 2.4-8 the appearance of the tent and the manifestation of the glory of God [rev 15.8], as at the time of Moses [Ex 40.34-35] and Solomon [I Kgs 8.10] wereexpected to mark the advent of messianic times and the restoration to dominance of the chosen people. II Macc 2 records that the prophet Jeremiah found the tent, the ark, and the altar of incense, and sealed them up in a cave. Some people followed him and tried to find the way but were not successful and Jeremiah rebuked them, saying, "the place shall be unknown until God gathers His people together again and shows his mercy. And then the Lord will disclose these things, and the glory of the Lord and a cloud will appear, as they were shown in the case of Moses, and as Solomon asked that the place should be consecrated." II Macc 2.7b-8. Ford,[271]257

8.5; 9.11-12 The author treats the law as typical foreshadowing of Christ, not as an agent of moral condemnation, as in Paul [Gal 3.21-24; Rom 5.20]. "Hebrews, in fact, answers closely to the OT book of Leviticus, in that it is the NT volume that is the most involved in the phenomenon of typical prediction: some 18 of its 52 prophetic topics, and almost half of its predictive verses, are concerned with the types of the OT. Indeed, Hebrews is the most important book in the Bible on the relationship of the OT to the NT: it emphasizes how the former is fulfilled in Jesus Christ, and it views the goal of the Sinaitic law as achieved through its being written upon men's hearts under the newer testament of the church [Heb 8.7-15].Correspondingly, this letter contains proportionately more about biblical prophecy than any other book in the NT, with the exception of Revelation: 47% of the verses [137 out of 303] of the book have to do with prediction, and these are scattered through all 13 if its chapters. The overwhelming majority consist of either references to or direct citations of OT prophecies. Hebrews, as a result, cites predictions that have accomplishments in all 18 of the periods of prophetic fulfillment as used in this study--from the flood of Noah in per.1 [11.7] to the New Jerusalem and the final lake of fire in par.18 [10.27; 12.28]--with the exception of five periods [5,8 and 10-12]. Payne,[272]572

8.6 'better': where does this appear in the book? What more can you add to observations already made about the comparative mode used to stress the superlative in this book? Why are they 'better'? is a transition verse, a transition to what subject? Covenant and promises are mentioned below.

8.7 Ex 3.8; 19.5 The first covenant from the start had faults, since the result did not maintain a relationship of trust and obedience it was designed for on the basis of thankful remembrance and reliance on God alone. From this text we suggest;

1. One generation of males who heard it could remember it not the next.;
2. The covenant was the Ten Commandments in the ark. No one had access to it even though later the king did to have his copy.
3. The details were written but detailed teaching would not be possible after the People dispersed in Canaan;
4. The application of God's will to all aspects of life was not in the ark and could have many interpretations.
5. The emotions of unbelief and anger from the carnal side of man would make reasonableness difficult to maintain.
6. The provisions for infractions were not directly linked to the Ten Commandments for which no forgiveness was available.
7. They needed circumcision of the heart, a new heart and spirit and life to be able to walk in his ways. Who sought for another covenant? Jeremiah spoke of it and Hosea predicted it. Paul never said there was anything wrong with the first covenant, meaning the one promulgated by Moses at Sinai. He does mention that to Abraham as a promise, which is a unilateral covenant. Neither does he mention the covenant to David or Levi as such. But this inspired writer in v.7 and 8, first in a negative sentence and then positive says 'God found fault with his people' meaning, he 'sought for another' covenant. By calling this one 'new' 'he has made the first one obsolete and what is obsolete and aging will soon disappear.' Precisely what was wrong with the first covenant is not specified directly and what may be inferred is that it was not suitable for the house of Israel. 'Founded on better promises' are those pertaining to the New Covenant in Jeremiah and in the Gospels. This becomes discontinuity with the older covenant since even in the predictions the foundations are different.

8.7 The author is saying that something was wrong with the first covenant, something Paul would not say. V.8 God finds fault with his people, which happened all the time. God calls this covenant 'new'v.13 and thus 'he made the first one obsolete.' The author adds the inference, that 'what is obsolete and aging will soon disappear.' But how can the very infrastructure of Judaism age and pass away and still have Judaism? At what point will the old covenant cease to be in effect? This must await all the promises being fulfilled mustn't it? The church admitted the ground of the new covenant was the old. Without the old the new, by contrast, has been reduced in meaning. But as types, signs, predictions are fulfilled one is left still with a basic revelation of God's will and a valid standard for behavior. But as law Jesus reduced all law to two. The Council reduced it to 3 or 4. So animal sacrifice, tithe, Sabbath, holy days, temple worship, and its admninistration were discarded largely for Judaism in 70 AD, while Sabbath and holy days continued for them, but gradually no longer for the church. But for those under the Law the whole as updated still is in effect. For those in Grace the broader concept of the Will of God is never supplanted and that includes both testaments. The law and covenant were moved from collective to individual and then reapplied, rightly or wrongly, to the church.

8.8 Jer 31.31-34 The citation is the only one possible from the OT. It is cited intactly. What is not cited is that it is a part of a return of Israel and results in a perfect word of obedience to God. What is wrong with the covenant v.7 and v.8? The people? Are both covenant and people the problem? Will the New Covenant be one or two or simply with two houses forever? Or does v.10 speak of a further new covenant with Israel alone? 'After this time". 'Declare this word' at the end of v.9 suggests two covenants. Or does v.10 simply make explicit what is in v.8-9? The limiting of the covenant to the house of Israel and house of Judah is not only from the quote but also v.10 that applies this to the present dispensation. Nothing suggests 'house of Israel' has changed as recipient of this covenant but the nature of the covenant still concerns laws in minds and hearts, knowledge of God in all classes, ages and genders, and forgiveness for all their sins and wickednesses. Paul goes a step further that the spiritual or true Israel is only those who have faith and faith in Christ. So Hebrews does not clearly have a vision of world evangelism or the split of Jewish Chreistianity and Gentile Christianity. How does 'Israel' and 'Judah' relate this prediction as a promise for the New Covenant believer? For the original recipients of this treatise there is no problem. For us using Gentile Church and Jewish Church is patently wrong since by the time of Hebrews Paul's approach to faith had been applied differently in different localities. But if 'People of God' is sunstituted and fulfillment extends from now onward through the Millenium, then realization is 'stepped' and not fully realized as yet. 'with the house of Israel and with the house of Judah' are one covenant but the two peoples are not always viewed in prophecy to remain separate. But in v.10 only Israel is mentioned. In the pre 70 AD situation is Judah viewed as a political entity, that which rejected the Messiah and is very shortly to be destroyed, while in. v.10 'Israel' is the total people? If the latteri s true the scope may be the same as Rom 9-11 for a future salvation of all Israel.

8.9 This implies God covenanted before bringing them out of Egypt and assembling them at Sinai. Cf. . Ex 1ff What two things happened? God forsook the rebels not his covenant.12? The admission of God that the first covenant was not suitable to the Israelite condition and its replacement by a newer one shows

1. The people's teaching plan was inadequate;
2. Their unspiritual hearts could not accept and appreciate the wisdom of God's laws;
3. The external law was good but seldom became internalized;
4. The historical salvation from Egypt was followed by historical breaking of the covenant although the validity and necessity of the Law continued as an instrumental device for teaching about God.
5. The rebellions folowed by God's turning from them, no longer being their God in blessing them.
6. 'After that time' indicates certain things had to come to pass before the will of God as expressed in the laws of God could be internalized and obedience become a second nature to them.
7. Nothing is said of Ezekiel ch.36's mention of removing the heart of stone and giving a heart of flesh, so in the cited verses the evil tendency would be still present but with the ascendency of the good tendency. 'The covenant I made with their forefathers' is more in keeping with Exodus' narrative than an angels tradition.

8.10 'They will be my people; is mutual, but repeated because it is a new covenant and relationship and dependent on knowing God and God's laws and will. Related passages in Ezekiel and Jeremiah declare that because of imparted grace the people will obey God. But this knowledge of God is not from phenomena and theophanies but an inner knowledge. Otherwise one might assume that education received is the key to an orderly society and this simply is not the case owing to the evil tendency in man. Here the laws are made part of man's very nature and not just one Servant of God's nature. What is one feature of the internalized covenant v.10-[273] When was 'after this time'? Dispensationalism of Dallas and Scofield counter the arguments of Bowman about the number of covenants. Hebrews seems to not call Abraham's a covenant but a promise plus oath. The first covenant of all is that of Moses and then the New Covenant period. The promise to Adam and to Cain are not called covenants. In Gen 15 'establish covenant' and Gen 17 'Confirm my covenant' are neither Moses' or Christ's but concern the People, land and Messiah, and clans of the world. Later this is assimilated into the New Covenant but not referred to by Jeremiah. "Bowman first observes that Scofield does not appear to have given a definition of his use of the word covenant, so he suggests "a pact imposed by a sovereign 'individual' (in the Bible, always God, of course) upon another or upon others over whom he has supreme authority." This is a generally acceptable formula, but ignores two important particulars: (1) Nothing is said about those with whom the covenants are made. The first three--Edenic, Adamic, Noahic--are made with all mankind; the next four--Abrahamic, Mosaic, Palestinian, Davidic--are made totally or primarily with and concerning Israel; the final one, the new covenant, is to be established with Israel upon their national repentance, but into its blessings present-day believers in Christ enter as being in the Seed. (2) Nothing is said about the possibility of a covenant being conditional or unconditional. All are unconditional except the Mosaic covenant. In this case, God proposed a relationship possibility. ("If ye will") to which Israel responded: "All that the LORD hath spoken, we will do" (Exod. 19:5-8). On the basis of their acceptance, the covenant was instituted (Exod. 19:9ff). All the other covenants were simply announced by God and/or imposed. All promised blessing for obedience and warned of discipline for disobedience. Bowman's threefold criticism of SRB in this matter is: (1) He feels only that may be called a covenant where the word covenant is used by Scripture. This comparatively inconsequential observation he follows with the argument that "Scripture nowhere opposes the Mosaic Covenant with the New Covenant." While using some of the verses cited by this reviewer in his discussion of law and grace under dispensations above, Bowman's case is not convincing. That God works harmoniously with diverse elements is admitted, but to argue that there is no distinction between the two covenants, that all is of grace, is to do violence to whole sections of Scripture, particularly Romans 3, Romans 4, Romans 7, Romans 9--Romans 11; 2 Corinthians 3; Galatians 3, Galatians 4; Philippians 3; Colossians 2; 2 Timothy 1, and the whole letter to the Hebrews.(2) He then contends that "there are at most but two covenants to be found in Scripture which are so different in fundamental conditions attaching to them as to render them distinguishable." This is a strange statement in the light of the argument under criticism (1) just concluded. Evidently the difference of emphasis is that in (1) it is argued both the Mosaic and new covenants were made with "a view to displaying God's grace and His purpose to save, " whereas (2) admits two but limits to two covenants those that can be distinguished. It must be objected that the Mosaic covenant was not given to display God's purpose to save, for the law can only condemn sin. It cannot give life (Gal. 2:15-21; Gal. 3:21-22).Further objection must be raised to his suave conclusion that the phrase "the covenants of promise" used in Romans 9:4 "can only mean to gather up under this plural use of the word those repeated occasions on which God renews His single covenant with His people under whatever form."[274] Both writers ignore the crux of where the word 'covenant' occurs and whether it is imposed as in a unilateral covenant or a parity treaty, and whether initially or only later conditions were imposed. A further issue is that both Mosaic and Christian required a response; in the case of the New covenant one of faith, obedience, covenant meal, washing feet, and love etc. There was also the covenant with David, Levi and the 'everlasting covenant' in Hosea. To reduce all of these to two or one shows systematizing tendenz. There are elements of overlap in most of these covenants, but recipients, scope, content, conditions(expressed or not) are different.

8.11 Christian education will be unneeded because they will all know God, where 'least to greatest' includes gender, age, class, and all other ponderables. This fulfillment has not yet come even though Pentecost came. The fulfillment of the promises is still awaiting the Second Coming. But teaching was the task of levites and priests or wise men. In exile or Diaspora it may be the elders and heads of household felt responsible to teach others. Forgiveness is linked to knowing God; In what way knowing God? From Heb 1.1 it is from knowing the Son and this fits John's message as well. 'a prophet like me' was possibly referring to the forerunner John or the Messiah.v. 11-12 Does this declare that God is known only in forgiveness? Joel also mentions the fact of universal knowledge of God among God's people.

8.12 But from Rom chs 9-11 we learn that God remembers transgressions. Is this promise conditional on response to God or does it concern millenial prophecy? Another possibility is that for God to remember is not what it means as pertaining to men. Rom 3.25 'forbearance' is a passing over of sin not forgiveness. So in Jesus' illustration of two stewards,. one who received forgiveness of debt and the subordinate other who would not remit it to his debtor; , the latter's debt was recalled and reinstated because he did not do to his debtor as he had received from his creditor. The command to believers in the Psalms and prophets is to remember the pit from which you were dug. But the focus of the Lord's Supper is not on remembering former sins but on remembering the Lord's grace. God actually can forget nothing and man, only by grace can put behind him former failures.

8.13 The Old Covenant [275]is obsolete and aging, will it soon disappear? Or has it? One viewpoint is that "In so far as a new covenant believer sins or is not faithful to the new covenant, or seeks to establish his own righteousness, he automatically comes under the full condemnation of the law." Only life actually lived " Christ" in living relationship to him is totally freed from the Old Covenant with its law. 'obsolete' is a logical conclusion. But Israel continued in that framework. It is only for those who have faith that can consider this correct. The Jewish-Christian community for their own faith must struggle with the significance of the covenant being obsolete. Paul used Abram's faith of Gen 15 and the establishing of the covenant, but not Abraham's faith and doubt of Geb 17 and circumcision in his argument. How can he reject circumcision which was the seal of the old covenant? But then, Paul does not tell the Jewsh-Christian people to cease becoming circumcised.

Chapter Nine:

Christ's Covenant, Blood, and Most Holy Place are Greater:

God's Glory, Eternal Life, Mediator and Presence.

9.1 What corresponds to these 'first regulations'[276] Note 9.10 speaks of 'external regulations' and 9.11. Besides Moses' regulations at Sinai and in Moab did Phiineas, David, Solomon, Jehoshaphat, Hezekiah, Josiah, introduce to procedures? Ahaz, Manasseh, Jeroboam did. Ezekiel has many features that don't correspond to the Pentatech. Note the Mishneh in the Talmud and the various tracts for data. The first covenant contained all the regulations for the building of the tabernacle and for the worship procedures. 'Earthly sanctuary' accentuates that whether tablernacle or temple it was still earthly as opposed to heavenly. For application what regulations are needed for worship today? Note that 9.12-14 in its application is to the cleansing of conscience.The focus isn't on temple but tabernacle that all knew about even those who could never make the trip to Jerusalem. For this reason there are texts that refer to the heavenly 'tabernacle.' Sharon Gritz[277] suggests that the old sanctuary consisted of a series of barriers between the worshipper and God. Approach to God was only through representatives. High priests would enter once a year to present blood and cleanse the conscience over and over again; But Christ entered once for all and secured eternal redemption through his own blood. Calvin said: . "Some copies read, prw>th skhnh< the first tabernacle; but I suspect that there is a mistake as to the word "tabernacle;" nor do I doubt but that some unlearned reader, not finding a noun to the adjective, and in his.172 ignorance applying to the tabernacle what had been said of the covenant,unwisely added the word skhnh< tabernacle. I indeed greatly wonder that the mistake had so prevailed, that it is found in the Greek copies almost universally.F136 But necessity constrains me to follow the ancient reading. For the Apostle, as I have said, had been speaking of the old covenant; he now comes to ceremonies, which were additions, as it were, to it. He then intimates that all the rites of the Mosaic Law were a part of the old covenant, and that they partook of the same ancientness, and were therefore to perish. Many take the word latrei>av as an accusative plural. I agree with those who connect the two words together, dikaiw>mata latrei>av for institutes or rites, which the Hebrews call µyqwj , and the Greeks have rendered by the word dikaiw>mata ordinances. The sense is, that the whole form or manner of worshipping God was annexed to the old covenant, and that it consisted of sacrifices, ablutions, and other symbols, together with the sanctuary. And he calls it a *worldly sanctuary,* because there was no heavenly truth or reality in those rites; for though the sanctuary was the effigy of the original pattern which had been shown to Moses; yet an effigy or image is a different thing from the reality, and especially when they are compared, as here, as things opposed to each other."[278] Calvin questions the text even the validity of the law for the period it was given. This approach does not see the good. Perfect law and in fact, sees the rituals as added at a later time. Since the rituals must substitute for both Egyptian and Canaanite they could not have been an afterthought, but designed as heuristic customary avenues of educating the Hebrew conscience and conscikousness..

9.2 The mishkan or 'ohel mo'ed or miqdash is found in Ex 25-40, where the pattern is revealed from heaven. Ex 25.9,40. But still it was earthly, a copy only. In this account the rebellion before building it, the offerings of materials for construction, and the glory dedicating it are not mentioned, Hebrews isn't speaking of the 'ohel mo'ed outside the camp where God met with Moses, but the one in the center of the camp. Hebrews doesn't seem to refer to either Solomon's, Haggai's or Herod's, but the original one, the tabernacle. The Courtyard was 46m by 23m. Curtains 2.3m high. The Tabernacle was 4.6m high, 4.6m wide and 14m long.[279] What is omitted? Is it the courtyard and altar or laver? There could be more about the laver if the temple worship was still in effect since this book stresses the uncleanness-cleansing paradigm even more than Leviticus does and focusses on the internal aspect.

The lampstand 2 Kgs 4.10 memra was a pedestal for oil-filled wick lamps or a stand for several of these small bowls holding oil into which a wick was placed, the latter would have several branches as in Zechariah. In the sanctuary it was golden, seven-branched, cynindrical in form Ex 25.31-40; 37.17-24; There were 10 in Solomon's temple 1 Kgs 7.49.In the post-exilic period temple it featured a bowl with seven seven-lipped lamps Zech 4.1-6,11-

14. Rev 1.12-13, 20; 2.1 shows seven singler lampstands. A representation is found on the arch of Titus in Rome.[280]

9.3 Where was' the first curtain' located? Exodus does not seem to have a first curtain. Ex 26.31-35; 40.3.There is no door as such. Ency Judaica notes "The sanctuary was divided into two unequal parts by means of the veil (or veil of the screen), which was a beautiful portiere, "skillfully worked," made of the same fabric as the curtains. It hung from golden clasps and was draped over four acacia pillars overlaid with gold and set in silver bases. This partition was placed 20 cubits from the entrance of the Dwelling exactly underneath the clasps that joined the two sets of curtains together. This inner room, a perfect cube of ten cubits, was called the "Holy of Holies" or the "Most Holy Place," while the outer room, measuring 10X20 cubits, was known as the "Holy Place." In Solomon's Temple the two compartments, designated respectively *devir* (the inmost sanctum) and *hekhal* (the outer sanctuary), were twice the size of the rooms in the Tabernacle, but in the same proportion of one to two."David Reagon represents a symbolical interpretation: "The Mercy Seat pointed to the fact that through the work of the Messiah the mercy of God would cover the Law. The blood foreshadowed the fact that the Messiah would have to shed His own blood to atone for our sins.

Jesus fulfilled every prophetic type of the Ark. He was God in the flesh (John 10:30). He had the Law in His heart (Matthew 5:17). He declared Himself to be the "Bread of Life" (John 6). He shed His blood on the Cross and was resurrected in power, atoning for our sins and covering the Law with Grace (Romans 3:21-26).

Mary saw the fulfillment of the Ark when she went to the tomb and discovered the body of Jesus missing. In John 20:11-12 its says she looked into the tomb and "beheld two angels in white sitting, one at the head, and one at the feet, where the body of Jesus had been lying." Do you understand what she saw? She saw the "mercy seat" where the blood had been spilled, with an angel at each end exactly like the Mercy Seat that covered the Ark!" [281]'The hilasmos cover to the ark covers the Law, and the Glory covers all.

9.4 How does this account differ from the account in the Book of Exodus? Is the point here 'incense'? In other descriptions the altar of incense was in front of the inmost veil but outside the Most Holy Place. "the golden altar, was about 1.5 feet square and 3 feet high, and was used to burn incense before the veil (Ex 30:1–10; 40:5)."[282] Harris said "Since incense was such a precious commodity, incense was a fitting offering to God (Mal 1:11). Incense offerings also provided tangible sense of God's holiness in which the people could experience atonement for sin (Nm 16:46, 47). The smoke rising to the sky symbolized the prayers of the people (Ps 141:2; Lk 1:10; Rv 5:8; 8:3, 4). At the same time the smoke in the temple symbolized the presence of God as it had been portrayed by the cloud in the wilderness (Ex 19:18; 33:9, 10; Nm 11:25). Together with the rising sun the smoke provided a powerful symbol for the glory of the Lord (Is 6:1–7). The significance of incense is further enhanced by NT allusions. The Christian's testimony about Christ is paralleled with the offering of incense (2 Cor 2:14, 15). The sweet smell of the gospel is contrasted with the smell of death which leads to death. Likewise, money from the Philippian Christians came to Paul in the spirit of an incense sacrifice (Phil 4:18), a costly expression of love and devotion. Finally, incense seems to sanctify and accompany the prayers of the saints into the presence of God[283] (Rv 5:8; 8:3, 4). None of the NT references call upon the Christian to offer incense, but rather to learn the devotion and dedication to holiness signified by the burning of this precious substance.J. Gordon Harris"[284] What is the thought connection between 'stone tablets' and 'covenant', the genitive of possession, partitive[part to whole], or equivalence? Or from the actual ritual of meal, sacrifice, oath, stipulations, benefits, and concluding parties, and finally the words of the promise and then the whole recorded? Or were the Ten Commandments in their simplest form the actual covenant? By breaking the tablets Moses performed hepu or breaking the covenant, an Assyrian word for breaking the covenant. In Rev 6.9 heaven has a golden altar where souls are.. There is a door Rev 4.1. A throne is not linked to the mercy seat Rev 4.2. There are seven lamps Rev 4.5. Scrolls, thunder, lkightning, crowns, harps, incense bowls, Rev 5.8, horses 6.2, the ark 'of his covenant' Rev 11.19 and a moment when the tempole of heaven is opened 11,19. The heavenly tabernacle of the Testimony Rev 15,5, was opened. The New Jerusalem follows last events including new heaven and new earth and this has no temple. If these pictures are homogenous then the pattern shown was based on the actual sanctuary in heaven. It is not clear that the burnt offering altar was there. Possibly, as Babel built to make a link point with heaven the altar on earth was the link point, and then the tent of meeting, not tabernacle, and the ark.

9.5 40.12 Greek hilasmos the means by which sins are forgiven — 'the means of forgiveness, expiation." '(Christ) himself is the means by which our sins are forgiven' 1Jn 2:2. 'God offered him as a means by which sins are forgiven through faith (in him)' Ro 3:25. Though some traditional translations render hilasterion as 'propitiation,' this involves a wrong interpretation of the term in question. Propitiation is essentially a process by which one does a favor to a person in order to make him or her favorably disposed, but in the NT God is never the object of propitiation since he is already on the side of people. hilasmos and hilasterion denote the means of forgiveness and not propitiation.-Louw-Nida. The OT word would be rather kippur [kpr[285] 123 times] [286].Jenni-Westermann take up the background in comparative semitics and different uses: (b) In the attempt at an etymological explanation, neither association with a non-Hebr. word nor the analysis of the biblical evidence has yet lead to a generally accepted result. For the time being, it is not possible to decide finally between the two possible derivations from another Sem. language: Akk. kuppuru "to uproot, wipe away" and also "to cleanse (cultically)" (AHw 442f.) and Arab. kfr "to cover, hide"[287]. The word is common in Arab. in the sense "to atone" only since Islamic times. Most assume a relationship between kpr pi. and Arab. kfr "to cover." The notion underlying this relationship would be that sin is covered,[288] or that the sinner must be covered against the effects of the sin-disaster sphere.[289] Objections to the derivation from Akk. kuppuru arise from ostensibly weak support in the OT evidence (only the problematic passage Isa 28:18); yet comparative materials would be much more extensive if more consideration were given to the notion of cleansing associated with kipper pi.; according to Lev 14:19; 16:18f.; Ezek 43:26, etc. "atonement" is simultaneously a cleansing. Often cited as the strongest OT support for the basic meaning "to cover" are Gen 32:21 (esp. in comparison with Gen 20:16) and Jer 18:23 (Cf. . Neh 3:37). Nevertheless, an argument against the meaning "to cover" also derives from Gen 32:21 (Jacob wants [lit.] to "atone" Esau's face): it could not have this sense here, because the statement that Jacob wants to see Esau's face follows immediately.[290] The discussion concerning this passage demonstrates the speculative nature of such inferences regarding an original meaning. The observation that Neh 3:37 cites Jer 18:23 and replaces kpr pi. with the verb ksh pi. "to cover" is noteworthy. A third option is the derivation of the verb from the old subst. koper "ransom," etc. it is usually refuted with reference to the observation that koœper has nothing to do with the cultic realm and should more likely be regarded as a secondary derivation from kpr pi. The Ug. texts have not yet clarified the etymological explanation of kpr pi. (UT no. 1289)[291]. (c) The subst. kippurim "atonement" derives from kpr pi. It is limited to P (Exod 29:36; 30:10, 16; Num 5:8; 29:11, and in the phrase yom kippurim "day of Atonement," Lev 23:27f.; 25:9; as in this term, kippurim occurs only in cs. relationships, apart from Exod 29:36, "for the atonement": "sin offering/ money/ram of atonement"). The Covenant Code and Amos already use koper signifiying "reparation, ransom" (Exod 21:30; 30:12; Num 35:31f.; Isa 43:3; Psa 49:8; Job 33:24; 36:18; Prov 6:35; 13:8; 21:18) or "bribe" (1 Sam 12:3; Amos 5:12). The derivation of kapporet from kpr pi. is a specialized term for the platform with two cherubim located above the ark. It seems to have originally been not the lid of the ark (Exod 25:17, 21) but an independent sanctuar. (d) The hapax legomena koper "asphalt" and kpr qal "to coat with asphalt" in Gen 6:14 represent another root; it has precise equivalents in Akk. (also in Gilg. XI:65, kaparu II "to coat with asphalt" (AHw 443a[292]) kpr pi. in the meaning "to atone" is always resultative in the OT ("never used to describe a current process, rather always with a view to the result to be achieved." The subj. is usually the priest; in most cases, the prep. points to an individual or a group to be atoned and corresponds—if kpr pi. is rendered "to effect atonement"—to Eng.[293] "for"..[294] Lev 16.2 Above the ark takes these cherubim as a canopy, but the hilasterion is taken as a cover only. In later thought it wasn't the ultimate place for atonement but the throne of God.

9.6 3 The outer tent also had restrictions, constant washings, changing clothes, and set times Num 18.2-6; 28.. The expanded tabernacle in the temple of Solomon of course had more space, larger staff, ad Herod's temple had the Court of the Gentiles' and 'Court of the women.' The 'service' latreia , in Rom 9 is temple worship [Jos 22.27; 1 Ch 28.13; 1 Macc 2.22; Philo, Decal. 157; Spec.Leg.2.167; Jos.War 2.409, but Paul spiritualized or secularized it in Rom 12.1.Cf. . Dunn,503n20.

9.7 'Himself' and 'sins' is there an adverbial objective case? 'Sins of ignorance' are the antithesis of 'rebellion' or willful transgressions of a known law for which no sacrifice had been possible, although in certain instances forgiveness with or without punishments was granted. The Encyclopedia of Religion notes:[295] "Old Testament Background. The Hebrew root for atonement is kpr, which probably means "to cover" or perhaps "to wipe away." The Greek equivalent is hilaskethai and its derivatives. The system of sacrifice that was practiced by the Israelites was regarded as an institution graciously provided by God and had atonement as its aim. Its rationale may be seen in Leviticus 17:11: "it is the blood that makes atonement, by reason of the life." On the solemn yearly Day of Atonement the high priest went into the holy of holies to the covering over the ark, the mercy seat (kaporet, hilasterion), where God was believed to appear and announce forgiveness of sins to his people. Some scholars would translate hilasterion in Romans

3:25 ("whom God set forth to be a hilasterion") simply as "mercy seat." Their feeling is that Paul meant to assert that the cross of Christ is now the place where God shows his saving mercy. Most translators, however, render the word in this context as either "propitiation" or "expiation," depending on whether they want to suggest that God's wrath must first be satisfied before he will forgive human sinfulness or locate the block to restored relationships not primarily in God but in the alienation that is created by the sin itself and is acted upon directly by Christ's atoning action. Strongly divergent theories of atonement were constructed later on the basis of this debate. The prophets constantly warned against any automatic assumption that sacrifice of itself would provide forgiveness; they preached that God desires mercy and repentance (Is. 1:10-17). The ritual system of sacrifice was spiritualized in the Old Testament in the prophetic view of a new covenant to replace the original, Mosaic covenant (Jer. 31:31) and was personalized in the actions of the suffering servant of Yahveh (Is. 53) sent by God to become an asham ("guilt-offering") and to bear the sins of many in a redemptive act of self-oblation. New Testament Foundation. The associations of atonement with animal sacrifice, the offering of incense, and payments of money disappeared in the New Testament except as vivid metaphors for elucidating the atoning life, death, and resurrection of Jesus Christ and, especially, the "once for all" (Heb. 10:10) event of Calvary. When Christians say that the cross is the crucial point of the early preaching of the gospel, they do not so much make a pun as testify that the Atonement, whatever else it has done, has changed our language. It was probably inevitable that sacrificial language would be emphasized in describing the Atonement simply because the contemporary institution of sacrifice was well known to the early Christians (as it is not to us today) and because the actual penal process of crucifixion with its attendant shedding of blood suggested at once the religious ritual of sacrifice." Why is there so much provision for and thus stress on 'sins of ignorance; for laity, levites and priests all alike? With the historical and prophetic books detailing so much corruption, murder, deception, false witness, desertion to the enemy and outright idolatry, unwillingness to change and repent, and incorporation of foreigners and foreign culture—which ultimately destroyed the nation –why emphasize the minutia? Was it to enhance conscience awareness of sin? Why is there no ritual approach to restore the rebel, murderer, lier, and outright rebellious? Warnings, exhortation, disasters all seemed so inadequate even as they still are.

Martin Hengel[296]notes that interest in Germany over the soteriological work of Christ revived the distinction of Hellenistic Christianity and Judaists

Christanity tracing Christ's death' for us' to the Hellenists.But if Palestinian and Aramaic in locus then how did it become the focus of the Greek missionary outreach. OT and Judaism had no glorification through death docrtrine as Greeks did, although the 'suffering servant' was in the Q document. Excet for Isa 53 vicareious death as a sacrifice does not appear till 1 Maccabees 2.50 death for the covenant or Jos Ant 12.281 death for the laws. He says Dt 24.16 makes every man responsible for his own sins and Ps 44.23 doesn't praise martys killed by the enemies of God but accuses God for refusing to help innocent people. But Hengel's argument builds on Paul's wrtings not Hebrews. Here cleansing of people and things, cleansing of conscience, atoning for the holy place, and the propitiation hilasmos cover for the ark are central to cleanse all things. The Day of Atonement with two sin offerings and two goat offerings, oneo n the altar, and one sent away expiate sin. The blood cleanses and atones as well as seals the covenant. But suffering is not related to expiation but rather to priesthood.

9.8 'The way ..had not been disclosed' But there is detail how the high priest would enter once a year, preparations for it and what he did once inside. Zechariah's entrance may have been such in the Gospels. But The connection was with a place, ark, cherubim, mercy seat, blood, but in total darkness, hence 'undisclosed.' This required a high level of faith, obedience and piety as well as performance, but in these times the glory was not apparent. The 'Holy spirit was showing by this' refers to the yearly entering of the high priest into the Most Holy place and the revelation derived from this observance and festival along with the particular actions of the priests was that of a separation from Israel and mankind and the highest degree of holiness possible aside from God himself. The way hadn't been opened yet for covenant people to fully participate in enjoying the presence of God. This enhanced the common belief that 'no man shall see God and live' although there were exceptions when God elected or called certain men like Gideon for special tasks. Judaism and Christianity have generally held strongly to concepts and rules concerning the holy and the profane. Only segments of these believers truly negate the concept and make all of life either holy or profane. Perhaps biblical antitheses require in a deep structure level that this contrast is always existing. The most remarkable case is the Book of Revelation that has a new heaven and earth and sacred city descending to earth. But the whole city is filled with God's glory and those inside are holy, while there are still profane and unholy people outside the open gates who will never enjoy this glory as part of the people of God. The way had been opened and many entered are within but unbelievers still exist. The way to the heavenly holiest place was not revealed while the tabernacle was standing. Is this a marker for the date of authorship that the temple already had been destroyed? Or was the way truly revealed not through Mosaic legislation but through the hymnology of the Solomonic Temple? But if 'tabernacle' stands for the temple the Solomonic temple was destroyed in 587 BC and the Haggai Temple had none of the glory of God's presence. But was there something in the exilic and post-exilic writings that disclosed the way? Ezekiel set forth a plan for a new temple with a great deal of focus on gates and altar, but almost nothing about the holiest place. Since Hebrews and v.9 contrast the past dispensation with the current one the centrality of Christ must mean that in Jesus the way is now disclosed and opened. Rom 5.1 says the same thing. V.12 declares he entered and and v.24 affirms this way is now open.

9.9 Offerings were not able to clear the conscience of the worshipper. Unless a priest declared his prayer answered as in Hannah's case or fire came down, or an angel spoke, or ascended in the smoke, or special words of affirmation were spoken to the one God had chosen, there would be no connection between forgiveness and acceptance of the believer. The very personal words often spoken to God's servants were not said to the ordinary worshipper. Without those words it would be hard to accept pardon, and know there is now nothing between the believer and God. As in Job's experience if things are not going well it may be because of sin and God might be angry, and the reasons for life or death are not clear from the data. Parabole in the NT means parable, but also 'comparison' or 'analogy'. Lk 5.36; Mk 3.23, 'symbol' Heb 9.9; 11.19; Mk 13.28; Lkl 4.23 ="proverb" or 'commonplace' 6.39 'proverb'; Mk 7.17 'riddle' and Lk 14.7 'rule' Cf. the linguistic background of Aramaic mathla that embrace metaphor, simile, parable, similitude, allegory, illustration and so on. Mathla can mean every sort of figure of speech such as parable b.Pes.49a; similitude b.Pes.49a; allegory Mech.Ex 21.19; fable proverb; apocalyptic revelation riddle symbol b.Sanh.92b; apology J.Keth.2.26c; refutation Git.9.9;b.Git.88b,89ab; Jest b.Pes.114a. Jeremias, 20[297]

9.9-10, The contrast of the present age to the age to come is also found in II Esdras 4.27 as an age 'full of sorrows' 1 John 5.19; 1 Enoch 48.7; and in Nag Hammadi writings.Myers, 174[298] 'External regulations applying until the time of the new order.' Many in the first century agreed with a promised and expected new order but considered the law and its detailsas eternal and unchangeable. By calling them 'external' the author considers them not essential to the basic matters of God's Will and Law. The question in Hebrews is what synthesis can be derived from the data as to what this new order would be? What was 'the new order'? If this is the Millenium then the law will continue till the king comes for those who don't receive the Lord not as alternate way of salvation but a way of accountability within which to seek God and turn to him. If the New Order is the New Covenant established by Jesus at Passover time then the whole of external regulations are now observed to an extent but without authorization since a new way is called 'I am the way. No man comes to the Father but by me.' Under the theory that all OT faithful were saved retroactively by the Redemption of Christ on the cross it was covenant faithfulness in what the types and laws represented. If the prostitute was saved by her 'loved much', and 'we are saved by hope' then the love of the law in Ps 119 and the heart of David all are completed in Christ. But what of Jews continuing without Christ and only hope in the Messiah or trust in obedience to the law as God's will ? Isaiah saw his glory and spoke of him, and prophets sought to understand the promises. Clearly they were saved by faith within the old order but without true knowledge of God. God can 'set aside' his divine order and words of God pertaining to it, but man cannot and must not. The human effort to imitate God and become God makes man seek to do those things that are only God's prerogative.

9.11, 'Holy Spirit' pneuma hagion in Matt 7.9-11 means the same as agatha eschatologically. Lk 1.53.In Matt his words are directed against a misinterpretation of his words and acts. Thus ta agatha 'good things', since Semitic lacks the superlative, really designates the gifts of the messianic age Rom 3.8; 10.15.Cf. Isa 52.7They could not comprehend the fatherliness and goodness of God. In the New Age God the Father gives good gifts to those who ask him. The present age 'you being evil, know' thus contrasts to the age to come.Jeremias,[299]145. the good things that are here already include the list of gifts received mentioned in ch.6, and the whole scheme of redemption and person of the Son detailed in this book. Can the phrase include the older testament including the law with the promises and the structures set up? According to this verse beginning with Christ's coming he became high priest of already existing structures. According to this book he entered into fulfilling the types, the promises, the conscience and the whole will of God, both previously revealed and presently revealed. Lane notes "The review of the Levitical liturgy in 9:1–10 is summed up in the statement that the old cultus consisted of regulations that were obligatory "*until* the time of correction" (v

10). That pregnant formulation prepares for the subsequent argument in 9:11–14, where the writer balances the presentation of the precedents of redemption with the description of redemption itself. The transition is announced in v 11, the δέ having an adversative sense ("but when Christ appeared as high priest"). The installation of Christ as high priest indicates that "the time of correction" has begun. This understanding of v 11*a* is confirmed by the parallel statement in v 26 that Christ "appeared at the climax of the ages," where the reference is clearly eschatological in character and corresponds to "the time of correction" in v 10. With the transition from 9:1–10 to 9:11–14, the writer draws a temporal contrast between two successive periods of redemptive history and their respective provisions for salvation".[300] The 'Time of Correction' could also correspond to Acts1.6 'restore the kingdom to Israel' in popular eschatology or Acts 3.19 'that times of refreshing may come from the Lord...until the time comes for God to restore everything.'Matt 19.29, If 'restore' is correct it may still represent an alternate eschatology to that of the epistles. Lane also notes "Christ appeared as high priest τῶ̂ν γενομένων ἀγαθῶ̂ν, "of the good things *that have now come*" (This would be a different eschatology)."The variant reading μελλόντων (of the good things "which are to come") would vitiate the contrast. That which was prefigured by the Levitical cultus had already begun to be experienced by the community for which the homily was prepared. The comprehensive expression τῶ̂ν ... ἀγαθῶ̂ν, "the good things," has reference precisely to those aspects of redemption that the old order could not provide, namely, decisive purgation and full access to God (see *Comment* on vv 8–9, 14)."[301] 'Good things' in Matthew corresponds to Holy Spirit in Luke, but Matthew's rendering really corresponds to an eschatology that is broader than that of Luke and, while Holy Spirit is in harmony with Lukan theology probably what Jesus said was more accurately recorded in Matthew. But see Matt 12.28' 12.32.13.38-39; Matt 7.9-11.

9.12 The Blood and the Covenant: "Moses took half the blood, and put it in bowls, and the other half he sprinkled on the altar. Cf. . v.18. Ex 24.6 Then he took the Book of the Covenant and read it to the People." But the blood never touches the ark, in this ritual, or the Covenant tablets. The victim becomes the atoner, and this is real forgiveness. "Moses then took the blood, sprinkled it on the People and said, 'This is the blood of the covenant that the Lord has made with you in accordance with all these words.'" These 'words' include the oath of response the People all made v.7. Zech 3.9 Dan 9.24[302] the 'in a single day' was when Jesus cried out 'it is accomplished' or when he reported in to the heavenly throne just before he allowed People to touch him in the post-resurrection days. Seventh Day Adventists place atonement on the heavenly altar within the prophet scheme at 1840 or somewhat later. But then the single day prediction would have nothing to do with the cross at all. It would solve the problem of why a cross, outside the city in an unclean place could serve as an altar when it completely is against the regulations for altars. But they key focus is that Jesus made atonement 'once for all' and if this is lost sight of the message of a completed redemption would fade. Jesus took his own blood to redeem mankind, but any other man cannot take his own blood and life to redeem himself, since in has no efficacy.

9.13 The dedication of sacrifices and priests did make them ritually pure for the worship or service to God. But what of their inward thoughts, feelings, memories? The ritual must be linked to the words of the worshipper in the Psalms where Ps 51 and the like cry out for a new heart, clean spirit, a washiing, a purging white as snow, a forgiveness and renewal. Especially in the Psalms of lament or confession is this inner state revealed. Note that some make their confession far from the sanctuary and some in a pilgrimmage procession. Faith to believe God has heard prayer is not equated with inner cleansing by the author of Hebrews:

If the ashes of an heifer - Consumed by fire as a sin - offering, being sprinkled on them who were legally unclean. Purified the flesh - Removed that legal uncleanness, and re - admitted them to the temple and the congregation.(Nu 19:17-19)".[303] Note the heifer, a young cow 'egla or 'eglat baqar had not produced offspring but could b used for milk Isa 7.21. Gen 15.9 and 1 Sam 16.2 shows their sacrificial role, designated in the ritual for the purging of bloodguilt in rural murder where the murderer is unknown Deut 21.1-8. In the ritual for purification of a person defileed by contact with a corpse Num 19.1-22, the 'red heifer' para, is slaughtered outside the camp and burned. The ashes are then mixed with spring water to produce the water of purification Num 19.17-19. "The sacrifice is unique in that it was performed away from the altar of the sanctuary and, though the process was intended to remove impurity, individuals who contacted the cow, its ashes, or the water of purification were considered unclean Num 19.7-10,21 Midr Rabbah, Num Rab 19.5-6. According to the Mishnah, the ashes were divided into three parts: one was kept on the rampart, one on the Mount of Olives, and one divided among the 24 courses of priests. M.Para 3.11. The water of purification was placed in a jar at the entrance to the temple court. According to m.Para 3.5, only seven, according to Rabbi Meie, or nine, according to sages, red heifers were actually burned, since after the destruction of the temple it was impossible to sacrifice more, but use of the ashes may have continued into the Talmudic period. Some later traditions hold that the Messiah willk prepare the last of the red heifers or otherwise emphasize an eschatological role for the sacrifice."[304] "Saying, This is the blood of the covenant which God hath enjoined me to deliver unto you - By this it is established.(Ex 24:8).

"Entered once for all into the Holy Place," Does he now ever leave except in the Eschatological sense? Is the throne also in the Most Holy place? Clearly the point is that he need not enter often. He is there for us. On an earthly analogy the ark was the throne for his shekinah presence, and it is there that reconciliation hilasmos takes place.

9.14 The purity of Jesus as a sacrificial offering is based not on Sonship but on obedience in this book. He was sinless or could nt be so offered. He offered himself much as volunteers in the army or work force, or Nazirites, or Levites who stood with Moses.

'Through the eternal Spirit': Only in this manner could the offering was completed, since the Spirit covers life and death and life again, so that the heavenly purification could take place.

The blood as purifying agent, not as life agent, cleanses deadness in conscience. Implied is that conscience not obeyed, that is influenced by works counter to it, dies while it still exists. So no one is without a conscience, but some are seared and others filled with dead works.

'Works [that lead to] death' of the NIV sounds like Paul, but is in keeping with the warnings of the book. But, choose rather, the translation 'dead works' as adjective describes works issuing from the flesh or sinful principle on Rom 7, is similar to the 'stony heart' of Ezekiel 36. A deadness of heart produces nothing positive, for the dead cannot produce or perpetrate life. Dead works in the conscience are destructive memories, fears, experiences, regrets and failures that resulted not from faith but fear. Having the 'perfect love which casts out fear' results in serving the living God acceptably. The OT rules for priests and levites are stringent about coming near any dead thing. The one serving God must 'choose life.' Thompson[305] notes the tendency to spiritualize sacrifice so that prophetic scriptures criticizing the validity of sacrifice became useful after the destruction of the temple. Thus they believed that true sacrifice did not demand the blood of animals nor a physical sanctuary.

Sanctuary and sacrifices. Ch.9 does discuss sanctuary and sacrifices together. The sanctuary is kosmikos 'belonging to this world' and transitoriness as in epi gets in 8.4, while regulations belong to dikaiwmata sarkos 'rules of humans' as in 7.16. Because these institutions are material they are not efficacious. The section then shows the contrast by which the blood of Christ and heavenly tabernacle are better.

9.15 In the OT the 'eternal inheritance' was the land and blessings of the covenant. Here the new covenant goes beyond this world so that David in Ps 23 desires to live in the sanctuary of God forever. The Psalms gives a person's life and this wish stands in the last phase of it.

The Covenant Mediator: Moses as Mediator appears often in Ex 19 mediating between God's holiness and the People's tendency to transgress the boundaries to the mount. In Ex 20 he is mediator of God's words to them. V.19. In Ex 21-23 he is mediator through procedures for interpersonal conflict cases. In Ex 24.1ff he mediates God's word and the People's and wrote it all down. In 24.8ff Moses mediates that seventy elders eat a covenant meal and are not slain in God's presence on the Mount. In Ex 23-31 he mediates the proper worship procedures and sanctuary. In Ex 32. He mediates between God and man by having Levites execute the golden calf offenders and then before God several times to have their lives preserved. 'Mediator of a new covenant' is separated from Jesus' intercessory role. In terms of 'will' he could be called executor. This role will never cease but it is the intercessory role that continues. Are other roles also continuing?[306]

"Conscience" (συνείδησις) is the human organ of the religious and moral life embracing the whole person in relationship to God (see *Comment* on v 9). It is the point at which a person confronts God's holiness. The ability of the defiled conscience to disqualify someone from serving God has been superseded by the power of the blood of Christ to cleanse the conscience from defilement. The purpose of this purgation is that the community may be renewed in the worship of God."[307]

9.16 There are no direct references to a 'Will' as such in the OT, but a great deal about the blessing of a father pronounced on his son or sons or the rights of the one designated as 'firstborn.'. From Nuzi orally transmitted wills even in the absence of corroborating testmony stood in court cases. On the other hand Joshua divided the land corresponds a little to distribution of assets before death and not a will; indeed Joshua did not leave a blessing either. But then, he never claimed the land was his to give. David's last words to Solomon and Bathsheba were a will not a blessing as such, and in them last minute directives are given. Moses did bless the People and left Deuteronomy as the last will and testament. It is when he dies that those words can be realized since he was the last survivor of the 40 years of rebellion. J.Barton Payne's theology uses the 'will' to translate diatheke since the covenant aspect is a parity treaty and the use as 'will' predominates Hellenistic usage. So this severs a link to the OT berith. But in fulfillment of prophecy the Messiah and lamb was also the servant of God, the Son, and God himself. So the death of this one fits the context of a Will precisely. Because of this believers 'inherit' not only on the word of promise of God but on His dying that the will be put into effect.

9.17 The question is who made the will and who died? The obvious answer is that Jesus made the will and died, not God. Therefore it is in effect. The switch from the covenant idea to the will idea is unique and forms the basis of Payne's Theology of the Older Testament. It links the idea of inheritance and heir to all that the Father had bestowed upon his Son, the second person of the Trinity. Then from a different perspective believers are joint heirs with Jesus.

9.18 To prove the death of the testator Paul and the Gospels had already written, especially 1 Cor 15. But it is going too far to say this is the death of God the Son. The physical human died totally, but, in line with the prophecy did not 'experience corruption' and this did not mean the mummification sense. His death is verified by Roman soldiers, Pilate the procurator, the flow of blood and water from his side, and the first person witness in the Gospel of John. He expired or gave up the spirit describes the inspired author's report. Those doing the burial Joseph and others are also witnesses. The fear of authorities wasn't that he wasn't dead but that he either would rise from the dead or disciples would steal his body. The actual death is integral to atonement just as resurrection is integral to justification by faith.

9.19 The will is effected by blood, and the declaration of every commandment of the law is sanctified by sprinkling on the scroll and all the people, not only those men old enough to be part of the assembly. The covenant is already holy and promises secure, but this is distinguished from the items of law and that distinguished from the scroll. The climax of the sprinkling of the blood for is the sprinkling of tabernacle, every utensil used, 'nearly everything.' What is added here is that Moses sprinkled the book and all the People. This assumes that in establishing covenant there was not just the 10 Commandments but also the book he had written. The blood cleanses or atones for all concerned so that they can properly enter into this Accord.

9.20 'This is the blood of the covenant, which God has commanded you to keep' How does this compare or contrast with Jesus' words ? Lk 22.20 reads "This cup is the new covenant in my blood, which is poured out for you.' For the bread 'this is my body given for you; do this in remembrance of me.'

1. The refocus is on the person through the blood.
2. The OT has no body in the covenant ceremony only in the First Passover, the lamb, but no one remembers that.
3. The commandment to observe the covenant is replaced with 'remember.'
4. God's command in Christ is to take and drink, illegal in OT law, iti s to participate in the life of God himself. Mk 14.24 changes it to 'for many.'
5. The OT is for a completed fact of covenant, but the NT covenant is not complete till Jesus drinks the cup anew with his disciples in the Kingdom of God. The pointer is past the present to the Final Goal of God's government on earth for all men not only Israel.

9.21 Ex 29.12,36 "Take some of the bull's blood and put it on the horns of the altar with your finger, and pour out the rest of it at the base of the altar." Offering the fat by fire follows.The fumes of the burnt offering and others was a propitiation to seek God's favor and reconciliation, and the blood was expiation, to remove sin and uncleanness. At the altar horns expiation corresponds to the base of the altar an ablution. This latter was probably instituted that people and priests alike would reverence life and might have had a carry over from ablutions to the dead. Survival of early pagan practices do occur from Moses onward, but are authorized 'because of their weakness' and to eliminate other practices. The all-encompassing system seems to legalize some practices and make them sacred and effective in the people's eyes, so family pagan practices could be discontinued.

9.22 Capital offences required execution or shedding of blood for the blood that had been shed. The killing of animals also had a ritual component to avoid sinning and atone for the shed blood through the draining or spraying of the blood. But forgiveness required the shedding of blood in sacrifices. It would be possible to come to God and not experience forgiveness, but after repentance and offering it was possible, not once for all, however. The goat sent away on the Day of Atonement did not involve blood but their the problem wasn't forgiveness but cleansing from impurity. Other things were cleansed with water or isolation, burning, or non-sacrificial killing of an animal to take away accountability for neighbors who experienced a capital crime but had nothing to do with it. The connection between cleansing 'nearly everything' with blood and shedding of blood for forgiveness isn't totally clear. Most of the Psalms of lament and confession allude to the ritual aspects of worship. The background for the prayers is public or private worship in a context where allusions to the public ritual abound. The provision for forgiveness for certain things is contained in the covenant. So along with the commands to be kept, and included in the means of grace found in Exodus and Leviticus, is the goal for forgiveness when those commandments are broken. While the covenant with the people cannot be broken by individuals but the individual in the covenant must obtain forgiveness.

9.23 Why are sacrifices needed in heaven? Why are they better than those Moses decreed. The earthly copies must be purified by sacrifices but why would heavenly altars also need purification? Is there a reciprocal action between heavenly and earthly and earthly and heavenly? Does the earthly sanctuary function as a shadow or copy of the heavenly? If so does an impure earthly sanctuary profane the heavenly one?

9.24 Heaven is where the true sanctuary is and presumably it approximates the earthly one. Christ has entered and not to offer himself again, but has entered to put away sin by the sacrifice of himself once for all. The putting away sin does not await either his return nor a gradual fulfillment historically, but has been accomplished. He already has taken away the 'sins of many people' so sacrifice is never again needed. But 'to bring salvation to those waiting for him' still awaits his return. The ambiguity of the 'many' versus the 'few' who await for him is similar to Rom 5 in Paul's contrast and comparison of Adam and Christ with sin and righteousness in justification by faith. Hebrews mentions the heavenly country 11.14,16, heavenly city11.10, heavenly tabernacle['house of God'10.21, heavenly altar and heavenly incense, while Revelations only has the eschatological, not current heavenly city, descending from heaven or suspended between heaven and earth. The original tabernacle was a copy of the heavenly. But that and Solomon's, Haggai's and Herod's were all manmade. This is stressed in the instructions of Moses, the plan of David, the administrative acts by Solomon, the contributions in the time of Haggai , and the time consumed in the inflationary times of Herod. No one compares to this mediatorship except Moses several times on the mount interceding with his own life for the People. In Canaanite thought the

'Mount' of Zaphon or later Zion corresponded to heaven where the Assembly of God was located. Moses was called to this office but gradually became so concerned that he put his own life on the line so that God would spare them. 9.24-28 have been used by partial rapturists, a position refuted by Walvoord.: "The entrance of Christ into heaven and his return when he "shall appear a second time, apart from sin, to them that wait for him, unto salvation" (Heb. 9:28) is the theme of this portion of Scripture. Partial rapturists seize upon the phrase, "to them that wait for him," as indicating that only such believers as are actively waiting for Christ will be raptured. The obvious answer is that those who are here described are Christians pictured in characteristic attitude of waiting or anticipating the completion of the salvation of which they now have the first fruits. All Christians worthy of the name anticipate the future completion of God's program of salvation for them. The phrase upon which partial rapturists put so much emphasis is more of an aside than the main revelation of the passage. The main point is that Christ is going to return and complete at his second coming the salvation which He provided in His death at His first coming. The figure is that of the priest who, having sacrificed, goes into the holy of holies and then appears the second time to those on whose behalf He has been ministering. In the sense used in this passage all true Christians are waiting for Christ in His second coming."[308]

9.25 'Again and again' points to the importance of the singular unrepeated and unrepeatable event. To celebrate this as a sacrifice is sacrilege; To celebrate it as a new covenant is a message and relationship in constant need of renewal. Historians seek patterns, repetitions, similarities, analogies and genre to explain events. Here is a singular event of meaning in and of itself. College NIV Commentary summarizes: "Christ is not forced to leave and return again for he is able to remain in God's presence. The difference is in the blood. Each former priest had entered with blood "not his own," a description which echoes the statement of v. 12 that Christ "entered the Most Holy Place once for all by his own blood" and anticipates the statement in v. 26 that "he has appeared once for all at the end of the ages to do away with sin by the sacrifice of himself."[309] The finality or once for all sacrifice has already been offered on the heavenly altar and accepted for all mankind. But the exhortations of the book stress that response and receiving the gifts and graces and so continuing in the faith is part and parcel of forgiveness, deliverance and cleansing.

9.26 'At the end of the ages' depends on how many ages are involved. The seven ages of dispensationalism has some connection to both Archbishop Usher's chronology and Jewish dating of universal history. The culmination of history was subsequently modified to include an era of millennium, but nothing specific for an era following that except for a new heaven and new earth. Grether notes "In the Hebrew Scriptures usually in the sense of the age of a person or of people. In this sense it renders a number of terms or expressions in Hebrew. While this meaning also is found in theGospel, much more often there it is used in the sense of one or both of the two ages of the world, as conceived in late Jewish thought. This meaning is found in expressions such as "this age," "the present age," "the end of the age," and "that age," "the age to come."Herbert G. Grether ABD Christ did not suffer and identify with the Tanakh sacrifices from the time of Adam's clothing, Abel's blood and Noah's whole burnt offering. They pointed to the one and only sacrifice made by Christ alone. He has appeared once for all to do away with sin by the sacrifice of himself. In the argument the purpose to do away with sins must not be stretched into an historical process since that diminishes from the one sacrifice and what it alone accomplished. This was accomplished and is complete. This portion of Hebrews says nothing about application or process, but only the completed and all-sufficient sacrifice. The allusion to history does not assume that the Son had come many times in history in one way or another but without offering himself except in this one time. The antithesis of past offerings and the self-offering of the Son is maintained by symbol and reality or shadow versus substance.

'many times.' [310]The parallel between OT and NT references to sacrifice is not one on one, nor between heavenly and earthly or shadow or form with reference to reality. The parallel is between historical fact and an extensive period of the sacrificial institution versus the one-time coming of Christ, who put away sin by the sacrifice of himself, a never-to-be- repeated event. Those speaking of a heavenly repetition of the event or who make it repeated in the Eucharist are failing to see the contrast of historical-process versus the historical-crisis. The singular, unique, event, can only be studied by historians, by analogies in other societies or events, and by classifications that cancel out the myriad of factors that make the solitary event unique. There is no method for studying the single event or a single unique event with the result in denial or refusal to believe it was unique. But to a lesser extent all events are unrepeatable, since science alone by means of methodology and controls can approach the control of factors and demonstrate a theory or law by means of a controlled re-enactment. But outside of the lab this is impossible. Humans only can be aware of some of the factors entering in to a given event. But this event coupled with divine revelation makes it unique to all of history so that all classifications or analogies fail, twn aiwnwn is an unusual genitive, but since the construct state omits the article Matthew does not use it. It occurs 5 times in Matthew[311] in sunteleia aiwnov Matt 13.39. [312] This is not necessarily dispensationalism as understood today, but at least includes the Antedeluvian Period and the Post-Deluvian Period. According to the covenants, perhaps sevent exist that might correspond to Aeons. A plural of majesty makes it simply the culmination that corresponds to the 'foundation of the earth.' Nor is there a concept of Transmigration or mere cyclical view of history. Jesus divided time periods into pre-John and Pst-John the Baptist leading into the kingdom of God. Daniel spke of four periods leading to an End Time and the Kingdom of God. The precise background for ths might be Ecclesastes 3 where 'olam is time eternally past and eternally future. This is not 'Days of the Son of man' that prophets desired to see.

9.27 Man is destined to die once corresponds to Jesus dying once and this hasn't changed. Nothing is said that death is due to sin or that some will be transfigured to heaven without death. The second destiny is the judgment for all men. In abab structure Christ's second coming corresponds to the judgment.v.28 , could nekra erga refer to the evil yetser inclination? II Esdras 7.128 'if he is defeated' and 'if he is victorious' can refer to the good impulse or inclination. Sir 15.14-17 "God from the beginning created man, and put him in the hand of his despoiler, and gave him into the hand of his inclinations. If you desire [to do so] you can keep the commandment, and it is understanding to do his delight; if you have confidence in Him, you will live." Myers,[313]240; The judgment "they must die" was issued in Gen 2-3 and II Esdras 8.58 Isa 22.13; Wisd.Sol 2.5f; 1 Cor 15.22; Rom 8.13; and here. In the OT many scriptures basically refer to physical death alone. Spiritual death is alluded to in Eph 2.1-4. Eternal death then needs a definition lest it become cessation of existence, which would be no punishment at all. Myers,[314]247,325

9.28 Spicq contrasts two possible meanings in this verse [see 12.26]: "Hapax usually is given the sense of once for all' in Heb 9.28; 1 Pet 3.18--Christ offered himself and died one single time for sins, and it is indeed true that this oblation was perfect and unique, so that there is no need for it to be renewed. But if this translation suggests the definitive quality of Christ's sacrifice, it does not sufficiently emphasize that it is absolute, complete; it takes hapax too exclusively as an adverb of quantity and inadequately reflects the word's etymology. Hapax may be an old nominative whose root is found in pegnymi 'to fasten by driving well in, to drive into the ground, fasten by assembling, fix by compacting, soidifying, crystallizing, jelling, being congealed."[315] "This quality of 'compactness' seems to be retained in Jos Ant.12.109 hapax...eis aei diamene2 18.172; and the papyri where an initial act includes its effects. In AD 54, when the prefect of Egypt, L. Lucius Geta, wrote that his orders and decisions had been formulated once, he means that they always remain binding and mst be applied by everyone everywhere just as on the first day. In a contract for a nurse, dating to 21 May 26:'When the year is up Paapis will pay her once for all 60 silver drachmas for the second year' P.Rein.103,14. 'Here eis hapax means not just 'one time only' but 'entirely, completely'; the sum will be paid in full. On the theological plane, to say that the sacrifice of Christ is 'compact' would mean that it includes all of its effects (and its commemorations?), like the spirng which contains potentially the whole river." Note in the OT that the covenant is one with Abraham, one with Israel, and with Levi and David, perpetually, and even after the nation is destroyed God still honors all the relationship and promises that were part of it, only that they can only be fulfilled on a future generation. It is the unique events, the miracles, that historians can't accept because they have few analogies, and scientists can't accept because they are not repeatable. But Paul in 1 Cor 12 asserts that all Israel participated in the Red Sea, of very generation, and in the same sense every NT believer participated in Christ's death and resurrection. [316] Christ came and will come again and no more. 'To bring salvation' remains future and is only for 'those who are waiting for him.' Does this apply to the many Jews who still look for the Messiah zealously even though he has already come and some of these may have rejected the Gospel message? In context the fact of atonement forms the ground of the waiting and the salvation. Much depends on what waiting means here. If the Tanakh word qawah is the background then hope, expectation, anticipation, looking and longing are all involved. the antithesis of the first coming of Christ as sin bearer or atonement for sin is with the second coming where He comes to bring salvation to those waiting for him. We look back at a finished work, but ahead for a full salvation. Nothing defines what the latter means in this book. Usually it includes a resurrection body, glorification, deliverance from weaknesses and an ugly environment, Satan, and evil men. Also is deliverance from the scars of sin and earthly existence including ignorance. The Second Coming will have nothing to do with bearing sin, but to bring salvation. The issue of sin and the issue of people are two issues not one. Nothing is said of what this salvation entails, but can be gleaned from the whole book. Isa 53.12 The connection with Isa 53 is brief declaring Christ came the first time was to bear the sins of many. In Isa 53 'our transgressions' is Israel. He 'was offered' is the sacrificial asham of that chapter. The second coming is 'to bring salvation'. Ths term is not used in Isa 53 or in Hebrews elsewhere. Most of the language is about redemption or atonement-reconciliation. But in Isa he intercedes for them and in ch.52 his appearing is to sprinkle many nations. From this standpoint salvation is a future event for the nations. But if we gain peace v.5, are healed, are atoned for v.10, God is satisfied v.11, and men are justified v.11, is it only the 'dividing of the spoil v.12 that must be accomplished? Salvation theology is purported by the Jews to be a Johannine and Pauline invention without basis in the OT. But Matt 1.21 asserts his name shall be called 'Jesus'= Joshua, 'because he will save his people from their sins.' This reflects not only the OT Joshua, but the role of Judges as 'saviours'. For the LXX use see Hatch-Redpath II,1331. Anderson,339 for 'save' 184 times; 'salvation' 36 times; 'be saved' 21 times. The participle is used to express Savior'. The usage appears mostly in Former and Latter Prophets and Psalms. Salvation from sins is not clearly mentioned in the OT, but may be included in some verses from the Psalms [317] But the king's role was t save Matt 27.17; lk 19.38. In Phil 2.9-10 and Jude 25 'the only God, our Savior' reflects OT usage. Ezek 34.22; 36.29; Isa 35.4; 63.1; 49.6 includes purification from sins to the ends of the earth. Zech 9.9 proclaims liberty in Christ. [318]

Chapter Ten:

Christ's offering of self is greater:

God's Will, Covenant, House and Awesomeness

10.1 'The law is only a shadow of the good things that are coming, not the realities themselves. This criticism counters the eternity of the law doctrine and that it precisely represents the laws that is in heaven. One possibilities is that the law is past time and the coming realities are largely unrevealed and in an on-going continuum of God's sovereign in what God desires to do in the future. The fact that sacrifices are repeated yearly demonstrates those offering them were not 'perfect' but still felt guilty because they were. People would not make sacrifices once their consciences had been permanently cleansed. Was the doctrine of a priest proclaiming forgiveness at Mass and the doctrine that the Mass is a sacrifice an outgrowth of the fact that those people knew their sins had not permanently been cleansed away? "make perfect" is not the Day of Atonement only but mainly the individual worshipper in daily worship. The link to v.2 implies the need of a sense of incompleteness, of guilt or alienation that never was satisfactorily resolved. In this perspective 'fear of God' is definitely a fear motive and not just a reverence-worship motive. The residue of guilt and concern about acceptance by god can only create the attitude expressed in Heb 12 concerning the awesomeness of God. Psalms of lament almost always reflect a sense of guilt even when no particular sin is mentioned. According to Hebrews vis a vis Psalm 51 the NT grace does cleanse the conscience from dead works to serve the living and true God. This verse does not compromise the Father's Sovereignty and the "throne of the Majesty in heaven" as found in Ps 2. But it does go beyond the OT in that high priests were never seated with royalty. The double role of throne and priestly service is unique. This priest has no dstance to the Majesty, nor is the throne associated with a Mercy seat here. Speaking of eikwn Spicq uses Philo, Alleg.Interp 3.96 "God is the image of his shadow, called shadow' skia. 'Image' eikwn appears in Gen 1.26-27. In Herodotus eikwn is an 'image, effigy, representation' whether a painting, statue, or figure on a coin. [Herod 2.130] Philo says "before a shining mirror, Glauke arranged her hair, smiling at the lifeless image of her person' Plato says " What I call image is first of all shadows [tav skiav] then appearances that show themselves in the water and those that form on surfaces that are dense, atractive, and shiny, and every other representation of this sort." Spicq,1.413; 418n26.

"Make perfect" is not the Day of Atonement only but mainly the individual worshipper in daily worship. The link to v.2 implies the need of a sense of incompleteness, of guilt or alienation that never was satisfactorily resolved. In this perspective 'fear of God' is definitely a fear motive and not just a reverence-worship motive. The residue of guilt and concern about acceptance by god can only create the attitude expressed in Heb 12 concerning the awesomeness of God. Psalms of lament almost always reflect a sense of guilt even when no particular sin is mentioned. According to Hebrews vis a vis Psalm 51 the NT grace does cleanse the conscience from dead works to serve the living and true God. This verse does not compromise the Father's Sovereignty and the "throne of the Majesty in heaven" as found in Ps 2. But it does go beyond the OT in that high priests were never seated with royalty. The double role of throne and priestly service is unique. This priest has no dstance to the Majesty, nor is the throne associated with a Mercy seat here. Speaking of <u>eikwn</u> Spicq uses Philo, Alleg.Interp 3.96 "God is the image of his shadow, called shadow' skia. 'Image' <u>eikwn</u> appears in Gen 1.26-27. In Herodotus eikwn is an 'image, effigy, representation' whether a painting, statue, or figure on a coin. [Herod 2.130] Philo says "before a shining mirror, Glauke arranged her hair, smiling at the lifeless image of her person' Plato says " What I call image is first of all shadows [<u>tas skias</u>] then appearances that show themselves in the water and those that form on surfaces that are dense, atractive, and shiny, and every other representation of this sort." Spicq,1.413; 418n26

'Only a shadow of things that are coming, not the realities.' This stands in contrast to the heavenly altar and sanctuary which are based upon the past and continuing heaven-earth parallels. But this is not a copy of the heavenly but only a shadow iof the future realities. Why can the law be only an imperfect copy of the heavenly and only a shadow of the future reality? Does this mean the Jewish concept of the law as being eternal before creation and to eternity means the future laws of the universe are still unknown? The 'good things to come' imply that either the future is not related to 'The Law' or else pertain to altogether different domains. The intent to show that in a sense the good things have arrived. Note 'good things' is Matthew's(Matt 7.11)version of the answer to prayer as opposed to Luke's where' Holy Spirit' is substituted. (Lk 11.13). The 'Age to come' has begun. The laws are not the realities and stand in opposition to the 'Will of God' which brings in the new reality and accomplishes salvation within.

'Make Perfect' is the motivation of the worshipper in the OT. In that context the Psalms of Lament reflect a wide range of the worshippers frm 1. sin and uncleanness in Ps 51; to 2. healing; 3. rescue from death; 4. from enemies; 5. from fear, guilt, shame; 6. from questions and doubts etc. But very seldom are the prayers reaching a break-through.Even then the problems still exist but no longer bother the worshipper. The vows and praise are confidence in God but seldom involve a deliverance. But life has recurring problems. So there are recurring sacrifices as part of worship and seeking God.

10.2 Sacrifices and offerings centering in a priest, sacred location, fixed calendar celebrations, a theology of sin reiterated in a multitude of different offerings and procedures all go to create a dependency on them and enhance the sense of sin and shame. The text reflects the first century CE. In the OT the pattern was different, the tendency rather to add foreign religious customs to guarantee fecundity and productivity, rain, children, security and blessing. Thus popular religion abandoned centralized singleminded worship with its focus on sin and restoration and sought out blessing through local acts of worship. 'Blessing' is a wisdom motif and villages had wisdom personnel. Wisdom, as in Ecclesiastes does mention temple and sacrifice and is not strongly influenced by the worship of 'YHWH. Still after Ezra's time the focus on sin returned and dependency on worship as obedience to the Law and avoidance of sin. If this society felt their conscience completely cleansed and righteousness confirmed they truly might have conceived some other form of worship. The latter did happen as soon as the temple was destroyed.

10.3 "annual remembrance of sins" contrasts to "once for all." V.10. What the offerings did was to provide a united public and authorized means to act out reliance on mercy and grace. Paul would speak of the role of the law to lead to grace and convince of sin. The text here makes the Day of Atonement a reminder, while in the OT it is an atonement of people and things comprehensibly including everything connected with worship of God. The worship component seems to be missing, while in Hebrews it is not, since in Heb 13 and ch.2 church worship and OT worship are contrasted stressing that worship itself has been transformed. Men are commanded to remember, the worship mode aided in this, because as Stephen's sermon shows God calls to mind all the sins of the past each time they again slip into sins. God remembers but also can intentionally 'forget.'

10.4 'Because' gives the reason for the annual 'reminders'. The sentence is gnomic or timeless in proverbial sense, that it is 'impossible' for sacrifices to take away sins' What then did sacrifices accomplish besides reminding people of sin? Does this apply to the Lord's Supper? Is the latter a reminder of sin? Or, has the church made it function in this way? Or does the Lord's Supper celebrate and communicate deliverance from sin by grace not sacrifice/ Wesley took the sacrament stance. The answer Hebrews gives is that Christ offered himself once fr all time to take away sins by the sacrifice of himself. This cannot be repeated. Or, is it repeated whenever communion is held? Isa 1.16 denies that God accepts worship and sacrifices and places the getting rid of sins and stains on the ground of thoroughgoing repentance and change alone. V.18 is a promise only fulfilled in the NT through the blood of Calvary. The sentence is gnomic or timeless in proverbial sense, that it is 'impossible' for sacrifices to take away sins' What then did sacrifices accomplish besides reminding people of sin? Does this apply to the Lord's Supper? Is the latter a reminder of sin? Or, has the church made it function in this way? Or does the Lord's Supper celebrate and communicate deliverance from sin by grace not sacrifice/ Wesley took the sacrament stance. The answer Hebrews gives is that Christ offered himself once fr all time to take away sins by the sacrifice of himself. This cannot be repeated. Or, is it repeated whenever communion is held? Isa 1.16 denies that God accepts worship and sacrifices and places the getting rid of sins and stains on the ground of thoroughgoing repentance and change alone. V.18 is a promise only fulfilled in the NT through the blood of Calvary. Clearly context is everything.4 In the NT, almost all the occurrences are religious, and we should compare our text closely with the response of Jesus to the problem of the salvation of the rich and of everyone: "with humans this is impossible, but with God all things are possible" (para anthropois touto adynaton estin, para de theo panta dynata).5 Or again: "It is impossible that the blood of bulls and goats should obliterate sins" (Heb 10:4) or that one could be pleasing to God without faith (11.6), because such is the providential disposition of the economy of salvation.6 In the case of apostates, it is not stated that they will not be pardoned, but they are denied the possibility of reforming themselves and repenting, given their spiritual bearing and the nature of their sin: having rejected God, after having seen the light of the faith, they are psychologically incapable of making another about-face; that would be contradictory to their apostate condition.7 The best parallel is perhaps Philo: "It is not easy, and perhaps even impossible, for a defiant spirit to be educated."8 Certainly, that which is impossible for humans is possible for God,9 and the whole gospel bears witness that divine initiative can change the spiritual condition of apostates, bring to them to a light and a power that will destroy the aforementioned impossibility.10 But on the one hand the context emphasizes the seriousness of the crime—"crucifying for themselves the Son of God and holding him up for public ridicule"—in order to conclude that such a soul is "rejected and close to destruction; its end is to be burned" (verse 8); on the other hand, it seems that this sin of apostasy can be assimilated to the sin against the light and the blasphemy against the Holy Spirit, which is forgiven neither in this world nor in the one to come.11. Spicq 5 Matt 19:26; Cf. . Mark 10:27; Luke 18:27. Salvation is beyond the power of humans; the inability of the creature is radical; God must intervene; Cf. . Rom 8:3—that which was impossible for the law, because it was without power, God has accomplished. Josephus, War 2.390: without God's help, it is impossible that such a vast empire could have been established. Spicq 6 On the other hand, "it is impossible for God to lie" (Heb 6:18) is an absolute impossibility which allows of no exception;[319]: "It is impossible that the gods should lose their incorruptibility"; Cf. . 104: "In pairs of opposites, it is impossible for one term to exist without the other[320] "it is impossible, even for a god, to escape destiny."[321] It has been taken in the softened sense of a great difficulty (Nicolas of Lyra, Erasmus); in the Middle Ages, theologians set aside the possibility of pardon after death[322] take this verse as a reference to the impossibility of receiving baptism again.[323]: "We cannot remain in Sicily without your concurrence").[324]: "It was impossible for him to continue his advance, because the land was crisscrossed with trenches"; 3.172; Cf. . Alcimus declaring to Demetrius that as long as Judas is alive it will be impossible to restore peace to the state (2Macc 14:10). The examples from Prov 30:18—to understand the course of the eagle in the sky or of the serpent on the rock—prove that adynaton is to be taken inits strict sense, even though it corresponds to the niphal of pala', "to be arduous, difficult." Spicq: 3 "Can a Cushite change his skin or a leopard its spots? And can you, who are addicted to doing evil, do good?"[325]: "Without obeying the laws of nature, nothing can last, not even for an instant"). To represent an impossible or implausible fact or action, one juxtaposes it with one or several natural impossibilities; this is comparison which lived on in the examples cited by Roman jurists of materially impossible conditions with respect to wills and stipulations. He distinguishes six kinds of impossibility, based on:

(1) powerlessness: a child cannot fight.:

(2) a condition ut in pluribus: a city locate on a mountain cannot be invisible;

(3) reason and propriety: the friends of the groom cannot fast while the groom is with them[326]: he saw the incapacity of his brother, who was supposed to succeed to the throne; War 7.144);

(4) the disposition of the will: at Nazareth, Jesus could not perform many miracles because of the unbelief of the people; he did not want to perform miracles;

(5) nature —but God can change nature: a camel entering through the eye of a needle (Cf. . Herodotus 1.32.39: "It isn't possible, so long as one is a human, to bring together all of the advantages of which I have spoken"; Josephus, Ant. 10.196);

(6) that which absolutely cannot be: that God should be evil, that two times two plus four should equal ten. We have to add scientific impossibility, as with a method that would not cover actual results Adunaton in the sense of "not powerful," "unable," "there is no means," is common in secular Greek, Cf. . Thucydides 1.32.5; 1.73.4.; 1.141.6.; 6.85.1; 6.12.2; 7.44; 7.64.1. Dio Cassius 1.114: "It is [psychologically] impossible for those who have not been raised with the same mores and who do not have the same ideas concerning evil and good to be united in friendship"; 45.26: "It is morally impossible that a person raised in such disorder and in such shamelessness should not ruin his life altogether"; 5.27; 55.14: "It is impossible to satisy the passions of the wicked"; 61.2, Domitius, father of Nero, talking about his wife Agrippina: "It is impossible for an honest man to be born to me and her." Philo, Alleg. Interp. 3.4: without allegory, the exegete cannot discover a valid meaning in the letter of a text; 3.10: humans are incapable of praising and thanking God adequately; Spec. Laws 1.32: of understanding God: "for some people doing good is impossible"; Change of Names 49: "It is not possible to wash and completely clean away the stains that soil the soul": those who are incapable of offering perfect sacrifices;: "I cannot pay on that which I have not sown."[327].

The Salvation of Israel: The hymn goes 'The Blood will never lose its power.' This is evident for the future as it was for Noah's generation. The New Covenant promises must be fulfilled for the whole house of Israel. "It has been observed that, in the age that is past, Jehovah's dealing with Israel's sins...was only a temporary covering of those sins, and that Christ in His death bore the judgment of those sins which Jehovah had before passed over;

but the final application of the value of Christ's death in behalf of Israel awaits the moment of her national conversion... It is then that, according to His covenant, Jehovah will 'take away' their sins. In Hebrews 10:4 it is stated that it is impossible that the blood of bulls and goats should 'take away' sin, and in Romans 11:27 it is promised that Israel's sins will yet be taken away... The induction to be drawn from these and other portions of Scripture is that Jehovah will yet in the future, in the briefest portion of time, and as a part of Israel's salvation, take away their sins... We conclude, therefore, that the nation Israel will yet be saved and her sins removed forever through the blood of Christ."[328](6)

"Can a Cushite change his skin or a leopard its spots? And can you, who are addicted to doing evil, do good?"[329] "Without obeying the laws of nature, nothing can last, not even for an instant").[330] To represent an impossible or implausible fact or action, one juxtaposes it with one or several natural impossibilities; this is comparison[331] (.), which lived on in the examples cited by Roman jurists of materially impossible conditions with respect to wills and stipulations,[332] "We cannot remain in Sicily without your concurrence"). Josephus, War 5.57: "It was impossible for him to continue his advance, because the land was crisscrossed with trenches"; 3.172; Cf. . Alcimus declaring to Demetrius that as long as Judas is alive it will be impossible to restore peace to the state (2Macc 14:10). The examples from Prov 30:18—to understand the course of the eagle in the sky or of the serpent on the rock—prove that adynaton is to be taken inits strict sense, even though it corresponds to the niphal of pala', "to be arduous, difficult."[333] Adunaton in the sense of "not powerful," "unable," "there is no means," is common in secular Greek, Cf. . Thucydides 1.32.5; 1.73.4.; 1.141.6.; 6.85.1; 6.12.2; 7.44; 7.64.1. Dio Cassius 1.114: "It is [psychologically] impossible for those who have not been raised with the same mores and who do not have the same ideas concerning evil and good to be united in friendship"; 45.26: "It is morally impossible that a person raised in such disorder and in such shamelessness should not ruin his life altogether"; 5.27; 55.14: "It is impossible to satisy the passions of the wicked"; 61.2, Domitius, father of Nero, talking about his wife Agrippina: "It is impossible for an honest man to be born to me and her." Philo, Alleg. Interp. 3.4: without allegory, the exegete cannot discover a valid meaning in the letter of a text; 3.10: humans are incapable of praising and thanking God adequately;[334]: "for some people doing good is impossible"; Change of Names 49: "It is not possible to wash and completely clean away the stains that soil the soul"[335]: those who are incapable of offering perfect sacrifices;[336]: "I cannot pay on that which I have not sown."[337] Spicq:7

Clearly context is everything—all inclusive In the NT, almost all the occurrences are religious, and we should compare our text closely with the response of Jesus to the problem of the salvation of the rich and of everyone: "with humans this is impossible, but with God all things are possible" (para anthropois touto adynaton estin, para de theo panta dynata).5 Or again: "It is impossible that the blood of bulls and goats should obliterate sins" (Heb 10:4) or that one could be pleasing to God without faith (11.6), because such is the providential disposition of the economy of salvation.6 In the case of apostates, it is not stated that they will not be pardoned, but they are denied the possibility of reforming themselves and repenting, given their spiritual bearing and the nature of their sin: having rejected God, after having seen the light of the faith, they are psychologically incapable of making another about-face; that would be contradictory to their apostate condition.v7 The best parallel is perhaps Philo: "It is not easy, and perhaps even impossible, for a defiant spirit to be educated."v8 Certainly, that which is impossible for humans is possible for God,v9 and the whole gospel bears witness that divine initiative can change the spiritual condition of apostates, bring to them to a light and a power that will destroy the aforementioned impossibility.v10 But on the one hand the context emphasizes the seriousness of the crime—"crucifying for themselves the Son of God and holding him up for public ridicule"—in order to conclude that such a soul is "rejected and close to destruction; its end is to be burned" (verse 8); on the other hand, it seems that this sin of apostasy can be assimilated to the sin against the light and the blasphemy against the Holy Spirit, which is forgiven neither in this world nor in the one to come.11 It has been taken in the softened sense of a great difficulty (Nicolas of Lyra, Erasmus); in the Middle Ages, theologians set aside the possibility of pardon after death (PeterLombard, Hugh of Saint Victor, Robert of Melun).[338] Almost all the Fathers, and recently A. Richardson[339] take this verse as a reference to the impossibility of receiving baptism again. On the other hand, "it is impossible for God to lie" (Heb 6:18) is an absolute impossibility which allows of no exception; Cf. . Philo, Etern. World 46: "It is impossible that the gods should lose their incorruptibility"; Cf. . 104: "In pairs of opposites, it is impossible for one term to exist without the other"; Herodotus 1.91.3: "it is impossible, even for a god, to escape destiny." Spicq 6. Salvation is beyond the power of humans; the inability of the creature is radical; God must intervene; Cf. . Rom 8:3—that which was impossible for the law, because it was without power, God has accomplished. Josephus, War 2.390: without God's help, it is impossible that such a vast empire could have been established. Spicq 5 Matt 19:26; Cf. . Mark 10:27; Luke 18:27. St.

Gregory of Nazianzus (Orations 30; PG 36.113–116) distinguishes six kinds of impossibility, based on;

(1) Powerlessness: a child cannot fight (Cf. . P.Lond. 971, 4: adunatos gar estin gune dia asqenian ths fusews, third-fourth century);

(2) A condition <u>ut in pluribus</u>: a city locate on a mountain cannot be invisible;

(3) reason and propriety: the friends of the groom cannot fast while the groom is with them (Josephus, Ant. 13.423: he saw the incapacity of his brother, who was supposed to succeed to the throne; War 7.144);

(4) The disposition of the will: at Nazareth, Jesus could not perform many miracles because of the unbelief of the people; he did not want to perform miracles;

(5) Nature —but God can change nature: a camel entering through the eye of a needle (Cf. . Herodotus 1.32.39: "It isn't possible, so long as one is a human, to bring together all of the advantages of which I have spoken"[340];

(6) That which absolutely cannot be: that God should be evil, that two times two plus four should equal ten.

(7) We have to add scientific impossibility, as with a method that would not cover actual results (Hippocrates, De Vetere Medicina 2.6; Cf. . Archimedes, On Spirals 16.9; 17.27; The Equilibriums of Planes 6; The Sand-reckoner 1, etc.; numerous examples in C. Mugler, Terminologie géométrique, pp. 41ff.). Spicq: 4

10.5 'A body you have prepared for me.,' Transmigrationists or re-incarnationists would read this one way of the babe, while the body could also be Mary's. But it is the body of Christ that is offered once for all not Mary's in this context. The miracle of the incarnation cannot be reduced to eastern belief in pre-existence of all souls and reincarnation of all life forms into other life forms. The only case of a preexistent person entering humanity for the first time occurs in the Christmas story. Is the context of past and present wonders and miracles tending toward the future and thus imply a prayer. V.5-6 and God's response in v.7-8 show no clear indication that God's response ends on v.8. If v.9-10 are the -pre-existing Christ's continuing response till v.10, then the forthrightness of Christ's public ministry in synagogue and temple on the subject of righteousness v.9 and the dialogue with the Father assert a message of faithfulness and salvation. V.10 deals with a message of God's love and truth. Then is v.11 the worshipper's response to the divine dialogue much as Isaiah 6 shows Isaiah's response to the antiphonal words of the Seraphim. A body you prepared form me. This must not be read apart from the Gospels and God's preparation of Mary, which is based on similar situations for Sarah, Rebecca, Manoah's wife, Hannah and others. If the 'body' is Jesus' own body the question of trasnmigration occurs, or that Christ as pure Spirit at the point of conception entered the human fetus. But Church Councils rejected this early on. The body is prepared for 'me' namely Christ and hence the parallel to the preceding line is incomplete, since that is the sacrifice offered to God. But then in v.16 it is this body sacrificed that makes men holy v.10. Ps 40.6-8. 'A body' is not transmigration into an earthly body, but the body of Mary. But this interpretation is disconnected from v.6 and the context that has to do with a sacrificial body. If at the moment of conception the soul/spirit is created in ordinary people, couldn't it be rhat at conception trhe 'I' of v.7 entered the fertilized egg and this plus the fertilized egg made up the person of Christ? V.5, seems to refer to body, soul and spirit. Cf. . Ps 40.6-8 in the LXX. Is the context of past and present wonders and miracles tending toward the future and thus imply a prayer. V.5-6 and God's response in v.7-8 show no clear indication that God's response ends on v.8. If v.9-10 are the -pre-existing Christ's continuing response till v.10, then the forthrightness of Christ's public ministry in synagogue and temple on the subject of righteousness v.9 and the dialogue with the Father assert a message of faithfulness and salvation. V.10 deals with a message of God's love and truth. Then is v.11 the worshipper's response to the divine dialogue much as Isaiah 6 shows Isaiah's response to the antiphonal words of the Seraphim. A body you prepared form me. This must not be read apart from the Gospels and God's preparation of Mary, which is based on similar situations for Sarah, Rebecca, Manoah's wife, Hannah and others. If the 'body' is Jesus' own body the question of trasnmigration occurs, or that Christ as pure Spirit at the point of conception entered the human fetus. But Church Councils rejected this early on. The body is prepared for 'me' namely Christ and hence the parallel to the preceding line is incomplete, since that is the sacrifice offered to God. But then in v.16 it is this body sacrificed that makes men holy v.10. Ps 40.6-8. Because of this this body' hardly is Mary's

10.6 In the OT such language that God is not pleased with offerings and sacrifices is because of injustices or social sins, and usually not because of the offerings in and of themselves. Compare Isa 1.10-17 In Isa 1.12 'Who asked this of you?' seems to deny that the arrangement set up by Moses included burnt offerings and blood. If v.12 and 11 are separated, then the reactin of God in this paragraph is because He has had enough of them and he cannot bear any more. 'I am weary bearing them' indicates the sacrifices in themselves cannot please God. But v.12 may refer to the offering of blood that Moses never institutionalized. The blood was to be sprinkled on people and holy things, poured out at the base of the altar, shot against its side, and essentially was never offered as a wave offering or on the altar. But now in Hebrews the interpretation is that the whole system cannot please God. has God grown or matured, or is the repetitive nature of ritual together with its ineffectualness in bringing people closer to God the real reason. Has the object lesson or the ritual education program not only failed in its purpose but really become a burden? Another possibility is that in a time of wealth, as in Uzziah's times, there was little trust and dependency on God. This is proven by the next kings as international pressures cause not a drawing closer to God but an all-out effort to use the world's ways to solve political crises. Find other texts critical of sacrifices in Amos and Micah.. In the OT such language that God is not pleased with offerings and sacrifices is because of injustices or social sins, and usually not because of the offerings in and of themselves. Compare Isa 1.10-17 In Isa 1.12 'Who asked this of you?' seems to deny that the arrangement set up by Moses included burnt offerings and blood. If v.12 and 11 are separated, then the reactin of God in this paragraph is because He has had enough of them and he cannot bear any more. 'I am weary bearing them' indicates the sacrifices in themselves cannot please God. But v.12 may refer to the offering of blood that Moses never institutionalized. The blood was to be sprinkled on people and holy things, poured out at the base of the altar, shot against its side, and essentially was never offered as a wave offering or on the altar. But now in Hebrews the interpretation is that the whole system cannot please God. has God grown or matured, or is the repetitive nature of ritual together with its ineffectualness in bringing people closer to God the real reason. Has the object lesson or the ritual education program not only failed in its purpose but really become a burden? Another possibility is that in a time of wealth, as in Uzziah's times, there was little trust and dependency on God. This is proven by the next kings as international pressures cause not a drawing closer to God but an all-out effort to use the world's ways to solve political crises. Find other texts critical of sacrifices in Amos and Micah. In the OT such language that God is not pleased with offerings and sacrifices is because of injustices or social sins, and usually not because of the offerings in and of themselves

10.7,9 'In the scroll' would be the Psalms not the heavenly Tablets of Destinies. The scroll is the inspired authority, not the author, and the words cited by Jesus were the words spoken by Him. 'I have come to do your will, O God' For the Son to use the expression 'O God' is not hard to accept in view to His submission to the Father of spirits and the words used on the cross 'My God.' Actually Stern notes Ps 40 reads differently:" Sacrifice and meal-offering Thou hast no delight in; Mine ears has Thou opened; Burnt-offering and sin offering hast Thou not required. Then I said: 'Lo, I am come with the scroll of a book which is prescribed for me; I delight to do thy will, O my God.' [JPS reading]. Ps 40.8 'I am now coming' or 'I come'hkw expresses the performative use of perfect and first person, a personal deliberative statement of choice that is acted upon in the act of stating it. 'a body you have prepared for me' in Greek is 'to mend, restore, create, strengthen.' Since v.10 refers to this body as the sacrifice v.5 replacing the types of sacrifices usually offered.

'The scroll' almost corresponds to the pre-existent Tablets of Destinies or the Eternal Torah. Here Jesus is obeying and volunteering for a task to do the will of God. This utter abandonment to God for total obedience is the real worship and corresponds to what is 'perfect.' But does this scenario take place in heaven before creation or just before the birth of Jesus when the 'scroll' of the Scriptures already existed. In this sense Jesus offered Himself, the Lamb offered from the foundation of the World, and intentionally to fulfill the predictions and words of Ps 40.6-8. Schonfield, The Passion Plot, operates on a thesis that most of Jesus words and actions and experiences were not lone happenings but all involved personal intentionality to fulfill what was written.[341]

10.8 The Son is speaking to God v.7, and declares that 'Sacrifices and offerings, burnt offerings and sin offerings you did not desire, nor were you pleased with them(although the law required them to be made)." This conversation between God the son and the Father took place late in the prophetic period after the law was in effect, not at creation. The prophets had oracles to the same effect. Were sacrifices only of heuristic value from the beginning and like the law of divorce was a condescension to the sinfulness of man? 'Which were being offered according to law' NIV read 'which were prescribed'. The lack of a definite article on nomon is unclear unless read 'legally' or 'according to torah' open-ended for the instruction of scriptures and oral tradition. Still of the 14 occurrences of nomoV in Hebrews those in phrases are still definite and once defined as 'law of Moses.' So here is an antithesis between the Law of Moses and the Will of God. To do what the written will of God commands may not fulfill the actual will of God, since the latter has to do with a relationship. Judaism and Pauline faith both concerned pleasing God and doing his will but the former identified this with fulfilling traditional applications of a limited number of crucial cultural observances, not total response to the living God who is now ruling. They considered what was written as the total will of God and thus had supplanted God Himself as the focus of the desire to please. In this way the desire to please men and appear pious to men replaced Good as the true object of love and piety. God's desire and v.9 God's will are two different entities. The first is the ideal and appears in Isaiah 1, where the sacrificial system is not cancelled by God's will but is not what he desires. But in Amos God's will declares punishments one after another that, through, petition, are cancelled. Finally the heavy punishments are announced and no alleviation is allowed. So even God's will is subject to the circunstances of human repentance or seeking in prayer. The contradiction is 'the law required' and' you weren't pleased'. In Isaiah 1, Amos and Micah the resolution usually adopted by scholarship is that those who offered the sacrifices were not sincere and repentant and society as a whole was included in the scope of God's non-acceptance of sacrifices, not that there was a radical discrepency per se. The other resolution is that of Jesus in speaking about divorce, that God permitted divorce due the hardness of their hearts. The question really is what Isaiah, Amos and Micah really meant; did they intend to state that God rejected the whole system per se? If so He was preparing them for the cessation of altar and temple worship in the Exile, and so the words must be taken in a Book-Period context only and not literally. But here the whole system is suspect. Does God authorize and require what he cannot be pleased with as an interim measure? The answer is yes! The contrast is with the one and only offering, the Son, that can please God. So the suggestion is dispensational and not a principle to understand God's ways in a broader sense as to authorize what He did not accept in the first place. But God allowed the census of David and then punished him. God "granted their request but sent leanness to their souls." Why require sacrifices when "God does not want them? Is this God's condescension to human weakness as illustrated in Jesus words about Moses' allowing divorce, because of the weakness of the flesh? The OT explains as sins wilfully done and the plea for mercy. Cf. . Mic 6.6-8. This does not cte the law, v.6, but asks questions about valid worship including child sacrifice v.7. By contrast and in answer is the revelation to 'everyman' 'what is good' corresponds to Gen 1, the original state of creation. 'Act justly, love mercy, and walk humbly with your God'. Here is no mention of blood, sacrifices or atonement. Or, is what is 'good' of a higher order than what God requires or of a different genre? The 'justly' or 'do justice' answers to the legal-moral sphere. "Love mercy" encompasses love of people that motivates one to make exceptions to the rigours of legalese. Then 'to walk humbly' recalls Amos' words about two walking together by agreement, appointment and covenant relationship along with 'with God' taking us into the context of Enoch 'who walked with God.'. Clearly the OT in many ways shines light on 586 and A.D. 70 in the ending of temple and sacrificial worship, so much so, that Jewish thought has now substituted study of Torah or the doing of good for the offering of sacrifices. , in a parenthesis, contrasts what the law required and the will of God. God's will did not desire sacrifice, but His law required it. On a higher level the law did not and could not require Christ to die for everyman. But raising the ante Jesus tells the Father, 'Lo I come to do your will O God.' The Jews, by limiting God's will to the written and oral traditions [plus their interpretations] were limiting the person of God. God is sovereign even over his revealed will. The law was old and established but a point was reached in Micah, Isaiah 1 and Amos that God rejects sacrifice. The ultimate rejection is the exile and in 70 AD the destruction of the temple. God is sovereign by making a substitution for the old law in the person of his son, not a new law. God's desire and v.9 God's will are two different entities. The first is the ideal and appears in Isaiah 1, where the sacrificial system is not cancelled by God's will but is not what he desires. But in Amos God's will declares punishments one after another that, through, petition, are cancelled. Finally the heavy punishments are announced and no alleviation is allowed. So even God's will is subject to the circumstances of human repentance or seeking in prayer. The contradiction is 'the law required' and' you weren't pleased'. In Isaiah 1, Amos and Micah the resolution usually adopted by scholarship is that those who offered the sacrifices were not sincere and repentant and society as a whole was included in the scope of God's non-acceptance of sacrifices, not that there was a radical discrepency per se. The other resolution is that of Jesus in speaking about divorce, that God permitted divorce due the hardness of their hearts. The question really is what Isaiah, Amos and Micah really meant; did they intend to state that God rejected the whole system per se? If so He was preparing them for the cessation of altar and temple worship in the Exile, and so the words must be taken in a Book-Period context only and not literally. But here the whole system is suspect. Does God authorize and require what he cannot be pleased with as an interim measure? The answer is yes! The contrast is with the one and only offering, the Son, that can please God. So the suggestion is dispensational and not a principle to understand God's ways in a broader sense as to authorize what He did not accept in the first place. But God allowed the census of David and then punished him. God "granted their request but sent leanness to their souls." Reflecting a historical progression in the OT it would appear that God decreed the sacrificial system but that only in a sinning society with concomitant 'pious' acts of worship was there a final rejection of sacrifice and not immediately. The end of the city of Jerusalem and temple was one juncture, and this was repeated in 70 AD before the sacrificial system ceased and acts of study, alms, etc substituted for sacrifice. But according to this text the pre-carnate Son said these words of recognizing the heart of the Father. The text doesn't say when these words were said to God, whether before creation, or in the junctures of history, or at the omment of the incarnation. The latter fits such a narrative the best. Why require sacrifices when "God does not want them? Is this God's condescension to human weakness as illustrated in Jesus words about Moses' allowing divorce, because of the weakness of the flesh? The OT explains as sins wilfully done and the plea for mercy. Cf. . Mic 6.6-8. This does not cte the law, v.6, but asks questions about valid worship including child sacrifice v.7. By contrast and in answer is the revelation to 'everyman' 'what is good' corresponds to Gen 1, the original state of creation. 'Act justly, love mercy, and walk humbly with your God'. Here is no mention of blood, sacrifices or atonement. Or, is what is 'good' of a higher order than what God requires or of a different genre? The 'justly' or 'do justice' answers to the legal-moral sphere. "Love mercy" encompasses love of people that motivates one to make exceptions to the rigours of legalese. Then 'to walk humbly' recalls Amos' words about two walking together by agreement, appointment and covenant relationship along with 'with God' taking us into the context of Enoch 'who walked with God.'. Clearly the OT in many ways shines light on 586 and A.D. 70 in the ending of temple and sacrificial worship, so much so, that Jewish thought has now substituted study of Torah or the doing of good for the offering of sacrifices., in a parenthesis, contrasts what the law required and the will of God. God's will did not desire sacrifice, but His law required it. On a higher level the law did not and could not require Christ to die for everyman. But raising the ante Jesus tells the Father, 'Lo I come to do your will O God.' The Jews, by limiting God's will to the written and oral traditions [plus their interpretations] were limiting the person of God. God is sovereign even over his revealed will. The law was old and established but a point was reached in Micah, Isaiah 1 and Amos that God rejects sacrifice. The ultimate rejection is the exile and in 70 AD the destruction of the temple. God is sovereign by making a substitution for the old law in the person of his son, not a new law.. 'God not pleased' is said of the offerings here so we judge Cain and Abel's sacrifices' differences were crucial as were their attitude and motivation and surrender to God's response. Only the perfect human being who is also God could offer the totally acceptable sacrifice and do it from the right attitde and motivation.

10.9 'He set aside the first to establish the second.' There are no multiple eras or covenants in this line of thought, but only two, the first and second. The First is put aside in order to have the second one. The 'He' should be the speaker in the preceding sentence, the Messiah. Similarly, in Samuel's ministry he could not conceive of setting aside the Theocracy of a Confederation of twelve tribes for a monarchy and wherever and whatever that would lead to. But God does set aside systems and supplant [Jacob] them. 'He sets aside the first' is the system of sacrifices, namely the present religious establishment. When was this done? Was it before creation? Or was it just before the incarnation took place? Or is this the logical conclusion by the author to what the scriptures record as the commitment of the Son to do God's will? The message of this author is therefore the use of the quotation from David to declare to the first century church and Judaism that the sacrificial system was already set aside regardless of whether the destruction of the temple had occurred or not. The quote here is said to be events immediately subsequent. 'Here I am, I have come to do your will.' Then 'He sets aside' the sacrificial system in order to establish the will of God. This 'He' is God. The will of God is living and dynamic not legalistic and a mere compilation of case laws. The reference to 'law' in v.8 could be a parenthesis and comment for the reader. If not, the contrast is of 'the law' or torah with God's will. The requirement is thus replaced by the self-offering of the Son of God. This establishes the second, which is one sacrifice once for all.

10.10 'by the body'. This is not Pauline theology where the body is the church. But in what sense is Christ's body redemptive. There are 253 occurrences of 'body' in the Bible. Which verse provides background for Heb 10.10 and which verse is illuminated most by this verse here? Isa 53.12 Isa 53 speaks of God's will as sanctifying once for all since it is God's will that is satisfied with the offering made. But Isa 53 focuses on the person not merely the body "He poured out his soul to death' and endured suffering beyond measure. The actual focus is on the offering of himself not on 'body' per se. This once for all sanctfication corresponds to the faith that is found in Rom 6 that all believers particpated in that one death and burial with resurrection, even as all Israel of every generation were baptized in the sea and in the cloud. 'day after day' includes 'every priest,' not only the High Priest. This is in contrast to 'This priest' v.12. The 'same sacrifices' contrasts to 'one sacrifice for sins', not for the person. In Ps 51.9 'to blot out my iniquity' interprets the 'Hebrew word kipper. Here the Psamist's self-awareness transcends the efficacy supposed for sacrificing v.10-12 and he declares that God does not delight in sacrifices v.16. the sacrifices of God are a broken spirit [plural not one sacrifice only]. But then v.18-19 speak of 'righteous sacrifices' and thus he is apparently holding on to the sacrificial system for worship not for redemption. His prayer is answered in Christ. But is the phrase possibly to be read 'sacrifices of Zadok?' But this would depend on re-installing a purified priesthood. If read as 'sacrifices of righteousness' the parallel does not allow taking them as equating a righteous lifestyle or works of beneficence as the equivalent to sacrfices, which is actually the thought, if not the interpretation of later Judaism. Does the above denial of the efficacy of sacrifices grow out of a situation in which there are no walls, structures, priesthood and sacrifices? 'day by day' stresses the monotony of sacrifice for the same sins, denying that real forgiveness or cleansing were ever obtained. The OT stresses the periodical festivals, whether in the agricultural calendar or in the monthly observances. Especially important is the Day of Atonement to take away and cleanse sins. Ps 51 clearly demonstrates that those sacrifices were not even suggested as a means to remove sins by David. The cry and hope is that God will do it directly and not through ritual, or else that something deep and spiritual will happen concomittantly with the ritual. 'never take away sins' summarizes the Hebrew Bible Period of Israel and beyond Israel since it is a principle. Exactly what then does the author suppose was the efficacy of sacrifices? The prophets declare their uselessness since the hearts of worshippers were hard and disobedient and so prayers and worship were rejected. The system encompassed the total religious life of Israel and should have excluded all else. This didn't happen because of centralized worship on one hand, assimilation to pagan peoples and their culture, and the failure of local elders, judges and levite leadership to provide justice and spiritual focus. The use of sacrifices was a pointer to the sacrificial lamb, opportunities for true worship, provision for needs of priests and levites, reminder that good acts don't redeem, only blood can, and remind the worshipper of his sins. It was an external prod that worked in tandem with tradition and conscience to urge Israelites to focus on God. When these became an end in themselves their function had already ceased. The continuity of the priesthood during the kingdom period and in the post-exilic period is not said to be continual ministry and service along with leadership in worship as things done by faith. But neither were these a matter of merit for salvation but obedience to the revealed will of God. If they are basically ineffectual and unpleasing to

God why did they continue except through faith that they were God's will? peri in emphasis, compound verb form: perielein amartias 'to take away sins completely.'[342] The sacrifice without the camp or the sending of the goat away from the camp or diisposal of ashes outside the camp all are to rid the camp of the pollutions of sin. If once for all the threat of backsliding is real until the church discovered that no one is unsavable.

10.11 The 'day by day' and 'religious duties' along with 'again and again' describe a drudgery but, more to point, the continuing nature of a commanded but ineffectual religious exercise for both priests and worshippers. The point wasn't lack of instruction, but the nature of the acts. Charles Finney instructed never tell a person to do what would leave him still unconverted. Senseless acts can be interpreted and an understanding gained that is truly spiritual, unless the act in itself had no present value except as a pointed to the future. Should these acts be done even without any use? If done the institution and priests with Levites could be maintained financially till the messiah came. But by putting faith in the institutions the same people would later reject the one and only Messiah.

10.12 Priests did not sit with kings, but here 'this priest ' did. Whereas Ps 68.18 corresponds to Heb 10.13, it goes one step further. The waiting period is over and the enemies have been reduced. Heb declares a time of waiting. V.18 declares 'you led captves in your train, you received gifts from/ for men, even from the rebellious, that you, O Lord God, might dwell there.' In the NT this is first said of the gift of the Spirit and the gifts of the Spirit and then of the ministers who have these gifts. In other texts this is connected with the 'ravishing of Hell' releasing souls there unto eternal salvation, The servant is to open blind eyes. "In the view of the faithful person, security is walking to God's light, that is, in conformity with his will.[343] 'Having offered once sacrifice for sins' his work as sacrifice is over because it is completed. But his work as high priest and king continues.

10.13 God is waiting: God and the Son Messiah along with believers of all ages continue to wait for final fulfillment. So Isa 40.31, where 'hope' or 'expectation' can also be translated 'wait' makes 'salvation by hope' a human and divine human as well as divine activity. The concept of the patience of man and God in waiting for the 'set time' or 'appropriate time' of Ecclesiastes ch.3 is a feature not studied in systematic theologies. We all acknowledge the time line but 'only the Father knows' may point more to sovereignty over events than simple foreknowledge. Qawah is one of those Hebrew significant words that point to history as the stage of divine action..Ps 110.1. God as a waiting one and Christ as a waiting one takes tarrying out of merely human and time-bound context. They are waiting for the church to preach the Gospel to every creature. While we wait in prayer for God to act, God is waiting and causing things to coordinate for that good pronounced at creation. Chronos does not limit God anymore than God's promises do. But 'everything must be done decently and in order' is a principle for church life and for God's dealings before the End. It is in times of judgment that chaos breaks loose when human systems and structures are terribly disrupted. God patience and endurance are to find a reflex in human patience as well.

10.14 'By one sacrifice...forever' parallels above in v.10 'through the body of Jesus Christ once for all'. Christ is the sacrifice here not only that he offered a sacrifice. This emphasizes the centrality of Christology and soteriology which depends on it. The one event in history 'makes perfect' a past completed event at the cross, and 'those who are being made holy' is the concommitant event in the heart happening on a continuing outpouring of grace. Thus 'perfect' and 'holy' are in parallelism. But one is completed and the other is not yet. Note that Job was perfect but man aspects of his life were not holy, especially his mouth, words, thoughts, feelings,reactions,hopes and especially his fears. But the cross of Job was making him holy by bringing more of him into a one to one relationship to God alone. The purpose of God in Job was not discipline or punishment but testing and proving to bring Job first to a mature faith, then a vision of the Almight, a redirection of his theology and a commitment to the Almighty sovereign. It is the one sacrifice that completes perfection for believers, who are described as 'being made holy.' They are perfect because of the blood, but not yet completely holy since the form of the verb is a process, but even this process is through the atonement. Jesus made them perfect. But God, expressed by the passive, is sanctifying believers. So the terms perfect and holy are not coextensive in usage. In 10.29 it is 'the blood of the covenant that sanctified him.' This is not the same concept since this making holy is already complete. As a matter of 'Religion' context there is a sociological matrix involved in sacrifices and bonding of people: "Encyclopedia of Religion, An Overview, Vol.1, p.66 Sacrifices are performed on a variety of occasions in seasonal, curative, life-crisis, divinatory, and other kinds of rituals, and always as isolable ritual sequences. Sacrifices that involve the sharing of the victim's flesh confirm the bond between the people and the spiritual power, to which a portion is given. Purifications may also be performed so that the participants may be cleansed of the potent sacred elements of the sacrifice. Major sacrificial rites usually have the following structure: consecration, invocation, immolation, communion, and purification. At the social level, sacrifices and offerings bring together individuals and groups and reinforce common moral bonds. Fundamentally, blood sacrifice is a reciprocal act, bringing gods and people together in a circuit of moral, spiritual, and social unity. In this way sacrifice restores moral and spiritual balance—the healthy equilibrium between person and person, group and group, human beings and spiritual powers—which permits the positive flow of life on earth. As a sacred gift of life to the gods, sacrifice atones for human misdeeds and overcomes the human impediments to the flow of life; thus it is one of the keystones of African religions." The African element may correspond to some elements in the Mosaic Period. 'By one sacrifice.' Is not genetic-unfolding in present time, a wrong analogy, but rather is the all encompassing efficacy of the Redemptive Atonement in Christ that encompasses the process of sanctifying every believer from now to eternity. In the OT God made people holy through laws that obeyed would separate them to God for a period of time, but the making holy must be done by the people. The contrast here in the NT period is that men are in the process of God making them holy This process is also missing in the OT.

10.15 'The Holy Spirit also testifies'. We have noted the Spirit's role as witness. But what does 'also' refer to? Either the actions of the priests or the human author behind the Psalm is the other witness. The structure of messages in Jeremiah show quotation supplemented by prophetic comment and exhortation. Both together constitute God's word. In Paul's thought 'The Spirit bears witness with our spirit/Spirit that we are the sons of God.' He does this through the word and inner guidance. So perhaps above the second rationale may be more objective. Even Psalms where the speaker is negative and lacks faith are witnesses to need that contrast with the fulness offered in the NT pages.

'I will put my laws in their hearts and write them on their minds.' The covenant is mentioned first as a collective covenant, one covenant. It has been predicted in Jeremiah so it is not 'new' but a fulfilling of prophecy and the original intent of believers' education from Moses onward. But the laws are a plural and must be written on each person's heart and mind. This is not only information, awareness, understanding, but a good tendency to believe and obey. The laws become part of human nature. This is not only the good tendency versus the evil tendency, since the Jeremiah and Ezekiel context is a transformation into obedience of life. The OT stressed 'remember' and 'do this in remembrance' in Sabath and Passover and other rituals. What is now remembered is the specifics and not merely cognitively but affectively, both heart annd mind. In psychological theory children are observed as growing when they talk to reach other saying' Mommy doesn't want you to do that' to 'don't do that, that's wrong. You shouldn't do that.' The social conscience become introjected and one's own.

10.16 The covenant is the internalized laws in hearts and minds Jer 31.33,34. The contrast of 'covenant' singular, and a new one, and 'my laws', apparently a given. The first is collective 'with them' and hence societal in span. The second, is individualized 'their [individual] hearts and minds'. The OT problem of the relationship of the covenant as a document and formal agreement with an outline structure and background in Hittite and Assyrian treaties, really can only be understood in terms of the function of the individual rules that form the 'stipulations' portion of the covenant. Apparently the covenant here is viewed as new but not the laws. But the very existence of two terms 'covenant' and 'laws' implies two separate distinct graces are bestowed. The analogy of the covenant is with the church, the new collective body of Christ. The analogy of the second is regeneration and sanctification so that the will of God becomes a very part of the human nature, both in heart and mind. Then v.17 is cited seemingly to indicate that forgiveness is based on transformation of the relationship to God and of the human nature. Peter calls this 'the engrafted word which is able to save your souls.'Jer 31.33,34. The contrast of 'covenant' singular, and a new one, and 'my laws', apparently a given. The first is collective 'with them' and hence societal in span. The second, is individualized 'their [individual] hearts and minds'. The OT problem of the relationship of the covenant as a document and formal agreement with an outline structure and background in Hittite and Assyrian treaties, really can only be understood in terms of the function of the individual rules that form the 'stipulations' portion of the covenant. Apparently the covenant here is viewed as new but not the laws. But the very existence of two terms 'covenant' and 'laws' implies two separate distinct graces are bestowed. The analogy of the covenant is with the church, the new collective body of Christ. The analogy of the second is regeneration and sanctification so that the will of God becomes a very part of the human nature, both in heart and mind. Then v.17 is cited seemingly to indicate that forgiveness is based on transformation of the relationship to God and of the human nature. For the laws, 'my laws', to be written on the heart the application must be even greater than the finger of God writing on the tablets of stone after first cutting and preparing those tablets. Congitive, affective, volitional and behavior therapy might assist but don't change one's basic nature and character. Wesley experienced this as a warm heart when suddenly God applied the truth to him and he realized he truly was forgiven through Christ alone. The prophecied act of God on Israelites, God's people, corresponds to an aspect of creation that was not done: God had used clay to form man and had breathed into him life, but had not used internalization by the Spirit of the laws of God. The beginning of history and its end correspond yet this is not a return to the beginning. The naming and classifying of things was necessary to understand moral right and wrong, but God did not make man's nature one that would automatically evaluate and obey, but only one that would evaluate and choose. This lack of determninism will make for a completed creation when the promises are fulfilled. But what of non-Israelites? Or is this a picture of Paul's conversion of all Israel mentrioned in Rom 9-11?

10.17 'Remember no more' is parallel to 'have been forgiven.' Similar usage is found in the Psalms. Jer 31.34; Heb 8.12. v.18 follows logically that sacrifices are no longer needed since sin has been purged. Jer. 31:34 No longer will a man teach his neighbor, or a man his brother, saying, 'Know the LORD,' because they will all know me, from the least of them to the greatest," declares the LORD. "For I will forgive their wickedness and will remember their sins no more." Heb. 8:12 For I will forgive their wickedness and will remember their sins no more."

10.18 Forgiveness in the NT sense means that any further sacrifice for sin is unnecessary, but serving people and the like are pleasing to God. The shift also took place in Judaism, from temple sacrifices to alms, called 'works of righteousness' or 'righteousnesses,' reading and study of the scripture, and other acts as substitutes. Most of this was necessitated by the destruction of the temple and state. But without accepting the sacrifice of Christ as full atonement there could be no coming to grips with accepting God's forgiveness or of extending and accepting forgiveness from people. Using the terminology Rom 12.1 makes the basic whole burnt offering the individual's body presented to God and the fire of the Spirit doing the medium of transformation into a form that is acceptable worship. NT books all urge the doing of good to all men and especially to those of the household of faith and the poor and distraught. 'No more sacrifice for sins' relates to a concluded transaction of forgiveness forever in a context of the actualization of the New Covenant where the laws are written in human nature. This phrase is also used in v.26, indicating that never again will any of the OT or similar corresponding sacrifices have anything to do with salvation, so it is useless to return to Judaism for salvation. This 'forgiveness' of individual and collective people of God follows from the new covenant in the heart. Does one forgiveness cover past, present and future and forever, just so they arei n the New Covenant? Is it like Rom 6 crucifixion, death and burial of Christ and the believer's participation in that one event in his own baptism? But v.22-23 speak of application of cleansing to the individual and a lively faith.What if they backslide? One writer suggested these Hebrews were Jews in relation to God not by faith in Christ but by virtue of fidelity to God, but the full assurance described is impossible apart from relation to Christ by faith.

10.19 'Have confidence' includes the writer and those readers, all are brothers, that is, believers. Cf. . Lev 16.2 'not to come' contrasts to 'draw near' in our passage. In Lev 16.2 'he will die' contrasts with confidence. Note the priesthood of all believers. Lev 9.7 'come to the altar to make atonement' and Heb 10.21 where there is no mention of a need for atonement, seeing it has already been accomplished in Christ. It was accomplishjed before the drawing near, not in order to draw near.

'We have confidence to enter' The Old Testament only allowed Moses to ascend the mountain; Levites and priests and one high priest to enter the Most Holy Place. It was shrouded in darkness and people listened for the continual sound of bells on the fringes of the high priest's robe, that if the sound died, surely God had punished him with death. The teaching of the OT and the Psalms of Lament occasionally arise to confidence. But the prophetic writings show a confident people in worship but the confidence is misplaced on God's election and covenant and ignores the fact that sin had cut off all grounds of false confidence, for surely inconsistency regarding covenant faith and life removes the grounds of confidence. Is this a subjective experience of guilt or shame that only removes the believer from intimate fellowship with God? Or is the very covenant placed in jeopardy for his own person? Is a lack of confidence a lack of understanding of God's word, or can it go back to the same kinds of sins of 'unfaith' /'unfaithfulness' that killed those in the wilderness. Is there any dispensation in which behavior doesn't matter, and sin is not a serious matter? The Most Holy Place[344] here is heaven itself that we enter in worship and prayer. The means of entry in practice are 1. Faith v.22; 2. Hope v.23; 3. Good deeds v.23; 4. Meeting for worship v.25; 5. Exhortation or sharing v.25; 6.continual unbroken exercise of belief v.39.

'have confidence' includes the writer and those readers, all are brothers, that is, believers. Cf. . Lev 16.2 'not to come' contrasts to 'draw near' in our passage. In Lev 16.2 'he will die' contrasts with confidence. Note the priesthood of all believers. Lev 9.7 'come to the altar to make atonement' and Heb 10.21 where there is no mention of a need for atonement, seeing it has already been accomplished in Christ. It was accomplished before the drawing near, not in order to draw near. 'We have confidence to enter' The Old Testament only allowed Moses to ascend the mountain; Levites and priests and one high priest to enter the Most Holy Place. It was shrouded in darkness and people listened for the continual sound of bells on the fringes of the high priest's robe, that if the sound died, surely God had punished him with death. The teaching of the OT and the Psalms of Lament occasionally arise to confidence. But the prophetic writings show a confident people in worship but the confidence is misplaced on God's election and covenant and ignores the fact that sin had cut off all grounds of false confidence, for surely inconsistency regarding covenant faith and life removes the grounds of confidence. Is this a subjective experience of guilt or shame that only removes the believer from intimate fellowship with God? Or is the very covenant placed in jeopardy for his own person? Is a lack of confidence a lack of understanding of God's word, or can it go back to the same kinds of sins of 'unfaith' 'unfaithfulness' that killed those in the wilderness. Is there any dispensation in which behavior doesn't matter, and sin is not a serious matter?

The Most Holy Place [345]here is heaven itself that we enter in worship and prayer. The means of entry in practice are 1. Faith v.22; 2. Hope v.23; 3. Good deeds v.23; 4. Meeting for worship v.25; 5. Exhortation or sharing v.25; 6.continual unbroken exercise of belief v.39. Note in Mal 3.16-17 "then those who feared the Lord talked with each other, and the Lord listened and heard. A scroll of remembrance was written iin his presence concerning those who feared the Lord and honored his name.'

10.20 'His body' is not the church but his dead and resurrected body, his person, with a possible hint of the bread in communion. The metaphor here is that it is the veil. There is still a veil but it is the person of Christ, and through him to the glory, the access, the Way, Truth and Life. David Ulansey[346] notes the Inclusio between the 'tearing of heavens at the baptism of Jesus Mk 1.10 and the 'tearing of the temple veil' at the death of Jesus Mk 15.38. He cites Motyer for four similarities.[347] While their arguments concern literary and motif matters, the ascension brings Jesus body together with entry into heaven, from which He will come again and receive believers to himself in the same manner.This becomes the last trek of the racecourse to heaven. Armerding notes the symbolism: "It is quite commonly held that the boards of the Tabernacle are symbolic of those who, by grace, "are builded together for an habitation of God through the Spirit" (Eph. 2:22). The significance of the veil is clearly stated in Hebrews 10:19-20 where we are told that it represents the flesh of our Lord. That being so, the four pillars in the church (Cf. . Rev. 3:12) who were specially honored in being chosen to portray the incarnate Son of God in the four Gospels. As a matter of fact, the whole of the structure is in some sense symbolic of "the church of the living God, the pillar and ground of the truth" (1 Tim. 3:15).[348]That church "hath many members, and all the members of that one body being many, are one body. "But all do not have the same function. "God hath set some in the church, first apostles, secondarily prophets, thirdly teachers" (Cf. . 1 Cor. 12:12ff). We have already suggested that the four pillars which supported the veil may

10.21 'Having a great high priest over the house of God' in a sense corresponds to Christ as head of the church, king over the kingdom, Lord of all, and head of the body, which is his body.. But the role is to make possible the believer's drawing near to God. Here body is in disjunction to 'have a great high priest' by virtue of the connective 'an since.' But even so the High priest here stands in relation to the house of God as in Pauline writings Christ stands in relation to the Christ. Since 'house of God' in 3.6 corresponds to the people of Israel, the reference here is to the church as 'House of God' namely God's temple. But the metaphor does not center on a building such as tabernacle or temple building but on the people of God as a collective 'place' in the sense of as a 'holy place.' It may also be from this background we could read Paul's expression 'in Christ' as referring to the 'place' of the individual believer. Here, however, the focus is on access through the 'House of God' the people in worship that one draws near. In Ezekiel 48 'YHWH is There/ is that sense of place being Jerusalem. But in Isaiah 6 YHWH's glory and holiness filling the universe makes Dahood's rendering of certain Psalms probable, that ma2qo3m is a term for God himself. Then 'No man cometh to the Father but by me' makes God himself the Ultimate Place in the universe. Note the OT focus on holy places at Gilgal, Jericho, Horeb-bush, Mount Zion, Shechem, Shiloh, Gibeon, etc. Davd sought to use one physical place to unify the people; Solomon, Hezekiah, Josiah and especially Haggai, Zechariah, Joshua, Ezra and Nehemiah sought to do the same. But the place of worship almost became a substitute for God himself in certain Psalms [15.1; 87.1;90.1 'our dwelling place';91.1-2 God as Refuge, in that temples were refuges; Ps 110.4. Here body is in disjunction to 'have a great high priest' by virtue of the connective 'an since.' But even so the High priest here stands in relation to the house of God as in Pauline writings Christ stands in relation to the Christ. Since 'house of God' in 3.6 corresponds to the people of Israel, the reference here is to the church as 'House of God' namely God's temple. But the metaphor does not center on a building such as tabernacle or temple building but on the people of God as a collective 'place' in the sense of OT as a holy place. It may also be from this background we could read Paul's expression 'in Christ' as referring to the 'place' of the individual believer. Here, however, the focus is on access through the 'House of God' the people in worship that one draws near. In Ezekiel 48 'YHWH is There/ is that sense of place being Jerusalem. But in Isaiah 6 YHWH's glory and holiness filling the universe makes Dahood's rendering of certain Psalms probable, that maqom is a term for God himself. Then 'No man cometh to the Father but by me' makes God himself the Ultimate Place in the universe. Note the OT focus on holy places at Gilgal, Jericho, Horeb-bush, Mount Zion, Shechem, Shiloh, Gibeon, etc. Davd sought to use one physical place to unify the people; Solomon, Hezekiah, Josiah and especially Haggai, Zechariah, Joshua, Ezra and Nehemiah sought to do the same. But the place of worship almost became a substitute for God himself in certain Psalms [15.1; 87.1;90.1 'our dwelling place';91.1-2 God as Refuge, in that temples were refuges; Ps 110.4 Moses, Aaron, Eli, Samuel in a theocracy were heads of the 'house'. But only from the Essenes onward do we visualize one person who is priest and king snce they conceived of two Messiah's. In Solomon's day he officiated in worship on dedication day. After that day Uzziah was stricken, Saul lost his anointing, Ahaz and Manasseh polluted the throne. Only Jesus has the blood line to be king of Israel and the priestly line to be an eternal Mediator.

10.22 The pre-requisite to worship is in view here, not the result of worship. The way is Jesus' blood.v.19 says it is non-repeatable. Cleansing in Hebrews is of body and heart, a merismus representing the whole person inside and out. Lev 8.11 mentions sprinkling of oil on the altar, anointing of Aaron v.12, and anointing the head. In 8.19 there is sprinkling of blood on the altar, and 8.30 blood from the altar is sprinkled on Aaron, his garments and hs sons and their garments. This is the consecration chapter. The body is emphasized, but Hebrews declares the body's purity is not enough. Cf. .Eli's sons' behavior. In Lev 13.6 there is washing of clothes and body. Lev 14.7 mentions sprinkling to cleanse of infectious diseases and it is by blood and promise, but in v.8 one must wash his clothes, bathe in water, so as to be ceremonially clean, plus a quarantine for seven days. The two-fold aspect of human nature, conscience and body , begin with baptism with 'pure water' and at the same time 'sprinkle the heart from a guilty conscience. To enter God's presence and to have hope depend on the witness of the Spirit to these cleansings. The reference in 6.2 to 'baptisms' could be read as physical baptism with water and Spirit baptism. Here in this verse both are joined. Anderson[349] notes only Lev8=ex 29 requires the priests to bring a bull during seven days of ordination, while 11Qtemple 15.15-16.1 requires this for priest and congregation. Also added to this is a cereal and drink offering. This addition does not fit Hebrews, but cleansing for priest and congregation does, but not for Jesus. But the congregation is being elevated to the role of a kingdom of priests unto God.

10.23 The focus on possibility of disobedience naturally recalls the history of Israel as sinning and of grace. "Hosea and Jeremiah reflect a minority view that there had been a golden age of obedience and devotion on the part of Israel in the early days befor the entrance into the land Hos 2.16-17[=RSV 2.14-15]; 9.10,15; 11.1-3; Jer 2.2-3]. But the Torah, as well as the other prophets, knows of no such tradition. According to them, although Israel had always been disobedient and recalcitrant, God's grace was not thwarted. Whatever evil Joseph's brothers, Jacob's eponymous sons, 'intended' against him, God could and did 'intend' it for good to the benefit of all[Gen 50.20]. Insistence on the faithfulness of the promiser [Heb 10.23] in some contexts [750-586 B.C.] apparently became deception and falsehood. Coats,[350]. 'to hope' is a goal and God is faithful. The key to explain the need for assembly in 10.24-25 is that hope must be held on to within a community of love, good works, meeting together and encouraging one another. Morale is important to maintain hope. Anything against fellowship and mutual encouragement is against hope and wrong and destructive and doesn't prepare one for the Lord's coming.. Ps 133 stresses unity as a morale factor. Ps 135.1-2 speaks of praise by ministers while recognizing God's sovereignty v.56. But at the same time this mind-set confirms hope v.14,18 for future days. The OT motif is more often fear than hope, as in Lev 22.3[351] Unknown in Josephus, attested by one late occurrence in the papyri,1 aklines, literally "which does not bend, is straight," signifies "stable, set," then "unmoving, at rest"; it is a synonym of bebaios. 2 It is used of an enduring friendship (Anth. Pal. 12.158.4) and above all to unshakable reason or judgment.3 The emphasis is on immutability.4 It is Philo who gave this adjective its religious and moral sense by attributing stability on the one hand to God, as opposed to creatures,5 and on the other hand to the perfectly regenerated human.6 From that point one can see how the term made it into the vocabulary of the Epistle to the Hebrews, which exhorts us to hold fast the homologia of our hope (Heb 10:23). This hope, which is "firmly founded" on the promise of God,7 must be guarded without wavering. Note that the content of faith is identical to its hope (Cf. . Heb 11:1), just as in 1Pet 3:15. Psa. 96:10 Say among the nations,

"The LORD reigns." The world is firmly established, it cannot be moved; he will judge the peoples with equity. Pss.96:10; Psa. 93:1. The LORD reigns, he is robed in majesty; the LORD is robed in majesty and is armed with strength. The world is firmly established; it cannot be moved. 'they were not afraid' really goes beyond the OT narrative, but what they did was against the king's whole policy for subject peoples and was based on the perception by faith that 'this was no ordinary child' and that meant God had things for him to do. They believed this and acted to preserve life.

'To hope' is a goal and God is faithful. They key to explain the need for assembly in 10.24-25 is that hope must be held on to within a community of love, good works, meeting together and encouraging one another. Morale is important to maintain hope. Anything against fellowship and mutual encouragement is against hope and wrong. Ps 133 stresses unity as a morale factor. Ps 135.1-2 speaks of praise by ministers while recognizing God's sovereignty v.56. But at the same time this mind-set confirms hope v.14,18 for future days. The OT motif is more often fear than hope, as in Lev 22.3. lines, S 186;; Unknown in Josephus[352], attested by one late occurrence in the papyri,1 aklines, literally "which does not bend, is straight," signifies "stable, set," then "unmoving, at rest"; it is a synonym of bebaios. 2 It is used of an enduring friendship (Anth. Pal. 12.158.4) and above all to unshakable reason or judgment.3 The emphasis is on immutability.4 It is Philo who gave this adjective its religious and moral sense by attributing stability on the one hand to God, as opposed to creatures,5 and on the other hand to the perfectly regenerated human.6 From that point one can see how the term made it into the vocabulary of the Epistle to the Hebrews, which exhorts us to hold fast the homologia of our hope (Heb 10:23). This hope, which is "firmly founded" on the promise of God,7 must be guarded without wavering. Note that the content of faith is identical to its hope (Cf. . Heb 11:1), just as in 1Pet 3:15. Psa. 96:10 Say among the nations, "The LORD reigns." The world is firmly established, it cannot be moved; he will judge the peoples with equity. Psa. 93:1 The LORD reigns, he is robed in majesty; the LORD is robed in majesty and is armed with strength. The world is firmly established; it cannot be moved

10.24 Proverbs and Ecclesiastes are examples of spurring men on, motivating through exhortation, a pattern followed more by Paul and James than Jesus. Samuel encouraged the crowds by seriously laying out options of commitment but more in detail than with Saul. Moses' words in Deuteronomy and others words in wisdom psalms are the same genre. These words are more personalized than laws are. The concerns and love of the individual speaker come through the words. " All the meanings discussed above have a part in the love of Christ that constrains us [2 Cor 5.14][353] This love suggests the Lord's seizing us to hold us and maintain us in his sovereign and exclusive possession. It takes possession of us so forcefully that it compels us to love in return. Cf. . The persistence in Mic 7.18; Ps 77.9, and wraps up our whole being. More than pressure, it is an compulsion[354] that orients our whole life and all our conduct. The fervor of this agape, which is suggestive of a fire [Matt 24.12], can be compared to a burning fever [Heb 10.24] paroxumos agapes and thus implies intense emotion, the giving of one's heart. Finally, since according to St.Paul; the agape of Christ is essentially linked to the cross, this love in a way oppressews the disciple, just as Christ was in anguish at the prospect of his passion; it judges him and convinces [krinw] him to die with his Savior. He is forced to it,as it were."[355] 'Consider how we may spur one another on toward love and good deeds' is a church business meeting, congregational meeting or elders council discussing not what we call business as opposed to ministry, but the essence of how to motivate and how to do good to all men . It is this question of 'How' that requires considered thought and planning.

10.24-25 A real-life note of the situation of the recipients is that some were not continuing to meet together to encourage one another. It was these that were vulnerable to persecution and arrest. The small cell that functions to spur one another to good deeds is normal for church or for a small synagogue sermon. The fact is that 'the Day approaching' was vital in their faith and not conceived of something remote.

10.25 The meeting together in the synagogue or home meeting was normal but in persecution this openness of confessing faith might have been avoided by some even as Esther was told not to tell about her Jewish background. Thos praying while Simon was in prison were also behind closed doors. One aspect, perhaps the first, that one was backsliding was absence in the meeting together.In Israel at the festivals every male 20 years and older was required to be present in worship. For Israel this was mandatory not optional. For the readers of Hebrews they might have thought it was optional. 'As often as you do this…in remembrance of me' were words oft repeated and called one back to basic faith in Christ. The role of testimony and encouragement were evidently more central to those receiving the letter than preaching. Of course, Hebrews is a model of how to use scripture for encouragement. Church Fathers had a similar method of preaching or exposition and application of Scriptures.

10.26 'Deliberately sin' for Jews involved no possibility of forgiveness through sacrifice but only punishment. But to the readership of this treatise they may have believed that in Christ all sins could be forgiven if there were confession and genuine repentance. But to not have now the only sacrifice that can save because it has been rejected makes for not a search for another religion or faith or philosophical means of renewal for these believer-backsliders since they would not want to turn elsewhere. They are caught with the check cashed, the money received –and thrown away.v.28 brings into the paradigm the OT judgment procedure before two or three witnesses, Perhaps these words apply to converted Jews who are now rejecting their faith and returning to the old sacrificial system, which, to those who have received Christ is no longer an effective procedure. So they are caught with no where to go. Usually this paragraph is applied to public denial of the faith to avoid martyrdom. But the simple language of knowing the truth implies conversion and now a return to deliberate sinning. Paul enforced the same in Galatians, that whatsoever one sows one will reap. 'How much more' makes the Gospel way much more productive and thorough but also much more stringent and dangerous for those who disobey.

'If we keep on sinning' seems broader than Jews or Gentiles or believers and non-believers. If once they had received the knowledge of the truth there was responsibility. But the following description is not that of inquirers only. But the list is not about sinning in general but about the real meaning of a given set of criminal actions some of which have nothing to do with the Law.:

1. 'keep on sinning after receiving the knowledge of the truth;' Inconsistency and flagrant behavior
2. 'enemies of God'; Anathema and under ban
3. 'rejected the law of Moses'; Apostasy
4. 'trampled the Son of God under foot'; Acted-out denial

5. 'treated as an unholy thing the blood of the covenant that sanctified him';. Desecration
6. 'insulted the Spirit of grace.' Blasphemy

Items 4-6 are only applicable to believers, since this language would only be significant to Christian believers. The items 1-3 could move from 'anyone' to an 'apostate Jew.' Clearly these Jewish-Christian believers in this antithesis structure would never reject the law of Moses. But to reject the Son, the blood and covenant, and Spirit is a total rejection. Deliberate sinning was not provided for under the OT regime. Does this mean that some recipients came from pagan or impious backgrounds to account for this being mentioned as a lead-in? This hardly seems to fit the obvious apostasy in the rest of this paragraph. But as a lead-in it has to function as tantamount to denying the Lord. The main treatment of apostasy seems to come in ch.12, yet even this is dealing with sin in the believer 12.1 and 'struggle against sin' and the danger of a root of bitterness 12.15 shooting up. The 'hardness' addressed earlier is not in the arena of public denial, although ch.11 does mention faithful believers who did face prison, exile, torture and death for their faith. So the issue in this paragraph may not necessarily be apostasy but the more insidious sinning of a general sort, albeit deliberately. John Wesley's definition of sin properly view is a willful transgression of a known law of God, and that is the kind addressed here. Elsewhere sins of ignorance are mentioned in connection with sacrifices for sinning.

10.26-31,Atonement: On Isa 53.10 North 'In Leviticus even the 'burnt offering' is said to 'make atonement' kipper Lev 1.4, while Gray prefers 'make expiation' and the same applies to the 'sin offering' chatta't 4.20 and guilt offering v.16. At the same time, for deliberate and 'presumptuous' sin Ps 19.13[14] there was, at least in theory, no remission by sacrifice Num 15.30f. the only remedy was for the sinner to cast himself upon the divine forgiveness Ps 32.5. Even the sin-offering only availed for sins committed in ignorance Lev 4.2 'unwittingly.' Nevertheless, the guilt-offering is said to cover such deliberate offences as breach of faith and robbery with extortion, and its purpose was to make restitution for injury done LEV 6.1-6. V.20-26] these are such crimes as the heathen may have committed and this is probably the reason for the choice of 'asham here North, 243

10.27 Dating evidence: Indicates the outbreak of hostilities between Jews and Rome and hence possibly the year CE 67. Payne,572 Note that 'raging fire' is spoken of as a final judgment as Gehenna was a metaphor for

Hades or the Lake of Fire. "Gehenna, is used to describe the eschatological hell of fire where the ungodly will be punished after death (Matt 5:22). There is one place, however, where Hades is described as a place of torment (Luke 16:23). Yet in contrast to much of later Christian literture, the "torments of hell" are not elaborated upon in the NT."[356] Theodeore J Lewis.Zeph 1.18. IIEsdras 13.10 'fiery blast' [357] corresponds to II Thess 1.7ff; Ps 14.4; Heb 17 and 10.27. Widengren sees Iranian influence here.[358] Myers,[359]38. Zeph 1.18. IIEsdras 13.10 'fiery blast' [360] corresponds to II Thess 1.7ff; Ps 14.4; Heb 17 and 10.27. Widengren sees Iranian influence here.[361] Myers,[362]308

10.28 The verb is used for the rejection of a law (Isa 24:16; Ezek 22:26; Heb 10:28—ton nomon), of a commandment (Mark 6:9—ten entolen), of a covenant (Gal 3:15—diatheken; 2Macc 14:28—ta» diestalmena), of an agreement (2Macc 13:25—peri twn sunthekwn). Cf. . 1Macc 15:27—"He revoked all that he had agreed with Simon." This corresponds to ma'as in the OT. 'reject' the English gloss has 32 occurrences in the OT both of God to men and men to God: Lev. 26:15 "and if you reject my decrees and abhor my laws and fail to carry out all my commands and so violate my covenant," Lev. 26:44 "Yet in spite of this, when they are in the land of their enemies, I will not reject them or abhor them so as to destroy them completely, breaking my covenant with them. I am the LORD their God." 1Sam. 12:22 "For the sake of his great name the LORD will not reject his people, because the LORD was pleased to make you his own." 2Kings 23:27 "So the LORD said, "I will remove Judah also from my presence as I removed Israel, and I will reject Jerusalem, the city I chose, and this temple, about which I said, 'There shall my Name be.'" 1Chr. 28:9 "And you, my son Solomon, acknowledge the God of your father, and serve him with wholehearted devotion and with a willing mind, for the LORD searches every heart and understands every motive behind the thoughts. If you seek him, he will be found by you; but if you forsake him, he will reject you forever. 2Chr. 6:42 "O LORD God, do not reject your anointed one. Remember the great love promised to David your servant." Job 8:20 "Surely God does not rejects a blameless man or strengthen the hands of evildoers." Psa. 27:9 "Do not hide your face from me, do not turn your servant away in anger; you have been my helper. Do not reject me or forsake me, O God my Savior". Psa. 36:4 "Even on his bed he plots evil; he commits himself to a sinful course and does not reject what is wrong." Psa. 44:23 Awake, O Lord! Why do you sleep? Rouse yourself! Do not reject us forever. Psa. 77:7 "Will the Lord reject forever? Will he never show his the wrong and choose the right." Hos. 4:6 my people are destroyed from lack of knowledge. "Because you have rejected knowledge, I also reject you as my priests; because you have ignored the law of your God, I also will ignore your children."

10.28 Men who scorned the offering to Yahweh; Often these were levites or priests with no spirituality whatsoever. 1Sam 2:17;Isa 63:8; Wis 5:1.'act faithlessly,' Cf. . Exod 21:8; Deut 21:14. Compare the apostates who trample on the Son of God and treat as common the blood that he shed (Heb 10:28-29), as opposed to Paul who does not treat the grace of God as nothing (Gal 2:21).Dt 17.2-6; 19.15. The rebel in Israel is compared to the apostate in the church. The latter has even less a chance of avoiding the death penalty. But in this case God judges directly. One might think that as a parallel the Gospel would have a theoretical base for salvation for anyone. But if it lacks the theoretical basis for mercy it doesn't lack the pastoral basis as in Gal 5 'if any one of you be overtaken in a fault...restore such an one...' However the apostolate basis is expulsion from the church and a handing over to Satan. This lack of uniformity seaks to adjustments to defectors in the church during the first three centuries in which gradually the church was enabled to forgive and restore such. Only biblical faith puts such a strong emphasis on faithfulness, loyalty, consistency in commitment. Note the the law of two or three witnesses is followed in law, historical narrative, poetry, prophecy and in Gospels and the epistles. In Rabbinic law the person himself is one witness and confession alone cannot convict anyone of a crime. The witnesses to the crime who testified are usually designated to take up the first stones. 'Rejected God's Law' points to an interpretation of Numbers and Exodus that Israel leaders did not just have difference of opinion and conflict with Moses, or usurpation of authority over Moses, but simply they had rejected the laws of God.

10.29 'How much more' is a biblical penology concept. While all have sinned, all sins are not equal. The sacrifices were for sins of inadvertence or ignorance. Presumptuous sins had no sacrifices, but forgiveness was granted on occasion through intercession or disciplinary punishments. The number of case types requiring execution were not only capitol offences of the laws of Israel. But still were not as many as in Assyrian law. The ultimate punishment for seeking to overthrow the government, in most ancient nations, was death or even 'laying hand on an anointed one,' as occurred to the Agagite at the death of Saul, but not Adonijah or Jonathan, who were not anointed. It may be Amorite kings were not anointed, hence their execution was in a holy war context, near Jerusalem and in a cave. To burn the bones of a king was grievous, even though cremation was recognized. But to kill the Son of God and 'trample his atonement as if there was non-burial. 'insult the Spirit of grace' is equivalent with what Jesus called the unpardonable sin in the Gospels. The context of the Son of God does not allow the 'blood of the covenant whereby he was sanctified' to refer to Moses' covenant, and that therefore these were backslidden Jewish catechumens, because them you would assume that the Day of Atonement re-enacted the establishing of the Covenant. 'He was sanctified' cannot either refer to Jesus, but to one deeply disrespecting the shed blood of Jesus that he has just proven established the New Covenant. Of course, their acts would undermine the link to the First Covenant as well and cut off logically, a person from Israel and God. But then in killing again the antitype they cut themselves off from both covenants as acts that reject the Law of Moses and the Movenant of Jesus.

Tapeinos [363] Humility in the NT comes from the OT and example of Christ Matt 1.29 "learn of me". It "combines the ideas of poverty, modesty, and mildness. [364] The humble are contrasted with potentates, the great, the arrogant, the rich, with all that is lofty, and glorious [Prov 29.23]." A profile:1. They are 'little people,' of modest circumstances, who are regarded with favor by the Lord; 2. They are unfortunate sufferers, whom God comforts [2 Cor 7.6; 12.21; Phil 2.8; Heb 6.6; 10.29]; 3. They are discreet and self-effacing [Ep.Arist. 257; Rom 12.16; Gal 6.1-3; Eph 4.2; 1 Tim 3.6; 1 Pet 3.8] 4. They are humble before the Lord and reserved with respect to their brethren, persuaded of 'the misery and emptiness of the whole creation.' [Acts 20.19; Jas 4.10; 1 Pet 5.5-6]. It is hard to separate social class, attitudes toward them, economic dependency at times, their oppression, from their spirituality since these circumstances create character. But pagans also considered this a virtue of modesty, or moderation, associated with prauthes, heshchia, metriotes, kosmiotes and sofrosyne the opposite of hybris, authadeia, and hyperephania. Spicq,3.370; Dt 32.35; 32.36, 'How much more' points to proportional punishment for the crime committed. In Egypt and Babylonia it was possible for the most extreme punishment to destroy the soul of man or god, leaving the future totally without the person of deity. <u>Ttapeinos</u> [365] Humility in the NT comes from the OT and example of Christ Matt 1.29 "learn of me". It "combines the ideas of poverty, modesty, and mildness. [366] The humble are contrasted with potentates, the great, the arrogant, the rich, with all that is lofty, and glorious [Prov 29.23].".[367]

10.30 Vengeance is alleviated in the OT only for the suspected killer involved in an accidental death Dt 32.35; 32.36. So Rom 12 orders believers not to seek personal revenge, the turniing of cheek ethic, because it might hinder the Gospel, but basically because God will deal with the criminal in his time and way. It is the Christian that truly knows the vengeance of God, He will repay, the Lord will judge his people' and 'dreadful thing'. 'we' know that the judgment of Christians to turn away from God means only a horrendous judgment for apostates. Even believers who apostasize have 'a fearful expectation of judgment and raging fire.' 'His people' originally was Israel and here the name is not used because the text is here applied to the church. Rom 12 reiterates this and urges Christians to never seek revenge. But vengeance is so basic for God in OT and NT and for all mankind. The OT law only controlled the reaction nature of man in the manslaughter law where there was doubt of culpability. Otherwise the human nature of man must be regulated by the Gospel. But God blessed Solomon because Solomon 'did not seek the life of his enemies.' Here was a quality going beyond the human 'base-line' character pattern. When the believer slips below the Gospel expectation he finds himself immediately not in the level of Spirit but of nature, and nature lacks self-control, forgiveness and the other qualities except for the prevenient grace of God. In a study of the 'thus says the Lord' formula legei kurios Ellis notes it often concludes the cited OT passage Rom 12.19; 1 Cor 14.11; 2 Cor 6.18; Heb 10.30a; Acts 7.49; 15.17; Evans,239. 'Insult to the Spirit of grace' is one form of the unpardonable sin the main form perhaps only form mentioned by Jesus in the Gospels. If the Spirit is manifest basically through believers and ministers anointed by God, sharing the Gospel, and seeking to do good to all men the rejection of all this as amounting to 'ulterior motives' is tantamount to this sin since what they are doing is what the Spirit is doing.

10.30-31 In the hands of God: In Ps 141.6 Dahood[368] reads "drop into the clutches of the Crag." Hebrews: "It is a terrible thing to fall into the hands of the living god." The crag or rock is YHWH sela' occurs also in Ps 18.3; 31.4; 71.3. He prays for his enemies to fall into the hands of the Rock or crag, but in v.9 prays that he himself might be protected from the clutches of the snare mide pach. The implication is that those who do not keep themselves in the way, close to the Lord, can become God's enemies, not only for discipline. The figure is 'falling into' God's hands not being seized by God.

10.31 'Fall into the hands of the living God' Nadab and Abihu did. Miriam and Aaron did. The idea is a sudden move by God unexpectedly to destroy such as those burned up or swallowed alive. Instead of tempting fates, or doing a foolish act that would bring normal consequences this expresses that what happens is truly an act of God. This is related to YHWH as kurios in the NT and some novels in which these verses appear. Parke-Taylor,[369] 106; 12.29

10.32-34; The Diaspora Christian Assembly: 13.24 seem to indicate the epistle is addressed at large to those who had formed congregations, or segments of a church, or a limited group of churches. They are apparently Jewish Christians, in danger of lapsing back into practices of Judaism 2.1; 4.1; 5.12; 10.19-39; 12.12. Payne,[370] 571. The great reward is that in Lk 6.23 'Your reward is great in heaven' It also speaks of obtaining a promise at the Lord's Parousia. Payne,[371] 37n The initial inquirer or catechument 'receives the light' and in the excitement of salvation stands his ground in great suffering. The behaviors that are mentioned are learned and shown in great conflict. Reputation besmerched, identification with the persecuted, sympathy for the imprisoned, and confiscation of property are all taken in good grace since life does not consist of the abundance of things one possesses. 'Those earlier days' point to an event of persecution in which these young believers stood firm and also stood together. The linking of events in 'the great contest' could refer to the arena but clearly it was not of short duration. The author knows the details of past victories and places these back to back with present dangers. Had attrition or atrophy set in? They had lost comfort, respect, honor, identity, freedom, property and possessions. To maintain solidarity they even identified with those who were so treated. They had learned sympathy.

10.35 Confidence is the crux of the danger facing these believers. This isn't because of not knowing the truth or shallow Christian experience but to to the laws of attrition tending toward physical and spiritual exhaustion. 'throw away confidence' is reflected in many Psalms that make the sufferer, the victim believe God doesn't truly care and know and if he did would give some kind of sign to show his presence. The message to them is that they must persevere in doing the will of God, and only then receiving what is promised. The rich reward is not life, liberty and the pursuit of happiness or even curvival. But they will receive what God has promised. The quote from Habakkuk affirm that 'He who is coming will come and will not delay.' As time went on they may have interpreted this in terms of historical events.

10.36 Paul said 'having done all stand.' Persevering is in relation to the will of God. Is this salvation by works? Perhaps this is a 'work of faith' but work nevertheless. The 'short time' is unspecified, so perseverance must continue till Jesus returns. All of this is unrelated to salvation by works since Jesus himself said 'I come to do your will O God.' Believers are to be imitators of Christ and the martyrs. In Paul's writings the antithesis of grace or faith and works are really about a merit system where one seeks to make up for sins and failures by acts of compensation somewhat as in the transgression or asham offering where there has been loss to be made up. Egypt had the full myth and cosmology of judgment after death, where the scale holds ma'at or justice-righteousness and punishment. on one side and the bundle of the quality of one's life on the other. If one's righteousness did not measure up judgement was pronounced. The paintings of the scales are well preserved and in full color with the various beings identified. The point of judgment isn't perfection but more good than bad. The Jewish system of merit entered the catholic church in a system of confessional, mass attendance, both mandatory, contributions and church work plus penance, the ultimate device to make God pleased. Alms or 'righteousnesses' as appear in the Gospels were similarly used. But neither Hebrews nor Paul have written off the OT, its God, prophecies, teachings, and in fact base faith on the God and Christ so predictedi n the OT. While 'law' in the NT Period Judaism really referred to the legalese of the torah plus their interpretation and application through rabbis and tradition for a number of years. The OT used them to enhance accountability of the Hebrew worshipper, and this became a method of control without ever having assurance of eternal life. But the will of God, all righteousness, along with the present decisions by the living God must be carried out by humans to fulfill them andate to rule, take possession, and control the created order under God and his Christ. But what God wants cannot be reduced to a system 'do this and you shall live.' Those words meant selling all, giving to the poor and following Jesus literally, in addition to keeping the commandments. But the focus is on God, loving God, seeking God, and living for him only. The closest approximation to this in the OT is Deuteronomy on loving God and fellow man and Psalm 119, except that the latter has all but placed God's revealed will in place of God Himself. 'This is the will of God even your sanctification' was written by Paul. 'That you may actualize/prove what is the good, perfect and acceptable will of God.' The response to justification and sanctification in Romans is a dedication as a sacrifice, following Jesus with the total offering up of oneself as a means to fulfill the will of God in spiritual service.

10.37 The so-called Delay of the Parousia begins not at a moment in Jesus life on earth or later in the century but with the prophecy in Habakkuk Hab 2.3,4. In that text it is probably Nebuchadnezzar not the real Messiah that is alluded to. But John 21 does suggest that the return is not to be immediiately. The delay in 2 Peter caused People to imagiine the resurrection was over or the time changed. But all the Gospels are not constrained by Daniel's sevens or any other factor, since times are in His hands

"The Coming one[372]' Rev 17.14, is found in Ps 118; Matt 121.8; 23.39; Lk 19.38; John 12.13; but as a title in the NT alone, and in the Gospels relating to John the Baptist and in Revelation. John proclaims the Coming One to be a judge holding a winnowing fork in his hand, separating the chaff from the wheat. Matt 3.12; Lk 3.17; Cf. . Rev 14.14-16, where one like to a son of man is holding a sickle to reap the earth. Acts 19.14 relates to the Baptist's disciples, but Heb 10.37 comes from Hab 2.3-4. Ford,[373]31,160. If the hope of the return of Christ waned perhaps they hoped an historical personage would arise bringing deliverance, such as esther did. The person of Emperor Claudius is ambiguous, sometimes for the Jews and sometimes against. ABD notes "The Acts of the Pagan Martyrs" which purport to give, *inter alia,* details of the trials in Rome of Greek nationalist leaders: In tone, they are violently anti-Roman and, at the same time, hostile to the Jews. Later, though, he expelled the Jews from Rome "for constant rioting at the instigation of Chrestus" (Suet. *Claud.* 25.4), where at least the reference to Christianity is unambiguous; the emperor's action is confirmed by an incident recorded in Acts 18:2, where two Jews, Aquila and Priscilla, expelled from Rome, came to Corinth and later met Paul. Finally an inscription said to come from Nazareth records a decree (possibly of Claudius) on the violation of tombs: scholars since 1930 have debated the possibility of an allusion to the burial and resurrection of Christ.[374] The final period sees him poisoned by Aggripina and thus establishing Nero on the throne. Had they expected a new emperor this one in 54 AD did not prove to be a Savior. They needed to turn their eyes on Jesus only, the 'coming one.'

10.38 There are many scriptures dealing with apostasy in OT and NT. As, for instance: Jer. 8:5 Why then has this people turned away in perpetual backsliding? They have held fast to deceit, they have refused to return. Ex. 32:8 they have been quick to turn aside from the way that I commanded them; they have cast for themselves an image of a calf, and have worshiped it and sacrificed to it...[375]Dt 9.12,16; 11.16,28; 31.29; Jud 2.17; 1 Sam 6.12; 1 Kgs 15.5; Ps 14.3; Mal 2.8; 3.7. The Idea of departing, turning aside is found both in a spiritual and concrete use throughout the OT. The oppisite is shub 'to return'. Both involve 'turning' hence 'conversion' and hence leaving the true God is conversion to another religion.. Jer. 2:19 Your wickedness will punish you, and your apostasies will convict you. Know and see that it is evil and bitter for you to forsake the LORD your God; the fear of me is not in you, says the Lord GOD of hosts.[376]

'My righteous one will live by faith' Evans remarks "Two classes of men are described in Habakkuk 2:4, which are in distinct contrast with each other. "Behold, his soul is puffed up, it is not upright in him; but the righteous shall live by his faith." The proud, puffed up Chaldean is contrasted with the righteous child of faith. The one lives in expectation of God's blessing while the other by implication must await God's judgment. Habakkuk 2:4 is quoted three times in the New Testament. It is used in Romans 1:17 to enforce the doctrine of justification by faith. It appears again in Galatians 3:11 where it is appealed to in order to set aside the interpolation of the law in opposition to grace. It occurs in Hebrews 10:38 to insist on faith as the power of life. The Chaldean invader is described as one who is proud and completely self-dependent without any thoughts of God. His soul is described as being "not upright in him." It is unsound and distorted. His judgment is unstated but implied. Such a being as the Chaldean is demands that he be judged. The antithesis of the statement describes the righteous and their being characterized not by pride but by faith."[377] The LXX inserts 'his faith' which could mean the faithful, habitual dealing of Nebuchadnezzar with rebellious kings and lands. The MT has no 'his.'

10.39 Contrasts to ch.11. 'those who draw back..and perish'. Saul was as was Ahithophel and Jonathan. The NT had Demas and others mentioned in the letters. David felt he was of this sort since; 1. He had rebelled against Saul's orders; 2. Implicated Nob; 3. Deceived the king by a lie with complicity involving Jonathan; 4. Made a covenant with foreigners, namely people of the land; 5. Lied to higher authority [his benefaqctor and covenant partner] about his activities; 6. Had no confidence in his survival: 'a step between me and death'; 7. Carmelites did the right thing to report on a criminal; 8. Offered to fight Saul with Saul's enemies; 9. Cut off Saul's robe, could have used I in magic; 10 challenged Saul and the rightness of his decrees, what Jonathan only did once; 11. Accepted fugitives from the law; 12. Engaged in frontier warfare. But he did not perish! Psalms reveal his longing for God and his 'sharing his heart' with Saul on two occasions showed a heart of love and respect for God's anionted. But at the time did his heart leave God? The ephod, Abiathar, families, arrangement with Moab, crisis at Keilah, two scares in the wilderness, and the turning point--the Nabal incident-- did turn him back to positive responsible behavior preparing him for a road upwards. The tenses are imnportant in relation to each other and the kind of action. 'Draw back' is done by and for oneself as if by a middle voice; 'those who believe' is a continuing characteristic and behavior. 'and are saved' is a passive where the believer is experiencer or patient in terms of case grammar. 'not of the shrinking back' hupostoles genitive is parallel to the pistews 'but of the faith pistewes' unto 'the preservation of [the soul].' Peripoesin ''possession, preservation.' The noun hupostoles < hupostellw 'state of being timid, timidity'according to BDAG is used in classical literature of holdng troops in a reserve position. This is in contrast to the earnestly committed. It takes daring and initiative to be saved. 'soul' can be read life. If this is simply survival of earthly life then those, while not denying the Lord still do not take the initiative to proclaim him will be executed also. Are there examples were denying the Lord in the arena did not save their lives?

Chapter Eleven:

FAITH IN CHRIST IS GOD'S GREATEST PLAN.

God's Command, Commendation, Pleasure, and Testing

11.1 'Faith' pistews :Is it possible that the NT meaning of 'trust, believe' is not intended, but the OT concept of hesed and 'emuna 'Faithfulness'" . The two stems in Greek are related grammatically and etymologically, but as opposites: pistoß and pivsti" only the first relates to the OT terms. This meaning could apply in verses 4,5,7,7 but v.6 uses the verb 'believe' and so the verbal meaning seems to carry over to the nouns. Does pisti include the idea of faithfulness. Perhaps the contrast is 'to have/use x' versus 'to x [that] y' or 'to x ...y' . If the object is a person, use 'trust'as the gloss. If the 'y' is a message, then 'believe' is x a psychological verb.; If the instrument-case uses z [while subject or topic of the grammatical sentence] then x is the verb of the sentence. [378379]. Spicq,3.112; 354n46, 421. Faith is the topic [subject of the sentence] but the content of the chapter illustrates v.2 which are God's commended ones. V.39; v.6. The emphasis of the chapter on those who finished the race course is reflected in the hymn, The Church's one Foundation: "Yet she on earth hath communion with God the Three in One, And mystic sweet communion with those whose rest is won. O happy [blessed] ones and holy, Lord give us grace, that we, like them the meek and lowly, On high may dwell with thee.' Heb 1.3 upostasis relates to epistaths as guarantee. In Acts 17.31 pietiß means guarantee :God has given guarantee through a man that he will resurrect the dead.' This is the meaning of hupostasiß in Heb 11.1 "Faith is the guarantee of things hoped for.' Pesh pyso. "The substantive hypostasis, literally 'that which is placed beneath' hence 'support, base,foundation' has already been used [Heb 1.3] in its philosophical meaning 'substance' as opposed to accidents. 'Reality' as opposed to appearances. [380] Faith is the topic [subject of the sentence] but the content of the chapter illustrates v.2 which are God's commended ones. V.39; v.6. The means to gain this faith is hidden within this chapter and is implicit not explicit.'commended' is a major topic of this chapter and approaches the matter of merit in which faith is the driving motivation and the following action carries through on what faith led him to do. Linking to v.2 faith is certainty of what has no proof and of what one hopes for. So in this reading, at the time of faith or as summary of a life at the time of using faith there was no external evidence or proof only this internal evidence which is faith. To act thus approaches daring, not the 'cowardly' that Revelation says will not be saved. To those standing by adventuresomeness has little to support it, to leave one's father, to go not knowing where, to believe God created to build an ark, all without precedent or analogy or other proof. So commended is not merit but the opposite since what was believed or done had no other motivation than to act by faith in God. Oswald Chambers notes "Faith in antagonism to common sense is fanaticism, and common sense in antagonism to faith is rationalism. The life of faith brings the two into right relation. Common sense is not faith, and faith is not common sense; they stand in the relation of the natral and the spiritual; of impulse and inspiration. Nothing Jesus Christ ever said was common sense, iti s revelation sense, and it reaches the shres where common sense fails. Faith must be tired before the reality of faith is actual. 'we know that all things work together for good,' then no matter what happens, the alchemy of god's providence transfigures the ideal faith into actual reality. For every detail of the common sense life, there is a revelation fact of God whereby we can prove in practical experience what we believe God to be. Faith is as tremendously active principle which always puts Jesus Christ first—Lorde, Thou has said so and so Cf. . Matt 6.33, it looks mad, but I am going to venture on thy Word. To turn faith into a personal possession is a fightr always, not sometimes. God brings us into circumstances in order to educate our faith, because the nature of faith is to make its object real. Until we know Jesus, God is a mere abstraction, we cannot have faith in him; but immediately we hear Jesus say 'Anyone who has seen me has seen the Father,' we have something that is real, and faith is boundless. Faith is the whole man rightly related to God by the power of the Spirit of Jesus Christ."[381]

> Wesley defined faith as follows: "BUT what is Faith? It is a divine "evidence and conviction of things not seen;" of things which are not seen now, whether they are visible or invisible in their own nature. Particularly, it is a divine evidence and conviction of God, and of the things of God. This is the most comprehensive definition of faith that ever was or can be given; as including every species of faith, from the lowest to the highest." ....

"Level 1: The heathen who live by sight is not faith at all. "The lowest sort of faith, if it be any faith at all, is that of a Materialist,— a man who, like the late Lord Kames, believes there is nothing but matter in the universe. I say, if it be any faith at all; for, properlyspeaking, it is not. It is not "an evidence or conviction of God," for they do not believe there is any; neither is it "a conviction of things not seen," for they deny the existence of such. Or if, for decency's sake, they allow there is a God, yet they suppose even him to be material."

"Level 2; The heathen in general "that there are four dispensations that are distinguished from each other by the degree of light which God vouchsafes to them that are under each. A small degree of light is given to those that are under the heathen dispensation. These generally believed, "that there was a God, and that he was a rewarder of them that diligently seek him." "The Second sort of faith, if you allow a Materialist to have any, is the faith of a Deist. I mean, one who believes there is, a God, distinct from matter; but does not believe the Bible. Of these we may observe two sorts. One sort are mere beasts in human shape, wholly under the power of the basest passions, and having "a downright appetite to mix with mud." Other Deists are, in most respects, rational creatures, though unhappily prejudiced against Christianity: Most of these believe the being and attributes of God, they believe that God made and governs the world; and that the soul does not die with the body, but will remain for ever in a state of happiness or misery." "The next sort of faith is the faith of Heathens, with which I join that of Mahometans. I cannot but prefer this before the faith of the Deists; because, though it embraces nearly the same objects, yet they are rather to be pitied than blamed for the narrowness of their faith. And their not believing the whole truth, is not owing to want of sincerity, but merely to want of light. When one asked Chicali, an old Indian Chief, "Why do not you red men know as much as us white men?" he readily answered, "Because you have the great Word, and we have not." "It cannot be doubted, but this plea will avail for millions of modern Heathens. Inasmuch as to them little is given, of them little will be required. As to the ancient Heathens, millions of them likewise were savages. No more therefore will be expected of them, than the living up to the light they had. But many of them, especially in the civilized nations, we have great reason to hope, although they lived among Heathens, yet were quite of another spirit; being taught of God, by his inward voice, all the essentials of true religion. Yea, and so was that Mahometan, and Arabian, who, a century or two ago, wrote the Life of Hai Ebn Yokdan. The story seems to be feigned; but it contains all the principles of pure religion and undefiled."

"Level 3: The Jewish people; "the Jewish nation; inasmuch as to them "were entrusted" the grand means of light, "the oracles of God." Hence many of these had clear and exalted views of the nature and attributes of God; of their duty to God and man; yea, and of the great promise made to our first parents, and transmitted by them to their posterity, that "the Seed of the woman should bruise the serpent's head." "By Jewish faith, I mean, the faith of those who lived between the giving of the law and the coming of Christ. These, that is, those that were serious and sincere among them, believed all that is written in the Old Testament. In particular, they believed that, in the fullness of time, the Messiah would appear, "to finish the transgression, to make an end of sin, and bring in everlasting righteousness."   It is not so easy to pass any judgment concerning the faith of our modern Jews. It is plain, "the veil is still upon their hearts" when Moses and the Prophets are read. The God of this world still hardens their hearts, and still blinds their eyes, "lest at any time the light of the glorious gospel" should break in upon them. So that we may say of this people, as the Holy Ghost said to their forefathers, "The heart of this people is waxed gross, and their ears are dull of hearing, and their eyes have they closed; lest they should see with their eyes, and hear with their ears, and understand with their hearts, and should be converted, and I should heal 217 them." (<442827>Acts 28:27.) Yet it is not our part to pass sentence upon them, but to save them to their own Master.

"Level 4: John the Baptist: "John the Baptist. To him a still clearer light was given; and he was himself "a burning and a shining light." To him it was given to "behold the Lamb of God, that taketh away the sin of the world." Accordingly our Lord himself affirms, that "of all which had been born of Women," there had not till that 215time arisen "a greater than John the Baptist." But nevertheless he informs us, "He that is least in the Kingdom of God," the Christian dispensation, "is greater than he."
"Level 5 "" By one that is under the Christian dispensation, Mr. Fletcher means one that has received the Spirit of adoption; that has the Spirit of

God witnessing "with his spirit, that he is a child of God." "Hitherto faith has been considered chiefly as an evidence and conviction of such or such truths. And this is the sense wherein it is taken at this day in every part of the Christian world. But, in the mean time, let it be carefully observed, (for eternity depends upon it,) that neither the faith of a Roman Catholic, nor that of a Protestant, if it contains no more than this, no more than the embracing such and such truths, will avail any more before God, than the faith of a Mahometan[Moslem]or a Heathen; yea, of a Deist or Materialist. For can this "faith save him?" Can it save any man either from sin or from hell? No more than it could save Judas Iscariot: No more than it could save the devil and his angels; all of whom are convinced that every tittle of Holy Scripture is true. 218 10. But what is the faith which is properly saving; which brings eternal salvation to all those that keep it to the end? It is such a divine conviction of God, and the things of God, as, even in its infant state, enables every one that possesses it to "fear God and work righteousness." And whosoever, in every nation, believes thus far, the Apostle declares, is it accepted of him." He actually is, at that very moment, in a state of acceptance. But he is at present only a servant of God, not properly a *son.* Meantime, let it be well observed, that "the wrath of God" no longer "abideth on him."Indeed, nearly fifty years ago, when the Preachers, commonly called Methodists, began to preach that grand scriptural doctrine, salvation by faith, they were not sufficiently apprised of the difference between a servant and a child of God. They did not clearly understand, that even one "who feareth God, and worketh righteousness, is accepted of him." In consequence of this, they were apt to make sad the hearts of those whom God had not made sad. For they frequently asked those who feared God, "Do you know that your sins are forgiven?" And upon their answering, "No," immediately replied, "Then you are a child of the devil." No; that does not follow. It might have been said, (and it is all that can be said with propriety,) "Hitherto you are only a *servant*, you are not a *child* of God. You have already great reason to praise God that he has called you to his honorable service. Fear not. Continue crying unto him, 'and you shall see greater things than these.'" And, indeed, unless the servants of God halt by the way, they will receive the adoption of sons. They will receive the *faith* of the children of God, by his *revealing* his only begotten Son in their hearts. Thus, the faith of a child is, properly and directly, a divine conviction, whereby every child of God is enabled to testify, "The life that I now live, I live by faith in the Son of God, who loved me, and gave himself for me."[382]

Commendation comes 'by faith,' not by works. Because both faith and works have actions how do they differ? Faith looks to the person of God while works look to the quality of an action. The world stresses 'performance, success and accomplishment,' but this chapter does also. What is the 'accomplishment' God is looking for? In this chapter 'survival' on earth is not a goal. Proper offerings, righteousness, pleasing God, belief in God's existence and rewarding, obedience, patience of a foreign residence, believing promises, looking for a city, being enabled, considering God faithful, confession of alien role, longing, reasoning that God v.19; blessing sons, conveying of a hope to sons v.22, hiding a son against an edict v.23, etc. NBC:

Hebrews shows the link between faith, hope, obedience and endurance, illustrating that it is more than intellectual assent to certain beliefs. God-honoring faith takes God at his word and lives expectantly and obediently in the present, waiting for him to fulfill his promises. Such faith brings suffering and persecution in various forms".383 :: Here we discover the essential characteristics of faith from the writer's point of view. Faith deals with things future (*what we hope for*) and things unseen (*what we do not see*). The NIV translation (*being sure of what we hope for*) puts the emphasis on faith as an expression of our confidence in God's promises. However, it is also possible to translate, 'faith is the substance of things hoped for' (AV), or 'faith gives substance to our hopes' (NEB). Such a rendering suggests that *what we hope for* becomes real and substantial by the exercise of faith. This does not mean that the gospel is true simply because we believe in it! Rather, the reality of what we hope for is confirmed for us in our experience when we live by faith in God's promises. Again, faith is being *certain of what we do not see.* It is the means of 'proving' or 'testing' invisible realities such as the existence of God, his faithfulness to his word and his control over our world and its affairs. If this definition seems abstract, its meaning becomes more concrete in the illustrations that follow. For such faith *the ancients were commended.* In the record of Scripture, God testified to their faith, and so made them 'witnesses' 12:1 of true faith for us."David Peterson,384. The emphasis of the chapter on those who finished the race course is reflected in the hymn, The Church's one Foundation: "Yet she on earth hath communion with God the Three in One, And mystic sweet communion with those whose rest is won. O happy [blessed] ones and holy, Lord give us grace, that we, like them the meek and lowly, On high may dwell with thee.' Vanhoye notes: "The meaning of the Pauline pistis Xristou= is the subject of much discussion. Is the genitive here objective: "faith of Christ" or subjective: "the pistis of Christ"? In the latter interpretation the problem is the meaning of pistis. "The *faith* of Christ" comes up against the fact that the act of believing is never ascribed by Paul to Christ, nor is it ascribed to him elsewhere in the New Testament. The "*faithfulness* of Christ" avoids this objection but is a weak alternative. The fact that pistis also has the meaning of "credibility" or "trustworthiness", is sometimes overlooked. This is the meaning which suits some texts because the "trustworthiness" of Christ is what makes the Christian's "faith" possible."[385] Buchanan[386] hypostasis 'grundwork' used to describe God's nature 1.3 and a Christian's faith. 'amunah 'faith' suggests solidarity, firmness, stability' while the verb means 'support' 'confirm.' "The one who has faith has support; if he believes in someone or something, he has supported himself in or found support from that person or object. Elegchos 'basis for testing' is a legal term used in debates or cross-examination. Hope is a major word in Hebrews 10.23; 6.11, 6.18, thus the groundwork of things hoped for is faith.' Are hupostasis 'guarantee' objectively and elegchos 'being sure' subjectively. Luther accepted Melanchthon's Zuversicht 'confidence' 'conviction' or 'proof.' Hupostasis has many uses depending on domains.[387] Elegchos in the verb means convicting, disciplineing, reproving, correcting or punishing. Cf. Prv 12.1; 13.18; 15.10; 15.32 but not relevant here. Objective use yields ' bringing to light Jn 3.20;demonstrating, proving Wis 1.9; Ep.Diog.9.6; disprosinge Ep.Deiog.2.9; Job reasoning 13.6; pleading 16.22; arguing 23.4. Subjectively: conviction, 'faith is the state of being concvinced' or 'faith conviinces one of the realty what one does not see.' Objectively' evidence, demonstration'. As a definition of faith several problems exist: 1. There is no mention of God or Christ. 2. Is it a definition or simply describing whart faith does: 'Faith binds the believer to the reality of what he does not yet see, but for which he hopes' (or has expectation). 3. Are two parts of the verse synonymous? There is no kai.4. If so it is a chiasmus. If not 'confidence' and then 'proof' would be a complete thought. [388] The author in 10.35, 10.36; 10.39,and 12.1-2 and elsewhere avoids mentioning the object of faith. Is this to avoid the name of God as was present protcol in Judaism? Or is faith in Christ and of Christ one that includes the trinity and entire revelation of God? In this where multiple causes are apparent authors frequently use the passive voice.

11.2 'Commended' 'attested' not 'condemned'. The 'commendation' corresponds to 'Well done, good and fathful servant' which is a direct link to verses like 'Noah was righteous in his generation' and 'Job was perfect' David 'a man after God's own heart' and 'Moses was meeker than..." In 11.2 presbuteroi are examples of saintly men, mainly from the OT. In the Apocalypse the elders are probably not angels, because

1. Angels are never said to occupy thrones; they stand in God's service;
2. Nor are crowns ever ascribed to angels;
3. The designation elders' is unparalleled if used for angels;
4. In Rev 19.4 they are redeemed.

The ascension of Isaiah 9.6-12 assigns thrones, crowns, robes to just men of the OT. Since they are dressed like priests, the number 24 could reflect the 24 classes of priests in Chronicles. But these features do not belong exclusively to priests! 1 QM 12.1-8 refers to saints in heaven. If elders are glorified saints and not angels they may be prophets or wise men. They do not have any Christian features., Ford,[389]72. OT elders and Greek society elders would not be the same. 'Perseverance' is the quality of endurance one side of which is faith and the other faithfulness. The latter is hard if there are entangling things. The ritual and doctrine of confirmation of children who had been baptized as infants, and of 'confirming grace' as another term for the grace of Entire Sanctification or Christian Perfection also deal with this issue. Last Rights or Last Unction in the Catholic Church also concern the soul's salvation as one approaches or enters into death. In all of this discipleship training is aiming at a more than 'in the door' believer, but one that can face bitter challenges and even pain, torture and martyrdom. 'surrounded by such a great cloud of witnesses' cannot refer to the living because it is in the context of martyrdom. Nor are these mere humans on earth observing the living habits of believers. Nor is it the dead whose spirits are roaming the earth. The point is that those who finished the race are with Jesus. But are they fully aware of what is going on in the lives of people on earth? This is not a question the context is asking or answering. But these witnesses are the context of contemporaneity for every believer, the track is the environment or place, and the direction is toward one goal out ahead, Jesus himself. 'things that hinder or sins that beset are in the analogy of a runner, but extend to whatever might make winning impossible. Greeks ran naked. But spiritually runners can be hindered by food, discipline, unhappiness, disease, vanity, and a whole gamut of emotional problems. According to Hebrews major hindrances are fear of dying,ch.2., neglect of the word 2.33; hardening heart 3.8; unbelief 3.19; coming short of a promise 4.3; disobedience 4.6; go on….not laying again 6.2; laziness 6.12; etc. To run with patience is either endurance or perseverance for the long run. This race is not one we choose but is 'marked out for us' by the one in charge of the race. 'Throw off': Did Elijah's need for the mantle till the very last need to be cast off in order for him to be carried off to heaven? Was his seeming unwillingness to transfer his ministry to Elisha symbolized in his mantle? Are dead believers present observers? Jesus spoke of a gulf between the unbelieving dead and heaven as well earth without saying what 'Lazarus' in heaven knew. Does the appearance of Elijah and Moses indicate their present involvement in earthly affairs as is indicate for angels? Jesus said God is not the God of the dead Abraham, Isaac or Jacob but of the living, meaning that these were still living. Is there soul sleep? These texts would indicate not. Only Daniel 12 might indicate sleep till the Day of Resurrection. But the souls of those who died as martyrs in Revelation, who pray beneath the altar day and night, their blood having been poured out beneath the altar that cries out as even Abel's blood cried out, are very aware of earthly affairs. All are crying for justice and vengeance. So are the 'witnesses' in 12.1 angels? From OT perspective witnesses were in 'the Gate' of the city not in an arena. This would make life here pursued as if in the very gateway to heaven. The OT does show observations about messengers and their running. Hindrances are obstacles. Jesus spoke of occasions of stumbling or rocks of offence, causing others to stumble. They are not sin but cause sin. For this reason Judaism as considered the instigator of sin to have the more serious offence. [The current evangelical theology does not recognize that the Bible has degrees of sin in both testaments and even in the words of Jesus]. Jesus said his own ministry will cause and has caused many to fall, but woe to any believer that causes people to stumble. For this reason hindrances are here listed with 'sins' as being equally injurious and punishable, but here basically they function as a drag or stumbling block toward finishing the race. There is nothing here about winning or being first, such as with some OT runners. Here the issue is simply finishing the race. The time factor is excluded because most will finish in martyrdom. Only one verse speaks of the runner in the OT: Job 9:25 "My days are swifter than a runner; they fly away without a glimpse of joy. But many[39 times] speak of messengers and runners as part of the news-bearers in the army.[390] In the ANE they served an important function but not in terms of observers but message. While the race course metaphor is used, the OT corresponding concept is 'way'/'ways', a motif not only in the Psalms, Proverbs but also in Deuteronomy and the prophets. "The way to life" in Prov 10.17 implies more than life here and now. Prov 10.29 "The way of the Lord is a refuge for the righteous but ruin to those who do evil." This is similar to those who preach, heal, cast out demons, that say 'Lord, Lord' but the Lord will not recognize them in that day, because they are in the way but are doing evil. Jesus divided life into two ways, a right narrow way and a broad wrong way, hence the doctrine of "two ways." Similarly, "the way of the wicked" in Prov 12.26 leads them further and further astray. But in 12.28 "In the way of righteousness there is life, along that path there is immortality" makes this, as in Heb 12.1, the way to heaven and not just one's career or life on earth.

11.2 In 7.8 God witnesses emarturethesan, as in v.4, and is the same as witness of scripture 10.15. 1 Clem 17.1ff; 1.18.1; 19.1; 30.7 Also there is man's testimony and to human works as good 1 Tim 5.10. God's witness and man's witness establish truth and reality. In the Scripture both are present. In the OT God also witnesses to sin and to the heart of man, and to every action done.

11.3 'God said let there be light' is taken as a command that invisible elements obeyed. Gen 1 really doesn't start creation with primaeval unseen elements such as water, wind, tohu-wa-bohu chaos but with physics and the basis of all things in light. 'The ages were put in order katartisthai tous aionas, not created. The faith needed for God to be creator is that he is a king whose orders are obeyed and not only by what is but by what isn't as yet. In Gen 18 this is what the Lord asked Abraham to believe that what isn't will be born 'next year at this time'.[391]

Faith is productive:

1. understanding the non-empirical;
2. of commendation by men and God;
3. of righteousness in individual character;
4. of communication effectiveness v.4;
5. of deliverance from earthly life v.5;
6. of pleasure to God v.6;
7. of theology, the study of God v.6;
8. of seeking God as earnest endeavor v.6;
9. of holy fear to obey and save one's own v.7;
10. of condemnation of evil men v.7;
11. of being heirs of righteousness v.7;
12. of obedience to leave security v.8;
13. of a vision of the unseen city v.10;
14, of enabling to conceive and descendents v.11;
15. of dying in the faith v.13;
16. of admission or confession of alien status v.13;
17. of longing for a better country v.16;
18. of offering Isaac the heir v.17;
19. of reasoning v.19;
20. of blessing both Jacob and Esau contrary to custom v.20;

21. of prophecy about the future v.22;
22. of instructions for the future v.22;
23. of perception, boldness and a plan v.23;
24. of refusal to identify with Egyptian identity v.24;
25. of choice to be mistreated with v.25;
26. of logical conclusion: disgrace was greater that treasures of the present v.26.
27. of travel, victory over fear, perseverance, keeping Passover v.27-28;
28. of hospitality, covenant, choice for God v.31.

This list could be extended, but many have to do with internal processes. The restatement of Gen 1.1 that 'the universe,' not solar system, was 'formed' at God's command, and clarified 'so that what is seen was not made out of what was visible,' acknowledges the original darkness, abyss, water and wind of Gen 1.1-2 but uses a naturalistic setting of the early morning sunrise and places it into a forming of invisible things into visible and forming these into the universe. This process cannot be observed and is not based on material evidence and must be based on faith. To start this chapter using 'we' transcends the generation gap from Abel [not Adam] to the NT believers and martyrs by starting with God, the Word, faith, and creation. The modern question is dealt with again in v.6 the belief God exists and that He rewards those who diligently seek him.' These were greater problems of faith under Greek thought that in the Semitic world. This insertion interrupts the illustrations that follow, but is not a digression. Creation of the universe precedes the 'are created', and secondly 'we understand' continues and carries over to v.4 and following. We 'see' the biblical record with the sins, errors. mistakes and also faith, but we 'understand' the heavenly record by faith alone. katartizw 'were ordered.'

"The superiority of the divine bara' over human creations is also shown in the fact that the object of this verb is never a substance, an intermediate stage, but always the result, the completed and perfect work. The originality inherent in this term does not, however, prevent its association with expressions borrowed from anthropomorphic speech; it is used as parallel to 'as1ah in Gen 1.26,27, with yatsar and konen in Am 4.13; Isa 43.1; 45.18; so that these can be used as evidence in favor of creation ex nihilo. This idea is foreign to the Old Testament, where God is content to mould matter without creating it, though the sovereignty he shows, in the readiness with which the elements bend to his orders, compel us to recognize that creatio ex nihilo was the only possible issue from the thought of the Old Testament in which the action of God increasingly tends to take a less material form, namely that of the word. Creation by a word is not an idea peculiar to Israel, but by presenting the diverse works of creation as a simple order from God, the Priestly writer gives unequalled expression to the divine sovereignty and to the marvelous character of creation."[392] These "show sufficiently the extent to which the line starting from Genesis 1 determined the teaching of Judaism." Jacob, 143. The overwhelming structure of this chapter is 'Instrumentation': 'by faith'. With the phrase occurring 5 times before the break in v.6 and 5 times after the break, including Abraham. A break occurs at v.13-16 and v.16-17 returns to Abraham. Note v.13 'living by faith' is a different structure. 5 patriarchs follow Abraham v.17, Isaac v.20, Jacob v.21, Joseph v.22; Moses' parents' v.23. 5 occurrences deal with Moses. 1 with Rahab. 6 are given names only v.32. vv 33-35 are the successful, of which 9 are men and 1 a woman, with 10-13 'others' mentioned. Contrastingly, v.36-37 lists the 'unsuccessful' with those 10-13 names. 'let heaven and earth be made' as a passive avoids the personal agent and corresponds to other passives or ergatives in Gen 1. Cf. . Ps 33.6,9; 2 Pet 3.5; 2 Bar 14.17. The words are added in Esdra:" your word accomplished the work' Myers,228. This interrupts the illustrations that follow, but is not a digression. Creation of the universe precedes the 'are created', and secondly 'we understand' continues and carries over to v.4 and following. We perceive the biblical record with the sins, errors, mistakes, and also faith, but we 'understand' the heavenly record by faith alone.

11.4 'Commended as a righteous man' implies God brought fire on his sacrifice to consume it since it is within the narrative action that God commended him and also later through the narrator. The partiality felt by Cain would thus be pertinent. God spoke well of his offerings is read from the narrator, and reflects that burnt offerings were basic to God's pleasure while grain offerings were not since there was no life for life and no blood. The OT stresses that Cain must do good, in order for his offering to be accepted and he must conquer the demon at the door. Abel offered 'a better sacrifice' and 'God spoke well of his offerings' [plural]. The double witness verifies God's commendation. Faith is not only internal but seen in behavioral attitude and choices as well. This kind of sacrifice was offered through the motivation of faith and seeking God. His commendation and speaking today are all by his faith. His righteousness was through his faith. Was it because he knew God that a blood sacrifice was required? So was his faith really faithfulness to what God asks of a person? It could not be trust in the sacrifice itself, but rather in God, who accepts a person of faith and faithfulness. 10.19 indicates that believers today as well as Abel have confidence to enter through the blood.

Peterson notes "v.4–6 Moving on through the pages of the OT, the writer notes that Abel's faith was expressed when he *offered God a better sacrifice than Cain did.* The difference was not in the substance of the sacrifices (Gn. 4:3–4), but in the attitude of the two brothers (as implied in Gn. 4:4–7). Cain was told that his offering would be acceptable if he did what was right (*Cf.* . Pr. 15:8). But God testified to the righteousness of Abel and to the faith that motivated him when he *spoke well of his offerings.* Abel *still speaks* in the sense that he witnesses to the faith that pleases God, 393" The faith is linked to character in both the cases of Cain and Abel. The faith of Abel has the extra component of God's witness to Abel and us as well as Abel's continuing witness to us. Nothing more was asked of him. But Cain 'if you do well' indicates a behavioral disorder, that sacrifice was a burden or a substitute for righteousness and therefore unacceptable to God. The faith 1.faith enabled him to offer a better sacrifice; 2. Spoke well of his offerings; God still speaks by his faith. The offering, as in Abraham, is the point of the revelation that he pleased God. The same is true of Enoch without being able to see how God enabled him. The first act of faith in history in Abel's. Here it is not a matter of 'accepting Abel and his sacrifice' but of 'accepting Abel's sacrifice and then Abel.' Note 'righteous' follows the offerings, does not precede them. The message of 'Abel' and every 'saint' speaks, he speaks through righteous character and his worship. 'By faith' is both his then and ours now. Rom 1.17 speaks of 'from faith to faith.' Ours because of what is heard 4.2 that must always be mixed with faith. Gen 4.3-5 Faith in addition to the sacrifice makes it a greater sacrifice. The OT account does not show this clearly except to say God accepted Abel and his offering. Apparently Cain did not offer with faith so neither he nor his offering were accepted. 'If you do right' and 'if you subdue sin' you will be accepted. By not having faith in God's bestowal of blessing in God's own way he could not accept his brother nor his responsibility. He did not believe in responsibility toward the family, and this in Israel is a major sin.

The faith:

1. faith enabled him to offer a better sacrifice;
2. Spoke well of his offerings; God still speaks by his faith. The offering, as in Abraham, is the point of the revelation that he pleased God. The same is true of Enoch without being able to see how God enabled him.

The first act of faith in history in Abel's. [394] Here it is not a matter of 'accepting Abel and his sacrifice' but of 'accepting Abel's sacrifice and then Abel.' Note 'righteous' follows the offerings, does not precede them. The message of 'Abel' and every 'saint' speaks, he speaks through righteous character and his worship. 'By faith' is both his then and ours now. Rom 1.17 speaks of 'from faith to faith.' Ours because of what is heard 4.2 that must always be mixed with faith. Emphatic concession, by the use of the participle.[395] 'By faith he was commended as a righteous man' may point to God's faith in him that elicited the commendation, or to Abel's faith by which God justified him. But what was the connection of his offerings, plural on many occasions??, or did he know the heart of God and his need and offer what pleased God to represent his heart's attitude?

11.5 'To please God' and to do works that bring attention from God or that make up for sins committed are two separate things. Forgiveness is a sovereign act of God and based on grace alone. But it is always the duty of man to please God and done in the way God accepts. The motivating power is to do right and the result is that he pleased God. To aim at pleasing God by specific acts approaches the self-acclaim that focuses not on God but self. Nehemiah approached this in mentioning all he had done for God in his prayer for divine assistance, but he knew that only divine assistance would allow the work to be accomplished. Gen 5.21-24 the text is only quoted, but his translation to heaven was 'by faith'. Did he believe that he need not die that God would take him alive? Thus Hebrews has shifted the stress from 'Enoch walked with God.' This is unique in the whole OT. The Enoch Pseudepigrapha bear witness to the productivity of this man of God. Selectivity can account for omitting Elijah, who also did not die.

11.6 'Faith' is parallel to 'believe' and the noun clause 'that' mentions two things, God's existence and his rewards, plus a subjective element that seeking God is efficacious. Implied it is that Abel had this faith and received his reward, while Cain evidently lacked in this respect. 'It is impossible" to please God: But the double negation defines it as possible to please God. Faith in God pleases God and the context is Pre-Jewish, Pre-Hebraic, Pre-Christian and hence Universal, hence without either Bible or Incarnation. In this kind of 'dispensation' it is possible to please God. The goal of faith is to please God as Abel did. This verse implies Abel earnestly sought God and was not simply engaged in fulfilling a religious obligation, entertained superstitions or carried out rituals; his heart was in it. "reward" God speaks to Ezra: "For this reason you alone have been informed: Because you have relinquished your [own interests], And devoted yourself to mine; You have explored my law, You have dedicated your life to wisdom, And you have called understanding your mother.. That is why I disclosed this to you, for there is reward with the

Most High." Myers,[396]313. 'It is impossible" to please God: But the double negation defines it as possible to please God. Faith in God pleases God and the context is Pre-Jewish, Pre-Hebraic, Pre-Christian and hence Universal, hence without either Bible or Incarnation. In this kind of 'dispensation' it is possible to please God. It isn't the passages on sacrifice that show the desire to please God but the Psalms as they transparently show the worshipper before God almost as if there was no temple mount, temple personnel or ark present. The goal of faith is to please God as Abel did. This verse implies Abel earnestly sought God and was not simply engaged in fulfilling a religious obligation, entertained superstitions or carried out rituals; his heart was in it.

'Without faith it is impossible to please God.' In the OT faith is included in hearing, obeying, acting, hoping, and not merely believing some doctrine. The basic need in the OT to please God has not changed for believer or unbeliever alike. So the writer makes this commendation and Hall of Fame with the understanding that persecuted believers still want to please God. Those that believed he existed and rewarded all pleased God. He doesn't deal with the situation of the prophetic period when people believed God existed and rewarded but disobeyed and compromised themselves. All the while they sacrificed and sought to please God they were disobeying His clear laws. To Ahaz 'If you will not establish[God's word] you will not be established.' The verb based on 'Amen' h'emin in Hiphil and Hophal is a leading word for 'have faith in'., "reward" God speaks to Ezra: "For this reason you alone have been informed: Because you have relinquished your [own interests], And devoted yourself to mine; You have explored my law, You have dedicated your life to wisdom, And you have called understanding your mother.. That is why I disclosed this to you, for there is reward with the Most High."[397] Faith in God's existence is the base faith required of all men to win approval from God. To not believe in God's existernce is the utmost in denial. The second and co-oborating faith is that God does reward those who diligently seek him. This is not only fo success, health, well-being, long life, and such selfish self-seeking, but simply the reward to those who are seekers after God. They are centered on God, who cannot be seen, proven, and who speaks sometimes seldom, yet rewards those wh patiently wait and seek with endurance. Chambers said worship, waiting, and work are not a series but simultaneous in the believer's life.[398]

11.7 'When warned about things unseen' pertains to faith not in person or processes or things with analogous record or evidence but faith in what does not yet exist. For the resultant fear to grip him and motivate to build for a

120 year old period is remarkable. Because of it he saved his whole family, but not based on two or three witnesses. Faith is the power and perseverance to build and the response in holy fear, that 'went', not merely 'reverence' in the OT sense, but' holy fear' paired with 'warned.' Reading into the OT from this it is obvious that pistis should never be totally lacking the sense of 'fear' to maintain the idea of 'reverence' since this text clarifies the basis for the proper translation. Faith is the power and perseverance to build and the response in holy fear, that 'went', not merely 'reverence' in the OT sense, but' holy fear' paired with 'warned.' Reading into the OT from this it is obvious that ary should never be totally lacking the sense of 'fear' to maintain the idea of 'reverance' since this text clarifies the basis for the proper translation. Noah's faith was to respond to a divine warning by holy fear and building of an ark to save his family. This was more than works or obedience, since it mobilized his whole being to do what he believed was an absolute necessity. The same act, perhaps with preaching also, condemned the world and thus he became heir of the righteousness that comes by faith. Action is not 'works' when it springs from obedient faith. Preaching and warning and building done in faith condemned the world. All these actions done by faith made him eligible for justification [righteousness] by faith at the end, while at first, as in Gen 6, he was righteous comparatively [in his generation,--a fact omitted by Hebrews] and was seen as righteous. At the end of the story the covenant and accepted sacrifice confirm that Noah was righteous and declared righteous.

Purpose or Intent in Noah's action is to save his family, not selfish, but a response to the warning and plan that came from God. John the Baptist preached similarly 'to escape from the wrath to come.' Peter warned the Penrtecost crowd to escape this wicked generation. Secondly, by so doing he 'condemned' the world [as Jesus said 'I I had not come that had not sin']. Thus thirdly, he became heir to the righteousness by faith, which is the result of this process and cause-effect chain of events. No one was saved by merit but rather by response to God's initiative.

Several verses relate to the topic of the illogicality of faith.

1. Here is the building of a huge ark, the first of its kind and probably on par with a modern freighter, all when there was as yet no indication it had rained as yet.
2. In v.8 the trip without a prior destination is also 'absurd'.
3. The 'reasoning' in v.19 contrasts with this topic, but the reasoning begins with the Creator and deduces that God can cause a resurrection. In the ANE the very concept existed in myth and legend, but not in doctrine, and not outside Baalism in Canaan.

4. V.25 mistreatment; v. 26 disgrace; v.35 torture; v.34 refusal to be released from prison; and then jeers etc. These are certain and are gladly accepted instead of comfort and security. It is obvious from this ideal that psychological testing and the so-called norm that is used would consider these people to be in need of deep long-term counseling. But the worldly 'norm' is simply the way of sight and not of faith.

   Fear as a motivator for and of faith.

Fear of God in the Bible, especially in Proverbs and Ecclesiastes and other wisdom literature, pertains to both a terror elicited by the Lord and felt by a person that enabled him to seek to please God, and an attitude of deep respect and submission that led to obedience and confidence in God's commands. Both are in the role of two witnesses to God's work in the soul; to avoid the appearance of evil and urge all men to do likewise, and to hasten to complete the work God has commited to one. Noah manifested both aspects. It was after the flood when crisis had melted away and sacrifices made, and God's word of promise was received that he was tripped up by his passions. After reconciliation with God it might be easier to not continue that self-control that is part of the fear of God.

11.8 'Called to go' links faith to the event by an act of obedience and going. This is applicable to the NT faith expressed in pisteuw bordering on peithw. Abraham was not called by a father, priest, preacher, king or prophet, but by God himself. The negative feature here is 'he didn't know' 11.7 says he 'condemned' but in 2 Pet 2.5 note the twice repeated 'even though' .v8,11. Here are given many challenges to faith. The negative feature here is 'he didn't know' 11.7 says he 'condemned' but in 2 Pet 2.5 note the twice repeated 'even though' .v8,11. Here are given many challenges to faith.

11.8-16 Here are many passives, men and women as agents, ergatives v.16 with 'experiencers.' God's role is in v.16 He is not ashamed of them nor are they ashamed of God. He has prepared for them; v.17 God tests them; God said to him. For many there was no command in the narrative but they knew what was God's will. The initiative to do what is right is what is lauded. Many of the situations were not because of God's arranging or their mistakes, but the unknown opposer and faith responds in faithfulness in these situations.

11.9 'By faith' is not 'by words' or 'by works of the flesh' or by' my Spirit'. The faith was to be able to continue [1] as a stranger after he has moved to the Land of Promise. But by means of altars, tents, buying the Cave Macpelah, and the Abimelech treaty, as well as the Melchizedek Tenth and Amorite treaty he was trying to not be a stranger. But in the feudalistic sense only Macpelah was exceptional and a faith compromise. If 'stranger' [2] is not the point of emphasis, then he really sought a place to live and stop trial and error places. But the reason for his movements in Palestine may have been that as a merchant and the seasonal needs of flocks he had to move about. In this reading God wanted him to settle down. If both the above factors are in mind, then the Promise stimulated efforts to settle down, to fulfill the plan, to own land and flocks, and yet be mobile in the sense of not making the current state of affairs and a permanent dwelling place. For the 'merchant' soher concept we have meta-textual [archeological] evidence only that a merchant could not live in one place all year around under Hittite law. Were Egypt and Philistia a part of this scenario, or foreign resident requirement or part of his business, Here two famines drove him to Egypt and Philistia; was this to discipline him because he was settling in, and hence forced to move over and over again, especially out of Egypt and Philistia where he had started to settle down? The message is that all three lived by tents and this proved their faith. The message is that all three lived by tents and this proved their faith.

11.10 'Foundations' are plural, not only one foundation. In the NT there is 1. Christ; 2. Prophets and apostles; and 3. 'Depart from iniquity.4. Revelation' Note that Jesus said he is going to prepare a place. In Rev.21 there is the heavenly Jerusalem, whose foundations are not on soil. Rev 21.2 since the gown of the heavenly bride covers the 'foundation' from sight. In 21.14 there are 12 foundations to the walls corresponding to the twelve apostles. But in 21.19 the foundations are precious stones, jasper, sapphire, chalcedony, emerald, sardonx, carnelian, chrysolite, beryl, topaz, chrysoprese, jacinth, amethyst. Sumerian archeology has a lot of information about foundations. Is this because the apostles became foundation sacrifices in the Sumerian sense? This brings up the motif of 'without hands' found in Daniel. The builder and maker is God [architect and builder]. This contrasts also to Nehemiah and all the hands that were engaged in that project. What city? It turned out not to be Shechem, Bethel, Jerusalem, Hebron or Beersheba. Apparently he never entered into any of the cities in the land. The reasons for rejecting these cities could be the aborigine populations. The Jerusalem [Salem] incident was the closest to accepting a place, person, religion, functionary of the land hence the parallel is that he was really looking forward to a heavenly Jerusalem. The same reference to the city appears in II Esdras 8.52[399] In 2 Esdras it is linked to Paradise being opened and tree of life planted. Myers,[400]246, Apocalyptic literature often refers to the new Jerusalem[401]. This brings up the motif of 'without hands' found in Daniel. The builder and maker is God [architect and builder]. This contrasts also to Nehemiah and all the hands that were engaged in that project. What city? It turned out not to be Shechem, Bethel, Jerusalem, Hebron or Beersheba. Apparently he never entered into any of the cities in the land. The reasons for rejecting these cities could be the aborigine populations. The Jerusalem [Salem] incident was the closest to accepting a place, person, religion, functionary of the land hence the parallel is that he was really looking forward to a heavenly Jerusalem. The same reference to the city appears in II Esdras 8.52; Sir 24.11; 2 Bar 4.2ff; Rev 3.12; 21.2,10; 2 Esd 10.42. In 2 Esdras it is linked to Paradise being opened and tree of life planted. Myers,[402]246, Apocalyptic literature often refers to the new Jerusalem Rev 21.10; 1 En 90.28-29.; 2 Esd 13.36; but it also appears in the Talmud in Tannith 5a; Baba Bathra 75b; Hermas Visions 3.4-5 and Nag Hammadi VI 1.line 24. 274,276. Does the plural 'foundations' correspond to the 12 patriarchs and 12 Apostles?

11.11 Abraham had Ishmael. So Abraham had no problem of sterility; Sarah did. She was barren. But it was Abraham whom God enabled. The one with faith was enabled. Sarah in Gen 18 lacked faith. This explains Gen 15.6 'he considered him [God] faithful who had made the promise' In 15.6 ' It/he was reckoned to him [God] as righteousness/vindication. God's faithfulness is to the promise. What was Sarah thinking through all of this? Did she ever come to true faith?

11.12 In 11.2 presbyteroi are examples of saintly men, mainly from the OT. Ellenworth,568 are not church leaders, senior members of community, nor patriarchs, but earlier generations in Israel. In the Apocalypse the elders are probably not angels, because;

1. Angels are never said to occupy thrones; they stand in God's service;
2. Nor are crowns ever ascribed to angels;
3. The designation elders' is unparalleled if used for angels;
4. In Rev 19.4 they are redeemed.

   The ascension of Isaiah 9.6-12 assigns thrones, crowns, robes to just men of the OT. Since they are dressed like priests, the number 24 could reflect the 24 classes of priests in Chronicles. But these features do not belong exclusively to priests! 1 QM 12.1-8 refers to saints in heaven. If elders are glorified saints and not angels they may be prophets or wise men. They do not have any Christian features., Ford,[403]72. OT elders and Greek society elders would not be the same, how great. [404] '..' a comparative idea James 3.5 and II Esdras 4.31"Because a grain of evil seed was sown in the heart of Adam from the beginning, how much wickedness it has brought forth until now and will yet bring forth by 'threshing time' Calculate now for yourselves how great a harvest of wickedness a [single] grain of evil seed has brought forth..." Myers,[405]175.

11.13 'what they did' is living by faith. This goes on beyond their years. The focus is on faithfulness through the point of death. The message of 12.4 permeates the death and offers a closure to Gen 5 the 'and he died' chapter that merely gives the world's 'seeing' perspective, except for Enoch. Hebrews ch.11 gives the 'faith-ing' perspective. Not everyone merely dies. 'They did not receive the things' which is repeated in v.39. Faith exists with or without miracles and fulfillments. The stress of the author's philosophy of history is on final fulfillment and thus the OT looked forward to the NT just as the NT looks forward to 'the world to come'. parepidemos is a foreigner temporarily in a place, a sojourner. In an city of Egypt foreigners were distinguished from natives as <u>katoikountes</u> but in Ex 12.45; Lev 22.10 as paroikoi. They had obtained right to domicile. The parepidemoi, or sojourners,[406] were foreigners who were only passing through the city, not establishing themselves there; i.e. they stayed only long enough to unload cargo or settle a business matter... Abraham at Hebron called himself a resident alien "I am a resident alien and a sojourner in your midst." Cf. . Heb 11.13. They were 'strangers and exiles on the earth." <u>Xenoi kao parepidemi eisin epi ten gen</u> Philo said "every wise soul has received heaven as its country, the earth as a foreign land; it considers the corporeal dwelling as someone else's property in which it must sojourn parepidemein" [407]Spicq: 3.40-43; see 1 Pet 1.1. Phil 3.20; 'I urge you as aliens and <u>paroikous kai parepidemous</u> to abstain from carnal desires'. Note Gen 23.4 <u>ger</u> <u>wetoshab</u> Dhorme: a foreigner who has been received as a resident in a neighboring country but does not have the rights of a native. "strangers in the earth' appears also in Ps 119.19; 1 Pet 2.11 here and II Esdras 16.41 "Listen to the word, O my people; prepare yourselves for the combat and in the [coming] calamities you must be just like strangers in the earth--he who sells as one who escapes, and he who buys as one who will lose..." Myers,[408]347.

'Did not receive the things' which is repeated in v.39. Faith exists with or without miracles and fulfillments. The stress of the author's philosophy of history is on final fulfillment and thus the OT looked forward to the NT just as the NT looks forward to 'the world to come' <u>Parepidemos</u> is a foreigner temporarily in a place, a sojourner. In a city of Egypt foreigners were distinguished from natives as katoikountes but in Ex 12.45; Lev 22.10 as paroikoi. They had obtained right to a domicile. The parepidemoi, or sojourners,[409] were foreigners who were only passing through the city, not establishing themselves there; i.e. they stayed only long enough to unload cargo or settle a business matter...Abraham at Hebron called himself a resident alien "I am a resident alien and a sojourner in your midst." Cf. . Heb 11.13. They were 'strangers and exiles on the earth." Xenoi kao parepidemi eisin epi ten gen Philo said "every wise soul has received heaven as its country, the earth as a foreign land; it considers the corporeal dwelling as someone else's property in which it must sojourn parepidemein"[410] Spicq: 3.40-43; see 1 Pet 1.1. Phil 3.20; 'I urge you as aliens and paroikous kai parepidemous to abstain from carnal desires'. Note Gen 23.4 ger wetoshab Dhorme: a foreigner who has been received as a resident in a neighboring country but does not have the rights of a native. Ps 39.12[411] The promises were larger than the times and involved a large population and processes that were predicted in Gen 15 and 17. There had to be a lapse of time for the stage to be set. So Abram had Isaac, he had a treaty with Abimelech, he bought a burial site in perpetuity, but he only received a pledge of what was to come.

11.13, 11.13,'Strangers in the earth' appears also in Ps 119.19; 1 Pet 2.11 here and II Esdras 16.41"Listen to the word, O my people; prepare yourselves for the combat and in the [coming] calamities you must be just like strangers in the earth--he who sells as one who escapes, and he who buys as one who will lose..." Myers,[412]347. v.13-14 The 40 years in the wilderness enabled Israel to recover the situation and faith of the Patriarchs, where Abraham's story has just been summarized. To create the drive and hope of a country, not an earthly one, they had to develop a mindset of the alien, the foreign resident and stranger or foreigner. It is this testimony that makes a person and people unashamed to acknowledge God and God unashamed to acknowledge them. For the Judges and kingdom period the drive for an earthly country, a king, and earthly kingdom overwhelmed the prime objective. It allowed them to fall from grace into Canaanite type feudalism, classed society, unequal distribution of wealth, employment of power moves by authorities and oppression legally and economically. It was the exile that made them briefly aliens again and this happened over and over again. Is the real test of faith to have a settled society and yet look for a city that is not Jerusalem and Mount Zion? Is it to have a country and to not make holding on to it the obsession and basic antagonism to looking for another land and city? V.14 'Seeking a country' v.16 'a city' v.10 an urban orientation; v.20 'a future; v.26 a reward. Did the fact that he never entered a city in Canaan have anything to do with seeking for a heavenly city? He approached only Shechem, Bethel, Jerusalem, Beersheba, Hebron, and Sodom

11.16 'God is not ashamed..' The OT does not attribute this emotion to God but to sinners and enemies under disciplinary judgment. But in a 'shame' not 'guilt' society shame is a strong motivation. Heb 2.11 Jesus s not ashamed to call them brethren. Lk 9.26 'The Son of man will be ashamed of him.' The latter is the glorified Son of man. polei theou zwntos Heb 12.22; 11.10; 13.14; Gal 4.26; Phil 3.20; Rev 3.12 is an urban or civic metaphor in the NT for the Christian life. Heaven is like a city polis; Christ is its sovereign kurios, and it has its own laws and constitution politeia, namely the Gospel and laws of the kingdom. Christians are its citizens politai. A fourth century Christian letter reads "for we believe that your citizenship is in heaven' pisteuomen gar ten politian sou en ouranw SB 2265,5 A certain pride attached to one's city "I am a citizen of Tarsus in Cilicia, no obscure city' Acts 21.39. A third-century inscription IGLAM,n.1480: "Tarsus, the first and greatest and most noble metropolis. The only city or district to which patriarchs seem to be drawn is to Harran. [413] Spicq,3.124n1. Citing Heb 11.10,16; 12.22; 13.14 Box translated Esdras.10.49 'her figure' as 'the [heavenly] pattern of her', a reference to the heavenly city. Cf. . Ex 25.9,40 the pattern or model of the tabernacle. Note that in Qumran tbnyt, as in 1 QMM 10.14, refers to the pattern or shape of Adam and 4Q.#40,#24.3 use the phrase tbnyt ksh hbkrm 'the model[or structure] of the throne chariot' In the OT it appears 15 times, especially in late documents. Vulgate uses exemplar for Ex 9.40. It was this heavenly pattern [the original] that was shown to Ezra in II Esdras 10.49.Myers,[414]276. Citing Heb 11.10,16; 12.22; 13.14 Box translated Esdras.10.49 'her figure' as 'the [heavenly] pattern of her', a reference to the heavenly city. Cf. .Ex 25.9,40 the pattern or model of the tabernacle. Note that in Qumran tbnyt, as in 1 QMM 10.14, refers to the pattern or shape of Adam and 4Q.#40,#24.3 use a phrase meaning 'the model[or structure] of the throne chariot' In the OT it appears 15 times, especially in late documents. Vulgate uses exemplar for Ex 9.40. It was this heavenly pattern [the original] that was shown to Ezra in II Esdras 10.49.Myers,[415]276

11.15

11.16

11.17 'One and only son' Ishmael and Hagar had both been disinherited and cast out. This was the only son God recognized as firstborn, but not son with the promise. From the ANE background 'firstborn' is a position of heir and not necessarily the firstborn. Especially is this true if the actual wife later gives birth to a son. God authorized and Abraham cast out Hagar and the firstborn that Abraham cared for very much and from that point on he only had one son. Note that apart from the plan through Abraham the OT proclaims God's plan, another plan, for the Arab descendants of Hagar and Ishmael. God tested but there is no mention of YHWH, saving v.18 which says 'he reasoned 'Elohim could raise the dead.' The passive 'he did receive indicates the action of YHWH. Note in the OT account it is 'elohim that commands the sacrifice and in Elohim Abraham has confidence they will all return from the altar of Moriah, but that it is the 'Angel of YHWH' that saves the 'only son'. Compared to Jesus, the Father did not spare him, but gave him up. Does this mean that the object of Abraham's faith as indicated by the name changed, or that the author of the story interpreted Elohim to be an earlier non-specific object of faith, and that YHWH from that point on was normalized orthodox faith, faith in the God who saves and does not allow human sacrifice. The layers even in the OT make it hard to decide this point.

The Testing of men occurs very frequently in the OT[416] Since the theme of backsliding and rebellion, apostasy runs throughout the book and those instances were due to God's testing, a few words are in order to clarify the purpose of those testings.

1. God tests the weak and prone to backslide for them to seek help from Him;
2. God focuses on establishing trust in the absence of all but the word of a servant;
3. God creates a situation of mere survival and sure disaster to wean men from the earth and the past;
4. God enables people to conceive of options, to think, evaluate, but does not force those people to choose the right.
5. God uses a crisis to raise up those leaders that in the future will lead Israel astray.

6. God is concerned to create a situation requiring personal prayer not prayer activity or political action;
7. God is creating history, memories of failures and grace long before the time of establishing a verbal agreement and written covenant.
8. God is causing people to unite for action, causing Moses to realize that a program is needed to develop leadership.
9. God models faithfulness to the covenant and the people who needed to perceive God as faithful to his word regardless of their faithfulness or its lack.
10. God established patience, self-control, fear of God, trust through the cycles of testing and punishment.
11. God causes Moses to intercede or fact a wilderness alone. 12. God is teaching the children. The theme of man testing God and God testing man is found in the Book of Hebrews. Heb. 3:9 where your ancestors put me to the test, though they had seen my works Heb. 11:17 By faith Abraham, when put to the test, offered up Isaac. He who had received the promises was ready to offer up his only son... Heb 11.17 does avoid the question of who did the testing that is clear in Gen 22 as done by μyhla But in Exodus, when God tests or tries it is usually following gross rebellion and unbelief. In Gen 22, along with the Greek indefiniteness, another reading would contrast Elohim with YHWH's angel who does not want to hurt the boy but saves him.

    The question in the Hebrew contrastive structure is how Abraham can recognize the voice of the true God from that of a demon that wants to put an end to salvation history.

1. He could confer with his wife;
2. As Gideon, he could ask for a sign;
3. He could pray a prayer of clarification;
4. He could appeal and plead on Isaac's behalf;
5. He could refer to the promises and the history of grace for Isaac in the first place;
6. He could treat this command as illogical;
7. He could search his heart for some sin that would cause God to do this;
8. He could make a visit to Melchizedek;
9. He could rise early and make a war march preliminary sacrifice;
10. He could confer with his son, since his son may have already been 25 years of age. But he did not. The Climax is not in Abraham's naive obedience to blindly do what ordered to do, but in the Angel of Yahweh who is gives the command of salvation. As applied to the Exodus and Moses

himself it was YHWH who sought to kill him, and circumcision of his son saved them all. It was God's Son Israel that Pharaoh would execute through genocide; it was Yahweh who saved them. The canonical message reflected here is that YHWH- the TETRAGRAMMATON is the Savior of his people! God tested but there is no mention of YHWH, saving v.18 which says 'he reasoned elohim could raise the dead.' The passive 'he did receive indicates the action of YHWH. Note in the OT account it is elohim that commands the sacrifice and in Elohim Abraham has confidence they will all return from the altar of Moriah, but that it is the 'Angel of YHWH' that saves the 'only son'. Compared to Jesus, the Father did not spare him, but gave him up. Does this mean that the object of Abraham's faith as indicated by the name changed, or that the author of the story interpreted Elohim to be an earlier non-specific object of faith, and that YHWH from that point on was normalized orthodox faith, faith in the God who saves and does not allow human sacrifice. The layers even in the OT make it hard to decide this point.

11.18 Gen 21.12 The specific promise had been repeated and enforced in different circumstances, places, times and ways. The promise did not change and, no doubt, he repeated it to his son. The inner contradiction of God's earlier promise and later command seems insurmountable. Had something happened in Isaac's life that disqualified him from inheriting the promises as happened in the case of Israel? Had the Abimelech incident in which Abraham was not faithful or a treaty with 'people of the land' reduced Abraham's use-ability? Or was the recognition that the god elohim who spoke the command was indeed Satan and the 'angel of Yahweh' that issued the second command to not kill his son was the true God? Or was this test necessary just before the death of Sarah in Gen 23, in which case Abraham the value and importance of Isaac was enhanced so that immediately he began to arrange for Isaac's bride. There probably is some truth in all of the above each on a different level.

11.19 'Abraham reasoned': This is important for the readership of the Epistle in Alexandria, possibly, to read and understand in the Greek-Roman Age. God's power and God's promises correspond. The Law said intent to kill involves full guilt of murder, even if opportunity did not present itself. Here "according to your faith" means that Abraham actually received Isaac back from death. The sentence had been passed by both God and Abraham. "In reference to the person of Isaac, at the time of his intended sacrifice by his father Abraham, the NAS of Heb 11.19 reads that 'he received him back from the dead as a type.' But its margin more accurately renders the Grk en parabole as 'figuratively speaking.' So while Isaac's restoration [Gen 22.13] served as a symbol, acted out, of resurrection, it was still not predictive; nor should Isaac be considered as a divinely devised type of Christ's resurrection on Easter." Payne,[417]53n "In reference to the person of Isaac, at the time of his intended sacrifice by his father Abraham, the NAS of Heb 11.19 reads that 'he received him back from the dead as a type.' But its margin more accurately renders the Grk en parabole as 'figuratively speaking.' So while Isaac's restoration [Gen 22.13] served as a symbol, acted out, of resurrection, it was still not predictive; nor should Isaac be considered as a divinely devised type of Christ's resurrection[418] on Easter." [419] At the time there was no Hebrew doctrine of resurrection, and nothing on immortality per se. Like Job his faith created through hope and expectation for his future. But Egyptian Osiris and Babylonian Tammuz and others throughout the ANE had heroic personalities who died and came back for a period of time. But Abraham had the obedience throughout his response to God's call and faith, at this juncture, foresaw, in the light of the promises death was not final. He probably was not thinking of the resurrection of all men but definitely of Isaac. Had Abraham made a distinction between the commands of God and the promises of God,. The first were immediate and the second was future. The future was in God's hands and still is.

11.20 Blessing him in v.21,22 was a deathbed ritual, with the power to effect the intended result. Note that it was not merely a ritual but a legal one and an intended one and one that is a pattern such as even Paul in 2 Timothy follows for his son in the faith. Gen 27.26-40 Both were blessed. His faith included both of them. This was done not by tradition or law of some custom but by faith since custom had only one blessing for one son. But Isaac didn't die immediately, and later after Jacob's return from Harran both sons attended the funeral. According to this text Isaac did accede to Esau's importunate cry to 'bless me only.' Because of Esau's blessing we have Gen 36 list of abundant descendants. Because of Jacob's we have his blessing on Ephraim and Manasseh and later each of his sons. Then Joseph blessed them. But then blessing skips to the final words of Moses.

11.21 About the last act of Jacob and Joseph is for the former to bless Joseph's sons , but in Gen 49 he makes predictions or prophecies about each of his sons. Evidently these were not considered the father's blessings, since the word for blessing only appears in the list in reference to Joseph, even though he is not firstborn nor last born. Nor is Judah blessed. Therefore, it seems Hebrews did not consider this chapter as a blessing document. The predictions are poetic in format, but v.38 is not in the third person each of them is blessed with a blessing appropriate to him. In this the writer in Genesis summarizes the section 1.28 as the blessing of the father to each of his sons, something which the poetic periscope did not do. The one instance and only one cited for Jacob was in contrast to conniving, deceiving, fearing, mistaking, and the moaning less-than-glorifying God testimony he gave to pharaoh, and centers on blessing each of Joseph 's sons, not just one of them. the blessing and prediction on each son is omitted since it belongs to what later Judaism would call the prophetic role of Jacob. It is at the time of leaning on his staff for support that he finally arises to the point of blessing his posterity and thus showing faith in the future as not limited to one son or the other or to the firstborn only. This is done as he worships leaning on top of his staff, not prostrate on the ground. This calls to mind the role of the twelve staffs and Moses and Aaron's staffs in the history of the Exodus, a mark of leadership that is depending on God. This links to v.22. The near-death blessing and worship and the passing on of the vision is a message found in all the literature, from the Torah, Abraham, Jacob, Joseph; to Historical Books: Samuel, David, Solomon; Psalms and Wisdom literature as in Job, Ecclesiastes and Proverbs, and especially in the father figure of Proverbs. This links to v.22. The near-death blessing and worship and the passing on of the vision is a message found in all the literature, from the Torah, Abraham, Jacob, Joseph; to Historical Books: Samuel, David, Solomon; Psalms and Wisdom literature as in Job, Ecclesiastes and Proverbs, and especially in the father figure of Proverbs. Temporal clause with participle.[420]

11.22 Gen 50.24,25 Hebrews misses the very personal communication of Joseph to his sons. God will bring 'aid' He will take you out of this land. He will fulfill his promise to Abraham, Isaac and Jacob. And then he made them swear an oath to carry his bones up.. He wasn't reciting. Hiding or seeking personal refuge, or David finding refuge for his family in Moab while he fled Saul among the badlands of Judah were never considered cowardly or forsaking responsibility. They hid Moses in faith because Miriam was on duty to respond to the baby's crying and the one who picked him up. She was there for him. In the OT Joseph's story as patriarch is detached from succession through Jacob's choice of Ephraim and Manasseh to replace Joseph as heirs with the other tribal leaders and tribes, because in the OT history it came to be Ephraim that represented Israel for much of the history. But what Manasseh did for the royalty is frequently mentioned in scripture, while what Ephraim did in breaking covenant is equally clear. But Joseph has narrative to support his record of faith and in a testament or last words in the form of a prophecy and command that expressed his faith in their leaving Egypt eventually. Joseph thus set in motion the direction of a new generation of Israelites to be willing to leave Egypt under the leadership of Moses. But it is not this that either testament stresses, only Joseph's vision and concern for the future of God's people. This also represents the pinnacle of Joseph's spiritual development, where he is committing himself, his bones, to his brethren as part of his faith in God's promise. In the OT Joseph's story as patriarch is detached from succession through Jacob's choice of Ephraim and Manasseh to replace Joseph as heirs with the other tribal leaders and tribes, because in the OT history it came to be Ephraim that represented Israel for much of the history. But what Manasseh did for the royalty is frequently mentioned in scripture, while what Ephraim did in breaking covenant is equally clear. But Joseph has narrative to support his record of faith and in a testament or last words in the form of a prophecy and command that expressed his faith in their leaving Egypt eventually. Joseph thus set in motion the direction of a new generation of Israelites to be willing to leave Egypt under the leadership of Moses. But it is not this that either testament stresses, only Joseph's vision and concern for the future of God's people. This also represents the pinnacle of Joseph's spiritual development, where he is committing himself, his bones, to his brethren as part of his faith in God's promise. Campbell studied ek pistou and dia pistou in Paul's writings.[421]He disagrees with Stowers that he cites to which I lend my credence. Stowers argues "a delicate case. Stowers distinguishes between very similar prepositional phrases that use both the same substantive, pistis, and the same case, and which tend to appear in the same contexts-if not side by side. In fact, they seem to vary only in their preposition. He argues that a noticeable semantic distinction can be made between these phrases: dia pistews is a singularly Gentile phrase referring to salvation for ta ethne, through the cross, whereas ek pistews may refer to Jews, Gentiles, both or ceither, but in a broader sense of faithfulness.' 'Faithfulness' could be substituted throughout Heb 11 with almost no loss of content.

11.23 Moses parents acted by faith that involved the timing of 3 months after birth, the observable fact he was no ordinary child, and they were not afraid of the king's edict. Thought about danger of discovery entered into the timing. Thought about the qualities of the child were not dismissed;

intuition may have been present here. But the third was the catalyst was no fear of the edict or fear that overcame the danger. That faith counters fear is in line with Heb 2.15 where fear is the instrument of Satan. Pharaoh is a Satanic figure and he was overcome.

11.24 This adds the remark that his faith was exercised or was born when Moses was grown up. If he belonged to pharaoh's household and he killed someone would that have been punished.? The Josephus tradition has Moses as a general in the Egyptian army that conquered Ethiopia, and thus in line for the throne, noting that "the Moses"= Ms in Egyptian for "Ra-Moses"= "Ramses" the pharaoh's kingly throne name.. Evidently there were other marks of non-submission and this act along with informers became the one he 'came out' that he identified with his people.

11.25 'Pleasures of sin for a season' are never identified. Naturally, in the pharaoh's court there would be pleasures of aesthetics, of idolatry, of art, of music and dancing, of thinly dressed transparent clothes for foreign slaves, the pleasure of the court and the competition for the throne with rewards of houses and lands and power. But the biblical text does not fill this in for us. Simply he chose the hard and uncertain way of alienation that was illogical in terms of his commitment to his people over the cozy secure position guaranteeing advancement in the pharaoh's court. Read Josephus about Moses' traditions as commander of Egyptian forces in southern Egypt and possible vows of loyalty to the living god—the pharaoh.

11.26 Historical writing can deal with motivation: The study of 'equivalences' needs to be careful, however, since the eras and covenants as well as revelations and available grace vary per covenant.

1. 'Refusal' .v24 is not clear from the Exodus text, may = refusal to rely on a court trial or the judge or pharaoh, in order to rely on God alone.
2. 'Chose' v.25 is not clear in the OT: possibly = he identified with the mistreated and thus was dragged down by this sympathy and mercy.
3. 'Enjoy' v.25 not clear in OT: possibly = he found himself where workmen were working.
4. 'Sake of Christ' not apparent in OT: possibly - he believed in the Messiah or the prophet or anointed one that would follow him, according to Deuteronomy.

5. 'Reward' not apparent in OT, but possibly = only at the border of the Promised Land did he really show how much really wanted to enter the land.
6. 'Left' not clear in Exodus, but could = faith that God wanted him alive and not dead.
7. 'Not fearing' not clear: possibly = in principle he feared Pharaoh, but not 'the king's decree.' The difference is between disrespect for a divinely ordained 'king,' and a 'pharaoh= 'Great-House' a title man-made and not God-made. The panegyris was the festal assembly, sacred festival, and sports meet. Isocrates, Paneg.1 "I am often amazed that the founders of panegyreis and the organizers of gymnastic competitions should think physical advantage to be worthy of such great rewards.' Philo: 'Work to be crowned...with a noble and glorious crown that no panegyris among mankind offers'. Spicq: 3.6n9. The panegyris was the festal assembly, sacred festival, and sports meet. Isocrates, Paneg.1 "I am often amazed that the founders of panegyris and the organizers of gymnastic competitions should think physical advantage to be worthy of such great rewards.' Philo: 'Work to be crowned...with a noble and glorious crown that no panegyris among mankind offers'. Spicq: 3.6n9

11.27 This is based on the record in Ex 33, but Moses waited there for God to show his glory v.18 and Presence v.14,15. God said he would reveal his Goodness which equals glory v.21. According to 11.27 Moses' perseverance after leaving Egypt onward was due to his vision [hope?] of seeing the invisible. Exodus does not tell us this fact. 'Him who is invisible.' When Titus marched into Jerusalem and discovered an empty inner sanctuary he was amazed. There was nothing to look at or loot. One cannot fight the invisible. Because God is invisible he belongs to references in Hebrews concerning things not seen as opposed to created things, things unshakeable, as opposed to those that will be shaken, the city 11.10 Abraham looked for whose builder and maker is God, the resurrection 11.19 that hadn't been revealed as yet, a whole realm of things 'welcomed from a distance'11.13. This makes faith in 11.6 based on believing that god is, and that He rewards those who earnestly seek Him. 13.14. 'Him who is invisible.' When Titus marched into Jerusalem and discovered an empty inner sanctuary he was amazed. There was nothing to look at or loot. One cannot fight the invisible. Because God is invisible he belongs to references in Hebrews concerning things not seen as opposed to created things, things unshakeable, as opposed to those that will be shaken, the city, 11.10 Abraham looked for whose builder and maker is God, the resurrection 11.19 that hadn't been revealed as yet, a whole realm of things 'welcomed from a distance'11.13. This makes faith in 11.6 based on believing that god is, and that He rewards those who earnestly seek Him. 13.14. 'not fearing' But Ex 2.14 says 'Moses was afraid' v.15 Pharaoh tried to kill Moses, but Moses fled'. He feared that the deed would become known, and it was. Perhaps only secondarily did he fear pharaoh since he knew the deed itself, its influence on Egyptians and Israelites and before God was not glorifying God. Moses also may have feared others connected with pharaoh who would urge execution. His father and mother did not fear the king v.13. Nor did the midwives. But they still hid the child. Life preservation does not always come from fear but from wisdom. Another viewpoint, is that because of faith God did not reckon his fear unto him, and hence Moses did not belong to the timid that find their portion in the Lake of Fire. All of this may simply mean we are failing to recognize that we lack full information on the whole confused realm of motivation and may not observe, because of it, that Moses is going through a process of growth that Scripture notes for Ishmael, Samuel and the boy Jesus. The passage does seemingly divide into those with faith who were successful and those with faith who were not so and died early; those delivered and those killed. But the focus is not on two kinds of faith! In Paul's thought, as opposed to the Book of Hebrews, it would be easy to posit 'from faith to faith' in Rom 1 and those with the gift of faith in 1 Cor 12-14, versus those with simple faith, little faith and say those with the gift had 'great faith'. These latter would be NT canon categories and acceptable as such. But they are not cateogories of this book! This Memorial lists all who made it spiritually, who are now heavenly spectators of our race on the heavenward track in 12.1. They all made it! karterew 'be firm and courageous, endure' as in Job 2.9; Sir 2.2; Philo, Husbandry 152; Epictetus 1.26,12; T.Job 4.10 meaning 'persevere' in 2 Macc 7.17.In Tob 5.8 a proskarterew reads 'be courageous' in Num 13.20. Elsewhere proskarterew moves in a different meaning domain. Spicq,3.191n1.

'Him who is invisible.' When Titus marched into Jerusalem and discovered an empty inner sanctuary he was amazed. There was nothing to look at or loot. One cannot fight the invisible. Because God is invisible he belongs to references in Hebrews concerning things not seen as opposed to created things, things unshakeable, as opposed to those that will be shaken, the city. 11.10 Abraham looked for whose builder and maker is God, the resurrection 11.19 that hadn't been revealed as yet, a whole realm of things 'welcomed from a distance'11.13. This makes faith in 11.6 based on believing that god is, and that He rewards those who earnestly seek Him. 13.14. 'not fearing' But Ex 2.14 says 'Moses was afraid' v.15 Pharaoh tried to kill Moses, but Moses fled'. He feared that the deed would become known, and it was. Perhaps only secondarily did he fear pharaoh since he knew the deed itself, its influence on Egyptians and Israelites and before God was not glorifying God. Moses also may have feared others connected with pharaoh who would urge execution. His father and mother did not fear the king v.13. Nor did the midwives. But they still hid the child. Life preservation does not always come from fear but from wisdom. Another viewpoint, is that because of faith God did not reckon his fear unto him, and hence Moses did not belong to the timid that find their portion in the Lake of Fire. All of this may simply mean we are failing to recognize that we lack full information on the whole confused realm of motivation and may not observe, because of it, that Moses is going through a process of growth that Scripture notes for Ishmael, Samuel and the boy Jesus.

The Exodus narrative states he did fear the king's anger Ex 10.28 . His flight was to preserve his own life. But larger issues were at stake, namely the People of God surviving and now alienated from Moses. Perhaps he feared them as well. Throughout the narrative he feared being stoned on numerous occasions.

The passage does seemingly divide into those with faith who were successful and those with faith who were not so and died early; those delivered and those killed. But the focus is not on two kinds of faith! In Paul's thought, as opposed to the Book of Hebrews, it would be easy to posit 'from faith to faith' in Rom 1 and those with the gift of faith in 1 Cor 12-14, versus those with simple faith, little faith and say those with the gift had 'great faith'. These latter would be NT canon categories and acceptable as such. But they are not cateogories of this book! This Memorial lists all who made it spiritually, who are now heavenly spectators of our race on the heavenward track in 12.1. They all made it! <u>karterew</u> 'be firm and courageous, endure' as in Job 2.9; Sir 2.2; Philo, Husbandry 152; Epictetus 1.26,12; T.Job 4.10 meaning 'persevere' in 2 Macc 7.17.In Tob 5.8 <u>proskarterew</u> reads 'be courageous' in Num 13.20 for the hiphil of Elsewhere <u>proskarterew</u> moves in a different meaning domain. Spicq,3.191n1

11.28 Ex 12.21 We would read it that he 'by obedience' kept the Passover and the sprinkling or was it by 'effective communication and the willing faith of the people in his arrangement.'? All of this is really a part of faith. Peithw and pisteuw are really related. Total success is reported, because every house of the Israelites was saved in Egypt, or does this verse only show Moses' purpose and motivation and not the results? [422] But compared to Noah, both Moses and Noah wanted to save their family. In this respect Abraham v.17 is a countermove, an act that is illogical. Ex 21.28, although his efforts to save Lot were multiple. Apparently the text of Hebrews declares that everyone did as Moses commanded and all were saved. 'The Destroyer' is often the name for Satan so the Death Angel is identified. Based on Job could there have been a challenge from Satan and permission granted, only that for Israel only a few plagues touched them, while the death of the firstborn had a plan for protection based on special revelation, and appropriation of faith and obedience to do as God ordered for their salvation. Harrison says "the statement in Heb 11:28 concerning Moses may be said to gain illumination from Exodus 12:48, just cited, where poiew is used in the sense of observance of the Passover.[423]

11.29 Is the 'dry land' account of the Exodus is this 'a metaphor, but the 'as' of equivalence? The 'drowned' perspective declares there was indeed a lot of water and so the Sea of Reeds theory is patently wrong.. Cf. . Ex chs 14-15. Thus, this miracle was not at a marsh with reeds. It was Moses and Aaron's faith, not all Israel's, yet under Federal Headship Theory all were believers. In 1 Cor 12 'all "Israel" went through the Red Sea, every generation participated. peira lambanw Classically means 'to make an attempt, to experiment' Deut 28.56 uses it for the woman 'who will not venture to put the sole of her foot on the ground' piel of nasah Here it is used for Egyptians who tried to cross the Red Sea and for martyrs who experienced derision and floggings.' The NT prefers peirazw, rare in secular Greek. The basic meaning is 'trial' translating the piel of nasah It is a question of trial and exploration. "Hence the religious and moral meaning, 'temptation,' which Spicq,3.82. It was Moses and Aaron's faith, not all Israel's, yet under Federal Headship Theory all were believers. In 1 Cor 12 'all "Israel" went through the Red Sea, every generation participated. peira lambanw Classically means 'to make an attempt, to experiment' Deut 28.56 uses it for the woman 'who will not venture to put the sole of her foot on the ground' piel of nasah Here it is used for Egyptians who tried to cross the Red Sea and for martyrs who experienced derision and floggings.' The NT prefers peirazw, rare in secular Greek. The basic meaning is 'trial' translating the piel of nasah It is a question of trial and exploration. "Hence the religious and moral meaning, 'temptation,'[424]

11.30 The faith that brought down the walls of Jericho was the command, explicitly explained in detail, arranged for administratively, carried out by all personnel of Israel Painstakingly through the seven times around on the seventh day. Was this a Sabbath? The element of superstition surrounding the seventh day has been studied and the suggestion from the usage of the full moon the 14th spread to the other sevenths, to avoid disaster by resting on that day. The walls fell by faith, the faith to precisely follow instructions to march around the walls for seven days. The key is the continuation of v.29 where 'the people' are those with the faith because they had the obedience.. But it was Moses that inspired this faith by his specific directions of exactly what God told him to do and say.

11.31 'She welcomed the spies.' Her faith was in her deed, one that allowed strangers inside, conversed with them, lied to police officers, hid them, accepted a plan to save them, entered into covenant, gave them a route to safety, and a sign and thus a way for the spies to fulfill their part of the contract. Lastly, she gathered her whole family to be ready for salvation. Note that she enunciated her faith in God and Israel and the future based on the promises of God. Afterward, she and her family became an integral part of the covenant people. 'She welcomed the spies.' Her faith was in her deed, one that allowed strangers inside, conversed with them, lied to police officers, hid them, accepted a plan to save them, entered into covenant, gave them a route to safety, and a sign and thus a way for the spies to fulfill their part of the contract. Lastly, she gathered her whole family to be ready for salvation. Note that she enunciated her faith in God and Israel and the future based on the promises of God. Afterward, she and her family became an integral part of the covenant people. Note the women in the chapter 1. Rahab [no Deborah]; 2. Moses' parents v.23; 3. The woman of Zarephrath/Elijah 1 K 17.23 and Shunemite woman/Elishah 2 K 4.32 all in .v35. 4. Sarah appears in v.11; The fifth is a counter-ploy, namely the pharaoh's daughter v.24, who fits the '5' structures as one who had faith in Moses not God. Rahab had the faith to welcome the spies that she knew all about what God had done for Israel, as if it had just happened a few months before. She confesses her faith so the initial act of faith was welcoming the spies. But this faith without action occurred earlier. Now her faith convinced the spies and the spies faith confirmed an arrangement. On this mutual faith and faith in God there was the follow-up of obedience which grows out of this faith. Covenants should be established between parties based on faith and this is true on both the horizontal and vertical. Traditions about Rahab are very varied: "

'by faith' here has a fear component in Rahab's words, Jos 2.1, as well as concern for the salvation of her whole family, a willingness to commit their lives to foreigners, to lie for their escape, to arrange for their security. All this is part of her faith. She, along with Abraham, did not consider it expedient to tell all the truth to the enemy.

Note the women in the chapter: 1. Rahab [no Deborah]; 2. Moses' parents v.23; 3. The woman of Zarephrath/Elijah 1 K 17.23 and Shunemite woman/Elisha 2 K 4.32 all in .v35. n 4. Sarah appears in v.11; 5. The fifth is a counterploy, namely the pharaoh's daughter v.24, who fits the '5' structures as one who had faith in Moses not God.

11.32 Gideon is included in spite of later self-seeking. Here the deliverance wrought covers up events later in life during which time he wanted and obtained the privileges of a king without the responsibility. But he did continue to judge Israel and it was a time of victory over foreign intrusions.

Jephthah is included in spite of his foolish vow, for God used him and continued to do so, for it was the vow that brought the power of God into the conflict. It was this earnest and complete commitment that changed the direction of his life from a leader of an outlaw band to the leader of a tribe. The sad result of the vow was that a very foolish girl impetuously, the definition of a fool, burst out of the gate to lovingly embrace her victorious dad.

Samson is here in spite of moral failures. All these were 'enabled' by faith. [425] Notice 'end-stress' that Samson's final act was not suicide but self-sacrifice for the covenant People and this covers up all the questionable things he did previously. Gideon is included in spite of later self-seeking. Jephthah is listed even though a bastard and the unfortunate incident of his vow and its consequence. But he is listed here because he did not renege on his vow and everyone knew it. He was a man of his word.

11.32-38 The cost of following Christ for various persons involves 1. No settled living place; 2. No respect; [426] The details are all included and skipped over as common knowledge,, and the one important thing is that they pleased God. Barak in the story of Deborah does not seem to be the one with faith and because of his dependence on Deborah does not receive the honor of victor, which Jael receives. But his faith was really confidence in Deborah the judge-leader, and it was this confidence and obedience to her battle plans that enabled the victory. Note that Gideon's latter years use of an ephod led Israel to sin and yet in spite of his son's atrocities and the murders of 70 sons which must have been a terrible loss, and also in spite of his request not to be made king and to be given the plunder, he is still listed here. Faith in God established him as the leader even though pride, covetousness, false humility, refusal of responsibility, use of a symbol, the ephod, which is basically for priests only, even though these were scars on his character and record because he was saved by faith all of these are not on his record before God. These things influenced history, destroyed his family, and many other unknown effects, but before God he remained justified by faith.

11.33 'ministering justice' involved Moses and Joshua, some judges, Samuel, and some kings, not all. Some prophets were involved as well. It took faithfulness for Samuel to kill the Jerusalem king, for David to kill the messenger of Saul's death, to giving refuge to Abiathar and so many from all Israel. 'Shutting the mouths of lions would be David, Samson and most probably Daniel and his friends. To be victorious over wild animals was a sign of kingship and power in Assyria and Babylon. Jephthah is listed but not Abimelech son of Gideon. Gideon is though later he caused Israel to worship an idol. Samson rose in his self-sacrifice which covers up many indiscretions. David, Samuel conquered kingdoms, but Abimelech did not. The commands in Jeremiah's call show him as a destroyer of nations. Samuel is not linked to the prophets and may have been the only priest in the list. Baraq fits a general's profile but Deborah is omitted. Solomon fought no wars.

Daniel shut the mouths of lions. Dan 6.22 The Daniel text does not say Daniel shut their mouths but that they were shut. But this happened because of Daniel's steady faith in God regardless of outcome. Solomon administered justice. David conquered kingdoms. Hannah gained what was promised. The genre is a listing. The actions illustrate what faith accomplishes in and through the person remembered. 'Through faith conquered' seems to take away from human initiative and ability or courage and from God's intervention. Actually faith was the bond in which victory was obtained.

11.34 Who quenched the fire? Dan 3.23-28 Is this interpreting the text to read that the fire was smothered? Or was Daniel the one that put it out? Saul escaped the edge of the sword but was he a hero of faith? David does count in his encounter with Goliath. 'strength in weakness' sounds like Samson's two cases. 'put foreign armies to flight' may be David, Jehoshaphat, Elisha, Jonathan and other kings. David was thirsty and so his warriors went to Bethlehem to get water for him at terrible risk, only to have David pour it out on the ground. David and Elijah both had seasons of depression, but God led them out to serve once more.

11.35 'Refused to be released' sounds like a death wish, where they are choosing death for the sake of the resurrection. Later in Christian history as in Islamic thought death for the sake of the Gospel or Allah brings merit of eternal life. In the purpose in choosing death a belief that somehow in this way they will gain the resurrection? Is death a means to an end? Note that in corporate incarceration a desire to not forsake fellow prisoners might be more forceful than release. Or is hiding an omitted line meaning that by denial of Christ they could be released but that they chose not to deny the Lord. Did they believe martyrdom was a direct route to heaven? In context their choice of remaining a prisoner instead of release is an illustration of faith. In the case of Joseph and John, Jeremiah and the Revelator there is desire to survive more than to be free, but in each case other considerations predominated, and no case is the equivalent to ethnic and religious persecution on a thorough and massive scale. A case might be made that Israel in Egypt was patiently obedient to foreign cruel masters in keeping with biblical injunctions to obey those' over you.' But when divine revelation came they gradually came to faith and obedience to that revelation through Moses. 'refused': possibly Paul in Acts 16.37. The issue of release or resurrection is the unspoken middle factor of denying the Lord. 'Better resurrection' may be that people reckoned them dead already, or their release is a kind of resurrection, or the First Resurrection on Revelations. This existential choice was freely made and in dissonance theory considered the better option, a very rational act. They did not view intimidation as the leading factor in determining their destiny but rather their own choice. The story of Elisha and Elijah contain a resurrection. From the OT it is a question of whether this was heat stroke or coma and not death. But Hebrews clarifies that these women received their sons back from the dead. Inner scriptural interpretation thus clarifies a moot point, here used to laud the way of faith. The women in Elijah and Elisha's life experienced these resurrections of sons. They are not named but still remembered as recipient's of grace. Others occurred in Gospel times through Jesus' ministry. , Ezra, in II Esdras faced a similar situation as Daniel did, and in prayer was troubled by, not the strangeness of the vision, but the dread of those who would not remain on earth in the last days to experience the new world order. Here is some of Paul's cry 'even so come Lord Jesus." The focus is on physical survival, without integrating this into a view of resurrection.[427] Myers,314. the verbs cannot be subserved under one category such as testing, temptation, training, or persecution. None of these negative experiences is clearly in the positive-divine initiative for the salvation of the world, or for the church, a group of believers, or single persons, yet each of them is caused by the enemies of God and does fulfill the divine plan and purpose. The reason for many of the cases is found in resistance to cultural assimilation.

11.36 Brings the history to the author's present time. Gen 39.20. His was a time of persecution and pressure from Greeks, Romans, tribes and ethnics and Diaspora Jews. He is preparing them for Nero's onslaught. The denigration of mankind has run parallel to scientific advances. War on a religio-ethnic group widely scattered makes no front line of attack. But the church was and is attacked simply because of their faith. The effort to remove religion and faith from the public scene could be seen in Hatti and Persia where law replaced divine edict, in Rome where kings deified themselves and ruled by fiat, in Egypt as security of eternal life of the old Kingdom gradually deteriorated into the New Kingdom, and then when massive and enforced migrations of people took place. Not many instances of genocide occurred in early history as have been attempted more recently through enforced assimilation or slaughter. The secular world has merely increased the devaluing of mankind.

11.37 'Sawed' in tradition was Isaiah. See the Martyrdom of Isaiah ch.5. 'They were stoned' might refer to many people, but probably not sinners as such. In the frame of this chapter one remembers Naboth's Vineyard, a just man who would not capitulate on forfeiture of land God had given his family in perpetuity. His faith said 'no.' In Israel to be stoned would be execution for a capital crime undescribed, and in the context of faith the execution had to be a miscarriage of justice. But in spite of that fact the person was faithful to the end, with the name known only to God. We think of Naboth but the point isn't a history of a person but of faithfulness. The nomadic or semi-nomadic lifestyle had been one background for the patriarchs and Israel. These, by definition' were 'Hebrews' 'Apiru, the unassimilated elements in any territory who could ally with anyone or no one. Such shepherds were despised in Mesopotamia as well as in Egypt and Greece called such Barbaroi. To re-enter this social class and lifestyle, to go back to one's roots, is not easy. 'Stoned' would be for a crime. 'sawed in two' was literally fulfilled in Isaiah's case according to tradition. Many died in wars by the sword. Sheepskins and goatskins could be the nomadic lifestyle adopted by Elijah and John the Baptist and many hermits to follow. 'Persecuted and mistreated' was because they lacked legal standing in the lands they reached or sought to live in. They were people without a country. Even today the people of Dafur are refugees,

Kurds are persecuted on all sides, and so many are without representation or legal recourse. Wearing skins was a mark of John the Baptist and Elijah. But as a step back in culture to a primitive lifestyle of mere survival it was a trial of patience. For Jeremiah to leave Anathoth to live in Jerusalem was a step up, but his family of priests had already lost employment. Amos was a successful dual-employment secular person when God called him to go to Bethel. Daniel had to adopt Babylonian and Persian dress, names, food, and protocols with his life and position in constant danger. Esther would not compromise her ethnic background till a crisis forced her to it. She was queen and top of the harem, so why expose oneself and one's family. Most of all, Jesus left glory for a manger, and a lifestyle without a pillow. The willingness to leave all for Christ comes down to the missionary who must consider on the field what can or must he give up, even the question of moving from a culturally advanced field to a backward one, or from urban ministries with hospitals and city life to a country town with its provincial attitudes towards outsiders. Abraham moved from culture to Canaan, and not city-state Canaan, but pasture land Canaan. Isaac tried sheep raising but was innovative to his hurt in farming. The call to 'in whatever state I am therewith to be content' is a mark of biblical faith. Why not mention Uriah the Hittite 'by the sword'? The reference to stoning is reflected in 1 Ch 24.21; Matt 23.37; Lk 13.34 and the two parables involving missions 21.34-36 in which the fate of the prophets is mentioned. Mark's reference is simplest, a single messenger. Gospel of Thomas is also simple. Jeremias,[428]72

'They were stoned' might refer to many people, but probably not sinners as such. In the frame of this chapter one remembers Naboth's Vineyard, a just man who would not capitulate on forfeiture of land God had given his family in perpetuity. His faith said 'no.' Zechariah was stoned in I Chron 24.21; 1 Kgs 21.13; 2 Kgs 1.8; Zech 13.4. Wearing skins was a mark of John the Baptist and Elijah. But as a step back in culture to a primitive lifestyle of mere survival it was a trial of patience. For Jeremiah to leave Anathoth to live in Jerusalem was a step up, but his family of priests had already lost employment. Amos was a successful dual-employment secular person when God called him to go to Bethel. Daniel had to adopt Babylonian and Persian dress, names, food, and protocols with his life and position in constant danger. Esther would not compromise her ethnic background till a crisis forced her to it. She was queen and top of the harem, so why expose oneself and one's family. Most of all, Jesus left glory for a manger, and a lifestyle without a pillow. The willingness to leave all for Christ comes down to the missionary who must consider on the field what can or must he give up, even the question of moving from a culturally advanced field to a backward one, or from urban ministries with hospitals and city life to a country town with its provincial attitudes towards outsiders. Abraham moved from culture to Canaan, and not city-state Canaan, but pasture land Canaan. Isaac tried sheep raising but was innovative to his hurt in farming. The call to 'in whatever state I am therewith to be content' is a mark of biblical faith. Why not mention Uriah the Hittite 'by the sword'? The reference to stoning is reflected in 1 Ch 24.21; Matt 23.37; Lk 13.34 and the two parables involving missions 21.34-36 in which the fate of the prophets is mentioned. Mark's reference is simplest, a single messenger. Gospel of Thomas is also simple. Jeremias,[429]72

'Sawn asunder' cited with 70AD as a year of Roman use: "Tertullian, *On Patience* 14; Origen, *Epistle to Africanus* 9; Hippolytus, *Concerning Christ and Antichrist* 30). The practice of sawing men in two was perpetuated by the Romans at the time of the Jewish War (*Gen. Rab.* 65.22: a certain Jose Meshita was sawn by the Romans on a sawhorse) and by certain Cyrenian Jews during the insurrection of A.D. 115 (Cassius Dio 68.32)."[430] The destitute are those who for their faith in preserving their relationship to God even if the people of God had no country, land, or structure, it is these who choose this life, not because they were simply the oppressed of earth. They were refugees by choice. Homeless by choice. Life meant witness, not mere survival, and this witness involved their faith, their children, and their history.

11.38 'Not worthy of the world' means worthy to God. These people don't fit, they are not one of the honorables of secular world history!.The world was not worthy of them is a reversal of values with the world; The present reality shows often illustrate the world's system of values, of assertiveness, decisiveness, struggle to be first, critical of others, pitting one against the other, and stressing success, monetary gain, position enhancement all at any cost. Therefore, in scripture there are worthy people and not only because they are now dead, were canonized because of miracles, and were elevated to sainthood.! Jesus instructed disciples as they entered a village to evangelize it, to enter the house of one who is worthy, which probably carries social, moral and religious undertones. This verse is not on merit for salvation, but because of salvation and leading to salvation. Cf. . Rom 8 for a non-specific scenario.

'World was not worthy of them' hangs on the meaning of axios.[431] Dative of specification: 'concerning whom the world is not worthy'. The context describes a lifestyle of the oppressed and persecuted and disenfranchised that the world looked down on. Actually they are those who really should be honored since all their troubles have come on them because of their tenacious faith in Christ alone. These do not follow the crowd, imitate, take opinion polls and have a relativistic ethics. They have principles. 1 Kgs 18.4,13; 19.9.

The pattern for the wanderer in the OT is Cain who went to Nod,[432] the land of wandering. But through worldly self-help he established the Sumerian civilization, and no longer wandered. Abraham's wandering was different in that he sought for a city and was expecting God to show him where in Canaan to settle. The foreign resident lifestyle is not one of wandering. Even Rechabites who were antisocial and unassimilated were not wanderers. Nomadic tribes are not either as the National Geographic study of Iranian tribesmen and their yearly migratory patterns clearly shows. Wandering could be because they were fugitives, but not because they were Hebrews, since the 'apiru were unassimilated residential peoples not wanderers. The Bible does not laud gypsy or rootless people per se. But for the sake of the faith many cannot become rooted. Under persecution the Psalms witness flight not fight. It is this refugee mentality that accounts for returning to a primeval lifestyle in caves far from humanity. Everything is reduced to simplicity and survival. So many of this category did survive, never to return to cities or civilization again.

11.39 The commendation is part of the motivation of God for writing the stories in Israel's history. The written and oral history is their commendation and earlier mistakes and sins don't count, because their sins were covered and only the final picture counted. But unfaithfulness excluded some from the list. Another reason for not including some persons has to do with unfaithfulness, as in the case of Abimelech, Solomon, Jeroboam, Asa, Uzzah, and many others. In the Greco-Roman world 'telling it like it is' was not the goal, but rather mentioning models for emulation. The chapter portrays some exalted patriarchs, military heroes, but also many who were victims, because of their faith or not, but they went through these tests and left a testimony of faith. Success was not measured in survival terms or in permanence of victories, or records of details, or even names and the names of their fathers, or even gender. Their situations all differed, but were within the providential will of God. Many of them received promises, some received what was promised in a limited way, while for all 'none of them received what had been promised.' This is a version of realized eschatology. 'commended for their faith.' Where did this happen? Was it in heaven? Or was it in Sirach (Ecclesiasticus)? Or was the biography of these people designed to proclaim God's acceptance and commendation? 'were commended' but was it to their face. Was there an inner witness to God's pleasure. Apparently Abel realized God was pleased but Cain did not. God did confirm Job to his face and through angels confirmed Daniel. But isn't most of the commending through people as their witness is used by God to confirm them? The other fact is that 'God is not the God of the dead but of the living.' The significance of this is that after they died and through sacred writings inspired by God, they did receive a personal commendation. Paul longed for the day when Jesus would say 'Come good and faithful servant, enter into the joy of your Lord.' The Lord himself received affirmation 'This is my believed son, hear him/ in whom I am well pleased.'

'commended for their faith' is an interpretation of the way the narrative was written and the subsequent tradition developed. It may be that they did not sense Abram's fear in going into Philistia and his misrepresentation of his wife as sister. Rather the tradition may have viewed his plan as believing firmly that he himself would have a son and that God would protect Sarah during those days apart from him. Note that Jewish tradition did not take Lot's daughters' acts of sex as incest but as faith and obedience to the mandate to continue the family line. The same was true of Judah and Tamar, where Judah was wrapped in fear for his last son while Tamar was heroic in seeking not only justice for herself but for the line of her first husband. Both acts would be considered incest from the male standpoint but faith from the woman's standpoint. Taking these narratives as a record of faith was their commendation. This contradicts 11.33 'gained what was promised'. The 'already/not yet' already existed in the OT period. There were promises fulfilled, but not totally or in accord with what the hearers were expecting. Thus those were not 'fulfillments' but types, shadows, pointers, appetizers, pointing to the full reality. Thus is Haggai 2.6-9 the Zechariah-Joshua temple was not a fulfillment of Isaian or Ezekielian prophecies. The Persian assistance for rebuilding [through local antagonistic indigenous peoples in Canaan] was not fulfillment of promises that all nations would bring their precious things to Jerusalem. The purpose of 'biography' in Scripture is to record, publish, testify to God's commendation on men of faith and thus put history in right perspective and eschatology in the domain of history. Some prophecies in the OT are ambiguously cited in the NT such as Acts 3.24 "all the prophets who have spoken, from Samuel and his successors onward, announced these days." Cf. . Rom 1.1-2; Eph 3.6; Here 'what was promised.' Acts 7.52 13.27,29; 13.23 and 2 Sam 7.13b with Acts 2.30. Payne,[433]38. 'They were commended' often by God, by kings, by writers of scripture, but often again the commendation must be an inference from a narrative. Later generations recount the commendation. Moses' commendations in the narrative by the author may be by Joshua, but Joshua's is unclear. Not so the Elijah and Elisha prophetic community anecdotes that reflect their deep confidence in their leader. 'None received what was promised' may be because they are awaiting the general resurrection or because later they lost out in terms of persevering in the faith, such as Saul, Eli, Jehoshapat, Judas, Demas, Asa, and others. Even Moses and Aaron's sons lost out. Melchizedek did not since 'he lives.' [434] Dallas Theological Seminary review their position and the dispensational position for OT saints: ""We believe that it has always been true that 'without faith it is impossible to please' God (Heb. 11:6), and that the principle of faith was prevalent in the lives of all the Old Testament saints. However, we believe that it was historically impossible that they should have had as the conscious object of their faith the incarnate, crucified Son, the Lamb of God (John 1:29), and that it is evident that they did not comprehend as we do that the sacrifices depicted the person and work of Christ. We believe also that they did not understand the redemptive significance of the prophecies or types concerning the sufferings of Christ (1 Pet. 1:10-12) ; therefore we believe that their faith toward God was manifested in other ways as is shown by the long record in Hebrews 11:1-40. We believe further that their faith thus manifested was counted unto them for righteousness (Cf. . Rom. 4:3 with Gen. 15:6; Rom. 4:5-8; Heb. 11:7)."[435]

11.40 'God had planned' indicates this did not happen just recently. The context is the whole of history and the unity of those of the past with those of the church age so that fulfillment of all the promises intended can only happen in the Second Coming, the resurrection,. Millennium, Judgment, new heaven and earth and establishment of the Kingdom of God.

'Perfect' success, completeness for OT persons, depends on the mission of God in the church being carried out through the preaching of the Gospel. "We" are the key to their fulfillment. This is an 'all Israel' theology as in the Book of Joshua and 1 Cor 12.13. People of God. links saints of OT and NT together as one continuum all saved through faith alone and all receiving what was promised as part of one covenant plan and eschatological fulfillment. This fulfillment could be taken as 'perfect' already in Christ's completed propitiation and from ch.11 could be taken as awaiting the last saint's completing his racecourse. But this verse says nothing about propitiation, only about 'us' and 'they' being perfected together. Is this a case of already and not yet? Based on the inherent eschatology of Hebrews 11.35 points to the resurrection as the time of perfecting. 11.40 The plan of God for the NT people is 'better for us' and hence worthy for OT people also to receive. 'Perfect' means that apart from resurrection [and martyrdom?] v.35 which has not yet occurred, they would not 'be made perfect'. Therefore, these onlookers were concerned about the race in ch.12. This interpretation implies that the onlookers also ran their race. Another interpretation makes the onlookers to be angels.

The plan of God for the NT people is 'better for us' and hence worthy for OT people also to receive. 'Perfect' means that apart from resurrection [and martyrdom?] v.35 which has not yet occurred, they would not 'be made perfect'. Therefore, these onlookers were concerned about the race in ch.12. This interpretation implies that the onlookers also ran their race. Another interpretation makes the onlookers to be angels. But is faith considered merit. The first verses of the chapter point to something else, evidence and substructure to life in God. The chapter shows faith as a motivator, inspirer of courage, daring, adventuresomeness, uncomplaining fortitude, perseverance, initiative, survivability, and so much more.

Chapter Twelve:

CHRIST IS THE GREATEST FORERUNNER, AUTHOR AND PERFECTOR OF FAITH.

God's Throne and Fatherhood

12.1 'Perseverance' is the quality of endurance one side of which is faith and the other faithfulness. The latter is hard if there are entangling things. The ritual and doctrine of confirmation of children who had been baptized as infants, and of 'confirming grace' as another term for the grace of Entire Sanctification or Christian Perfection also deal with this issue. Last Rights or Last Unction in the Catholic Church also concern the soul's salvation as one approaches or enters into death. In all of this discipleship training is aiming at a more than 'in the door' believer, but one that can face bitter challenges and even pain, torture and martyrdom.

'Sin which entangles' makes one think of Ps 18.16 'He reached down and took hold of me and drew me out of deep waters.' 69.14 mire; 69.21 miry depths; and Jonah 2.5 'seaweed wrapped around my head.' Absalom's hair got entangled in a tree which made escape impossible. The competition of runners to report on Absalom's death was not a matter of encumbrance or speed but of route followed. David fled Absalom and sent several people away so that their lives would be saved and he and his could safely escape with encumbrances.

'Throw off': Did Elijah's need for the mantle till the very last need to be cast off in order for him to be carried off to heaven? Was his seeming unwillingness to transfer his ministry to Elisha symbolized in his mantle?

The Witness observers? Are dead believers present observers? Jesus spoke of a gulf between the unbelieving dead and heaven as well earth without saying what 'Lazarus' in heaven knew. Does the appearance of Elijah and Moses indicate their present involvement in earthly affairs as is indicate for angels? Jesus said God is not the God of the dead Abraham, Isaac or Jacob but of the living, meaning that these were still living. Is there soul sleep? These texts would indicate not. Only Daniel 12 might indicate sleep till the Day of Resurrection. But the souls of those who died as martyrs in Revelation, who pray beneath the altar day and night, their blood having been poured out beneath the altar that cries out as even Abel's blood cried out, are very aware of earthly affairs. All are crying for justice and vengeance. So are the 'witnesses' in 12.1 angels? The great cloud of witnesses may correspond to Deut 33.2 'He came with myriads of holy ones from the south.' Rev 5.11; 1 Cor 4.15 ten thousand guardians in Christ' and Dan 7.10 'A river of fire was flowing, coming out from before him. Thousands upon thousands attended him. Ten thousand times ten thousand stood before him. The court was seated and the books opened.' But as a missionary Gospel tract the author may also have had in mind the arena where martyrs were born and the boisterous howling crowds waiting to see if the believers will recant. Actually all men are witnesses when God's servants are made into a drama on a stage. Because of the encouragement of those gone before and the influence on those following and currently observing there is the highest incentive to not take personal persecution as unique to the person.

From OT perspective witnesses were in 'the Gate' of the city not in an arena. This would make life here pursued as if in the very gateway to heaven. The OT does show observations about messengers and their running.

Hindrances are obstacles. Jesus spoke of occasions of stumbling or rocks of offence, causing others to stumble. They are not sin but cause sin. For this reason Judaism as considered the instigator of sin to have the more serious offence. [The current evangelical theology does not recognize that the Bible has degrees of sin in both testaments and even in the words of Jesus]. Jesus said his own ministry will cause and has caused many to fall, but woe to any believer that causes people to stumble. For this reason hindrances are here listed with 'sins' as being equally injurious and punishable, but here basically they function as a drag or stumbling block toward finishing the race. There is nothing here about winning or being first, such as with some OT runners. Here the issue is simply finishing the race. The time factor is excluded because most will finish in martyrdom.

Runners: Only one verse speaks of the runner in the OT: Job 9:25 "My days are swifter than a runner; they fly away without a glimpse of joy. But many[39 times] speak of messengers and runners as part of the news-bearers in the army.[436] In the ANE they served an important function but not in terms of observers but message. While the race course metaphor is used, the OT corresponding concept is 'way'/'ways', a motif not only in the Psalms, Proverbs but also in Deuteronomy and the prophets. "The way to life" in Prov

10.17 implies more than life here and now. Prov 10.29 "The way of the Lord is a refuge for the righteous but ruin to those who do evil." This is similar to those who preach, heal, cast out demons, that say 'Lord, Lord' but the Lord will not recognize them in that day, because they are in the way but are doing evil. Jesus divided life into two ways, a right narrow way and a broad wrong way, hence the doctrine of "two ways." Similarly, "the way of the wicked" in Prov 12.26 leads them further and further astray. But in 12.28 "In the way of righteousness there is life, along that path there is immortality" makes this, as in Heb 12.1, the way to heaven and not just one's career or life on earth.[437] The motivation is provided by the great cloud of witnesses which surround us. The antecedent is chapter 11, and the numbers show that this chapter only mentions a few illustrations from OT history. But does this mean the deceased are ghosts that surround the individual believers, or that they are witnesses to what is happening on the track? What are these witnesses witnessing to but for the faithfulness of God during their time on earth. Or do they continue to witness in their role as witnesses to the struggles of believers? In church history the implications of these questions has been officially extended to include these witnesses, angels and the deceased believers, continuing to pray and witness what happens on earth, so that prayer to angels and saints is justified. The whereabouts of the deceased who 'surround' us is really in the spiritual not physical realm. Or is this unseen multitude the fellowship of the saints who, like the Israelites marching around Jericho, are contributing their faith to the concluding events of history? While disciples on Galilee and in the upper room considered Jesus to be a ghost, and Saul believed Samuel rose up to answer him, the scriptures have not been clear. Those who hold soul sleep are on one end of a continuum while on the other 'absent from the body, present with the Lord.' Between these are Paul's position of immediately receiving a spiritual body 2 Cor 5.2-4, and only later a new body in the general resurrection. Sarles sites Hiebert's reflection on the 'excluded middle' of western thought. "Hiebert equates the second level of reality in the Eastern world view with the "excluded middle" in the Western world view. Reflecting on his own experience as a missionary in India, he notes: "I had excluded the middle level of supernatural but this-worldly beings and forces from my own worldview. As a scientist I had been trained to deal with the empirical world in naturalistic terms. As a theologian, I was taught to answer ultimate questions in theistic terms. For me the middle zone did not really exist. Unlike Indian villagers, I had given little thought to spirits of this world, to local ancestors and ghosts, or to the souls of animals.(40)."[438] Kuemmerlkin-McLean notes " 1. Deut 18:10–11. Interpreters generally agree that Deut

18:10–11 provides the most basic and inclusive list of magic terminology in the OT. However, understandings of these terms frequently differ since it is difficult to determine the precise practices to which the terms refer (e.g., the OT often sees divinatory practices as a subcategory of magic, and interpreters often appeal to different etymologies to explain the same Hebrew term). Further, translations frequently project back into biblical times practices seen as "magical" at the time of the translation.

a. One who makes his son or his daughter pass through the fire"). Interpreters debate the meaning of this phrase and its relationship to the other terms in Deut 18:10–11. This phrase has been taken to refer both to child sacrifice and to a type of "oracle ordeal." As a reference to child sacrifice, it is often interpreted as "propitiatory" and so divorced from the other magical/divinatory practices in the text. As a reference to a type of oracle ordeal, it is more frequently associated with either divination or magic.
b. Diviner, augurer"). Translations tend to equate *qsm* with divination. Commentaries, however, tend to view *qsm* as a more general term referring to the whole complex of magical and divinatory practices in ancient Israel. Arguments for understanding *qsm* as a very general term are based (1) on the Deuteronomistic tendency to list a general term first in a series with subsequent terms providing clarification and nuance, (2) on comparative etymology, and (3) on uses of *qsm* elsewhere in the OT (Cf. . Num 23:23; 1 Sam 15:23; 2 Kgs 17:17; Mic 3:6)
c. Soothsayer, observer of times, one who looks for omens, sorcerer, enchanter"). The term the first in the series of seemingly specialized terms for various types of magical and divinatory practices. The diversity in translation of this term reflects lack of scholarly consensus regarding the practice(s) to which it refers and its primary focus (magic or divination). Interpretations have relied strongly on etymological comparisons, variously equating with divinatory practices such as observation of clouds, the "evil eye," "eyeing" or observing "the times," the humming sound associated with diviners, as well as with magic practices such as conjuring up spirits.
d. Augur, diviner, enchanter"). The precise meaning and focus of *meńnah\ eṇsû* are also difficult to determine because interpreters associate it with two different roots. Those emphasizing the connection with it as a denominative from ('snake') and associate it with some form of divination related to snakes. Those emphasizing this connection tends to associate it more with magic—particularly with the use of charms and "enchantments" (Cf. . Isa 3:3; 3:20; 26:16; Jer 8:17; Eccl 10:11).

e. Sorcerer There is general agreement regarding the meaning of the term usually translated "sorcery." However, there has been a tendency on the part of some interpreters and translations to use the negative and antisocial term "sorcery" for references to female practitioners of while employing the more neutral term "magic" for references to male practitioners. The unequal distinction between female and male practitioners seems present in the OT itself. The commandment in Exod 22:18—Eng 22:17 requires the community to put the female to death. However, in texts referring to the male either no precise penalty is given (Deut 18:10) or the judgment and punishment are left to God (Jer 27:9; Mal 3:5).
f. Charmer, one who casts spells, one who uses charms"). Interpreters generally agree that the root *hbr* is related to the use of charms and spells. This connection arises from the widely recognized association of the root *hbr* with the idea of "uniting, joining, weaving." Many interpreters relate this concept to the practice of tying or wrapping magical knots or threads around people or objects, understood either to bind the gods to do one's will or to bind (disable) the object or person to be affected. Another interpretation relates the term to the idea that words are woven together in the spell itself. An alternative derivation of the term however, relates it to the Akk term *abarum*—to be noisy, to make an indistinguishable clamor. Here, the is seen as a "mutterer" (one who makes indistinguishable noises).
g. 'an inquirer' of an *yidde'oni* "a medium or a wizard, one who traffics with ghosts and spirits, one who consults ghosts or spirits"). These are two of three terms in Deut 18:11 seemingly related to the practice of necromancy (divination by inquiring of the dead).439." Do the laws of Israel and Hatti deal with a reality belonging to the occult, that must be eliminated at all cost? The OT crux is probably the account of the witch of Endor, what she heard and saw and what Saul heard and saw. Samuel did add somewhat to his former messages, but the message of death sounds like the death angel. Through this means Saul would be unable to mount an effective defense. The common beliefs in the ANE and OT, even those expressed in Job, Psalms and Ecclesiastes in poetic form are a large part of the data. Isa 14.3-21, 8.19-20; 28.18, 29.4; Ezek 28 have poetic and satirical elements in them but form a major data base. Abel's blood crying out to God from the ground, laws about burial by sundown, David's words' I shall go to him he will not come to me' support the belief.

12.1-2 The scenario is unusual since one race is finished and the track only has one runner with witnesses or observers not only on the outside or inside but all around the runner. There does not appear to be a team effort. Each is running in his solitariness. Thus this does not seem to be a matter of time or competition with others but of survival—a survival course. If this is linked to the Esau-Jacob story, then we have two 'courses' and the link is 'the course set out before us' is personal and individualized. There obstacles on one's own person that can hinder. As in the Olympiad meet where a runner was down due to being tripped up accidents do occur in close running, but was there incompetence? The problem with Esau was his sense of injustice and outrage, anger hate and jealousy leading to murderous design was a choice involving his own lifestyle, his delay in return so that shame and guilt are part of the 'baggage' that he had; but also his 'course' never was the same as God lay out for his brother. He forfeited the birthright and the blessing and murder would have left the family destitute. The blessing-power to enable Esau and his descendants was lost but God's protection was not. In other ways, viewed as part of the race metaphor there are obstacles, and the greatest are not environmental but inside. Endurance depends on accepting adverse happenings and injustices; the opposite is the bitter root of original sin that finds opportunity to spring up leading to defilement. Such an integrated reading makes the role of legal and interested, committed and experienced witnesses .Sometimes since they know precisely what each person is going through. Fortunately, due to Jacob's absence Esau woke up to the unhappiness of his parents and changed in that he took a wife they could accept. The many years of absence sees the eldest son as leading a procession to their father's funeral, as being blessed with manpower and goods and living the kind of lifestyle he was used to—his course in life laid out for him. He, at some point, forgave his brother. Accepted his excuses, and returned to his home and later moved to the Petra region. In Hebrews the case is not so presented. Rather Esau only had one chance and he lost it, and even through seeking forgiveness and a second blessing was not heard. Genesis makes this an impossibility of receiving a second blessing due to the nature of the dying speech act. The Hebrew makes the blessing and curse of Jacob and Esau almost identical in language, the only real difference for a non-urban lifestyle was subordination to Jacob's descendants. Reading Hebrews one is inclined to see Esau from the standpoint of the demise of Edom, the sins of the late Divided Kingdom period and time of Esau, and to reflect that opposed to the sins of Abraham, that were not recorded due to his faith, we see the repentance and blessed life of Esau as not being recorded in God's eternal Book of Life. Preacher's Commentary succinctly notes :" *—Hebrews 12:2–3:* For the Christian disciple there is only one way to run this race successfully and that is to look to Jesus, whom our author describes first as *"author"* (*archegonia*) and then as *"finisher"* (*teleiōtēn*) of our faith. *Archēgos* can mean founder, leader, or pioneer, a prince or ruler. The meaning here is that of founder, the first, even the designer of this race. As a leader or pioneer, Jesus is meant to be followed. He is not the one and only, but the first of many. He has set the course and we are to follow hard after Him. He is also the first one to finish the race, the perfecter in terms of having completed it. The word *teleiōtēs* is used nowhere else in the New Testament, the LXX, or the classical writers. Again, is our author coining a usage?" Archegon as pioneer fits the metaphor and 'finisher' makes a pair. But these are not actions performed on believers but the focus on Christ alone. He is the first and last, the beginning and end of our faith. [440]

12.2 'The Joy' is part of the pattern for us. Phil 2 speaks of the joy in a context of humiliation and glorification. It is also in the context of the bridegroom returning and the Kingdom of God There was no joy in Gethsemane, but there was at the birth of Christ and the giving of the Spirit. Hope saves because it can visualize joy at a future point. 12.1-4 sounds 'hard' since this is the time of waiting for the bridegroom and joy comes in the morning. In the Psalms the laments anticipate a time of joy. But Paul declares rejoice always and again I say rejoice, and this is from prison. Every OT Festival was a joyous time except for the Day of Atonement. But the laments probably do not reflect national holidays but personal need. This text allows us to look carefully at the Songs of exhuberance in the Psalter and even at Christ's own life in terms of moments of joy. His hearing the reports of miracles his disciples wrought caused him to express joy. The excited realization of foreigners having strong faith brought praise to them. Peter's confession of Christ was one moment. The 'joy in the presence of the angels over one sinner that repents' reflects Christ's joy in the return of one to give thanksgiving. "That your joy may be full" gives the true meaning of prayer in a context of promises and gifts. Especially important in the OT is the Song of Deborah, of Miriam, exhuberance of David, and the words of Hannah."Author and Perfector": Both the initial awakening[Wesleyan] and new birth[Calvinism] as well as the gift of dying grace[faith] complete the life. In 11.40 those who are in heaven are not perfect, and he is the perfector of their faith. Or, does it only mean they aren't perfect apart from the fullness of the number of NT believers? When faith is perfected, as seen from a different angel, it is no longer needed, since the eye will see and heart know. Neither those in heaven now nor those on earth now see what is prepared for them, since "that which is perfect" who will come has not come as yet. Isa 64.4; 65.17 are used in 1 Cor 2.9. Here' love' characterizes both those in heaven and those on earth since the title for Jesus is given as "Lord of Glory." The revelation in 2.10 Paul says has already been given, but in 1 Cor 13 he says it is still hoped for. In the OT passages there is also the need for the individual 'O man' who needs to be aware of the collective significant 'others' that love God, in the same sense that the readers of Hebrews need to know about the many witnesses. Katafronew and perifronew are often synonymous. "Audacious and arrogant false teachers 'despise authority' 2 Pet 2.10; this is rejection and rebellion. Eleazar and the Maccabeus brother despise pain 2 Macc 6.9; 14.1. Christ despised the shame of the cross' Papyri of the 7-8th century show more than mere negligence or abstention is involved:" I had to abandon my humble occupation." Jos Ant 4.260 Dtp.Apoll. 27.5; 21.18 Cf. . 5.200 'Their troubles were due to their contempt for the laws.' Spicq:3.104;

"Author and Perfector": Both the initial awakening[Wesleyan] and new birth[Calvinism] as well as the gift of dying grace[faith] complete the life. In 11.40 those who are in heaven are not perfect, but he is the perfector of their faith. Or, does it only mean they aren't perfect apart from the fullness of the number of NT believers? When faith is perfected, as seen from a different angel, it is no longer needed, since the eye will see and heart know. Neither those in heaven now nor those on earth now see what is prepared for them, since "that which is perfect" who will come has not come as yet. Isa 64.4; 65.17 are used in 1 Cor 2.9. Here' love' characterizes both those in heaven and those on earth since the title for Jesus is given as "Lord of Glory." The revelation in 2.10 Paul says has already been given, but in 1 Cor 13 he says it is still hoped for. In the OT passages there is also the need for the individual 'O man' who needs to be aware of the collective significant 'others' that love God, in the same sense that the readers of Hebrews need to know about the many witnesses. Ps 68.18; 69.7,19. anti 'instead of the joy' Dana-Mantey,100. Moses made a similar choice to leave Egypt which might imply he had decided to leave before the crisis of his crime being discovered.

'Joy set before him'does not appear in the Gospel account of the last events in Jesus' life or show this as a motivating force. But as in the Christian's hope it is an objective fact, not subjective realization and it is through much tribulation that one must enter the kingdom. Heb 2 shows Jesus in the assembly rejoicing along with the disciples in God's presence. 'Scorning the shame' is really bearing a cross, and cognitively, emotionally, coming to grips with the fact of one's relationship to God and not allowing shame to destroy one's mind or service to mankind.

12.3 "Let the Lord guide your hearts toward the love of God and the endurance of Christ.': a call to participate in the sufferings that Christ endured Rev 1.9, or constancy to wait for Christ or simply hope that has Christ as its object. Cf. 2 Thess 3.5; Spicq:3.420n28. 'endured' is an aspect of faith, as is seen by example after example in ch.11. In James Job is lauded not for 'patience,' which he did not have, but for 'endurance' and 'perseverance' under all that pressure. The King James' translation of 'patience' belies the meaning to remain and continue to remain 'under' hupomone. This is really endurance. 'opposition endured' can cause attrition, weariness, losing of heart [stomach] for the enterprise. It is possible, as in the experience of Job, for patient endurance [Job 2] to suddenly collapse in a devastating torrent of self-pity. 'opposition from sinful men' applies to most prophets, Jesus and the apostles, but here is the situation in much of Jesus ministry, from birth to death. Confrontational dialogues are with sinful opposing men, the Sadducees, Zealots, Pharisees and officials of Judaism. Here Jesus is identified with the 'poor' who are usually also the 'pious poor.' 'weary and lose heart.' In Daniel the antichrist wears out the saints of the most high.' The role of emotions, the affective and feeling domain and faith is an area Evangelicals have tended to set aside since one should live by faith and not feeling. The OT also stresses physical and psychosomatic phenomena of sickness or stress in many of the Psalms. In v.4 'struggle' is a wrestling metaphor, where one's 'resisting' can reach a point of exhaustion. The prime example is Jacob at Peniel, where an injured Jacob still would not let go. Did he consider himself doomed to death anyway and hence his faith simply would not let go even thought he had wrestled all night? Paul in his Corinthian epistles mixes affective domain matters with all the external pressure references as part of a package of suffering for Christ. He also more clearly than in the Psalms of lament shows the means he personally used to restore equilibrium to a nearly burnt-out servant of God. The OT and Paul in Rom 5.5 speaks to the emotion and mental-state of shame. Here opposition is defined as those things suffered by the hand of sinful men. 'Consider him' is a barrier against losing faith. The life model of Jesus in this book somewhat harks back to the wisdom books and certain OT personalities that are taken as models, such as God's comparisons of all the kings to David. Weariness and discouragement hinder the 'running' and perseverance and v.4 'the struggle'. The only solution is 'to consider Him'. The OT frequently uses *zakar in this sense to 'recall, visualize, focus on" the

Lord. Dt 29.29 is a focus on divine revelation, not on the unknown things where God alone is in total control. Dt 8.18 'remember the Lord your God' is opposed to 'forget'. The focus on sinful men [not idols] may bring them down in Heb 12.2. 'endured' is an aspect of faith, as is seen by example after example in ch.11. In James Job is lauded not for 'patience,' which he did not have, but for 'endurance' and 'perseverance' under all that pressure. The King James' translation of 'patience' belies the meaning to remain and continue to remain 'under' hupomone. This is really endurance.. 'opposition endured' can cause attrition, weariness and losing of heart [stomach]. It is possible, as in the experience of Job, for patient endurance [Job 2] to suddenly collapse in a devastating torrent of self-pity. 'weary and lose heart.' In Daniel the antichrist wears out the saints of the most high.' The role of emotions, the affective and feeling domain and faith is an area Evangelicals have tended to set aside since one should live by faith and not feeling. The OT also stresses physical and psychosomatic phenomena of sickeness or stress in many of the Psalms. In v.4 'struggle' is a wrestling metaphor, where one's 'resisting' can reach a point of exhaustion. The prime example is Jacob at Peniel, where an injured Jacob still would not let go. Did he consider himself doomed to death anyway and hence his faith simply would not let go even thought he had wrestled all night? Paul in his Corinthian epistles mixes affective domain matters with all the external pressure references as part of a package of suffering for Christ. He also more clearly than in the Psalms of lament shows the means he personally used to restore equilibrium to a nearly burnt-out servant of God. The OT and Paul in Rom 5.5 speaks to the emotion and mental-state of shame. Cf. 2 Thess 3.5 "Let the Lord guide your hearts toward the love of God and the endurance of Christ.'[441] Eiv ten hypomonen tou xristou a call to participate in the sufferings that Christ endured Rev 1.9, or constancy to wait for Christ or simply hope that has Christ as its object.[442] Here opposition is defined as those things suffered by the hand of sinful men. 'Consider him' is a barrier against losing faith. The life model of Jesus in this book somewhat harks back to the wisdom books and certain OT personalities that are taken as models, such as God's comparisons of all the kings to David. Weariness and discouragement hinder the 'running' and perseverance and v.4 'the struggle'. The only solution is 'to consider Him'. The OT sometimes. uses zkr in this sense to 'recall, visualize, focus on" the Lord. Dt 29.29 is a focus on divine revelation, not on the unknown things where God alone is in total control. Dt 8.18 'remember the Lord your God' is opposed to 'forget'. The focus on sinful men [not idols] may bring them down in Heb 12.2. 'Endured such opposition' is not merely patience, but stamina, quietness of spirit, perseverance, calmness, and the ability to hupomenw 'to remain underneath' and not seek a way out. 'Grow weary and lose heart' describes victims of a war of attrition, exhaustion, rethinking, seeking an honorable way out, and about to give up.The struggle has become a tool of Satan in psychological warfare, and the allies are tired of fighting. Only by considering Jesus in a similar situation can one avoid burn out.

12.4 'Shed blood'. Resistance here is not suicide, but martyrdom, hardly rebellion against Rome or authorities, a cause for arrest that Peter warned against. The phrase is usually used in the OT of murder. But here it is induced by resistance to evil men and authorities. In Hebrews martyrdom is the norm; the race is shorter for some than for others.

'Struggle against sin' could use Satan, instead of sin, but does not. Nor does the author speak of the inner law of sin, an evil force abiding in the body. The next line defines the situation that to not compromise in anything might lead to death and the shedding of blood or someone else's blood, as in the Maccabean revolt. But envision a situation where a white lie could save one's life. As when Micaiah tells Jehoshaphat to go up in battle but then corrects the message? The question is 'the whole truth and nothing but the truth.' This is biblical even though some say it is not right at certain times to be blatant about the truth. 'Struggle against sin' could use 'Satan,' instead of 'sin', but does not. Nor does the author speak of the inner law of sin, an evil force abiding in the body. Besides 'buffeting one's body' and 'standing against the Devil' and the image of the fully equipped warrior and wrestling, boxing, there is the race in which only one wins. None of this is called works but faith at work as in the phrase 'work of faith.' The next line defines the situation that to not compromise in anything might lead to death and the shedding of blood or someone else's blood, as in the Maccabean revolt. But envision a situation where a white lie could save one's life. As when Micaiah tells Jehoshaphat to go up in battle, but then corrects the message? The question is 'the whole truth and nothing but the truth.' Wisdom dictates to speak the truth in love so as to 'do good to all men' while speaking the whole truth may injure instead of doing good. Temporal clause using prepositions introducing a phrase rather than a clause. [443]

12.5 The readers are familiar with this passage from Proverbs probably because wisdom literature of this type was used in the schools. Prov 3.11,12 But the metatextual aspect takes this beyond the literature and page in that it is now God speaking through a page in the curriculum to specific persons, and saying things that must never be. The two reactions which are temptations and tests as well, are to 'make light of the Lord's discipline' and not perceive its reason or gravity, and seek to find joy in the hard going. Typical examples of this are in experiencing loss when believers surround the bereaving person and put the pressure on them to behave as a Christian and present a good testimony to the world, while in actuality the person must go through the grief in order to not treat the events lightly and miss the opportunity for spiritual growth. The second temptation is to 'lose heart' when receiving a rebuke from the Lord through another human being. Depression is again a reaction and does contain unbelief and alienation, deprecation of self-worth and unworthy thoughts about God. As in Paul's testimonies it is from despair one arises stronger than before, not by by-passing the despair. 'You have forgotten that word of encouragement' is from a minister or passage of scripture but is recognize in an experience as applied to one's self. But the power of the word of exhortation and comfort is often negated by failure to remember the whole passage of scripture that meant so much at one time because one had worked his way through it cognitively. Faith interprets this struggle against sin , tiredness of the race, as a father's discipline, not for mistakes or sins, but for the good of a child of God. Sons, the world children is not used here, in relation to fathers always have aspects of thinking, behavior, talking, expressing, obsessing, and emoting that the father wishes would become more mature. Aldrich notes "In the Epistle to the Hebrews the author points out that submission to the loving chastisement of the family of God proves and preserves life: "If ye endure chastening, God deals with you as sons" (Heb. 12:6-10). Submission to the teaching and corrective process of fatherly discipline as evidenced by keeping His Word, is proof that we belong in the family. Certainly no father seeks to discipline his neighbor's children, and the neighbor's child will not submit himself to the chastisement of any other father but his own.[444]

12.6 Why should sons God accepts be punished as a normal thing. Jesus learned obedience through the things he suffered, taking 'through' as not merely 'path' but 'means.' In Galatians Paul gives the argument that under the law believers are in a state of immaturity and subject to an overseer-teacher and thus his status is nothing different from a slave until he comes of age. But here 'son' indicates not an immature childhood status, but the fact of sonship regardless of public recognition of this fact. Acceptance as a son simply means discipline and punishment for the sake of partaking in God's holiness. Thus the parallel to human fathers breaks down at this point. The question is not disobedience but respect and subjection. Islam means submission, and here believers must learn submission. Proverbs has several verses that stress the same thing.[445] 'Submit' is used 24 times in the Bible.[446] As in protocol before earthly kings men must bow before God Almighty: "Psa. 72:9 The desert tribes will bow before him and his enemies will lick the dust. Rom. 14:11 It is written: "'As surely as I live,' says the Lord, 'every knee will bow before me; every tongue will confess to God.'" II Esdras 16.20 mentions "lashes for correction" Cf. . Hab 1.12; Prov 3.11,12, a prophetic conception. The context is apocalyptic. Myers,[447]346 Musar or discipline correction is not always through a whip or cane, but may be through speech of the sort that is found in these books as in Prov 1. Note Acts 15.4; 16.21; 22.18; 1 Tim 5.19; Heb 12.6 for paradexesthai. Mk 4.13-20 is thus related to this text. Jeremias,[448]78. Subordinate causal clauses introduced by relative pronouns[449] God 'accepts as a son' because this is adoption to a legal status and personal relationship and not due to natural or supernatural birth per se. The son must expect punishment, rebuke, discipline, and it is in this way the father prepares his son for living a spiritual life. The application of this truth is in the biblical pattern of father and mother, not just a mother. It is only this relationship and none other that has the discipline, because it has the acceptance.

12.7 "Know then in your heart that as a man disciplines his son, so the Lord your God disciplines you.' Hebrews applies this to persecution that God is doing and by so doing shows himself as a Father who trusts his son to learn something, Dt 8.5. Christ endured the cross so each disciple must 'consider what he endured from sinners' hypomone is related to serious trials in Paul and Revelation 2 Cor 1.6; Heb 10.32; 12.1; 'let us run with endurance the trial before us' Cf. .12.7 Christ endured the cross so each disciple must 'consider what he endured from sinners' hypomone is related to serious trials in Paul and Revelation 2 Cor 1.6; Heb 10.32; 12.1; 'let us run with endurance the trial before us' Cf. .12.7 eis paideian hypomonete imperative as in the Peshitta:bear,submit yourself, or a present indicative. Eis has causal value: calamities endured by the community are inflicted by God so as to educate [musar education through correction] those dear to Him. Paideia comes from pais. Jas 1.3-4 "The trial of your faith produces endurance. Let endurance come to full flower.' Job in Jas 5.11; Rev 3.10; 13.10 and 14.12 "This is the endurance and the faith of the saints.'Spicq,3.420n27;Dt 8.5

12.8 'Illegitmate children' in the biblical world had many laws to define rights and limitations and these entered western consciousness and a depreciating of these victims. In Babylonian law illegitimate children could be adopted and even made heirs. Rabbinical mamzer[illegitimate child] laws pertained especially to the priesthood. But were they not disciplined? Or was the prejudice and privilege so great that their role in history was ignored and therefore they were not disciplined? Jephthah seems to be the only obvious case and he is listed among the faithful in ch.11. 'illegitimate sons' are presumed to be only loosely cared for with fewer demands than sons in a descending order from the firstborn. Today the bastard is looked down on and the word is more and more in disuse, since the worth of the individual does not depend on the route of his birth or background. Today we would be more concerned with misuse and ill-feelings, alienation and cruelty toward these members of society. But the argument holds. God values very highly his sons and therefore disciplines them. From Isa 41.4 "I, the Lord, am the first...'. A statement of fact, not an answer to the questions in 2-4a, which are rhetorical and imply their own answers. The meaning is not exactly that Yahweh is 'eternal' but that He is contemporary with all history, from its beginning to its eschaton.

'I am He 'ani hu' This 'monotheistic formula' recurs in Isa 43.10,13,25, 46.4; 48.12; Ps 12.28,28, where 'Thou art the same' is lit. "Thou art He'. Indeed, 'I am one and the same' would be a permissible rendering here' GK 135a,N.1. Heb 13.8 'Jesus Christ is the same yesterday and today and forever.' There is no copula in the Hebrew and Rev 1.4,8, "who is and who was and who is to come," is only drawing out the implications of these two equated personal pronouns. That 'personality' is attributed to Yahweh is clear from them both. Yet another translation could be 'I am God' [Arab. Huwa, of God]. OT theism is in strong contrast with Hindu pantheism: the one has Yahweh say to man 'I am He than whom there is none other.'; the other bids man say to himself, 'thou art That One than which there is naught else." But 'everyone undergoes discipline' and 'children' extend this to more than males. The phrasing is that 'if one is not disciplined one is illegitimate' seems reversed but isn't. the evidence of the new birth is precisely in the disciplines of the Father. This is not to say that fathers should treat illegitimate children as such, but that he should rather accept them as his own and discipline them as such. The foster child is an anomaly; adoption is the biblical pattern. This is because in human society a foster family will rear a child with little bonding, love and concern, and may only meet out punishments. That is not a biblical pattern.

12.9 'Submit to the Father of our spirits and live.' The context is not stoning of rebellious children, nor overly zealous discipline, nor psychological pressure. The issue is discipline suffered within the context of martyrdom. To endure this discipline rightly means death but then also life. Some people in church history considered martyrdom the quickest route to heaven as do the Moslems. But the issue is not a choice of death but a choice of eternal life. 'We all'...respected them' is appealing to a cultural norm among the writer and his constituency that would not be true today. Not all are disciplined out of love, but reaction, and many are not disciplined at all. More, many who are respect their fathers less and less. If the father is not a good person, an honorable and upright and especially towards the mother, his wife is not fair and loving, how can the application of this verse be meaningful? "We have our fathers according to the flesh as correctors eixomen paideutas and we inclined toward them' Pss.Sol. 8.29. Cf. Hos 5.2 'I am the one who punishes you." Job 12.10[450]. 'We all'...respected them' is appealing to a cultural norm among the writer and his constituency that would not be true today. Not all are disciplined out of love, but reaction, and many are not disciplined at all. More, many who are respect their fathers less and less. If the father is not a good person, an honorable and upright and especially towards the mother, his wife is not fair and loving, how can the application of this verse be meaningful?

"We have our fathers according to the flesh as correctors eixomen paideutas and we inclined toward them' Pss.Sol. 8.29 su paideuthes hmwn ei Cf. Hos 5.2 'I am the one who punishes you." Egw de paideuthes humwn.[451] 12.9 Job 12.10. A proper family relationship is discipline that yields respect.. If one's relationship to the heavenly father does not do so when one is punished, and instead doubts, fears, accusations result, it means that the discipline was really needed and the Father had the confidence in him that he could handle the test.

12.10 'For a little time'. The age of children needing discipline is through elementary school. Once the 'young adult' graduates and is in the work world parents don't usually discipline them, although they may need it. By contrast God the Father disciplines his child throughout life. Lev 11.44. But the earthly father's discipline is relative to 'as one sees best' and often grows out of anger, despair, worry, fear, and is to handle a specific out-of-control situation. The heavenly Father is the model since he disciplines 'for his good.' The earthly father disciplines 'for a little while' and therefore is not continuous and consistent. The ultimate use of discipline by God is that 'we may live' and this is in a context of eternal life not just skills in living or physical life. The goal is holiness, not merely correction. It is sharing in God's holiness, and only the relationship to God can cause this outcome. The lesson on the human sphere is that the father is modeling for the child and therefore the evil tendency in the father must be the factor that makes an earthly father unlike the heavenly one. This evil tendency must give way to holiness such as God is. How is holiness attained through painful discipline? Holiness in this sense is not dealing with sin or failures but a development of spiritual character through one's response to the adverse happenings. The proper response will produce good fruit. But training is needed for this to happen. Discipline may not be for sin but for positive growth in holiness. Often in deep crisis of unbearable pain or trouble a person comes to complete surrender to God and acceptance of whatever God grants or takes away, and the result is holiness, defined as righteousness and peace. V.9 is the focus 'Submit!'

12.11 Righteousness and peace as in Rom 5.1-4 and 2 Peter 1.3-6 discipline and hardship produce a harvest of fruit ——for those trained by it. Paul speaks of the fruit of the Spirit. The whole picture is that at the time of faith in Christ and linked to baptism the Holy Spirit is granted, but then as victory is gained over the world, flesh and devil the suffering as a believer including seeing one's family suffer and die horrendous deaths all goes to produce these fruits. The aphoristic saying guaranteeing fruit assumed that this discipline is ministered by God and not some inconsistent earthly father. The goal of discipline should not be punishment, cruelty, repaying debts, enforcing submission, seeking to show who is in charge, and destroying a relationship. God does not discipline except to bring forth good and fruit. The difference between punishment for misbehaving and discipline isn't clear, especially in light of 12.6 where discipline, rebuke, punishment, hardship are all linked together.

The justification for discipline is not sins, but

1. Instruction in attitude 12.5; 'Allowing criticism from people, who are in God's control, to destroy relationships' error.
2. Training in acceptance of rebuke from God ; 'Unwillingness to admit one is wrong' error
3. Accepting hurt from God as love; 'Failure to deconstruct' error
4. Assuming a son role that has a job description of one the Lord punishes. 'inconceivable role description' error.
5. Enduring hardship as of God v.7; .'viewing hardship as of Satan' error
6. Training in respect for and submission to the heavenly Father 12.9; 'viewing submission as giving in and surrender' error

7. 'For our good' indicates not vengeance or venting wrath or paying a debt, but rehabilitation. 'Attributing wrong motives to God' error, as Israel did.
8. 'For our holiness' is for the development of character. 'God's and man's' incomprehensible relationships error
9. Realizing that discipline in its nature is painful, that it is a given. 'Pain can't be good' error.
10. Discipline is training to produce fruit of righteousness and peace, that Paul calls two out of three features of the Kingdom of God. 'Enforced new behavior' seemingly unrelated to morals attitude and affective realm.
11. Perception while discipline is happening is often misunderstood. 'Forest for the trees' error
12. The harvest of good is not immediately discoverable. 'Immediate gratification' childishness error

12.12 Weakness and strength: Isa 35.3 The quotation is quite precise. The use is that suffering weakens one and the recovery does not come from time or complaint. It comes from consciously facing the weakness with inner strength and going forward. As one acts in this way, 'do not fear,' words to Joshua, put strength from God into ones' inner self. It is God who is commanding and repeated to oneself it becomes God's grace giving power now. He returns to the 12.1-2 metaphor of the runner in a long race whose arms and knees become weak. But the track and challenge go on. The strengthening 'of the things which remain' must precede 'make level paths for your feet.' In the church some who are lame could easily become disabled. Clearly it is not all sons that need healing, but those in persecution and injured emotionally do need healing. Isa 35.3 Depression and discouragement besides over-exertion can leave one weak in arms and knees. The nearest life-context is the race track or the life of a slave serving a master, who having done all is still an unprofitable servant.

12.13 Permanency and Temporality: Here the Sinai experience is contrasted to the End Time when heavens and earth will be shaken. But in 12.27-28 there is a kingdom which cannot be shake. This is defined as created things in v.27. All the created things will be removed so what cannot be shaken will remain. We are receiving this kind of kingdom which is contrasted to his speaking from heaven and shaking heaven and earth. 'My kingdom is not of this world' could mean 'not of the people and of the created material of this world.' 'Make level paths for your feet' appears to be an exhortation to not choose the hardest route, but to pay attention to a life style in which tripping and falling would not likely happen.

12.14 'Root of bitterness' The analogy can apply to the carnal nature, original sin or also to events of injustice, jealousy, hatred, and hurt that have not been accepted and in memory begin to fester once more when a similar event occurs. Here the root was planted long ago. But roots grow down and not up! The figure is possibly that the nourishment for the root comes from above within memory and consciousness and it fruit or results lies even deeper in the unconscious. This exhortation goes beyond v.12-13 to include 'all men' a mandate elsewhere stated as 'doing good to all men.'

Live at peace is the theme of reconciliation found in Mal 4.1 in connection with the Messiah's forerunner and a major theme of Paul, reconciliation to God does imply reconciliation with all men. 'Every effort' is sufficient not the actual accomplishment, which is impossible. 'and to be holy' may be simply Hebrew style where 'and' need not be translated. But it also can point out a limitation to peace with all men when it comes to being holy.

'Without holiness no one will see the Lord' goes beyond John 3 which says that without the birth from above no man shall see God. In this latter context 'see' is spiritual seeing of what God is doing as ruler in history and the present tense and what God is doing right now in the world. But the same all-inconclusive language here is used not limiting it to believers. Here is not the beneficent vision just before death, but the 'seeing him as he is.' No man has seen God at any time, but the Son has revealed him, and will to whoever He wills. Holiness is the prerequisite and the obligation, as in the OT, is on the individual to 'be holy.' Of all men Moses was closest to God, and the mount of transfiguration in 1,2 Peter was the closest Peter came to it. John declares Jesus said he had seen and heard heavenly things. Believers will see him as he is. Peace with men is probably the horizontal aspect and holiness the vertical and thus the pair brings the stress on the second item. Without imparted holiness the unfolding of the invisible God will never be experienced.

12.15, The watchman metaphor: 1 Cor 1.7 It is necessary to watch lest any brother be deprived of grace. Dt 29.18 Note 'sinners are deprived of the glory of God. Rom3.23. Spicq,3.430n19 . The husbandman metaphor 1 Cor 3.6f, Matt 15.13 has many variants. IV Ezra 9.31 reads "Today I am sowing my law in your heart,, which will bring fort fruit in you.' The OT does not speak of the divine message as seed?? Is this an influence of logos spermatikos a Hellenistic conception? But IV Ezra 8.41 reads "For as the husbandman sows much seed upon the ground, and plants many trees, and yet not all that is sown shall come up in due season, neither shall all that is planted take root; even so they that are sown in this world shall not all be saved." Thus the community of God is God's planting as in Isa 61.3; Eth. En 62.8; Ps.Sol. 14.3f; Jub 1.16; 21.24; 36.6; Dead Sea Scrolls; Rabbinical Numbers r.16; and the NT. Jeremias,[452] 'So that no one misses the grace of God.' The 'root of bitterness' corresponds to the need for 'eradication' of original sin as taught by some holiness teachers. Here the root exists, and the danger is a connected series of aggravations causing it to' grow up' and 'cause trouble' and then 'defile many.' In biblical terms as in medical defilement is a living, active, growing, possessing and controlling force and contagion not only in a ritual or symbolical meaning, and thus Satan can have his way by using this evil to destroy the individual and all those he contacts. James 1.19 deals with anger, while 1.13-15 with evil desire and 3.16 with earthly wisdom interacting with envy and selfish ambition. In each reference the stepped progression and spread of defilement is explicitly mentioned. Hence the OT focuses on impurity not only to maintain health, and propriety in worship but to teach the lesson that sin in this form needs atonement and cleansing 1 John 1.7,9, and must be replaced with heavenly wisdom and the Spirit of God James 4.5.

12.16 'Godless like Esau' means that his act of selling his rights as eldest son were despising a birth order that God had arranged. But it was arranged that the blessing was to be given to Jacob, as announced early on to his mother. Getting both blessings involved conniving and deceit, taking advantage of Esau and his basic human nature. Even so God's gift was snubbed for something of very little and very temporal value. The end of the story does not justify what Esau did any more than what Jacob did. The world would say Jacob had initiative, means, goals, assertiveness, and learned more with Laban, Isaac and Esau. Jacob over-valued getting ahead, while Esau under valued it. Impiety treats the gift of God with contempt, and barters everything to meet immediate needs. Jacob carried fear of Esau for a long time, while Esau had dealt with his anger. Often the slow learner is taken advantage of and awakes up to anger, jealousy, and a spirit of retaliation and this describes Esau who woke up to reconciliation. 'No one' in inclusive and to not perceive God and grace in the adversities means to miss out receiving the grace such a discovery would provide. 'no bitter root grows up' Often this is used to describe original sin or the carnal nature or evil tendency. It exists unseen till something occurs, causes trouble, and defiles the person and everyone in touch with him. This only happened in Esau's case after the second deception when, very angrily, he awoke to the extent of his loss, the tragedy of deceiving his father, the irrevocableness of Isaac's blessing. Rebecca wouldn't allow this to result in the death of her two sons and so Jacob was sent to Harran. Compared to the Genesis account there is no indication Isaac knew of Esau selling his birthright, or whether, on discovery, he could have voided it, since the sons were still living at home. Does this continue the rather passive behavior of Isaac from marriage, to well drilling and moving episodes? 'Sexually immoral' seems out of context with a discussion of Esau, but is linked to 'godless.' Actually Esau's marriages to Hittite and Canaanite women was immoral within the patriarchs' mores. It was unacceptable to both parents and finally Esau woke up to this fact and sought to rectify it. Had he divorced his previous wives when he married a third, an Ishmaelite, Mahalath? Did this constitute adultery as in later moral laws? The grounds for adding a wife were largely bound by whether the earlier wife produced a male heir or not. But Gen 36.2-3 indicates he had several wives: Adah a Hittite, Oholibamah a Hivite, Basemath, daughter of Ishmael. Adah did have a son. So marrying Basemath was done so as to please his parents.

12.17 "He[Esau] could bring about no change of [Isaac's] mind, though he [Esau] sought the blessing[of Isaac] with tears.' Isaac only had one blessing, he said, , while 11.20 says he blessed both Jacob and Esau.

'Unable to repent" for those who want to repent, is a grace denied them according to II Esdras 7.82. Beginning from line 75 Ezra rays: " If you please, Lord, Lord, also make this clear to your servant; whether after death, or when each one of us has to surrender his soul, we will really be kept in repose until those times when you are to renew the creation, or [whether] we will be tormented immediately? He replied to me as follows:" I'll show you this too. But you must not get entangled with scorners nor reckon yourself with those who are tormented. For indeed you have a treasure of words stored up with the Most High but it will not be revealed to you until the last times. For the conception of death is this: when the final sentence of death has emerged from the Most High that man is to die, when the spirit withdraws from the body, to return again to him who gave it, it first of all entreats the glory of the Most High. If it should be one of those who scorned, 'Who did not adhere to the ways of the Most High, Who held his law in contempt, Or who hated those who feared God;' such spirits will not enter habitations but will roam around henceforth in torment, ever unhappy and sad, in seven ways. The first way: because they have spurned the law of the Most High. The second way: because now they are unable to truly repent that they may live. The third way: they will see the reward deposited for those who were faithful to the covenants of the Most High. The fourth way: they will contemplate the torment deposited for themselves in the last [times]. The fifth way: they will see the habitations of others guarded by angels in complete freedom from disturbance. The sixth way: they will see how immediately[some] of them will pass over into torment. The seventh way: which is worse than all the above mentioned ways: 'because they will languish in confusion, they will be consumed in shame, and they will pine away in fears' when they see the glory of the most high before whom they sinned and before whom they are to be judged in the last times." The next paragraph gives the contrast for those saved, and asserts there can be no intercession for people in the next life. Note "while the place of repentance was yet open to them' indicates this was not an isolated case but valid for all time.[453]. But the one unable to repent here is Isaac, while in ch.6 it is the apostate person. To view these statements as consistent with the Genesis account it must be that Isaac's blessing on Esau did occur but was not the same as that on the one designated with primogeniture.

12.18 Deut. 4:11 "You came near and stood at the foot of the mountain" while it blazed with fire to the very heavens, with black clouds and deep darkness.; Deut. 5:22 "These are the commandments the LORD proclaimed in a loud voice to your whole assembly there on the mountain from out of the fire, the cloud and the deep darkness; and he added nothing more. Then he wrote them on two stone tablets and gave them to me. Holy mountains, such as Horeb, Sinai, Nebo, Carmel, Zion, reflect a mythological mountain of the north where God reigns with his heavenly court. The physical mountain was replicated in Sumer by building over 40 towers of Babel, ziqqurauts, where the top level contained a room for sacred marriage rites and heaven and earth met when the divine came down. Similarly, in Canaan and Ugaritian culture the mountain of the north, under various names, was important. Even in Christian hymnology and vocabulary it comes to us largely through the Psalter.

12.18-22, Heavenly and earthly mountains also appear in Rev 16. Ford,[454]264. Another reading is that the spiritual realm has theophanies that aren't located at Horeb or Sinai and may reflect Zaphon or Zion as an abstract quantity as in ancient Semitic poetry. 'Mountains' in Akkadian <u>shadu</u> use a sign from Sumerian KUR read as a classifier or logogram read but not pronounced: <u>'mat'</u> meaning 'land, country, nation' in Akkadian. Here the mountain is the Kingdom of God and the People of God, where the king and judge reign over all things. In David-Theology Zion or Jerusalem is the focus of future events. But discontinuity with earthly history faces all men as all must be judged.

12.19 "When the people saw the thunder and lightning and heard the trumpet and saw the mountain in smoke, they trembled with fear" Ex 20.18-26:. They stayed at a distance; and said to Moses, "Speak to us yourself and we will listen. But do not have God speak to us or we will die." Moses said to the people, "Do not be afraid. God has come to test you, so that the fear of God will be with you to keep you from sinning." The people remained at a distance, while Moses approached the thick darkness where God was. Then the LORD said to Moses, "Tell the Israelites this: 'You have seen for yourselves that I have spoken to you from heaven: Do not make any gods to be alongside me; do not make for yourselves gods of silver or gods of gold. "'Make an altar of earth for me and sacrifice on it your burnt offerings and fellowship offerings, your sheep and goats and your cattle. Wherever I cause my name to be honored, I will come to you and bless you. If you make an altar of stones for me, do not build it with dressed stones, for you will defile it if you use a tool on it. And do not go up to my altar on steps, lest your nakedness be exposed on it.'

The 'trumpet blast' corresponds to the type in Exodus and antitype in the Eschaton. In Deuteronomy Moses asserts that all Israel was there and heard the voice of God and this together with the sights of that day at Sinai brought the demand for Moses to relay the message instead of God speaking directly to them. The medium of glory put Moses prostrate before God in fear in more than one instance. Cf. the mount of transfiguration which Peter recalls that even transcended the resurrection or ascension as an evidence of the faith. Isaiah ch.6 has Isaiah first hearing angels' voices as did Ezekiel.

While the witness of both testaments is uniform in this fear, still Paul says that believers will see God as he is since 'we shall be like him'. There must be more than imputed holiness to live in God's presence. Imparted holiness through the indwelling Spirit and presence of Jesus turns our eyes away from the fearful to the praiseworthy, as in the next paragraph v.22-24.The use of the 'test' isn't to find out what their reaction would be, but to instill in them the fear of God and thus has instructional function. 'Those who heard begged that no further word be spoken,' yet God did not take this as an affront. It is not a modern phenomenon that church people ask the minister to discontinue speaking on certain topics or in a certain manner. 'They could not bear what was commanded' corresponds to the Gospel where Jesus could not share some things with disciples for they were 'not yet able to bear it.' The reaction to the test was further alienation, dissatisfaction with God's plan, earnestly seeking a substitute for God's voice, and asking God to change his plan.They may have learned to negotiate with God but did not learn the fear of God.

v.20 seems to place the cordoning off of the mount immediately after their request that God not speak to them directly. While ch.2.2 describes the law given through angels, this account of God initially speaking directly to Israel has all the elements of theophany and a hint that the world could end now. All of these phenomena were dangerous to superstitious people, but in fact, were dangerous.. However, God seeks not to rebuke their fears, but to establish a relationship with the people based on His Word so that they become his People. Moses and then God's Word through law, promise, threat, and covenant because the mediator between God and man.

12.20 'An animal,' not directly killed, but through men to teach holiness. Ex 19.12-13 includes whoever 'whether man or animal' is stoned, but not by hand. This is judicial execution for man or beast alike. It is off-limits and taboo." It shall be stoned' could be a passive where God acts, but normally stoning is done by the adult males of the assembly. A parallel would be summary execution in a military tribunal since in the crowd at the foot of the mountain it would appear military law was in effect. In addition, the chronology shows the covenant had not been adopted as yet, so procedures for judging cases had not been proclaimed. Cf. . V. 21-23.

'Set it apart as holy' v.24. The prime lesson is holiness of place and holiness of theophany. The means of teaching this is by imposed limitations and disciplined behavior, the means of enforcing the rule is through warning and execution of offenders, while the provision for approach is through blood of the covenant and person of the high priest. Ex 19.12,13 Put limits for the people around the mountain and told them, 'Be careful that you do not go up the mountain or touch the foot of it. Whoever touches the mountain shall surely be put to death. He shall surely be stoned or shot with arrows; not a hand is to be laid on him. Whether man or animal, he shall not be permitted to live.' Only when the ram's horn sounds a long blast may they go up to the mountain."There is no record that the long blast sounded for the people in general to ascend the mountain. Holiness of God is taught through holiness of place, and through separation.Gen 1.7, when God separated day from night, and waters above and beneath, and separated the waters only then God saw it was good. Separation as part of basic infrastructure is 'good.' Nothing is 'good' but God, Jesus said, but God and men can be holy. The fact is that the idea of energy-charged holiness has not been lost on those who produce movies, as in Raiders of the Lost Ark. The lessons of apartness, otherness, holiness of places, objects, times, procedures, people and events was a major lesson that Israel had to learn. Death, directly from God or through societal leaders or judges was a powerful lesson, that sometimes caused alienation through terror and fear which didn't inspire trust in God but an understanding of God's sovereign will..

The parallel here is coming not to a physical mountain but to 'A consuming fire' v.28. Reverence and awe, thanksgiving and worship are a natural response to 'receiving' a kingdom that cannot change. Why should the animal be responsible, accountable and liable for encroachment on a boundaried area? The Hebrew background where animals, slaves, foreigners, ger-residents often were integral to the family unit and obedience was required of all, accounts for this liability.[455] The similar case is encroachment into the temple by anyone who is not a priest, or touching or looking at the ark by anyone at all. The rules of isolation, separation, distance, and holiness were indeed strict and punishment was not based on whether the person 'knew to do good and did it not,' or sinned accidentally. Rules of taboo operate apart from intention. For instance, the law against murder is reduced to involuntary manslaughter, but when Samuel killed the king of Jerusalem he was operating on rules of a holy war situation, otherwise as priest he could not have slaughtered them. Laws forbade killing an anointed king, but common sense and wisdom made this condemned king confess the punishment was 'just' because it was based on their own laws and practice heretofore. Samuel was a priest who must not approach dead things. But the command of God to fight the enemy took precedence in order to establish a precedent and a model for the army to follow..

'Could not bear what was commanded'; The initial revelation only commanded them to not ascend the mountain and was part of preparation for God's appearance; they had to wash bodies, clothes and abstain from marital relations, but possibly not food. Did they reject the Ten Commandments which appear in v.20.1ff as the direct speech of God? Did they thus reject monotheism and iconless religion even before the covenant was established? Or was this rejection of a supreme being and any imposition of rules over them? Moses repeats this in 20.23, and this seems to be the point they balked at.

12.21 Personal vulnerability; 'I feared the anger and wrath of the LORD, for he was angry enough with you to destroy you. But again the LORD listened to me.' Dt 9.19. This setting is not Moses' mere absence, or long delay in returning, but Israel's rebellion in the golden calf incident. Moses testifies he interceded with trembling and offered himself to be the substitution for their sin; Hebrews does not stress Moses as intercessor, only as covenant mediator. But in the initial year Moses is strong, he doesn't show any vulnerability, which may have helped in bonding with the people, or may have been disastrous to maintaining respect for God. God had said he would exalt Moses so the people would follow him. So to reveal any weakness had to wait 40 years. This was the beginning of identification of Moses with the people in a deeper way. The second generation needed to know the length Moses went to save them. But it also makes a setting for those, who just now are believers in distress, who are beginning to rebel against God's word, to know that approach to God was purchased only through the Son and that it was available now. Moses can't help them now. None of this grace is for license to sin, disbelieve or rebel.

12.22 Victory celebrations: "Given the abundant, quasi-technical usage of panegyris for the Olympic, Isthmian, Pythian, Nemean,etc, games, we must include a sports meaning in Heb 12.22; These competitions not only attracted the largest crowds, they also celebrate a victory[456] and here a reward. In effect, Hebrews defines the Christian life as an athletic trial, describes the conditions for training and winning, points to the prizes offered and the crowd of spectators who admire and encourage the athletes of faith 12.1-2. So it is not surprising that the epistle uses a compatible metaphor to evoke the glory and joy that are in store for the victors, namely, the metaphor of the jubilant polis, of a panegyris at which the whole assembly of the elect celebrates and sings the praises of the garlanded competitors." Spicq,3.7. This recalls David returning from the slaying of Goliath and Psalm 9, 21, 66. In contrast to Rome Israel celebrated victory at the temple, which was in the same building complex as the palace. Josephus War.5.230 mentions that the high priests ascended the altar only on the Sabbath, the new moon, the celebration of a national festival, or a public observance.' 'The panegyris.[457]is so described. The New Jerusalem was always in the plans as seen from the Zohar: "When Israel left Egypt, God desired to make them on earth like ministering angels above, and to build for them a holy house, which was to be brought down from the heaven of the firmaments, and to plant Israel as a holy shoot after the pattern of the celestial prototype. Thus it is written, "You shall bring them in and plant them in the mountain of your inheritance, the place, O Lord, which you made for you to dwell in"- this is the first Temple- "the sanctuary, O Lord, which your hands have established" (Ex. Xv, 17)-this is the second Temple; and both were to have been the work of the Almighty. But as they provoked God in the wilderness they died there and God brought their children into the land, and the house was built by human hands, and therefore it did not endure. In the days of Ezra also on account of their sins they were forced to build it themselves and therefore it did not endure. All this time the first building planned by God had not yet been set up. Now of the future time it is written, "The Lord builds Jerusalem" (Ps.147.2)-He and no other. It is for this building that we are waiting, not a human structure which cannot endure. The Holy One, blessed be He, will send down to us the first House and the second House together, the first in concealment and the second openly. The second will be revealed to show all the world the handiwork of the Holy One, blessed be He, in perfect joy and gladness. The first, which will be concealed, will ascend high over that which is revealed, and all the world will see the clouds of glory surrounding the one which is revealed and enveloping the first one which ascends to the height of the glorious heavens. It is for that building that we are waiting. Even the future city of Jerusalem will not be the work of human hands, all the more so then the Temple, God's habitation. This work should have been completed when Israel first went forth from Egypt, but it has been deferred to the end of days in the last deliverance."[458] "Huge throng on Mount Zion" appears also in Rev 4.1; 7.9 and II Esdras 2.42. In the latter case Mount Zion is rather the heavenly Jerusalem, where the Lamb and the 'sealed' dwell. [459]. Mount Zion only occurs in Rev 14.1 of that book. Seven times in the NT, five from OT quotations. It is the highest mountain of the world in Isa 2.2; Mic 4.1; Ezk 17.22; 50.2; Zec 14.10; Ps 48.1-2 and associated with the water of life in Ps 48.7. It is a symbol of rejoicing and security. "As the Abyss is the place of evil, so the mountain is the place of revelation and security."[460]. , Mountains of Zion argues that the Christian approaches a Mt.Zion destiny' 'come to a Mt Zion'. Use of the article for quality or character.[461] Spicq notes "Mountains always have had supernatural significances: the throne of God, a cultic center, a place of sanctuary—'Our fathers worshipped on this mountain' John 4.20. Thus, according to the Hymn to Isis of Isidorus, at the New Moon the royal statue was paraded <u>en orei</u>, i.e. in the desert. According to the NT, not only did Jesus climb a mountain 'to be apart' Matt 17.1; Mk 9.2; Lk 9.28; 2 Pet 1.18 'alone in that place' Matt 14.23; Mk 6.46; Lk 6.12; John 6.15,i.e. to see solitude for prayer; but it was also there that he taught the sermon on the mount Matt 5.1; 8.1; 15.29; John 6.3, chose his disciples Mk 3.13, and appeared to them after his resurrection Matt 28.16. The mountain is the place for communications from God Gal 4.24-25; Heb 8.5; 12.20 and the symbol of heaven Heb 12.22; Rev 14.1;21.10. Note Horeb:[462] appears 17 times: But Sinai appears 39 times:[463]Mount Zaphon appears 6 times[464] 'mount' 146 times from Ex 19.11 to Rev 14.1; Mount Zion 22 times 2 K.19.31 to Rev 14.1; Only once in Hebrews. 'Mountain' 154 times Gen 22.14-Rev 21.10; 'Mountain of the Lord' Gen 22.14-Zech 8.3 6 times. Sinai 39 times. 'Mount of God' Ezek 28.6; 'Holy Mount' Ezek 28.14= Eden. 'Ebal' appears 7 times; 'Gerizim' 4 times; 'Nebo' 13 times; Carmel 27 times but not all are the mount' Only 5 times are Mount Carmel. 'Hermon' 16 times. The Zion Theology in the prophets is a backdrop for both temple imagery and throne imagery.

12.22 Josephus war. 5.230 mentions that the high priests ascended the altar only on the Sabbath, the new moon, the celebration of a national festival, or a public observance.' 'the panegyris' [465] The New Jerusalem was always in the plans as seen from the Zohar :" When Israel left Egypt, God desired to make them on earth like ministering angels above, and to build for them a holy house which was to be brought down from the heaven of the firmaments, and to plant Israel as a holy shoot after the pattern of the celestial prototype. Thus it is written, "Thou shall bring them in and plant them in the mountain of your inheritance, the place, O Lord, which thou hast made for thee to dwell in"- this is the first Temple-"the sanctuary, O Lord, which thy hands have established" (Ex.15.17)-this is the second Temple; and both were to have been the work of the Almighty. But as they provoked God in the wilderness they died there and God brought their children into the land, and the house was built by human hands, and therefore it did not endure. In the days of Ezra also on account of their sins they were forced to build it themselves and therefore it did not endure. All this time the first building planned by God had not yet been set up. Now of the future time it is written, "The Lord builds Jerusalem" (Ps.147.2)-He and no other. It is for this building that we are waiting, not a human structure which cannot endure. The Holy One, blessed be He, will send down to us the first House and the second House together, the first in concealment and the second openly. The second will be revealed to show all the world the handiwork of the Holy One, blessed be He, in perfect joy and gladness. The first, which will be concealed, will ascend high over that which is revealed, and all the world will see the clouds of glory surrounding the one which is revealed and enveloping the first one which ascends to the height of the glorious heavens. It is for that building that we are waiting. Even the future city of Jerusalem will not be the work of human hands, all the more so then the Temple, God's habitation. This work should have been completed when Israel first went forth from Egypt, but it has been deferred to the end of days in the last deliverance."[466] The Zohar belongs to Jewish Kabala literature.

"Huge throng on Mount Zion" appears also in Rev 4.1;7.9 and II Esdras 2.42. In the latter case Mount Zion is rather the heavenly Jerusalem, where the Lamb and the 'sealed' dwell[467].Mount Zion only occurs in Rev 14.1 of that book. Seven times in the NT, five from OT quotations. It is the highest mountain of the world in Isa 2.2; Mic 4.1; Ezk 17.22; 50.2; Zec 14.10; Ps 48.1-2 and associated with the water of life in Ps 48.7. It is a symbol of rejoicing and security. "As the abyss is the place of evil, so the mountain is the place of revelation and security."[468] 61. Tsiwn orei argues that the Christian approaches a Mt.Zion, a 'destination' and thus one 'comes to the Mt Zion'. Use of the article for quality or character. Dana-Mantey, 138. Mt Zion has been transferred and transformed into a heavenly location altogether. The contrast between Moses' fear and the believer's experiencing heavenly joy among the angels is precisely the point.

12.22-24 Spicq notes various terminology for the Christian hope of 'heavenly inheritance' Rom 8.17; 1 Cor 15.50; Eph 1.18; Titus 3.7, 'kingdom' 2 Thess 1.5; 2 Tim 4.18; 'vision of God' 1 Cor 13.12; 1 John 3.2, not now 2 Cor 4.18. It all .depends on what is not seen. They are summed up in 'Christ our Hope' 1 Tim 1.1. He will lead the .sometimes of the children of God to glory Heb 2.10; 10.22; to be with him Phil 1.22-23.Spicq,I,488. 'Hope' in English appears in the Bible 166 times but hwqt in the OT only 36 times. There other terms in the OT so translated. The word can also mean 'thread' or rope. Is this another stem or does Rahab's life-line symbolize the believer's hope?[469]

The lists of Hebrews are in a variety of domain-contexts.In contrast to Mount Sinai and all that entailed the Christian believer has come and is now at

1. The heavenly Jerusalem, city of the living God. No mention of the sacred name.
2. To thousands upon thousands of angels in joyful assembly, corresponding the book of Revelation's picture.
3. To the church of the firstborn, whose names are written in heaven;
4. To God, the judge of all men;

5. To the spirits of righteous men made perfect;
6. To Jesus the mediator of a new covenant;
7 To the sprinkled blood. These perfect-seven are the basis to not refuse him who speaks. This is the situation of final judgment and the removing of every material and stable thing. When it comes to everything being removed only these things are eternal and transcend life and death.

12.22f, 'Jerusalem' in Deutero-Isaiah stands not only for a geographical location, but for an idea, the community of God's people. There is little difference between 'my people' Jerusalem,' and 'Jacob-Israel.' Jerusalem is already on the way to becoming a symbol and has become a type in the NT[470] In the language of Christian devotion it has become almost synonymous with the Church." [471] But here it is a heavenly Jerusalem as in Revelations where it is descending or suspended between heaven and earth. What longing would be created in Gentile Christians is unknown, but for the Diaspora and those who experienced Jerusalem's destruction yet again, a heavenly one coming down would not be subject to destruction ever. This seems to be a tacit rejection of the kingdoms of this world, their cities and social order, much as is found in the Major Prophets in regard to Babylon, Tyre, Thebes, Damascus and others, and in the NT Period would likewise place Athens, Babylon, and other great cities as not part of the new world order.

12.23 'Spirits of righteous men made perfect' does not refer to 'perfect' as used elsewhere in the book, which is for the living. It doesn't refer to death as Savior and Perfector, since Jesus is the author and finisher of our faith, and faith, according to 1 Cor 13, is for this life, before we can see things as He does. Nor does it refer to resurrection or immortality, since these have not happened as yet. Does this refer to 2 Cor 5, where the dead are clothed upon in an event occurring before the first resurrection, clothed with a body something like Jesus' resurrection body? Perfected spirits no longer are concerned about personal matters, but like those beneath the altar in the Apocalypse of Revelation are supremely concerned that the just judgment of God be carried out on earth and approaches vengeance. "Spirits of righteous men made perfect " are spirits which are not in soul-sleep, since they are aware of and following events even as prophets are aware. The resurrection is still future, but spirits are already made perfect in heaven, or does it simply mean they have been martyred? Heb 11 says they are not perfect apart from 'us' and in this context they are perfected, but still await a new body. Unrighteous men are not the topic, but are excluded, in that they may not actually have a spirit-life. Eph 2.1-6. Only righteous believers have a 'resurrected spirit' in their mortal lives. "Perfected" is thus not clarified, but could be the negation of Job 17.13-16; Job 14.13-17; Job 31.35-37. These are all questions of spirit. 1 Thess 5.23, on the other hand, 'sanctify them through and through [namely] may your whole spirit soul and body be kept blameless' is currently available and not yet available in OT times. Cf. . Ps 51.10-12. 'steadfast spirit' v.12 'willing spirit'; v.17 'broken spirit'; v.11 'Holy Spirit'. All of these are a heart cry for God to perfect the inner work of God in the soul. 'The assembly of the firstborn' ekklesia prwtotokwn "exegetes take to mean the patriarchs, or Christians who have already died, or the first converts and martyrs, or all the members of the church militant, or the angels in heaven. In all cases, prwtotokos is a title of honor." Sir 36.11 applied the term to Israel:" Have pity, O Lord, on the people called by your name, and on Israel whom you have made like a firstborn." Progonw corrected in Sinaiticus to prwtokw.[472]. 'Zion' here and in II Esdras 2.40 refers to the church. Myers,[473]152,348. The book of life appears in Rev 13.8; 17.8; 20.12; 21.27 and Lk 10.20; Phil 4.3; Heb 12.23;Ford,[474]84,409,413. The crowns in Rev 2.10 and 4.4; 4.10 "symbolize heaven's glory, the reward beyond the grave for those 'faithful unto death' [Jas 1.12; Heb 12.23; on the perfection attained by the blessed dead]. Payne,[475]49. 'Church of the firstborn' is still on earth, but their names are already written in heaven. The church is the 'firstfruits' but the 'Firstborn' is the Lord Jesus. 'To God, judge of all men' moves from

1. a mountain;
2. to Heavenly Jerusalem;
3. to thousands of angels;
4. to Church of firstborn;
5. to God
6. to spirits of righteous men made perfect;
7. to Jesus the Mediator. This movement of thought does not stop with God the judge, but moves on to Jesus, and that name is significant in covenanting context.' Church of the firstborn' who are the first generation believers in other NT passages. But here it appears to be all those whose names are written in heaven. The term 'firstborn' is thus shared by Jesus and the church making it his church and theirs. 'Judge of all men' does not seem to recognize a divided judgment when Christ comes for his saints in the rapture, and later to rule in the parousia. As in Wesley's sermon 'The Great Assize' all texts about the final judgment are linked in narrative form; It was preached before a court house. One of his points

is that all God's judgments and justice will be vindicated before billions of angels and humans in all world history. Then, the linking of God as judge is followed by the 'spirits of righteous men made perfect' which might indicate a judgment immediately on death and not waiting till a later time.

12.24 'Mediator of a new covenant' here is not the same as the high priest's role to have mercy for those who are weak and failing as an intercessor. Now it is not Moses but Jesus that stands between God and man. This position is not only intercessor but also mediator of the covenant who guarantees it. Jesus as covenant Mediator is a different role from Jesus as High Priest although both have to do with blood. Aaron had little to do with the first covenant but Moses did, and Jesus corresponds to Moses. In ch.2.18, Jesus as high priest 'helps', is 'merciful and faithful,' and 'frees' those bound in sin and temptation. But this assumes prayer to this high priest but not the high priest as a mediator to God. He 'sympathizes with our weakness' 5.15 and is available at the throne of grace to bestow mercy grace and help. He deals gently with the ignorant. He enters behind the curtain, where heaven evidently still has a curtain, 'and entered on our behalf.' It is as priest he saves 'those who come to God through him, because he always lives to intercede for them.' 7.25; 9.24 'He entered heaven itself, now to appear for us in God's presence.' But nothing says prayer to God directly is improper, for whoever calls upon the name of the Lord will be saved. But now we have Jesus by God's right hand and so the doubts in the Psalms about God's presence or absence, His willingness to hear and grant, or the fear that sin will cancel the prayer, are now absence since the blood deals with the conscience(9.14) and the high priest and Spirit(Rom.8) facilitate the praying. Jesus has become the 'Way' to the Most holy place of God's presence, while many Psalms seem to convey that they weren't sure of the way. The Mediator of the New covenant' is a different role from that of intercessor. Jesus as Mediator fulfills Moses not Melchizedek's role and this Mediator loves forever. He is a principle to the contract and it is in his blood. Mesites in Heb 8.6; 9.15; 12.24 is close to eggus for which see 7.22 Spicq,1.394n20; misten does not appear in Classical Greek. In the Hellenistic period it is common, more in literary than in papyri. It derives from mesos, one who stands "or walks in the middle, between two persons or groups: the context indicates the reasons for this intervention. Herod, in Jos Ant 16.24, intervened on behalf of those who were seeking something from Agrippa. He had influence in persuading Agrippa to perform good deeds and reconciled the inhabitants of Ilium with Agrippa when he was angry with them. The term usually has legal connotations. In the LXX it only occurs in Job 9.33 and in the papyri krites mesites and can be translated 'judge-arbiter.' P.Rein 44.3. 2nd cent.AD. In a business transaction he is 'negotiator' and 'peacemaker' or 'mediator-conciliator' mediating two states at war and bringing them to sign a treaty. The word is also used for 'witness' legally, as in a marriage, questions of a debt, or 'surety' engyos.He is the guardian of oaths, deposits,contracts. Philo first gave the word a religious meaning in referring to angels as mediating and conciliating. [Dreams 1.142-143] and Moses as making prayers for the forgiveness of sins. [Moses 2.166]. Paul, in 1 Tim 2.5 asserts ''there is one mediator between God and humans, the human Christ Jesus." He is the sole intermediary. In Job several categories of possible mediators come to the arguments but are later dropped; In 4.18 'servants and angels' appear, but Eliphaz asserts God doesn't trust them. 'Judge' appears in 9.15 but would he give a hearing?. 9.32-34 seeks an arbiter, a man, 'to lay his hand upon us both," someone before whom one could speak up without fear. In Job 15.15 Eliphaz suggests 'holy ones' but as unacceptable to God. In 16.19-21; Job cries out for 'my witness' 'my advocate' and 'my intercessor' 'on behalf of a man he pleads with God as a man pleads for his friend.' Job 16:20 My intercessor is my friend as my eyes pour out tears to God. Then in 19.25 "My Redeemer" is the living one, and implied is that he does not pursue as God does 19.22. Job 19:25 I know that my Redeemer lives, and that in the end he will stand upon the earthJob 33.23 also seeks for a mediator, but then God appears without such an one as Mediator: Job 33:23 "Yet if there is an angel on his side as a mediator, one out of a thousand, to tell a man what is right for him. 'The sprinkled blood' here is not the OT ritual but Jesus' blood, implying that sprinkling was on the cross and ground as an altar of a type not allowed in the OT. How does this speak a better word than the blood of Abel? Is it not that Abel's is evidence of Cain's crime, while Jesus' blood through the living Lord is interceding, not crying out for vengeance? The contrast is of a condemning blood versus an atoning blood.

12.25 Capitulates 2.2-4 'refuse him' is stronger than 'ignore'. The 'we' includes speaker and hearer, any man. Warned on earth as YHWH and the prophets v.25, and in contrast is 'from heaven' through Jesus, as reflected in John 3.11-12. The 'on earth' and 'from heaven' antithesis appears in John 3 concerning a birth from above as well as a message contrast between that of John the Baptist and Jesus. Mount Sinai was from earth, according to this paradigm that probably considers the revelation as mediated through angels. Jesus message is from heaven, from the father, for 'I am the Father are

One'. While the covenant is mediated the message is not, since it is the Son mediating this message. It is still possible to turn away from the one warning us from heaven. The antithesis is to 'receive such a kingdom that cannot be shaken. The ultimate authority is the one who speaks, not writes, and the ultimate responsibility is to listen to Him. Even the blood of Abel speaks. Perhaps the antithesis is between the letter and the message. The avoidance of law or Torah and focus on speaking is notable throughout. It is 'hearing' and the connection to God 'speaking' are not on a par with 13.22 'a short letter' which is an exhortation. This reflects worship centered in grateful praise for all God has give them. In this it corresponds to Psalms of Thanksgiving in the Book of Psalms that recount basically God's favor to Israel, and in individual Psalms the memory of a deliverance, a healing, or a special sense of God's presence among His people. Philo, Drunkenness 94 "The brotherhood of the Levites: those who sing the hymn of thanksgiving" ton eucaristetikon humwn Spicq, 505n23. 'did not escape' indicates there is no escape to the wicked, unless one like Abraham, Moses and Samuel interceded. Here 'one from heaven' warning is Jesus and the contrast is to the warning of angels. Jesus did have a prophetic role of warning but largely to disciples, Saduccees, lawyers, and priests. This verse has a similar structure to John 3.12-13 and Rom 10.6-8 based on Deut 30.12.

12.26-27 'Once more' is making a parallel between Sinai and the End of the Age. Here is part of Hebrews' Eschatology. We read Exodus as a theophany of a new beginning and the end of servitude in Egypt, and this entailed the formation of a People of God. The 'shaking' in the OT is so awesome the people thought the end of their world had come. Hag 2.6 "This is what the LORD Almighty says: 'In a little while I will once more shake the heavens and the earth, the sea and the dry land. The predicate adjective can be added to the predicate, corresponding to an adverb or prepositional phrase in English 'I am not content with shaking the earth alone" is not un-Greek;[476]. Hapax can mean 1. Once,one time, first, 'first and second' can mean at various times'; 2.it is the opposite of multiplicity, one time or often but not 'once again'. 3. One single time, unique' Heb 9.26; 9.27. 'a single bite'; 'once a year'. Cf. 9.28;1 Pet 3.18; [477] the shaking of earth is an earthquake with loud sounds but shaking of earth and heaven is a forerunner of the End. Nothing here is revealed about a new heaven and earth, but that is the next progression of revelation in 1 Peter and revelations. Heaven and earth is a merism, a phrase that encompasses everything. The Revelation of Jesus Christ in the parousia corresponds to that at Sinai. There was no shaking in the Transfiguration. Occasional voice from heaven in the Gospels has evidential value to the wise and understanding, but not to those who thought it was thundering. Sinai is the allusion, but 'again' for a shaking may be forecast by the earthquake at Golgotha when Jesus died. These are types of the final shaking.

12.27 'Shaken' is a merism in this context, interpreted as meaning the removal of created things. What remains? The Isaiah doctrine of the 'remaining' Remnants finds a new form here. Isa 6.12-13; 7.22; But in 1 Cor 13.13 [Cf. . 8-13] only love survives. Part of the strong language of the epistle is that not only political or physical changes will occur, but total changes. Only the believer rooted in his faith can survive these changes. Everything material created by God can be shaken and removed, but there seem to be some things that 'will remain' even in a new heaven and new earth. The law of physics that matter can only be transformed but not destroyed could be involved here. The Sinai or Mount Horeb shaking or earthquake phenomena are forerunners and omens of the last times. Scholars have pointed out that the Sinai account may not necessarily report an earthquake at the time, but also that the Sinai peninsula had no seismic activity either by earthquake or volcano, but that Midian did, and Hab 3.3. Even so earthquakes and volcanic activity along with dark skies, clouds, lightning, hail, rain, thunder and fire are all part of theophany of God's coming and presence. Everything material created by God can be shaken and removed, but there seem to be some things that 'will remain' even in a new heaven and new earth. The law of physics that matter can only be transformed but not destroyed could be involved here.[478] Ford,274,[479]

12.28 'Things created' is antithesis to 'what cannot be shaken.' Does this concept exist in the OT? Ps 139.16 approaches this. But the visible versus invisible as in Heb. 11.3 is a development of theology and cosmology under the influence of then current Platonic philosophy, while proportion wise still stressing the visible world. Does this mean that there is an invisible world that was not created or simply an invisible world that cannot be shaken? Dan 2.44 "In the time of those kings, the God of heaven will set up a kingdom that will never be destroyed, nor will it be left to another people. It will crush all those kingdoms and bring them to an end, but it will itself endure forever, eulabeia is associated with aidws that has many meanings. Anaideia 'shamelessness' 1. The sense of adornment with decency in 1 Tim 2.9; 2. From aidomai 'fear, respect' the word goes back to Homer, and expresses the respect and secret fear that one feels toward oneself. "With the Stoics it became a leading virtue."[480] Plutarch said aidws 'often allows itself to be led by reason and places itself under the same laws."The opposite is 'shame' 'whose hesitations and delats are contrary to reason.' "In the first century AD, this sentiment is sometimes that of shame, notably the shame of soldiers who are in flight and know that they are defeated, hence awareness of guilt; it is sometimes that of respect for others, the consideration owed others. It is then a restraint, a dignity, a modesty, or a discretion that keeps one from excess; thus a self-respect and a sense of honor that is often identified with modesty."[481]Spicq,1.43; 269; This virtue finds its highest expression in women. Philo explains why there was a wall of separation between Therapeutai and Therapeutrides, "to respect the modesty appropriate to the feminine nature," and he personifies the virtue as a woman who has "colors which are those of modesty . . . simple clothing, but more precious than gold, wisdom and virtue for her finery" (Sacr. Abel and Cain 26). This is the closest parallel to 1Tim 2:9.

Eulabeias is associated with aidwn that has many meanings. Anaideia 'shamelessness' 1. The sense of adornment with decency in 1 Tim 2.9; 2. From aidomai 'fear, respect' the word goes back to Homer, and expresses the respect and secret fear that one feels toward oneself. "With the Stoics it became a leading virtue."[482] Plutarch said aidws 'often allows itself to be led by reason and places itself under the same laws."The opposite is 'shame' 'whose hesitations and delats are contrary to reason.' "In the first century AD, this sentiment is sometimes that of shame, notably the shame of soldiers who are in flight and know that they are defeated, hence awareness of guilt; it is sometimes that of respect for others, the consideration owed others. It is then a restraint, a dignity, a modesty, or a discretion that keeps one from excess; thus a self-respect and a sense of honor that is often identified with modesty."[483]Spicq,1.43; 269; This virtue finds its highest expression in women. Philo explains why there was a wall of separation between Therapeutai and Therapeutrides, "to respect the modesty appropriate to the feminine nature," and he personifies the virtue as a woman who has "colors which are those of modesty . . . simple clothing, but more precious than gold, wisdom and virtue for her finery" (Sacr. Abel and Cain 26). This is the closest parallel to 1Tim 2:9. 'Worship God acceptably with reverence and awe' is not an excited manner, but one in keeping with the larger society for the expression of piety. These recipients are not like Corinth at all. The worship manner toward the larger society does have an a level of accountability that will be viewed as proper and pious. The worship expresses thankfulness. And this, in keeping with certain psalms, involves testimony.

12.29 To the Israelites the glory of the LORD looked like a consuming fire on top of the mountain Ex 24.17. ,Cf. . 5.12 kai gar meaning etenim 'for' so that kai has lost its force. [484] God is a consuming fire can be seen in Isa 6 and Ezekiel 1-8 and here is linked to God's self-manifestation at Mount Sinai and we can add the burning bush. On the other hand fire is linked in 10.27 to the raging fire of judgment but not in 12.27 to the final shaking of the earth and heavens of the final events. Nothing really speaks of a new heaven and new earth. But God is a consuming fire in the kingdom which cannot be shaken. In 13.11 Jesus goers forth to the place outside the camp or city gate to the place where the bodies of the sin offering are burned. 'God is a consuming fire' seems to be quote. But in this context of eschatological events it doesn't directly speak of love but of theophany and the destruction of the earth by fire. Fire was seen in Ezekiel's vision of the chariot-throne and the divine glory and John the Baptist's message 'He is the one who will baptize with Holy Spirit and fire.'

Chapter Thirteen:

CHRIST IS THE SAME YESTERDAY, TODAY AND FOREVER.

God of Peace

13.1 'Keep on loving one another as brothers' may reflect ethnic and linguistic diversity as well as various parties in the church, and if this book is prior to AD 70 may reflect pro-zealot and anti-zealot attitudes. There may also be feelings toward Nero 54-68, the burning of Rome in 64, and as the revolt in Judea approached in 66-70. During Paul's stay in Rome many had forsaken him in Asia and party-politics may have arisen elsewhere as well. Some believers may have compromised within limits and others fallen so the command to continue loving AS brothers may be in this context as well as Gentile-Jewish context. Could 'brothers' include unbelieving Jews? In time of crisis infighting among Jews of whatever persuasion would not make for a strong church.

'Love of the brethren' contrasts to 'hospitality to strangers.' This is not a monastery or holy order but in contrast to marriage indicates a problem in the church of continual good relations between the men. In the Greek world and more so in the OT world where men 20 and older were part of the assembly the harmony between brethren was part of the power to keep Israel and now the church, together. From Cain and later the army of Saul and David as well as the Israel struggles that never established a long hereditary dynasty the need was for love. This implies covenant.. Is there a concept or word like 'brotherly love' in the OT? Or, does this grow out of a NT society called the church? None in OT, Josephus but in 4 Macc 13.23,26; 14.1 Rom 12.10; 1 Th 4.9; Heb 13.1; 1 Pet 1.22; 2 Pet 1.7. Can the Maccabean small group of utterly devoted and mutually committed men for the background for the disciples relationships? 13.1-3

'Loving 'each other' is illustrated by 1. entertaining strangers; 2. remembering those in prison. 3. remembering those who are mistreated. The command 'as brothers' may be needed since 'strangers' may actually include non-Christians. 'Brothers' would not be needed for fellow-Jews, but would be for strangers. Three situations are concerning fugitives on the run with no refuge who need someone to keep them. Those in prison can be forgotten or lost through multiple transfers, unless someone keeps track of them. Those mistreated are closely observed by Roman authorities and assisting them may involve implication. Role modeling for these tasks involves understanding what fellow prisoners are going through and not distancing oneself too far from the former time of being mistreated.

13.2 Gen 18.1-22;19.1 "The two angels arrived at Sodom in the evening, and Lot was sitting in the gateway of the city. When he saw them, he got up to meet them and bowed down with his face to the ground." The duty of believers to entertain strangers goes back to the desert Bedouin ideal as noted in the Abraham story. Among Arabs eating together is part of a covenant though unwritten. So to kill one attending a feast was dastardly indeed as in Abimelech's case and Jesus's Last Supper and reflected in Psalms and elsewhere. 'Entertaining angels' is definitely in the Abraham story and Gideon's. Several other stories concern the faith to open one's door to an apparent stranger. Joshua faced the Commander of the forces. There many references to angels in the Apocrypha[485] and Pseudepigrapha.[486] Note Jeremiah's Message on Angels.[487] 'To be hidden,' 'to be manifest, evident' in langanein the supplementary participle with verbs denoting a modified sense of to be or to do[488] The admonitions to the Hebrews about the ger-foreign residents, slaves and foreigners to care for them, treat them justly, because they had the same role in Egypt, could easily open the door to compromise and in corporation into Israel, a fact early opposed by both Ezra and Nehemiah. But these were hardly viewed as 'angels.'

13.3 'Those in prison' are fellow Jews or Christians indicating a background of severe persecution to the point of some denying the faith to save their lives. But immediately we think of Joseph and Jeremiah and the words of Jesus in Matthew. Prisoners are worthy of loving care and that care is reckoned to be performed on Jesus himself. From these words it appears that a general command such as this reflects a time before the Nero persecution, and those in prison were not especially Christians or Jews. It is a general command

and along with Deuteronomy and the Gospels form part of the drive toward humanitarian laws and practice.

13.4 A ruling about marriage and the contrast of adultery and all sexually immorality, are part of Christian ethics, not Jewish law. 'God will judge' is in the context of 12.18-28 'the judge of all men.'Ecclesiastes also does not invoke law but the judgment of God. There is no indication of a believer's judgment apart from the judgment on all the others. One is tempted to see an ascetic movement starting and abstinence become a mark of the perfect. Greek thought regarding impurity of body and sex along with all material things began to permeate even the church as seen in ! John and Colossians. Greeks confined women to the second floor, not allowing them to mingle or even go into the market, creating a large gay population. Abnormalities in this regard were more in Greek society than in Roman, where the women were free to be business people. 'undefiled' could refer to a kind of contraception or extra-marital liaison. The need for specific instruction must have been felt among ascetic millenarians, who did not want marriage in view of Christ's early return. Prov 5.18,19; Prov. 5:18 'May your fountain be blessed, and may you rejoice in the wife of your youth. A loving doe, a graceful deer — may her breasts satisfy you always, may you ever be captivated by her love.' Two categories of sexual sin are involved, one illicit affair outside of the marriage vows, and one involving a kind of forbidden activity including fornication. The recipients had to be Jewish to fill in the background to this. Rom 1 is much more explicit and detailed because it is not directed only to Jews. The 'bed' could also involve the prohibition against intercourse during a menstrual period. The early Gnostics and monastic ideals had begun even earlier, and Paul often rebuked believers for not working or marrying because they believed the Lord would come right away.

13.4, Heb 7:26 writes of Christ the heavenly high priest, "Such is the high priest that we needed, holy, innocent, undefiled" (hosios, akakos, amiantos),10 this means absolute perfection in the sense of the Book of Job, with an extreme insistence on the absence of any stain, for in heaven he is even "separated from sinners." Hence the redundancy of these adjectives, which amounts to a superlative. Hosios implies:

(1) consecrated to God as a priest;
(2) holy in the cultic sense, possessing the qualities necessary for the accomplishment of the sacred functions; 11

(3) holy in the moral sense, possessing a perfection that is lacking in nothing, carrying God's will completely. Akakos means that like an innocent lamb (Jer 11:19), Christ is the spotless victim, acceptable to God (Job 8:20). Amiantos means without stain, pure, is the adjective used for the chaste (Heb 13:4), for a consecrated temple (2Macc 14:36; 15:34), for authentically religious acts (Jas 1:27). The perfection of the Christ-Priest is thus consummate, absolute, religious, and moral.[489]

13.5 Love..contentment are word pairs and the focus is on money, the same as when Jesus said the love of money is the root of all evil or the problem of mammon. Only 1Tim. 6:10 "For the love of money is a root of all kinds of evil. Some people, eager for money, have wandered from the faith and pierced themselves with many griefs." The lack of a similar verse in the OT may be due to the influence of Deuteronomy and Proverbs that these things are blessing from God and should be received as such. mimneskomai[490] 'remember' zakar is a key OT word as treated so well in Spicq's article. Here "remember prisoners, as if you were imprisoned with them" means we must feel and share in their misfortune and through compassion become 'co-prisoners'. The sense of 'memorialize' is found in Acts 10.31. Rev 16.19 "Babylon the great was memorialized before God" in the sense of having an eternal record against the day of judgment. In the NT 1. The Virgin Mary Lk 1.54; Zacharias Lk 1.72; as in Ps 98.3; 16.8; 3. Heb 2.16 from Ps 8.5' what is man that you should remember him' and 4. Heb 812 citing Jer 31.34 'I will remember their sins no longer.'[491] This Scripture citation, identical to that of Philo,[492] is not from Josh 1:5 but from Gen 28:15, supplemented with Deut 31:6, 8 (Cf. . P. Katz, "Hebr. 13, 5. The Biblical Source of the Quotation," is in Biblica.[493] The promise quote is frequent in the OT and usually linked to fear, which occurs in v.6, the next quote. One meaning of YHWH is that God is the ever-present one. But by and large the Psalms and prophets show the contrasting emphasis in the OT, that God does leave his people when sin increases and then later He returns to bring salvation and a blessing..13.5, Spicq: Thus we can see the message of Heb 13:5 to its readers as being "Let your ways, or conduct, be free of all greed (aphilargyros ho tropos); be content with what you have."6 The Greek Fathers supposed that the Hebrews had suffered or been threatened with the loss of their goods (10:34) and must have been trying too eagerly to rebuild their resources or guarantee their material security.7 At any rate, trusting in Providence excludes any preoccupation with tomorrow, and one must be self-sufficient (arkew, Matt 25:9; Luke 3:14; John 6:7; 1Tim 6:8) with that which one currently has at one's disposal. In moral theology, aphilargyria and tharreo theo are linked. St. Paul requires that the candidate for overseer at Ephesus be aphilargyros (1Tim 3:3), that the Cretan overseer not be eager for shameful gain, me aischrokerde (Titus 1:7), and similarly the deacons (1Tim 3:8). St. Peter urges the presbyters to shepherd the flock of God "not for sordid gain (aischrokerdos), but out of devotion." The office of the presbyter is above all pastoral and is not a sincere: watchfulness and continual care for the sheep, providing food, guiding the movements of the flock (Num 27:17; Ps 80:2), leading them to pasture (2Sam 5:2; Isa 40:11; Ezek 34:15; Ps 23; 95:7), keeping the sheep from dispersing and bringing back the strays (1Kgs 22:17; Isa 53:6; Zech 11:16; 13:7; Ps 119:176), defending them against savage beasts (Exod 22:13; 1Sam 17:34; Amos 3:12; Isa 31:4) and thieves (Gen 31:39; Job 1:17). Much courage and self-denial is therefore necessary in a "good shepherd" who seeks only the good of the flock and does not exploit them to his own profit.9 All shepherds are susceptible to the degeneration of the hireling who is transformed by the spirit of lucre into a shameless profiteer.10 This probably explains why, in discussing ministers of the church, St. Paul and St. Peter substitute for the simple aphilargyros the highly pejorative aischrokerdes. 11 A "steward" in the household of God has a subordinate function. He will have to turn over his accounts to his Kyrios (Luke 12:42-48); his uprightness, which must be beyond suspicion, is an essential element of the "ethic of the oikonomos " prescribed by the Lord to his servants.12 This ethic opposes the service of mammon to the service of God (Luke 16:10-13). Xenophon had already defined it: "a good manager must not touch the goods of his master or steal them."13 The Christian steward will be disinterested, no doubt in accord with agape (1Cor 13:5), but first of all in the name of honesty. His freedom from lust for money will guarantee not only his uprightness in the management of material goods but also his compassion toward all the miseries of his neighbors, because it is avarice that hardens the heart.14Spicq,1.46; 245; 400. 'love of money' and 'contentment with possessions' are not capitalist and economy based advisories. Demas had left Paul 'having loved this present world.' But focused on God's promise 'Never will I leave you' making God one's full sufficiency is a point of Satanic attack. Security v.5-6 is in the Lord 'my helper; I will not be afraid.' When the market falls or war displaces one discovers the truth of these words.

13.6 Ps 27.1 "The LORD is my light and my salvation — whom shall I fear? The LORD is the stronghold of my life — of whom shall I be afraid?" ; Ps118.6 "The LORD is with me; I will not be afraid. What can man do to me?" The subject of being courageous, without fear, is the theme of a book and contains the words directed to male leaders, including Joshua in ch.1 of his book."We can say courageously qarrountas 'The Lord is my help, I will not fear'. Moule, Idiom Book 10,22 elects 'be afraid' linear, than 'become afraid' punctiliar. Dio Chrysostom 32.21 and a first century hymn speaks of God who strengthens and gives divine power in the midst of wars and crimes, but there are few who receive courage oligoisi de qarsos edwke The Stoic use is found in 2 Cor 7.16; 10.1-2 where the apostle rejoices at "being able in all things to be bold with' the Corinthians, to speak to them undiplomatically, with evangelical liberty and authority, and thus to communicate to them painful truths. He is accused of being timid in person, but bold, inflexible, assertive from a distance, so he protests that he is ready to demonstrate his boldness if circumstances require." Note that Joshua dispatched two kings[Jos 10.26] but Gideon appeared to lack the courage in Jud 8.21.Saul preserved Agag [1 Sam 15.20],but before yielding to Saul Samuel dispatched Agag at Gilgal 1 Sam 15.33. In the body of the story it is Saul and the army that preserve condemned things, and as another time at Gilgal Saul feared the army. 'To melt' speaking of men's hearts as God prepares them to be defeated, is the verb of contrast.[494]

13.7, Spicq: Etymologically, hegoumenos means "leader, guide"[495] but in usage is refers to a head or chief, for example the Roman authorities[496] the princeps[497] the governor of the Thebaid[498] the heads of a village[499] the president of the council of elders governing the Jewish community at Alexandria[500] the head of a school[501].Note that this corresponds to the shofetim in tribal Israel, the elder in village Israel, the nasi' or nagid in pre-Kingship Israel. The use in Hebrews is broad enough to include different kinds of social structures, much as ro'sh in Israel could transcend changes in societal structure and even be used of Christ the 'head' of the church.[502]

13.8 This gives a direct translation and interpretation of YHWH such as is also found in Revelations 1 'Yesterday today and forever'. So while time changes but yet is contiguous, God never changes and is always the same. The initial self-introduction in Ex 4 uses 'I am' while the time that Moses asked how he should explain God to the people the form is third person 'He is'. The contrast is obvious and no need exists to appeal to the fact Isbell observed that the alef and yod can be interchangeable in not a few cases. The argument that YHWH is a closure formula 'I am that I am' indicating God did not wish to discuss the matter any further. Here the meaning is the important thing, since it is taken out of a dialogue speech situation. The function of YHWH in a speech narrative indicating 'closure' needs to be separated from the lexeme usage where the meaning is the chief thing. This is the central point .This takes the name as from hayah in the Qal conjugation 'He who [always] is [present]. By so doing the sacred name is not pronounced.

13.9, To varied and strange doctrines do not let yourself be led': The exhortation uses the figurative passive: "." Or "do not be carried off, away from the right path' para- is used in paraferw and elsewhere to express a deviation, a turning aside, a marring, a positioning next to the right place. Cf. 2.1; 6.6; 12.25; 3.8,15-16; 6.6. It is used as 'bring' in Judg 6.5 for Midianites who are bringing their tents beyond the borders of their kingdom.[503]. The exhortation uses the figurative passive: "to varied and strange doctrines do not let yourself be led." Or "do not be carried off, away from the right path' para- is used in paraferw and elsewhere to express a deviation, a turning aside, a marring, a positioning next to the right place. Cf. 2.1; 6.6; 12.25; 3.8,15-16; 6.6. It is used as 'bring' in Judg 6.5 for Midianites who are bringing their tents beyond the borders of their kingdom. [504] in the OT 'strange' as in 'strange woman' or 'strange gods' means 'foreign.' In this context it may refer to cults in the Greco-roman empire that are cults that depart from practice in the larger community.

13.11 The sin offering here only involves taking the blood into the Most Holy Place, while the bodies are burned outside the camp.

13.12, ta idia can refer to the eye Lk 6.41; blood Acts 20.28; Heb 9.12; 13.12; a nurse's milk, the hands 1 Cor 4.12; Eph 4.28; Jos.War 4.47; 6.216,m346; 7.243.[505] Spicq,2.207n11; 372n3, Matt 21.39 and Lk 20.15 represent the Son as being first cast out of the vineyard and then slain. Cf. . John 19.17.Jeremias,[506]73

13.13 In Israel, Rome and Greece as in most cultures disgrace or shame is a stronger motivating force than sin and guilt. In Rome 'honor' was foremost. But 'disgrace' is central to the incarnation and submission just as in Phil ch.2. The believer then endures and 'bears the disgrace he bore.' The cross is not a thing of beauty and honor in the world where it was the electric chair. The ability to do this comes from many sources that are mentioned in the book. In v.14 it is from looking 'for the city which is to come.' In 12.2; 10.33; 11.26 "The author exhorts Christians to behold Jesus, who endured the ignominy of the cross, despising the shame [aisxunes katafronesas]. The emphasis is not on suffering, but on the humiliation of this punishment, which was reserved for slaves and criminals [Cf. . Oneidismos] . It is also an allusion to the mockery, the ridicule, and the insults to which the saint par excellence was subjected by 'sinners'. Nothing could be more abject! Precisely 'to scorn' is 'to laugh at' 'mock'[507] The OT parallel is Ps 70.2 and similar Psalms where the worshipper's enemies are particularly trying to put him to shame. Spicq,2.282; 587

13.13, In 12.2; 10.33; 11.26 "the author exhorts Christians to behold Jesus, who endured the ignominy of the cross, despising the shame [aisxunes katafronesas]. The emphasis is not on suffering, but on the humiliation of this punishment, which was reserved for slaves and criminals [Cf. . Oneidismos] . It is also an allusion to the mockery, the ridicule, and the insults to which the saint par excellence was subjected by 'sinners'. Nothing could be more abject! Precisely 'to scorn' is 'to laugh at' 'mock' [Jos Life,337,347] Cf. 1 Cor 11.22; The OT parallel is Ps 70.2 and similar Psalms where the worshipper's enemies are particularly trying to put him to shame. [508] The disgrace of Christ was 1. conviction; 2. death sentence; 3. naked parading to the hill; 4. failure of the hope in believers; 5. their forsaking him at the cross; 6. The Deuteronomic passage 'cursed is everyone hanging on a tree' but not 7. the denial of burial before night time. Disgrace is the opposite of honor, which was the superior human quality in the Roman world. Disgrace brought dishonor or followers, family and even village.

13.14 'looking for a city' is linked to Abraham, who probably never entered any city, including Sodom, Gomorrah, Hebron, Jerusalem, Beersheba, except for Harran. But the city that is to come now is part of revelation to the Christian believer and it endures. In an urbanized world this contrasts so drastically with the non-urban, rural, agricultural world of the OT in Palestine demographics, the system of laws, and the concern for inherited land and progeny. The goals have changed. The hope is not the OT hope. Can 'looking for an enduring city' be equated with seeking for a refuge? Heb 6.18 speaks of Christians as exiles and pilgrims, so heaven as a place of asylum would be appealing. Spicq notes "The persecuted, the oppressed, the fugitives seek refuge, security and justice wither with an authority [Jos. Ant 1.131; Life,113] or in a place, notably in a temple that has the privilege of inviolability. This custom perhaps allows us to specify the sense of the aorist participle 'we refugees' in Heb 6.18, which could be seen as a term for Christians. They are, after all, exiles and pilgrims on this earth, whose hope of heaven has all the appeal of a city of refuge or place of asylum. This figurative meaning can be compared to the Philonian framework,, with which this epistle--addressed, it would seem, to a group of persecuted exiles--has so many other points of contact:"The law permitted a murderer to take refuge not in the temple, since he was not yet purified...but in a holy city, an intermediate place between the temple and profane soil, a sort of secondary temple...The law aims to take advantage of the prerogatives of the city or reception to assure the refugee of the most secure safety 'Those who do not have solid faith in God their Savior first of all seek refuge in the help of creatures; then if someone says to them, 'Fools, Seek refuge with the only physician for the diseases of the soul' in spite of them, the wretches turn late and not without trouble to seek refuge with the only Savior, God. Philo,Sacr.Abel and Cain 70-71.Viewed from perspective Heb 12 contrasts Heavenly Zion to Sinai as a place of refuge, and Jerusalem as refuge in war as also in the Psalms. But did the patriarchs at Shechem, Bethel, Hebron, Mamre, seek refuge or avoid entanglements. Only Jacob at Shechem and Abram in Philistia and Egypt, where no city is mentioned, were seeking a refuge. But was David, who was involved with Jerusalem from the viewpoint of possible Jebusite connections, was he even at Keilah and elsewhere, seeking a city? The move on Jerusalem seems precipitous, but was it? Obviously those in exile were thinking of Jerusalem, but in an ideal sense.[509].

'Looking for an enduring city' Can this be equated with seeking for a refuge? Heb 6.18 speaks of Christians as exiles and pilgrims, so heaven as a place of asylum would be appealing. Spicq notes "The persecuted, the oppressed, the fugitives seek refuge, security and justice wither with an authority[510] or in a place, notably in a temple that has the privilege of inviolability. This custom perhaps allows us to specify the sense of the aorist participle hoi katafeuontes 'we refugees' in Heb 6.18, which could be seen as a term for Christians. They are, after all, exiles and pilgrims on this earth, whose hope of heaven has all the appeal of a city of refuge or place of asylum. This figurative meaning can be compared to the Philonian framework,, with which this epistle--addressed, it would seem, to a group of persecuted exiles--has so many other points of contact:"The law permitted a murderer to take refuge [katafeugein] not in the temple, since he was not yet purified...but in a holy city, an intermediate place between the temple and profane soil, a sort of secondary temple...The law aims to take advantage of the prerogatives of the city or reception to assure the refugee of the most secure safety [bebaiotaten asfaleian] 'Those who do not have solid faith in God their Savior first of all seek refuge in the help of creatures [katafeugousin epi tas en genesei boetheias]; then if someone says to them, 'Fools, Seek refuge with the only physician for the diseases of the soul [katafeugete...epi ton monon iatron]' in spite of them, the wretches turn late and not without trouble to seek refuge with the only Savior, God [katafeugousin...epi ton monon swthra theon" Philo,Sacr.Abel and Cain 70-71.Viewed from perspective Heb 12 contrasts Heavenly Zion to Sinai as a place of refuge, and Jerusalem as refuge in war as also in the Psalms. But did the patriarchs at Shechem, Bethel, Hebron, Mamre, seek refuge or avoid entanglements. Only Jacob at Shechem and Abram in Philistia and Egypt, where no city is mentioned, were seeking a refuge. But was David, who was involved with Jerusalem from the viewpoint of possible Jebusite connections, was he even at Keilah and elsewhere, seeking a city? The move on Jerusalem seems precipitious, but was it? Obviously those in exile were thinking of Jerusalem, but in an ideal sense[511] 'Do not have an enduring city' could allude to the expulsion of Jews from Rome in the time of Claudius and Nero and persecution even of those in Alexandria. Rome burned, but these believers were prepared for it.

13.15 anaferw,[512] In the classical language, this verb means "to carry up" or "back".[513] In biblical Greek, it is used for everything that ascends, physically or metaphorically, from the flower of the vine (Gen 40:10), incense (Exod 30:9), or smoke (Judg 20:38), to anger (1Macc 2:24) and hymns (2Macc 10:7). Hence: to ascend or to carry from one place to another. Thus before the transfiguration Jesus made Peter, James, and John ascend a high mountain (Matt 17:1; Mark 9:2); and after the resurrection he himself "ascended into the sky."

The 'sacrifice of praise' is to continue. In the OT Psalms the thanksgiving Psalms are few, and the praise Psalms are late. There is so much in the worship of Israel that is not praise Confessing his name, praising him both convey the sense of yadah but Hebrews moves beyond the call to come and praise, to the actual praise. This sacrifice of praise is' through Jesus' Apart from Him praise is a culture matter in Judaism. The OT reference uses the Thanksgiving offering and the precise details of a process of preparing it to express thanksgiving. Hebrews, for the same even of thanksgiving offers up 'a sacrifice of praise, the fruit of lips that confess his name.' Confession is essential for salvation Rm. 10. The central fact of the church is verbalization and sharing. This is worship. The OT has Thanksgiving Offerings, but on Psalms designated as praise offerings as such. Lev 7.12; Hos 14.2. Christians "a holy company of priests" offer spiritual sacrifices 1 Pet 2.5, their continual praise, to God.

Anaferw 'cause to ascend' thus means 'to offer' and is a synonym to prosferw In classical language 'to carry up, back' Ep.Arist.268;Jos.War 4.404;Ant. 1.16; Ag.Apion 2.162; In the Bible it is used for anything that ascends, physically or metaphorically. Flowers Gen 40.10; incense Ex 30.9; Smoke Jud 20.38; anger 1 Macc 2.24; hymns 2 Macc 10.7. Jesus, Peter, James and John ascended a high mountain Matt 17.1; After the resurrection he 'ascended into the sky'. In the OT it is uniquely used for 'raise a levy' 1 Kgs 5.27; 'dress up in garment with jewelry' 2 Sam 1.24; 'bring something' 'present a matter to Moses Dt 1.17 or God. In sacrifice both testaments refer to the priests who " carry and transport the victim, raise it to place it on the altar, and offer it for sacrifice' 1 Macc 4.53. Jesus offered himself once Heb 9.28; 7.27. [514] The OT reference uses the Thanksgiving offering and the precise details of a process of preparing it to express thanksgiving. Hebrews, for the same even of thanksgiving offers up 'a sacrifice of praise, the fruit of lips that confess his name.' Confession is essential for salvation Rm. 10. The central fact of the church is verbalization and sharing. This is worship. The OT has Thanksgiving offerings but on offerings designated as praise offerings as such. Lev 7.12; Hos 14.2. Christians "a holy company of priests" offer spiritual sacrifices 1 Pet 2.5, their continual praise, to God. In Rom 12.1-2 the believer is to offer himself holy on the altar and thus be transformed.

13.16 'Doing good' [515] "1 Pet 4.19 Because verse 18 has touched on the perfection of the judgment of God, one may include in agaqopoiia the works of mercy, according to Matt 25.31-46; Acts 9.36; Heb 13.16; Tjos 18.2; and Epictetus 4.1.122 "It is human nature to do good, to be useful to others." Note that this relates directly to the creation and YHWH revealing not his glory but his Goodness' to Moses in Ex 33. Spicq,1.2n9; 2.133; 137n1; Doing good to people and sharing with them is accounted an acceptable sacrifice even though it has nothing to do with temple or religious establishment. God is pleased has nothing to do with justification by faith, but rather with the main goal of believers to please God that is more basic than any legal system of observances. Serving people is serving God. It is the privilege of all believers. Sharing with others is a sacrifice to God which God is pleased with. Jews at the same period would also say about the same thing.

13.17 Obedience is motivated by the accountability the shepherds have for their flock Leaders have authority and 'keep watch' just as 'watchmen' are mentioned in Isaiah and Ezekiel. Obedience makes their work a joy, not a burden and this makes their work an advantage to the church. The leaders' joy makes for everyone having joy. 13.24; 1 Clem 21.6:"let us honor those who preside over us." Jos War 1.271 "He died as a hero by an end that matched the conduct of his whole life." The term in the Hellenistic period was a technical term for the person in charge of a city, responsible for its defense and protection, and also the president of an assembly, esteemed by all. Lk 22.26 is the only parallel;'leader, president' The head of weavers, religious bodies, town assemblies. He was appointed because of his great competence. "He had responsibility for the overall administration of the association and wielded authority, called and presided over meetings, supplied the drinks for the monthly dinner, managed finances, gave orders and was owed obedience." This seems to be the role Samuel conceived for Israel's king in 1 Sam 8.10ff.,but it appears rather in 1 Sam 15.17 var; 22.1 25.30. Note also the noun hegemwn

13.17 Twn hegoumenwn hymwn Also appears in 13.24; 1 Clem 21.6:"let us honor those who preside over us." Jos War 1.271 "He died as a hero by an end that matched the conduct of his whole life." The term in the Hellenistic period was a technical term for the person in charge of a city, responsible for its defense and protection, and also the president of an assembly, esteemed by all. Lk 22.26 is the only parallel;'leader, president' The head of weavers, religious bodies, town assemblies. He was appointed because of his great competence. "He had responsibility for the overall administration of the association and wielded authority, called and presided over meetings, supplied the drinks for the monthly dinner, managed finances, gave orders and was owed obedience." This seems to be the role Samuel conceived for Israel's king in 1 Sam 8.10ff.,but it appears rather in 1 Sam 15.17; 22.125.30 Note its appearance also in 2 Sam 2.5; 3.38; 4.2 5.2; 6.21; 7.8 The latter is frequent as a noun in Jeremiah and Ezekiel. Note also the noun hegemon in Hatch-Redpath,I,64.[516] .

13.17, kopos, kopiaw 'work hard' refers to:

1. Constant, exhausting manual labor;
2. The fatigue of long incessant missionary wanderings;
3. Blows, wounds, and suffering endured in the course of stonings and riots;
4. Slanders and insults by enemies, the humiliations of imprisonments;
5. The difficulties of governing and exercising apostolic authority;
6. The preparation of sermons, speeches given in the open air, the editing of epistles;

7. Care for all the churches and for each soul 2 Cor 11.28-29; Heb 13.17 "who will not be saved on the steep path except through costly endurance and violence Matt 11.12."Note that 1 Tim 5.17 "In the primitive church 'working priests' were preachers of the gospel'.[517] Particles with a future participle 'as men who' 'with the thought that.'[518] peithw meaning 'obey' refers to obeying leaders:"obey your leaders and be in submission' and in Jas 3.3 "We put bits in horses' mouths so that they will obey us.' "One obeys the truth [Gal 5.7] or unrighteousness [Rom 2.8]; that is to say, one conforms to certain moral principles, submits to and remains faithful to their requirements, just as one joins with, is won over by certain persons Acts 4.36-37. 'one is brought to obey, persuaded so' [519]

13.18 This sounds so much like Paul as do other things in this final chapter. The last of Romans is an epistle and a closure to the book Most argument for Pauline authorship don't first discount this final chapter and consider only the thought content of chapters 1-12. 13.18, and 13.7 "Remember your leaders...and meditate carefully on the outcome of their manner of life, imitate their faith" the scholar who wrote this letter certifies that he himself wishes to conduct himself well in all things.". Cf. . Jas 3.13 "Who is wise and experienced among you? Let him manifest his works by a noble comportment with amiable wisdom" Ep.Arist.130 'You see the influence of conduct and company.' Note that moral and religious meanings are not confined to the OT, but abound in secular literature,[520] papyri[521] and honorific titles; "Menander, in the magistracies to which he was elected, has shown himself irreproachable by his noble and splendid conduct."[522] "I respect this man, who conducts himself so generously in all things.' I.Cor vol.8,n.306,8 2nd century AD]. In I.,Car: "In all his embassies, he has conducted himself properly and managed affairs justly." Spicq,1.112n7; 113; 3.74n63; 335. ,Peithometha [523]'we are convinced' or 'we keep hopefully persuading ourselves' But pepoithamen The pres. Is not perfective in those cases where the duration or repetition of an act up to and including the present is to be designated [a temporal expression indicates the intended period of the past] The perfective present. BDF,§322,Verbs of believing can use hoti or accusative 397[2]

13.18, and 13.7 "Remember your leaders...and meditate carefully on the outcome of their manner of life, imitate their faith" The didaskalos who wrote this letter certifies that he himself wishes to conduct himself well in all things." Kalws qelontes anastrefesthai. Cf. . Jas 3.13 "Who is wise and experienced among you? Let him manifest his works by a noble comportment "with amiable wisdom"[524] 'You see the influence of conduct and company.' Note that moral and religious meanings are not confined to the OT, but abound in secular literature,[525] papyri[526] and honorific titles; "Menander, in the magistracies to which he was elected, has shown himself irreproachable by his noble and splendid conduct."[527] "I respect this man, who conducts himself so generously in all things.'[528]. In I.,Car: "In all his embassies, he has conducted himself properly and managed affairs justly." [529] Peithometha 'we are convinced'[530] or 'we keep hopefully persuading ourselves' But pepoithamen The pres. Is not perfective in those cases where the duration or repetrition of an act up to and including the present is to be designated [a temporal expression indicates the intended period of the past] The perfective present.[531]

13.19 Paul often asks the churches to pray for him personally and sometimes mentions his co-workers as well. Ch.13 has this personal characteristic of letter writing that is missing elsewhere in the book. 'Restored' appears to mention some restraint or imprisonment. God can release him but prayer of the churches is needed.

13.20 The book clearly distinguishes God from the Lord Jesus except in the divine dialogues. The God of peace is involved in the plan of salvation from beginning to end. Here God brought back from the dead the Lord Jesus 'through the blood of the eternal covenant.' God equips the believer with everything to do his will and he works in believers what is pleasing to himself through Jesus Christ, 'to whom be glory for ever and ever'. The use of 'Father' for God is evidently avoided. Shalom is the reconciliation Paul speaks of. The 'eternal covenant' is either the all-encompassing covenant from Abel on or else the New Covenant this book speaks of, which is eternal. While Payne's theology adds a seventh or eighth covenant for the millennium or after it this book seems to focus on this eternal covenant established through the blood of Jesus. mega[532] "In Hebrew, the attributive adjective follows the noun [Sir 39.6] Heb 4.14 exontes oun arcierea megan. Here, this modifier, commonly used in antiquity for sovereigns and divinties exalts the King-Priest above Moses and all the other hegoumenoi who have died and not yet been resurrected. On the participial construction, which is common in the Hellenistic preaching [533] mega "In Hebrew, the attributive adjective[534] follows the noun [Sir 39.6] kurios ho megas Heb 4.14. Here, this modifier, commonly used in antiquity for sovereigns and divinties exalts the King-Priest above Moses and all the other hegoumenoi who have died and not yet been resurrected. The participial construction, is common in the Hellenistic preaching[535] 'God of peace' is a play of words on covenant, blessing, Solomon, Jerusalem, and the theme of reconciliation. The usage is Christian Rom 15.33; 16.20; Phil 4,9; 1 Th 5.23; Heb 13.20. although 'covenant of peace' occurs four times Num 25.12;; Isa 54.10; Ezk 34.25; 37.26. 'Eternal covenant' and its blood are single, one covenant. Redemption is through this covenant blood celebrated in the Lord's Supper by shed on the cross. Was it presented in the heavenly temple? God brought Jesus from the dead, not himself. He is the Great Shepherd of the sheep with many shepherds under him.

13.21, doxa "There is nothing to do but give glory to God after the fashion of Abraham [Rom4.20], do everything for God's glory [1 Cor 10.31; 2 Cor 8.19], as an expression of our gratitude and adoration, homage to the almighty and faithful God [2 Cor 1.20; Phil1.11;v 2.11]. Here glory is verbal expression out loud for God to hear. The fact is that the whole economy of salvation in God's intention has as its goal to draw from the saved a hymn 'to the praise of the glory of his grace'. Hence more or less developed doxologies acclaim either God's excellence, nature, and activity, or Christ as king, heavenly priest, archegos, shepherd: 'Jesus Christ, to whom be glory for ever and ever.'"[536] "There is nothing to do but give glory[537] to God after the fashion of Abraham [Rom4.20], do everything for God's glory [1 Cor 10.31; 2 Cor 8.19], as an expression of our gratitude and adoration, homage to the almighty and faithful God [2 Cor 1.20; Phil1.11;v 2.11]. The fact is that the whole economy of salvation in God's intention has as its goal to draw from the saved a hymn 'to the praise of the glory of his grace'. Hence more or less developed doxologies acclaim either God's excellence, nature, and activity, or Christ as king, heavenly priest, archwn, shepherd: 'Jesus Christ, to whom be glory for ever and ever.'"[538] katartisai[539] 'to prepare, outfit in/with every good.' 'for doing his will, working in us every good that is well pleasing before Him.' NIV adds 'and' to join the clauses and make it a wish prayer 'and may he work in us what is pleasing to him.' The reason for the 'and' is the switch of pronoun from 'you' pl to 'us' pl. the prayer is thus for the recipients and for the missionary team. Do the recipients need something restored or merely equipped? Doing God's will in the first case is parallel to 'working in us what is pleasing' 'good,' 'will of him,' and 'pleasing' are word pairs. For either to happen both must happen. 'Good' reflects Gen 1, where God saw that everything was good. . The nearest similar text is Phil 2.13 'continue to work out your salvation with fear and trembling, for it is God who works in you to will and to act according to His good purpose.'

13.22 Occasion: Bruce suggests along with A. Gulding that Hebrews was a sermon referring Pentecost since Gen 14 and Ps 110 "were prescribed for the season of Pentecost in the triennial lectionary of Palestinian and western synagogues."[540] Along with Stephen he avoids the current temple and chooses the tabernacle in the wilderness to teach his lessons.. The writer calls the letter a word of exhortation and 'a short letter'. Clearly this points to ch.13, which sounds like Paul. But the rest of the book is a dissertation of Christ, Son of God. What are similarities in this chapter to Paul's writings.

1. His mention of coworker Timothy;
2. His saying he himself wrote it.
3. Awareness of his own movements coordinated with Timothy's with destination the recipients.
4. v.1 focus on loving the brethren.
5. Exhortation to contentment;
6. Urging imitation of leaders.
7. stress on faith.
8. fear of false doctrines;
9. Communion as eating from an altar.
10. Do good and share.
11. request for prayer'
12. concern for immorality. Many of these are common pastoral issues applicable anywhere. But concern for conscience sounds like Paul. 12.29 sounds like a closure.

13.23 [541]'The author was a friend of Timothy, but was he also his colleague. In the analogy of writing for a friend did Moses write for Joshua and Joshua for Caleb or Othniel? Samuel could have written for David and we know that prophets wrote for and alluded to earlier prophets. Theophilus is the clearest treatise for a friend in Luke-Acts. Epistles are naturally so but the theory of clay tablets forming the structure of Genesis where one side had narrative and another side had names or witnesses following a mid-eastern pattern, shows the person writing to be the last mentioned name in the tablet, and the one written for the person who followed him.

13.24 Could indicate the epistle is directed to Rome[542] since those away from Italy send greeting. Payne,[543] or it could mean the author was writing from Italy 571. In the OT Kittim referred to the Mediterranean islands or Aegean and later the term refers to the Greeks and still later, in the Qumran sect, to Rome. The OT mentions many place names on a near-distant deixis showing the place from which the author is writing. Perspective is thus shown and this is one factor in interpretation. If Ezekiel was at many places including the Tyre he describes of passionately and vividly almost reacting to this pagan culture as Paul did to Athens, then various perspectives must be accounted for in the book. This is explicitly stated in Jeremiah, which has both a Palestine and Egyptian orientation. Samuel functioned in basically three places. The many places of Abraham account for many perspectives on his character and personhood.

13.24, The hegoumenos leader' 'guide,commander' and in Matt 2.6 refers to the Messiah 'the leader who will shepherd my sheep' from Mic 5.2 the same as arcontos Gen 49.10. Acts 15.22 presents Barsabbas and Silas as 'leading men among the brethren' Cf. Dan 6.2; 2 Ch 7.18; 1 Ch 7.40. These are glorious men, wise in counsel and prudence 2 Ch 17.7; 1 Macc 9.35;13.8. Cf. . Lk 22.26; Phil 2.3; Dt 1.13; Sir 9.17 the king, and general. In Hebrews they are similar to proistamenoi 1 Theee 5.12; 1 Tim 3.4-5, who can administrate kybernesis 1 Cor 12.28; Rom 12.8., who care for believers as shepherds epimeleomai 1 Tim 3.5, or as oikonomoi of the house of God They are worthy of respect. Heb 13.17,24. 1 Clem 21.6; Josephus war 1.271` "He died as a hero by an end that matched the conduct of his whole life." Spicq,2.168

13.25 Meta' pantwn hymwn. God is the creator of the universe which of itself has no divine quality. He brought all into existence, out of nothing, as a divine act of will (Ps. 33:9). This implies that the entire universe from subatomic particles to meteor galaxies constitutes a unity, with the same laws of nature holding uniformly throughout the cosmos. However, the universe has no independent existence outside of God who constantly infuses it with life. If it could be imagined that God should cease to exist, the universe would immediately collapse into nothingness. God is the Lord of universal history Who manifests Himself in the affairs of nations and particularly in the history of Israel. After completing the creation of the world of nature, God continues to guide the course of history (Deut. 32:8). Though in fashioning the physical world God had no opposition, in history He must contend with man's freedom, which often turns to rebelliousness. The prophets affirm however, that ultimately in the "end of days," God's Will be done. Having given man freedom, God does not overwhelm him, either in personal relationship or in His direction of history. In creating man, God, as it were, accepts a certain self-limitation in order to preserve man's freedom. God relates to man more as a loving father, that is to say, as an educator rather than as a king. For 'Glory' as heaven the following reference is quite clear: " through Your abundant kindness I will enter Your house, and filled with awe for You I will bow down toward Your holy Temple. O Lord, I love the house of Your abode, the dwelling place of Your glory. the clearest OT verse speaks of being "taken to glory." "Psa. 73:24 You guide me with your counsel, and afterward you will take me into glory." There is no directional preposition or terminative. The bet could over-reach the two clauses. In the case of 'glory' an adverbial phrase would be set up 'with glory' or 'gloriously.' Both would be on earth. But in poetry directional prepositions are not too abundant. Glory appears 295 times and so this is a major study in itself. Luke 24:26 Did not the Christ have to suffer these things and then enter his glory?" This does speak of both a state and quality of being as well as heaven. A good many OT meanings are unknown in the NT: "raise a levy" (1Kgs 5:27), "to dress up a garment with jewelry" (2Sam 1:24), "to bring something,"3 "present" a matter to Moses (Deut 1:17) or to God.4 But in both testaments,5 ascend or cause to ascend has above all a sacrificial usage and figures in the cultic vocabulary. The priests carry and transport the victim, raise it to place it on the altar, and offer it as a sacrifice (1Macc 4:53). In this sense, the high priest of the new covenant offered himself once to take away the sins of the many (Heb 9:28) and has no need to offer himself anew (Heb 7:27). Abraham offered his son Isaac on the altar (Jas 2:21), and Christians, "a holy company of priests," offer spiritual sacrifices (1Pet 2:5), their continual praise, to God (Heb 13:15); anapherw is in this sense synonymous with prospherw, 6 meaning "to offer."If aidos (Latin verecundia) keeps one from committing an act unworthy of oneself, makes one avoid that which is base, anaideia (NT hapax) is effrontery or impudence that shrinks from no means of achieving its goals.17 It is the anaideia of the importunate friend who gets the three loaves that he asks for in the middle of the night.18 This noun is rare in the papyri: it is found in a list of words (P.Cair.Zen. 59534, 21); in the complaint of Kronion, priest of Tebtunis in the second century, victim of the extreme insolence of Kronios;19 in the complaint of Aurelius, attacked in the third century by a basely impudent woman;20 and finally in an elegiac poem on Meleager.21 If the Lord praises this boldness, it is because he has just instructed his disciples to pray to the heavenly Father and ask that his name be sanctified. But in accordance with aidos —the religious fear that one experiences in the presence of the sacred—believers would be careful about being too free with their demands, would be hesitant to hail the holy God in an impetuous fashion, with too little concern for propriety. In truth, a child knows nothing of this timidity, but "pours out her heart" (1Sam 1:15) before her Father, and the tradition of Israel validates this importunity.22 It is a form of parresia. If aidos is sometimes associated with the agreeable equilibrium that is epieikeia, 14 it much more frequently connotes fear15 and even eulabeia, the feeling of reverence that one experiences in the presence of majesty, whether of the emperor16 or of God himself. It is in this sense that Christians offer worship to God (latreuein meta aidous kai eulabeias, Cf. . Heb 12:28). There remains 1Pet 2:24—"He bore our sins in his body on the cross,"7 where most commentators see a reference to the LXX of Isa 53:12 and understand 1Pet in the same sense: bear sins = undergo punishment for sins. But A. Deissmann objects that quotations do not often have the same sense in their new context as in the original,8 and that to undergo punishment on the cross would have been expressed by epi to xylwi (the dative case), while the accusative in 1Pet, epi to xylon, evokes the idea of removal. He cites P.Petr. I, 16, 2 (vol. 1, p. 47) from 230 BC, in which the litigant protests against the debts that have been transferred upon him and submits his case to Asclepiades. It is true that, in the papyri and the inscriptions, anapherw often signifies "transfer, pay money"10 and that one can here get some idea of substitution. But Moulton-Milligan (on this word) rightly observe that nothing turns our thoughts in this direction in 1Pet 2:24, where the accusative that follows epi is a person, which weakens considerably the parallel cited by A. Deissmann.

Bibliography for the Epistle to the Hebrews[544]

Ahern, A. A. "The Perfection Concept in the Epistle to the Hebrews." JBR 14 (1946) 164–67.

Aldrich, Willard M., "Assurance: Traits of the Family of God," BSac 114 #456, 313

Aldrich, Ray L. "An Apologetic for Dispensationalism," BSac 112 (1955),51.

Alexander, J. P. A Priest for Ever: A Study of the Epistle Entitled "To the Hebrews." London: Clarke, 1937.

Allegro, J.M., "Further Messianic references in Qumran Literature," JBL 75[1956],174f.

Anderson, C. P "The Setting of the Epistle to the Hebrews." Dissertation, Columbia University, 1969.

Anderson, C. P. "Hebrews among the Letters of Paul." SR 5 (1975–76) 258–66.

Anderson, C. P. "The Epistle to the Hebrews and the Pauline Letter Collection." HTR 59 (1966) 429–38.

Anderson, C. P. "Who Wrote 'The Epistle from Laodicea'?" JBL 85 (1966) 436–40.

Anderson, Gary A, 'The Interpretation of the Purification Offering hat't in the Temple Scroll (11Qtemple) and Rabbinic Literature,' JBL 111/1(1992)17-35.

Anderson, R. The Hebrews Epistle in the Light of the Types. London: Nisbet, 1911.

Armerding, Carl, 'the Atonement…" BSac 15 (1958),338

Arndt, William F,.and F.Wilbur Gingrich,A Greek-English Lexicon of the New Testament [Chicago: University of Chicago Press,1979]138.

Atkinson, B. F. C. The Theology of Prepositions. London: Tyndale, 1944.

Attridge, H. W, "Heard because of his reverence,' Heb 5.7 JBL 98.1(1979),90-93

Attridge, H. W. "Paraenesis in a Homily (λόγος παρακλήσεως): The Possible Location of, and Socialization in, the 'Epistle to the Hebrews.'" Semeia 50 (1990) 211–26.

Attridge, H. W. A Commentary on the Epistle to the Hebrews. Hermeneia. Philadelphia: Fortress, 1989.

Aune, D. The New Testament in Its Literary Environment. Philadelphia: Westminster, 1987.

Ayles, H. H. B. "The References to Persecution in the Epistle to the Hebrews." Exp 8th ser. 12 (1916) 69–74.

Ayles, H. H. B. Destination, Date, and Authorship of the Epistle to the Hebrews. London: Clay, 1899.

Bacon, B. W. "The Doctrine of Faith in Hebrews, James and Clement of Rome." JBL 19 (1900) 12–21.

Badcock, F. J. The Pauline Epistles and the Epistle to the Hebrews in Their Historical Setting. London: SPCK, 1937.

Baigent, J. W. "Jesus as Priest: An Examination of the Claim that the Concept of Jesus as Priest May Be Found outside of the Epistle to the Hebrews." VoxEv 12 (1981) 33–44.

Barclay, W. The Epistle to the Hebrews. Daily Study Bible. Philadelphia: Westminster, 1957.

Barnes, A. S. "St. Barnabas and the Epistle to the Hebrews." HibJ 30 (1931–32) 103–17.

Barnes, A, Barnes Notes on the Bible Vol.16, the Ages Digital Library Commentary 1.0, 2000.

Barrett, C. K. "The Eschatology of the Epistle to the Hebrews." In The Background of the New Testament and Its Eschatology. ed. W. D. Davies and D. Daube. Cambridge: Cambridge UP, 1954.

Barth, M. "The Old Testament in Hebrews: An Essay in Biblical Hermeneutics." In Current Issues in New Testament Interpretation. ed. W. Klassen and G. F. Snyder. New York: Harper & Row, 1962.

Bartlet, J. V. "The Epistle to the Hebrews Once More." ExpTim 34 (1922–23) 58–61.

Bartlet, V. "Barnabas and His Genuine Epistle." Exp 6th ser. 6 (1902) 28–30.

Bartlet, V.. "The Epistle to the Hebrews as the Work of Barnabas." Exp 6th ser. 8 (1903) 381–96.

Barton, G. A. "The Date of the Epistle to the Hebrews." JBL 57 (1938) 195–207.

Batdorf, I. W. "Hebrews and Qumran: Old Methods and New Directions." FS F. Wilbur Gingrich. ed. E. H. Barth and R. E. Cocroft. Leiden: Brill, 1972.

Bateman, Herbert W., Early Jewish Hermeneutics and Hebrews 1.5-13: the Impact of Early Jewish Exegesis on the Interpretation of a Significant New Testament Passage.American University Studies, Series 7- theology and Religion,193.NY: Peter Lang, 1997.

Bates, W. H. "Authorship of the Epistle to the Hebrews Again." BSac 79 (1922) 93–96.

Batto, B.F, Zedeq,' Dictionary of Deities...The West Semitic deity Zedek, 'Righteousness'

Beare, F. W. "The Text of the Epistle to the Hebrews in P^{46}." JBL 63 (1944) 379–96.

Black, D. A. Linguistics for Students of New Testament Greek: A Survey of Basic Concepts and Applications. Grand Rapids: Baker, 1988.

Black, D. A. "The Problem of the Literary Structure of Hebrews." GTJ 7 (1986) 163–77.

Black, M. "The Christological Use of the Old Testament in the New Testament." NTS 18 (1971–72) 1–14.

Bligh, J. "The Structure of Hebrews." HeyJ 5 (1964) 170–77.

Bligh, J. Chiastic Analysis of the Epistle to the Hebrews. Heythrop: Athenaeum, 1966.

Borchet, L. "A Superior Book: Hebrews." RevExp 82 (1985) 319–32.

Bose, W. P. du. High Priesthood and Sacrifice: An Exposition of the Epistle to the Hebrews. New York: Longmans, Green, 1908.

Bourke, M. M. The Epistle to the Hebrews. Englewood Cliffs, NJ: Prentice Hall, 1990.

Bousset,W. Kyrios Christos Göttingen: Vandenhoeck & Ruprecht,1913. trans J.E.Steedyt[NT:Abingdon,1970.

Bowman, G. M. Don't Let Go! An Exposition of Hebrews. Phillipsburg: Presbyterian & Reformed, 1982.

Bowman, J. W. Hebrews. Richmond: Knox, 1962.

Bristol, L. O. "Primitive Christian Preaching and the Epistle to the Hebrews." JBL 68 (1949) 89–97.

Bristol, L. O. Hebrews: A Commentary. Valley Forge, PA: Judson, 1967.

Brooks, W. E. "The Perpetuity of Christ's Sacrifice in the Epistle to the Hebrews." JBL 89 (1970) 205–14.

Brown, J. V. "The Authorship and Circumstances of 'Hebrews'—Again!" BSac 80 (1923) 505–38.

Brown, R. "Pilgrimage in Faith: The Christian Life in Hebrews." SWJT 28 (1985) 28–35.

Brown, R. Christ above All: The Message of Hebrews. Downers Grove, IL: Inter-Varsity Press, 1982.

Browning,Jr Daniel C.,, 'Heifer,' Eerdmans Dictionary of the Bible. Ed. David N Freedman et.al., Grand Raids: Eerdmans, 2000, 571

Bruce, A. B. The Epistle to the Hebrews, The First Apology for Christianity: An Exegetical Study. 2nd ed. Edinburgh: Clark, 1899.

Bruce, F. F. "'To the Hebrews' or 'To the Essenes'?" NTS 9 (1963) 217–32.

Bruce, F. F. "Recent Contributions to the Understanding of Hebrews." ExpTim 80 (1969) 260–64.

Bruce, F. F. "Christianity under Claudius." BJRL 44 (1961–62) 309–26.

Bruce, F. F. "Kerygma of Hebrews." Int 23 (1969) 3–19.

Bruce, F. F. The Epistle to the Hebrews. NICNT. Grand Rapids: Eerdmans, 1964.

Bruce, F. F.. "The Structure and Argument of Hebrews." SWJT 28 (1985) 6–12.

Buchanan, G. W. "The Present State of Scholarship on Hebrews." In Judaism, Christianity and Other Greco-Roman Cults. FS Morton Smith. ed. J. Neusner. vol(s). 1. Leiden: Brill, 1975.

Buchanan, G. W. To the Hebrews. AB 36. Garden City, NY: Doubleday, 1972.

Bullock, M. R. "The Recipients and Destination of Hebrews." Dissertation, Dallas Theological Seminary, 1977.

Burch, V. "Factors in the Christology of the Letter to the Hebrews." Exp 47 (1921) 68–79.

Burch, V. The Epistle to the Hebrews: Its Sources and Its Message. London: Williams & Norgate, 1936.

Burns, D. K. "The Epistle to the Hebrews." ExpTim 47 (1935–36) 184–89.

Burtness, J. H. "Plato, Philo, and the Author of Hebrews." LQ 10 (1958) 54–64.

Burton, E. D. Syntax of the Moods and Tenses in New Testament Greek . 3rd ed. Edinburgh: Clark, 1898.

Caird, G. B. "The Exegetical Method of the Epistle to the Hebrews." CJT 5 (1959) 44–51.

Calvin, John. "The Commentaries on the Epistle of Paul and Apostle to the Hebrews," The Ages Digital Library Commentaries. 1.0, 1996.

Calvin, J. The Epistle of Paul the Apostle to the Hebrews. tr. W. B. Johnston. Grand Rapids: Eerdmans, 1963.

Campbell, A. G. "The Problem of Apostasy in the Greek New Testament." Dissertation, Dallas Theological Seminary, 1957.

Campbell, D.A., "The Meaning of pistis and nomos in Paul: A Linguistic and Structural Perspective," JBL 111.1(1992),91-103

Campbell, J. C. "In a Son: The Doctrine of the Incarnation in the Epistle to the Hebrews." Int 10 (1956) 24–38.

Campbell, J. Y. Three New Testament Studies. Leiden: Brill, 1965

Carlston, C. "Eschatology and Repentance in the Epistle to the Hebrews." JBL 78 (1959) 296–302.

Carlston, C.. "The Vocabulary of Perfection in Philo and Hebrews." In Unity and Diversity in New Testament Theology. FS G. E. Ladd. ed. R. A. Guelich. Grand Rapids: Eerdmans, 1978.

Carson, D.A.; et al., The New Bible Commentary, (Downers Grove, Illinois: Inter-Varsity Press) 1994.

Casey, J. Hebrews. Dublin: Veritas Publications, 1980.

Casey, R. P. "The Earliest Christologies." JTS 10 (1959) 253–77.

Cason, D. V. "ΙΕΡΕΥΣ and ΑΡΧΙΕΡΕΥΣ (and Related Contexts) in Hebrews: An Exegetical Study in the Greek New Testament." Dissertation, Southern Baptist Theological Seminary, 1931.

Caudill, R. P. Hebrews: A Translation with Notes . Nashville: Broadman, 1985.

Chadwick, G. A. The Epistle to the Hebrews. London: Hodder & Stoughton, –

Chambers, Oswald, My Utmost for His Highest, NIV edition. (New Jersey: Barbour and Company,Inc.,1935,1963.

Chapman, J. "Aristion, Author of the Epistle to the Hebrews." RBén; 22 (1905) 50–64.

Chilstrom, H. W. Hebrews: A New and Better Way. Philadelphia: Fortress, 1984.

Chirichigne, G. Old Testament Quotations in the New Testament. Chicago: Moody, 1983.

Chisholm, Robert B. Jr., 'Does God Change his mind?' BibSacra 152(1995),60-71

Chrysostom, J. Homilies on the Gospel of John and the Epistle to the Hebrews. tr. P. Schaff and F. Gardiner. NPNF 14. New York: Scribner's, 1889.

Clarkson, M. E. "The Antecedents of the High Priest Theme in Hebrews." ATR 29 (1947) 89–95.

Cleary, M. "Jesus, Pioneer and Source of Salvation: The Christology of Hebrews 1–6." TBT 67 (1973) 1242–48.

Clements, R. E. "The Use of the Old Testament in Hebrews." SWJT 28 (1985) 36–45.

Clines, David J.A., The Dictionary of Classical Hebrew, III [Sheffield: Sheffield Academic Press, 1996] 155 under h5eber I

Cockerill, Gareth Lee, 'Heb 1.1-14; 1 Clem 36.1-6 and the High Priest Title,' JBL 97/3(1978)437-440

Cody, A. Heavenly Sanctuary and Liturgy in the Epistle to the Hebrews: The Achievement of Salvation in the Epistle's Perspectives. St. Meinrad, IN: Grail, 1960.

Collins, R. F. Letters That Paul Did Not Write: The Epistle to the Hebrews and the Pauline Pseudepigrapha. Wilmington, DE: Glazier, 1988.

Combrink, H. J. B. "Some Thoughts on the Old Testament Citations in the Epistle to the Hebrews." Neot 5 (1971) 22–36.

Conner, W. T. "Three Types of Teaching in the New Testament on the Meaning of the Death of Christ." RevExp 43 (1946) 150–66.

Conner, W. T. "Three Theories of the Atonement." RevExp 43 (1946) 275–90.

Constable, T. L. "The Substitutionary Death of Christ in Hebrews." Dissertation, Dallas Theological Seminary, 1966.

Cockerill, Gareth Lee, "Heb 1.1-14, 1 Clem 36.1-6 and the High Priest title,' JBL 97.3(1978),437-440.

Cockerill, Gareth L.Hebrews.A Commentary in the Wesleyan Tradition. Indianapolis: Wesleyan Publishing House, 1999.

Corbishley, T. Good News in Hebrews: The Letter to the Hebrews in Today's English Version. Cleveland: Collins & World, 1976.

Cotterell, P., and Turner, M. Linguistics and Biblical Interpretation. Downers Grove, IL: Inter-Varsity, 1989.

Cox, W. L. P. The Heavenly Priesthood of Our Lord. Oxford: Blackwell, 1929.

Craddock, F. B. The Pre-Existence of Christ in the New Testament. Nashville: Abingdon Press, 1968.

Croy, N.Clayton, "A Note on Hebrews 12.2," JBL 114(1995),117-119

Cullmann, O. The Christology of the New Testament. rev. ed. Philadelphia: Westminster, 1963.

Culpepper, R. H. "The High Priesthood and Sacrifice of Christ in the Epistle to the Hebrews." ThEduc 32 (1985) 46–62.

Cundall, Arthur E. 'Zadok,' Elwell, W. A., & Beitzel,B. J. 1988. Baker encyclopedia of the Bible. Map on lining papers. Baker Book House: Grand Rapids, Mich.

Custer, S. "Annotated Bibliography on Hebrews." BV 2 (1968) 45–68.

D'Angelo, M. R. Moses in the Letter to the Hebrews. SBLDS 42. Missoula, MT: Scholars, 1979.

Dahms, J. V. "The First Readers of Hebrews." JETS 20 (1977) 365–75.

Dahood, M., The Psalms vol.3,[NY: Doubleday,1970],313

Dale, James W, Classic Baptism. (Phillipsburg, NJ: Presbyterian and reformed Publishing Co.,1867, 1989).

Daly, R. J. "The New Testament Concept of Christian Sacrificial Activity." BTB 8 (1978) 99–107.

Dana,H. E, Julius R. Mantey, A Manual of the Greek New Testament[NY: Macmillan,1957].loc.cit.

Daube, D. "Rabbinic Methods of Interpretation and Hellenistic Rhetoric." HUCA 22 (1949) 239–64.

Davidson, A. B. The Epistle to the Hebrews. Edinburgh: Clark, 1882.

Davies, J. H. "The Heavenly Work of Christ in Hebrews." SE 4 (1968) 384–89.

Davies, J. H. A Letter to Hebrews. Cambridge Bible Commentary. Cambridge: UP, 1967.

De Young, J. C. Jerusalem in the New Testament. Kampen: Kok, 1960.

Déaut, R. le. "Apropos a Definition of Midrash." Int 25 (1971) 259–82.

Decker, Rodney J., 'The Church's Relationship to the New Covenant,' Bib Sacra

Delitzch, F. J. Commentary on the Epistle to the Hebrews. 2 vol(s). tr. T. L. Kingsbury. Edinburgh: Clark, 1871–72.

Dey, L. K. K. The Intermediary World and Patterns of Perfection in Philo and Hebrews. SBLDS 25. Missoula, MT: Scholars, 1975.

Dickie, J. "The Literary Riddle of the 'Epistle to the Hebrews.'" Exp 8th ser. 5 (1913) 371–78.

Dimock, N. The Sacerdotium of Christ . London: Longmans, Green, 1910.

Dimock, N. The Sacerdotium of Christ. London: Longmans, Green, 1910.

Dinkler, E. "Hebrews, Letter to the." IDB 2 (1962) 571–75.

Dodd, C.H. According to the Scriptures. NY: Scribners, 1953.

Dodd, C.H. The Authority of the Bible. Glasgow: William Collins Sons, 1929, 1960.

Dukes, J. G. "Eschatology in the Epistle to the Hebrews." Dissertation, Southern Baptist Theological Seminary, 1956.

Dunbar, D. G. "The Relation of Christ's Sonship and Priesthood in the Epistle to the Hebrews." Dissertation, Westminster Theological Seminary, Philadelphia, 1974.

Dyck, T. L. "Jesus Our Pioneer: ΑΡΧΗΓΟΣ in Heb 2:5–18; 12:1–3, and Its Relation in the Epistle to Such Designations as ΠΡΩΤΟΤΟΚΟΣ ΑΙΤΟΣ, ΠΡΟΔΠΟΜΟΣ, ΑΡΧΙΕΡΕΨΣ ΕΓΓΨΟΣ, ΜΕΣΙΤΗΣ, ΠΟΙΜΗΝ and to the Recurring Theme of Pilgrimage in Faith along the Path of Suffering Which Leads to Glory." Dissertation: Northwest Baptist Theological Seminary, 1980.

Eagar, A. R. "The Authorship of the Epistle to the Hebrews." Exp 6th ser. 10 (1904) 74–80, 110–23.

Eagar, A. R.. "The Hellenistic Elements in the Epistle to the Hebrews." Her 11 (1901) 263–87.

Eccles, R. S "The Purpose of the Hellenistic Patterns in the Epistle to the Hebrews." In Religions in Antiquity. FS E. R. Goodenough. ed. J. Neusner. Leiden: Brill, 1968.

Eccles, R. S. "Hellenistic Mysticism in the Epistle to the Hebrews." Dissertation, Yale University, 1952.

Edgar, S. L. "Respect for Context in Quotations from the Old Testament." NTS 9 (1962–63) 55–62.

Edwards, T. C. The Epistle to the Hebrews. New York: A. C. Armstrong and Son, 1903.

Ellingworth, P. "The Old Testament in Hebrews: Exegesis, Method and Hermeneutics." Dissertation, University of Aberdeen, 1977.

Ellingworth, P. and Nida, E. A Translator's Handbook on the Letter to the Hebrews. New York: United Bible Societies, 1983.

Ellingworth, Paul, Commentary on Hebrews, NIGTC (Grand Rapids: Eerdmans, 1993)268.

Ellis, E. E. "Midrash, Targum and New Testament Quotations." In Neotestamentica et Semitica. FS Matthew Black. ed. E. E. Ellis and M. Wilcox. Edinburgh: Clark, 1969.

Ellis, E.Earle, "Traditions in the Pastoral Epistles,' ," Early Jewish and Christian Exegesis. Studies in Memory of William H. Brownlee. [Atlanta: Scholars Press, 1987]235

Elwell, W. A., & Beitzel, B. J.. Baker encyclopedia of the Bible. Map on lining papers. Baker Book House: Grand Rapids, Mich, 1988

English, E. S. Studies in the Epistle to the Hebrews. Traveler's Rest, SC: Southern Bible House, 1955.

Etheridge, J. W., ed. The Targums of Onkelos and Jonathan ben Uzziel on the Pentateuch . London: Longmans, Green, 1962–65.

Etheridge, J. W., ed. The Targums of Onkelos and Jonathan ben Uzziel on the Pentateuch. London: Longmans, Green, 1962–65.

Evans, Craig A., "Obduracy and the Lord's Servant," Early Jewish and Christian Exegesis. Studies in Memory of William H. Brownlee. [Atlanta: Scholars Press, 1987]235

Evans, L. H. Hebrews. The Communicator's Commentary 10. Waco, TX: Word, 1985.

Evans, L. H., Jr, & Ogilvie, L. J. Vol. 33: The Preacher's Commentary Series, Volume 33 : Hebrews. Formerly The Communicator's Commentary. The Preacher's Commentary series . Thomas Nelson Inc: Nashville, Tennessee,1985.

Evans, J. Elwood, "The Song of Habakkuk III," Bsac 113(1956),60

Fairhurst, A. M. "Hellenistic Influence in the Epistle to the Hebrews." TynBul 7–8 (1961) 17–27.

Farrar, F. W. The Epistle of Paul the Apostle to the Hebrews. CGTC. Cambridge: UP, 1894.

Fensham, F. C. "Hebrews and Qumran." Neot 5 (1971) 9–21.

Fenton, J. C. "The Argument in Hebrews." SE 7 (1982) 175–81.

Ferrin, Hward W., 'All Israel shall be saved.' Bibsacra 112(1955),235

Feuillet, A. The Priesthood of Christ and His Ministers. Garden City: Doubleday, 1975.

Field, F. Notes on the Translation of the New Testament. Cambridge: Cambridge UP, 1899.

Field, J. E. The Apostolic Liturgy and the Epistle to the Hebrews London: Rivertons, 1882.

Filson, F. V. "Yesterday": A Study of Hebrews in the Light of Chapter 13. SBT 2nd ser. 4. Naperville: Allenson, 1967.

Filson, F. V. "The Epistle to the Hebrews." JBR 22 (1954) 20–26.

Filson, F. V.. "Yesterday": A Study of Hebrews in the Light of Chapter 13 . SBT 2nd ser. 4. Naperville: Allenson, 1967.

Fitzmyer, J. A. "The Use of Explicit Old Testament Quotations in Qumran Literature and in the New Testament." NTS 7 (1960–61) 297–333.

Fitzmyer, Joseph A., Essays on The Semitic Background of the New Testament [Atlanta: Scholars, 1974]loc.cit.

Floor, L. "The General Priesthood of Believers in the Epistle to the Hebrews." Neot 5 (1971) 72–82.

Ford, J.Masseyngberde, Revelation. The Anchor Bible[NY: Doubleday,1975],loc.cit.

Ford, J. M. "The Mother of Jesus and the Authorship of the Epistle to the Hebrews." TBT 82 (1976) 683–94.

Ford, J. M. "The First Epistle to the Corinthians or the First Epistle to the Hebrews." CBQ 28 (1966) 402–16.

Forkman, G. The Limits of the Religious Community. Lund: Gleerup, 1972.

Freedman, David Noel, ed., The Anchor Bible Dictionary, (New York: Doubleday) 1997, 1992.

Galinsky, G. K. The Herakles Theme. Leiden: Brill, 1972.

Gamble, J. "Symbol and Reality in the Epistle to the Hebrews." JBL 45 (1926) 162–70.

Gammie, J. G "Paraenetic Literature: Toward the Morphology of a Secondary Genre." Semeia 50 (1990) 41–77.

Gammie, J. G. "A New Setting for Psalm 110." ATR 51 (1969) 4–17.

Gardiner, F. "The Language of the Epistle to the Hebrews as Bearing upon Its Authorship." JBL 7 (1887) 1–25.

Garrard, L. A. "The Diversity of New Testament Christology." HibJ 55 (1956–57) 213–22.

Gayford, S. C. Sacrifice and Priesthood. 2nd ed. London: Methuen, 1953..

Gilbert, G. H. "The Greek Element in the Epistle to the Hebrews." AJT 14 (1910) 521–32.

Giversen, S. "Evangelium Veritatis and the Epistle to the Hebrews." ST 13 (1959) 87–96.

Glaze, R. E. No Easy Salvation: A Careful Examination of Apostasy in Hebrews. Nashville: Broadman, 1966.

Glaze, R. E. "Introduction to Hebrews." ThEduc 32 (1985) 20–37.

Gooding, D. An Unshakeable Kingdom: Studies on the Epistle to the Hebrews. Toronto: Everyday Publications, 1976.

Gooding, D. An Unshakeable Kingdom: The Letter to the Hebrews for Today. Grand Rapids: Eerdmans, 1989.

Goodspeed, E. J. "First Clement Called Forth by Hebrews." JBL 30 (1911) 157–60.

Goodspeed, E. J.. "The Problem of Hebrews." JBR 22 (1954) 122.

Gordon, V. R. "Studies in the Covenantal Theology of the Epistle to the Hebrews in Light of Its Setting." Dissertation, Fuller Theological Seminary, 1979.

Gotaas, D. S. "The Old Testament in the Epistle to the Hebrews, the Epistle of James, and the Epistle of Peter." Dissertation, Northern Baptist Theological Seminary, 1958.

Gotton, J. H. "The Epistle to the Hebrews." IB 11 (1955) 575–763.

Graham, A. A. K. "Mark and Hebrews." SE 4 (1968) 411–16.

Gray, Patrick, "Brotherly Love and the High Priest Christology of Hebrews," JBL 122.2(2003)335-351

Greer, R. A. "The Antiochene Exegesis of Hebrews." Dissertation, Yale University, 1965.

Greer, R. A.. The Captain of Our Salvation: A Study in the Patristic Exegesis of Hebrews. BGBE 15. Tübingen: Mohr, 1973.

Griffin, H. "The Origin of the High Priestly Christology of the Epistle to the Hebrews." Dissertation, University of Aberdeen, 1978.

Grogan, G. W. "The New Testament Interpretation of the Old Testament." TB. 18 (1967) 54–76.

Gromacki, R. G. Stand Bold in Grace: An Exposition of Hebrews. Grand Rapids: Baker Book House, 1984.

Grothe, J. F. "Was Jesus the Priestly Messiah? A Study of the New Testament's Teaching of Jesus' Priestly office against the Background of Jewish Hopes for a Priestly Messiah." Dissertation, Concordia Seminary, 1981.

Gudorf, Michael E., "Through a Classical Lens: Hebrews 2.16," JBL 119.1(2000),105-108

Guilding, Aileen JTS n.s. 3[1952],53 in F.F.Bruce,"Hebrews,' Peake's Commentary on the Bible [London:Nelson, 1964]1008

Guinan, Michael D., "Lampstand," Eerdmans Bible Dictionary, Grand Rapids: Eerdmans, 2000 787-788.

Guthrie, D. "The Epistle to the Hebrews." In New Testament Introduction. vol(s). 3. Chicago: Inter-Varsity, 1962.

Guthrie, D. The Letter to the Hebrews. TNTC. Grand Rapids: Eerdmans, 1983.

Guthrie, G. H. "The Structure of Hebrews: A Textlinguistic Analysis." Dissertation, Southwestern Baptist Theological Seminary, 1991.

Guttmann,,Joseph ed. The Image and the Word, (Missoula: Scholars Press, 1977).

Hagen, K.. A Theology of Testament in the Young Luther: The Lectures on Hebrews. Leiden: Brill, 1974.

Hagner, D. A. The Use of the Old and New Testaments in Clement of Rome. Leiden: Brill, 1973.

Hagner, D. A. "Interpreting the Epistle to the Hebrews." In The Literature and Meaning of Scripture. ed. M. A. Inch and C. H. Bullock. Grand Rapids: Baker, 1981. 217–42.

Hagner, D. A. Hebrews. Good News Commentaries. San Francisco: Harper & Row, 1983.

Hagner, D. A.. Hebrews. NIBC 14. Peabody, MA: Hendrickson, 1990.

Hamerton-Kelly, R. G. Pre-Existence, Wisdom, and the Son of Man: A Study of the Idea of Pre-Existence in the New Testament. SNTSMS 21. Cambridge: Cambridge UP, 1973.

Hammer, P. "The Understanding of Inheritance (κληρονομία) in the New Testament." Dissertation, Heidelberg University, 1958.

Hanna, R. A Grammatical Aid to the Greek New Testament. vol(s). 2: Romans to Revelation. Hidalgo, Mexico: Saenz, 1979.

Hanson, A. T. "Christ in the Old Testament according to Hebrews." SE 2 (1964) 393–407.

Hanson, A. T. "The Gospel in the Old Testament according to Hebrews." Theol 52 (1949) 248–52.

Harnack,A, Probabilia uber die Adresse und den Verfasser des Hebraerbriefs," ZNW 11 (1900),16-41/

Harris, J. R. "An Orphic Reaction in the Epistle to the Hebrews." ExpTim 40 (1928–29) 449–5

Harris, J. R. "Menander and the Epistle to the Hebrews." ExpTim 44 (1932–33) 191.

Harris, J. R. "Side-Lights on the Authorship of the Epistle to the Hebrews." In SideLights on New Testament Research. London: Kingsgate, 1908.

Harrison, E. F. "The Theology of the Epistle to the Hebrews." BSac 121 (1964) 333–40.

Harrison, M. P. "Psalm 110 in the Epistle to the Hebrews." Dissertation, Southern Baptist Theological Seminary, 1950.

Harrison, Everett F., "the Importance of the Septuagint Part I," BSacr 112. n.y.

Harrop, C. K. "The Influence of the Thought of Stephen upon the Epistle to the Hebrews." Dissertation, Southern Baptist Theological Seminary, 1955.

Harvill, J. "Focus on Jesus: The Letter to the Hebrews." SpTod 37 (1985) 36–47.

Harvill, J.. "Focus on Jesus (Studies in the Epistle to the Hebrews)." ResQ22 (1979) 129–40.

Hatch, E., and Redpath, H. A. A Concordance to the Septuagint and the Other Greek Versions of the Old Testament. 2 vol(s). Oxford: Clarendon, 1897.

Hatch, W. H. P. "The Position of Hebrews in the Canon of the New Testament." HTR 29 (1936) 133–51.

Hay, D. M. Glory at the Right Hand: Psalm 110 in Early Christianity. SBLMS 18. Nashville: Abingdon, 1973.

Henderson, M. W. "The Priestly Ministry of Jesus in the Gospel of John and the Epistle to the Hebrews." Dissertation, Southern Baptist Theological Seminary, 1965.

Heris, C. V. The Mystery of Christ, Our Head, Priest and King. Cork/Liverpool: Mercier, 1950.

Hession, R. From Shadow to Substance: A Rediscovery of the Inner Message of the Epistle to the Hebrews Centered around the Words "Let Us Go On." Grand Rapids: Zondervan, 1977.

Hewitt, T. The Epistle to the Hebrews. TNTC. London: Tyndale Press, 1960.

Higgins, A.J.B. "The Priestly Messiah." NTS 13 (1967) 211–39.

Hill, D. Greek Words and Hebrew Meanings. SNTSMS 5. Cambridge: Cambridge UP, 1967.

Hill, H. E. "Messianic Expectation in the Targum of the Psalms." Dissertation, Yale University, 1955.

Hillers, Delbert R., "Delocutive Verbs in Biblical Hebrew," JBL 86(1967)320-325.

Hillmer, M. R. "Priesthood and Pilgrimage: Hebrews in Recent Research." ThBullMDC 5 (1969) 66–89.

Hoekema, A. A. "The Perfection of Christ in Hebrews." CTJ 9 (1974) 31–37.

Holbrook, F. B., ed. Issues in the Book of Hebrews. Silver Spring, MD: Biblical Research Institute, 1989.

Hoppin, R. Priscilla, Author of the Epistle to the Hebrews and Other Essays. New York: Exposition, 1969.

Hoppin, R., Priscilla's Letter: Finding the Author of the Epistle to the Hebrews. Fort Bragg: Lost Coast Press, 2000

Horton, C. D. "The Relationship of the Use of Tenses to the Message in the Epistle to the Hebrews." Dissertation, Southern Baptist Theological Seminary, 1953.

Hoskier, H. C. A Commentary on the Various Readings in the Text of the Epistle to the Hebrews in the Chester Beatty Papyrus P^{46}. London: Quaritch, 1938.

Houlden, J. L. "Priesthood in the New Testament and the Church Today." SE 5 (1968) 81–87.

Howard, G. "Hebrews and the Old Testament Quotations." NovT 10 (1968) 208–16.

Howard, W. F. "Studia Biblica, XIII: The Epistle to the Hebrews." Int 5 (1951) 80–91.

Howell, Jr.,Don N. "The Center of Pauline Theology," Bibliotheca Sacra 151:601 (January-March 1994): 50-70

Hudson, J. T. The Epistle to the Hebrews. Edinburgh: Clark, 1937.

Hughes, G. Hebrews and Hermeneutics: The Epistle to the Hebrews as a New Testament Example of Biblical Interpretation. SNTSMS 36. Cambridge: Cambridge UP, 1979.

Hughes, P. E. "The Blood of Jesus and His Heavenly Priesthood in Hebrews." BSac 130 (1973) 99–109, 195–212, 305–14; 131 (1974) 26–33.

Hughes, P. E. A Commentary on the Epistle to the Hebrews. Grand Rapids: Eerdmans, 1977.

Hughes, P. E.. "The Christology of Hebrews." SWJT 28 (1985) 19–27.

Humphrey, J. F. "The Christology of the Epistle to the Hebrews." LQHR 14 (1945) 425–32.

Hunt, B. P. W. S. "The 'Epistle to the Hebrews': An Anti-Judaic Treatise?" SE 2 (1964) 408–10.

Hunter, A. M. "Apollos the Alexandrian." In Biblical Studies. FS William Barclay. ed. J. R. McKay and J. F. Miller. Philadelphia: Westminster, 1976. 147–56.

Hurst, L. D "Eschatology and 'Platonism' in the Epistle to the Hebrews." SBLASP (1984) 41–74.

Hurst, L. D "The Background and Interpretation of the Epistle to the Hebrews." Dissertation, Oxford University, 1981. [Published as The Epistle to the Hebrews: Its Background of Thought. S

Hurst, L. D. "Apollos, Hebrews, and Corinth: Bishop Montefiore's Theory Examined." SJT 38 (1985) 505–13.

Hutaff, M. D. "The Epistle to the Hebrews: An Early Christian Sermon." TBT99 (1978) 1816–24.

Huxhold, H. N. "Faith in the Epistle to the Hebrews." CTM 38 (1967) 657–61..

Jackson, Howard M. 'The death of Jesus in Mark and the Miiracle from the Cross,' NTS 33(1987)23,27,31

Jeffrey, P. J. "Priesthood of Christ in the Epistle to the Hebrews." Dissertation, University of Melbourne, 1974.

Jeremiah David,, What The Bible Says About Angels (Multnomah Publishers, Inc., 1996).

Jerusalem Post December 10, 2004 www.rabbiwein.com/jpost-index.html

Jewett, R. Letter to Pilgrims: A Commentary on the Epistle to the Hebrews. New York: The Pilgrim Press, 1981.

Joachim Jeremias, The Parables of Jesus [NY: Scribners, 1963] rev.ed. loc. cit.

Johnson, S. L. "Some Important Mistranslations in Hebrews." BSac 110 (1953) 25–31.

Johnson, W. G. "Defilement and Purgation in the Book of Hebrews." Dissertation, Vanderbilt University, 1973.

Johnson, W. G. "The Cultus of Hebrews in Twentieth-Century Scholarship." ExpTim 89 (1977–78) 104–8.

Johnson, W. G. "The Pilgrimage Motif in the Book of Hebrews." JBL 97 (1978) 239–51.

Johnson, W. G.. "Issues in the Interpretation of Hebrews." AUSS 15 (1976–77) 169–87.

Johnsson. W. G. Hebrews. Knox Preaching Guides. Atlanta: John Knox, 1980.

Jones, C. P. M. "The Epistle to the Hebrews and the Lucan Writings." In Studies in the Gospels. FS R. H. Lightfoot. ed. D. E. Nineham. Oxford: Oxford University, 1957.

Jones, E. D. "The Authorship of Hebrews xiii." ExpTim 46 (1934–35) 562–67.

Jones, P. R. "The Figure of Moses as a Heuristic Device for Understanding the Pastoral Intent of Hebrews." RevExp 76 (1979) 95–107.

Kallenbach, W. D. The Message and Authorship of the Epistle "To the Hebrews." St. Paul: Northland, 1938.

Katz, P. "The Quotations from Deuteronomy in Hebrews." ZNW49 (1958) 213–23.

Keck, L. E. "The Presence of God through Scripture." LexTQ 10 (1975) 10–18.

Kee, Howard Clark, Jesus in History.NY: Harcourt and Brace, 1970.

Kennedy, G. A. New Testament Interpretation through Rhetorical Criticism. Chapel Hill, NC: University of North Carolina Press, 1984.

Kennedy, H. A. A. "The Significance and Range of the Covenant-Conception in the New Testament." Exp 8th ser. 10 (1915) 385–410.

Kent, H. A. The Epistle to the Hebrews, A Commentary. Grand Rapids: Baker, 1972.

Kidner, D. "Sacrifice--Metaphors and Meaning." TynBul 33 (1982) 119–36.

Kilpatrick, G.D, "The Order of Some Noun and Adjective Phrases in the New Testament," Donum Gratulatorium Eth. Stauffer [Leiden: Brill, 1962],111ff.

Kirkpatrick, E. "Hebrews: Its Evangelistic Purpose and Literary Form." Dissertation, Southern Baptist Theological Seminary, 1941.

Kistemaker, S. J. Exposition of the Epistle to the Hebrews. New Testament Commentary. Grand Rapids: Baker Book House, 1984.

Kistemaker, S. The Psalm Citations in the Epistle to the Hebrews. Amsterdam: Van Soest, 1961.

Kitchens, J. A. "The Death of Jesus in the Epistle to the Hebrews." Dissertation, New Orleans Baptist Theological Seminary, 1964.

Knox, E. A. "The Samaritans and the Epistle to the Hebrews." TCh 22 (1927) 184–93.

Knox, W. L. "The Divine Hero Christology of the New Testament." HTR 41 (1948) 229–49.

Koester, Craig R., "Tabernacle," Eerdmans Dictionary of the Bible," 1270

Koester, H. Introduction to the New Testament. vol(s). 2: History and Literature of Early Christianity. Philadelphia: Fortress, 1982.

Koester, Helmut, "Jesus the Victim," JBL 111.1(1992),3-15

Koester, Craig R., Hebrews.The Anchor Bible.NY: Doubleday, 2001

Kuemmerlin-McLean, Joanne E., 'Magic,' ABD, loc.cit.

Kürzinger,BZ 1958,294-299. A. R. .Leaney,"Conformed to the Image of His Son," NTS 10[1964]470-479.

Lampe, G. W. H. "Hermeneutics and Typology." LQHR 190 (1965) 17–25.

Lampe, G. W. H.. "Typological Exegesis." Theol 56 (1953) 201–8.

Lane, W. L. "Hebrews: A Sermon in Search of a Setting." SWJT28 (1985) 13–18.

Lane, W. L. Call to Commitment: Responding to the Message of Hebrews. Nashville: Nelson, 1985.

Lane, W. L. Hebrews 1-8: Word Biblical Commentary. Vol. 47A: (electronic ed.). Logos Library System; Word Biblical Commentary. Word, Incorporated: Dallas, 1998.

Lang, G. H. The Epistle to the Hebrews. London: Paternoster, 1951.

LaSor, W. S. "The Epistle to the Hebrews and the Qumran Writings." In The Dead Sea Scrolls and the New Testament. Grand Rapids: Eerdmans, 1972. 17990.

Legg, J. D. "Our Brother Timothy: A Suggested Solution to the Problem of Authorship of the Epistle to the Hebrews." EvQ40 (1968) 220–23.

Lehne, S. The New Covenant in Hebrews. JSNTSup 44. Sheffield: JSOT, 1990.

Leivestad, R. Christ the Conqueror: Ideas of Conflict and Victory in the New Testament. New York: Macmillan, 1954.

Lenski, R. C. H. The Interpretation of the Epistle to the Hebrews and the Epistle of James. Columbus, OH: Wartburg, 1946.

Leon, H. J. "The Jews of Rome in the First Centuries of Christianity." In The Teacher's Yoke. FS H. Trantham. ed. E. J. Vardaman and J. L. Garrett. Waco, TX: Baylor UP, 1964.

Leonard, W. The Authorship of the Epistle to the Hebrews. London/Vatican: Polyglott, 1939.

Leschert, D. "Hermeneutical Foundations of the Epistle to the Hebrews: A Study in the Validity of Its Interpretation of Some Core Citations from the Psalms." Dissertation, Fuller Theological Seminary, 1991.

Lewis, T. W. "The Theological Logic in Hebrews 10:19–12:29 and the Appropriation of the Old Testament." Dissertation, Drew University, 1965.

Lewis, W. M. "St. Paul's Defense before King Agrippa, in Relation to the Epistle to the Hebrews." BW 13 (1899) 244–48.

Liddell, Henry George and Robert Scott, A Greek-English Lexicon [Oxford: Clarendon Press,1977]398.[L-S]

Lidgett, J. S. Sonship and Salvation: A Study of the Epistle to the Hebrews. London: Epworth, 1921.

Lightfoot, N. R. Jesus Christ Today: A Commentary on the Book of Hebrews. Grand Rapids: Baker, 1976.

Lindars, B. "The Rhetorical Structure of Hebrews." NTS 35 (1989) 382–406.

Lindars, B. New Testament Apologetic: The Doctrinal Significance of the Old Testament Quotations. London: SCM, 1961.

Linss, W. C. "Logical Terminology in the Epistle to the Hebrews." CTM 37 (1966) 365–69.

Loader, W. R. G. "Christ at the Right Hand: Ps cx. 1 in the New Testament." NTS 24 (1977–78) 199–217.

Loane, M. L. "The Unity of the Old and New Testaments as Illustrated in the Epistle to the Hebrews." In God Who is Rich in Mercy. FS D. B. Knox. ed. P. T. O'Brien and D. G. Peterson. Homebush West, NSW: Lancer, 1986. 255–64.

LoBue, F. "The Historical Background to the Epistle to the Hebrews." JBL 75 (1956) 52–57..

Longenecker, R. N. Biblical Exegesis in the Apostolic Period. Grand Rapids: Eerdmans, 1975.

Louw, J. P. The Semantics of New Testament Greek. Philadelphia: Fortress, 1982.

Lövestam, E, .Son and Savior: a Study of Acts 13.32-37[ConNeot 18;Lund,1961]15-37.

Lussier, E. Christ's Priesthood according to the Epistle to the Hebrews. Collegeville, MN: Liturgical, 1975.

Luther, J. H. "The Use of the Old Testament by the Author of Hebrews." Dissertation, Bob Jones University, 1977.

Lyonnet, S. and Sabourin, L. Sin, Redemption and Sacrifice. AnBib 48. Rome: Pontifical Biblical Institute, 1970.

Maar, O. " Philo und der Hebräerbrief ." Dissertation, Vienna, 1964.

MacDonald, W. The Epistle to the Hebrews: From Ritual to Reality. Neptune, NJ: Loizeaux, 1971..

Mack, B. L.. Rhetoric and the New Testament. Minneapolis, MN: Fortress, 1990.

MacKay, C. "The Argument of Hebrews." CQR 168 (1967) 325–38.

MacLeod, David J., 'The Cleansing of the True Tabernacle,' BibSacra 152(1995),60-71

MacLeod, David J., "The Present work of Christ in Hebrews: the Commencement of Christ's Ministry," BSac 148(1991),185

MacNeil, H. L. The Christology of the Epistle to the Hebrews. Chicago: Chicago University, 1914.

MacRae, G. W. "Heavenly Temple and Eschatology in the Letter to the Hebrews." Semeia 12 (1978) 17999.

Madsen, N. P. Ask and You Will Receive: Prayer and the Letter to the Hebrews. St. Louis: CBP. Press, 1989.

Manson, T. W. Ministry and Priesthood: Christ's and Ours. Richmond: John Knox Press, 1958.

Manson, T. W.. "The Problem of the Epistle to the Hebrews." BJRL 32 (1949–50) 1–17.

Manson, W. The Epistle to the Hebrews: An Historical and Theological Reconsideration. London: Hodder & Stoughton, 1951.

Mantey, J.R. 'Is Death the Only Punishment for unbelievers,' Bibsacra 112(1955),340.

Marchant, G. J. C. "Sacrifice in the Epistle to the Hebrews." EvQ 20 (1948) 196–210.

Marshall, I. H. Kept by the Power of God: A Study of Perseverance and Falling Away. London: Epworth, 1969.

Mauro, P. God's Apostle and High Priest. New York: Revell, 1912.

Mauro, P.. God's Pilgrims: Their Danger, Their Resources, Their Rewards. rev. ed. Boston: Hamilton Brothers, 1918.

Maxwell, K. L. "Doctrine and Parenesis in the Epistle to the Hebrews, with Special Reference to Pre-Christian Gnosticism." Dissertation, Yale University, 1952.

McCasland, A.V. "The Image of God according to Paul," JBL 1950, 87.

McCaul, J. B. The Epistle to the Hebrews: A Paraphrastic Commentary with Illustrations from Philo, the Targums, the Mishna and Gemara, etc. . London: Longmans, Green, 1871.

McCown, W. G. "Ο ΛΟΓΟΣ ΤΗΣ ΠΑΡΑΚΛΗΣΕΩΣ: The Nature and Function of the Hortatory Sections in the Epistle to the Hebrews." Dissertation, Union Theological Seminary, Richmond, 1970.

McCown, W. G. "Holiness in Hebrews." WesThJ 16 (1981) 58–78.

McCullough, J. C "Some Recent Developments in Research on the Epistle to the Hebrews." IBS 2 (1980) 141–65.

McCullough, J. C. "Hebrews and the Old Testament." Dissertation, Queen's University, Belfast, 1971.

McCullough, J. C. "The Old Testament Quotations in Hebrews." NTS 26 (1979–80) 363–79.

McDonald, J. I. H. Kerygma and Didache: The Articulation and Structure of the Earliest Christian Message. SNTSMS 37. Cambridge: Cambridge UP, 1980.

McGaughey, D. H. "The Hermeneutic Method of the Epistle to the Hebrews." Dissertation, Boston University, 1963.

McKay, Johnston R and James F Miller. Biblical Studies: Essays in Honor of William Barclay. Phil.:Westminster, 1976

McNamara, M. The New Testament and the Palestinian Targum to the Pentateuch. AnBib 27. Rome: Pontifical Biblical Institute, 1966.

McNamara, M.. Targum and Testament: Aramaic Paraphrases of the Hebrew Bible, A Light on the New Testament. Shannon: Irish UP, 1972.

McNicol, A. J. "The Relationship of the Image of the Highest Angel to the High Priest Concept in Hebrews." Dissertation, Vanderbilt University, 1974.

McNicol, J. "The Spiritual Value of the Epistle to the Hebrews." BibRev 15 (1930) 509–22.

McRay, J. "Atonement and Apocalyptic in the Book of Hebrews." ResQ 23 (1980) 1–9.

Mealand, D. L. "The Christology of the Epistle to the Hebrews." MCM 22 (1979) 180–87.

Meeter, H. H. The Heavenly High Priesthood of Christ. Grand Rapids: Eerdmans-Sevensma, 1916.

Metzger, B. M. "The Formulas Introducing Quotations of Scripture in the NT and the Mishnah." JBL 70 (1951) 297–307.

Metzger, B. M.. A Textual Commentary on the Greek New Testament: A Companion Volume to the United Bible Societies' Greek New Testament (third edition). London/New York: United Bible Societies, 1971.

Michel, J., "Quelques formules primitives de serment promissoire et l'origine de la comparaison par adynaton," in RIDA, 1957, pp. 139–150.

Mickelsen, A. B. "Methods of Interpretation in the Epistle to the Hebrews." Dissertation, University of Chicago, 1950.

Milgrom, Jacob, Leviticus,. The Anchor Bible. [NY:Doubleday,1991],loc. cit.

Miller, P. D. The Divine Warrior in Early Israel. Cambridge, MA: Harvard UP, 1973.

Miller, Merland R, "Seven Theological Themes in Hebrews," GTJ 8.1 Spring n.y.

Milligan, G. The Theology of the Epistle to the Hebrews with a Critical Introduction. Edinburgh: Clark, 1899.

Milligan, G. "The Roman Destination of the Epistle to the Hebrews." Exp 4 (1901) 437–48.

Milligan, W. The Ascension and Heavenly Priesthood of Our Lord. London: Macmillan, 1891.

Minear, P.S New Testament Apocalyptic. Nashville: Abingdon, 1981.

Minear, P.S. "An Early Christian Theopoetic?" Semeia 12 (1978) 201–14.

Moffatt, J. Jesus Christ the Same. The Shaffer Lectures for 1940 in Yale University Divinity School. New York: Abingdon-Cokesbury, 1940.

Moffatt, J. "The Christology of the Epistle to the Hebrews." ExpTim 28 (1916–17) 505–8, 563–66; 29 (1917–18) 2630.

Moffatt, J. A Critical and Exegetical Commentary on the Epistle to the Hebrews. ICC. Edinburgh: Clark, 1924.

Montefiore, H. A Commentary on the Epistle to the Hebrews. HNTC. New York: Harper, 1964.

Morris, L. Hebrews. Bible Study Commentary. Grand Rapids: Zondervan, 1983.

Morris, L. The Apostolic Preaching of the Cross. Grand Rapids: Eerdmans, 1955.

Motyer,S, 'The Rending of the Veil: A Markan Pentecost,' NTS 33(1987)155-57;

Moule, C. F. D. "The Influence of Circumstances on the Use of Christological Terms." JTS ns 10 (1959) 247–63.

Moule, C. F. D. "The Influence of Circumstances on the Use of Eschatological Terms." JTS ns 15 (1964) 1–15.

Moule, C. F. D. An Idiom-Book of New Testament Greek. 2nd ed. Cambridge: UP, 1960.

Moule, C. F. D. "Commentaries on the Epistle to the Hebrews." Theol 161 (1958) 22832.

Moule, C. F. D. "The Influence of Circumstances on the Use of Eschatological Terms." JTS ns 15 (1964) 1–15.

Moule, C. F. D.. The Sacrifice of Christ. Greenwich: Seabury Press, 1957.

Moxnes, H. Theology in Conflict. NovTSup 53. Leiden: Brill, 1980.

Murray, J. "Jesus the Son of God." In Collected Writings of John Murray. vol(s). 4. Edinburgh: Banner of Truth Trust, 1982. 58–81.

Murray, J. "The Heavenly, Priestly Activity of Christ." In Collected Writings of John Murray. ed. I. Murray. vol(s). 1. Edinburgh: Banner of Truth Trust, 1976. 44–58.

Murray, R. "Jews, Hebrews and Christians: Some Needed Distinctions." NovT 24 (1982) 194–208.

Myers Jacob M.,, I and II Esdras[NY: Doubleday, 1974]loc.cit.

Myers, F.B., The way into the Holiest. London: Oliphants,1968

Nairne, A. The Epistle to the Hebrews. Cambridge Bible for Schools and Colleges. Cambridge: UP, 1921.

Nairne, A. The Epistle of Priesthood: Studies in the Epistle to the Hebrews. Edinburgh: Clark, 1913.

Nakagawa, H. "Christology in the Epistle to the Hebrews." Dissertation, Yale University, 1955.

Narborough, F. D. V. Epistle to the Hebrews. Clarendon Bible. Oxford: Clarendon, 1930.

Nash, R. H. "The Notion of Mediator in Alexandrian Judaism and the Epistle to the Hebrews." WTJ 40 (1977) 89–115.

Neeley, L. L. "A Discourse Analysis of Hebrews." OPTT 3–4 (1987) 1–146.

Neighhour, R. E. If They Shall Fall Away: The Epistle to the Hebrews Unveiled. Miami Springs: Conlay & Schaettle, 1940.

Neil, W. The Epistle to the Hebrews. 2nd ed. TBC. London: Black, 1959.

Nestle, E. "On the Address of the Epistle to the Hebrews." ExpTim 10 (1898–99) 422.

Neufeld, V. H. The Earliest Christian Confessions. NTTS 5. Grand Rapids: Eerdmans, 1963.

Neusner, Jacob. First Century Judaism. Nashville: Abingdon, 1975.

Newell, W. R. Hebrews: Verse by Verse. Chicago: Moody Press, 1947.

Nicole, R. "C. H. Dodd and the Doctrine of Propitiation." WTJ 17 (1955) 117–57.

Nida, E. A Translator's Handbook on the Letter to the Hebrews. New York: United Bible Societies, 1983.

North, Christopher R., The Second Isaiah [Oxford: Clarendon, 1964]loc. cit.

Olson, S. N. "Wandering but Not Lost." WW 5 (1985) 426–33.

Osborne, G. "Soteriology in the Epistle to the Hebrews." In Grace Unlimited. ed. C. Pinnock. Minneapolis: Bethany Fellowship, 1975.

Oudersluys, R. C. "Exodus in the Letter to the Hebrews." In Grace upon Grace. FS L. J. Kuyper. ed. J.I. Cook. Grand Rapids: Eerdmans, 1975. 143–52.

Owen, J. An Exposition of the Epistle to the Hebrews. 7 vol(s). Edinburgh: Ritchie, 1812.

Parker, H. M., Jr. "Domitian and the Epistle to the Hebrews." IlRev 36 (1979) 31–43.

Parke-Taylor, G.H., Yahweh: The Divione Name in the Bible[Waterloo,Ont.: Wilfrid Laurier Univ Press,1975]loc.cit.

Payne, J.Barton, Encyclopedia of Biblical Prophecy [NY:Harper and Row, 1973] lo.cit.

Pentecost, J Dwight, "The Nature of Savation in the Old Testament. Bsac 115 #457 (1958),54

Perdue, L. B. "The Social Character of Paraenesis and Paraenetic Literature." Semeia 50 (1990) 5–39.

Perkins, D. W. "A Call to Pilgrimage: The Challenge of Hebrews." ThEduc 32 (1985) 69–81.

Perowne, T. T. Our High Priest in Heaven. 2nd ed. London: E. Stock, 1894.

Perry, M. "Method and Model in the Epistle to the Hebrews." Theol 77 (1974) 66–74.

Peterson D.,, 'Hebrews,' in Carson, D.A.; et al., The New Bible Commentary, (Downers Grove, Illinois: Inter-Varsity Press) 1994.

Peterson, D. G. "An Examination of the Concept of 'Perfection' in the 'Epistle to the Hebrews.'" Dissertation, University of Manchester, 1978. [Published as Hebrews and Perfection: An Examination of the Concept of Perfection in the "Epistle to the Hebrews." Cambridge: Cambridge UP, 1982.]

Peterson, D. G.. "The Ministry of Encouragement." In God Who Is Rich in Mercy. FS D. B. Knox. ed. P. T. O'Brien and D. G. Peterson. Homebush West, NSW: Lancer, 1986. 235–53.

Peterson, D. G.. "Towards a New Testament Theology of Worship.' RTR 43 (1984) 65–73.

Pfitzner, V. C. Chi Rho Commentary on Hebrews. Adelaide, S. Australia: Lutheran Publishing House, 1979.

Philo: A., & Yonge, C. D. 1996, c1993. The works of Philo : Complete and unabridged. Hendrickson: Peabody.

Pittard, C. R. "The Person and Work of Christ in the Epistle to the Hebrews." Dissertation, Southern Baptist Theological Seminary, 1926.

Plessis, P.J. du. ΤΕΛΕΙΟΣ: The Idea of Perfection in the New Testament. Kampen: Kok, 1959.

Plooij, D. Studies in the Testimony Book. Amsterdam: NoordHollandsche, 1932.

Plumptre, E. H. "The Writings of Apollos." Exp ns 1 (1885) 329–48, 409–35.

Pollard, E. B. "Notes on the Old Testament Citations in the Epistle to the Hebrews." CrozQ 1 (1924) 447–52.

Powell, C. H. The Biblical Concept of Power. London: Epworth, 1963.

Powell, D. L. "Christ as High Priest in the Epistle to the Hebrews." SE 7 (1982) 387–99.

Prince, A. "An Investigation into the Importance of Perseverance in the Christian Life as Presented in Five Warning Passages in Hebrews." Dissertation, Southwestern Baptist Theological Seminary, 1980.

Purdy, A. C "The Purpose of the Epistle to the Hebrews in the Light of Recent Studies in Judaism." In Amicitiae Corolla. ed. H. G. Wood. London: University of London, 1933.

Purdy, A. C. "The Purpose of the Epistle to the Hebrews." Exp 8th ser. 19 (1920) 123–39.

Purdy, A. C., and Cotton, J. H. "The Epistle to the Hebrews." IB 11 (1955) 575–763.

Ramsay, W. M. "The Date and Authorship of the Epistle to the Hebrews." In Luke the Physician. London: Hodder & Stoughton, 1908.

Rawlingson, A. E. J. "Priesthood and Sacrifice in Judaism and Christianity." ExpTim 60 (1949) 116–21.

Reid, R. "The Use of the Old Testament in the Epistle to the Hebrews." Dissertation, Union Theological Seminary, New York, 1964.

Rendall, F. The Epistle to the Hebrews. London: Macmillan, 1888.

Rendall, F. Theology of the Hebrew Christians. London: Macmillan, 1886.

Rendall, R. "The Method of the Writer to the Hebrews in Using Old Testament Quotations." EvQ 27 (1955) 214–20.

Rice, G. E. "Apostasy as a Motif and Its Effect on the Structure of Hebrews." AUSS 23 (1985) 29–35.

Richardson, A., An Introduction to the Theology of the New Testament, London, 1958, pp. 33, 348ff.

Riddle, D. W. "Hebrews, First Clement, and the Persecution of Domitian." JBL 43 (1924) 329–48.

Rienecker, F. A Linguistic Key to the Greek New Testament. Grand Rapids: Zondervan, 1976.

Robertson, A. T. A Grammar of the Greek New Testament in the Light of Historical Research. Nashville: Broadman, 1934.

Robertson, O. P. "The People of the Wilderness: The Concept of the Church in Hebrews." Dissertation, Union Theological Seminary, Richmond, 1966.

Robinson, J. A. T. Redating the New Testament. London: SCM, 1976.

Robinson, T. H. The Epistle to the Hebrews. 8th ed. MNTC. London: Hodder & Stoughton, 1964.

Robinson, W. "The Eschatology of the Epistle to the Hebrews: A Study in the Christian Doctrine of Hope." Enc 22 (1961) 37–51.

Robinson, W. The Eschatology of the Epistle to the Hebrews. Birmingham, AL: Overdale College, 1950.

Rogers, E. W. Him That Endured. London: Pickering & Inglis,1965.

Ross, A. "The Message of the Epistle to the Hebrews for Today." ExpTim 51 (1942–43) 161–68.

Rowell,J. B. "Our Great High Priest." BSac 118 (1961) 148–53.

Rylaarsdam, J. C. "Jewish-Christian Relationships: The Two Covenants and the Dilemmas of Christology." In Grace upon Grace. FS L. J. Kuyper. ed. J. I. Cook. Grand Rapids: Eerdmans, 1975.

Sabourin, L. Priesthood: A Comparative Study. Leiden: Brill, 1973.

Salmon, G. "The Keynote of the Epistle to the Hebrews." Exp 2nd ser. 3 (1882) 81–93.

Salom, A. P. "Ta Hagia in the Epistle to the Hebrews." AUSS 5 (1967) 59–70.

Sandegren, C. "The Addressees of the Epistle to the Hebrews." EvQ 27 (1955) 221–24.

Sanders, J. T. The New Testament Christological Hymns. SNTSMS 15. Cambridge: Cambridge UP, 1971. Sanford, C.J. "The Addressees of Hebrews." Dissertation, Dallas Theological Seminary, 1962.

Sanders, James A. , Hermeneutics in True and False Prophecy. Canon and Authority[Phil.: Fortress,1977]21-41.

Sarles, Ken L. , 'An Appraisal of the Signs and Wonders Movement,' Bibliotheca sacra 145 #577(Jan 1988).

Saydon, P. P. "The Master Idea of the Epistle to the Hebrews." Mel Theol 13 (1961) 19–26.

Schaefer, J. R. "The Relationship between Priestly and Servant Messianism in the Epistle to the Hebrews." CBQ 30 (1968) 359–85.

Schiele, F. M. "Harnack's 'Probabilia' Concerning the Address and the Author of the Epistle to the Hebrews." AJT 9 (1905) 290–308.

Schierse, F. J. The Epistle to the Hebrews. tr. B. Fahy. London: Burns & Oates, 1969.

Schildenberger, J. " Psalm 109 (110): Christus, König und Priester." BenM 20 (1938) 361–74.

Schmidgall, P. "The Influence of Jewish Apocalyptic Literature on the Book of Hebrews." Dissertation, Western Kentucky University, 1980.

Schneider, J. The Letter to the Hebrews. tr. W. A. Mueller. Grand Rapids: Eerdmans, 1957.

Schonfield, Hugh Joseph, The Passover Plot: New Light on the History of Jesus, n.p., 1966,

Schoonhoven, C. R. "The 'Analogy of Faith'and the Intent of Hebrews." In Scripture, Tradition, and Interpretation. FS E. F. Harrison.

ed. W. W. Gasque and W. S. LaSor Grand Rapids: Eerdmans, 1978. 92–110.

Scott, E. F. "The Epistle to the Hebrews and Roman Christianity." HTR 13 (1930) 205–19.

Scott, E. F. The Epistle to the Hebrews: Its Doctrine and Significance. Edinburgh: Clark, 1923.

Scott, W. M. F. "Priesthood in the New Testament." SJT 10 (1957) 399–415.

Segal, Philip, "Further Reflections on the 'Begotten' Messiah," Hebrew Annual Review 7(1983)221ff.

Selph, B. K. "The Christology of the Book of Hebrews." Dissertation, Southwestern Baptist Seminary, 1948.

Shneider, J. The Letter to the Hebrews. tr. W. A. Mueller. Grand Rapids: Eerdmans, 1957.

Shulam, Joseph. With Hillary Lecornu. A commentary on the Jewish Roots of Romans..Baltimore: Messianic Jewish Pub., 1997.

Siegman, E. F. "The Blood of the Covenant." AER 136 (1957) 167–74.

Silva, M. "Perfection and Eschatology in Hebrews." WTJ 39 (1976) 60–71.

Silva, M. Biblical Words and Their Meanings: An Introduction to Lexical Semantics. Grand Rapids: Zondervan, 1983.

Simpson, E. K. "The Vocabulary of the Epistle to the Hebrews." EvQ 18 (1946) 35–38, 187–90.

Smalley, S.S. "The Atonement in the Epistle to the Hebrews." EvQ 33 (1961) 36–43.

Smith, J. A Priest for Ever: A Study of Typology and Eschatology in Hebrews. London/Sydney: Sheed and Ward, 1969.

Smith, L. "Metaphor and Truth in Hebrews." NB 57 (1976) 227–33.

Smith, R. B. "Apostasy in the Book of Hebrews." Dissertation, Southern Baptist Theological Seminary, 1959.

Smith, R. H. Hebrews. Augsburg Commentary on the New Testament. Minneapolis: Augsburg, 1984.

Smith, R. W. The Art of Rhetoric in Alexandria: Its Theory and Practice in the Ancient World. The Hague: Nijhoff, 1974.

Snell, A. A. New and Living Way: An Explanation of the Epistle to the Hebrews. London: Faith, 1959.

Solari, J. K. "The Problem of Metanoia in the Epistle to the Hebrews." Dissertation, Catholic University of America, 1970.

Soncino Zohar, Bereshith, Section 1, Page 6a

Sowers, S. G. The Hermeneutics of Philo and Hebrews: A Comparison of the Interpretation of the Old Testament in Philo Judaeus and the Epistle to the Hebrews. Richmond: Knox, 1965.

Spence-Jones, H.D.M. The Early Christians in Rome. London: Methuen, 1910.

Stagl, H. "Pauline Authorship of the Epistle to the Hebrews according to Mt. Sinai Arabic Manuscript 151." RefRev 21 (1961) 14, 51–53.

Staples, A. F. "The Book of Hebrews in Its Relationship to the Writings of Philo Judaeus." Dissertation, Southern Baptist Theological Seminary, 1951.

Stibbs, A. M. So Great Salvation: The Meaning and Message of the Letter to the Hebrews. Exeter: Paternoster Press, 1970.

Stine, D. M. "The Finality of the Christian Faith: A Study of the Unfolding Argument of the Epistle to the Hebrews, Chapters 1–7." Dissertation, Princeton Theological Seminary, 1964.

Stott, W. "The Conception of 'Offering' in the Epistle to the Hebrews." NTS 11 (1962–63) 62–67.

Stuart, M. A Commentary on the Epistle to the Hebrews. 4th ed. Andover: W. F. Draper, 1876.

Stuart, S.S. "The Exodus Tradition in Late Jewish and Early Christian Literature: A General Survey of the Literature and a Particular Analysis of the Wisdom of Solomon, II Esdras and the Epistle to the Hebrews." Dissertation, Vanderbilt University, 1973.

Swetnam, J. "Form and Content in Hebrews 7–13. Bib 55 (1974) 333–48.

Swetnam, J. "On the Literary Genre of the 'Epistle' to the Hebrews. NovT 13 (1969) 261–69.

Swetnam, J. Jesus and Isaac: A Study of the Epistle to the Hebrews in the Light of the Aqedah. AnBib 94. Rome: Biblical Institute Press, 1981.

Swetnam, J. "Form and Content in Hebrews 1–6." Bib 53 (1972) 368–85.

Synge, F. C. Hebrews and the Scriptures. London: SPCK, 1959..

Talbert, Charles H. "The Problem of Pre-existence in Philippians 2.6011," JBL 86(1967),141-153

Tasker, R. V. G. "The Text of the 'Corpus Paulinum.'" NTS 1 (1954–55) 180–91.

Tasker, R. V. G. The Gospel in the Epistle to the Hebrews. London: Tyndale, 1956.

Taylor, C. D. "A Comparative Study of the Concepts of Worship in Colossians and Hebrews." Dissertation, Southern Baptist Theological Seminary, 1957.

Tenney, M. C. "A New Approach to the Book of Hebrews." BSac 123 (1966) 230–36.

Thayer, J. H. "Authorship and Canonicity of the Epistle to the Hebrews." BSac 24 (1867) 681–722.

Thiselton, A. "Semantics and New Testament Interpretation." In New Testament Interpretation: Essays on Principles and Methods. ed. I. H. Marshall. Grand Rapids: Eerdmans, 1977.75-104.

Thomas, J. "The Use of Voice, Moods and Tenses in the Epistle to the Hebrews." Dissertation, Western Kentucky University, 1980.

Thomas, K.J. "The Use of the Septuagint in the Epistle to the Hebrews." Dissertation, University of Manchester, 1959.

Thomas, K.J. "The Old Testament Citations in Hebrews." NTS 11 (1964–65) 303–25.

Thompson, J. W. "The Underlying Unity of Hebrews." ResQ 18 (1975) 129–36.

Thompson, J.P. "Structure and Purpose of Catena," CBQ 38(1976),352-363

Thompson, J. W. Strategy for Survival: A Plan for Church Renewal from Hebrews. Austin, TX: Sweet, 1980.

Thompson, J. W. "'That Which Abides': Some Metaphysical Assumptions in the Epistle to the Hebrews." Dissertation, Vanderbilt University, 1974.

Thompson, J. W. The Beginnings of Christian Philosophy: The Epistle to the Hebrews. CBQMS 13. Washington, DC.: The Catholic Biblical Association of America, 1981.

Thompson, J. W. The Letter to the Hebrews. Austin: Sweet, 1971.

Thompson, J. W."Hebrews 9 and Hellenistic Concepts of Sacrifice.' JBL 98.4(1979),567-578.

Thurston, R. W. "Philo and the Epistle to the Hebrews." EvQ 58 (1986) 133–43.

Tiede, D. L. The Charismatic Figure as Miracle Worker. SBLDS 1. Missoula, MT: Scholars, 1972.

Toorn, K. v. d., Becking, B., & Horst, P. W. v. d. (1999). Dictionary of deities and demons in the Bible DDD (2nd extensively rev. ed.) (Page 14). Leiden; Boston; Grand Rapids, Mich.: Brill; Eerdmans.

Torrance, J. B. "The Priesthood of Jesus." In Essays in Christology for Karl Barth. ed. T. H. L. Parker. London: Lotterworth Press, 1956. 153–73.

Torrey, C. C. "The Authorship and Character of the So-Called 'Epistle to the Hebrews.'" JBL 30 (1911) 137–56.

Toy, C. H. Quotations in the New Testament. New York: Scribner's, 1884.

Trites, A. A. The New Testament Concept of Witness. SNTSMS 31. Cambridge: Cambridge UP, 1977.

Tucker, M. A. R. "The Gospel according to Prisca." Nineteenth Century 73 (1913) 81–98.

Turner, G.A. The New and Living Way: A Fresh Exposition of the Epistle to the Hebrews. Minneapolis: Bethany Fellowship, 1975.

Turner, N. A Grammar of New Testament Greek: IV. Style. Edinburgh: Clark, 1976.

Turner, N. A Grammar of New Testament Greek: III. Syntax. Edinburgh: Clark, 1963.

Ulansey, David, "The Heavenly Veil Torn: Mark's cosmic Inclusio" JBL 110.1(1991),123-125

Unger, Merrill, "The Significance of the Sabbath – BibSacra Vol 123 #489 -- Jan 1966 – 53

Unger, Merrill F., "Historical Research and the Church at Thessalonica," Hebrews in the Greek NT BSac 119(1962),46.

Van den eynde, S., "Crying to God: Prayer and Plot in the Book of Judith" Biblica 85(2004)217-231

Vanhoye, A. A Structured Translation of the Epistle to the Hebrews. tr. J. Swetnam. Rome: Pontifical Biblical Institute, 1964.

Vanhoye, A. Our Priest in God: The Doctrine of the Epistle to the Hebrews. Rome: Biblical Institute Press, 1977.

Vanhoye, A. Structure and Message of the Epistle to the Hebrews. Rome: Pontificio Instituto Biblico, 1989.

Vansant, A. C. "The Humanity of Jesus in the Epistle to the Hebrews." Dissertation, Southern Baptist Theological Seminary, 1951.

Vaughan, C. J. The Epistle to the Hebrews. London: Macmillan, 1890.

Vis A. The Messianic Psalm Quotations in the New Testament. Amsterdam: Hertberger, 1936.

Vos, G. "The Priesthood of Christ in the Epistle to the Hebrews." PTR 4 (1907) 423–47, 579–604.

Vos, G. "Hebrews–the Epistle of the Diaqh̄kh" PTR 13 (1915) 587–632; 14 (1916) 1–61.

Vos, G. The Teaching of the Epistle to the Hebrews. ed. and rev. J. Vos. Grand Rapids:Eerdmans, 1956.

Waal, C. van der. "The 'People of God' in the Epistle to the Hebrews." Neot 5 (1971) 83–92.

Waddell, H. C. "The Readers of the Epistle to the Hebrews." Exp 8th ser. 26 (1923) 88–105.

Walden, H. E. "The Christology of the Epistle to the Hebrews." Dissertation, Southern Baptist Theological Seminary, 1944.

Walvoord, John F., 'The Present work of Christ. Part 1 Ascension of Christ.' Bibsacra 121(1964),3ff

Walvoord, John F., "Present Work of Christ-Part VII: Present Work of Christ in Heaven" (Part 5) --BibSacra 122 #487 -- Jul 1965 – 195

Walvoord, John f. "Premillennialism and the Tribulation." Part V; Partial Rapture Theory. BSac 112(1955),209

Walvoord, John F., "The Present Work of Christ: Part 10 Propitiation." Bibsacra 119(1962),99

Walvoord, John F.,'The Incarnation of Christ.' Bibsacra 117(1960),195

Warfield, B. B. "Christ Our Sacrifice." In The Person and Work of Christ. ed. S. G. Craig. Philadelphia: Presbyterian and Reformed, 1950. 391–426.

Webster, J. H. "The Epistle to the Hebrews." BSac 85 (1928) 347–60.

Wengst, K. Christologische Formeln und Lieder des Urchristentums. SNT 7. Gütersloh: Bertelsmann, 1972.

Wenschkewitz, H. " Die Spiritualisierung der Kultusbegriffe Tempel, Priester und Opfer im Neuen Testament. " Angelos 4 (1932) 70–230.

Werner, E. The Sacred Bridge. London: Dobson, 1959.

Westcott, B. F. The Epistle to the Hebrews: The Greek Text with Notes and Essays. 3rd ed. London/New York: Macmillan, 1903.

Whitley, W. T. "The Epistle to the Hebrews." RevExp 3 (1906) 214–29.

Wickham, E. C. The Epistle to the Hebrews. London: Methuen, 1910.

Wiefel, W. "The Jewish Community in Ancient Rome and the Origins of Roman Christianity." In The Romans Debate. ed. K. P. Dornfried. Minneapolis: Augsburg, 1977.

Wikgren, A. "Some Greek Idioms in the Epistle to the Hebrews." In The Teacher's Yoke. FS H. Trantham. ed. E.J. Vardaman and J. L. Garrett. Waco, TX: Baylor UP, 1964.

Wikgren, A. "Patterns of Perfection in the Epistle to the Hebrews." NTS 6 (1959–60) 159–67.

Williams, A. H. 'An Early Christology: A Systematic and Exegetical Investigation of the Traditions Contained in Hebrews.' Dissertation, Mainz, 1971.

Williams, S. K. Jesus' Death as Saving Event: The Background and Origin of a Concept. HDR 2. Missoula, MT: Scholars, 1975.

Williamson, R "Hebrews and Doctrine." ExpTim 81 (1969–70) 371–76.

Williamson, R "Platonism and Hebrews." SJT 16 (1963) 415–24.

Williamson, R. "Philo and New Testament Christology." In Studia Biblica 1978 III. JSNTSup 3. Sheffield: JSOT Press, 1980. 439–45.

Williamson, R. Philo and the Epistle to the Hebrews. ALGHJ 4. Leiden: Brill, 1970.

Williamson, R. "Hebrews and Doctrine." ExpTim 81 (1969–70) 371–76.

Williamson, R. "Philo and New Testament Christology." In Studia Biblica 1978 III.

Williamson, R. "Platonism and Hebrews." SJT 16 (1963) 415–24.

Williamson, R. "The Background to the Epistle to the Hebrews." ExpTim 87 (1975–76) 232–37.

Williamson, R. "The Eucharist and the Epistle to the Hebrews." NTS 21 (1974–75) 300–12.

Williamson, R. The Epistle to the Hebrews. London: Epworth, 1965.

Willis, C. G. "St. Augustine's Text of the Epistle to the Hebrews." sup6 (1962) 543–47.

Wilson, R. McL. "Coptisms in the Epistle to the Hebrews?" NovT 1 (1956) 322–24.

Wilson, R. McL. Hebrews. New Century Bible Commentary. Grand Rapids: Eerdmans, 1987.

Winter, A. "ἅπαξ, ἐφάπαξ im Hebräerbrief" Dissertation, Rome, 1960.

Worden, T. "Before Reading the Epistle to the Hebrews." Scr 14 (1962) 48–57.

Worley, D. R. "God's Faithfulness to Promise: The Hortatory Use of Commissive Language in Hebrews." Dissertation, Yale University, 1981.

Wuest, Kenneth S., 'When Jesus Emptied Himself' BibSacra 115(1958),153

Wuest, Kenneth S.,'Hebrew Six in the Greek NT,' BibSacra 119(1962),45

Wuest, Kenneth S.,'the Deity of Jesus in the Greek text of John and Paul,' Bib sacra 119(1962),216

Yadin, Y "The Dead Sea Scrolls and the Epistle to the Hebrews." ScrHier 4 (1958) 36–55.

Yadin, Y. The Art of Warfare in Biblical Lands in the Light of Archaeological Study. 2 vol(s). tr. M. Pearlman. New York: McGraw-Hill, 1963.

Young, F. M "The Use of Sacrificial Ideas in Greek Christian Writers from the New Testament to John Chrysostom." Dissertation, Cambridge University, 1967.

Young, F. M Sacrifice and the Death of Christ. London: SPCK 1975.

Young, F. M. "Christological Ideas in the Greek Commentaries on the Epistle to the Hebrews." JTS 20 (1969) 150–63.

Young, J. A. "The Significance of Sacrifice in the Epistle to the Hebrews." Dissertation, Southwestern Baptist Theological Seminary, 1963.

Zuntz, G. The Text of the Epistles: A Disquisition upon the 'Corpus Paulinum.' Schweich Lectures, 1946. London: The British Academy, 1953.

Zupez, J. "Salvation in the Epistle to the Hebrews." TBT 37 (1968) 2590–95.

Study and Discussion Questions for Each Chapter:

Chapter One

1. What is God like and what does He do?
2. What is the Son like and what does he do or say?
3. Are there in 1.7 two kinds of angels represented by winds and fire, as for instance creating and destroying? Gen 1.1-2
4. Is'My Son…your father' a formula of adoption so that the believer is adopted based on the sons? Or is this repeating on Jesus the words said to David about Solomon, the only other place in Hebrew Scriptures where these words are used of any individual?
5. Does 1.6 allude to the heavenly choir on the occasion of the birth of the Son?
6. Why is the Son so called but in v.8 is called 'O God'? Are these two Gods or simply recognition of divinity?
7. Who are the companions of 1.9?
8. Was there any other servant of God filled with joy 1.9
9. Why doesn't 1.10-12 mention a new heaven and new earth?
10. Is 1.13 saying the Father' consummates complete victory in history for the Son?
11. In 1.14 is it implied that every believer has an angel as ministering spirit?

Chapter Two

1. The Scriptures used in ch.1 were known and the Messianic interpretation also known. Do these texts give reason for endeavoring not to drift away? What is implied in 'drifting away'?
2. Where do angels appear in the Sinai narrative?
3. In what sense was every sin in the BCE era? How is this statement true?
4. What is there to escape from if we ignore such a great salvation?
5. Does 2.3 tell us whether this message is for Christians, inquirers, Jews, or anyone who has heard the message, or any of the above?
6. From 2.4 what are the evidences of Christianity?

7. In 2.6 does 'testify' and the use of 'some one' 'there is a place' detract from the authority of the quotation?
8. In 2.3: In what sense was 'this salvation' never announced before Christ's coming?
9. Gen 1 limits man's ruling to the Zoological realm of animals and ch.2 extends his rule to naming and classifications and seeking solutions that lack the object of the solution. But here man is given authority to rule and manage over everything that is and an unspecified realm of the future 'everything'. Does this imply a change from the original mandate or a different reading of it?
10. in 2.6 is mentioned God's care for man but v.8 man's complete authority. What kind of 'care' is this?
11. How does 2.9 differ from Phil.2's statement of the same sequence of ideas?
12. Was 'glory and honor' because he suffered death? Is this a martyr's model or encouragement 2.9
13. How can what is perfect be made 'perfect.'?
14. 2.17 'that he might make atonement' seems to point to the future as some cults maintain, but is there a distinction between atonement on the cross and atonement in the heavenly temple?

Chapter Three

1. In Greek-Roman society honor is very important and respect for those in position are part of the value system. How does this fit the viee all men are sinners/
2. In 3.6 is there a shift of 'house' from family or society to kingdom or clan?
3. How in 3.6 are courage and hope related to faith?
4. 3.10 speaks of a particular generation, not all men, whose hearts are always going astray. What factors entered in to this proneness to wander for that generation?
5. According to 3.16 all those led out of Egypt rebelled and died but Numbers shows the women and immature did survive. Was this mercy and thus a denial of the use of collective guilt?
6. The 3.12 interactiveness of people can either further hardening through deceit or the encouraging of one another can establish people in the faith. Does this mean both groups must be actively doing in order to fight evil men?

7. Has in 3.13 the daily small group meeting and encouraging one another now substituted for the morning or evening sacrifices? Or is there more evidence to link it to the love feasts.?
8. Can you relate 3.18-19 together in terms of God and man, or cause-effect, or the lack of faith is cause and the judgment on them is effect?

Chapter Four

1. What are the implications of 'none of you' for the use of 'we' in the book Cf. . 4.1? Is the only collective 'Israel' and al else is individuals?
2. What Gospel in v.2 had elements in common for people of both covenants?
3. Suggest why different tenses are used for v.3 'We..enter that rest', 'never enter that rest,' v.6 'some will enter that rest' 'if Joshua had given them rest' and v.11 'make every effort to enter that rest'
4. What is implied in 'God rested from his own work' on the seventh day?
5. Do 4.12-13 have any function of the word of God to reveal God or are its functions only to reveal our own spiritual condition.?
6. Is there an antithesis between the use of 'seventh day' and 'today.'?
7. How did Jesus experience all the kinds of tests and temptations and yet without sin? This cannot be because God cannot be tempted by evil.
8. Does v.16, in referring to 'with confidence' and in contrast to 'without sin,' imply that the mercy and grace in time of need or temptation may imply sin?

Chapter Five

1. Does 5.1 'priest is selected' imply the human process in choosing a descendent of Aaron to become priest, perhaps an interactive God and man coordination?
2. To what extent is weakness necessary 5.2 in order to be people related to the ignorant and those going astray? As interpreter and applier of the law how can he be gentle against lawlessness?
3. What is the role of the equivalence today of the priest offering for his own sins, in order to be gentle to the ignorant and those going astray?
4. In 5.4 is the author assuming that after the time of Aaron the priests all had a sense of God's call before assuming office?
5. How did Amos' testimony to the king correspond to 5.5 in denying any family connection to the calling of prophet?
6. Must 5.7 only relate to the prayer in the Garden of Gethsemane?

7. If in 5.7 God heard Jesus' prayer, at the same time he submitted to God, yet he still died on the cross, what was the essence of the prayer?
8. In 5.9 what is the range of meanings possible to 'being made perfect'?
9. Soteriology usually stresses confession, repentance, faith etc. What has happened through the resurrection and glorification whereby obedience to Jesus is now the only avenue of salvation?
10. In 5.8 relate 'Son' to 'learning obedience' and to 'suffering.' Why should Jesus need to learn obedience which doesn't seem at all related to his atoning sacrifice?
11. Does 5.10 suggest that chronologically Jesus was appointed high priest subsequent to his glorification.?
12. Does 5.11 separate Jesus Savior function and his priestly function as seen in the connective 'and'?
13. Are there other analogies in scripture for praying with a loud voice?
14. How do the 'elementary teachings' in 6.1-3 relate to 5.12? The crux is that infants need milk and mature need meat so as 'to distinguish good from evil.' How do the elementary teaching provide or not provide a foundation for this skill?

Chapter Six

1. Except for changing educational subject material is there any other way apart from apostasy to leave the elementary teachings? 6.1-3
2. In 6.6 the impossibility is expressed for those who have already received all these graces? What is impossible?
3. In 6.6 the problem is disgrace to the Son of God, but Jesus said that only sin against the Holy Spirit was unforgiveable. What is the key idea in this verse? Is it a logical conclusion to the act or is it a theological personal identitification with the Son that creates the taboo?
4. in 6.8 if the land needs plowing and weeding or anything else why simply burn the land/
5. Does 6.10 indicate that God's knowing a person's good works counts, but counts for what?
6. In 6.16 how exactly did Abraham received what was promised.?
7. In 6.18 If God cannot lie, why emphasize promise and oath? Can the promise-plan be altered if there is no oath? Or is the oath merely for our encouragement? Or is it to show that the Law can be altered but not this particular promise?

8. Gen 12 is the general promise. In 15.4 the heir would come from Abraham's body, which could apply to Ishmael. But the general promise of 17.1 but in 17.16 the son must be through Sarah. Does this narrowing of the promise consist of changing the plan? If so, then by contrast, what God promised by oath would not be changeable? Does this relate to the Gentile church in relation to Israel after the flesh?

Chapter Seven

1. Was the offering of the tithe a thank you for receiving the blessing of Merlchisedek?
2. What motivation do you suppose a priest like Merlchisedek would have to bless Abraham in the first place and not the others?
3. In what ways does Gen 14 differ in style, content, profile of Abraham, and detail from all the other chapters referring to Abraham in Genesis?
4. In 7.6 the 'blessed him' may be because he knew that Abraham had received promises. What would indicate that this might be so?
5. Could the tithe be for services rendered to Merlchisedek who blessed him? If so it is a type of thanksgiving offering.
6. In 7.12 what is the validity and position of law and its resultant institution in view of the fact it can be changed? God cannot lie. God only speaks the truth and real; the major plan cannot change and God cannot lie what status does the law have to allow changes in it?
7. The basis for Jesus and Merlchisedek's priesthood 'in the power of an indestructible life..' What made Merlchisedek's life indestructible? Was a lack of a death record, a burial site, or his eternal life that allowed this connection.
8. In 7.18 the weakness and uselessness of a set of regulations of the law is declared set aside. Paul said man was weak through the flesh but the law was perfect, but not designed to make men righteous. Does this mean that weak laws such as prohibition or abortion should be set aside because they are weak?
9. In 7.25 'Therefore' in what way connects a permanent priesthood to a complete and eternal salvation? Will Jesus be interceding for his children forever and ever?

Chapter Eight

1. What is the significance of sitting at the right hand of God?
2. What does 8.2 mean that Jesus 'serves' in the sanctuary in heaven?
3. Does 8.2 'was set up' indicate a point of time when the heavenly sanctuary was set up? Is this important?
4. In 8.3 why does it say the high priest does all the offering when any priest could do this?
5. What information is there to see the function of 'gifts' as offerings? 8.4
6. In 8.6 'Better promises' refers to what things?
7. In 8.7-8 'wrong with the first covenant' is // .or in form parallel but in referent not so. One is covenant and one is people. Both the covenant and people have something wrong about them. How is this impass or chasm in infrastructure of the system of society and law plus the people who don't know God or remain faithful to be breached to bring a good covenant and good people?
8. Is 8.7,10 indicating the covenant is only for ethnically and geographically located descendents of Israel and Judah as the physical descendents of Jacob? How is it relevant to the NT believer?
9. In 8.10 what kind of inner transformation is prerequisite to being God's people and He being their God.
10. Has v.11 been fulfilled as yet?

Chapter Nine

1. Besides criminal law and covenant law what two aspects of the covenant are mentioned here? How are these integral to the covenant?
2. How does the golden altar of incense inside the second curtain relate to the ark of the covenant contrary to the record in the Torah? There it was in front of the second curtain.
3. Based on the three object in the ark what kind of function did the ark eventually attain?
4. Some pictures of the ark show the cherubim of the Glory as of one piece with the atonement cover. Here they are separated. Is this theologically or historically significant?
5. 9.6-10 record the offering of blood only in the Most Holy Place, no sacrifice of flesh. How does the offering of blood for sins differ from the offering of the carcass of an animal or its innards?

6. 9.9 Gifts and offering were not able to clear the conscience of the worshipper. So what did allow the worshipper to sense God's presence, approval, forgiveness and leave the sanctuary in peace as seen in the Psalms?
7. When and how did the offering of the heifer occur in the OT? How did it differ from other offcerings?
8. In 9.15 Christ is a ransom to set men free. To whom is the ransom paid? This was a conflict in theology for some time in church history. In this verse is the analogy of slavery governing the meaning?
9. In 9.15 does 'eternal inheritance' as the goal of the New Covenant point out that the Old Covenant had no connection to eternal life but simply long life?
10. In 9.16ff the one making the Will is Jesus and so he must die for the will to be in effect. The first covenant also requires a death. But then the topic switches to cleansing. The use of blood in .v20 is connected to covenant but not the death of a testator. Could the death of the Firstborn or of the Exodus generation, or Moses be the Testator in the OT?
11. 9.22 If blood is for forgiveness what of the non-blood offerings in the OT?
12. 9.27 ignores the Second Death found in Revelations. Presumably this is because in God's plan one death and judgment not many were the plan. Is there room in this for incarnation to a new life on earth?

Chapter Ten

1. Heavenly thing are the 'real' or 'true' while the Law is only a shadow of good things to come. It is thus transitory, representative, referrentive and inadequate to communicate completely God's will. Does this mean the Law scriptures only partially communicate God's will and continuously effect reconciliation?
2. Does this mean 10,2 that worshippers in the act of drawing near to God are made perfect for that moment but because of later sinning must yearly repeat the ritual?
3. 10.3 Does guilt function positively as an incentive to draw near to God for renewal? What of the NT believer?
4. 10.4 Does this teach that sacrifice is only a reminder of sin and on a yearly basis? Is this referring to the Day of Atonement?
5. 10.5 Does this 'body' refer in context to Jesus' body or Mary's? Does the former suggest pre-existence while the latter suggest incarnation?
6. In 10.7 does 'Will' of God form another contrast to 'Law'?

7. 10.8 How can 'the Law required them' and at the same time God was not pleased with them?
8. 10.9 Is the free offering of himself 'I come to do your will O God' the chief way that this offering differed from the burnt offering and the others that were offered by others and not voluntarily.?
9. 10.10 In what sense does the sacrifice of Christ make believers holy once for all? Or does it mean that through the once for all offering 'we have been made holy.'? Is this the same as 'perfect' in v.14?
10. Does 10.15-17 add anything to 8.8-12?
11. What is the chief significance of water baptism in 10.22? How does the internal aspect dominate over the external aspect?
12. In 10.24-25 what is the importance of assembling together to worship?
13. In 10.26ff How does this 'deliberately sinning' differ from the corresponding willful sin in the OT Law? Are the consequences the same?
14. In 10.32 what descriptions of these believers indicate they are not really new believers?
15. Does the theme of perseverance' in10.36ff provide a leading means to understand ch.11 as faith which perseveres and endures?
16. How does the antithesis of 'live by faith' with 'shrinks back' define faith? How are 'my righteous one' and 'I will not be pleased with him' relate to each other?

Chapter Eleven

1. In what sense is faith both objective and subjective? 11.1
2. From 11.2 describe how faith is a creative force?
3. How are 'a righteous man' and 'spoke well of his offerings' related as two factors in being accepted by God. How does faith enter into this?
4. 'Commended as one that pleases God' 11.5 is the same as justification by faith. How does faith relating to being taken out of this life relate to this?
5. Based on 11.6 could you say that faith in God is enough to please God? Today?
6. How did Noah's fear move positively into he becoming a preacher of righteousness?
7. What was the initial way Abraham's faith manifested itself?
8. Does this chapter require that receiving what was promised is a necessary proof that faith existed before death?
9. In which cases is hope intertwined with the subject of faith?

10. Based on v.19 could we say that in many cases reasoning is a necessary component of faith?
11. Faith enabled Moses' parents to 'see' and to 'to not fear' but what else?
12. What is implicit in 11.27 about Moses faith up through the time of his flight? Why?
13. In 11.40 perfect is not so far as perfect or cleansed conscience, so what is perfect in this context?

Chapter Twelve

1. Hindrances and sins are linked together as entangling forces in the believer's life. 'Turning from' and 'turning to' are a process or only a decision here?
2. 12.2 How is a believer to deal with public shame before believers and non-believers alike? Can this be done apart from Christ's example and the power cof grace?
3. Why, contrary to ch.11 where OT saints looked for a city or country is the NT believer to look on Jesus being aware of the multitude of witnesses 'surrounding' us?
4. What verbs or words express the idea that faith is a continuing struggle and challenge?
5. How can punishment and discipline be distinguished if they are from the Lord?
6. For the depressed person how does 12.12ff teach one to once more be strong?
7. How did Esau's 'bitter root' plant itself, grow, become mature and almost destroy him?
8. What are elements of heaven in the picture portrayed in this chapter.?

Chapter Thirteen

1. What elements of difference are in this chapter compared with the rest of the book?
2. What stories form the background for 'strangers' possibly being angels in actuality?
3. Does 13.4 allude to making love during one's period or some other forbidden practice such as Onanism, along with Adultery and other immoral acts?
4. How does v.8 relate to the preceding context?

5. Is the grace for strengthening derived from God's presence, and the teaching of the Word through various leaders and their life example?
6. Why did Jesus suffer outside the gate and die there identifying himself with the body of the sin offering burned outside of the camp?
7. In what ways does this chapter, in brief, reinstate 'sacrifices' in a spiritual way?
8. God is giving grace for two important aspects of the needs of believers. From 12.20-21 explain how these two aspects complement all that a believer needs.

Endnotes

1 Baker Encyclpedia of the Bible CD-ROM. 1988

2 Aileen Guilding, JTS n.s.3(1952),53. See also W. Manson, The Epistle to the Hebrews, 1951.

3 Girdwood, J., & Verkruyse, P. 1997. *Hebrews*. The College Press NIV commentary . College Press: Joplin, Mo.

4 Girdwood, J., & Verkruyse, P. 1997. *Hebrews*. The College Press NIV commentary . College Press: Joplin, Mo.

7 See Andrew Trotter, *Interpreting the Epistle to the Hebrews* (Grand Rapids: Baker), pp. 187–196.

5 Girdwood, J., & Verkruyse, P. 1997. *Hebrews*. The College Press NIV commentary . College Press: Joplin, Mo.

6 Elwell, W. A., & Beitzel, B. J.. *Baker encyclopedia of the Bible*. Map on lining papers. Baker Book House: Grand Rapids, Mich. 1988

7 F.F. Bruce, "Hebrews," Peake's Commentary on the Bible. Ed. M.Black and H.H.Rowley. (Ontario: Nelson, 1962, 1977), 1008-1019

8 Harnack, 'Probabilia uber die Adresse und den Verfasser des Hebraerbriefs,' ZNW 11 (1900),16-41

9 James Trimm, Semitic Light on Hebrews, www.nazarene.net/frhebrews.htm., 1997.

10 Trimm, 1997. "For a number of reasons this author is persuaded that Paul was the author of Hebrews. The Church Fathers; Clement of Alexandria (150-212 C.E.) and Eusebius (315 C.E.) maintain Pauline authorship of the book (see quotations below under Language). In addition, the most ancient New Testament manuscripts place Hebrews with the Pauline Epistles, as does the Peshitta Aramaic New Testament. From 2Peter 3:15 it appears that Paul had written a letter to the Hebrews (compare 2Pt. 1:1 and James 1:1). Pauline authorship is supported by the fact that the author was in bonds (10:34) in Italy (13:24) and Timothy was one of his companions (13:23). Further support for Pauline authorship may be found in the fact that Heb. 6:1-2 gives an outline for the whole of the General Pauline Epistles (see note to 6:1-2). The author treats the subject of inheritance in detail, Paul had been commissioned to teach on the topic of inheritance (Acts 26:12-18) and only in the Pauline epistles is the concept of inheritance dealt with in such detail. Finally, the authors' expert

use of the Seven Rules of Hillel and complex forms of Homiletic Midrashic Exegesis point to Paul (Saul), who had been a student of Gamliel (Acts 22:3) the grandson of Hillel."

11 Elwell, W. A., & Beitzel, B. J. *Baker encyclopedia of the Bible.* Map on lining papers. Baker Book House: Grand Rapids, Mich., 1988.

12 Bruce, Peake,1008.

13 Bruce, Peake, 1009.

14 Elwell, W. A., & Beitzel, B. J.. *Baker Encyclopedia of the Bible.* Map on lining papers. Baker Book House: Grand Rapids, Mich, 1988

15 Transcription protocols are as follows; 1. w =omega; 2. e= episolon 3. e= eita; 3. h= chet; 4. '=ayin 5.'= alef; for chet use ch; for tsade use tz; for samekh or sin use s; for tet or tau use t; for bet use v or b. for qof or kaf use k; theta is th; xi =x; u=y; for X use ch; psi uses ps; Most of these are based on Plaut q.v.

16 The arguments that 'Angel of Yahwe' is the Son in the OT are sound and variously based on the Gospels and 1 Corinthians. But the writer of Hebrews is focusing on the Son and intentionally using hyperbole to stress this point. By contrast it was men versus the historical God-man in reveling truth.

17 Ex. 15:20 Then Miriam the prophetess, Aaron's sister, took a tambourine in her hand, and all the women followed her, with tambourines and dancing. Judg. 4:4 ;2Kings 22:14 2Chr. 34:22 Neh. 6:14 Is. 8: Luke 2:36 Rev. 2:20 2Sam. 14:2 So Joab sent someone to Tekoa and had a wise woman brought from there. He said to her, "Pretend you are in mourning. Dress in mourning clothes, and don't use any cosmetic lotions. Act like a woman who has spent many days grieving for the dead. 2Sam. 20:16 a wise woman called from the city Prov. 14:1 The wise woman builds her house

18 Heb.1:1; 1.6;1/8;1/9;2/4;2.9;2.13;2.17;3.4;3.12;4.4;4.9;4.10;4.12;4 14;5.1;5.4 ;5.12;6.1;6.3; 6.6; 6.7; 6.109; 6.13; 6.17; 6.18; 7.1; 7.3; 7.19; 7.25; 8.10; 9.14; 9..20; 9.24; 10.7; 10.12; 10.12; 10.21; 10.29; 10.31; 10.36; 11.3; 11.4; 11.5; 11.6; 11.10; 11.16; 11.19; 11.25; 11.40; 12.2; 12.7; 12.15; 12.22; 12.23; 12.28; 12.29; 13.4; 13.7; 13.16; 13.20;

19 CE=Common Era; BCE 'Before Common Era. These Jewish labels avoid mentioning the Lord.

20 Mt 12.27,28,Dana-Mantey, 106

21 H.E. Dana, Julius R. Mantey, A Manual of the Greek New Testament[NY: Macmillan,1957].loc.cit.

22 George Wesley Buchanan, To the Hebrews [NY:Doubleday,1972],3 [=Buchanan].

23 Buchanan,3 stresses the beautiful alliteration of the Greek, which would not be possible fully in Hebrew where canon of writing poetry were two worlds and

languages apart. Thus polymerws, polytropws, palai, patrasin, prophetais all begin with 'p'.

24 A 'Period' as in Lk 1.1-4,is, by definition "the organization of a considerable number of clauses and phrases into a well-rounded entity." Here is a two-member period with appended 2b, 3, a period with four clauses, an appended two-member period.Other occurrences are Acts 15.24-6 BDF,§464

25 Joseph A.Fitzmyer,Essays on The Semitic Background of the New Testament [Atlanta: Scholars, 1974]loc.cit.

26 Buchanan,4

27 ep' eschatou twn hmerwn : epi with the genitive. BDF,234[8]

28 Called Hebraizing, BDF,§234[8], ep' escatou twn hemerwn in the use of epi and genitive. BDF classify this as 'contemporaneity' in classical use Mk 2.26;

29 note Delling,TDNT 6.305 and 1QpHab 7.2.

30 Boyarin, USQR 47[1993]47-80

31 Dunn, 144n83

32 Dunn,240n22

33 Dana-Mantey,102,

34 Spicq.loc.cit.

35 F.F. Bruce, Peake's Commentary....1009

36 Ps 77.10; Matt 26.64; Mk 14.62; 16.19;Lk 22.69; Acts 233; 7.55; 7.56; Rom 8.34; Col 3.1; Heb 1.3; 8.1; 1012; 122; Rev 5.1; 5.7

37 Rev. 5:1 Then I saw in the right hand of him who sat on the throne a scroll with writing on both sides and sealed with seven seals. Rev. 5:7 He came and took the scroll from the right hand of him who sat on the throne. These refer largely to accession to the throne. The terminology of sitting at the right of one on a throne is confined to the following verses: Heb. 8:1 The point of what we are saying is this: We do have such a high priest, who sat down at the right hand of the throne of the Majesty in heaven, Heb. 12:2; . Rev. 3:21;. Rev. 5:1;. 5:7

38 Psa. 89:42 You have exalted the right hand of his foes; you have made all his enemies rejoice. Psa. 109:31 For he stands at the right hand of the needy one, to save his life from those who condemn him. _

39 Spicq,I,371n50.

40 J.Kürzinger,BZ 1958,294-299. A. R. .Leaney," Conformed to the Image of His Son," NTS 10[1964]470-479.

41 A.V.McCasland, "The Image of God according to Paul," JBL 1950, 87.Spicq,418n27

42 Holladay, Lexicon,77 "weight, power, splendour, height, majesty, posessed by: 1. Nature: thunder, snorting horse; olive trees; God: Ps 8.3; 3. Men: the king Ps 21.6; Messiah Zc 9.1`3; Moses Nu 27.20; complexion Dn 10.8 and metaph

use ‘bloom in Pr 5.9. Apparently this is natural and not conferred. Glory in doxa could have too much connection with dokew ‘to seem, appear’ hence phenomena, appearances, stressing the externals as viewed and appreciated by men.

43 It is used for the majesty of cedars Zech 11.13; of a city Jer 33.9; En 98.2; of a king Theod. Dan 4.19,33; 5.18-19; 1 Macc 9.22; of the ‘great thing’ accomplished by God 2 Sam 7.21,23; 1 Ch 17.19.In the meaning of majesty it appears in Ps 145.3 En 5.4 ‘You offend his majesty.’ Wis 18.24 ‘your majesty was on the diadem of his [Aaron’s] head.’ T.Levi 3.9 ‘the face of his majesty’ 18.8.

44 Spicq,460n20 Ep.Arist,192 “God does not smite those whom he does not hear according to their sins or according to the greatness of his might; mildness epieikeia is God’s demeanor.”

45 Spicq,2.459; 2 Pet 1.17

46 Xenophon Ap.32 “Socrates, praising himself before the tribunal”; Plutarch Lyc.14.6 “exalted by their praises” Lys 7.5 “exalting justice when it profited him to do so.” Thucydides 8.81.2 “Alcibiades, exaggerating his influence over Tissaphernes” An epigram of 200 BC “Do not glory in your ships alone.” Clearly in a biblical sense and even from the wording the writers considered this kind of praise to be too extravagant and inappropriate, and biblically bordering on idolatry.

47 Spicq,2.460n21;

48 Beginning here in 1:5 and continuing through 1:13, the writer strings together seven quotations from the Old Testament: (1) Psalm 2:7, (2) 2 Samuel 7:14, (3) Deuteronomy 32:43 (v. 6), (4) Psalm 104:4 (v. 7), (5) Psalm 45:6–7 (vv. 8–9), (6) Psalm 102:25–27 (vv. 10–12), (7) Psalm 110:1 (v. 13). All but two are found in the Greek Psalter, the hymnbook of the synagogue and early church.”[49] Bruce, Life Application Bible. loc.cit.

50 Dunn,246n60

51 13.3. Myers,[52] 38. 1.3,Similar to Wis 7.25-26; Cf. . Philo Plant.50; Dreams 1.72; Spec Laws 4.123.

53 Spicq, 1.371n50,371n51, 374n68;

54 Winston, 69,187,299

55 Oswald Chambers, My Utmost for His Highest, NIV edition. (New Jersey: Barbour and Company,Inc.,1935,1963.is the husk of the personal life. Individuality is all elbows, it separates and isolates. It is the characteristic of the child and rightly so; but if we mistake individuality for the personal life, we will remain isolated. The shell of individuality is God’s created natural covering for the protection of the personal life; but individuality must go in order that the personal life may come out and be brought into fellowship with God.

Individuality counterfeits personality as lust counterfeits love. God designed human nature for himself; individuality debases human nature for itself. The characteristics of individuality are independence and self assertiveness. It is the continual assertion of individuality that hinders our spiritual life more than anything else. If you say 'I cannot believe,' it is because individuality is in the road; individuality never can believe. Personality cannot help believing. Watch yourself when the Spirit of God is at work, He pushes you to the margins of your individuality, and you have either to say—I shan't' or to surrender, to break the husk of individuality and let the personal life emerge. The Holy Spirit narrows it down every time to one thing Matt 16.23-24/ the thing in you that will not be reconciled to your brother is your individuality. God wants to bring you into union with Himself, but unless you are willing to give your right to yourself. He cannot. 'he must deny himself'—deny his independent right to himself, then real life has a chance to grow.'

56 Joseph A.Fitzmyer,Essays on The Semitic Background of the New Testament [Atlanta: Scholars, 1974]l125..

57 Joseph A.Fitzmyer,Essays on The Semitic Background of the New Testament [Atlanta: Scholars, 1974]loc.cit.

58 Soncino Zohar, Bereshith, Section 1, Page 6a

59 Dana-Mantey,90,108,273, 276

60 W.Bousset, Kyrios Christos [Göttingen: Vandenhoeck & Ruprecht,1913] trans J.E.Steedyt[NT:Abingdon,1970. His theory is that "The uttering of the name is probably only a weakened sacramental form for the more original, more robust custom of branding or etching upon the person being initiated the sign [name, symbol] of the appropriate god, to whom he was consecrated." He uses Gal 6.17 in interpreting the stigmata of Paul. E.D.W.Burton, ICC Galatians, 1921,361 "refers to the practice of branding slaves, and sees this as the metaphor by which Paul, as a slave of Jesus, is marked by the scars of his suffering."

61 G.H.Parke-Taylor, Yahweh: The Divine Name in the Bible[Waterloo,Ont.: Wilfrid Laurier Univ Press,1975]loc.cit.

62 J.Barton Payne, Encyclopedia of Biblical Prophecy[NY:Harper and Row, 1973] lo.cit.

63 Joseph A.Fitzmyer, Essays on The Semitic Background of the New Testament [Atlanta: Scholars, 1974]loc.cit.

64 Elements belonging together are here separated for emphasis, namely -agg. And onoma. On links this to the following clause. V.5 does the same thing. BDF,§473[2]

65 J.M. Allegro, "Further Messianic references in Qumran Literature," JBL 75[1956],174f. "The holy and sure blessings of David" were fulfilled in Christ according to Acts 13.34.

66 J.Masseyngberde Ford Revelation. The Anchor Bible[NY:Doubleday,1975],loc. cit.

67 Jacob M.Myers, I and II Esdras[NY: Doubleday, 1974]loc.cit.

68 Barnabas Lindars, "The New look on the Son of Man." BJRL 63.2()1981),437-62.

69 Raymond E. Brown, the Birth of the Messiah. (NY: Doubleday, 1979).

70 J.Barton Payne, Encyclopedia of Biblical Prophecy[NY:Harper and Row, 1973] lo.cit.

71 Joseph A.Fitzmyer,Essays on The Semitic Background of the New Testament [Atlanta: Scholars, 1974]loc.cit.

72 130 times in the LXX, usually literal, of firstfruits of human or animal mother's womb. The religious connotation is that the firstborn is always dedicated to God. The qualitative connotation is that 'it is the firstborn of the father's vigor.' Gen 49.3; Num 1.20; Ps 78.51. It is the best or most excellent. Ezk 44.30; Philo. Prelim,Stud.98. It is best-loved. It has an honorific connotation, with birthright, and hence sharing the father's authority and property. 2 Kgs 3.27; 1 Chr 5.1-2; 2 Ch 21.3. Ps 89.28. "Israel is my firstborn' Ex 4.22 expresses this honor. Luke 2.7 'she gave birth to her firstborn.' The firstborn could claim messiahship. As a title it could be given to later offspring, but in Jesus' case it was given immediately on birth. Ex 13.2; 34.19. It can only be a child, as seen in the inscriptions. "At Leontopolis in Lower Egypt, the epitaph of a Jewish woman of Arsinoe in 5 BC mentions that she died bringing her firstborn into the world;'Fate, through my labor pains with my firstborn child, brought me to the end of my life.'"

73 Philip Segal, "Further Reflections on the 'Begotten' Messiah," Hebrew Annual Review 7(1983)221ff. Contrariwise: Joseph Klausner, Messianic Idea in Israel. London, 1956..Brown, The Birth of the Messiah (Garden City, NY:Doubleday, 1977).

74 Delbert R.Hillers, "Delocutive Verbs in Biblical Hebrew," JBL 86(1967)320-325. Notes that many times verbs 'justified', 'clean'. 'unclean' are not declarative piels but consist of the word itself that constitutes the fact. 'to call a person x' as in 'happy,' pure', perverse' etc., is an illocutionary act that consists in the speech act, the factual content, the reality of the new situation so constituted. The same delocutive as in 'hail' or 'welcome' So it is not 'to make a person just' or 'show a person x' or 'behave justly' but to say a person is in the right..'

75 Note: E.N. Gardiner, Olympia: Its History and Remains[Oxford,1925]; Gardiner, Athletics of the Ancient World[Oxford, 1930]. M.P.Nilsson, "Festivals," Oxford Classical Dictionary,p.435. Herodotus,2.59f; Strabo 5.2.9; 5.3.5; Isocrates, Paneg. 43;"It is right to praise those who established the panhgureis because, thanks the practice they left behind after libations and the abolishing of existing hatreds, we come together and then, pooling our prayers and sacrifices, we recall how we are related to each other.' Note there were liturgical ceremonies of procession, songs, sacred rites. ET History of Greek religion. For the OT see Josephus War, 5.230; Amos 5.21 qusias en tais panhguresin Herod 2.62; Strabo 10.5.2; 14.1.20; Pausanias 10.32.14-16; Philo,Moses 2.159: "Many sacrifices were of necessity celebrated each day, and especially in the panhgureis and festivals, either of private individuals or publicly on behalf of all." Decalogue 78; Spec. Laws 3.183; Nicolas of Damascus,frag.62 ed. C.Müller vol.3,p.396; Note that in the 6-7th centuries Menos wrote to Theodorus urging him to guard hid health so as to celebrate the panegyris feast of Holy Epiphany for many long years. P.Oxy.1857,5. Philo understood the spirituality of Judaism: "Work to be crowned...with a noble and glorious crown that no panegyric among humankind offers." Alleg.Interp.2.108. Cf. Dio Cassius 53.1; Manetho 4.74.

76 labor [C.Or.Ptol. 53,49=P.Tebt.5; P.Cair.Zen. 59604,5,

77 Spicq,2.382n16

78 pros meaning 'with reference to, pertaining to' Dana-Mantey,110

79 J.Masseyngberde Ford Revelation. The Anchor Bible[NY:Doubleday,1975],loc. cit.

80 It would be easy to find an earthly kingdom in Ps 2, which grew out of an accession ceremony. But in Ps 66.2-3 God's deeds are not through Israel's armies, but through his 'in-process' and 'intervention' miracles, especially in the fears of the enemy 66.3.The illustration in 66.6 is from the Exodus at the Sea, but v.7 "He rules forever by his power, his eyes watch the nations; let not the rebellious rise up against him." Clearly has little to do with the nation of Israel, even though v.13-15 show the temple and sacrifices are still on-going. Note that Ps 93 is synchronic in speaking of the normalities of tides and waves, but diachronic in that past statutes are always valid v.5. 93.5 is more than an earthly temple since the prophets always proclaimed the uncleanness of that place, and its temporality. 'For endless days' proclaims a holy perfect house and law that never changes. Note also that 93.1-2 link God's rule and majesty not to Jerusalem or Zion, but to the world and eternity. When Jesus said "my kingdom is not of this world" the crux is the genitive, either of 1. From this worldly system's authorization 2. Belonging to the world of men; 3. Not made up

of this world's people; 4. Not belonging to the kosmos sphere. Descriptive use is impossible although partitive 'not part of this larger whole' would be feasible.

81 J.Barton Payne, Encyclopedia of Biblical Prophecy[NY:Harper and Row, 1973] lo.cit.

82 Joseph A.Fitzmyer,Essays on The Semitic Background of the New Testament [Atlanta: Scholars, 1974]loc.cit.

83 Craig A.Evans," Obduracy and the Lord's Servant," Early Jewish and Christian Exegesis. Studies in Memory of William H. Brownlee. [Atlanta: Scholars Press, 1987]235

84 Ex. 25:6 olive oil for the light; spices for the anointing oil and for the fragrant incense; Ex. 29:7 Ex. 29:21 Ex. 30:25 Ex. 30:31 Ex. 31:11 Ex 35:8 Ex. 35:15 Ex. 35:28 . Ex. 37:29 Ex. 39:38 Ex. 40:9 . Ex. 40:15 Lev. 8:2 Lev. 8:10 Lev. 8:11 Lev. 8:12 Lev. 8:30 Lev. 10:7 Lev. 21:10 Lev. 21:12 Num. 4:16 1Chr. 29:22 Psa. 45:7 Heb. 1:9 1John 2:20 1John 2:27

85 Spicq,2.478n3

86 para with accusative:to the side of, beside, along, beyond. Dana-Mantey,108; Spicq,1.331n51

87 David J.A.Clines, The Dictionary of Classical Hebrew, III [Sheffield: Sheffield Academic Press, 1996] 155 under cheber I, 'company, association, council, community, gang, guild, while company, community all are collective singulars. This is obvious since ben- must be used to indicate the individual. Would this come into Greek as a plural, though? Cf. Hos 6.9; Neh 3.8; Pr 21.9; 25.24 and fem in Jer 13.23. Clines Bibliographical notes do give J.Neusner I 'join' and companion but based on TDOT,ZIV,193-97. Or rb,j, in the collective sense. See p.387.

88 Joseph A.Fitzmyer,Essays on The Semitic Background of the New Testament [Atlanta: Scholars, 1974]loc.cit. Cf. Pirqe Aboth 2.5; Oxy P 1.15

89 Joseph A.Fitzmyer, Essays on The Semitic Background of the New Testament [Atlanta: Scholars, 1974]loc.cit.

90 Joachim Jeremias, The Parables of Jesus [NY: Scribners, 1963] rev.ed. loc.cit.

91 dia in perfective sense: 'you remain endlessly'; 'but you abide through' Dana-Mantey,101

92 12.27 Fulfilled per 17; Ps #47 Payne,[93]573

94 J.Masseyngberde Ford, Revelation. The Anchor Bible[NY:Doubleday.1975],loc. cit.

95 Matt. 5:35 or by the earth, for it is his footstool; or by Jerusalem, for it is the city of the Great King. The word pair is with 'Jerusalem' as a part to the whole. This is not prospective but described as actual. Luke 20:43 until I make your enemies a footstool for your feet." This is again the same as Hebrews and forms part of

NT and OT Eschatology. The one addressed in the OT is not only the current king but the Messiah's eventual triumph. Paul declares the last enemy is Death [1 Cor. 15] Acts 2:35 until I make your enemies a footstool for your feet."' Acts 7:49 "'Heaven is my throne, and the earth is my footstool. What kind of house will you build for me? says the Lord. Or where will my resting place be?

96 Joseph A.Fitzmyer, Essays on The Semitic Background of the New Testament [Atlanta: Scholars, 1974]loc.cit.

97 J.Barton Payne, Encyclopedia of Biblical Prophecy[NY:Harper and Row, 1973] lo.cit.

98 Joseph A.Fitzmyer, Essays on The Semitic Background of the New Testament [Atlanta: Scholars, 1974]loc.cit.

99 Henry George Liddell and Robert Scott, A Greek-English Lexicon [Oxford: Clarendon Press,1977] 398.[L-S]

100 [Herodotus 4.154;Plato,Plt.290a;

101 Spicq,3.7; Cf. on swzw see Spicq 3.350n32

102 Gareth Lee Cockerill, 'Heb 1.1-14; 1 Clem 36.1-6 and the High Priest Title,' JBL 97/3(1978)437-440

103 L-S 1512 show the meaning is determined by the phrase-level noun. If 'ship' it means to bring to port, land'; if 'mind' nous then to turn towards a thing, be intent on, turn one's mind to'; 'to give heed to' . Without noun 'to be on your guard' 'to attend to' 'to devote oneself to'[Herod.9.33] 'continue' and 'to take orders from' Polybius 6.37,7.

104 BDF 60[3]

105 A.Barnes, "Hebrews," Notes on the Bible vol.16. The Ages Digital Library Commentary 1.0 2000.

106 Jay Snell, http://jaysnell.org/Book1Htm/chapter_one.htm.

107 William F.Arndt and F.Wilbur Gingrich,A Greek-English Lexicon of the New Testament [Chicago: University of Chicago Press,1979]138.

108 The sequence of events is not clear. If Hezekiah earlier had sought alliances with Babylonia or Egypt and these were rebuffed, it may be that his sickness was recompense. Following mercy he became strong to face the 701 B.C. challenge. But another 'recompense' can be inferred in the life and acts of Manasseh, possibly formed under the 15 year period of grace that Hezekiah was given. The time was needed for Manasseh was still a child at the time. But the less-than-manly and aggressive father, Hezekiah, may have set a pattern for submission and non-involvement rather than what might have been perceived as a dangerous policy of insecurity.

109 3rd cent. AD: Sotas writes "Believe it, it is sure, because it can be seen.' Philo, Sacr.Abel and Cain 93: "the simple words of God, in their certitude, differ not

at all from oaths...it is because of God that an oath itself is sure." orkos bebaios. For other illustrations see Spicq,I,280.

110 but also Jub.1.29-2.1; Philo,Som.1.143; Apoc. Mos; Jos.Ant.15.136; JBL 99[1980]549-67. Acts 7.38,53;

111 A-G 247 from Homer on, LXX and papyri. Probably Josephus Ant.2.341, Acts 16.27; Sir 16.13; 1 Th 5.3; Heb 12.25 and Jos.Bell.1.65 are closer to the times of Hebrews. Herod 5.95 'he escapes by flight' is not dealing with God's judgment.

112 A-G 855-56 1. Flee for safety Matt 3.7 fygein is closest to the usage here in fleeing the wrath to come.2. Escape; 3. Avoid, shun morally some evil; 4. Guard against threats and their punishments 5. Vanish, disappear; 5. Flee from the face of the Lord fugein apo proswpou Kurou Ctesias.Pers.2.

113 amelew verb.aor.act.part.masc.pl.nom. 'to neglect' A-G,44 'be unconcerned, disregard, neglect, care nothing about,

114 Heb. 2:2 Heb. 4:2 Heb. 4:12 Heb. 4:13 Heb. 5:11 Heb. 5:13 Heb. 6:1 Heb. 7:28 Heb. 12:19 Heb. 13:7 Heb. 13:17 Heb. 13:22 Heb. 1:14 Heb. 2:3 Heb. 2:10 Heb. 5:9 Heb. 6:9 Heb. 9:28 Heb. 11:7

115 Deut. 22:1 You shall not watch your neighbor's ox or sheep straying away and ignore them; you shall take them back to their owner. Deut. 22:4 You shall not see your neighbor's donkey or ox fallen on the road and ignore it; you shall help to lift it up. Prov. 12:16 Fools show their anger at once, but the prudent ignore an insult. Prov. 15:32 Those who ignore instruction despise themselves, but those who heed admonition gain understanding. 2Pet. 3:5,8

116 There appears leveling of o and w in some ms, as ekfeuxwmeya in P46. BDF,28

117 Spicq,1.87; 88n5; 292; 2.554; 3.350n30

118 Example of vowel quantity leveling in w for o in ekfeuxwmeqa BDF,§28P46, which looks like but is not a future subjunctive.

119 Christopher R.North, The Second Isaiah [Oxford: Clarendon, 1964]loc.cit.

120 Spicq,1.282n4;

121 Jacob M.Myers, I and II Esdras[NY: Doubleday, 1974]loc.cit. Matt 11.4f; Lk 7.22; Ps 96.3; Dan 4.2; Acts 2.22; II Esdras 2.48;

122 : S 1926; BDB 214a; HALOT 1:240a; TDOT 3:335–41; TWOT 477b; NIDOTTE 2077

123 Cf. . H. Donner, ZAW 79 (1967): 331n.57

124 W. J. Gerber, Die hebr. Verba denominativa [1896], 163f.; BLA 273

125 Cf. . BL 552; HAL 230a),

126 Ahw. 207; Cf. . DISO 63

127 G. Widengren, Sakrales Königtum im AT und im Judentum [1955], 103n.22)

128 A. Caquot, Syria 33 [1956]: 37–41; E. Vogt, Bib 41 [1960]: 24; W. H. Schmidt, Königtum Gottes in Ugarit und Israel [19662], 56) over against the translation "revelation, appearance" (F. M. Cross, BASOR 117 [1950]: 19–21; Kraus, Psa, CC, 1:344f.; UT no. 752; P. R. Ackroyd, JTS 17 [1966]: 393–96) H. Donner, ZAW 79 (1967): 331–33

129 (BH 3; HAL 230a;

130 (Cf. . H. Gross, FS Junker 96; H. Wildberger, TZ 21 [1965]: 481f.).

131 (von Rad, Theol. 1:364–67

132 BDF, 103

133 MT elohim is translated aggelos in the LXX and so used in the NT.

134 Dunn,284n.80 para in comparisons 'than';Dana-Mantey,108 3.3. Spicq,1.370n49; 470

135 The aorist infinitive en tw hypotaxai = hypotaxas A preposition with the dative in a sense not purely temporal,Cf. Heb 8.13 en tw legein 'in speaking, in that he says' BDF, 404[3], de used as alla 'but' also in 4.13; 6.12; Here 'however' 447[1]

136 Spicq,3.424n3

137 Spicq,2.480.

138 Dana-Mantey,111,225

139 Spicq,I,371.

140 The use of dia for the originator instead of agent. BDF, 223[2]

141 Spicq,1.324n22; 371; 395; 451n70; 488; 2.384; 3.350; 355

142 Spicq,2.426n12; 480;

143 Spicq,1.394

144 Note that if the last enemy is Death then this is a personification of Satan without giving free press to such a personality within the theological mainstream. While Ugaritic scholars take Mot as a judge of the netherworld or of grain with a role of judge, clearly the root is the same as 'Death.' Ps 23 'valley of the shadow of Mot' would then be situations in which Satanic power is the greatest. The fear is not for death but 'I will fear no evil'. Clearly Mot is not Death only but is Evil in a proper name.

145 BDF, 398,

146 James W Dale, Classic Baptism. (Phillipsburg, NJ: Presbyterian and reformed Publishing Co.,1867, 1989). This was part of four parts that includes Judaic Baptism, Johannic Baptism, and Christian and Patristic Baptism.

[147] Instrumental of cause, the instrumental dative, "because of fear..." Dana-Mantey,90,209,213

[148] "Encyclopedia of Religion, PASSOVER, Vol.11, p.205

[149] Encyclopedia of Religion, ANGELS, Vol.1, p.284

[150] Encyclopedia of Religion, UNDERWORLD, Vol.15, p

[151] Dana-Mantey,261, 263 Spicq,2.494

[152] Patrick Gray, "Brotherly Love and the High Priest Christology of Hebrews,' JBL 122/2(2003) 335-351.

[153] Michael E. Gudorf, 'Through a Classical lens: Hebrews 2.16,' JBL 119/1 (2000)105-108

[154] Spicq, 478n27;

[155] en w 'while, because, here 'wherefore' BDF, 219[2]

[156] Subordinate causal clause, by a subordinating conjunction; Dana-Mantey,274

[157] The double use of the preposition is a feature of the use of apposition. It is rather forced and needing a lot of demonstration to translate "speak against my servant [who is] in Moses" The point of the text is not to make 'my servant' a special use of continuity with a history of those who were servants of God, but the contrary, to show that Moses this person has been given a unique status, experience, power and authority beyond everyone before and after that time till Jesus appeared transformed on the mount.

[158] efoson as long as' Dana-Mantey,113

[159] Dana-Mantey,183; locative of sphere with adjectives Dana-Mantey,88,230

[160] twn lalesomenwn the only fut.pass ptcp in the NT BDF, 351[2]s

[161] Heb. 2:2 For if the message spoken by angels was binding, and every violation and disobedience received its just punishment, Heb. 2:3 Heb. 3:6 Heb. 3:7 Heb. 3:14 Heb. 3:15 Heb. 3:18 Heb. 4:7 Heb. 4:8 Heb. 6:6 Heb. 7:11 Heb. 7:15 Heb. 8:4 Heb. 8:7 Heb. 10:2 Heb. 10:26 Heb. 10:38 Heb. 11:15 Heb. 12:8 Heb. 12:20 Heb. 12:25 Heb. 13:3 Heb. 13:23

[162] Deut. 4:25 ¶ After you have had children and grandchildren and have lived in the land a long time — if you then become corrupt and make any kind of idol, doing evil in the eyes of the LORD your God and provoking him to anger, Deut. 4:29 But if from there you seek the LORD your God, you will find him if you look for him with all your heart and with all your soul. Deut. 4:42 to which anyone who had killed a person could flee if he had unintentionally killed his neighbor without malice aforethought. He could flee into one of these cities and save his life. Deut. 5:24 And you said, "The LORD our God has shown us his glory and his majesty, and we have heard his voice from the fire. Today we have seen that a man can live even if God speaks with him. Deut. 5:25 But now,

why should we die? This great fire will consume us, and we will die if we hear the voice of the LORD our God any longer. Deut. 6:25 And if we are careful to obey all this law before the LORD our God, as he has commanded us, that will be our righteousness."

163 Joseph A.Fitzmyer,Essays on The Semitic Background of the New Testament [Atlanta: Scholars, 1974]loc.cit.

164 E.Earle Ellis, "Traditions in the Pastoral Epistles,' ," Early Jewish and Christian Exegesis. Studies in Memory of William H. Brownlee. [Atlanta: Scholars Press, 1987]235

165 Dana-Mantey,171

166 Locative case with verb: 'he was made strong in faith.' Dana-Mantey,88

167 use of ei as negative. Dana-Mantey,247

168 Spec.Laws 2.214

169 Genitive of reference. Dana-Mantey,78

170 Apath here and in Eph 4.22; Col 2.8; 2 Pet 2.13 and genitive Mk 4.19; 2 Thess 2.10;

171 Preposition per as part of another particle eiper Rom 8.17; 'if we really suffer together' Cf. . 5.4,8 Dana-Mantey,262

172 para used in compounds for emphasis, with adverbial overtones. Dana-Mantey,108

173 Here rarely ei=mh but here mh for ei. Hebrew uses the coinditional particle in the negative occasionally;Dana-Mantey,246

174 Liddell-Scott,195.

175 as in Alexander Suter, A Pocket Lexicon to the Greek New Testament,n.p., 1974 .Liddell-Scott list I.1. leave behinbd one, be left,remain, a force left behind the rest.2. bequeath, leaving behind a will when going into the service 3. Leave in a certain state; II. Forsake,abandon, leave many on the field, 2. Let drop, give up, III. Leave remaining;remainder in calculations; 2. Left alone;b. Leave undisputed; admit, allow the truth of a doctrine c. Omit with Heb 4.1 passive: of to be left.

176 Jacob M.Myers, I and II Esdras[NY: Doubleday, 1974]loc.cit.

177 Robert North, "The Derivation of Sabbath' Bib 36(1955)182-201

178 Michael Morrison, "Sabbath and Sunday in Early Christianity,"online. 1999. Maxwell, an Adventist l ists areas of agreement among the church fathers 1. Sabbath eschatology typical of age of sinlessness; 2. Moral typology of a godly life' 3. One of Ten Commandments not binding on Christians. 4.. It is not part of natural law; Matriarchs before Moses did not observe the Sabbath. But Tertullian and others insisted on a spiritual Sabbath of the soul, perpetual repentance from sin and life devoted to the deliverance of the soul. D.

Brinsmead, "sabbatarianism re-Examined; the Reality of the sabbath. Ch.12 an undated paper. Samuele Bacchiocchi 'Sabbath-keeping not required for slaves' cf. reg-forum@skognet.com, 1997. chatroom discussion Matitiahu Tsevat, "the Basic Meaning of the Biblical Sabbath,' ZAW 84(1972)447-459 sees the sabbath as 'neutral structuring empty time.' All daylight derives from the sun, but God differentiated seasons and festivals, some blessed and declared holy and others ordinary. George h. Williams, 'the Sabbath and the Lord's Day,' Andover Newton Q,NS 121-128 address given at Harvard University ?Conference on Common Motifs of Jewish and Christian Worship April 6, 1978. the Babylonian Sabbath in Miscellaneous Inscriptions.The monthly tablets from the time of Cambyses record 7th, 14th, 21st, 28th and record cf 1 uritsu tsihru hi-it-pi 'one young kid, an offering' W.M. Muller says htp is old Egyptian 'offering, 'something to quiet' and ah-ta-ti-ip 'I cut down, or destroyed' BA 2, p.628 and tahtipu 'oppression.' These seventh days are offering days. Another text CT 18.23;17 'day of rest of the heart' yom nu-uh lib-bi = sha-bat-tum/ It might be the name of a day in hemerology. If so it wasn't a day of rest but appeasement prescribing dutues for the king on these days. But shabattum also in a syllabary was a synonym for gamaru 't be full' the name of the 15th of the month, but nothing to do with hemerology. Assyriology doesn't seem to have a root but sh-b-t 'to cut off, desist, put an end to, destroy' is in S and Western semitics. In Hemerology Second Elul and Marchesvan 7,14,21,19,28 are dasys for king, diviner, physician and imprecator. A text can be translated 'An evil day. The shepherd of great peoples shall not eat flesh cooked over coals on an oven; he shall not change the garment of his body; he shall not put on clean clothes; a sacrifice he shall not offer; the king shall not ride in his chariot; he shall not speak as a king; the diviner shall not gve a decision in the secret place' the physician shall not lay his hand upon the sick; it is not suitable to pronounce a curse. At night the king shall bring his gift before Marduk and Ishtar; he shall offer a sacrifice. The lifting up og his hands is pleasing to the god.'cf Ezek 46.4.[Note that htp may relate to ht' 'sin, sin offering, expiatory sacrifice' but not through any phonetic law of interchange. 'to destroy' occrs in Rawlinson IV 2,32,33. Cf. Jastrow, Hebrew and Babylonian traditions,p.168.

179 indicates a dative of instrumentation, location, association, or material.

180 Dana-Mantey,72,232,276

181 Dana-Mantey,247

182 In some contexts this pertains to the pre-creation creation of the unseen world of the cosmos, terrestial and celestial structures. But by taking it out of the Gen 1 context it is set free to apply not to the Sabbath day but to a Sabbath rest of soul.

183 Dana-Mantey,293

184 Jacob M.Myers, I and II Esdras[NY: Doubleday, 1974]loc.cit.

185 Either predictive or descriptive of what happened in 592 when the temple ceased to be a sign of the gracious presence of the Lord."

186 J.Barton Payne, Encyclopedia of Biblical Prophecy[NY:Harper and Row, 1973] lo.cit.

187 North 187,260

188 J.Masseyngberde Ford Revelation. The Anchor Bible[NY:Doubleday,1975],loc. cit.

189 Ford: 385

190 J.Masseyngberde Ford Revelation. The Anchor Bible[NY:Doubleday,1975],loc. cit.

191 Jacob M.Myers, I and II Esdras[NY: Doubleday, 1974]loc.cit.

192 J.Masseyngberde Ford Revelation. The Anchor Bible[NY:Doubleday,1975],loc. cit.

193 Jacob M.Myers, I and II Esdras[NY: Doubleday, 1974]loc.cit.

194 George Wesley Buchanan, To the Hebrews. The Anchor Bible. (NY: Doubleday, 1972).

195 J.Masseyngberde Ford Revelation. The Anchor Bible[NY:Doubleday,1975],loc. cit.

196 Principal T. C. Edwards, " Hebrews," Expositor's Bible. Ages Software®, Inc. • Www.Ageslibrary.Com •Rio, Wi Usa • © 2001

197 Paul Ellingworth, Commentary on Hebrews, NIGTC (Grand Rapids: Eerdmans, 1993)268.

198 Philo, o. A., & Yonge, C. D. 1996, c1993. *The works of Philo : Complete and unabridged*. Hendrickson: Peabody. Sinlessness of the logos cited by Ellingworth p.269 but not found in Philo Fuga 109f, Spec.Leg.1.293; and of the Messiah in Ps Sol.17.41.

199 Jacob Milgrom,Leviticus. The Anchor Bible. [NY:Doubleday,1991],loc.cit.

200 Jacob Milgrom,Leviticus. The Anchor Bible. [NY:Doubleday,1991],loc.cit.

201 Dana-Mantey,218

202 E.Lövestam,Son and Savior: a Study of Acts 13.32-37[ConNeot 18;Lund,1961]15-37.

203 Ps 110 possibly has messianic overtones, because it is a royal psalm, David or his descendant is addressed as hero, and is associated with Melchizedek. Along with Ps 2 it reflects the dynastic covenant oracle of Nathan [2 Sam 7.8-16]. But this king is not simply an historical king but a religious person who "incorporates in himself the kingdom of Israel and its hope for a future in which the kingship of

Yahweh will become universally effective. In this sense the Ps is messianic since it repeats the messianic outlook of the dynasty of David.. It has been maintained that v.4, in which the Israelite mnarch is presented as a king-priest, is a gloss, because it is unique in the OT. However, the excision of it has to be based on something more than a hunch, and the otherwise early date of the Ps pointsto its composition in the time of David or Solomon, whwen the connection of the Davidic dynasty with the city of Melchizedek was still fresh and when many of thei nhabitants were not Israelites. Ps 110.4 thus presents the king as the heir of Melchizedek, succeeding him as a priest forever."

204 1. Arrangement, fixed order,succession;' Hellenistic: office,post' of priest; 3. 'Character,quality' 2 Macc 9.18.

205 Joseph A.Fitzmyer,Essays on The Semitic Background of the New Testament [Atlanta: Scholars, 1974]loc.cit.

206 E.Lövestam,Son and Savior: a Study of Acts 13.32-37[ConNeot 18;Lund,1961]15-37.

207 Ps 110 possibly has messianic overtones, because it is a royal psalm, David or his descendant is addressed as hero, and is associated with Melchizedek. Along with Ps 2 it reflects the dynastic covenant oracle of Nathan [2 Sam 7.8-16]. But this king is not simply an historical king but a religious person who "incorporates in himself the kingdom of Israel and its hope for a future in which the kingship of Yahweh will become universally effective. In this sense the Ps is messianic since it repeats the messianic outlook of the dynasty of David.. It has been maintained that v.4, in which the Israelite monarch is presented as a king-priest, is a gloss, because it is unique in the OT. However, the excision of it has to be based on something more than a hunch, and the otherwise early date of the Ps pointsto its composition in the time of David or Solomon, whwen the connection of the Davidic dynasty with the city of Melchizedek was still fresh and when many of the inhabitants were not Israelites. Ps 110.4 thus presents the king as the heir of Melchizedek, succeeding him as a priest forever."

208 1. Arrangement, fixed order,succession;' Hellenistic: office,post' of priest; 3. 'Character,quality' 2 Macc 9.18.

209 Joseph A.Fitzmyer,Essays on The Semitic Background of the New Testament [Atlanta: Scholars, 1974]loc.cit.

210 Harold W Attridge, 'Heard bewcause of his reverence'Heb 5.7' JBL 98/1(1979)90-93 cop Sahidic version
NT New Testament
cop Sahidic version

[211] Lane, W. L. 1998. *Vol. 47A*: *Word Biblical Commentary : Hebrews 1-8* (electronic ed.). Logos Library System; Word Biblical Commentary. Word, Incorporated: Dallas

[212] Dana-Mantey,87,219

[213] Joseph A.Fitzmyer,Essays on The Semitic Background of the New Testament [Atlanta: Scholars, 1974]loc.cit.

[214] BDF,§165

[215] [Menander,Dysk.722]

[216] Dana-Mantey,78

[217] Jacob M.Myers, I and II Esdras[NY: Doubleday, 1974]loc.cit.

[218] Bruce, Peake,1012 citin g A. Nairne, the Epistle of Priesthood, 1913,15.

[219] Jacob M.Myers, I and II Esdras[NY: Doubleday, 1974]loc.cit.

[220] Joachim Jeremias, The Parables of Jesus [NY: Scribners, 1963] rev.ed. loc.cit.

[221] Dunn,431n.100

[222] Kenneth S Wuest, 'Hebrews Six in the Greek NT,' Bib sacra 119(1962),45ff.

[223] Joseph A.Fitzmyer,Essays on The Semitic Background of the New Testament [Atlanta: Scholars, 1974]loc.cit.

[224] Spicq,1.36n6; 489; 2.276;

[225] J.Barton Payne, Encyclopedia of Biblical Prophecy[NY:Harper and Row, 1973] lo.cit.

[226] It also uses midrash technique to introduce phrases from Ps 110 into Gen 14 [7.11,15,17,21,28] similar to 4Qflorilegium, a text that begins with the formula midrash., that comments on 2 Sam 7.10-14 and Ps 1.1 and 2.1 but introducing into the commentary verses from Ex 15.17-18 and Am 9.11; Isa 8.11 and Ez 37.23 into Ps 1.1. While Hebrews does this implicitly the Qumran text does it explicitly. Note Hebrews avoids the extreme allegorical speculation found in Philo, Josephus, some gnostic writers and the Rabbis.

[227] Joseph A.Fitzmyer,Essays on The Semitic Background of the New Testament [Atlanta: Scholars, 1974]loc.cit.

[228] It also uses midrash technique to introduce phrases from Ps 110 into Gen 14 [7.11,15,17,21,28] similar to 4Qflorilegium, a text that begins with the formula midrash., that comments on 2 Sam 7.10-14 and Ps 1.1 and 2.1 but introducing into the commentary verses from Ex 15.17-18 and Am 9.11; Isa 8.11 and Ez 37.23 into Ps 1.1. While Hebrews does this implicitly the Qumran text does it explicitly. Note Hebrews avoids the extreme allegorical speculation found in Philo, Josephus, some gnostic writers and the Rabbis.

[229] Joseph A.Fitzmyer,Essays on The Semitic Background of the New Testament [Atlanta: Scholars, 1974] 221-n, 253-4,n, 267. .

[230] Jacob M.Myers, I and II Esdras[NY: Doubleday, 1974]loc.cit.

231 Toorn, K. v. d., Becking, B., & Horst, P. W. v. d. (1999). *Dictionary of deities and demons in the Bible DDD* (2nd extensively rev. ed.) (Page 14). Leiden; Boston; Grand Rapids, Mich.: Brill; Eerdmans.

232 Grolier Encyclopedia. Loc.cit.

233 B.F.Batto, Zedeq,' Dictionary of Deities....The West Semitic deity Zedek, 'Righteousness', is found in the Bible only in the personal names →Melchizedek (Gen 14:18; Cf. . Ps 110:4; Heb 5:6; 6:20–7:17) and Adonizedek (Josh 10:1.3), both Canaanite kings of pre-Israelite Jerusalem. Zedek is probably to be identified with the deity known as Išar among the Amorites and Kittu in Babylonia, and thus a hypostasis or personification of the sun god Shamash's function (→ Shemesh) as divine overseer of justice. The cult of Zedek appears to have been well established in pre-Israelite (Jebusite) Jerusalem. Some aspects of this cult apparently were translated into Yahwism; in a number of texts Righteousness appears either as a member of →Yahweh's court or as a personification of Yahweh's concern for justice.[234]

235 Arthur E. Cundall, 'ZADOK,' Elwell, W. A., & Beitzel,B. J. 1988. *Baker encyclopedia of the Bible.* Map on lining papers. Baker Book House: Grand Rapids, Mich.

236 Joseph A.Fitzmyer,Essays on The Semitic Background of the New Testament [Atlanta: Scholars, 1974]loc.cit.

237 Fitzmyer,239. Melchizedek: Soncino Zohar, Bereshith, Section 1, Page 87a:

238 ... Soncino Zohar, Bereshith, Section 1, Page 87a.

239 Joseph A.Fitzmyer,Essays on The Semitic Background of the New Testament [Atlanta: Scholars, 1974]loc.cit.

240 Soncino Zohar, Bereshith, Section 1, Page 87a:

241 Robert W. Smith and Albright, W. F. 1924. Some observations Favoring the Palestinian Origin of the Gospel of John. *HTR* 17:189–95.

242 Robert W. Smith and Albright, W. F. 1924. Some observations Favoring the Palestinian Origin of the Gospel of John. *HTR* 17:189–95.

243 Bruce, Peake, 1013.

244 Read in CBQ 22[1960]291; O.Eissfeldt "El and Yahweh",JSS 1[1956]29n.1 takes YHWH as secondary. J.A.Fitzmyer,The Aramaic Inscriptions of Sefire[Rome: Pontifical Biblical Institute,1967]37-8; R.Lack,CBQ 24[1962]44-64. Böhl,ZAW 36[1916]72-3; H.Gunkel,Genesis HKAT 1/1 Gottingen, 1922,284-5; B.Vawter, Path through Genesis [NY,1956]132. Other Bibliography is in Fitzmyer,p.234.

245 He is called kohen, a proper priestly title, yet lacks the genealogy that from Ezra onward was crucial, to be traced from Levi via Aaron and Zadok. But these are not types of the perfected son, and while typos is not used the expression

'made like to trhe son of God' afwmoiwmenoß de tw huiw tou qeou makes the Christ the real and Melchizedek the antitype. He is a pointer, and a point in the argument. But if the 'Son' is part of the heavenly 'real' world than Melchizedek was raised up to be a counterpart and hence a type of the heavenly 'Son' .

246 W.F.Albright,AASOR 6[1926]63.

247 1 Macc 14.41; Jos Ant 16.6.2,¶162. Assumptio Mos. 6.1; Jub. 32.1; T.Levi 8.14-15;

248 JW 6,10,1;¶438. Ant.1.10.2 ¶181.

249 De legum allegoria 3,79.

250 Joseph A.Fitzmyer,Essays on The Semitic Background of the New Testament [Atlanta: Scholars, 1974]loc.cit.

251 Read in CBQ 22[1960]291; O.Eissfeldt "El and Yahweh",JSS 1[1956]29n.1 takes YHWH as secondary. J.A.Fitzmyer,The Aramaic Inscriptions of Sefire[Rome: Pontifical Biblical Institute,1967]37-8; R.Lack,CBQ 24[1962]44-64. Böhl, ZAW 36[1916]72-3; H.Gunkel,Genesis HKAT 1/1 Gottingen, 1922,284-5; B.Vawter, Path through Genesis [NY,1956]132. Other Bibliography is in Fitzmyer,p.234.

252 He is called kohen, a proper priestly title, yet lacks the genealogy that from Ezra onward was crucial, to be traced from Levi via Aaron and Zadok. But these are not types of the perfected son, and while typos is not used the expression 'made like to trhe son of God' afwmoiwmenoß de tw huiw tou qeou makes the Christ the real and Melchizedek the antitype. He is a pointer, and a point in the argument. But if the 'Son' is part of the heavenly 'real' world than Melchizedek was raised up to be a counterpart and hence a type of the heavenly 'Son' .

253 W.F.Albright,AASOR 6[1926]63.

254 1 Macc 14.41; Jos Ant 16.6.2,¶162. Assumptio Mos. 6.1; Jub. 32.1; T.Levi 8.14-15;

255 JW 6,10,1;¶438. Ant.1.10.2 ¶181.

256 De legum allegoria 3,79.

257 Joseph A.Fitzmyer,Essays on The Semitic Background of the New Testament [Atlanta: Scholars, 1974]loc.cit.

258 Lane, W. L. 1998. *Vol. 47A*: *Word Biblical Commentary : Hebrews 1-8* (electronic ed.). Logos Library System; Word Biblical Commentary. Word, Incorporated: Dallas

259 Modern scholars note 1. that some Davidic kings held some priestly functions while the Levitical priesthood took care of the ark and its shrine. 2. The Testament of the Twelve Patriarchs and Qumran texts would cause reflection that the mother of Jesus was related to ?Elizabeth, who was 'of the daughters

of Aaron.' Lk 1.5. But Ps 110.4 is prediction and its fulfillment is duly noted in connection with the Messiah.

260 Joseph A.Fitzmyer,Essays on The Semitic Background of the New Testament [Atlanta: Scholars, 1974]loc.cit.

261 BDF,§113[2]

262 Spicq,3.241n50

263 Joseph A.Fitzmyer,Essays on The Semitic Background of the New Testament [Atlanta: Scholars, 1974]loc.cit.

264 Elwell, W. A., & Beitzel, B. J. 1988. *Baker encyclopedia of the Bible*. Map on lining papers. Baker Book House: Grand Rapids, Mich. Article 'Aaron and Priesthood,' by Charles Feinberg.

265 Adam Clarke Commentary on the Bible, in his notes.

266 Bruce, Peake, 1013.

267 Dana-Mantey,113

268 There may be allusion here to the Rabbinic belief that every generation has one righteous person without which the world would end. Jesus is 'the righteous one' and thus the end of the world is in his hand. But the fear the cross observers experienced along with earthquake, eclipse and thunder just at the death of Jesus may have been because they recognized Jesus as that generation's one righteous person.

269 BDF,§235[3]

270 Adjective agrees with the noun it modifies in gender,number and case; Dana-Mantey,116

271 Voluntative result clauses: one intended or contemplated. Dana-Mantey,273,284

272 J.Barton Payne, Encyclopedia of Biblical Prophecy[NY:Harper and Row, 1973] lo.cit.

273 Jacob M.Myers, I and II Esdras[NY: Doubleday, 1974]loc.cit.

274 (Ex 25:40" J Wesley notes.

275 J.Masseyngberde Ford Revelation. The Anchor Bible[NY:Doubleday,1975],loc. cit.

276 J.Barton Payne, Encyclopedia of Biblical Prophecy[NY:Harper and Row, 1973] lo.cit.

277 1. Monergistic: God not Moses or one's father; 2. Internal, not stone, although hearts can be come as stone. 3. Interpersonal, open to people but not co-dependent on them.

278 Clarence E. Mason, Jr.,A Review of Dispensationalism by John Wick Bowman-Part I -- Vol 114 #453 -- Jan 1957 – 10 Part I

279 BDF,§404[3]

280 BDF,§443[2]

281 Sharon G Gritz, 'Hebrews,' The IVP Women's Bible Commentary. Ed. Catherine Clark Kroeger and Mary J Evans (Downers Grove: Intervarsity Press,2002).

282 John Calvin, The Commentaries on the Epistle of Paul the Apostle to the Hebrews. The Ages Digital Library Commentaries 1,0, 1996.

283 Craig R. Koester, "Tabernacle," Eerdmans Dictionary of the Bible," 1270.

284 Michael D.Guinan, "Lampstand," eerdmans Bible Dictionary, 787-788.

285 David R Reagon, Types of Prophecy and Prophecy Types. Lamb and Lion Ministries, 1996-2004.on line.

286 Elwell, W. A., & Beitzel, B. J. 1988. *Baker encyclopedia of the Bible.* Map on lining papers. Baker Book House: Grand Rapids, Mich.
NT New Testament

287 "The altar of incense (30:1–10) may have been deliberately played down to give greater prominence to the sacrificial altar in the outer court, which is frequently referred to as "*the* altar" (vv 18, 20). In order to distinguish the altar of incense from the bronze altar of sacrifice, it was called "the golden altar" (40:5). The altar of incense was located in the holy place, immediately opposite the ark but just outside the veil, between the table of the "Bread of the Presence" and the lampstand (vv 1–5, 20–27). Made of acacia wood overlaid with gold, it was 18 inches square and 3 feet high, with horns and a golden molding around the four sides. Like the ark, it was made readily portable by the provision of rings and carrying poles. The altar was used for the offering of incense every morning and evening and for anointing the horns for the yearly atonement (30:7, 8). The incense from a special recipe was forbidden for secular use (vv 34–38). Originally, incense indicated something that ascended from a sacrifice, a pleasing aroma to God. Incense acknowledged God in worship (Mal 1:11), and at an early date signified the prayers of the godly (Ps 141:2). It also concealed God from human eyes (Lv 16:13)."

288 Arthur E. Cundall .

289 Elwell, W. A., & Beitzel, B. J. 1988. *Baker encyclopedia of the Bible.* Map on lining papers. Baker Book House: Grand Rapids, Mich.

290 *kpr* pi. to atone; S 3722; BDB 497a; *HALOT* 2:493b; *TDOT* 7:288–303; *TWOT* 1023; *NIDOTTE* 4105 1. (a) A number of investigations concerning the origin and meaning of the verb are available. The following are esp. thorough: D. Schötz, *Schuld- und Sündopfer im AT* (1930), 102–6; J. Herrmann, *TDNT* 3:302–10 (Cf. . id., *Die Idee der Sühne im AT* [1905], 35–37); J. J. Stamm, *Erlösen und Vergeben im AT* (1940), 59–66; L. Moraldi, *Espiazione sacrificale e riti espiatori nell} ambiente biblico e nell} AT* (1956), 182–221; S. Lyonnet, "De

notione expiationis," *VD* 37 (1959): 336–52; 38 (1960): 65–75 (on *kpr* pi.: 37 [1959]: 343–52); K. Koch, *Die isr. Sühneanschauung und ihre historischen Wandlungen* (1956); Elliger, HAT 4, 70f.

291 Gen. 6:14 So make yourself an ark of cypress wood; make rooms in it and coat it with pitch inside and out. Gen. 32:20 And be sure to say, 'Your servant Jacob is coming behind us.'" For he thought, "I will pacify him with these gifts I am sending on ahead; later, when I see him, perhaps he will receive me." Ex. 21:30 However, if payment is demanded of him, he may redeem his life by paying whatever is demanded. Etc.

292 WKAS 1:261–64; Lane 1/7:2620f.

293 Thus e.g., Wildberger, Isa 1–12, CC, 270 on Isa 6:7

294 Elliger, HAT 4, 71

295 Cf. . J. Herrmann, TDNT 3:304

296 DISO 126

297 AHw 509.

298 Dative; GKC §119bb; BrSynt 106f.

299 In the phrase "the priest effects atonement for him" (Lev 4:26, 31, 35; 5:6, 10, 13, 18, 26; 14:18, 20; 15:15; 19:22), which occurs 12x—together with the following "so he will be forgiven"—R. Rendtorff (*Studien zur Geschichte des Opfers im Alten Israel* [1967], 230) sees the "Grundform" or basis of the *hΩat√t√aœ}t* and *}aœs¥aœm* rituals.

P associates *kpr* pi. *{al* with the altar 6x (Exod 29:36f.; 30:10[bis] [horns of the altar and altar]; Lev 8:15; 16:18), once with the temple (*qoœdes¥* and *}oœhel mo®{eœd*, Lev 16:10), and once with the house cleansed from leprosy (Lev 14:53). Lev 16:10 directs that the goat be presented live before Yahweh "in order to effect atonement for it (the scapegoat)"; this is "senseless" (Elliger, HAT 4, 201). It could be interpreted, however, as "in order to carry out the atonement rites through it"; this expression would, however, be formally and substantively unusual; the passage is usually regarded as secondary.

300 "Encyclopedia of Religion, Christian Concepts, Vol.1, p.495.

301 Martin Hengel, "the Expiatory Sacrifice of Christ.' BJRL 62.2(1980),454-75.

302 Joachim Jeremias, The Parables of Jesus [NY: Scribners, 1963] rev.ed. loc.cit.

303 Jacob M.Myers, I and II Esdras[NY: Doubleday, 1974]loc.cit.

304 Joachim Jeremias, The Parables of Jesus [NY: Scribners, 1963] rev.ed. loc.cit.

305 Lane, W. L. 1998. *Vol. 47B: Word Biblical Commentary : Hebrews 9-13* (electronic ed.). Logos Library System; Word Biblical Commentary. Word, Incorporated: Dallas. (Cf. . Bover, *Bib* 32 [1951] 235; N. H. Young, *NTS* 27 [1980–81] 204)

306 Lane, W. L. 1998. *Vol. 47B: Word Biblical Commentary : Hebrews 9-13* (electronic ed.). Logos Library System; Word Biblical Commentary. Word, Incorporated: Dallas

307 indirect-middle voice 'he himself secured eternal redemption' Dana-Mantey,159,230

308 From J Wesley notes

309 Daniel C. Browning,Jr, 'Heifer,'eerdmans Dictionary of the Bible. Ed. David N Freedman et.al. (Grand Raids: Eerdmans, 2ooo) 571

310 James W Thompson, "Hebrews 9 and Hellenistic Concepts of Sacrifice,' JBL 98/4(1979)567-578

311 Some SDA materials indicated Christ offered the heavenly sacrifice in 1840 or thereabouts. This runs counter to a completed atonement taught in Hebrews. Their hermeneutic confuses the narrative description of Jesus work on earth as described in the Gospels and Epistles with the prophetic scriptures. This is a genre confusion and defective orientation, mixing Christology and Soteriology with eschatology and the inner-scripture of dating End-Time events which Jesus said were never to be revealed.

312 Lane, W. L. 1998. *Vol. 47B: Word Biblical Commentary : Hebrews 9-13* (electronic ed.). Logos Library System; Word Biblical Commentary. Word, Incorporated: Dallas

313 John F Walvoord, Premillennialism and the Tribulation-Part V: Partial Rapture Theory -- Vol 112 #447 -- Jul 1955 -- 204

314 Girdwood, J., & Verkruyse, P. 1997. *Hebrews*. The College Press NIV commentary . College Press: Joplin, Mo.

315 Dana-Mantey,105

316 Jeremias, 84

317 Joachim Jeremias, The Parables of Jesus [NY: Scribners, 1963] rev.ed. loc.cit.

318 Jacob M.Myers, I and II Esdras[NY: Doubleday, 1974]loc.cit.

319 Jacob M.Myers, I and II Esdras[NY: Doubleday, 1974]loc.cit.

320 P.Chantraine, Dictionnaire etymologique under phgnumi.

321 Spicq I,141;

322 Deut. 32:15 Jeshurun grew fat and kicked; filled with food, he became heavy and sleek. He abandoned the God who made him and rejected the Rock his Savior. 2Sam. 22:3 2Sam. 22:47 1Chr. 16:35 Psa. 18:46 Psa. 24:5 Psa. 25:5 Psa. 27:9 Psa. 38:22 Psa. 42:5 Psa. 42:11 Psa. 43:5 Psa. 65:5 Psa. 68:19 Psa. 79:9 Psa. 85:4 Psa. 89:26 Is. 17:10 Is. 19:20 Is. 43:3 Is. 43:11 I, even I, am the LORD, and apart from me there is no savior. Is. 45:15 Is. 45:21 Is. 49:26 Is. 60:16 Is. 62:11 Is. 63:8 Jer. 14:8 Hos. 13:4 Mic. 7:7 Hab. 3:18

323 Spicq:3.354n46

[324] Cf. . Philo, Etern. World 46

[325] "; Herodotus 1.91.3:

[326] Spicq: 1 Cf. . C. Spicq, Hébreux, vol. 2, pp. 167ff.; J. Héring, Hébreux, pp. 59ff. = ET pp. 45ff.

[327] (PeterLombard, Hugh of Saint Victor, Robert of Melun). Almost all the Fathers, and recently A. Richardson (An Introduction to the Theology of the New Testament, London, 1958, pp. 33, 348ff.)

[328] Spicq: 2 2Macc 4:5 (Cf. . Thucydides 6.86.3

[329] Josephus, War 5.57

[330] Dio Cassius 41.33

[331] (Josephus, Ant. 13.423

[332] Ag. Apion 5.442; P.Oxy. 2479, 19

[333] J.Dwight Pentecost, "Tribulation"- Vol 115 #457 -- Jan 1958 -- 54

[334] Spicq: 3

[335] Dio Cassius 41.33:

[336] E. Dutoit, Le Thème de l'adynaton dans la poésie antique, Paris, 1936, pp. ix, 50, 167ff

[337] J. Michel, "Quelques formules primitives de serment promissoire et l'origine de la comparaison par adynaton," in RIDA, 1957, pp. 139–150.

[338] Spicq: 2 2Macc 4:5 (Cf. . Thucydides 6.86.3:

[339] Spec. Laws 1.32: of understanding God; Alleg. Interp. 1.34

[340] (Cf. . Spec. Laws 1.103); Josephus, Ant. 3.230

[341] Ag. Apion 5.442; P.Oxy. 2479, 19

[342] J. Ebert, Griechische Epigramme, p. 69.

[343] Spicq: 1 Cf. . C. Spicq, Hébreux, vol. 2, pp. 167ff.; J. Héring, Hébreux, pp. 59ff. = ET pp. 45ff.

[344] An Introduction to the Theology of the New Testament, London, 1958, pp. 33, 348ff.

[345] Josephus, Ant. 10.196

[346] Hugh Joseph Schonfield, the Passover Plot: New Light on the History of Jesus, n.p., 1966, Jacob Neusner, First Century Judaism (Nashville: Abingdon, 1975). Joseph Guttmann,ed. The Image and the Word, (Missoula: Scholars Press, 1977).

[347] Dana-Mantey,109

[348] Spicq,3.354n46

[349] , BDF,§163

[350] , BDF,§163

351 David Ulansey, 'The Heavenly Veil Torn: Mark's Cosmic Inclusio.'JBL 110/1(1991)123-125.

352 S.Motyer, 'The Rending of the Veil: A Markan Pentecost,' NTS 33(1987)155-57; Howard M Jackson, 'the death of Jesus in Mark and the Miiracle from the Cross,' NTS 33(1987)23,27,31

353 Carl Armerding, "The Atonement Money," BSsacra -- Vol 115 #460 -- Oct 1958 -- 338

354 Gary A Anderson, 'The Interpretation of the Purification Offering hat't in the Temple Scroll (11Qtemple) and Rabbinic Literature,' JBL 111/1(1992)17-35.

355 James A. Sanders, Hermeneutics in True and False Prophecy. Canon and Authority[Phil.: Fortress,1977]21-41.

356 Lines, S 186; EDNT 1.49; MM 18; L&N 31.80; BAGD 30;

357 EDNT 1.49; MM 18; L&N 31.80; BAGD 30

358 Spicq,341n36 says "In St.Paul's usage, agaph with a person in the genitive means the love that belongs to that person.[2 Thess 3.5; Eph 2.4], so tou xristou would be a subjective genitive [Cf. .Rom 5.5; 8.35,39; Gal 2.20]; but here the context in v.13 suggests an objective genitive, love for Christ. In reality, these two meanings should not be separated; we have here a comprehensive or 'general' genitive, Cf. . M. Zerwick, Biblical Greek,§36.

359 St.Ambrose: "I am fastened as by nails of faith, I am confined by the good fetters of love' Lk 5.27.

360 Spicq,3.341

361 Freedman, D. N. *The Anchor Bible Dictionary*. New York: Doubleday. (1996, c1992).

362 VTS,IV,237(1996, c1992).

363 BDF,§301[1]

364 VTS,IV,237(1996, c1992).

365 Jacob M.Myers, I and II Esdras[NY: Doubleday, 1974]loc.cit.

366 BDF,§301[1]

367 VTS,IV,237

368 Jacob M.Myers, I and II Esdras[NY: Doubleday, 1974]loc.cit.

369 Secular Greek, in contrast to the Bible, viewed the tapeinos as base,ignoble or despised. [P.Oxy.79,verso 2] The person is servile aneleuqeroß, working at a humble occupation, held in low esteem, and can refer to lowliness ofheart.[Epictetus 3.2,14; 4.1,2 tapeinofronew 'having a low opinion of oneself' tapeinoomai 'be in an inferior condition' [Plutarch Sol. 22.2]: 'degrade oneself'; In Diodorus Siculus 19.67.3:" Cassander decided that it would be worthwhile to weaken [tapeinwsai] the Aetolians." Plutarch, Mulier.virt. 20: 'not in a pitiable

and lowly fashion.' In the early church the self-depreciatory tone continued as seen in a monk named Psoïos to his superior: "I pray my master to remember my humble self' [th emh tapeinwsei] in his holy and efficacious prayers."

370 Spicq,370n7 "The verb, substantive, or adjective usually translates the Hebrew 'anah or one of its derivatives, which connote misery, usually poverty, affliction, defeat. Hebrew kana' 'be confounded' shapel 'be abased' are in the same domain.

371 Secular Greek, in contrast to the Bible, viewed the tapeinos as base,ignoble or despised. [P.Oxy.79,verso 2] The person is servile aneleuqeroß, working at a humble occupation, held in low esteem, and can refer to lowliness of heart.[Epictetus 3.2,14; 4.1,2 tapeinofronew 'having a low opinion of oneself' tapeinoomai 'be in an inferior condition' [Plutarch Sol. 22.2]: 'degrade oneself'; In Diodorus Siculus 19.67.3:" Cassander decided that it would be worthwhile to weaken [tapeinwsai] the Aetolians." Plutarch, Mulier.virt. 20: 'not in a pitiable and lowly fashion.' In the early church the self-depreciatory tone continued as seen in a monk named Psoïos to his superior: "I pray my master to remember my humble self' [teh emeh tapeinwsei] in his holy and efficacious prayers."

372 Spicq,370n7 "The verb, substantive, or adjective usually translates the Hebrew 'anah or one of its derivatives, which connote misery, usually poverty, affliction, defeat. Hebrew kana' 'be confounded' shapel 'be abased' are inthe same domain.

373 Spicq,3.370

374 M. Dahood, the Psalms vol.3,[NY: Doubleday,1970],313

375 G.H.Parke-Taylor, Yahweh: The Divione Name in the Bible[Waterloo,Ont.: Wilfrid Laurier Univ Press,1975]loc.cit.

376 J.Barton Payne, Encyclopedia of Biblical Prophecy[NY:Harper and Row, 1973] lo.cit.

377 J.Barton Payne, Encyclopedia of Biblical Prophecy[NY:Harper and Row, 1973] lo.cit.

378 BDF,§127[2],304

379 J.Masseyngberde Ford Revelation. The Anchor Bible[NY:Doubleday 1975],loc. cit.

380 Freedman, D. N. 1996, c1992. *The Anchor Bible Dictionary.* Doubleday: New York

381 Ex. 32:8 Num 16.26 does use the root in the sense of turning from evil

382 Jer. 2:19

383 J Ellwood Evans, "The Song of Habakkuk,"Part III, BSac 113 #449 (June 1956)-60

384 pistis" in Hatch and Redpath usually translates Dt 32.20; and more frequently in 1 S 21.2; 26.23; 2 K 12.15[16]; 22.7; 1 Ch 9.22; 9.26; 9.31; 2 Ch 31.12,15,18; 34.12; Ps 32[33].4; Pr 12.17,22; 14.22; Ho 2.20[22]; Hb 2.4; Jer 5.1,3; 7.28; 9.3[2]; 15.18; Lam 3.23; It is in Ne 9.38[10.1]; Ct 4.8 possibly; in Pr 3.3; 14.22; 15.27[16.6]; Jer 35[28].9; 39[32]41; 40[33].6

385 pistos appears to translate the LXX in Nu 12.7; Dt 7.9; 28.59; 32.4; 1 S 2.35,35; 3.20; 22.14; 25.28; 1 K 11.38; Ne 9.8; 13.13; Jb 12.20; Ps 18.[19].7; 88[89].28; 88.37; 100[101].6; 110[111].7; Pr 11.13; Pr 25.13; Ho 5.9; Isa 1.21,26; Isa 8.2; 22.23,25; 33.16; 49.7; 55.5?; Jer 49[42].5. Translating Dt 32.4; Translating Pr 13.17; 14.5; 20.6; Translating Pr 14.25; Translating aphel Dan 2.45; 6.4[5]; By Pr 17.7; By Jb 17.9; By in Pr 2.1 phrase. Meden piston

386 Spicq,3.112; 354n46, 421

387 Oswald Chambers, My Utmost For His Highest NIV version. (Westwood: Barbour and company, Inc.,1935 and 1963 224-225

388 Complete Works of John Wesley, 14 vols, Sermons of John Wesley, 'On Faith,' Sermon 106. Heritage Master Christian Library. Ages Software Inc., Rio, WI, 2000-2003.

389 Carson, D.A.; et al., *The New Bible Commentary*, (Downers Grove, Illinois: Inter-Varsity Press) 1994.

390 D.Peterson, 'Hebrews,' in Carson, D.A.; et al., *The New Bible Commentary*, (Downers Grove, Illinois: Inter-Varsity Press) 1994.

391 Vanhoye, A., «Pi/stij Xristou=: fede in Cristo o affidabilità di Cristo?», Vol. 80 (1999) 1-21.

392 Buchanan, To the Hebrews,182.

393 Bauer 'substantial nature, essence, being, reality' under appearances. LXX support as one sinks in the mire Ps 69.2LXX 68.3], no foundation to stand on. Foundation of building in Na 2.7; Ezk 43.11; Dt 11.6. A support in Ezk 26.11, resources to support human line Jdg 6.4; Job 22.20. Army camp 1 Sam 13.23. Classical: one must suppose' or basis for calculation 1 Sam 13.21, and for hope Ezk 19.5. and confidence Ps Sol 15.5; These uses point beyond mere subjectivity to that which gives grounds of confidence.

394 Ellenworth, op.cit566.

395 J.Masseyngberde Ford Revelation. The Anchor Bible[NY:Doubleday,1975],loc. cit.

396 1Sam. 23:27 a messenger came to Saul, saying, "Come quickly! The Philistines are raiding the land." 2Sam. 11:19 2Sam. 11:22; _2Sam. 11:23; 2Sam. 11:25; 2Sam. 15:13

397 BDF,§491

[398] Cf. Ecclus 42.15; Apoc.Baruch 21.4f; Hebs 11.3; 2 Pet 3.5,6

[399] Carson, D.A.; et al., *The New Bible Commentary*, (Downers Grove, Illinois: Inter-Varsity Press) 1994.

[400] BDF,§405[1,2]

[401] Dana-Mantey,293

[402] Jacob M.Myers, I and II Esdras[NY: Doubleday, 1974]loc.cit.

[403] Myers,

[404] 313

[405] Oswald Chambers, My Utmost for his Highest, Jan 5.

[406] Sir 24.11; 2 Bar 4.2ff; Rev 3.12; 21.2,10; 2 Esd 10.42.

[407] Jacob M.Myers, I and II Esdras[NY: Doubleday, 1974]loc.cit.

[408] Rev 21.10; 1 En 90.28-29.; 2 Esd 13.36; but it also appears in the Talmud in Tannith 5a; Baba Bathra 75b; Hermas Visions 3.4-5 and Nag Hammadi VI 1.line 24. 274,276

[409] Jacob M.Myers, I and II Esdras[NY: Doubleday, 1974]loc.cit.

[410] J.Masseyngberde Ford Revelation. The Anchor Bible[NY:Doubleday,1975],loc. cit.

[411] BDF,§269[5],425[1],442[9]

[412] Jacob M.Myers, I and II Esdras[NY: Doubleday, 1974]loc.cit.

[413] Plutarch,Tim.38.2 "they led the foreign travelers into his house.' Twn xenwn pous parepidhmountas agontes eisten oikian. In Alexandria Ep.Arist.110 Peasants passing through the city stayed too long to the neglect of their farm work, hence "the king forbade sojourning in the city perepidhmein for more than twenty days."

[414] Philo, Husbandry,65; Heir,267.

[415] Jacob M.Myers, I and II Esdras[NY: Doubleday, 1974]loc.cit.

[416] Plutarch,Tim.38.2 "they led the foreign travelers into his house.' Twn xenwn pous parepidemountas agontes eis ten oikian. In Alexandria Ep.Arist.110 Peasants passing through the city stayed too long to the neglect of their farm work, hence "the king forbade sojourning in the city perepidhmein for more than twenty days."

[417] Philo, Husbandry,65; Heir,267.

[418] kata 'in' Dana-Mantey,107,196

[419] Jacob M.Myers, I and II Esdras[NY: Doubleday, 1974]loc.cit.

[420] Jacob M.Myers, I and II Esdras[NY: Doubleday, 1974]loc.cit.

[421] Jacob M.Myers, I and II Esdras[NY: Doubleday, 1974]loc.cit.

[422] Ex 15.25□ 16.4 17.2 20.20□ Testing God: Dt 6.13 God testing men: Dt 8.16 Judg 2.22□ 3.1; 6.39 [of the fleece]; 1 Kgs 10.1 queen of Sheba of Solomon; 2

Chr 32.31 God of Hezekiah "God left him to himself [Rom 1 in order to test him and to know all that was in his heart." Job 7.18 of all men; [Weigh: Ps 7.9 hearts Ps 26.2 'test my heart and mind; [God tested: Ps 16.14]. 'test me and know...'. Jer 6.27 'test their ways' Jer 9.7 'test them'▯ Jer 12.3 'test me'▯ Jer 17.10 Jer 20.12;

423 J.Barton Payne, Encyclopedia of Biblical Prophecy[NY:Harper and Row, 1973] lo.cit.

424 Payne53n

425 J.Barton Payne, Encyclopedia of Biblical Prophecy[NY:Harper and Row, 1973] lo.cit.

426 Dana-Mantey,282

427 D.A. Cambell, 'the meaning of istis and nomos in Paul: A Linguistic and Structural Perspective,' JBL 111/1(1992)91-103

428 BDF,§342[4]

429 Everett F.Harrison, "The Importance of the Septuagint for Biblical Studies-Part I -- Vol 112 #448 -- Oct 1955 -- 350

430 Spicq,3.82

431 BDF,§444[4]m473[2],475[2],495[1]

432 BDF,§491,494

433 Jacob M.Myers, I and II Esdras[NY: Doubleday, 1974]loc.cit.

434 Joachim Jeremias, The Parables of Jesus [NY: Scribners, 1963] rev.ed. loc.cit.

435 Joachim Jeremias, The Parables of Jesus [NY: Scribners, 1963] rev.ed. loc.cit. Gen. Rab. *Midraš Rabbah* on Genesis or *Genesis Rabba*
Gen. Rab. *Midraš Rabbah* on Genesis or *Genesis Rabba*

436 Lane, W. L.. *Vol. 47B*: *Word Biblical Commentary : Hebrews 9-13* (electronic ed.). Logos Library System; Word Biblical Commentary. Word, Incorporated: Dallas,1998

437 Liddell-Scott,171 Basic: counter-balancing, hence: weighing as much as, of like value, worth as much as' Used of money "worth one Hector'; 'not worth much' 'will bring you a return'; a 'goodly price'; of persons: peers, those of one's own rank; 'sufficient for'; Hom.: moral relations: worthy, estimable, of persons and things; 'worthy of, deserving' 'worth her while'; 'tis meet in the eyes of Hellas'; 'deserved,meet,due': suffering for fit deeds'.

438 Is there a Code where the reverse reads dn for 'judge' or the tribe of Dan that wandered and migrated north and then much further.?

439 J.Barton Payne, Encyclopedia of Biblical Prophecy[NY:Harper and Row, 1973] lo.cit.

440 Jerusalem Post December 10, 2004 www.rabbiwein.com/jpost-index.html Lasting Heroes http://rabbiwein.com/column-851.html One

of the tendencies of modern historiography is to debunk past heroes. Revisionist historians have blackened the name of some of the great people of the past by dwelling extensively on their human foibles and personal difficulties. Not only does this attitude reinforce the false idea that there are no real heroes in the world, it indirectly absolves all of us from ever attempting to be a hero to one's family, commun-ity or nation. One of the sources of this problem is the confusion of true heroism with infallibility. The Torah taught us that there are no perfect people. Only God is perfection incarnate. Heroes, as the Bible points out to us regarding the greatest people of our nation, may have faults and can make errors in judgment. Nevertheless, they remain heroes due to their accomplishments in life and their leadership of the Jewish people. It is essential beyond word to preserve the concept of human heroism in our =age. It has been cheapened by the elevation of celebrities and sports figures as heroes. There is a great difference between being well known and being heroic. The currently well known are soon forgotten as they are replaced by another generation's well-known celebrities and sports figures. True heroes weather the ravages of time and are exemplary and inspiring for generations after their actual departure from this world. Joseph's first dream comes to realization in this week's parsha. His brothers come down to Egypt and prostrate themselves before him. The dream of the sheaves of the brothers bowing to Joseph's sheaf is at last fulfilled. But strangely, Joseph does not feel himself satisfied. It is human nature that the expectation of the realization of events is alwaysgreater and more exciting than the fulfillment of the realization itself. No vacation or event that we plan for our-selves can live up to our imagination and expectation regarding it. And Joseph is further burdened by the enormity of what has transpired. He has the brothers, who sold him as a slave and were deaf to his shouts and tears and pleas for mercy, in his hands. But what is he to do with them now? And what of his beloved father, the old man,broken in grief, whom he has not seen or communicated with for twenty-two years? Are the brothers telling him the truth about his father's condition? And what about Benjamin, his younger brother? Is he like the other brothers in attitude and belief or is he different? Does he mourn for his lost brother Joseph or is he sanguine about his fate, as his ten older brothers seem to be? All of these questions plague Joseph at the moment of his seemingly great triumph when his brothers are in his power and abjectly bow before him. His triumph therefore seems somewhat hollow to him at that moment. Joseph comes to the great realization that his ultimate triumph over his brothers lies not in punishing them - though he will certainly cause them great anguish on their road of repentance - but rather to eventually conciliate them. Vengeance is momentarily more satisfying than is conciliation. But in the long run, vengeance lies not in human hands. And it will only continue to widen the rift within Jacob's family. Joseph's greatness and heroism lies in the fact that he chose the road of healing and conciliation rather than that of punishment and vengeance. Joseph, out of all of the avot and the brothers is called tzadik - righteous and holy. This is certainly due to his behavior in escaping from the clutches of Potiphar's wife.But Joseph's righteousness and piety is exhibited not only in that incident. It is apparent in his treatment of his brothers after his dream of their bowing down to him has been realized. He will protect his brothers from thePharaoh and the ravages of Egyptian society. He will support them physically, financially and spiritually for the rest of his life. He still weeps at the gulf of suspicion that yet exists between him and the brothers. Conciliation is a long and difficult road to traverse. But Joseph realizes that it is the only hope for his family's continuity and purpose..Shabat shalom. Rabbi Berel Wein

441 Roy L.Aldrich, 'An Apologetic for Dispensationalism,' BSacra 112 #445 Jan 1955-51 from CD.

442 1Sam. 23:27 a messenger came to Saul, saying, "Come quickly! The Philistines are raiding the land." 2Sam. 11:19 He instructed the messenger: "When you have finished giving the king this account of the battle, 2Sam. 11:22 ¶ The messenger set out, and when he arrived he told David everything Joab had sent him to say. 2Sam. 11:23 The messenger said to David, "The men overpowered us and came out against us in the open, but we drove them back to the entrance to the city gate. 2Sam. 11:25 ¶ David told the messenger, "Say this to Joab: 'Don't let this upset you; the sword devours one as well as another. Press the attack against the city and destroy it.' Say this to encourage Joab." 2Sam. 15:13 ¶ A messenger came and told David, "The hearts of the men of Israel are with Absalom." 1Kings 19:2 So Jezebel sent a messenger to Elijah to say, "May the gods deal with me, be it ever so severely, if by this time tomorrow I do not make your life like that of one of them." 1Kings 22:13 ¶ The messenger who had gone to summon Micaiah said to him, "Look, as one man the other prophets are predicting success for the king. Let your word agree with theirs, and speak favorably." 2Kings 5:10 Elisha sent a messenger to say to him, "Go, wash yourself seven times in the Jordan, and your flesh will be restored and you will be cleansed." 2Kings 6:32 ¶ Now Elisha was sitting in his house, and the elders were sitting with him. The king sent a messenger ahead, but before he arrived, Elisha said to the elders, "Don't you see how this murderer is sending someone to cut off my head? Look, when the messenger comes, shut the door and hold it shut against him. Is not the sound of his master's footsteps behind him?"Job 1:18 ¶ While he was still speaking, yet another messenger came and said, "Your sons and daughters were feasting and drinking wine at the oldest brother's house,

443 Hortatory subjunctive 'let us hold fast' Dana-Mantey,171

444 Ken L. Sarles, 'An Appraisal of the Signs and Wonders Movement,' Bibliotheca sacra 145 #577(Jan 1988).

445 Freedman, David Noel, ed., *The Anchor Bible Dictionary*, (New York: Doubleday) 1997, 1992.

446 Evans, L. H., Jr, & Ogilvie, L. J. 1985. *Vol. 33*: *The Preacher's Commentary Series, Volume 33 : Hebrews*. Formerly The Communicator's Commentary. The Preacher's Commentary series . Thomas Nelson Inc: Nashville, Tennessee

447 BDF,§342[5]

448 Spicq:3.420n28

449 Dana-Mantey,279

450 Willard M Adrich, "Assurance. Traits of the Family of God,' Assurance -- Vol 114 #456 -- Oct 1957 -- 313

451 1Chr. 29:24 All the officers and mighty men, as well as all of King David's sons, pledged their submission toKing Solomon. Dan. 11:43 He will gain control of the treasures of gold and silver and all the riches of Egypt, with the Libyans and Nubians in submission. 1Cor. 14:34 women should remain silent in the churches. They are not allowed to speak, but must be in submission, as the Law says. . 1Pet. 3:22 who has gone into heaven and is at God's right hand — with angels, authorities and powers in submission to him.

452 Gen. 16:9 ¶ Then the angel of the LORD told her, "Go back to your mistress and submit to her." Gen. 41:40 You shall be in charge of my palace, and all my people are to submit to your orders. Only with respect to the thronewill I be greater than you.". Job 22:21 "Submit to God and be at peace with him; in this way prosperity will come to you .

453 Jacob M.Myers, I and II Esdras[NY: Doubleday, 1974]loc.cit.

454 Joachim Jeremias, The Parables of Jesus [NY: Scribners, 1963] rev.ed. loc.cit.

455 : Dana-Mantey,275

456 Spicq:3.3n12; 236n28; 424n4; 425; 483n59;

457 Spicq:3.3n12; 236n28; 424n4; 425; 483n59

458 Joachim Jeremias, The Parables of Jesus [NY: Scribners, 1963] rev.ed. loc.cit.

459 II Bar 85.12' I En 63; 65.11; Sanh 97b; Apocryphon of John 70 15. Wisd. Sol.12.10. 1 Clemen ch.7. Myers,[460]237,249

461 J.Masseyngberde Ford Revelation. The Anchor Bible[NY:Doubleday 1975],loc. cit.

462 Saul found this out in assuming a priestly role in making a sacrifice. What of Solomon at the dedication? Uzzah and Uzziah were others. Ananias and Saphira

are NT examples. Philistines discovered the holiness of the ark and Belshazzar the holiness of the temple utensils.

463 [Strabo 5.2.7],

464 Spicq:3.4,5,6,7,8; 124n1; 125; 486n70

465 Soncino Zohar, Bemidbar, Section 3, Page 221a.

466 Jacob M.Myers, I and II Esdras[NY: Doubleday, 1974]loc.cit Myers, 153,196,276.

467 J.Masseyngberde Ford Revelation. The Anchor Bible[NY:Doubleday,1975],loc. cit. Ford, 233,333,361

468 Dana-Mantey,138

469 Ex. 3:1 Now Moses was tending the flock of Jethro his father-in-law, the priest of Midian, and he led the flock to the far side of the desert and came to Horeb, the mountain of God. Ex. 17:6 I will stand there before you by the rock at Horeb. Strike the rock, and water will come out of it for the people to drink." So Moses did this in the sight of the elders of Israel. Ex. 33:6 So the Israelites stripped off their ornaments at Mount Horeb. 2Chr. 5:10 There was nothing in the ark except the two tablets that Moses had placed in it at Horeb, where the LORD made a covenant with the Israelites after they came out of Egypt. Psa. 106:19 At Horeb they made a calf and worshiped an idol cast from metal. Mal. 4:4 "Remember the law of my servant Moses, the decrees and laws I gave him at Horeb for all Israel.

470 Ex. 16:1 The whole Israelite community set out from Elim and came to the Desert of Sin, which is between Elim and Sinai, on the fifteenth day of the second month after they had come out of Egypt. Ex. 19:1 In the third month after the Israelites left Egypt — on the very day — they came to the Desert of Sinai.

471 Josh. 13:27 and in the valley, Beth Haram, Beth Nimrah, Succoth and Zaphon with the rest of the realm of Sihon king of Heshbon (the east side of the Jordan, the territory up to the end of the Sea of Kinnereth). Judg. 12:1 The men of Ephraim called out their forces, crossed over to Zaphon and said to Jephthah, "Why did you go to fight the Ammonites

472 Spicq:3.4,5,6,7,8; 124n1; 125; 486n70

473 Soncino Zohar, Bemidbar, Section 3, Page 221a

474 Jacob M.Myers, I and II Esdras[NY: Doubleday, 1974] Myers, 153,196,276 by Meshullam and Shabbethai the Levite, opposed this..

475 J.Masseyngberde Ford, Revelation. The Anchor Bible[NY:Doubleday,1975], Ford,233,333,3.

476 Gal 4.26; Heb 12.22f; Rev. 21.2,10

477 North, 74

478 Spicq, 3.212; 1.150; 325; 3.129; 485n67

479 Jacob M.Myers, I and II Esdras[NY: Doubleday, 1974]loc.cit.

480 J.Masseyngberde Ford Revelation. The Anchor Bible[NY:Doubleday,1975],loc. cit.

481 J.Barton Payne, Encyclopedia of Biblical Prophecy[NY:Harper and Row, 1973] lo.cit.

482 BDF,§243

483 Spicq,1.140

484 Fut.participle. BDF,§ 425[3]

485 J.Masseyngberde Ford Revelation. The Anchor Bible[NY:Doubleday,1975],loc. cit.

486 aidwß swfrosunh see Xenophon Cyr.8.1.31; Symp.1.8; Thucydides 1.84.3; Diotogenes "When, in his appearance, his thoughts, his sentences, his character, his deeds, his walk, and his carriage' the king enfolds himself in such decorum and pomp that he has a psychological effect on those who behold him, affected as they are by his dignity and his moderation" B. Snell,Lexikon. Philolgus Suppl.30,1937. TDNT .169-171; EDNT 1.37; NIDNTT 3.826-827, 829; etc. It is called "a beauty remarkable for its modesty and propriety, beauty...truly virginal' "If with an older companion at his side a young man adorns himsewlf with modesty and restraint." Change of Names,217 See Spicq I,41.n.2.

487 Plutarch, On Ethical Virtue 8; Epictetus, Against Eicurus in Stobaeus 6.37 vol.3. 300. Jos.Ant 3.19,156; 4.285; 5.118; 6.20; plutarch Tim.7.1 "Timoleon was ashamed before his mother." Jos Ant 2.52; war 2.351; Jos.Ant 1.201; 2.23; 5.108; 6.262; 19.102; war 2.496; 2.317; 4.311; 5.33; .587; 6.262; Ant 19.97; plutarch Cleom.32.4; Philo said [Contemp.Life 33] "Young girls who stay in their rooms out of modesty to avoid being seen by men"; Glight 5; Spec Laws 3.5 "The republic of Moses has no room for the prostitute, to whom decency, chastity, modesty, and the other virtues are foreign." Jos War 2.465 "women from whom even the last veil of modesty has been taken away" etc.

488 aidws swfrosune see Xenophon Cyr.8.1.31; Symp.1.8; Thucydides 1.84.3; Diotogenes "When, in his appearance, his thoughts, his sentences, his character, his deeds, his walk, and his carriage' the king enfolds himself in such decorum and pomp that he has a psychological effect on those who behold him, affected as they are by hisdignityand his moderation" B. Snell,Lexikon. Philolgus Suppl.30,1937. TDNT .169-171; EDNT 1.37; NIDNTT 3.826-827 ,829; etc. It is called "a beauty remarkable for its modesty and propriety, beauty...truly virginal' "If with an older companion at his side a young man adorns himsewlf with modesty and restraint." Change of Names,217 See Spicq I,41.n.2.

[489] Plutarch, On Ethical Virtue 8; Epictetus, Against Eicurus in Stobaeus 6.37 vol.3. 300. Jos.Ant 3.19,156; 4.285; 5.118; 6.20; plutarch Tim.7.1 "Timoleon was ashamed before his mother." Jos Ant 2.52; war 2.351; Jos.Ant 1.201; 2.23; 5.108; 6.262; 19.102; war 2.496; 2.317; 4.311; 5.33; .587; 6.262; Ant 19.97; plutarch Cleom.32.4; Philo said [Contemp.Life 33] "Young girls who stay in their rooms out of modesty to avoid being seen by men"; Glight 5; Spec Laws 3.5 "The republic of Moses has no room for the prostitute, to whom decency, chastity, modesty, and the other virtues are foreign." Jos War 2.465 "women from whom even the last veil of modesty has been taken away" etc.

[490] BDF,§452[3]

[491] Tobit 5.4; 5.17; 5.22; 6.2,4,5,7; 11.14; 12.15,22. Add to Esther 15.16; Wisd Solomon 16.20; Letter of Jeremiah 6.7; Song of the three 1.26,37; Susanna 1.4435,55,59,60-62; Bell and Dragon 1.34,36,39; 1 Macc 7.41; 2 Macc 11.6; 15.22,24; 3 Macc 6.18

[492] Bk of Jubilees 1.25; 2.1; 4.15; 5.1; [Charles 2.27,34]; 15.27; 17.11; 27.21; 31.14; 32.21; Bk of Adam and Eve 4.2; 12.1; 13.2; 14.1; 15.1; 16.1; 21.1; 25.3; 31.1; Apoc Moses 17.1; 22.1; 27.1; 29.2; 31.3; 32.2; 33.1; 35.2; 42.2; Martyrdom Isaiah 2.2; Bk Enoch 1.2; 6.2; 10.7; 14.21; 18.5; 19.1; 20.1; 21.5; 22.3; 23.4; 24.6; 27.2; 32.2; 33.3; 36.4; 39.5; 40.2; 41.9; 42.2; 43.2; 46.1; 51.4; 52.3; 53.3; 54.4; 55.3; 56.1; 60.1; 61.1; 62.1; 63.1; 64.2; 65.6; 66.1; 67.2; 68.2; 69.2; 70.3; 71.3; 72.1; 74.2; 75.3; 80.1; 84.4; 93.2; 91.15; 97.2; 99.3; 100.4; 12.3; 14.1;16.6; 108.5; Testament of Reuben 3.15; 5.3; Test Simeon 2.8; Test Levi 2.6; 3.5; 5.1; 9.6; 18.5; 19.3; Test Judah 3.10; 10.3; 15.5; 21.5; 25.2; Test Issachar 2.1; Test Dan 5.4; 6.2; Test Naphtali 8.4; Test Asher 6.4; 7.1; Test Joseph 6.6; 19.9; Test Banjamin 6.1; Secrets Enoch 6.1; 7.2; 8.8; 10.3; 10.4; 12.1; 14.2; 15.3; 16.7; 19.1; 23.1; 24.3; 29.3; 30.1; 31.2; 33.6; 36.2; 40.3; 67.2; Syriac Apoc Baruch 6.4; 7.1; 8.1; 21.23; 51.5; 55.3; 56.10; 59.11; 63.6; 67.2; 80.1; Greek Apoc Baruch 1.3; 2.4; 3.1; 4.2; 5.1; 6.2; 7.2; 8.1; 9.3; 10.4; 11.1; 12.1; 13.1; 14.2; 15.2; 17.2; Fourth Ezra 4.1; 5.15; 6.3; 7.1; 10.28; Fourth Maccabees 4.10; 7.11; Zadokite Work Fragments 2.4; 20.2

[493] David Jeremiah, What The Bible Says About Angels (Multnomah Publishers, Inc., 1996).

[494] BDF,§414[3]

[495] Spicq,1.55

[496] From Homer on the middle voice means 1. Have in one's head, think abut, remember, mention' with genitive of object of memory. A. Put oneself in mind of, recall' 'farewell, and remember the things that I have said' P.Mert.12 .16. 'inform, make appeal' b. To mention is to evoke memory, recall, commemorate'

on tomb inscriptions. C. To take care, concern oneself with' a reason for acting. All are found in the LXX. 1. Psychological meaning of the past Num 11.5; Ezek 23.27; Ps 137.1,6; Wis 19.10; Tob 4.1; 6.15; God remembers to put away evil and bless his people He remembers his covenant in answering prayers Ex 2.24; Ps 15.8; 16.45; 111.5. He remembers men are flesh Ps 78.39; 88.5; 89.47; 13.14. Ps 8.4 On the human side to think of Yahweh: tobias "I remembered God with all my soul." Dt 7.18; 8.2; 9.7; 15.15; 16.3;etc.

497 Spicq: n.7 13:5-6).

498 Conf. Tongues 166,

499 1952, pp. 523–525.

500 Spicq,2.192n14

501 Cf. . C. Spicq, Hébreux, vol. 2, on this text

502 SEG XVIII, 143, 5; in AD 43,

503 ZPE, vol. 17, 1975, p. 144, n. 14,

504 P.Panop.Beatty 1, 78, 126, 143, 385,

505 P.Bon. 20, 21; P.Yale 62, 1,

506 Ep. Arist. 309–310),

507 P.Petaus, p. 166; Dionysius of Halicarnassus, Amm. 1 7); Cf. . I.Car., n. VI, 9; p. 107, n.1

508 Spicq,1.112n7 ;

509 Spicq:3.39

510 Spicq:3.39; Spicq,1.282; 286; 2.557n14; Spicq,1.282; 286; 2.557n14;

511 It can refer to all the things that a person owns or has use of: fruits, olive tree, a munt, sheep and flocks, organs of the body, a meal, pay, all that is personal. Territorial:a field,country, city, village,residence. The motif of owner- ship is clear regarding God and Israel and Israel of the land. Yet the land is in trust and not with a clear title; the title is the covenant and this is in Gods safe-keeping. The fact of private ownership enhances the concept of steward-ship, the proper use of what is truly one's own.

512 Joachim Jeremias, The Parables of Jesus [NY: Scribners, 1963] rev.ed. loc.cit.

513 Philo, Moses 1.102; Decalogue 85.'shame those who have nothing' is the result of a class conscious love feast. Philo said "One cannot take part lightly in a sacred ceremony, because that would be to profane it, commit an impiety, and incur mortal punishment." See also Matt 18.10; Eph 4.22; [Jos Life,337,347] Cf. 1 Cor 11.22;

514 Spicq,2.282; 587

515 Spicq,2.277n10; 3.124n1

516 Jos.Ant 1.131; Life,113

517 Spicq,2.277n10; 3.124n1

[518] S 399; TDNT 9.60–61; EDNT 1.94; MM 39; L&N 15.176, 15.206, 53.17; BAGD 63;

[519] Ep. Arist. 268; Josephus, War 4.404; Ant. 1.16; Ag. Apion 2.162)

[520] Spicq,1.118

[521] Dative of cause toiautoiß qusiaiß euaresteitai especially with verbs of emotion, here in a more refined style. 'On account of' BDF,§196

[522] Spicq,2.168; 500n62

[523] Spicq,2.329; 592n5;

[524] BDF,§425[3],

[525] Spicq,3.77

[526] Polybius 4.81.1 "Philip attracted admiration beyond his years for his conduct in general." Epictetus 1.9.24 "God has established for us a line of conduct." Jos Ant.15.190.

[527] 2nd century BC there is a formula 'if your conduct is not better' ouk apo tou beltistou anastrefomenou. BGU 1756, 12; 1769,4; P. Tebt.786,15; 904,10. Etc.

[528] L.Delos 1498.7 159-151 BC

[529] BDF,§336[3]

[530] Ep.Arist.130

[531] Polybius 4.81.1 "Philip attracted admiration beyond his years for his conduct in general." Epictetus 1.9.24 "God has established for us a line of conduct." Jos Ant.15.190.

[532] 2nd century BC there is a formula 'if your conduct is not better' ouk apo tou beltistou anastrefomenou. BGU 1756,12; 1769,4; P. Tebt.786,15; 904,10. Etc.

[533] L.Delos 1498.7 159-151 BC

[534] I.Cor vol.8,n.306,8 2nd century AD]

[535] Spicq,1.112n7; 113; 3.74n63; 335

[536] BDF,§336[3]

[537] BDF,§322,Verbs of believing can use oti or accusative 397[2]

[538] BDF,§118[2]

[539] see Feuillet, CBQ 1959,472. Delling, ST,17[1963] 23ff. G.D Kilpatrick, "The Order of Some Noun and Adjective Phrases in the New Testament," Donum Gratulatorium Eth. Stauffer [Leiden:Brill, 1962],111ff. Spicq,1.207n7; 394; 432 n40; 2.350n58

[540] BDF,§118[2]

[541] Feuillet, CBQ 1959,472. Delling, ST,17[1963] 23ff. G.D Kilpatrick, "The Order of Some Noun and Adjective Phrases in the New Testament," Donum

Gratulatorium Eth. Stauffer [Leiden:Brill, 1962],111ff. Spicq,1.207n7; 394; 432 n40; 2.350n58

542 Spicq,1.373n59; 2.20; 274.

543 "This glory is God in the splendor of his majesty and the omnipotence of his interventions, the Father of glory. But this predicate doxa, which is peculiar to God, is attributed also to Christ, "the Lord of Glory." Heb 1.3 adds the description 'the Son (of God), the effulgence of his (the Father's) glory [apaugasma thß dochß autou] and the image of his sub-stance. If Christ is the refulgence of God's doxa, it is because his origin is divine: he has the same nature as the Father while having his personal independence. The Council of Nicea would give the definition 'light from light' In proclaiming Jeus as His Son at Tabor, God conferred honor and glory upon him 2 Pet 1.17, [timhn kai doxan]; but as a human, Jesus--after the shame of his passion--was glorified by his resurrection, and at the end of time he will appear as an almighty sovereign and in blinding light. His disciples await 'the appearing of the glory of our great God and Savior Jesus Christ, for they will participate in it 2 thess 2.14." read Spicq,I,370ff and notes.

544 Spicq,1.373n59; 2.20; 274

545 BDAG under #1 to cause to be in a condition to function well, to put in order, restore. Sub categories: restore to a former condition, put to rights, clean nets, mend and fold 'restore in a gentle manner' Gal 6.1. Sub b 'put into propecondition, adjust, complete, trained, practiced. Under #2 to prepare for a purpose, prepare, make. Create, outfit.

546 Aileen Guilding JTS n.s. 3[1952],53 in F.F.Bruce,"Hebrews," Peake's Commentary on the Bible [London:Nelson,1964]1008

547 BDF,§244[1]

548 BDF,§437

549 J.Barton Payne, Encyclopedia of Biblical Prophecy[NY:Harper and Row, 1973] lo.cit.

550 This Bibliography ignores abbreviated items in the footnotes, and items taken from older resources, for which see footnotes.It is not complete.

JBR *Journal of Bible and Religion*

SR Studies in Religion/Sciences Religieuses

HTR *Harvard Theological Review*

JBL *Journal of Biblical Literature*

Exp *The Expositor*

ser. series

SPCK Society for the Propagation of Christian Knowledge

VoxEv *Vox Evangelica (London)*

SWJT *Southwestern Journal of Theology*
BJRL *Bulletin of the John Rylands University Library of Manchester*
Int *Interpretation*
NICNT New International Commentary on the New Testament
ab Anchor Bible (New York: Doubleday)
LQ *Lutheran Quarterly*
CJT *Canadian Journal of Theology*
tr. translation, translator(s), translated by, transpose(s)
JTS *Journal of Theological Studies*
NPNF P. Schaff (ed.) Nicene and Post-Nicene Fathers
ATR *Anglican Theological Review*
TBT *The Bible Today*
Neot Neotestamentica
rev. revised, reviser, revision, or reverse
ThEduc *Theological Educator*
BV Berkeley Version (The Modern Language Bible)
SBLDS Society of Biblical Literature [SBL] Dissertation Series
MT The Masoretic Text [of the Old Testament] (as published in BHS)
JETS *Journal of the Evangelical Theological Society*
BTB *Biblical Theology Bulletin*
HUCA *Hebrew Union College Annual*
UP University Press
IDB G. A. Buttrick (ed.), *Interpreter's Dictionary of the Bible* 4 vols. (Nashville: Abingdon, 1962-76)
Her *Hermathena*
SC Source chrétiennes
TynBul Tyndale Bulletin
CGTC Cambridge Greek Testament Commentary
SBT Studies in Biblical Theology (London/Naperville, IL: SCM/Allenson)
SBT Studies in Biblical Theology (London/Naperville, IL: SCM/Allenson)
CBQ *Catholic Biblical Quarterly*
AJT *American Journal of Theology*
ST *Studia theologica*
IB *The Interpreter's Bible*, ed. G. A. Buttrick (12 vols.; Nashville: Abingdon, 1951-57)
BGBE Beiträge zur Geschichte der biblischen Exegese
TNTC Tyndale New Testament Commentaries
NIBC New International Biblical Commentary
SNTSMS Society for New Testament Studies Monograph Series

Theol *Theology*
SpTod *Spirituality Today*
ResQ *Restoration Quarterly*
SBLMS Society of Biblical Literature [SBL] Monograph Series
CTJ *Calvin Theological Journal*
NovT Novum Testamentum
LQHR *London Quarterly and Holborn Review*
SBLASP Society of Biblical Literature Abstracts and Seminar Papers
SJT *Scottish Journal of Theology*
CTM *Concordia Theological Monthly*
AUSS *Andrews University Seminary Studies*
LexTQ *Lexington Theological Quarterly*
TCh *The Churchman*
EvQ *The Evangelical Quarterly*
JSNTSup *Journal for the Study of the New Testament* Supplement Series
JSOT *Journal for the Study of the Old Testament* Biblical Studies
BW *Biblical World*
SCM Student Christian Movement
Ps Psalms
AnBib Analecta biblica (Rome: PBI)
CQR *Church Quarterly Review*
WesThJ *Wesleyan Theological Journal*
IBS *Irish Biblical Studies*
BibRev *Biblical Review*
MCM *Modern Churchman*
NT New Testament
ICC International Critical Commentary (Edinburgh/New York: Clark/Scribner's)
HNTC Harper's NT Commentaries
ns new series
NovTSup Supplement(s) to *Novum Testamentum*
WTJ *Westminster Theological Journal*
OPTT *Occasional Papers in Translation and Texlinguistics*
TBC Torch Bible Commentaries
NTTS New Testament Tools and Studies
WW *Word and World*
IlRev *Iliff Review*
RTR Reformed Theological Review
CrozQ *Crozer Quarterly*

MNTC Moffatt NT Commentary
Enc *Encounter*
Mel *Melita Theologica*
BenM *Benediktionische Monatschrift*
AER *American Ecclesiastical Review*
NB *New Blackfriars*
RefRev *Reformed Review*
CBQMS Catholic Bible Quarterly—Monograph Series
PTR *Princeton Theological Review*
HDR Harvard Dissertations in Religion or History of David's Rise
ALGHJ Arbeiten zur Literatur und Geschichte des hellenistischen Judentums (Leiden: Brill)
sup Samaritan Pentateuch
Scr Scripture
ScrHier Scripta hierosolymitana

About the Author

William Bicksler grew up and was converted to Christ in the Evangelical Congregational church where he was first licensed to preach in 1951. He is a graduate of Houghton College B.A (1955), Asbury Theological Seminary MDiv (1958), Wheaton Graduate School M.A (1964), Brandeis University Department of Mediterranean Studies MA, PhD (1973), researching and successfully defending his Ph.D dissertation on "Slavery Documents of Old Babylonia" available from University Microfilms.. In 1957 he was ordained elder in the Free Methodist Church and held Annual Conference relation in New York and in Taiwan. He has pastored churches in Kentucky and Vermont, is ordained, and served both as missionary and professor in Taiwan from 1958 to 2003 with times in the states for graduate studies. He has taught at Holy Light Theological Seminary 1959 to 1969, China Evangelical Seminary 1973 to 2003, Soochow University 1973 to 1977; and Indiana Wesleyan University 1978 to 1982. In graduate studies he completed three dissertations. He also has contributed to three Festschrift published by China Evangelical Seminary. The seminary also published a biography including few collected short papers in 2002. He has published a *Commentary on Daniel* through the China Evangelical Seminary Press, in Chinese, 2001, *Commentary on Galatians 2004.and a Commentary on Romans 2005. This Commentary on Hebrews* owes its existence to several courses taught on the seminary level. *A Commentary on Job* has been submitted for publication 2005. At present he is completing the manuscript for a *Commentary on the Psalms.*

Printed in the United Kingdom
by Lightning Source UK Ltd.
108826UKS00001B/69

9 781420 855937